S0-ALC-247

1980

ari and Paul begin a conversation about how ann arbor could use a traditional Jewish deli like the ones they grew up with in detroit (Paul) and chicago (ari).

Paul notices that the building on the corner of kingsley and detroit is available. he calls ari to see if he's ready to open the deli that they had talked about.

march 15, 1982

zingerman's opens its doors for the first time. ari and Paul are behind the counter making sandwiches and cutting bread and cheeses.

1986

the 700-square-foot addition to the original zingerman's building is completed. the pie-shaped wedge houses the sandwich line and provides expanded room for dry goods.

1997

the new bread bag from zingerman's bakehouse earns national design recognition from "Print" magazine. zing artists become "Print" favorites, receiving similar recognition the next three years in a row for four other zingerman's design projects.

"America's very best rye? No contest. We found it in Ann Arbor, Michigan ... It comes from Zingerman's Bakehouse, which makes loaves of rugged rye that are dense and springy, laced with the taste of hearth smoke."

jane and michael stern, "saveur"

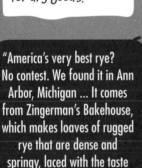

1999

Led by managing partners tom root and toni morell, zingermans.com goes online.

as demand for zingtrain seminars and workshops continues to grow, Stas' kazmierski joins zingtrain as maggie's co-managing partner.

1998

food gatherers delivers over 2,000,000 pounds of food to help feed those in need in washtenaw county.

jude walton and maurice (mo) frechette make the jump to full-fledged managing partners of zingerman's mail order.

2000

amy emberling, one of the original bakers and founder of the pastry kitchen, returns to zingerman's bakehouse as co-managing partner.

Zingerman's

Guide to Good Leading, Part 4

A Lapsed Anarchist's Approach to

THE POWER OF BELIEFS IN BUSINESS

Ari Weinzweig

Zingerman's
PRESS
2016

Copyright © Ari Weinzweig 2016

All rights reserved
Published in the United States of America by Zingerman's Press
Manufactured in Michigan, United States of America

First Edition, First Printing

2019   2018   2017   2016   4   3   2   1

Cover illustration: Ian Nagy
Cover design: Nicole Robichaud
Interior illustrations: Ian Nagy and Ryan Stiner
Text design: Raul Peña
Text font: Adobe Caslon Pro

This book may not be transmitted or reproduced in any form or by any means without prior written permission from the publisher. Brief excerpts for review purposes are fine. Please direct requests for permission to Zingerman's Press, 3756 Plaza Drive, Ann Arbor, MI 48108. We're friendly.

ISBN: 978-0-9893494-6-8

www.zingermanspress.com

Printed, bound, and warehoused locally, in southeastern Michigan.
Printed on FSC certified paper with a recycled content of 100 percent postconsumer waste.

FOUR WARNINGS

In the interest of shared understanding, I believe it's productive to begin with a few diligent disclaimers to make sure we're all in alignment on a few of the basics of and behind this book. Four brief warnings before you read:

1. Having spent the last few years paying close attention to the strange workings of my own mind, I'll share that studying one's own subconscious is an exercise in imperfect, if ultimately productive, impossibility. As E. F. Schumacher said, "Every thought can be scrutinized directly except the thought by which we scrutinize." Beware then, that as you read and reflect on what follows, it's likely that some of your beliefs will be challenged—even changed. My own beliefs have been impacted significantly through the challenge of working on this book. The good news is that my life is much better for it.

2. The essays in this book are not a unanimous declaration of philosophical unity at Zingerman's. Paul and everyone who's a part of our organization will each have their own perspectives. We may share many points of alignment, but our beliefs aren't exactly alike. What follows are, as usual, my views alone.

3. By the time you will have purchased (or borrowed) this book, I will probably have already altered some of my views. Knowing that makes it hard for me to let go of these words, but I try to live by writer Rebecca Solnit's charge: "Leave the door open for the unknown, the door into the dark. That's where the most important things come from . . ."

4. My hope is that what follows gets you thinking in new ways and about some new things. The idea here is to have a conversation—you with yourself; you with me; you with others you care about in your life; you with people you don't know yet who might be wondering about the same sorts of things. In that sense, the Guide to Good Leading *books have turned out be an old-school sort of social media. I work, you think, we talk, I think, I write, I work, we talk, I write some more, and so on. In fact, many of your comments and insights have already altered beliefs I used to hold back when I began this work, and I look forward to more to come. Thank you for the opportunity to be part of such a caring and thoughtful collaboration.*

the building rocco disderide built on detroit street in 1902—
it's been the home of zingerman's delicatessen since 1982

CONTENTS

Preface: Beliefs, Beads, and Buildings   9

Foreword: A View from Across the Street by Claude Steele   31

Introduction: Roots, Ecosystems, and Art   35

Cast of Characters   53

The "Secrets"

#40 The Power of Beliefs in Business   67

#41 Leading with Positive Beliefs   117

#42 It's All About Alignment   167

#43 A Recipe for Changing a Belief   211

#43.5 What I Believe About Anarchism and Business   249

#44 Building a Hopeful Business   281

#45 A Six-Pointed Hope Star   319

#46 The Spirit of Generosity   359

#47 Visionary Roots   413

#48 One + One = A Lot!   441

#49 Why (Paul or) I Still Teach Orientation
for New Staff Members   461

Epilogue: The Art of Business   493

Extra Bonus Stuff

More Notes from the Front Porch   508

More Notes from the Back Dock   516

Suggested Reading   522

What is Zingerman's, Anyway?   530

Paul and Ari's University of Michigan
Commencement Address   533

A Handful of Organizational Recipes   539

Time to Eat! Nine Recipes to Cook
in Your Own Kitchen   545

    Rocco's Spaghetti with Basil and Butter   556

    Chocolate-Dipped Espresso Stars   558

    Macaroni and 3 Peppercorn Goat Cheese   560

    Octopus and Couscous (Octo-cous)   563

    Tomato 'n' N'duja Sauce   565

    Zingerman's Challah   566

    Pisoni Salad   568

    Fine e Mezzi   570

    Grilled Halvah and Chocolate Sandwich   573

An Epicurean Epilogue: Anarchist Eating
in Greenwich Village   574

Endnotes   577

Appreciations   586

Beliefs, Beads, and Buildings

Each time I sit down to do one of these prefaces—this is the fourth in the series—I struggle. It's not easy (for me, at least) to strike a creative balance between sharing enough to help you understand our organizational ecosystem and boring you with the same old story that Zingerman's veterans have heard—or been part of—so many times before. The challenge is laid out beautifully by writer Rebecca Solnit's so-poetically put question: "Where," she wonders aloud, "does a story begin? The fiction is that they do, and end, rather than that the stuff of a story is just a cup of water scooped from the sea and poured back into it." Her query, like all good questions, gives me pause. Clearly, the book starts here, at its beginning. But the story goes back quite a way. Which piece, I begin to wonder, is the one to properly put forward first? It's hard to know the ideal answer.

In fact, there isn't one. Years ago that reality probably would have proven fatal; my perfectionism would have put an end to the project before it ever began. I would have gotten stuck in my own uncertainty, believing that there surely must be some right answer (or at least a near-ideal option), but that I just wasn't wise enough to work out what it was. I would surely, if quietly, have alternated between agonizing and being angry, getting next to nothing done in the process. "Anxiety," Anaïs Nin notes, "is love's greatest killer." Worry leads nowhere, I've learned, at least nowhere I want to go. The critical voices we internalize along the way almost always impede the expression of our innate creative spirit. I know, because it happened to me.

Fortunately, per what follows in the rest of this book, we can effectively alter our beliefs to align with the way we want to live. Or in this case, write. There are, I now believe, no perfect answers. Only imperfect people like me putting forth imperfectly formed ideas in the hope that others around us will complement and perhaps complete our original thoughts; the dialogue that has emerged from the essays in these books has made all the difference. As Walt Whitman said, "the audience writes the poetry." Although I can still hear a bit of a grumble from the persistently perfectionist voices in my head, I can use my now strongly held belief in the benefits of creative, caring, and well-crafted imperfection to push ahead and be productive anyway. I believe now that all of us—me included—have the ability to do amazing things.

Happily, over the years, I've learned to shift out of active worry into more rewarding writing. The insightful Brenda Ueland observed: "Creative power flourishes only when I am living in the present." These days, I've come to believe that the best thing I can do when I start to stress is simply to keep typing. It works. Instead of stopping, I just need to go faster! Even writing words that feel foolish while I'm putting them down is far better than *not writing*. I can block out writer's block, I've learned, by just continuing to type. My fingers, if I keep them moving, can usher out my unproductive energy. As Ueland adds, "I learned that you should feel when writing, not like Lord Byron on a mountain top, but like a child stringing beads in kindergarten—happy, absorbed and quietly putting one bead on after another." In the end, insights emerge, doors open, beliefs change, and—all the way along—it's far more fun.

Which is why I'm going to begin building *this* version of the Zingerman's story with beads, with Ueland's reminder at hand, pulling from a pile that's been gathering in my mind over the last 34 years. I'll start this time with the little two-story orange brick building where we first opened in 1982. Though we've added onto it three times so that the original building is only about a quarter of the Deli's current square footage, it's still at the spiritual center of our organization. In that context, the story of Zingerman's here will begin not with me, or Paul, or a Reuben sandwich, but with Rocco Disderide, the man who had the building built in the spring and summer of the year 1902.

Can a Great Building Build a Great Business?

The idea isn't as strange as it first seemed when it entered my mind. Now that I have this bead in hand, I'm wondering whether buildings might play a much bigger spiritual and inspirational role in creating great businesses than most of us suspect.

While I believe we live best by moving forward into our desired futures, it's also true, as Søren Kierkegaard says, that "life can only be understood backwards." With the benefit of hindsight, I wonder now, as I pick up the bead of the building, if maybe the main reason we were able to establish the community-focused business that we've built is because we were lucky enough to begin our project in a space that's both unique and yet just another part of the neighborhood. You might walk right by it without noticing. Or if you're paying close attention, you might find a wealth of interesting, one-of-a-kind details to draw you in. In that sense, the building was wholly aligned with the aesthetics of what we wanted to create when we first envisioned what the world now knows as Zingerman's.

In a sense, the store was nothing remarkable—just another corner grocery in a country that was once filled with them. Ann Arbor, back then, had a population of about 15,000 (it's nearly ten times that today), and probably a dozen similar stores were spread around town. And yet the building was, like you and me, completely unique. There is truly no other, anywhere in the world, that's exactly like ours—or I should say like Rocco Disderide's. The building is, I believe, one of those that architect Christopher Alexander is imagining when he writes that great buildings are "beautiful, ordered, harmonious—yes, all these things. But especially, and what strikes to the heart, they live." And, I humbly hope, so too does the business that we built within and, later, out from it.

Can a building impart its life force to the business opened within it? Solnit refers to that kind of spirit as "genius of place." While we might well have made a successful go of it in another location, most people's visual image of Zingerman's remains the building at the corner of Detroit and Kingsley in which we started. Zingerman's day still begins there, at 7:00 a.m., with the smell of Nueske's applewood-smoked bacon in the air and the sun rising to the east behind us, every single morning. "Every love has a landscape," Solnit says. This was the place where my career and I had our first date. Nearly 34 years later, our love affair is still going strong.[1]

Rocco Disderide was an immigrant, born in 1859 into a farming family to the east of Genoa in the Italian region of Liguria (the same year the modern Italian state was first unified). In 1882, he came to New York, where he worked as a day laborer on building projects and his wife, Catherine, gave birth to their five daughters. They moved to Ann Arbor 10 years later—he'd heard that Michigan was a good place to find work and raise a family. The mountains in Liguria start close to the sea, so farming is done on small, tightly terraced plots to make growing crops possible on the steep inclines. It must have been quite a change to become part of the overwhelming hustle and intensity of New York City, and then equally shocking to emerge into the flat, wide, squared-off streets of small-town America.[2]

11

Things were far less settled in Ann Arbor then than now. For context, consider that the country was only a bit over 100 years down the road of independence from England—and Michigan, while not quite wild, was still referred to by people such as Malinda Russell, author of *A Domestic Cook Book* (the first African American cookbook in print), as "the garden of the West." After a failed attempt to get to Liberia, Russell moved to the town of Paw Paw, Michigan, where she published her book in 1866 in an effort to raise funds to return home to Tennessee where she had once operated a pastry shop.

Mid-19th-century Paw Paw seems to have been a place welcoming of progressive beliefs. In 1850, sixteen years before Russell's now historically significant publication, Jo Labadie was born in the same town. Of French and Native American heritage, young Labadie lived on what was still considered the western frontier, at times among the Potawatomi people who remained in the area. Since they were both in the town at the same time, it's not unlikely that a teenage Labadie and a middle-aged Mrs. Russell could have walked past each other, or even spoken, at some point during their years in Paw Paw. Given his progressive beliefs about people of all backgrounds, I'd like to think Jo would have treated her far more respectfully than many others of European origin might have done in that era.

In 1872, Labadie moved to Detroit where he became a labor activist known locally as "the gentle anarchist." In the summer of 1911—while still alive and relatively well—Labadie offered to contribute his large collection of anarchist pamphlets, books, and posters to the University of Michigan, where 65 years later, I sat and studied his work. One of the three original copies of Malinda Russell's cookbook is stored down the hall in the Janice Bluestein Longone Culinary Archive, where I've also spent a fair bit of time studying over the years. Perhaps I'll add the bead of the University of Michigan Graduate Library to this history then—many of my own most strongly held beliefs have begun with books found in its stacks.

Not long after arriving in Ann Arbor, the Disderides lived at 424 East North Street (now known as Kingsley), a few doors to the east of where he later built the grocery building. That first Disderide house had educational roots—well before the family bought it and moved in, it had been the neighborhood school. Then in 1895, Rocco and Catherine purchased the property at the corner of Detroit Street that stands at the center of this story. The building that already stood there belonged to her brother, Charles Caramella, the first Italian immigrant to settle in the town, and housed a small grocery shop.[3]

It was a good spot for a store. There was a popular farm implement business across the street. The building kitty-corner from the Deli was built in
1899 by Frances Stofflet, designed as apartments for his children to live in. (In
1981, Rick and Deann Bayless, who would later go on to found the Frontera
Grill in Chicago—one of my favorite restaurants anywhere—lived in one of
those apartments while Rick was getting his PhD in linguistics at U of M.)
And the train station, considered the finest on the rail line between Buffalo
and Chicago, was just two blocks up; the corner of Detroit and Kingsley would
have been right on the walking route from the station into downtown. The
building was in the heart of Ann Arbor's Catholic neighborhood—the first
mass said in the city was held on the other side of Detroit Street in 1835. The
new St. Thomas church had just been built a couple of blocks up Kingsley
Street in 1899. The church was designed by Spier and Rohns, the same Detroit-
based architects who designed the train station. The Disderides, always good
Catholics, were very active members. Of course, beliefs and behavior change—
if you ask people in town today where to find the "Catholic neighborhood,"
they will surely look at you quite quizzically.

In 1901, Rocco decided to build a new two-story brick building on the
same spot to house the grocery he envisioned. Artisan mason Bill Suchman,
who recently did some restoration work on the old bricks, estimated it went up
quickly. "They probably had it built in a month. Maybe two," he told me. I was
surprised. "Could any construction move that quickly?" I was mistakenly applying my modern-day beliefs to a world chronologically and culturally quite far
from my own. "Codes then were nothing like they are today," Bill responded.
"You could build pretty quickly. Back then they were getting a thousand bricks
down in a day. Now it might be five hundred."

Cleaning the weather-worn bricks a century later is much slower work. A
skilled mason can restore and replace only 100 or so in a day. After 40 some
years of renovation work, Bill has an impressively intuitive feel for what he
works on. Talking to him, I felt like he could see right into the soul of the
building and understand it in a way that I, who'd spent years working *in* it, had
not. He pointed out what I wasn't knowledgeable or attentive enough to have
noticed. We stood together out front on a sunny spring morning 113 years
after Bill's bricklaying brethren completed their work. "They did a nice job on
it," he said. Although I'd always liked the building, and I'd certainly walked past
the details he was pointing out thousands of times, I realized I'd never *really*
seen the building as it actually is. And that while I'd most certainly spent more

time inside that place than in any other structure I've been in my whole life, I never understood it.

Although he speaks quietly, Bill's passion for the building is palpable. "Look at the quoins," he said, pointing at the rows of bricks on the corners of the structure that are alternately set in and then layered back out. In case you (like me) know nothing about brickwork—I had to look up the term to know what he was talking about—the word is pronounced *coins*. He showed me the granite blocks at the base of the front windows and also the copper flashing that frames them. "That detailing above the windows on the second floor is nice, too." As is true for everything in life, when you *really* look, you notice the nuance.

A few months after this conversation, Paul shared with me the Disderides' original 113-year-old construction contract. It looks as if the building work began in May and was done by the end of July. The shop would then have opened the first week of August. Coincidentally—or not—our fiscal year at Zingerman's begins on August 1.

Back at the Beginning

Building Disderide's grocery did require a good bit of rearranging: the old wood-frame house that originally stood on the corner had to be hauled to the back of the lot to make room for the new brick building. Skids would have been set down and the house jacked up off the foundation. A capstan (a vertical drum that can be rotated to pull a rope) would have been set up beyond the new resting place of the house. Horses were then hitched up and walked around the capstan, tightening the cables attached to the house. With the men guiding the process, the building was slowly shifted back a few hundred feet to the oddly angled spot it still sits on today, nearly 120 years later. I can imagine the Disderide and Caramella families standing by, the men helping the workers push as the horses strained to pull the older structure to its new spot.

Today you hardly ever hear of a house being moved unless it has great historical value. This was the opposite—it gained historical value mostly *because* it was moved to a seemingly strange location. Such a scenario would never happen today. Beliefs about buildings have changed. We're at the heart of one of Ann Arbor's historic districts, and I can't imagine anyone ever allowing a wood-frame house to be set at the back of a lot at an acute angle to the street and a two-story building of a totally incompatible architectural style to be built in its place. This odd setting, I've realized, is a good metaphor for beliefs. Our beliefs often develop without us knowing what's happening at the time. But once they've formed, they remain with us, frequently for the rest of our lives. We assume that their perhaps odd orientation is, in fact, "normal." Over time, they're taken as facts.

Although the old house can't now be repositioned, our beliefs most definitely can. A core belief may stay as is, but other beliefs can—and probably should—shift around it. For years, we believed we were stuck with that strange and fairly impractical configuration created in the spring of 1902. We used the house—by then probably a century and a half old, sagging in most every part of the floor—mostly for storage. But again, beliefs change. Grace Singleton, one of the managing partners at the Deli, decided not to let past precedent keep the Deli from growing and set her mind to getting permission from the city to add on to the building again. It had taken two years to get the okay back in 1986 when we added on to Disderide's building. This time it took four years just to get the go-ahead and then—in contrast to the three months it took to construct the original building—another three years to build. But the work eventually allowed us to renovate much of the old foundation and infrastructure that Rocco's crew had put in. The house now holds the Deli's cash and pick-up station for call-ahead orders and is connected literally, not just spiritually, to the brick building that was built in its place.

Hope, Generosity, and Jawbreakers

Backing up again to 1902, I can see Rocco standing out front as the construction comes close to completion. It is the end of July, so the sun is high and hot. I imagine him watching and wondering, hopeful, but maybe a bit anxious, smoking a cigar (as he loved to do), excited, envisioning success, believing that he has done the right thing. Who would construct a building without positive beliefs about the future? Immigrants like Rocco who head out from home by choice to find a better fit for themselves in the world are almost always full of hope. If they didn't believe there was a better place to put down new roots, they wouldn't have emigrated in the first place, right? (Refugees, on the other hand, often depart under duress, and many long to return to the home they hold in their hearts for years, even generations, after leaving.) Rocco, leaving Italy, clearly had a vision: first, of a better place to live; then, of a better way to make a living. It worked. Twenty years after arriving in America, he was building the two-story orange brick home of his soon-to-be business.[4]

On January 1, 1902, while I'm sure Rocco was already thinking of constructing his building, the first Tournament of Roses game ever was played in Pasadena's Tournament Park. It took the Michigan team eight days to travel to California; they would have left from the train station at the end of Detroit Street. It was worth the trip. National champion Michigan beat Stanford a whopping 49 to 0. Stanford's team completely lost hope and conceded the game with eight minutes left to play. You can imagine the excitement back in Ann Arbor—the Disderides and their neighbors laughing and smiling as the news made its way back to Michigan. And beliefs change, even in football. That field was 110 yards long; a team needed to move five yards, not ten, to get a first down, and forward passes were prohibited. Eight thousand people attended the game, and three-quarters of those had to stand throughout.

The energy in Ann Arbor after the big win must have been outstanding: 1,500 people (10 percent of the town) greeted the Michigan players at the train station when they got back. Positive beliefs go up when good things happen. I'm imagining 1902 as a very upbeat year in Ann Arbor history. Hope is contagious, and when we're hopeful, we're far more likely to make decisions to move forward than when we're suffused in fear. In fact, the flood of good civic energy that emerged from the tournament game might have been the thing that convinced Rocco to finally pull the trigger on his construction project. Who knows? If the football team hadn't been so good, maybe the building would never have been built.[5]

Having held this bead of the building in my mind a good bit of late, I grew increasingly interested in the man behind the building. I decided it was time to find out who Mr. Disderide really was. I got ahold of Diann Boik, Gayle Pastorino, and Steve Pastorino, three of his great-grandchildren, to learn more. Rocco was a tall man—over six feet—with a big mustache and a happy, upbeat attitude towards life. He never spoke English all that well, but he insisted that his children, grandchildren, and great-grandchildren use it every day. "He was quite a character," Diann told me. "He used to sing to us in Italian. He liked posing for the camera. He would get with my great uncle and they would pose for all these kooky pictures with silly hats on." He was also a handy guy. "Everyone called him Mr. Fix-it," she said. "He loved art, dancing, and singing. He was all about that."

Rocco seems like a guy Paul and I would have gotten along with quite well. Milo Ryan grew up in the neighborhood in that era and remembers Disderide's shop in his book, *A View of the Universe*. The store, he says, was "the neighborhood's favorite institution." Its "variety and range of two-for-a-penny candy has never been matched in the history of retail marketing." It seems like a spot I'd have happily shopped in. Ryan recalls that the Disderides "lived behind and above the store, which itself served as their family room. They slept upstairs, when they slept. The store was open from early morning, to sell milk, butter, and eggs, until late at night, for those who needed tobacco." Rocco is described as a "florid, full-cheeked" man who "cared more for love than for money." Eighty years before Zingerman's opened, he was doing, it seems, what we now refer to as "extra miles" for his own customers. "More than once," Ryan writes, "he would slip in a jawbreaker or a piece of peanut brittle into the stack of groceries, or hand it to us with the change."

Rocco Disderide was hardly a household name anywhere other than here in the Kerrytown neighborhood or maybe in his family's village back in northern Italy, but here in Ann Arbor he was something of a local hero. I like his story because it's what I believe history is made up of: a significant act, sandwiched around millions of small decisions, visions, risks, insights, and accidents that might get little notice from anyone other than the people who are making them or who happen to be directly impacted at the time. Bricks and mortar, laid one atop the other, copper-trimmed windows, and candy and peanut brittle shared with kids aren't the stuff of history books, but that's the kind of history that wins my heart.

The tale of Rocco Disderide, in whose spiritual and commercial footsteps we clearly, if unknowingly, followed, is one of the main messages of this book—that stories rarely start where they seem to at first glance, and that we would do well to dig deeper and learn more about what's going on and why it's happening. Would Zingerman's still have become Zingerman's if it had opened in a building other than this odd, well-suited-to-our-unconventional-outlook, trapezoidal orange brick building, with its catchy, then-state-of-the-art quoins on its anything-but-right-angle front corners, that Rocco built just after the turn of the 20th century?

Did You Ever Imagine . . .

People regularly ask me if I knew when I graduated from U of M that I'd eventually be part of creating the unique Community of Businesses that Zingerman's has become nearly one-fifth of the way through the 21st century. The flippant part of my personality wants to say, "Yeah, exactly!" But the only thing I truly knew for sure about the future was that I didn't want to move back home to Chicago. Although I didn't honestly believe it, I assured my mother that after a while I'd go back to school and get another, more advanced degree. The next bead to add to the story is the one that unexpectedly became the beginning of my vocation. After graduating with a degree in Russian history, I got a job as a dishwasher in a local restaurant. Neither food, nor business, nor anarchism was particularly in the front of my mind. In the words of Terry Tempest Williams, "only uncertainty was certain." I guess in that sense I was a small bit like Rocco Disderide after he arrived in the United States. We were each determined not to go back to where we'd come from. And although we both had high hopes for our new homes, neither of us had much sense of how things were actually going to work out.

It helped that I got to start learning my craft with some great people at that restaurant—Paul was the general manager, Frank Carollo (one of the managing partners at the Bakehouse) was a line cook, and Maggie Bayless (managing partner of ZingTrain) was a cocktail waitress. Paul left a few years later, but we stayed in touch. Four years of pretty good restaurant work down the road—most of which was spent cooking, running kitchens, and learning the basics of the food business—Paul and I reconnected and opened the Deli. It was a cold Monday morning—March 15, 1982, to be exact. It would have been the opposite of the day Disderide's opened in the first week of August, 80 years earlier. Rocco got rolling in the sun; we started in the snow. No leaves on the trees, just a bit of brown grass showing through in the space between the street and the sidewalk, and that dim, gray sort of sky that barely lights the day around here in the last week of winter. The weather, coincidentally, reflected much of the country's mood: the economy in 1982 was not in good shape, and interest rates were at 18 percent, the highest, by far, that they'd been in the 100 years since Rocco Disderide disembarked, possibly at Castle Clinton. To make matters even worse, Michigan had lost a close game to Ohio State the previous autumn while we were in initial discussions about the Deli and, consequently, failed to make the Rose Bowl that year. None of which did much for the energy of the town as we embarked on our new little venture.

When we opened in 1982, we most definitely did *not* envision—or even imagine—anything on the scale of a Community of Businesses. You might as well ring up Rocco Disderide in retail heaven and ask him if he could tell in 1902 that his building would come to house a nationally known shop selling specialty foods from all over the world, including many from the land he left to come to the United States; that the pesto his grandmother probably pressured him to eat so often would become a menu item in posh restaurants; and that the president of his adopted country would one day walk in the same front door he did every day, to sit down and have a sandwich.

We did, however, have a clear sense of what we wanted to do. To be sure, what we imagined was a much narrower scope than what we have going today. But like Rocco Disderide, and anyone else who's started anything, we definitely had a vision. It wasn't written down the way we now do it, but we knew from the get-go that we wanted a unique deli serving tasty, traditional fare—Jewish and otherwise—in a down-to-earth setting that featured great food, great service, and a great place for the few people we could afford to hire to work. Our dreams were modest by the world's standards, but they sure felt big to us. We knew that we wanted it to be a cornerstone of the community, in much the same way—as I've since discovered—that Disderide's had been. As I'm sure was true for Rocco, everything we had to our names was on the line. I tried to act nonchalant about it at the time, but unlocking that old front door for the first time at seven on the morning of March 15 was, for us, a monumental occasion.[6]

A few years after we opened, we took over the apartment in which the Disderides had lived above the store and set up our offices there. In 1986, we added on to the building, putting another 700 square feet along its south wall. In 1991, we renovated an additional house built in the 1860s that sits about 100 feet to the south on Detroit Street. By the time we got it, the house had served alternatively as student apartments and then one-room retail shops. We weren't able to connect the two buildings because of Historic District regulations, which meant that we ended up with the rather absurd setup of having to walk outside to bring guests their sandwiches in what we came to call Zingerman's Next Door, a situation that continues to this day. We've never liked doing it that way, but we made it work. To show you how much people's beliefs can be influenced by the way "successful people" do things, we've seen other restaurants replicate the system, assuming it to be a critical piece of the Zingerman's experience. I can only smile and wonder. The Caramella building—the one that had been on the corner before Rocco got his own project going—remained pretty much as it was. Run-down, a mere 600 square feet with not a flat spot to be found on its floor, we used it minimally for storage.

Lost and Found

The concept of the Community of Businesses came to us a couple years later. Looking back, we knew much more clearly than I realized at the time what we were going for when we opened in 1982. We didn't call it a vision, but in essence we had one, based on beliefs we'd both spent a lifetime living with.

We knew, from the beginning, that we wanted only one store: a unique shop that would be as much a positive part of the community as Disderide's was in its day. In a sense, this idea was more in synch with the way things were done in 1902 than in 1982. Single shops run by an onsite owner and deeply connected to the community were the norm at the turn of the 20th century. Small-scale grocers didn't open their businesses back then with the belief that success would mean going public or spreading units across the country.

By 1993, we'd built the Deli into what was already being recognized as one of the best in the country. Our original vision had come to fruition. But we weren't done, we weren't rich, and we weren't at all sure where to go from there. This stage, I've come to realize, is quite common for people who open their own business and then succeed and survive long enough to get lost. The clearest form of confusion in business—and the most commonly discussed—concerns the years of uncertainty when one is trying to figure out whether to open. Or maybe it's how to handle the chaos that usually comes right after the business gets going. But there's another sort of confusion, a kind of losing one's way, that generally gets little attention but can be spiritually lethal and, ultimately, a commercial killer as well. It's what happens when you've finally arrived at the place you were headed for so long, but you're totally unsure of where to go next. It is, per Natural Law of Business #9, a good problem. (See page 306 for the Natural Laws.) But it's not easy.

One day at a time, we kept moving "forward," but without any clear sense of where we were really going. That's not a terrible thing—sometimes we need to be able to work through the wilderness (literally or metaphorically) to get where we're meant, and want, to go. Everyone who makes something great happen pushes through the uncertainty that goes with being lost, through an array of ups and downs and in-betweens, and continues to move forward even when they're unsure of where they actually are at any given time. It's not a great feeling—trying to stay focused, unsure of what's next, fighting panic, trying to figure out how to trust your gut and listen to the advice of others at the same time.

The experience is universal. Whether it's us, Martin Luther King Jr., the Spaniard Cabeza de Vaca, or Rocco Disderide, I believe that it's a productive blend of positive belief, hope, generosity, vision, and a whole lot of hard work that gets you through. As historian Aaron Sachs explains, "Explorers were always lost, because they'd never been to these places before. They were never expected to know exactly where they were. Yet, at the same time, many of them knew their instruments pretty well and understood their trajectories within a reasonable degree of accuracy. In my opinion, their most important skill was simply a sense of optimism about surviving and finding their way." [7]

History, I suppose, would have it that Paul and I and our organization successfully survived being lost. With the benefit of hindsight, 20-plus years later, you might well say that we found our future. On a midsummer morning, roughly 91 years to the week that Rocco opened his shop, Paul and I sat on the wooden bench in front of Zingerman's. (The bench, I believe, has been there since the building was built—I can imagine folks in the neighborhood hanging out there as they do now, though the photo taking so common today would have been almost unheard of at the time.) With no warning whatsoever, Paul asked me (rather intently, as I remember) where I imagined the business would be in 10 years. The question threw me off completely. I had no idea how to answer it, other than by telling him how busy I was and that I didn't have time for that sort of abstract discussion when I had "real" work to do back inside the building.

As most of us do when we're caught off guard, I treaded conversational water and asked him what he was asking. Eventually he got his point—or, really, his question—across: What did I envision our business would be like a decade down the road? Ten years would place us in the year 2003. I couldn't even conceive of it, but my lack of imagination didn't slow him down in the least. "Come on!" he said. "This is important! What are we doing in ten years?" He was, as he nearly always is, very persistent. Would it be crazy to hold to our initial intention of having only one store, turning down all the offers to open elsewhere? Would we have sold the business? Would we still be here? I was close to clueless.

It took us about a year to come up with an effective, shared solution to Paul's challenge—lots of dialogue, discussion, disagreement, doubt, a decent bit of eye rolling, and, dare I say, a good deal of cursing. Ultimately it led us to a passionate rededication to each other and to our business. I didn't know it when he asked, but his willingness to stop and pose the question and have the ensuing conversation ended up changing my life, our organization, and, later, through the visioning process we now use and teach, a whole lot of other lives and businesses in the process.

While the two of us had no trouble making our way to and from work every day, Paul, intuitively and insightfully, knew that we'd lost our long-term direction. It was, in Solnit's sense, accepting that we were lost (though not a lost cause) and then doing the work to get clear on where we wanted to head. In hindsight, we did what Solnit says of the Spaniard Cabeza de Vaca: he "ceased to be lost not by returning but by turning into something else."

So, it turns out, did we. We could have taken any of the many frequently followed paths to the future: franchise, flip, open a second store, stick with the status quo, sell out. But none of those appealed. After all our conversations, like Cabeza de Vaca we finally figured out a new, previously uncharted, way—as unusual as Disderide's building—through the organizational wilderness. We stayed true to our origins and values but found creative ways to put old things together, and we ended up forging a very different vision of the future.

Things played out so positively in good part because we were able to effectively capitalize on the creative tension between us. Paul wanted to grow, but I hated the idea of multiple copies of our so-carefully-crafted creative original. He was adamant about offering opportunity for others in the organization; I was intent on improving our food and our service. He wanted to expand our community giving; I was driven to increase quality. None of what we wanted was particularly in conflict, but neither was it easy to arrive at a quick consensus. As we've done from day one, we kept coming back to the table until we could come up with a way to assemble all our aspirations and dreams into one coherent, creative future. It turned out that with a lot of dialogue, deep breathing, and healthy disagreement, we were able to turn turmoil into something truly terrific. Figuring it all out was, I would say now, akin to aligning an organizational version of a Rubik's Cube.

Our new vision, called Zingerman's 2009, was the first one we formally wrote out in the style we now use so regularly. We decided to create a Community of unique Zingerman's Businesses, all located in the Ann Arbor area, each with its own distinctive specialty, each run by a managing partner or partners, all operating synergistically as one food-and-service-focused organization. This plan was just one of the beads we put onto the thread of our existence, but in hindsight, it was an important one—bigger, bolder, and brighter, I suppose, than most of the beads that came before and those that would follow. I would not be here writing this book without it.

There are many other beads that could be added to the string of our organizational story. Each person who works here (probably Paul most of all) would surely string them their own way, putting each piece in place with a different set of contextual priorities. Which is exactly as it should be. Most of what we call history is impacted enormously by our beliefs—we include the things that support those beliefs and leave out what doesn't fit. But since this is my writing, I'll just keep picking up the beads that pop into my mind and allow others the chance to string their own necklace elsewhere.

Building a Bakery

In 1992 we opened Zingerman's Bakehouse. There's something special to me about being able to bake great bread for our community. Given that our main focus for the Bakehouse was to bake for the Deli, and only later to consider wholesaling to others, we looked for three things we didn't have downtown when we were searching for a place to put it: lots of space, low rent, and easy access for trucks. Eventually, Paul found us a spot on the south side of town in an industrial park about four miles away. The structure couldn't have been more different from Disderide's—an industrial complex, with long rows of identically shaped rectangular buildings made out of square cinder block painted a rather pallid off-white.

Of Loaves and Wishes

Starter cultures in bread bring me back to Rebecca Solnit's statement about how impossible it is to sort out with certainty where a story really starts. When we prepared to open the Bakehouse, we got our starter and our recipes from Michael London. Michael had grown up in New York working in the old Jewish bakeries and also trained extensively in France. Frank remembers how it all "started."

> Back in 1992, we could still meet travelers at their plane. Michael flew into Detroit Metro on a Continental Airlines flight and got off the plane carrying a Coleman cooler under his arm that contained five pounds of dough from his bakery in Saratoga Springs. That night, we fed that dough flour and water, and that turned it into our sourdough starter. So every day since September 12 of 1992, we've fed a piece of dough to create starter so we can continue to bake our sourdough breads (now over 8,500 consecutive days).

So when you buy a loaf of Bakehouse bread, you might take a moment, as I now do, to ponder: "Where did the bread begin?"

Two hundred years earlier, the land the Bakehouse is now located on was primarily forest filled with wild food sources. It would have been home primarily to Anishinaabe people, mostly Ojibwe, the Native tribes who'd been living intricate and interesting lives long before Europeans arrived to "discover" them. The name Michigan comes from the Ojibwe *michigaama*, meaning "large lake." If you asked an Ojibwe scholar to string the beads of the state's story, you'd get a very different historical necklace than the one most Michiganders are aware of. Beads, my friend Meg Noodin told me, "were considered a kind of cross between currency and artistry. Using them to draw or write on wearable items allowed images of the culture and history to be recorded and celebrated." The word for bead in Ojibwe is *manidoominens*, which (significantly, in this context) means "little spirit seed." Perspective changes everything. It could well be that the plot on which Disderide built in 1902, the spot where, 80 years later, we opened the Deli, was a significant site in Native history.[8]

Slowly but surely, Europeans (mostly French at first, then, later, English) came into the open land the Ojibwe had been living on for so many centuries. Depending on whom you ask, it's estimated that there were as many as 18 million Native people living in North America before the arrival of the Spanish, English, and French. The Treaty of Detroit in 1807 created seven reservations and removed Native Americans to those locations so that settlers willing and able to pay the federal government could maintain residency in the new territory of Michigan. Ann Arbor was formally founded in 1824, when land speculators John Allen and Elisha Walker Rumsey purchased 640 acres for $800. Michigan became a state 13 years later, in 1837. By the time Rocco Disderide purchased the land to build his store, the number of Native Americans counted on the census had been drastically reduced—only 5,600 souls out of a total Michigan population of 2,420,982. Today, trails near Ann Arbor mark areas where the Huron and Potawatomi peoples once traveled so routinely. There are approximately 69,000 Native Americans in the state, which now has a total population of just under 10 million people.

Africans also arrived in the area. In 1817, 40 years before Rocco was born, Mary Aray, a woman of mixed African American, Native American, and French Canadian ancestry, settled just outside of Ann Arbor. Along with her husband, she owned and worked a large piece of farmland east of town. Mary's son, Asher Aray, later become a prominent conductor on the Underground Railroad, which ran through Michigan en route to safe haven in Canada. His work, and the efforts of others with similar beliefs, gave a glimmer of hope to those seeking freedom from enslavement in the United States.[9]

The spot where we opened the Bakehouse is to the southwest of where the Arays' farm was located. It seems to have stayed farmland, mostly for corn, until Jake Haas (pronounced "Hayes") bought it in the 1970s. A few years later, he started putting up the industrial buildings that house a series of businesses, including what we now know as "Zingerman's Southside." In 1994, ZingTrain got going in Maggie Bayless's attic on Cambridge Street, a residential neighborhood a couple of miles to the south of the Deli. Nearly two decades later, ZingTrain moved into its own space down the block from the Bakehouse. Into that mix, we added the Creamery and the Coffee Company. A few years later, we opened the Candy Manufactory, making artisan candy bars and peanut brittle, hand-crafted confections that would have been in vogue in high-end shops back when Disderide's opened. (I often slip an "extra" bit of each to good customers, the way Rocco apparently did back in his day.) Each business is located on that same unglamorous industrial-park strip and works to produce old-school, artisan offerings and sell them to specialty shops and restaurants in the region and around the country.

Zingerman's Mail Order started, unofficially, around the same time as the Bakehouse. Calls would come from customers who'd moved away and weren't able to find what they'd been buying at the Deli. They wanted to know if we'd ship these things to their new locations. Of course, we said yes. In 1999, we started our website, zingermans.com. We were late to the Internet world by many people's standards, but going slowly as you move into unknown territory can turn out to be a plus. When most dot-coms met a rapid demise, we kept modestly and steadily moving forward through the wilderness of the web. What began as a box or two per day packed in the Deli's basement is today a $14-million business that fills a warehouse and a half about a mile east of the Bakehouse.

Farming and Road Food

Meanwhile, on the west side of town, we opened Zingerman's Roadhouse in 2003. The building, up until a few years earlier, had been a Bill Knapp's. If you're not from this part of the Midwest, the name probably means nothing. But Bill Knapp strung some interesting, mid-20th-century business beads of his own, opening his first restaurant in Battle Creek, Michigan, in 1958. His vision was to open all his establishments right off the exits of the then newly emerging Interstate Highway system.[10]

Bill Knapp's belief was that the nascent highway would soon reign supreme and that travelers would want dependable dining spots that were easy to access from the Interstate. Although his idea was a bit "out there" at the time he began, it worked—Knapp went on to open a chain of 60 or so spots, spread across Michigan, Indiana, Illinois, and Ohio. In his own way, he was a community institution, blending belief, hope and vision, risk taking, generosity, and a whole lot of hard work. His son-in-law, Jerry Hill, who ran the business for years, said, "Mr. Knapp was good with people and terrific with food." Even as the company grew, he insisted on quality. Three commissaries "which paid excruciating detail to ingredients and quality" provided the food to the five-dozen restaurants. After he passed away, quality standards collapsed, a fancy new marketing campaign created an image problem, and the whole company closed in 2002. We took over the empty space, renovated the entire building, and opened up as Zingerman's Roadhouse, serving an even higher quality of regional American comfort food. In 2011, the restaurant won a James Beard award. You can see a couple of the old Bill Knapp's dinner plates on display in the foyer, gifts from caring customers. I'd like to think that his customer- and quality-focused spirit lingers on at the Roadhouse.

Backing up just a bit . . . a year or so after we opened the Roadhouse, managing partner and chef Alex Young started to grow heirloom tomatoes in a small garden plot behind his family home on his day off. He, his wife, and kids were living in Dexter, 20 minutes west of the Deli. The land had been in his wife Kelly's family for four generations—her ancestors had been farming there nearly half a century before Rocco Disderide arrived in the area.

At the time that Kelly's ancestors were getting going, tomatoes did not generally appear on American dining room tables. Tomatoes are native to Central America, but before they arrived in the area of what is now Ann Arbor, they were taken first to Europe and then brought back to North America by European colonists. In order to be eaten regularly, they had to be bred away from the wild, mostly hollow fruits to the juicy, meatier, "modern" types we know today. Much of the breeding work was done by A. W. Livingston in the second half of the 19th century, in the town of Reynoldsburg in central Ohio, about four days by horse to the south of Ann Arbor.

By the end of the 19th century, the tomato tide had turned. In 1897, Campbell's introduced its new condensed tomato soup in tins. Three years later, the soup won a gold medal at the Paris Exposition. It's easy to imagine Rocco Disderide putting a couple dozen cans of this cutting-edge new product on the shelves for modern housewives to buy when he opened his shop. Further down the tightly packed aisle, he might have stocked a newly introduced packaged biscuit that had just been put on the market as "Barnum's Animals." They were sold in the now famous cardboard box with the string on it, creatively designed to be hung as ornaments on Christmas trees. I can hear Rocco chuckling at the novelty of them and then shaking his head in dismay as they flew off the shelves. The retail food world is always full of surprises.

Over the years, we bought more land near Alex's home and named it Cornman Farms (in reference to the anthropomorphic "corn man" that decorated the uniform shirts of the Roadhouse's servers). Gradually Alex and crew expanded the garden rows to include potatoes, peppers, and an array of root vegetables. Most all are grown from heirloom seeds that would likely have been in use back in Rocco Disderide's day. Later, we added cows, pigs, and sheep to the mix. Interestingly, the organic form of livestock management Alex has maintained is probably more similar to what would have been going on in Rocco's day than the factory farming you'd have found by the time we opened the Deli in 1982. Through the work of everyone on the farm, the soil has been restored, possibly to much the same state as when Kelly's ancestors, the Arnolds, first settled in.

On to 2020

In 2007, another big bead slid onto our string when we put together our next (and still current) vision—Zingerman's 2020. It was true to the concept of the Community of Businesses we'd written about in 1994, but we added to it by talking more about opportunity and responsibility, diversity, the environment, the idea of being a learning destination, and more. Like the 2009 vision, it commits us to opening only in the Ann Arbor area: 12 to 18 businesses by the year 2020. It aims for increased employee ownership, improved food and service, enhanced educational efforts, greater diversity, and an increase in fun. It mentions the books we wanted to write. Today, we're past the halfway mark— and only a year or so away from starting the next long-term vision for the organization.

In 2012, we purchased the land adjacent to our farm. The new acreage included an 1834 house and a barn that was likely raised in 1837, the same year Michigan became a state. The U.S. government at the time was actively engaged in getting the Native peoples, primarily Ojibwe, off the land so Europeans could claim it. Unacknowledged differences in beliefs, we know, can quickly lead to conflict, feelings of deception, fear, distrust, and ulti- mately violence. One of the tools of removal the American government used was to "purchase" land from people who never believed land could actually be "owned," any more than you or I would imagine we could charge you for the air you breathe when you walk down the sidewalk in front of the Deli.[11]

In 1827, there were 741 African Americans living in Ann Arbor and 12 free black families farming in the county. In 1837, slavery became illegal in the newly recognized state of Michigan—you could no longer legally own slaves, but escaped slaves were still considered the property of those who had owned them elsewhere and were often caught and returned. Four years earlier, in 1833, the British Empire had abolished slavery. Since Canada was still a colony, slavery was ended there as well, and it quickly became a destination for African people who had escaped enslavement. Ann Arbor was on one of the most prominent routes towards freedom, and the Underground Railroad had a strong presence in the area. In addition to Asher Aray, Dr. Nathan Thomas and Pamela Thomas were conductors on the Underground Railroad near their home, 90 miles west of here, near Kalamazoo. The Thomases' great-great-great-granddaughter, Ali Garrison, worked at the Deli in our early years in business. (The stage production about the Thomases' lives, which Ali worked on with Von Washington Sr., is called *In Search of Giants*.)

People who were sheltered by the Thomases would almost certainly have continued east towards Canada. Many could well have stopped at Gordon Hall, the stately mansion across the road from Cornman Farms. It was the home of Samuel Dexter, the man for whom the town of Dexter is now named. Kelly Young's ancestors lived on the land a bit north of Mr. Dexter's residence and a bit to the west of the barn. "The Arnolds," Chuck Bultman, our barn architect, told me, "had settled there in the 1820s. I immediately realized that if the Arnolds lived only a half-mile away from this property in 1837, they would have probably participated in the original barn raising; it was expected that anyone who could lend a hand would help with all raisings." Barn raisings, like businesses openings, depended on many of the same themes that run through this book—positive belief (why build a barn if you didn't believe in the future?), hope (if you had no hope for a better future, why bother?), vision (barn owners probably imagined themselves and their descendants being on the land for a long time to come), generosity (friends and neighbors always helped), and a whole lot of hard work. Today, after long and loving restoration, that barn is now a Zingerman's business that's helping us make our 2020 vision a reality. In 2015, it was named "Michigan Barn of the Year," a recognition that approximates an Oscar in the world of barn restoration.

As much as we've grown, I believe that we've stayed true to who we were back when we opened. Perhaps one of the nicest compliments we've received was from Boona Pobst, who worked at the Bakehouse within the last few years but was also with us back in the early years. "Having worked at the Deli twenty-five-plus years ago and coming back has been quite an experience," she said. "The difference between then and now is astounding. But what's really impressive is how much the same it is!"

Tying Up the String

It's hard to know where a story begins, and it's equally difficult to determine where it ends. Working with Brenda Ueland's image, I'll just say that at some point the last bead goes on, the string is tied, and the necklace will be worn as it is. The last bead on this thread, at least for now, is Rocco Disderide's death in 1962. Years ending in the number 2 were clearly critical in his life—he arrived in America in 1882, moved to Ann Arbor in 1892, built the building in 1902, retired in 1922, and died in 1962. (The Deli followed that legacy—we opened in 1982.) Rocco was 105 years old when he passed away; at the time, he was Ann Arbor's oldest citizen. In line with what follows in this book— maintaining positive beliefs, staying hopeful, sustaining moderate but manageable levels of concern without descending into gloom and doom—according to his granddaughter Nancy Kindel, Rocco credited his longevity to "never worrying." At the time Rocco opened the shop, the average American's life span was 47 years. He doubled it and then some!

Today, 40 years after Rocco passed away, 170 years after the barn at Cornman Farms was first raised, 114 years after the Disderides built what's now the Deli building, 34 years after Paul and I opened the Deli, Zingerman's is a forward-focused Community of 10 businesses, with nearly $60 million in annual sales and over 700 staff members. We continue to work hard to make and sell traditional food and provide exceptional service, all the while working to be both spiritually and financially healthy, contributing caring experiences to everyone—customers, coworkers, vendors, community—that we interact with. I believe that we have added positively, if always imperfectly, to many lives, both by feeding millions of food-loving people and by employing many thousands of others.

As I write, there are over two dozen partners including three "staff partners" (three staff members who are now full members of the Partners' Group consensus). I believe that thanks to their creative work, our organization will be around for many years to come, hopefully long after Paul and I have left the planet. We're now working on our next business—a restaurant serving traditional Korean food. We've just begun implementing the staff-ownership plan that we wrote into our 2020 vision back in 2007. The bricks on the original building that Bill Suchman restored last year should now last for another century. I can't say that I believe Paul and I will make it to 105 the way Rocco did, but we can hope, right? Whatever happens, it's been a wild and amazing ride.

As always, I'm reluctant to let this book, imperfect as it is, out into the world. In the words of William Butler Yeats, "I have spread my dreams under your feet." I've learned to move forward, through the fear, hoping that the book might be of help, in the belief that people who read books like these care deeply, like to learn, and strive to live lives that are as unique and impactful as Rocco Disderide's building.

A View from
Across the Street

How do you make something immaterial like an idea or a dream into a reality? I don't mean just any idea. I mean those ideas that are important to you, that seem to grow out of who you are, ideas that could set your life path. How do you make that kind of idea a material reality?

All of us would love to know. If you read this book, you will find a case study of just how to make it happen: the creation of Zingerman's Community of Businesses. And more than that, you will find a deeply thoughtful attempt to spell out the thinking and practices needed to accomplish a dream—in this case, a Community of Businesses that enriches an entire community, including the lives of its employees. This is Ari Weinzweig's fourth book about the principles and strategies behind Zingerman's and is, perhaps, his deepest on the subject. Its focus is on the relationship between belief and action, the role our beliefs play in enabling or frustrating our dreams, in clarifying or confusing how we achieve our goals, and in shaping the nature of our relationships. It even contains a delving discussion of how to identify and change any troublesome beliefs. Yet it is an accessible read. You will enjoy and benefit from it even if you don't care a wit about business. All you need are dreams you seek to make real.

Through the good fortune of having Paul (Ari's partner) and Lori Saginaw as dear friends, my family and I have had the accompanying good fortune of seeing much of the Zingerman's story unfold. In the fall of 1987, as we moved from Seattle to Ann Arbor so that I could join the University of Michigan psychology department, we moved into the periwinkle house that faces what is now Zingerman's loading dock. It was also, I know from reading Ari's book, almost directly across from the home that the Disderide family moved into when they first arrived in Ann Arbor. They say the first people you meet when you move to a new place become your best friends. That's what happened to us and the Saginaws. And through that friendship, we got to know a lot of the Zingerman's family—Frank, Maggie, and Ari chief among them. Thus, we gained our vantage point on the development of what I believe is the greatest deli in the nation. Yes, that's my opinion, and I stand by it—the great New York delis notwithstanding. We left Ann Arbor in 1991, but still come back often and . . . well . . . still feel part of the Zingerman's family.

During our time living in Ann Arbor, Paul would sometimes wander across the street for a coffee or a sit on the front porch. A cigarette might occasionally be involved. We'd talk life decisions. Mine seemed so academic. I was more interested in his—moving millions around, devising personnel practices, finding suppliers. Paul's decision making had an efficiency that I admired: make the best one you can, prepare for the consequences, and move on.

This was when he and Ari, as this book describes, were thinking hard about the kind of business they wanted the Deli to be. It had become hugely successful. It had upgraded the entire food and restaurant culture of southeastern Michigan and beyond. Its products and cultural influence—as they are now—were everywhere, from dinner parties to university receptions to weddings. Looking over their shoulders, so to speak, I could see that when success like this arrives, so do lots of questions: Should they franchise? Should they sell? Should they expand their product lines? Did the business offer employees enough opportunity for advancement? Just exactly how should they grow? Ari describes Paul and him feeling a bit lost during this period. Maybe. I just thought that after the stunning success of their original vision, they had a lot of questions to figure out.

Something struck me about how they did this: They didn't cede the design of their business to the principles of the market alone. They didn't ignore these principles; analyses and projections were made, and long, deeply analytic meetings were held. But accompanying all this and, from my vantage point, dominating all of it, was a constant self-examination of their beliefs and values—an examination of the kind of business they wanted and of the kind of businesspeople they wanted to be. As Ari describes here, there were differences between them—Paul focusing relatively more on the spirit of community within and outside of the organization, and Ari focusing relatively more on product and service. But they came together in rigorously applying values to their decision making. To my knowledge, that is how the concept of a "Community" of Zingerman's businesses was born—an idea that triumphed over such promising alternatives as franchising and even outright sale. It was a triumph of values and of a persistently hard look at how a business can further a community. And it has become a powerful model, influencing businesses throughout the nation.

In this book, Ari—the scribe of the partnership—describes how self-examination and understanding the role that beliefs play in shaping our lives and our behavior can build a better business and a better you. In this book, beliefs are conceptualized as nothing less than our understanding of reality. Some beliefs are highly conscious, as in the beliefs that are a prominent part of a strongly held ideology. Other beliefs are deep assumptions about the nature of the world and about ourselves that are buried so far beneath consciousness as to require therapy to access. Yet all of our beliefs shape our perception and understanding of reality and, in so doing, shape our behavior, our reactions to events, our level of cynicism, our ability to persist in the face of challenge, our habits, our happiness, and—to Ari's point here—how we function at work.

Accordingly, some beliefs lead to more constructive behavior in an organization than others do. The revelations in this book are about what those constructive beliefs are, especially as Paul and Ari and the Zingerman's family discovered them over the years. But Ari's larger how-to point is that if you want to have a better organization or a better self—if you want to see your ideals realized, your dreams come true—identify the beliefs that are shaping your experience, get rid of the bad, disadvantaging ones, and replace them with better, more enlightened ones. Bravely he shows you how he has done this in his own life. But most thoroughly, he shows you how this process has been integral to Zingerman's success and development—its "secret sauce"—and how it can be used in business more generally. It is rare that someone so deeply involved in business itself takes the time to so completely probe the psychological substrate of successful business and personal decision making.

This book does that. It provides a rare window into the functioning that underlies good, values-based decision making—going well beyond the typical how-to book on the subject. It is a generous book and an empowering one. Have at it. Enjoy this compelling tale of how self-examination by self-examination, belief change by belief change, an idea of a Community of Businesses was brought to life. And from this tale learn more about how you can bring your ideals to life. You will emerge at the other end of a good read both a better businessperson and a better person.

Claude Steele is a pioneering social psychologist; former provost at the University of California, Berkeley; and author of Whistling Vivaldi and Other Clues to How Stereotypes Affect Us.

rocco disderide and charles caramella standing out front
of disderide's new grocery, circa 1902

INTRODUCTION

Roots, Ecosystems, and Art

One Saturday morning this past summer, I had coffee with a very nice guy, David Nugraha. He'd just recently graduated from the University of Michigan and heard Paul and me speak at the spring commencement ceremony in early May (see page 533). Another bead on the Zingerman's string: It was the first time in U of M history that locals had given the commencement talk. Paul and I politely went at it for a few weeks trying to figure out how the two of us were going to give a coherent, meaningful, 15-minute speech to 50,000 people. We decided to build our talk around the subject of beliefs, how they've informed our growth and success over the years. And to stress our all-important belief: *Everyone has the power to choose the beliefs that will best get them to the life they want to lead.*

If you haven't spoken to that many people at one time, I can tell you, it's a little intimidating. It's not easy to figure out what to say to a football stadium full of people you don't know. I think we pulled it off: no slips of the tongue, no embarrassing gaffes. Paul offered up his passionate belief—which I share—that joy and generosity are critical components of living a great life. I spoke about my belief in the ongoing value of learning, of owning our choices, of appreciating the little things, making kindness part of our everyday existence, and going after greatness in all we do. Finally, I talked about how visioning (as we do it here at Zingerman's) is a tool that I'm totally convinced can help anyone create the life they would like to have. Wanting to lead with the spirit of generosity that Paul had touched on, I offered to get together with any one of the 6,500 graduates in the stadium who wanted help with understanding how they could put visioning to work in their own lives. David Nugraha was one who took me up on the offer.

Three months after the graduation ceremony, we got together for coffee at the Deli. It was my kind of morning—the sun shining (as it had been the morning of commencement); lots of customers eating out on the patio; kids playing behind me; the farmers' market packed with produce; and an energetic, curious person—David—to talk to while sipping a cup of really good Ethiopian (my favorite) coffee. I'd already been at work for a couple of hours when David arrived for our 9:00 a.m. appointment, which meant that books, bread, journals, pens, and pads were spread across the table. I cleared some space and he sat down to chat. After a bit of casual pleasantry, he opened his backpack and took out his copy of the *Guide to Good Leading, Part 1* so I could sign it. In my socially awkward kind of way, interested to learn but unsure of where to start the conversation, I asked if the book had been of help. "It's been really interesting," David said enthusiastically. "I mean I've always loved coming here. The food and the service were always really great. But until I started reading the business books, I just never really thought about why they were so great, or understood all the things that were going on behind the scenes."

He's not alone. Most of our customers, of course, aren't coming to Zingerman's to get a masters in organizational studies—they just want to enjoy a great Reuben, buy a good loaf of bread or a Magic Brownie. It's much the same when we buy an heirloom tomato or a ripe peach at the farmers' market. They look lovely, we appreciate the opportunity to purchase them, and later we'll enjoy eating them. But most of us have little or no sense of what's gone on behind the scenes, or more accurately under the ground, to make that delicious thing what it is.

Uncovering the Power of Beliefs

This brings me directly to the subject of beliefs. For as much as I've studied, taught, and written about both business and self-management over the years, up until recently I'd hardly paid a coffee cup's worth of attention to the ways in which beliefs were impacting my world. In the course of *Parts 1, 2,* and *3* of the series, I wrote 39 separate "Secrets" that I've learned about organizational life. I've covered mission, vision, values, culture, Servant Leadership, self-management, creativity, anarcho-capitalism, and a whole lot more. And yet it's only now, in four of the Secrets that follow—#40 through 43—that beliefs are finally getting their just due.

It turns out that I'd "discovered" a major player in the drama and dreams that make up my life, both personally and professionally. It was as if I'd been focusing on the play itself, the lines of the script, and the way actors sounded from the stage, but altogether ignoring the playwright who wrote the words and set the stage—literally and figuratively—for them to all be there doing what they do. That changed when I began to dial into the details and depths of what I believe, and to look into what others around me believed as well. It blew my mind. It was as if I'd walked through a door in the house I'd long lived in, but with a slight turn to the left instead of going straight ahead, I ended up exploring a suite of magical rooms I never knew existed. The reality wasn't so different from what it had been all along—what had changed was what I saw, felt, and experienced. And understood. Beliefs had always been there, below the surface. As soon as I realized their import, my interest was piqued. In fact, I was fascinated. I started studying them, and I haven't stopped since.

One of my core beliefs, it turns out, is that if I study hard enough, I can learn a lot about almost anything, and that what I learn will then significantly enhance the quality of my life and work. So just as with other subjects that are close to my heart—bread and olive oil, oysters, and anarchists—I began reading every book that seemed relevant, asking questions of anyone who might know more than I did, engaging with others whose values I respected, and reflecting regularly on all of it. The more I learned, the more captivated I became; I wanted to know where beliefs came from, how to bring out the best in them, how to modify my own and help others access theirs. That work has led me to change many of the beliefs that I had before I began. If you keep reading, as you take notes and reflect, converse with others you care about, and then read some more, many of yours will likely be altered as well. Both you and your beliefs, I'm confident, will be better off for the experience. Over time, I'd forecast, your life will grow ever more graceful, more congruent, more coherent.

While you're doing it, though, it won't be easy to track what's happening. As William James observed, "The attempt at introspective analysis . . . is in fact like . . . trying to turn up the gas quickly enough to see how the darkness looks." I had to think about his statement five or six times before I could fully grasp James's point. But now I smile at the idea: Studying our own subconscious is a fascinating exercise in imperfect, if ultimately productive, impossibility. Just making mental inquiries into what's happening in our heads and hearts, it turns out, will alter all our experiences ever after.

I don't regret a minute of the many months of work I've done on the subject. It's been a truly excellent use of my time and my energy. What's so great about it? Every single thing we do, every single thing we experience, everything others around us do is being radically influenced—and, more often than not, initiated—by beliefs. Yours, the people you work with, your staff, your customers, the community. Most of the time we don't even realize that they're at work. Beliefs, I've come to realize over the course of the last few years, are a really big deal. When we ignore them, we pay the price every day. By contrast, when we acknowledge and mindfully manage them, everything in our world starts to make a whole lot more sense, and we stand a far better chance to create the life that we truly want to lead.

Strongly held beliefs are at the core of everything we experience. Every time you eat at Zingerman's or buy one of our products, you're interacting with our beliefs. Whether you share our beliefs is, of course, for you to decide. But since our beliefs underlie most of what follows in the coming pages and also impact everything you taste and everyone you talk to here at Zingerman's, it seems right to get them out in the open now.

If You Want Roses, Plant Rose Bushes

Although they don't have their own line on the balance sheet, beliefs abound in the business world. But since few of us actually acknowledge them for what they are, or understand their import, they're essentially invisible. Beliefs, though, are where almost every action, conscious and unconscious, begins. Whether we know it or not, our beliefs create—for better and for worse, for richer and for poorer—the complex reality in which we struggle to succeed every day.

Thinking agriculturally (as I'm wont to do, given our work with food), I've come to see that beliefs are basically the root systems of our organizations. What shows up above the surface, in "real life," is a reflection of what's already been going on below ground. As anarchist Alexander Berkman writes, "You can't grow a rose from a cactus seed." This statement is so obvious that it seems almost silly to say it aloud. Unfortunately, many of us try to do exactly what Berkman poetically points out won't work—our beliefs are, all too often, out of alignment with what we're trying to attain. Yet we're still surprised each time the "wrong" plant sprouts from the soil. We get angry, frustrated, and depressed. We feel defeated. In response, many of us go out to cut the offender off at the root line. But you know what happens then, right? The same darned plant soon pops up again.

The real work isn't to cut out bad behavior; it's to change the beliefs that put it in motion, to set a different root system in the soil. If we want to grow roses, we'd best begin by getting rose bushes in the ground. So building on the image of beliefs as the root systems of our lives, here's more of what I've been imagining. As you'll see, what started as a small seed of a new belief has grown, blossomed, and begotten an entire metaphorical organizational ecosystem. It looks like this:

- If beliefs are roots, then new beliefs, ideas, products, and people are like seeds planted in our garden. Some, but never all, of those will successfully sprout, and a smaller number still will thrive.

- When beliefs, ideas, and people have already "worked" or existed elsewhere for a while, they arrive in our ecosystem as transplants. Like plants that are dug up and moved to different soil, they will likely take time to acclimate to their new surroundings. Frustrating as it is for the gardener, a good number of them won't survive the shock.

- Over time, strongly held, frequently-acted-upon beliefs become substantial roots. The more energy that flows through them, the bigger they grow. They're rarely fully formed in a fortnight; it takes time for them to develop. As my thoughtful and creative colleague Jenny Tubbs explains, "These beliefs start slowly, and as we gather evidence towards them, they build exponentially." The healthier and deeper the roots, the healthier and more resilient the plants that grow from them will likely be, the more oxygenated the soil, the more flavorful the fruit, the more welcoming the ecosystem to other positive arrivals.

- Positive beliefs tend to yield more positive outcomes; negative beliefs, more negative results; neutral beliefs don't really do either. The more positive and healthier the root system, the less-welcome pests and problems will be. The bigger and more extensive the root (belief) system, the more stable it is, the less subject to erosion, the harder to make change happen. That root system can, of course, be stable in a negative way or stable in a positive way—most organization ecosystems, more than likely, will contain a mix of the two. Long-held, oft-reinforced beliefs are hard to eliminate; leaders who want to pull those beliefs out of long-standing cultures very often fail.

- The beliefs that are most integral to our ethical existence, that we aren't willing to violate even when it would be more convenient to abandon or ignore them, become our values or guiding principles. I imagine them, in this context, as the massive roots one sees on very old trees—the ones that grow up out of the ground and gradually merge, quite marvelously, into the trunk of the tree. They're the roots and beliefs that are most visible to the world, reflected in our everyday behaviors—the ones we advocate for, organize around, and give of ourselves, our time, and our money to support.

Working in a Sustainable Ecosystem

There is, of course, a lot more to a business than the boss and their beliefs. An ecologically sound garden isn't just a big bed of roses. (Even roses have sharp thorns that can prick you if you're not careful.) As in nature, some organizations are healthy and sustainable; others are depleted, even downright depressing. In either case, every element of the system impacts, and is impacted by, the others. Permaculturist Toby Hemenway writes, "Interconnections are what turns a collection of unrelated parts into a functioning system, whether it's a community, a family, or an ecosystem." I see it the same way with business: an organization is also an ecosystem, equally as complex and nuanced as any woods we'll ever walk through or any ocean in which we'll swim. The tomatoes, the sandwich, the staff members, the marketing materials, all the other things we come into contact with are entry points to experience the other elements in play behind the scenes or, in the case of our beliefs, underground. Years of visioning, customer-service training, ingredient study, open-book finance, quality management, and so much more go into every sandwich we serve, brownie we bake, or tomato we pluck from the vine.

A healthy, sustainable organization, I believe, operates much as one of Hemenway's healthy ecological gardens would: in harmony with nature, sometimes self-organizing, a bit messy by modern industrial standards, but with an organic elegance that comes together to create something cutting edge, almost magical. Wendell Berry writes, "An ecosystem, the web of relationships by which a place and its creatures sustain a mutual life, ultimately is mysterious, like life itself." Berry is writing here about nature, but he could just as well be talking about business. If you're thinking "Well, how does it all fit together?" you're asking a good question. Berry wonders the same thing: "We appear to be deficient in learning or teaching a competent concern for the way that parts are joined. We certainly are not learning or teaching adequately the arts of forming parts into wholes, or the arts of preserving the formal integrity of the things we receive as wholes already."

The work on this book has helped me piece together an organizational "whole," a sustainable, ecologically sound metaphor for all of this. It's my humble attempt to do the work that Berry is challenging us to do. To make elegant "wholes" out of parts, to take the elements of the organization that the industrial world typically tends to view only in isolation and integrate them instead into a more holistic model. The question in this context is this: *How do the beliefs, the roots, fit with the rest of the ecosystem in which we're operating?* What follows is my effort to carry this metaphor all the way through, to examine how parts are formed into wholes, and how we can influence each part to make our organizations into flourishing ecosystems.

Organizational culture, as I've come to view it in this context, can be considered as the soil. Hemenway declares, "An exuberantly healthy soil is the cornerstone of a sustainable garden." It's also, I believe, the basis for a sustainable business. Everything—people, ideas, products, even other beliefs—grows in, and is influenced by, it. When the soil is poor, only the most resilient of seeds—or those that do well in poisoned or damaged settings—will survive. The healthier the soil, the more nutrients it contains, the better everything growing in it will do.

It's much the same in our workplaces as it is in the woods. Writing early in the 20th century, William Albrecht said, "[R]ebuilding and conserving our soils is the surest guarantee of the future health and strength of the nation." He viewed the soil as "the 'creative material' of most of the basic needs of life." A rich, positive organizational culture can do wonders for the quality of life of anyone working within it.

"Feeding the soil engages us in a partnership that benefits all," Hemenway says. "Life builds on life. Whatever we plant in this rich earth will have a far greater chance of thriving; whatever we hope to feed, whether wildlife, ourselves, or perhaps just our senses, will be deeply nourished. And serendipities we never hoped for—a surprising new wildflower, a rare butterfly . . . —will grace our lives almost daily." If you want to develop more positive beliefs in your organization, one of the best ways to do that is to enrich the culture. The stronger and more positive we make it, the more we stay away from pesticides and poisons, the better everything we plant in it will do. Culture building is critical work. Organic-gardening guru Eliot Coleman charges growers to "feed the soil, not the plant."

Looking up from there, hope is the sun. It lights our lives, drawing us towards its bright, soul-enriching warmth. As John Todd explains, all natural organic plant communities "have the ability to self-organize in the presence of sunlight." Hope helps pull people and ideas up, moving us forward—expansively and effectively—to a better future. Just as you see plants in nature leaning radically to one side to seek the sun, so too people will shape their behaviors and direction in life to lean towards the steadiest sources of hope that appear. With hope, much is possible.

The spirit of generosity is the water we need to moisten and enliven things in our cultural soil. Better quality soil is able to hold much more water than parched, essentially dead conventional soil. In nature, good soil contributes to plant growth and the plants return the favor; in the forest, tall trees and their root systems hold moisture in the soil. The corollaries in business? A healthier culture is always a more generous one. And the best people in an organization will effectively preserve and enhance generosity in the workplace.

The Needle and the Damage Done

You can't grow a rose from a cactus seed, but you can grow a cactus. I got to thinking the other day about what type of plants grow best in dry, difficult climates. Here in the United States, we all know it's cacti. It makes perfect sense that plants—or people—raised in harsh, ungenerous settings tend to develop prickly needles to protect themselves. It's practical for the plant, but it can prove painful to others who try to connect.

The people and products that make up our day-to-day existences are the plants that grow in our ecosystems. They're the presences that are tangible and visible to the casual observer: the people we hire and work with, the products we sell and serve, the services we deliver. All have beliefs beneath the surface, are informed by the soil/culture, are aided in growing through hope, and are nourished by the spirit of generosity.

Our most effective people are like tall trees in a natural ecosystem. They're rooted in the soil but shoot high up into the sky. They contribute to every element of the organization, hopefully at a high level. As Hemenway says,

> Trees reach deep into the earth for nutrients and water, and far and wide into the sky for solar power. They are life's largest, most effective, natural collectors of energy and matter. So by incorporating trees as

integral elements of the garden, we're putting heavy hitters on our team. Trees, though they share space with many other species, define the forest garden and distinguish it from other landscapes.

In the same way, effective leaders have deep roots in the cultural soil; they grow upward, collecting energy and then offering it to the rest of the organization. Through their presence, they enhance the entire ecosystem.

Systems are simply processes that help the ecosystem operate more effectively. I suppose in a garden they might be trellises or pruning routines. Here, in this book, they include the recipe for changing our beliefs, our Six-Pointed Hope Star, and our work around vision writing. They help us keep our culture rich and our levels of hope and generosity high.

Our mission statement, in this model, stays as we've so long described it. (See Secret #5, in *Part 1*, for more on missions.) It's the North Star. When it's dark out, when we've lost our sense of direction, tracking towards it can help any of us keep moving in the right general direction.

Purpose is embedded within our mission statement; it's in the first question missions are meant to answer: "Why do we do what we do?" In this context, purpose is the air we all need to breathe. We can't see it, but it's essential to our existence. When there's little purpose, breathing—or functioning at work—becomes difficult. When it's completely absent, we suffocate and slowly die.

The more I work with this idea of organization as ecosystem, with all of these interlocking elements well ensconced in natural beauty, the deeper the root of my belief has grown. I've begun to teach it, to explain it to friends and colleagues, to repeatedly turn it over in my mind. I feel more at peace, more grounded with it all the time. Living in harmony with nature makes sense.

Life on the Edge

Toby Hemenway writes of nature: "Edges are where things happen. Where a forest meets the prairie, where a river flows into the sea, or at nearly any other boundary between two ecosystems.... The edge is richer than what is on either side." The same is generally true for creativity. Robert Bilder, a psychiatry and psychology professor at UCLA's Semel Institute for Neuroscience and Human Behavior, writes, "The truly creative changes and the big shifts occur right at the edge of chaos." In everyday language, we even call it the "creative edge." Why? Because one of the key components of creativity is connecting things that aren't otherwise connected. Where does that happen most? On the edge—where otherwise unconnected concepts and communities meet up in new and interesting ways. Interestingly, G. K. Chesterton described anarchism as "the borderland of thought."

Crafting a Healthy Ecosystem Takes a Long Time

So, you might wonder, which element of this ecosystem is most important? What's the secret to making it work? What's that single thing smart CEOs are supposed to start with?

The simple answer, per my anarchistic wont, is that there isn't one. *Everything and everyone matters.* Without any single element—even the small ones—the ecology of the system will be altered. In the wild, the loss of a seemingly insignificant type of insect can eventually lead to a complete crop collapse. It's the same in business. While we can theorize and measure all we want, the truth is that every part of our work, every person we employ, matters, and each is impacting, even if quietly, everything else we do.

Crafting a business with beauty and elegance takes patience and persistence. And there's always much more happening behind the scenes, below the soil line, than the average consumer imagines. While I can show up with no notice at the farmers' market to buy an heirloom tomato, the farmer spent a year cleaning the fields, preparing them for the winter, making a plan for spring planting, ordering seeds, prepping the soil, fertilizing, planting, watering, weeding, watching, waiting . . . all with the hope and belief that by the time the peak of summer arrives, the vines will have a lot of wonderful, fully ripe, fantastically flavorful tomatoes to be picked and taken to market.

The story starts years earlier still. Building healthy soil, studying seeds, monitoring growing patterns, and managing the soil takes a long time. Some of the seed varieties we plant at Cornman Farms are over a hundred years old. And it all comes together somehow in the tomato I take home. As third-generation farmer Mas Masumoto writes, "It's almost a mantra for small, sustainable organic farmers . . . Farming stories means you bring in the entire complex—working with nature, the land, the family, the larger social issue of the history of the farmworkers, their wages, and one's own personal legacy." The same is true here at Zingerman's for a slice of Jewish rye bread; a syphon pot of Brazilian Sweet Yellow coffee; a pinch of semiwild, freshly ground Tribal black pepper from India; and all the people who have a part in producing, packing, and preparing them.

When We Violate Nature, We Pay a Big Price

The idea of an organization or business as a working ecosystem might seem mysterious. But I believe there is a coherent method and model to the magic. As you might already know if you've read the earlier volumes in this series, I'm a big believer in what I've come to call the "Natural Laws of Business." Having worked with, and on, them for a decade now (with the help of Paul, who conceived of the construct in the first place), I'm convinced that *all* successful organizations (and actually all successful human beings) are basically living in harmony with those laws. The more we honor them, and hence nature, the better we feel, the stronger our energy, the more sustainable our ecosystem, the better off everyone involved will be.

Wendell Berry writes, "The health of the context—the body, the community, the ecosystem—would reveal the health of the work." When we do good work, in harmony with nature, everyone benefits. Life remains imperfect, but a whole lot of good things are likely to happen. When we're out of synch, when we perceive our business as a series of parts instead of as a whole, things will begin to come apart. When industrialists try to study the organizational ecosystem, they often do it in pieces, slicing things into statistically separate sections, disconnecting what's naturally connected. And then, data in hand, they use what they've learned to discard seemingly inefficient elements and keep only the most productive. I believe that trouble follows from this strategy. As Masanobu Fukuoka writes in his wonderful book *The One-Straw Revolution*, "Now scientists just see the leaves and fruit instead of seeing the whole plant, especially the root. The farmer just sees the fruit. Some people just see the rice. That is why the soil is depleted."

In my business as ecosystem setup, when we isolate people and processes from each other, the culture is poorer for it. People in unhealthy organizations approach their work as if it were unrelated to what's going on around them. They never connect what happens in their daily lives to the beliefs that underlie their behaviors. They view work as an annoyance they need to tolerate to make a living. They don't see the connection between the quality of their work and the quality of their lives. You can see the symptoms in their surroundings. When we violate nature, we end up paying a big price. As Fukuoka says, "If we throw mother nature out the window, she comes back in the door with a pitchfork."

When we do our work selfishly, without regard for the elegance of our ecosystem and all its elements, we end up with erosion rather than good energy, disease instead of delight. The ecosystem becomes vulnerable, its elements competing for scarce resources. New plants don't do well. Insects invade and pests proliferate. "And what, precisely, is destroyed?" author Stephen Cope asks. And he answers, "Energy is destroyed first. Those shining eyes. And then faith. And then hope. And then life itself."

What Cope is describing can be seen all over the country. The industrial world works hard—too hard, and to a fault—to simplify and separate, put things into silos and prioritize the "key elements," the "top people," the "highest priorities." That approach, quite simply, doesn't work. This situation is endemic. I experience it as the "Energy Crisis in the American Workplace" (see Secret #19, in *Part 2*), with disengagement, apathy, even anger ruling the day. Toby Hemenway believes that "[c]onventional landscapes have torn the web of nature. Important threads are missing." It's the same, I'm convinced, in business. Having traveled the world a fair bit, I believe this is an international issue. It ought, by all rights, to be cause for great concern. But it rarely seems to come up. And when it does, hardly anyone seems to pay attention.

I reflect regularly on a story told by the insightful economist E. F. Schumacher. A *London Times* article, he said, had reported on the "mindless, repetitive boredom of working on a factory assembly line." The article argued that this work "destroys initiative and rots brains, yet millions of British workers are committed to it for most of their lives." If the report, Schumacher observed, were about birds being killed by oil spills, workers' bodies poisoned by petrochemicals, or employees physically beaten by their bosses, it would inspire an immediate outcry, with lawsuits likely to follow. But the article (and others like it) seemed to evoke no anger. The degradation of spirit caused little consternation. "Workers' brains, minds and souls," Schumacher laments, must be "a different matter."

Schumacher's story gets me thinking back to Wendell Berry's bold statement: "The difference between blasting in the coal fields and erosion in the corn and soybean fields is only that erosion is slower." I believe that Schumacher is right to wonder aloud why hardly anyone seems bothered by bad, spirit-deadening work? Is it only because "erosion is slower"? And if so many people are now, rightfully, working on raising minimum wage, why isn't there also a movement, as Ron Lippitt advocated, to "raise the appreciative and spiritual standard of living"?

Living the Natural Laws, Doing Business in a Sustainable Way

I believe we can do better. While it may take a bit more work in the here and now, a belief in the efficacy of the Natural Laws of Business (see page 306 for a refresher on what they are) begets a different, more rewarding set of ecologically sound results. It's about viewing our work as a positive thing; about embracing *all* the elements of the ecosystem; about appreciating everyone who works here, every customer, and every product; about learning, vocation, love, hope, and generosity; about synergy and sustainability. One generous act brings positive energy back in return. Instead of everyone involved feeling exhausted and drained, we can head home most days feeling better than when we got out of bed.

Working in a holistic way like this requires adjusting some long-held, socially accepted beliefs. This Sunday morning, for example, I went to work at 7:00 a.m. It's something most people in the typical business world would slough off as workaholic silliness, or maybe an unhealthy example of control issues. But I didn't feel burdened at all, nor did I go into work because I was worried about anything going wrong. I felt good when I got there. I drank good coffee and took a break to journal for half an hour. Then I interviewed a long-time staff member who's applying for a new position in our organization, and her enthusiasm and excitement left me feeling super energized. She texted me after the interview: "I was nearly skipping to my car! High five!" I also met with a former staffer who's now working to create a cooperative garden where people in need in the community can reground and learn to grow their own produce. By the time we were done with that conversation, I was jazzed. He wrote me an hour after we'd finished to say, "The pleasure in our meeting today is beyond words." When I left for home later that morning, I felt fantastic, which, to me, is what sustainable business is all about. It's not ever easy, and it takes years of steady, patient, imperfect, mindful, collaborative effort. But when it goes well, it is rewarding—good energy builds on itself, and everyone comes out a winner.

Work, in this context, isn't something one puts up with just to get paid; it's a productive, positive, soul-enhancing activity that helps all involved to feel and do better. It works. Hemenway believes, "We can restore many of those broken links, and work with nature to lessen our own load, not to mention the cost to the environment." It's energizing, not exhausting. And ultimately, "the garden becomes less work, less prone to problems, and vastly more like the dynamic vibrant landscapes found in nature."

What follows in this book is the opposite of the typical "flavor of the day" management that's so endemic in the mainstream business world. Leaders who believe the "magic answer" is just around the corner shift their business philosophy every six months, looking for a quick, unnatural fix. Fukuoka poses the question, "I wonder how it is that people's philosophies have come to spin faster than the changing seasons." I share his concern. I believe the real answers, aligned with nature, are much more complex and take a lot longer to implement. They require us to change a lot of what we believe about work and business. And, often, about ourselves as well.

Fukuoka's approach to farming is a productive one for us to learn from. The business world at large looks for fast food; Fukuoka wants to work slowly. They want easy solutions; Fukuoka looks for ways to work hard at what he believes matters. They want to know the "secret"; Fukuoka knows there isn't one. They ride roughshod over nature; he lives in harmony with it. His approach is to watch, read, and respond in a respectful and productive, ecosystem-sensitive way. It's a framework that feels right to me, one that's aligned with human nature and reinforces my positive beliefs in humankind. Fukuoka looks at his work as part of one world, one life, one community, one sustainable farm. He writes, "My natural farming has no distinction of trees, leaves, roots." Life comes together nicely when we can see things more holistically. When it's working well, it's a wonderful thing.

Sixty days or so after he and I had coffee at the Deli that morning, David Nugraha, newly earned business degree in hand, accepted a position in the retail shop at the Bakehouse. He's proven a wonderful new addition to our organizational ecosystem. At the end of the day, we evaluate the effectiveness of our work at Zingerman's on the impact we have on others, the quality of the experience we deliver to customers and the community. And to coworkers. Four weeks after he started, David sent me this email:

Today I noticed that I've been working at Zingerman's for one month and I wanted to thank you (along with Tracie Wolfe from HR and a few other people) for making all of this possible for me! Every day I learn something new, whether it's about great food, about positive business, about excellent customer service, or about myself. Being a part of Zingerman's encourages me to continuously improve. Above all, I've had

*a tremendous amount of fun and joy working at the Bakeshop. Work
actually cheers me up—something that I never thought was possible!*

As you would imagine from his note, David's presence in the Bakeshop
has been really positive. As shop manager John Rolfe-Chin says, "David is a
pleasure to work with." Everyone in the ecosystem is doing better for it. As in
nature, we're all impacting each other. David and I, and you and everyone here
at Zingerman's—all of our beliefs and our actions, our personalities and our
principles, are, it seems clear to me now, totally interconnected. The enthusiasm
that David brings when he waits on guests begins with his own beliefs, which
have now been impacted significantly by the rich and positive culture at the
Bakehouse. He was also, it sounds like, influenced by my beliefs, which were,
in turn, touched by Paul's, whose were affected by probably hundreds of other
people including his grandfather, who as he mentioned in our commencement
address was particularly important in the formation of his grandson's beliefs.
When David or one of his colleagues waits on you when you come in to buy
a loaf of bread or maybe a couple of Magic Brownies, we hope that you will
benefit also. And, when he moves on at some point, he will have gained from
the experience as well. As John says, "I think David will leave here with a lot of
the firsthand experience he was looking to gain to apply towards his personal
vision!"

Hemenway supports that view. "Each organism," he writes, "is tied to
many others. It's this interconnectedness that gives nature strength. Think of a
net or a web: Snip one thread, and the net still functions, because all the other
connections are holding it together." A *holistic* approach to organizational life,
then, sees beliefs not as a separate sidebar to be studied in our spare time but
as an integral component of the living, breathing businesses in which we go to
work every day. The correlation is clear. The more positive our beliefs, the more
positive the likely outcomes. The healthier our cultural soil, the better everything and everyone in it are likely to be. When we do our work well, I believe,
we can *all* win.

The bottom line is that when you buy our bread, you're also buying our
beliefs. When people like David choose to work here, they're buying our beliefs,
too. Somewhere in the mix, maybe Rocco Disderide's building has bestowed a
bit of a spiritual blessing on us all as well. If these images and ideas resonate,
then this book will, I'm confident, benefit you as well. We, in turn, will benefit
from you being part of it all. I'm honored to welcome you into our ecosystem.

Eco-quivalents

The parallels between Toby Hemenway's holistic views on permaculture and the way that we're striving to work here are just too striking not to place side by side. Here you go.

Hemenway's Characteristics of a Healthy Sustainable Ecosystem in Nature	Our Organizational Version of a Healthy Ecosystem at Zingerman's
"Deep soil that is rich in nutrients and organic matter."	A rich, positive, appreciative culture.
"Plants that draw fertility from deep in the earth, from the air and from rainwater."	People and processes that emerge from deeply held positive beliefs, a strong sense of purpose, and a spirit of generosity.
"Many layers of vegetation to create niches for other creatures."	Diversity and inclusion.
"Mutually helpful relationships among plants, insects, birds, microbes, mammals, and all other inhabitants, including people."	A collaborative, caring, synergistic environment.
"Increasingly closed cycles; that is, over time, the garden should require fewer supplies from outside, producing most of its own fertilizer, mulch, seeds, new plants, and so on. Except for the harvest, little from the garden is lost by leaching and erosion—it's all recycled."	Creating a sustainable energy cycle within the organization. By living in harmony with the Natural Laws of Business, we build each other's energy every day; there's not a big need for outside "enthusiasm builders." Bringing out the creativity of all involved, ideas and people are usually developed from the inside.
"Nothing in nature does just one thing."	Open-book finance, open meetings, and our One + One work, where we encourage people to get involved in other parts of the organization.
In the sustainable garden, "[c]ontinuity is the rule, unlike the annual garden. Most of nature remains standing through the changing years."	Building a business that's meant to last, one that can be creatively passed on, that can continue to contribute to the community for decades.

Jim Dorman, Accountant, Zingerman's Mail Order

I think everyone should work at Zingerman's at some point. How Zingerman's integrates belief in the mission of running a profitable business and individual development and care is amazing. Zingerman's says the individual is important, as many businesses do, but Zingerman's backs this up with big investments in training, development, and allowing people the time to make things better.

biLL Suchman repairing the bricks on the deLi building in 2015

Cast of Characters

What follows is intended to help you keep track of the characters I reference regularly in the book. If you're starting the series here with Part 4, you may not be familiar with them all. I like to think of it also as a nod to my roots as a student of Russian history—these sorts of lists are commonly found in the front matter of 19th-century Russian novels.

Adam Grant: A University of Michigan PhD in organizational psychology. Grant's book *Give and Take: A Revolutionary Approach to Success* has helped shape the thinking of many progressive business leaders in regard to generosity. He currently teaches at the Wharton School of Business.

Alexander Berkman: Late-19th- and early-20th-century anarchist. Born in Russia, lived for 30 years in the United States before being expelled in 1917 along with his colleague, friend, and former lover, Emma Goldman. He edited *Mother Earth*, the anarchist monthly from New York for many years, and later published his own journal, *The Blast*, from San Francisco. His book *Prison Memoirs of an Anarchist* is still considered one the best examples of prison literature.

Álvar Nuñez Cabeza de Vaca: A Spanish explorer of the New World in the early 15th century. He traveled extensively among the Native peoples of the American Southwest. He wrote extensively about his cultural learnings. Later he was appointed governor of what is now Argentina.

Anaïs Nin: Author, poet, and diarist. Considered one of the best-ever writers of erotica.

Anese Cavanaugh: Leadership coach and expert on the development of positive organizational culture. Anese is the woman who first taught me about the idea of energy management (see Secrets #20 and 21, in *Part 2*). Her recently released book is titled *Contagious Culture*.

Ashanti Alston: Former Black Panther, a provocative thinker, writer, and advocate for anarchism and the African American community.

Ashley Montagu: Born Israel Ehrenberg, Montagu was a British American anthropologist who became one of the leading advocates for humanism. His studies on race and gender were highly influential.

Bill Suchman: Ann Arbor mason and specialist in old brick restoration.

Bo Burlingham: Business writer and editor-at-large for *Inc.* magazine. He coauthored *The Great Game of Business*, the seminal work on open-book finance, with Jack Stack, and then wrote *Small Giants* and *Finish Big*.

Bob and Judith Wright: Educators, speakers, coaches, and proponents of transformational leadership. They write, teach, and run the Wright Institute with the stated goal of helping their clients live spectacular lives.

Brenda Ueland: A formidable feminist, writer, and free thinker. Born in 1891 in Minnesota, Ueland's 1937 book *If You Really Want to Write: A Book about Art, Independence and Spirit* literally changed my life. Carl Sandburg called it "the best book ever written on how to write." She lived her life by two rules: to tell the truth, and to not do anything she didn't want to.

Buenaventura Durruti: A central figure of Spanish anarchism. He died in battle during the Spanish Civil War.

Carl Jung: Pioneering Swiss psychologist and writer who developed some of the core approaches of modern psychology, including the idea of archetypes, introversion and extroversion, and the psychology of the unconscious.

Carl Rogers: Rogers grew up in suburban Chicago and is generally considered to be one of the most important psychologists of the 20th century. His work focused on the importance of positive self-concept and his belief that "unconditional positive regard"—accepting a person as they truly are—was critical to well-being. His work on learning-centered teaching is one of the foundations of the Bottom Line Training approach we use at Zingerman's.

Carl Sandburg: Illinois-born, Chicago-based late-19th- and early-20th-century American poet. His poems about Chicago were a prominent part of my early exposure to writing. Sandburg had strong radical and anarchist roots and spoke and wrote regularly for the cause of the common man in society. In his early years, he drove a milk wagon and worked as a porter, farmer, and coal carrier before becoming a journalist, writer, and professional poet. Sandburg was the first white man to be honored by the NAACP. He has gained great acclaim for his children's books, biographies, newspaper journalism, and poetry.

Carol Dweck: Psychologist and author, and one of the country's leading experts in the study of motivation.

Christopher Alexander: Austrian-born architect and author of many books, including *A Pattern Language: Towns, Buildings, Construction* and *The Timeless Way of Building*. He advocates for design based on a holistic, human-centered approach.

Claude Bristol: Born in 1891, Bristol was a journalist and author of the ahead-of-its-time book *The Magic of Believing*.

Claude Steele: Social psychologist and author of *Whistling Vivaldi*. Claude served as provost and vice chancellor at the University of California, Berkeley. He taught at the University of Michigan in the late 1980s when he and his wife, Dorothy, lived on Kingsley Street, a few doors down from the Deli and directly opposite the Disderide family's original Ann Arbor home. Born and raised in Chicago, he got his undergraduate degree at Hiram College in Ohio, where anarchist Ammon Hennacy had done the same half a century earlier. He has written extensively and insightfully on race and ethnicity, stereotyping, and the importance of sound self-image.

C. L. R. James: Radical Trinidadian historian, journalist, author, and social theorist.

Colin Ward: One of the great British anarchist thinkers and writers of the 20th century. His focus on self-managed, nonhierarchical forms of organization is highly relevant for progressive business thinkers.

Czesław Miłosz: Nobel Prize–winning Polish poet, writer, and diplomat.

Dan Barber: Award-winning chef and founder of Blue Hill restaurant in New York City and Stone Barns in upstate New York. His book, *The Third Plate*, is an insightful look into our food system.

David Graeber: Anthropologist, anarchist, and author. He currently teaches at the London School of Economics.

David Whyte: Poet, writer, and advocate for the power of conversation. His books are all powerful insights into the modern-day work world; *Crossing the Unknown Sea* is one of my favorites.

Dean Tucker: A former Boeing systems engineer who went on to found the Center for Teleocracy (purpose-driven management). His book *Using the Power of Purpose* is highly recommended.

Edgar Schein: Former professor at the MIT Sloan School of Management and one of the earliest advocates for the study of organizational culture.

E. F. "Fritz" Schumacher: One of the most influential economists of the late 20th century. He took a very different tack from most of his colleagues, encouraging the development of human-centered economics. His books—*Small is Beautiful: A Study of Economics as if People Mattered* and *Good Work*—remain at the cutting edge of creative business thinking.

Eli Genisio: A lifelong Zingerman's customer and friend. Eli was five years old at the time this book was published.

Élie Reclus: French anarchist, ethnographer, and writer.

Élisée Reclus: Younger brother of Élie, anarchist, writer, and geographer who studied and wrote about non-European cultures around the world. He was a vegetarian who advocated for ecology and respect for nature long before the urgency of those issues came to the fore.

Émile Armand: Late-19th- and early-20th-century French individualist anarchist. He wrote extensively about the import of living and thinking freely in the here and now and not waiting for a large-scale social revolution to begin being true to oneself.

Emma Goldman: Known by the tongue-in-cheek title "Queen of the Anarchists." Goldman arrived in the United States from her native Lithuania in 1885 at the age of 16. She went on to become one of the world's most renowned anarchist speakers and writers, an outspoken advocate for freedom, women's rights, and social equity. Her creative thinking was, I believe, far ahead of its time.

Errico Malatesta: Late-19th- and early-20th-century Italian anarchist who spent a good deal of time living in both the United States and Britain. His writing and speaking were highly influential.

Étienne de La Boétie: 16th-century French writer, jurist, and anarchist. His

"Discourse on Voluntary Servitude" is one of the great early essays to take an anarchist approach to traditional society.

Francisco Ferrer: Late-19th and early-20th century anarchist educator and founder of the Modern Schools. In the fall of 1909, he was executed by the Spanish government, causing an international outcry. The New York Ferrer Center Modern School, where Emma Goldman and Robert Henri taught, was named for him.

Gary Snyder: Pulitzer Prize–winning poet whose colleagues included Allen Ginsberg and Jack Kerouac. Lawrence Ferlinghetti called him "the Thoreau of the Beat Generation." Gary studied and practiced Buddhism with great seriousness and in 1961 published the essay "Buddhist Anarchism."

Gina Athena Ulysse: Performance artist, poet, professor of anthropology at Wesleyan University, and creative advocate for the people, culture, and traditions of her homeland, Haiti.

G. K. Chesterton: English writer, humorist, poet, and philosopher, often referred to as the "Prince of Paradox."

Gustav Landauer: A pacifist anarchist from Germany whose late-19th- and early-20th-century writings have been hugely inspirational to me and others. His grandson was the film director Mike Nichols.

Hadley Cantril: A pioneer in the fields of social psychology and statistical polling. He designed a self-anchoring scale for measuring hope, which came to be known more commonly as Cantril's Ladder. He also published a book about the public reaction to Orson Welles's *War of the Worlds* radio broadcast, called *The Invasion from Mars.* Cantril was one of the people who noticed the paradoxical polling result that a majority of Americans opposed "big government" but were simultaneously supportive of expanding social programs.

Henry David Thoreau: 19th-century poet, abolitionist, anarchist, and one of the great American thinkers of his era.

Howard Ehrlich: Author and anarchist. Long-time editor of the journal *Social Anarchism.*

Howard Zinn: American professor of political science, with a bit of an anarchist approach. He wrote many books, including *A People's History of the United States.*

Hugh MacLeod: British author and cartoonist. He wrote one of my favorite books, *Ignore Everybody*.

Isaac Asimov: Russian-born, American-raised science-fiction writer. I read his work extensively in my early teen years but discovered his insightful views on life and writing only recently. In Russia, his family were millers, and their last name, Asimov, is adapted from the Russian word for winter wheat. In the United States, his family owned candy stores, where Asimov read the many magazines available for sale and became fascinated with the written word. Asimov authored over 500 books in his lifetime.

Jay Sandweiss: Ann Arbor–based physician, a student of both Western and Eastern medical practices and a nationally known lecturer on the subject of integrative medicine.

Jim Morrison: Songwriter, poet and lead singer of the Doors. He studied and referenced the surrealist poets, of whom Suzanne Césaire was one.

Jo Labadie: Michigan-born, Detroit-based anarchist printer, writer, and speaker. In 1911, he donated his collection of books, pamphlets, and other printed material to the University of Michigan. Today, the Labadie Collection is on the seventh and eighth floors of the University's Graduate Library. It's there that the seeds of anarchist insights were first planted in my mind.

John Todd: A biologist who has become known for his creative ecological design work—looking to nature to find ways to holistically design solutions for things such as water treatment and waste management.

Joseph Ishill: Rumanian-born Jewish anarchist who immigrated to the United States in 1909 and went on to start Oriole Press. Ishill printed and published some of the most beautiful books I've ever seen. All were hand-printed and bound, and they reflected the anarchist ethos in both their aesthetic sense and their provocative content.

Julia Cameron: Chicago-born teacher, speaker, and author of *The Artist's Way*, which advocates effectively for the power of the creative spirit in helping us lead more engaged, rewarding, and interesting lives.

Kevin Bermingham: British project manager and author of *Change Your Limiting Beliefs*. His mission is "to help people take control of their life by planning ahead and then achieving a significant goal within ninety days. My first step is always to help people change the beliefs that have held them back for so long."

Larry Lippitt: Author of *Preferred Futuring* and the son of Ron Lippitt, the man who developed the original thinking behind what we now refer to at Zingerman's as "visioning."

Leda Rafanelli: Early- to mid-20th-century Italian anarchist. Born Catholic, she converted to Islam at age 20 and developed her own version of anarchism, Islam, feminism and individualism.

Lewis Richmond: Zen Buddhist teacher, monk, and writer. His most recent book is *Aging as a Spiritual Practice*.

Maia Genisio: A lifelong Zingerman's customer, colleague, and friend. My conversations with Maia have inspired many insights over the years. At the time of publication, Maia was nine years old.

Margaret Wheatley: Progressive business thinker, organizational behavior expert, and author. All her books are thought provoking; *Turning to One Another: Simple Conversations to Restore Hope to the Future* is one of my favorites.

Marge Piercy: Poet, science-fiction writer, feminist, forcefully creative thinker, and also a University of Michigan graduate.

Maria Popova: Bulgarian-born, New York–based blogger, writer, and essayist who started the insightful online weekly *Brain Pickings*.

Martin Luther King Jr.: Baptist minister and humanitarian leader of the American Civil Rights movement.

Martin Seligman: Generally acknowledged as the father of positive psychology. His books and articles on the subject offer great insight into how to build a positive workplace.

Masanobu Fukuoka: Japanese farmer and philosopher whose focus on natural, no-till farming has inspired many modern-day sustainable growers. He's the author of *The One-Straw Revolution*.

Matthieu Ricard: A French-born Buddhist monk who now lives in Nepal. Ricard has written extensively and insightfully on human happiness and well-being. His father was the French philosopher and writer Jean-François Revel. They coauthored the book *The Monk and the Philosopher*, which became a bestseller in Europe.

Meg Noodin: Ojibwe language teacher, poet, writer, editor, and all-around insightful leader at the University of Michigan, and now in her new position at the University of Wisconsin–Milwaukee.

Melvin Parson: Former Zingerman's staffer who started the We the People Growers Association in Ypsilanti, Michigan.

Mikhail Bakunin: 19th century Russian anarchist. Along with Peter Kropotkin, among the most important early contributors to anarchist thinking.

Mohatma Gandhi: Late-19th- and early-20th-century leader of the Indian independence movement. An advocate of decentralization and direct democracy.

Murray Bookchin: A mid- to late-20th-century American anarchist and radical advocate for positive ecology and the environment.

Oana Branzei: Professor of strategy at Ivey Business School, University of Western Ontario. She did a two-year stint as a visiting professor at the University of Michigan's Ross School of Business and Center for Positive Organizational Studies.

Oscar Wilde: Late-19th-century Anglo-Irish writer, poet, and playwright. After reading the work of Peter Kropotkin, he adopted an anarchist approach, best presented in his essay "The Soul of Man under Socialism." His *Ballad of Reading Gaol*, a long and powerful poem written from prison, was his last formal work.

Osho: Indian mystic, guru, and teacher. His many books (transcribed from his talks) are provocative and very anarchistic in their orientation.

Patrick Hoban: Good friend, conversation partner, and founder of Probility Physical Therapy.

Paul Avrich: Perhaps the most prominent modern-day writer about anarchists. He sought to show his students at Queens College, City University of New York, and his readers his "affection and sense of solidarity with anarchists as people, rather than as militants." For me, at least, he succeeded. His oral history book, *Anarchist Voices*, is one that greatly resonated with me.

Paul Cudenec: Anarchist writer, born in England, now living in France.

Paul Goodman: 20th-century American anarchist, poet, playwright, philosopher, and creative antagonist.

Paul Hawken: Cofounder of Smith & Hawken and author of *Growing a Business.*

Paul Saginaw: The cofounding partner of our organization. Paul and I have worked together for nearly 40 years, the last 34 of them as partners at Zingerman's. Paul's insight, guidance, patience, generosity of spirit, and everything else are imprinted all over our organization, my beliefs, and this book.

Paul Watzlawick: Austrian-born philosopher, psychiatrist, and leading exponent of Constructivist theory. I love his insight that "one cannot not communicate."

Peter Block: Speaker, trainer, and author of many books. His work has had a huge impact on our approaches here at Zingerman's. A powerful thinker, writer, and teacher.

Peter Drucker: Probably the most prolific and insightful 20th-century business writer.

Peter Koestenbaum: An insightful advocate for a philosophical, free-thinking approach to business.

Peter Kropotkin: Born a Russian prince, he later renounced his royal birthright and went on to become an internationally recognized scientist and one of the world's most mindful anarchists. His work *Mutual Aid* put forward the belief that natural selection favors the most collaborative, not the cutthroat and competitive. His advocacy for local agriculture and free thinking were well ahead of his time.

Peter Senge: Systems scientist, lecturer at MIT, and author of *The Fifth Discipline: The Art & Practice of the Learning Organization.*

Philippe, Ethné, and Marika de Vienne: Having traveled the world for nearly 30 years now, their knowledge of spices combined with their support for growers in the producing countries is yielding great results, both culinarily and culturally. If you visit Montreal, head to their Épices de Cru shop.

Ralph Waldo Emerson: 19th-century writer, poet, and presenter. Emerson established the Transcendentalism movement, speaking of the import of the individual. He influenced many, including his friend and colleague Henry David Thoreau.

Rebecca Solnit: Writer, anarchist, and author of a range of really good books, including *The Field Guide to Getting Lost* and *The Faraway Nearby*.

Rich Sheridan and James Goebel: Cofounders of Ann Arbor–based Menlo Innovations, whose mission is to "end human suffering as it relates to technology." Rich is the author of *Joy, Inc.*

Charles R. "Rick" Snyder: A positive psychologist who did pioneering work on the study of hope theory at the University of Kansas.

Robert Greenleaf: The author of *Servant Leadership* and one of the great business thinkers of the 20th century.

Robert Henri: American art teacher, author, and painter. His book *The Art Spirit* is inspirational. He was well connected with anarchism and taught at the Ferrer Modern School in New York City for many years.

Robin D. G. Kelley: Historian and author whose work has explored African American history and alternative social movements. He taught at the University of Michigan in the 1990s. His work on jazz and hip hop, his creative and often critical approaches to mainstream thinking, and his focus on the surrealists make him one of the country's most provocative thinkers and writers.

Rocco Disderide: The man who had the Deli's building built back in 1902. Born near the Italian port city of Genoa, he came to New York in 1882 and to Ann Arbor in 1902. He lived to be 105 and, at the time of his death, was Ann Arbor's oldest citizen.

Rollo May: One of the most fascinating psychologists of the 20th century. May's work on existential, humanist approaches was groundbreaking. His many books include *Man's Search for Himself*, *The Courage to Create*, and *Freedom and Destiny*.

Ron Lippitt: A social scientist who came to work at the University of Michigan in 1946. His pioneering work on what he called "positive futuring" is at the core of what we do with visioning here at Zingerman's.

Rosabeth Moss Kanter: Michigan PhD; author of many books and articles, including one of my favorites, *Confidence*; and former editor of the *Harvard Business Review*.

Sam Keen: Author, poet, psychologist, and philosopher. His writings have been a major influence on my thinking over the years. Among his many insightful works are *Hymns to an Unknown God, To Love and Be Loved, Inward Bound,* and *Fire in the Belly.*

Shane Lopez: Gallup senior scientist in residence and research director for the Clifton Strengths Institute at the University of Nebraska. Former professor at the University of Kansas. Lopez has written extensively about the importance of hope.

Shawn Askinosie: Chocolate and change maker. Based in Springfield, Missouri, Shawn's generous work with cacao growers is yielding higher levels of hope and positive belief. And great chocolate as well.

Simon Sinek: Business writer and speaker.

Søren Kierkegaard: One of the 19th century's most compelling philosophers, the essential Christian existentialist, and anarchist.

Stas' Kazmierski: Paul and I first engaged Stas' in the early 1990s to help guide us in the process of writing a mission statement and guiding principles. The name is Polish; Stas' is short for Stanislaus, and is pronounced like "posh." He joined ZingTrain as a second managing partner in 2000 and retired in 2013. The core of what we know about visioning and effective organizational change all originated from the teachings of Stas'.

Stephen Cope: Psychologist, yoga teacher, and author of *The Great Work of Your Life.*

Suzanne Césaire: Martiniquean surrealist poet and writer.

Tammie Gilfoyle: My long-time, loving, and lovely girlfriend and co-adventurer in life, who brings positive belief and a plethora of hope to my world every day. She models the spirit of generosity in ways that inspire me to ever greater heights.

Terry Tempest Williams: American author and conservationist.

Thomas Merton: Mid-20th-century American Catholic monk, mystic, and author of over 70 books. Merton was born in France to a pair of artists—his father was a painter from New Zealand, and his mother a Quaker and artist from the United States.

Toby Hemenway: Educator, writer, speaker, gardener, and one of the country's leading advocates for permaculture.

Tom Asacker: Creative business thinker and writer. His books include *The Business of Belief.*

Viktor Frankl: Austrian psychiatrist and neurologist who managed to teach about positive living while incarcerated in the brutal setting of Nazi concentration camps. His book *Man's Search for Meaning* chronicles his survival in the camps and his focus on purpose and meaning.

Voltairine de Cleyre: Late-19th- and early-20th-century American poet, writer, feminist, and passionate believer in anarchism.

Walt Whitman: 19th-century American poet and essayist, considered the "father of free verse." His work inspired many, including Emma Goldman and other anarchists.

Wendell Berry: Born in 1934, he's been writing insightfully and often controversially about America's rural heritage, ecological preservation, and traditional agriculture for over 60 years. His poetry, fiction, and nonfiction are all fine examples of American free thinking. Berry's letter to the editor of *The Progressive Magazine* is what got me thinking about the idea of "bad work" and "good work."

William Albrecht: Born in central Illinois, Albrecht taught at the University of Missouri. He was one of the early advocates for soil conservation and sustainable farming.

William Butler Yeats: Late-19th- and early-20th-century Nobel Prize–winning Irish poet and writer.

William James: One of the most influential 19th-century American philosophers. He has been referred to as the "father of American psychology." His brother was the writer Henry James.

The "Secrets"

The essays that follow aren't really secrets, but they are, in essence, the "secrets" that so many people have been asking us for. Secrets #1 to 18 are in Zingerman's Guide to Good Leading, Part 1. *Secrets #19 to 29 are in* Part 2, *and Secrets #30 to 39 are in* Part 3. *Included here are Secrets #40 to 49. Each is an important element of what makes Zingerman's Zingerman's. Read and use each on its own or adapt them all to your organization. Many thanks to all the insightful folks—both within and outside our organization—who have contributed ideas, comments, stories, edits, and advice!*

corn sprouting in the hoop house at cornman farms

The Power of Beliefs in Business

How Our Beliefs Alter
What Happens at Work Every Day

In 1908, six years after Disderide opened his shop on Detroit Street, anarchist Emma Goldman published a pamphlet called "What I Believe." As is often the case, I agree wholeheartedly with Goldman's words: "'What I believe' is a process rather than a finality." Understanding the thought and the action behind her statement is what this essay is all about. Beliefs, I've come to realize, are one of the most powerful forces in our lives. They impact how well we work together, the quality of our products, our organizational culture, our community, our relationships. Everything in our lives is likely to have its roots in beliefs. I believe, though, that as we become more mindful of our beliefs and the impact they have on us, we can steadily shape our lives to be as we would like them to be.

Times change. And so have I. Our beliefs may be akin to the root systems of our lives, but they're definitely *not* written in stone. Many of my beliefs have changed significantly from what they were in the past. And what I believe today is not necessarily what I'll believe in the future.

Forty years ago, I believed that business was mostly about doing bad things. Business meant big companies where profits took top priority, where people put on suits, sat in offices, and conspired to do evil deeds against consumers and the folks who worked on factory floors. In that context, I never would have even considered opening one of my own.

Thirty years ago, I believed I wasn't very good at writing. I was sure that there was some near-perfect way to put together every paragraph, and that if I were as skillful as I should be, words would flow freely and naturally onto the page. From that impossible-to-attain, perfectionist place, I used to sit and agonize over every sentence, tear up paper, erase over and over again, and grow ever more exasperated with my inability to express myself. I spent more time fighting with words than I did actually writing what I wanted. Writing seemed like a good idea, but it was hardly a whole lot of fun.

Twenty-five years ago, I believed that trying to determine what one was going to be doing a decade or so down the road seemed silly, naïve, and overly controlling. Which left me with an uncomfortable and awkwardly ineffective lack of vision. It turns out I was projecting. I was the one who was silly, naïve, and overly controlling.

Three years ago, I believed . . . well, I really didn't have many strong beliefs about beliefs. I hadn't ever given them much thought. I certainly didn't believe that beliefs would be worth spending a couple years of my life studying.

I'm excited to report that all those beliefs have changed completely, 180 degrees.

Although beliefs can shift in a split second, more often than not they change slowly. Some small thing happens, usually unexpected, that makes us take pause and wonder. We listen to a different perspective, see something surprising, read an insightful book, hear a new song, or meet a particularly interesting person. Any or all of these occurrences can present us with beliefs that are not aligned with our own. When these outlooks differ from those we've been holding, new insights may start to loosen the grip that our old beliefs hold on our hearts and our minds. Sometimes the soil is broken up, and an old belief is gently washed away. In other instances, the cause is more extreme—something drastic happens, and our beliefs are significantly altered in a matter of minutes. Other times, a new seed is planted but yields no immediate results. As "new" evidence is allowed into our thought processes, this novel belief steadily grows stronger. Seemingly small shifts in beliefs can develop over time into deep roots, from which enormous benefits—or if your beliefs pull you in a negative direction, potentially big problems—may eventually grow. One day, whether we fully realize it or not, our belief has changed. In some cases, this new belief could be the complete opposite of what we'd once thought to be truth.

That was the case for me with the examples I've mentioned above. The change was slow, but it was also steady. And it stuck. No cataclysm, catechism, economic crisis, or emotional collapse contributed to my learning. It all happened quietly, a few degrees, a few insights at a time. Today, my beliefs on all four of those counts couldn't be further from what they once were.

If my own beliefs hadn't changed, Zingerman's would surely never have happened. Even if we'd opened the Deli in 1982, we wouldn't have transformed into the thriving, engaging, imperfect, and interesting Community of over 700 people that we've become. You certainly wouldn't be holding this—the fourth book in this series, the eighth book I've written—in your hands. The visioning process we now use and teach so passionately never would have been implemented so widely. And I'd most definitely never have spent so much time studying beliefs and working so hard to write about them. The changes have paid big dividends. My life is about 1,800 times more rewarding and in alignment than it ever would have been had I held tightly to those original beliefs.

Beliefs may be the biggest single force at work in our organizational lives. Economics, education, the environment, and employee engagement are all important, but beneath the surface-level discussion, most of what's in play is really about the beliefs of the various folks whose views are being bandied about. While everyone has some beliefs that they're conscious of—politics, religion, sports, and popular social issues seem to provoke speedy expressions of support or scorn—we actually have far, far more beliefs at play in our lives than that. The difficulty is that those beliefs are frequently framed as facts, certitudes, thoughts, theories, norms, shoulds, and should nots. Most of us fail to recognize them for the beliefs they are. They're down there in the dirt, below the surface, sitting solidly in our subconscious minds. Many are so far below our levels of consciousness that we never even realize we have them. Whether we know it or not, though, our beliefs are almost always calling the shots. As William James wrote: "Belief creates the actual fact."

Stages of Learning a Skill

At ZingTrain, we teach these Four Stages of Learning a Skill:

Unconsciously	Competent
Consciously	Competent
Consciously	Incompetent
Unconsciously	Incompetent

Before we begin learning any skill, we're at the bottom level. After some initial explanation and/or demonstration, we shift to the second level up, conscious (i.e., "we're now aware") incompetence ("but we still aren't good at doing it"). With practice and training and more practice still, we can move to conscious competence—we now know what we're doing, and we're mindfully monitoring our own performance while we're in action. Finally, if we do the same skill repeatedly, over an extended period of time, we will likely end up being unconsciously competent. We're able to effectively complete the required task without even thinking about it. We can "do it in our sleep." There's no value judgment placed on any of this, by the way—all the levels have merit.

If you want to see how these levels come together, take any skill that you're good at. It could be as simple as cooking your favorite dish, selling your product or service, driving, or even reading books. Take a minute to reflect back to the beginning. Actually, go back before the beginning, before you'd ever considered developing this skill. And then, as best you can, track what's happened over the years to help you get to where you are. You'll need to adopt what Buddhists call "beginner's mind." What was it like when you first started? How did you feel in the beginning? Was it awkward? What did you do to start improving? How long did it take to get good? How long have you been doing it, all told? And when you've done this thing recently, how much thought—or how little—did you give to the task? My guess is you'll be able to see how you moved through the various stages, which I hope will give you a better sense of what they're about.

The interesting thing, though, is that learning on the subject at hand happens only when we're at the two middle levels. When we're unconsciously incompetent or unconsciously competent, we might do many things, but *one thing we're not doing is learning about the skill in question.* Carl Jung warns us accordingly: "Until you make the unconscious conscious, it will direct your life and you will call it fate." The point of this piece is to move us from unconscious to conscious in the management of our beliefs. Because it's only from a place of conscious attention that we can learn more about what our beliefs actually are, or about how to choose and manage them appropriately and effectively.

After living most of my life with beliefs that I barely even realized I had, the last few years of studying this subject have been life and business altering. While in the past I paid a lot of attention to actions, arguments, and analysis, I gave little or no thought to beliefs. That, too, has changed nearly 180 degrees. I work hard almost every day to be in touch with my own beliefs. I've also become far more sensitive to others' beliefs. I now watch the way that beliefs are being reflected—for better or worse—in relationships, projects, problems, profits, and, perhaps most importantly, the growth and success of the people who are part of our organization.

While specific beliefs may come and go (the world, it turns out, isn't flat), the role of beliefs has surely been in place for all of human history. Belief has always been at the core of organized religion, to take one powerful example. Psychologists have been studying this subject in depth for decades. But in my experience, beliefs are rarely discussed in the context of business, a place where logic and reason and strategy are generally said—or I could say "believed"—to dominate the dialogue. I suppose this isn't surprising. Most of us are trained to focus on the tangible: strategy, science, profit, product quality. Of late, subjects such as vision and values—here at Zingerman's especially—have also become high priorities. So too, appropriately, has organizational purpose. We like long-term planning, LEAN management, and low-cost change initiatives. All are interesting, and all are important. But if you haven't already picked up on my theme, it's worth recognizing that particular beliefs underlie them all. I've come to the conclusion that belief needs to be an area of focus unto itself.

All too often, we aren't cognizant of what we believe. As Rebecca Solnit puts it, "Some ideas are new, but most are only recognition of what has been there all along, the mystery in the middle of the room, the secret in the mirror." Our beliefs will be at work regardless, but unless we pay attention they remain a mystery to us and we lose the magic. I believe that reflection, understanding, and increased consciousness can change all that. As Isaac Asimov writes, "Knowledge is not only power; it is happiness." *I believe* that if we raise awareness of the role beliefs play in our lives, we can make a whole lot of good things happen for ourselves and for everyone around us. It's certainly worked well for me.

Business Changes Baker's Beliefs

The relationship between beliefs and business works both ways. What we believe underlies every single thing we do, every day, in every part of our organization. At the same time, our businesses impact the beliefs of the people who come to work with us. There's much more on this to come in this essay and in Secrets #41 to 43. But to give you a small taste of the kind of influence we can have on the beliefs of those we employ, check out these thoughts from Bakehouse baker Ben Lewis. Here's what he had to say after I sent out a request to our crew to share thoughts on how their beliefs about business and themselves might have changed since coming to work with us:

> *Looking back on previous job experiences, I know for sure I thought every employee in food service was expendable. Being replaced or moving on was inevitable. I was cheap labor, with little to gain from my employer. After all, "Anyone can cook!" After being here for two years, I've seen that everyone from the top to the bottom—not that there is a bottom at Zingerman's—was invested in my success not only as a baker, but as a person. An immediate shift in beliefs began from day one (with a little help from positive media and knowing previous employees). And it does not stop there. The more I invest in myself, the more support I receive. I have never before talked to the owner of a company I was employed at about my personal life goals. The owners of Zingerman's not*

only reinforce them, they pay me to take classes to make them happen. Literally, they pay me to better my personal life. That's totally crazy.

Crazy good, I'd say.

Where Beliefs Begin

I was born with brown eyes, but I wasn't born with beliefs. Like you and everyone else you know, I was trained into them. Whether we acknowledge it or not, our beliefs were bestowed upon us, often unintentionally or unconsciously, passed on through repeated interactions with parents, priests, professors, politicians, poets, and many others whose views of the world we saw, heard, or experienced (and later assimilated) at various points in our lives. Those we trust most—the people we believe, and believe in—usually have the greatest likelihood of influencing us. People we look up to—and people we don't—send us messages that become the basis for what we believe. [12]

The messages from which our beliefs form can come both directly and indirectly. Czesław Miłosz writes, "We construct our private mythologies throughout our lives and those from the earliest years last longest." Every small and large element of our early lives contributes to our learning. It could be an event we experience in the here and now that completes an unfinished picture from a much earlier period of our lives. Or maybe it's something that's well aligned with what's in our hearts but that we never heard spoken by anyone else. And then, bam! Spiritual synchronicity! At "just the right time," we hear someone speak with passion, read an amazing book, watch an incredible film, or meet a charismatic new person, and for some reason, a message resonates. Anyone could set the seed—a teacher, a cousin, a musician, an athlete.

Often, the seeds of new belief are planted when we experience a change of context: meeting a new friend, going to work for a new boss, moving to a new city, getting married or divorced, having kids, or getting promoted can all turn the trick. More than one person I know has told me that they were raised in a racist setting, but they switched gears completely within a few weeks of going away to college.

It's also about intensity. Charisma, passion, high energy, and excitement can anchor beliefs or cause us to alter them. When we hear an assumption repeatedly and dynamically asserted from a source we trust—or, perhaps, don't know enough to *dis*trust—that belief becomes a part of our own mental fabric. When we've heard or seen or felt it enough, it's so well ensconced in our psyches that we don't question its veracity—"it" is just the way it is.

In some cases, the beliefs we take on as kids can lead to great success later in life. Children who are raised to believe in themselves, in the world, in their ability to convert hard work into happy lives, in learning and contributing to others around them, often have an edge over those who were raised with negative beliefs. There are many unspoken advantages that we may have in life: economics, gender, race, education, and intellect are all certainly relevant. But I'm starting to think that perhaps the biggest form of privilege may be growing up surrounded by people who believe in themselves, who believe in you, who believe in what they're doing, and who believe that if you stick with things, you can push past the obstacles that others—often unfairly and inappropriately—may put in your path. It certainly seems to be a common theme as I read about individuals who grew to greatness, even, in many cases, after starting with significant disadvantages. Money and privileged social positions may get you more money and more privilege, but I don't think they get you to personal greatness and gratification unless they're combined with positive beliefs in self, in the world around you, and in the value of caring and giving to others.

That sense of things is summed up by the mantra of one of our good customers, Michael Chappell:

> *I will reach my goal.*
> *I will because I can.*
> *I can because I know.*
> *I know because I believe.*
> *I believe because my parents told me so.*

Of course, the beliefs we learn from our parents can turn out to be wrong, at least wrong for us if not for the world. Unlike gravity, which is a natural fact, beliefs are what we perceive, not necessarily what really *is*. As writer Kevin Bermingham says,

> *Beliefs are simply a feeling of conviction or certainty that something is real or true. They're based on our past experiences and what others have taught us. Beliefs are our best guess at reality—our mental model of how the world appears to work. . . . Our knowledge of the real world is limited. So to get by, we rely on our beliefs instead. They're the principles and rules by which we assume the world works.*

Many of us cling to our beliefs, even when the data tell us these beliefs are inaccurate.

A lot of the beliefs I came away with from my childhood were clearly positive. I discovered early on that I could read and learn; that giving to others was a good thing to do; that if you work hard, you can achieve just about anything; that it's smart to save money. I was taught that being kind and considerate is the best way to be in the world. All of which have helped me to effectively manage my life as an adult. But it wasn't *all* good. I also learned that it wasn't appropriate to express anger; that the world isn't a particularly trustworthy place; that businesses are generally, fundamentally bad. Somewhere I also picked up the belief that if I couldn't do something I cared about perfectly, then something was wrong, probably with me.

Incongruity, especially over extended periods of time, causes crises of consciousness. When what we hear from others continually fails to align with what we ourselves are experiencing, trouble will surely follow. It becomes almost impossible to make peace between what we feel and what others tell us is taking place. At times, the gap between what we've been taught and what's true can be terrifically large, in which case the tension can be terrible. As the Indian mystic Osho said, "Every child understands it, that he sees the world in a different way from his parents. . . . The only problem is, he is afraid to assert that he is right."

I believe that most of our parents did the best they could; sometimes they succeeded in passing along positive beliefs, and other times they stumbled. My mother stating firmly and angrily "I'm not angry!" didn't do much for my childhood beliefs about anger, nor did it help me learn how to express my own. The message I received was clear: Anger isn't something we should acknowledge, and it's best kept out of the conversation. The belief was that if we just deny that it's happening, then the angry feelings will go away. It won't shock you to know that as an adult, I had (and sometimes still have) a hard time expressing or assimilating anger. It took me a long time and a lot of outside help to realize that anger was a normal element of human emotion and a healthy piece of any meaningful, long-term, positive relationship. While I've learned to handle anger much more effectively, those early beliefs are still in there. To manage myself effectively, I will probably always need to give careful thought to how to handle anger every time it comes up.

Our beliefs even extend backwards—the history we hold in our heads is built up almost exclusively around what we *believe* happened. As Rosabeth Moss Kanter writes, "History and context shape interpretations and expectations." We can conveniently forget difficult family stories, business failures, and social outrages but still manage to remember the "good old days" with great fondness. Or, conversely, bad feelings and fear might be so deeply embedded that the positive aspects of past events have been long since forgotten. Ever wonder why personal, social, or political feuds last so long? One reason is that people have completely conflicting beliefs about what happened in the first place. What we believe about what happened in turn shapes what we do going forward. That can cause problems. As G. K. Chesterton writes with his usual thought-provoking wit, "The past is not what it was."

Perception plays—often not nicely—with reality. As Haitian poet Lenelle Moïse says (quoted in Gina Athena Ulysse's essay "Rasanble"): "I don't think memory is real. It's just a game we play with ourselves. We remember what we choose to." When we're feeling overwhelmed, our memory choices may help us to stay stable, "to feel sane." The problem is that this sort of self-editing—or to use a harsher term, denial—can later cause big problems for us and for others.

Do the Movies Make Reality?

Over the last hundred-plus years, movies, and later television, have had a huge impact on our beliefs. Many Americans' sense of history is based more on stuff they saw on big screens than anything that necessarily ever happened. Rebecca Solnit paints the picture powerfully in words in *River of Shadows*:

> And the movies themselves made fictions out of history, made up a South and a West that never existed, specialized at various junctures in westerns that turned a place into a genre that could be made anywhere, that prompted the sense of self of generations of American men, even politicians, that even generated a president who remembered as reality things that had happened only in movies. And from movies women learned how to look, how to love, how important looking and loving were.

How many of our beliefs, I wonder, were formed by watching actors playing parts that were created by men and women who themselves had only a limited sense of what once really happened? And then, taking the question further, how many of our actions are based on those beliefs?

If we understand that our memories are selective, we can at least start to explore our pasts more carefully than we might otherwise have done. Wendell Berry says, "When you remember the past, you are not remembering it as it was. You are remembering it as it is. It is a vision or a dream, present with you in the present, alive with you in the only time you are alive." The pressure we experience to conform to the beliefs of a dominant group can be difficult to withstand. When everyone around us expresses beliefs about a particular point of view, it's alarming how many of us will just go along. (See the film *A Class Divided* for more on this.) But as Bertrand Russell writes, "The fact that an opinion has been widely held is no evidence whatever that it is not utterly absurd; indeed, in view of the silliness of the majority of mankind, a widespread belief is more likely to be foolish than sensible."

Pick a belief. Any belief. About your business. The world. Yourself. Take a minute or two and try to track it back to the beginning. Who planted the seed? What happened to reinforce and strengthen the roots that grew from it? How long have you held it? Do you know anyone who holds a different belief about the same subject? What impact is the belief having on your life? If you held the opposite belief, what sort of things would you be doing differently?

In and Out of Alignment

Over the last few years, I've come to believe that belief is the barely acknowledged Achilles' heel of organizational behavior. It's invisible to the untrained eye and ignored by the average intellect, but it is, nevertheless, imperative to what we see going on all around us every day.

It's a lot like the alignment on your car. When everything is as it should be, driving goes smoothly, your stress level is lower, the risk of accidents is reduced, and the life of the vehicle is longer. As long as things go well, you generally give little thought to just how smooth the ride is. It's actually the absence of that quiet calm that clues you in to trouble—when the alignment is off, everything gets more difficult. Excess wear builds up on the engine and drive shaft, fuel efficiency goes down, and the driver expends a lot of extra energy just to keep the vehicle moving in the right direction. If you stop paying attention, even for a few seconds, the car can slide off course, resulting in a serious collision.

The same goes for us as individuals, and for our organizations. When our beliefs aren't aligned with our work, or with those of our coworkers, effectiveness will erode, and stress will skyrocket. Similarly, when our beliefs are incongruent with our values, vision, or mission, or totally out of touch with reality, trouble will also surely follow. Lack of alignment can slowly but surely lead us astray. If we don't figure out how to compensate for this lack of congruency, our beliefs will steadily, if surreptitiously at first, pull us off course. Despite our best efforts, we just can't keep things moving in the right direction. As Errico Malatesta makes clear, "Whoever sets out on the highroad and takes a wrong turning does not go where he intends to go but where the road leads him." Most of us will blame "the road" and try to change lanes, shift strategies, rebrand, write new policies, complain about others or reprogram our computers, but nothing seems to work. Attempting to lead in an organization in which beliefs are out of alignment with the mission or vision is confusing, exhausting, and, at worst, disastrous. So too is working in a setting in which *your* belief system runs counter to almost everyone else's.

On the other hand, when beliefs *are* in alignment with all those other important organizational constructs, everything flows more fluidly. When our beliefs are true to our vision and values, congruent with reality, and well aligned, or at least liberally overlapping with those of our coworkers, nearly any experience will be enhanced. The work being done is basically the same, but things seem to progress, somehow, far more smoothly. Pretty much everything goes better when we believe in the products, principles, processes, and people we work with. And in ourselves. Statistics show that positive beliefs help patients recover more quickly, assist athletes in winning, make students more likely to succeed, and make relationships more likely to blossom. Positive, well-aligned beliefs are good for business.

"Agreed, But Still Out of Alignment"

It was a small-scale instance of things being out of alignment that got me thinking about beliefs in the first place. We'd put together a work group to deal with an organization-wide quality issue we were struggling with.

By all rights and reasoning, it should have been a big success. The problem was clearly solvable—we knew we could do better. Quality is at the core of all we do and always has been. It's in our vision, our values, our mission. The people in the group were mostly upper-level folks, with a range of financial and emotional ownership in the organization. They had assigned additional staff members to the group as requested. We agreed on a vision of success and laid out action steps. But no matter how I tried to get the group going—pushing harder, pulling back, putting others in charge—it just never made much progress. Something was still wrong. It took me a long time to figure out what it was. In hindsight, I can see that although people went along with it, they didn't believe that the project would work, or was worthwhile. Did they believe in the value of quality? Of course. Each just believed that other people involved were the ones who were falling short. And they didn't believe that the group's work was going to lead to any improvement.

I still haven't totally figured out a way to keep this problem from happening. It happened again just last week. A group of really good, highly committed, well-compensated, caring, and intelligent folks had agreed by consensus to an element of a long-term vision for their group. The group's leader had advocated for it but not all that forcefully. All of the members had agreed to include it in the vision. Six months later, when the time came to start putting the idea in the vision into action, people started balking. The leader was confused. What, he wanted to know, had appealed to the group members about the approach when they'd agreed to put it in the vision?

Shockingly, hardly anyone had anything to say.

"But you must have wanted it, right? You agreed to it," he said. "Let's start with the positives. What got you excited about it?"

They sat there. I could see that they were searching for a good answer but were unsure of what to say. Finally, someone said, "Well, it was your idea. We went along because it was what you wanted. We want to know what *you* like about it."

To his credit, the leader remained firm. "I know why *I* liked the idea. But we decided by consensus. I'm asking what *you* liked about it. What motivated you to include it in the vision?"

Finally, the group started to talk, and they ended up with a productive discussion. But it was clear that they'd struggled to move forward because even though they'd made a common decision, they didn't, at least at the time, have commonly held beliefs.

Alignment Around Concepts

Let me pause to make sure we're all speaking the same language here. If you want to read further on any of these subjects, there's much more on mission, vision, culture, systems, and guiding principles in *Zingerman's Guide to Good Leading, Part 1*. As always, I'm not here to assert that our definitions are "correct"—only trying to be clear on what we mean here at Zingerman's when we use the terms.

A *Mission Statement*, as we see it, is meant to answer four questions: "What do we do?" "Why do we do it?" "Who are we that's doing it?" and "For whom are we doing it?" We view it like the North Star; though we can't ever actually arrive at it, it provides a good sense of long-term direction.

A *Vision* is a description of success at *a particular point in time in the future*, written out with a good bit of richly engaging detail and emotionally meaningful descriptions. A vision, as we see it, gets very specific about what we want to do at that point in the future: how we'll feel about it, how others might feel about us, etc. Our vision for Zingerman's 2020 is about nine pages long. Our mission, on the other hand, is short, just six sentences.

Guiding Principles, or values, are not *where* we're going or *why* we're going there but rather a detailed description of *how* we're going to relate to each other and the world around us while we're doing this work. They are, I suggest, the most closely held of our beliefs, the ones that we don't want to change even when holding true to them might cause us significant pain. (We could, I suppose, call the main owners of the business Guiding Principals. To be clear, if the principles of the principals aren't in alignment, the organization will also suffer.)

Systems are the processes we use to produce products, maintain sanitation, develop our services, sign up new staff, make potato salad, etc.

Culture is really everything about our day-to-day existence. It's the way our lives at work really work—not what we say we're going to do but what we actually *do*. It's the way we dress, talk, learn, and listen. The music we play, the clothes we wear, the food we eat, the frequency with which we laugh and with whom, the way we hold meetings, and the way we run the organization.

Reality is what's happening right now as you read. At least, I believe that's what it is. I'll come back to that in a bit.

Fantasy is just what it sounds like—a dream that's totally disconnected from reality, an imaginary situation that's super inspiring but has no real hope of happening.

Beliefs are, of course, what we're talking about here.

The boundaries between all of these constructs are porous. They can and do overlap at any given point. But it's good to be clear on a common language.

Beliefs Make a Big Difference

Whether we know it or not, belief is an essential element of creating excellence in everything, from parenting to project management to poetry—all of which makes a reading of what we believe a good way to forecast the future. Where belief is low, poor results are to be expected. Where belief is high, that which is believed in stands a good chance of succeeding.

This piece, then, is about how belief impacts the health of any organization or, for that matter, the health of any of us, as humans. It's about whom we believe in—ourselves, our boss, our lover, LeBron James, Barack Obama, Buddha, the woman working across the hall. You can take your pick. All matter. And it's about whether we believe (or not) in our products, our organization, the future, or anything else in our lives. What we believe alters everything, including our future as it unfolds. We also want to be mindful of who—and what we *don't* believe in. Whatever we don't believe in—a project, a partner, a particular part of our organization, or ourselves—is highly likely to fall flat.

I'm not saying that just "buying into" the "right" beliefs will assure you of overnight success; while the power built by belief may look like magic, it isn't. Belief won't overturn nature. The sun will rise, the rain will fall, winter will come, and spring too, regardless of how we feel about any of it. Things will continue to fall down and not up; the Natural Laws of Business still apply. But when it comes to stuff *we do*, work we undertake, and action plans we decide to implement, beliefs are a big factor in all of them.

I have this fantasy of inventing a belief-tracking machine, like a Geiger counter. But instead of checking for radioactivity, this gadget would measure belief. When belief is high, it would click loudly. When belief is faint, it would register little more than a murmur. People could still, as they have for centuries, loudly proclaim their allegiance to a particular program, or political party, or policy, but the belief tracker would reveal the reality. We can fake it at the board meeting or in a performance review or a job interview, but we couldn't fool this new machine. When someone's *stated* beliefs are totally out of alignment with their *actual* beliefs, the apparatus would be silent.

Life itself is a lot like my make-believe machine. If we start with what's working, or not working, more often than not we can track back to what we or others around us believed. Without belief, we will never build a great business, develop a great manager, successfully roll out a new product, or complete a big project on time or on budget. When we don't believe in ourselves, in our organizations, what we're making and selling, in our bosses, our coworkers, and our community, the odds of living a rewarding life, having fun, learning a lot, and feeling fulfilled will drop as well.

All of the above holds true for us as individuals as well as for any group of which we're a part. Disbelief in what we're doing or with whom we're doing it will lead, directly or indirectly, to bad business, bad energy, and eventually burnout and boredom. And as Christian anarchist philosopher Søren Kierkegaard tells us, "Boredom is the root of all evil—[it is] the despairing refusal to be oneself." Staying in a job or a relationship we don't believe is right for us is anything but inspiring. Going after a future we don't believe in is guaranteed to be frustrating. Working at something we don't believe in degrades our spirit. We may, perhaps, please others, but we will limit our own lives in the process.

To get by when we *don't* believe, we fool ourselves, spin stories, or sell ourselves short. We deceive our customers or our community, or we flee in the often-mistaken belief that a change of setting will change our results. It doesn't work. Beliefs, unacknowledged, are dangerous, if not downright deadly. As Slovenian philosopher Slavoj Žižek writes, "The real dangers are in the disavowed beliefs, suppositions, and obscene practices that we pretend not to know about."

Disbelief is a burdensome road to nowhere. Unfortunately, it's endemic in the kind of work that many people are engaged in. As Albert Camus writes, "[W]hen work is soulless, life stifles and dies." It will drag down pretty much any business. If you look closely, you can assess what's going on below ground by tasting the "fruit" of our organizational labors. As farmer Klaas says in Dan Barber's excellent book, *The Third Plate*, "Before yield declines, before weed and pest pressures, you can taste it. The doom before the doom." You can feel the soullessness in the energy you experience when you walk into a shop, see it in the faces of frontline staff, read it in the emails you get back when you send an inquiry, long before the financial statements tell the bank that there's trouble.

The upside of beliefs, by comparison, is enormous. Beliefs can take us to levels of attainment that the skeptics in our lives might never have imagined possible. Grounded, shared, passionately held beliefs are a strong starting place to reshape our organizational (or personal) realities. When our beliefs are aligned with our dreams, our visions, and our values, amazing things start to happen. Positive beliefs build energy, enthusiasm, love, caring, and creativity. They also build sales, improve resiliency, and inspire better bottom line results. They're the emotional foundation for excellence.

The Equine Belief Detector

It turns out that nature seems to have already beaten me to my science-fiction fantasy of developing a belief detector. In talking to Kim Cardeccia about her Equine Assisted Self-Growth practice, I learned that horses have an innate and intuitive ability to help tell us how true we are to our own beliefs and how positive those beliefs really are. A trained therapist and long-time riding instructor, Cardeccia creatively and effectively combined her two passions into one compelling career. Essentially she employs horses to help clients increase their understanding of their own beliefs. Kim explained,

> Horses are genetically "designed" to be ultrawary of predators. Their only real defense mechanism is their sensitivity and their speed. They're wired to follow the leader of the pack. If they pick up anxiety from the leader, it means there's probably a predator nearby and then they'll barely budge. When people are working with them, we're basically the leaders of the pack. So when we have anxiety—even when it's so below the surface that we ourselves don't even know it—they'll still pick up on it and balk.
>
> As part of our work, we lay down poles in the ring. We have the client tell us an obstacle that they're struggling with in their lives, and then ask them to imagine the pole as that obstacle. Then we have them walk the horse over the pole. It seems easy, but if their beliefs are negative and not in alignment, the horse will pick up on their internal anxiety. The dissonance creates a tension that the horse wants to hold back from.

While we might fool ourselves or other humans by pretending assurance when we don't truly feel it, horses won't fall for our ruse. "If you come out of congruence in some way," Kim says, "the horse reacts to that." The horse's "emotional antennae" are so finely honed that they can pick up on any incongruity. When we announce "A" to the world but believe "B" in our hearts, they can feel our uncertainty. "Sometimes," she says, "the issue is personal. Other times the issue is about what they expect from the horse. But in the end they usually end up dealing with their issues." I'm thinking about posting a full-time position for an in-house equine advisor to sit in on meetings (I guess it would actually stand in), performance reviews, visioning sessions, and the like.

See confidencethroughconnection.com for more on Kim's amazing work.

This I Believe

Beliefs can be about anyone, or anything, in our lives. They might center around

- What things mean or don't mean
- Who we are or are not
- Why things have happened or not happened
- What's possible or not possible
- What's important or not important
- Why we care or don't care
- What matters and what doesn't
- How we should be living our lives
- What it means to be successful
- The nature of authority
- Business in general
- The nature of our own organization in particular

How do we find out what we believe? One way I've learned to discover my beliefs is to do this simple exercise: Begin writing the statement, "This I believe . . ." Then keep writing for 10 or 15 minutes. Even five minutes will get you going. Basically, you keep writing without stopping for the entire time allotted. Writing straight through keeps you from overthinking. If you want, you can focus the exercise on a particular subject—yourself, your work, your significant other, your mother, society, the world. (See page 107 for detailed instructions).

What follows is what I wrote about my own beliefs about business during one of these exercises. After the initial throwdown, I did a bit of minor editing to clean it up; otherwise, it's as I originally laid it down. (The quotes, to be clear, were added later, because they resonated with my beliefs.) These beliefs are the root system of the way I work. If you want to understand why I do what I do, here are the answers.

When it comes to the workplace, or, for that matter, the world at large, I believe that

- People are generally good and want to do the right thing; they want to work hard and do great work; as Emma Goldman said, "No one is lazy."

- It's far more fun to work hard at something you believe in than it is to work less hard doing something you don't really care about.

- Training is a helpful tool, and when it's well managed, it's hard to do too much of it.

- The leader's job is to serve the organization.

- Everyone has insight to offer; I'm confident that I can learn from everyone.

- Just because someone is higher up on an org chart, has a terrific title, upper-level education, or a long résumé doesn't mean they're more capable or more intelligent.

- Organizations work better when everyone in them takes responsibility for leadership.

- Customers aren't always right, but we're going to act like they are anyway because it's better service and also better business.

- Freethinking and free choice will make for more rewarding lives and more productive and positive organizations.

- With that in mind, I believe that I can freely choose—despite the inevitable external and internal pressures—to act, think, and live my life as I want within the realities of the world as it is.

- I'm highly imperfect, but more often than not, I manage to do a good job.

- Quality makes a meaningful positive difference. As Gary Snyder writes, "The preserver of abundance is excellence."

- Any of us can learn to do almost anything if we're willing to do the work and stick with it over a long period of time.

- How hard we work at improving on something over the years is highly likely to lead to some level of success (much more than any "innate" ability).

- Meaningful personal change takes a long time.

- And meaningful, lasting organizational change usually takes even longer.

- You *can* taste the difference between good and great food and drink.

- The value of reading in gaining personal success (and, through the personal, organizational) is big and is often underestimated. (And for those who have a hard time with the written word, video and tape learning can, of course, work well, too.)

- Learning is energizing. Good teaching is even more so.

- Money is a helpful tool, but it's rarely the be-all and end-all.

- The anarchists were onto something significant, and I'm lucky to have studied them many years ago and to now be able to bring their insights out to the world.

- Success means you get better problems.

- Celebrating everything you have, with great regularity, creates a much more rewarding existence.

- If we work well together, there will be more than enough to go around. Working for win-win solutions is infinitely more rewarding and also much more effective.

- The visioning process works and can make a hugely positive difference in the lives of individuals and organizations that use it.

- Getting older is far better than the alternative, and I believe I'm doing a pretty good job of growing older with grace.

- People are trustworthy, for the most part, and life is more rewarding when one starts from a position of trust.

- From these beliefs, I *choose* to start out by trusting most everyone. As Osho said: "If you want to learn anything, learn trust—

nothing else is needed. If you are miserable, nothing else will help—learn trust. If you don't feel any meaning in life and you feel meaningless, nothing will help—learn trust. Trust gives meaning because trust makes you capable of allowing the whole to descend upon you."

- Choosing *not* to trust people ultimately poisons the spirit of the person who distrusts far more than it hurts the person from whom trust has been withheld.

- Diversity creates a healthier ecosystem in business and in agriculture and everything else. As anarchist Colin Ward writes, "Diversity, not unity, creates a tolerable society." And he clarifies, "In other words, it is diversity and not unity, which creates the kind of society in which you and I can most comfortably live."

- Speaking of diversity, I believe that stereotyping or assigning identities based on what "group" someone is perceived to be a part of *always leads to trouble*. While a free and caring choice to associate can be a plus, assignment by others is never productive. As Kierkegaard says, "Once you label me you negate me." And as anarchist anthropologist David Graeber wrote more recently, "For the most part, what we call 'identities' here . . . are forced on people." Even seemingly benign positive characterizations will later cause problems. When we assign "good characteristics" to groups—"women are more sensitive," "African Americans are great dancers"—it sets up the belief that assigning identities to groups makes sense. It also implies that other groups are less qualified than those who've been "praised"—men then must, by definition, be less sensitive. It's only a matter of time before trouble comes, through the assignment of some equally inaccurate negative trait to an entire group.

- Rather, I believe that each person is a unique individual with a one-of-a-kind personality, passion, past history, and skill set. Breaking free of roles, stereotypes, and social expectations to be true to oneself is usually a more challenging but infinitely more rewarding way to live and work.

- Anything we plan to be great at—project management, painting, pastry making—requires a lot of work.

- Work can be rewarding.

- Worrying is basically a big waste of time, or at worst, downright destructive. When it comes down to it, it's essentially "negative visioning."

- An organization's work is to help everyone who's a part of it to be themselves, and to encourage them to go for greatness and then help them get there.

- Preparing everyone in the organization to lead is sound business. As Henrik Ibsen wrote, "A community is like a ship; everyone ought to be prepared to take the helm."

- With that in mind, the more we teach people to lead, the more they lead the way in making their own lives what they want them to be.

- "Any normal human being," as anarchist Murray Bookchin believed, "is essentially capable of learning to run any organization of which they're a part." Or more to the point here at Zingerman's, as socialist Trinidadian historian C. L. R. James says, "Every cook can govern."

- Teaching people at every level of an organization how to run the business makes a big difference. As Paul Goodman posits, "[T]he only way to educate cooperative citizens is to give power to people as they are," not to wait until they get promoted.

- If I/we spend time with good people who are going after good things, then things are likely to work out well.

- Positive relationships make everything work more effectively.

- Making mistakes is a normal and healthy part of existence, both personally and organizationally. It's more about how we recover from them that counts. It's much as Errico Malatesta said: "Freedom coupled with experience is the only way of discovering the truth and what is best; and there can be no freedom if there is denial of the freedom to err."

- When we write out and actively share a vision of the future that we really believe in, it significantly increases the odds of it happening.

- The Natural Laws of Business are an accurate and real representation of the way the world works. As Osho said, "The essence of wisdom is to act in harmony with nature." Fighting nature, other than trying to hold off or survive a natural disaster, never results in good things.

- When we live in harmony with the Natural Laws, we bring out the best in everyone involved. Creativity follows naturally. As Paul Goodman wrote, "Those who draw on natural powers find it easy to be inventive." And "The persons who separate themselves from nature have to live every minute of their lives without the power, joy, and freedom of nature."

- The world is a complex place and trying to force superficial simplification onto what is naturally complicated can cause severe problems for all involved (see Secret #43).

- The world and life are out of control, and all we have are varying degrees of influence.

- It's all one life—not a struggle between work and what we do outside of work. And the more congruent our values, beliefs, passions, and vision are in all elements of our existence, the more rewarding our lives are likely to be.

- With that in mind, I believe that living life well is a creative act. As John Cowper Powys posits, "The art of life consists in the creation of an original and unique self." Or, as Émile Armand argues, "I consider life as an experience, or rather a series of experiences, lived to secure the richest, the most abundant, the most varied possible."

- It's unhelpful to hold an idea accountable for the behavior of the person from whom I heard it. In other words, the behavior of a great teacher or writer may lower their personal integrity, but it doesn't invalidate the concepts I learned from them. As Malatesta said, "We follow ideas and not men, and rebel against this habit of embodying a principle in a man." Ideas for me stand alone, or at least stand free, not for the taking but for taking off, using, building on, and, of course, believing in.

- The more mindfully we make free choices, the more positive our energy and our lives will be.

- Solitude is little appreciated but imperative if we're to achieve excellence.

- We can all choose what energy to bring to any setting and relationship of which we're a part.

- Happiness is a choice we all can make daily, and we can choose to be happy even when things aren't going as we'd like.

- Infusion of positive belief, hope, and the spirit of generosity into an organization will always help it to be healthier and will improve the quality of almost everything it does.

And last on this list, but certainly not least,

- I believe that we can change our beliefs.

This last bit of belief, it's ever clearer to me all the time, is a key to living free. As Ashanti Alston, an African American anarchist, writes, "living to the fullest is to win"—not *against* others, but *for* ourselves. Productive living is not about defeating anyone else but rather about attaining our own internal freedom—freedom to be ourselves and make a positive difference for the world around us in the process.

What You Believe Is (All Too Often) What You Get: Bob and Judith Wright's Self-Limiting Belief Cycle

If you take the word "belief" and swap around the second "e" and the "f," you get "be life": *our beliefs are the basis for the way our lives are going and are going to go in the future.*

Whether we realize it or not, what we believe in our heads is highly likely to happen in the world around us. Good beliefs often beget good outcomes. If we believe things are going to be bad, it's likely that they will be. In which case it will be as authors Bob and Judith Wright tell us in their very fine book *Transformed!*: "In fact, what we believe limits our reality and keeps us from realizing our potential. We think, *This is how it is, this is who I am,* rather than *This is how I'm programmed, this is what I believe, but it is not necessarily the full truth.* It causes us to believe, *I can't be assertive like that* or *I'm kind and thoughtful; I can't be angry.*"

Let me elaborate with a visual model that I learned from the Wrights. I give them full credit for the construct, and I share it here with their permission and active support (and my recommendation to buy their books and check out their work at the Wright Institute in Chicago). It connected for me as soon as I read it, and it has already helped thousands of others that we've shared it with here at work and through ZingTrain.

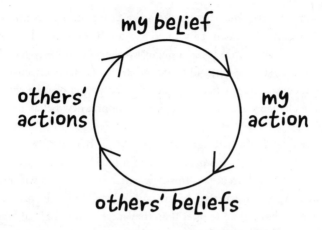

my belief

others'
actions

my
action

others' beliefs

It works like this: When we have a belief, it's likely that belief will lead us to take some sort of associated action. For instance, let's say we believe that our ideas aren't worth much and no one really cares about what we think. The action that follows might be that we rarely voice our views at work. That behavior will likely feed the belief in others that we have little to offer, or perhaps aren't very committed to the company's success. Which will then lead those coworkers to take action accordingly—they might not ask us for our views on important issues or include us in discussions. Which will then reinforce our original belief that others don't value our views.

The cycle will surely continue onward from there. Imagine what it will feel like after 20 or 30 years. We start to believe that the reality we're experiencing is "who we are" rather than a result of how our beliefs have been acting steadily—if surreptitiously—on our reality. We know from studies of brain change and development that when we think in a certain way for a long period of time, the "routes" in our brain grow ever more deeply embedded. The deeper they get, the more we follow along the same path onto which our beliefs long ago led us. And on and on the cycle goes, each element reinforcing the existing beliefs of others in the cycle. As author, psychologist, and professor of social theory at Swarthmore Barry Schwartz says, "These effects can arise because sometimes when people act on the basis of ideology, they inadvertently arrange the very conditions that bring reality into correspondence with the ideology."

All of which made clear to me how we each contribute to our own crises—both of conscience and of construct. It showed me that if I was frustrated with an action taken by others, I would do well to look away from them and turn back instead to inspect my own beliefs about the subject because, quite simply, our own beliefs are very often the cause of actions we don't like by others. Most importantly, it showed me that if I wanted to alter the outcomes I was getting in any situation, I would do well to begin by checking out my own beliefs about the other person, myself, and the world. Mindful effort, effective understanding, and consistent practice over an extended period of time *can* reverse the cycle. The change starts with a decision to adopt a new belief, or if you're thinking big, a whole new set of them.

In the scenario above, we might decide to change our belief by telling ourselves, "What I have to say *does* have value." Although it may be awkward and difficult at first, we start to act on this new belief. Rather than withhold our thoughts, we start to constructively share with others. As we do, people begin to believe that we have more to offer than they might have originally thought. In turn, *their* new belief will change *their* actions—they now start to ask for our opinion more often. That action begins to impact what we believe about ourselves, and our self-image slowly but surely starts to improve. Over time, we might become one of the most well-thought-of thinkers in the group.

Having become mindful of this dynamic since reading the Wrights' work, I can identify any number of situations in which I've unintentionally done damage to myself and to others around me over the years. Damn if I didn't contribute quantitatively to my own demise! Our beliefs, in that context, are part of what's called a "reflexive reality"—what happens around us is altered by our belief about what's going on, which only reinforces our beliefs. If we believe our boss is out to get us, we're on edge; our work quality decreases from the anxiety; the boss reads our uncertainty as apathy or a lack of commitment and begins to invest time in others, which just reinforces our belief that the boss is trying to be done with us.

Just recognizing the nature of this simple cycle is incredibly powerful. Our beliefs lead us to take certain actions, which inform the beliefs of others, which lead them to almost always act in ways that reinforce our original beliefs. It's what Claude Bristol wrote over half a century ago in *The Magic of Believing*: "Every person is the creation of himself, the image of his own thinking and believing. As individuals think and believe, so they are."

Kinds of Beliefs

Beliefs can be negative, neutral, or positive. In each case, I believe, they are essentially self-fulfilling.

Negative beliefs, whether we're conscious of them or not, can quickly poison our lives. They are the dark side of a situation, the shadow side of the street of belief that we all may walk on any given day or maybe pass through at night while we're dreaming. They're beliefs that ultimately hold us back and undercut work that we already may be doing on the surface to improve things. We might believe that training is a total waste of time and that we only tolerate it because corporate says we should; that having employees is a drag, the hardest thing about being in business; that most people are just out for themselves and couldn't care less about anyone else; that young people have a poor work ethic; that customers can't tell the difference; or that we have no influence on what goes on around us.

At the worst extreme, as Thomas Merton writes, "[W]here minds are full of hatred and where imaginations dwell on cruelty, torment, punishment, revenge and death, then inevitably there will be violence and death." Sadly, the cycle he describes plays out in so many parts of the world. Negative beliefs lead to violent actions that then inform the beliefs of others, which, in turn, lead others to take revenge. Where the cycle started no one may even remember. What we do know—and you can pick almost any regional/religious/racial conflict—is that negative beliefs are clearly leading to hurtful, harmful, horrible consequences.

Getting Rid of the ANTS

Giuseppe Del Giudice is married to Boona Pobst, one of our long-time staffers. He's done a great deal of his own professional work on beliefs (you can see more of it at realpotentialtoday.com). One practical tip he taught me has helped me (and others) to overcome longstanding negative beliefs. He calls them ANTS—"automatic negative thoughts." His approach is simple and effective. Let's say you catch yourself immediately thinking negatively about a coworker that you've long had trouble with. It's barely even conscious. That person starts to speak and you immediately roll your eyes and think to yourself, "Here they go again." Giuseppe's approach is to simply invert the belief. Instead of thinking that "Jack is a jerk," you flip it over and come out the other side. You turn the reaction around and tell yourself, "Jack is a really good guy." At the least, the technique will make you stop and reflect. And I bet you a couple of loaves of Bakehouse bread, it will likely lead to some interesting insights and a lot more positive outcomes.

Belief neutrality is what happens when we just haven't given an issue much thought and have received little input from others about it. We may be selling something that we don't feel super great about but neither are we actively down on it. Or we meet someone we know nothing about and have no preconceived notions about them. Or there's some issue in the news that we're totally unfamiliar with. Neutrality is, I suppose, akin to agnosticism in organizational behavior. We're not true believers but neither are we naysaying. We just let things be. While belief neutrality won't bring down a project as quickly as an actively negative set of beliefs, it also won't do much to make it play out positively. This neutrality may manifest as a lack of momentum, the failure to do the all-important little extra things that can make so much difference to a product, a project, or a person's long-term success. At other times, though, neutrality may be a way to rest or idle our emotional engines. Ignorance may not really bring bliss, but it can, in the right situations, help us to stay calm.

Positive beliefs occur when we actively take an optimistic outlook on whatever issue is at hand. I believe that our organization can make a lot of constructive contributions to the community and to the lives of the people we work with. I believe that although our prices may be higher than others, we're charging what we should in order to make our business sustainable. I believe that our organization is doing important work that matters. I believe that training is critical to the success of our organization. I believe our people are a huge asset and that the more we involve everyone here in running the business, the better we're going to do. I believe that my coworkers really care about me as a person. I believe that every little act has meaning. I believe that although everyone we work with makes mistakes, they're all basically good people. (I believe that we're all human!) I believe that I'm a good—if ever imperfect—person. I believe that I can learn almost anything. I believe that after you finish reading this essay—or better still, while you're in the process of reading it—you'll begin to examine what you believe and take a closer look at how your beliefs (both big ones and little ones) are impacting your life.

When we believe good things, good things are more likely to happen. As

Tina Seelig, author of *inGenius: A Crash Course on Creativity*, says, "Essentially, if you believe something is possible, then it is." Positive beliefs yield desirable, flourishing plant life above ground. And the deeper positive beliefs are rooted in our cultural soil, the harder it will be for negative beliefs to enter our ecosystem. If they do, it will be in moderate increments only, since there's too much positive energy to be quickly overcome by a few "weeds." As editor Lillian Watson wrote in *Light from Many Lamps*, "Good thoughts bear good fruit, bad thoughts bear bad fruit—and man is his own gardener."

Beware the Pretty, but Poisonous, Plants

Please note: Beliefs that might seem positive in one sense but are actually built upon negative foundations are likely to produce suboptimal long-term outcomes. This is often the case in competitive contexts. "I'm the best in my class at math." "We're the best business in town." "I'm the best baker in the building." These beliefs *sound* positive, but their positivity is built on a win-lose approach to work and life that's all based on the hierarchical thinking so common in the work world. "I'm the best baker in the building" implies negative beliefs about the other bakers. The "I" here may likely do well but only at the expense of others. The individual person might prosper, but their beliefs are likely to cause problems in the ecosystem. Here's an insightful comment from Matthieu Ricard that may sound all too familiar: "If we sow the seeds of poisonous plants along with those of flowers, we should not be surprised when the harvest is mixed. If we alternate between selfless and harmful behaviors, we ought to expect to get a sharply contrasting blend of joys and sufferings." Ultimately, the situation isn't sustainable.

What's the alternative? A more productive approach seems, to me, to shift your beliefs to a more positive, win-win, noncompetitive position: "We're doing great work in this area." "I'm doing a good job of teaching." "Our team is meeting and beating its goals." When we're focused on our own health or improvement for its own sake, not in the context of some ranking in relation to others, we're sure to get a more grounded, healthier outcome.

Belief Building

Taking all this to heart, it's become quite clear to me that a lot of what we do as an organization impacts the beliefs of those we bring into it. For openers, we attract people who share at least some of our beliefs. For them, I hope, working here reinforces the positive beliefs they brought with them. For others who have neutral or negative beliefs, I hope we slowly shift them to the positive. As Arianna Tellez says after three years at Zingerman's:

> *Now I believe that a business really can make a difference in the world. A positive difference. It can bring people together in so many ways, from a daughter bringing a special pie home to her mother to a business owner who challenges her employee to write a vision of greatness, not because it earns the business more money, but because it's the best thing for both of them. It's when a business doesn't just give a bulk of money to charity to show the world it "cares," but carefully decides how to invest in the health of its own employees, or raises its minimum wage to a degree that inspires other small businesses. I believe a business, with careful considerations of the "why," can establish the principles, systems, and culture that have a positive impact on its employees, its community, and the world.*

It's clear to me now—and there will be much more on this throughout the book—that getting our staff's beliefs into alignment is an important part of our work. As with everything else in life, the more mindfully, caringly, and respectfully we approach that work, the better it's likely to go! (For much more on this, see Secret #41.)

Weeding Out Bad Beliefs Before They Take Over the Garden/ Leading Through Weeding

Unproductive beliefs—or maybe I should say unaligned beliefs, which then by definition stand a high likelihood of becoming unproductive—can start to cause problems quickly in an organization. Unlike email blasts from headquarters, these generally appear more discreetly, but they can turn out to be very damaging.

On the bright side, these grumblings and disagreements may actually offer us a fresh way to look at things. There may be something interesting in an outlier's experience that we can all benefit from. One of Paul's sayings—"when furious, get curious"—is hugely helpful here. There's almost always some insight to be gained from going deeper, asking a few questions, and pausing to listen, reflect, and reevaluate. Dan Barber says that in sustainable agriculture, "If you pay attention to which weeds proliferate, the soil will tell you what it needs." Translating his statement into my metaphor here, if we pay attention to the problems that pop up, we'll see that our culture is telling us what it lacks. Sometimes a small shift in perspective can prove to be really positive. It doesn't have to take an all-day offsite meeting to address—it could simply involve a couple of minutes of off-the-cuff conversation. Perceived problems can be turned into positive improvement. As Gary Snyder writes, "Shall I not rejoice also at the abundance of the weeds whose seeds are the granary of the birds?"

But if, after inquiry and examination, we still feel that these beliefs are unproductive and unhealthy for the organization, it's probably better to weed them out quickly—the beliefs at this point, not the people—before they take over our "garden." As Toby Hemenway writes, "If these weeds are left alone, in a few seasons the short, early annuals are crowded and shaded out." Some beliefs can be like invasive weeds: "That customer is just trying to take advantage of us." "That new hire is never gonna make it—he's too old." "I shouldn't have to apologize to that customer. He was clearly wrong." If we let them continue, negative beliefs like this can quickly start to dominate our organizational ecosystem.

Here's a concrete example of something quite subtle that happened at Zingerman's, arising from a particular negative belief. For background, we've been systemically documenting customer comments for over 15 years now. (See *Zingerman's Guide to Giving Great Service* for more on the subject). I believe it's one of the best things we've ever done. In a bigger organization such as ours, it allows us to track input, look for systemic problems, and correct course quickly. Early on, someone observed that by looking at customer comments as data, we were effectively "escaping from the tyranny of emotion"; in other words, the documenting process diminished the power that one person's emotional response—either of the customer who made the comment or of the staff person who heard it—would have on how we handled a situation. A particular incident might feel severe at the time, but if it turns out from our tracking work that it was an isolated occurrence—say, the only one of its kind all year—it comes to seem minimal.

What I've realized here, though, is that what documenting customer comments can't do is eliminate the influence of beliefs. I'm sure you can tell what the beliefs of the well-meaning, intelligent, and loyal staff member are from the way this report was written up. Since these write-ups go to all of the staff member's coworkers, guess what influence it will have on others' beliefs? And if one or two of these coworkers already share the negative views, guess what will soon be happening in the shop? Here is an excerpt:

What happened:
Our front counter was bowing under the weight of new products—cheese, crackers, olive oil. Two different regular guests said it was over-whelming and that, in general, throughout the shop, we "just have too much stuff."

How it was handled:
I agreed, and said that we the staff were also seeking a way to be less overwhelmed in stuff, and we want to streamline our presentation. I let them know that their feedback would help make this happen!

From the perspective of the staff member who wrote this, the conclusions to be drawn from the customer comments are "correct." And this point of view may have some merit. There's certainly something to be gleaned by considering it. It's great, too, that they thanked the guest for voicing their concern.

But I happen to believe differently. Which is, of course, why the write-up caught my attention so quickly. I believe that our space actually has much *more* room than we're now using. I believe customers have been asking for more culinary alternatives, and while we can definitely clean up the counter areas to streamline our service, there's plenty of room for more shelves, more display tables, and more products. And from that increase in offerings, we will both improve service to guests and help sales, which will positively impact profit, bonuses, etc.

So with those quite different beliefs in my mind, here's how I might have written up the same customer comment:

Guest was concerned about how many products we had on the counter today. I acknowledged the complaint and apologized, and assured her we'd be working on ways to reduce clutter on the counter. I let her know that we were working hard to fulfill a number of requests from regu-lars to add to our culinary offerings and apologized for our short-term struggle to figure out where to put everything. I thanked her for men-tioning it and assured her we'd have things sorted out soon!

Like weeds and unwanted pests, negative beliefs can appear at any time and from any direction. They come with new staff members, from employees whom we've allowed to grow disenchanted, from the press, or from popular mythology. If we're not on our game, we ourselves can contribute to the problem. It could be that we fail to follow through on commitments, and maybe sales start to sag significantly, and nothing we do seems to fix the problem. Then we encounter a long series of disheartening setbacks, and people in the organization who aren't super mindful will lose their drive. They'll become discouraged, sometimes drastically so.

The interesting thing is that these small "weeds" will only be noticed if the leaders are literally "present." The bigger the distance—whether hierarchically, physically, or emotionally—between the boss and the front line, the longer the weeds will proliferate. By the time they're "discovered," we've got a big problem. Which is why I believe it's best to have supportive, hands-on leadership on site. (You can read more on this in *Part 2*, Secret #25: "Managing by Pouring Water.") In agriculture, Wendell Berry poetically refers to this concept as having a reasonable ratio of "eyes to acres." It's quite simple really—the further we are from an issue, the less likely it is we'll spot it. Conversely, the closer we are, the more quickly (and easily) we can act to correct the problem before it gets out of hand. As Hemenway writes, "When we're chatting in the yard over a cup of coffee, it's nothing to stoop and yank a couple of tiny weeds. They don't get much beyond tiny, because we're always there to spot them."

It's not always easy to know which beliefs to take out and which we'd do best to let run their course. This is true in nature, too. Looks can be deceiving, and things that may seem to be helping the ecosystem can turn out to have grave negative consequences. Writing about ill health in a local forest, Berry explained, "The culprit was the beautiful hay-scented fern, whose rhizomes and roots grow so thickly in the top layer of the soil that they cannot be penetrated by the roots of seedlings, and whose fronds steal the light from other plants." If we're not organizationally careful, what starts as a small statement—a seed of a negative belief—will catch hold and take over. And then over time we will end up in a big internal conflict over something that initially seemed insignificant enough to disregard.

Beliefs Filter Information

En route from belief to action, there is another "action" that few of us are even aware is occurring, an additional component of the self-fulfilling belief cycle. *It turns out that we generally only allow in information that will support our already existing beliefs.*

Conversely, *we will often unconsciously filter information to exclude what doesn't support our beliefs.* "When people are believing or not believing in something," Anese Cavanaugh explains,

> *they'll find evidence to support "their facts." No matter what—they'll find the evidence. If they believe something is "great and important," or that someone is "good," they're going to consciously—and subconsciously—work to find evidence that supports that belief. The same is true in reverse—if they think something or someone is "bad," they'll find the proof for that as well.*

Armed with more data to back up what we believed in the first place, we then take "appropriate" action. Which, of course, informs others' beliefs and then their actions, which nearly always reinforce the tenor of our original beliefs.

Don't believe me?

Read the study by sociologist Monica Prasad from Northwestern University and her colleagues. Their paper, "There Must Be a Reason: Osama, Saddam, and Inferred Justification," presents some powerful statistics that, I suppose one could say, reinforce this belief about beliefs. Shortly after 9/11, the United States invaded Iraq, claiming that Saddam Hussein was connected to the attacks and that we needed to go after Iraq in order to set things straight. Later, of course, as further data came in, even President Bush admitted that this belief had been inaccurate. Evidence showed that despite his other misdeeds, Saddam Hussein had played no part in 9/11.

That I knew before reading Prasad's paper. But what it revealed was that, shockingly, even after all the evidence—and Bush's statement—showing Saddam had *not* been involved, hardly anyone who had previously believed that Iraq was behind the attacks ended up changing their minds. Let me restate this, just to clarify—the President himself agreed that there had been a mistake and that Saddam Hussein had not been behind the horrors of that September day. But this and other significant data were quickly dismissed by nearly all of those who believed otherwise. Prasad's study suggested that 98 percent of those who'd believed the original supposition about Saddam's role stuck with that belief in the face of the overwhelming evidence that it was inaccurate.

What we filter, what we fit, and what we focus on will have a huge influence on how our lives play out. Howard Zinn writes, "What we choose to emphasize . . . will determine our lives. If we see only the worst, it destroys our capacity to do something." But it doesn't have to be that way. Believing the best, focusing on the positive, and maintaining hope have been shown to bring much better results. As Zinn says, "If we remember those times and places— and there are so many—where people have behaved magnificently, this gives us the energy to act, and at least the possibility of sending this spinning top of a world in a different direction." Someone I know pointed out that while people routinely say, "I'll believe it when I see it," what this all demonstrates is that it's actually the opposite. We'll only see it if, and when, we believe it.

A Shift

The beliefs through which we view the world can radically alter the conclusions we draw about what we experience. I love the quote from artist Paul Klee: "A line is a dot that went for a walk." How many other examples of this world-altering shift in perspective might we benefit from?

Between Stimulus and Response, You'll Find Beliefs

All of which brings me back to Viktor Frankl's brilliant insight about self-management and mindfulness in *Man's Search for Meaning*. "Between stimulus and response," he wrote, "there is a space. In that space is our power to choose our response. In our response lies our growth and freedom." Beliefs all too often operate unrecognized within that space—they're the pathways along which the stimuli travel en route to our actions. Most of the world believes that its beliefs are pretty much the equivalent of "objective reality." In some cases, as with gravity, those views may be accurate. But more often than not, our beliefs are only filters through which we view and then respond to the world.

Much of what we believe to be true says significantly more about our own beliefs than it does about what's actually happening. As Anaïs Nin noted, "We don't see things as they are, we see them as we are." Beliefs, you might say, form the basis of our relationship to reality. In that sense, it's *all* personal. As is the choice to address—or not to address—what's going on inside our heads. Nin warns, "While we refuse to organize the confusions within us we will never have an objective understanding of what is happening outside." We all have beliefs that shape our decisions, learning, and actions.

Which brings me back to the beginning of the essay. My objective is to help move us into a higher level of consciousness about our beliefs so that we can actively learn to effectively manage them. The alternative is that our beliefs manage *us*. As Robert Henri writes, "Very few people know what they want, very few people know what they think. Many think and do not know it and many think they are thinking and are not thinking." If that sounds confusing, it is. I guess that's the point. Beliefs, unacknowledged, are like that road sign in Tennessee that Sam Keen references: CHOOSE YOUR RUT CAREFULLY, it says. YOU'LL BE IN IT FOR TEN MILES. Studies of neuroplasticity would indicate that this image is all too accurate, except we might be in the rut for 10 years. Or 20, or the rest of our lives.

After years of "practice" letting our beliefs channel the pathways of our decision-making into a particular routine, the routes in our brains really do become like well-worn ruts in the road. Staying in "the groove" is easy. Kevin Bermingham writes that beliefs "shape the boundaries of our thinking." This book is about reversing that flow, mostly by *mindfully letting our thinking reshape the boundaries of our beliefs*. Once we understand how they work, we can break through old limits and cross into a much more rewarding way of life. The charts below might help you process the point visually.

Without Mindful Self-Management

Stimulus		THE SPACE IN BETWEEN	Response	
Strong emotional reaction	Typical triggers	Long-standing unacknowledged beliefs	Typical past behavior	Past outcomes

Moving mindfully into this space is a wonderful thing. Often awkward in the beginning, it relatively quickly becomes both freeing and energizing. The results can be impressive. Instead of unintentionally making a mess of things so much of the time, and then expending enormous amounts of energy to clean up after ourselves, we manage to match our outcomes with our vision and values. And with reality. As we pay more attention, we gain a broader perspective, an extra dimension with which to live our lives and do our business. As Frankl's compatriot Rollo May writes, "Human freedom involves our capacity to pause between the stimulus and response and, in that pause, to choose the one response towards which we wish to throw our weight. The capacity to create ourselves, based upon this freedom, is inseparable from consciousness or self-awareness." It's a wonderful world to be part of. When we're mindful of our beliefs, it's as if we're playing three-dimensional chess while the rest of the world is still working on a flat board.

With Mindful Self-Management

Stimulus		THE SPACE IN BETWEEN	Response	
Strong emotional reaction	Typical triggers	New beliefs	New behavior	New outcomes

Spending some healthy time in "the space," paying attention, taking stock of what you see and feel and experience, choosing not to go down undesirable paths, and then resetting beliefs to align with what you really want, can be one of the most empowering things you'll ever experience.

I started to imagine myself lying on the ground and someone rolling balls at my brain. For the first half of my life, I just let the balls go into the "usual" paths and continue on apace without paying much attention to any of it. Stimuli came, I responded, outcomes arrived. I didn't see it happening, but the cycles pretty much just continued as they always had. But over time, with a good bit of reading, reflection, and readjustment, I started to change the game. In essence, I realized that I could actually pick up each ball just before it entered my mind, pause for a second—or a minute or a day—to consider its import, and then carefully and consciously choose which path I wanted it to continue on.

To pull this off requires a high degree of mindfulness and a regular dose of reflection. For me, daily journaling (see Secret #31, in *Part 3*) has been hugely helpful. Knowing that beliefs are the roots beneath the surface of anything I'm struggling with, I can now direct my mind towards them during my morning period of reflection. They're hardly the only thing I journal about, but beliefs have begun to make regular appearances over the last few years. More often than not, a few minutes of looking into the beliefs below the surface yields interesting, and usually helpful, insights. I've come across any number of conflicts in which it's now clear to me that the cause is not a difference in values or vision, nor are either of the parties "bad" people. But different beliefs lead us to different conclusions, which, when we're not mindful, lead us quickly into conflict.

The clock ticks at the same pace whether I do this work or not, but it *feels* like time seems to slow when I choose where to set each "belief" down in the field of my brain. By making fewer poor decisions, I avoid a whole lot of awkward and unproductive situations. I actually save a *lot* of time by doing this work! On top of which, better decisions simultaneously help to improve the ecosystem in which I'm working. Which of course helps everyone around me at the same time. And by mindfully making choices, rather than just reacting, my own energy level goes up. As my friend Daphne Zepos said a few weeks before she passed away (see Epilogue, *Part 3*), I was "owning my life." It's like liberating territory in your head, making a strong move to reclaim what you had all along but often failed to take advantage of: your freedom.

Small Decisions, Big Implications

How about a bit of a role-play to clarify how this can work? Say, for instance, that Sam is heading down the hall at work. His new coworker Wanda is walking towards him. When she gets within about 20 feet, she looks the other way and doesn't make eye contact. Sam has a longstanding belief that his coworkers don't like him. He knows Wanda is new, but he's sure she's already heard from others that he's not a popular person. Without even thinking about it, he reacts with hurt feelings, quickly followed by anger. He scowls with frustration.

The problem is that his assessment of what's happening is wholly inaccurate. Wanda happens to be shy and self-conscious and is anxious about making eye contact with someone who's been working in the business for such a long time. She sees Sam's scowl and feels a sense of shame. "He must really be put off by me," she thinks to herself. The odds of these two connecting positively in the future, after that seemingly insignificant interaction, are now *very* low. What's really happened is that each of the two has experienced the other's action incorrectly, through the filters of their own beliefs. Going forward from there, nothing good is likely to evolve. At best, the two don't talk much to each other. At worst, they get caught up in conflict and start to take up a lot of time of the HR department.

More mindful management of the space between stimulus and response might look like this: Sam is walking down the hall, notices Wanda look the other way, and starts to get upset. But then he pulls his brain back from the negativity that he's cultivated for so long. He "steps" into that space "between stimulus and response," and then quietly and quickly considers his beliefs: "Wanda is new. Even if the others don't like me, she doesn't have any sense of who I am." He takes a deep breath. Instead of scowling, he stops, extends his hand, smiles, introduces himself, and welcomes Wanda to the team. She's relieved and happy to be treated in this way. Sam, she sees clearly, is a super nice guy. Her shyness starts to soften; a positive connection has been made. Good things are likely to follow.

Small decisions like these—based, of course, on our belief systems—can ultimately lead to big things. *Consciousness is the key to making Frankl's equation effective.* If we don't even realize we have the freedom to choose our responses, we move reactively through our lives. And if we aren't aware of the role beliefs play in shaping those choices, how can we ever improve the quality of our responses? Now that I've become cognizant of this, I realize we run the risk of missing out on great opportunities to make our lives into something special when our beliefs are negative and exclusive. Opportunities are everywhere, but only optimists—people with positive beliefs—are likely to see them.

Like Paul. He and I met at a restaurant nearly 40 years ago. It was the first day in my new job as a dishwasher, and he'd just started as general manager. Few new general managers would concern themselves with making meaningful connections with dishwashers, who aren't—to most people's perceptions and accepted industry norms—the most upwardly mobile members of an organization. But because Paul believes that every person has value and is of equal import in the world, he treated me as what I was, an intelligent human being with high potential to contribute, and engaged my assistance in cleaning out the office, where we began to get to know each other.

Good people like me, I believe, are passed by all the time. There could be a couple in your own company right now. As Van Gogh said a century ago, "There may be a great fire in our soul, yet no one ever comes to warm himself at it, and the passers-by see only a wisp of smoke." Paul's act of asking me to help him with a task opened the door to opportunity. Had he believed differently—say, "dishwashers are the dregs of the restaurant world"—he would have treated me as most managers treat dishwashers, with mild disdain or, at best, disregard. Instead, on that first day, Paul struck up a dialogue. Nearly four decades later, that connection is still going strong.

Fixed Mindsets Versus Growth Mindsets

In her book *Mindset*, Carol Dweck breaks people into two groups around opposing core beliefs. One group has what she refers to as a "fixed mindset." People in this group believe that "they are what they are," and that others are who *they* are, essentially for the rest of their lives, and there isn't much you can do about it. It's the "geniuses/leaders/artists are born not made" approach to the world. The other group has what she refers to as a "growth mindset," which she explains is "based on the belief that your basic qualities are things that you can cultivate through your efforts." I've long believed that any of us can do pretty much anything we want and that one of the keys to making that happen is the willingness to work long and hard over an extended period of time.

In Dweck's frame, people with the fixed mindsets will have a much harder time finding long-term success and happiness. They feel stuck with the way things are. The growth mindset she describes is at the core of this book, the belief that we have the ability to freely choose what we believe, that if we open up and work hard at it, we can make a huge difference in both our own lives and the lives of those around us.

I Believe That This Is the End!

There's a Hasidic saying: "The teacher learns five times as much as the student." Working on this Secret has radically increased my understanding of the importance of beliefs. With a lot of work, small seeds can grow into beautiful big trees. Here, my initial introspection about why one of our work groups wasn't getting their work done somehow turned into four essays, a recipe for changing beliefs, an addition to our interview process, a new unit of ZingTrain teaching, and a section of an internal class. I have high hopes that this work around belief will help us here at Zingerman's and will help you and many others around the world. I hope that through better understanding each other's beliefs, we can and will ultimately also change the way we interact to create more meaningful and rewarding encounters for all involved. While our beliefs may change slowly, I'm convinced that in a supportive setting, we can more quickly adjust the way we act. I believe ever more strongly that doing the work to clarify and agree upon organizational beliefs can help all of us. And that the more positive stuff we can put on the balance sheet of our beliefs, the better we—and everyone around us—are going to do.

We have the power. It is, I believe, up to me to manage my own beliefs to help do as much good work as I possibly can. I believe it will make—and already has made—a big difference. In the words of Ralph Waldo Emerson, "Nothing can bring you peace but yourself."

This I Believe: An Exercise with "Hot Pen"

In 1951, just about half a century after Rocco Disderide opened his business, CBS radio host Edward R. Murrow began a five-minute radio show under the title *This I Believe*. The show encouraged people from all walks of life—famous or not—to share what motivated them by reading short essays they'd written on the air. In essence, each guest was sharing beliefs about his or her own life, or about life in general. They had up to 500 words to accomplish this task. Producer Edward P. Morgan made it clear to participants up front that the beliefs shared should be positive—the show was not a place for put-downs. It was, as is this book, a forum featuring folks who had begun the process of taking their beliefs from the unconscious to the conscious, from the critical to the constructive.

In 1952, a book was published that pulled together 100 different segments from the show. Its sales were phenomenal, exceeded in that era only by the Bible. On the back cover is written:

> *This book is the further extension of an idea that has already exploded into the most widely listened to radio program in the world. That idea is simple. It is that men and women will live happier and richer lives if they deliberately decide what they want from life—what they want in material things and the relative importance of moral and spiritual things. You, like most people, undoubtedly have certain rules by which you run your life. But, again like most people, you've probably never tried to formulate them, even to yourself. That's where the men and*

women in this book differ from you. They have at least tried to do so. They have "looked in their hearts and written," humbly and hesitantly, upon the invitation of the distinguished radio and television news analyst, Edward R. Murrow. "After all," says he, "the only way of discovering what people believe is to ask them." What these thoughtful people, in all walks of life, have written is here for you to read and ponder, and perhaps to emulate — in this collection of the 100 of the best of the personal philosophies of life which Mr. Murrow has discovered among the many hundreds contributed to This I Believe—*on the air and in newspapers.*

The series was later revived in 2005, and two *This I Believe* books followed. It's from those two books that I first encountered the series. This exercise is a way to carry Murrow's good work forward into our own lives. The success of the exercise in this format depends—as it does with our visioning recipe—on using the "hot pen" technique that I learned from Stas' Kazmierski many years ago. It's an absolutely essential element of what makes the visioning process as we do it here work so well (see Secret #47 for more on the subject). Because it requires us to keep writing, it pushes us through what I call the "thought barrier"—the self-conscious thoughts, self-censorship, and self-doubts that are sure to sneak in when we're going after what we really believe in.

Using the "hot pen" means that when we sit down to write, we just keep writing without stopping for whatever time period we've decided upon. When we keep writing, our true, unguarded thoughts and feelings will fast outpace the self-editing. Time and again, people who use the "hot pen" technique tell me that ideas, insights, dreams, and desires emerged during the writing that they had only barely—if at all—acknowledged to themselves.

If your conscious mind starts to grow concerned over what you're writing, override it. Keep your fingers moving. The faster you write, the better it works. Remember, what you're writing at this stage is only for yourself, not for national publication. The exercise is an excellent way to get in touch with what we really believe and to separate that from what we believe we "should believe." While what comes up may seem scary at first, the good news is that, per Secret #43, with a fair bit of mindful effort, we can change our beliefs when we want to.

Sam Keen says, "To ask the simple question 'What do I really want?' is not merely risky, it is revolutionary." I'll piggyback on Sam's bold statement: To ask the question "What do I really believe?" can lead to life-altering actions.

Reflection is the best route I know to track our beliefs. The challenge is to push ourselves to take time for some introspection—to really become mindful of what it is we believe and then to correlate that with what we want. If the two are out of synch, something, of course, needs to give; if what I believe is out of whack with what I want, the odds of me getting to where I want to go are slim, maybe none. And while believing that better things are to come doesn't alone get rid of poverty, pestilence, or poor job performance, it sure does increase the odds of that happening. So I challenge myself, and invite you, to reflect for a few minutes. What do we believe about the following?

- Ourselves
- Our lives
- Our livelihood
- Our friends
- Our staff
- Our boss
- Our customers
- Our family
- Our future

To get going, simply settle on any subject that's on your mind. (Don't worry—you can address other areas of interest later.) Get out some blank paper or open a new file on your computer and pick a subject to focus on: yourself, a colleague in the company you work for, some issue the country is facing. With your specific subject in mind, start things rolling by writing out the simple statement: "This I believe about X . . ." And then just keep writing for at least 15 to 20 minutes. The "hot pen" technique—both with this free-form examination of beliefs and in the visioning process—works wonders.

exercise Backtracking on Beliefs

If you want to take a different tack on things, try tracking the Wrights' belief cycle (see page 91) in reverse. Start with the actions others are taking that reinforce your beliefs and then head back up through the cycle (going counter-clockwise instead of clockwise). See if it doesn't shed some light on otherwise unconscious beliefs you might hold.

exercise Build Beliefs from Our Vision

If you're intrigued by our thought processes at Zingerman's, you could try taking the Zingerman's 2020 vision, reading it through, and then making a list of what you believe our beliefs are! (See *Part 1*, or email me at ari@zingermans.com for a copy.)

exercise Build Beliefs from Your Own Vision

Better still, if you've drafted a vision for yourself or your own organization, make a list of the beliefs you would need to hold to help make it a reality. Compare that list to what you currently believe. Adjust accordingly. Add sea salt and fresh ground pepper to taste.

Chris McKee, Managing Partner, Venturity, Dallas, Texas

We rolled out our Venturity Vision of Greatness for 2020 to our team in late 2014 after nine months of working together as a team to create and finalize it. We expected that this Vision would immediately propel us to great things.

What transpired instead was one of the most difficult periods since the founding of our business. This included the departure of one of the earliest partners, the loss of one of the best salespeople we've ever had, and the departure of several other team members as well. In addition, we had an issue with our technology platform that was almost fatal to our business.

In spite of all that, when we convened for our annual partner retreat in late 2015, we found ourselves more energized about the future than ever. How could that be? First, sharing our Vision had little to do with most of the problems that arose over the last year. Most were just the things that you deal with in business, and we just had a lot of them happen in quick succession.

Secondly, in rereading our Vision to kick off that partner retreat, we realized how many things we had already accomplished in spite of all of the issues we faced over the previous year. We looked back and realized that several team members who had stayed had stepped up to help push the Vision forward because they saw themselves as part of that Vision. And lastly, we realized that the Vision had been quietly working on us in the back of our minds, driving our decision making through whatever winds buffeted us because we knew ultimately where we were headed. I shudder to think how far off course we might have gotten if we hadn't had a Vision guiding us.

Thanks to ZingTrain and the entire ZCoB, really, for teaching us about Visioning and being there to support us on the journey. We've grown as a business not just in revenue, but most importantly we've grown emotionally and in maturity as a business as a result of working with you guys.

Arianna Tellez, Zingerman's Deli Supervisor, now ZingTrain Event Concierge and Staff Partner

I. I Believe in the Pages of Learning and Wonder Why

My primary intention for working at Zingerman's Delicatessen was to learn something while having fun. I wanted to gain some "experience," something to write on a résumé that would get me on track for a "career." I wanted a job that involved doing something completely different from my previous résumé-writable experiences, which were namely school and office related. I wanted it because I heard that it was a good idea. I didn't really believe in it. I only intended to stay for a short while because what I believed was that the next step towards a career was graduate school. What can you really *learn* from memorizing 100 sandwiches?

The Deli's passport system was the first experience to change my mind. Just looking at the path to learning fascinated me. The first page was no surprise, classes, key training shifts, tests. Exactly the process that was ingrained in me as "learning." But that first passport was approximately a million pages long! The next pages included environmental learnings: where things were in the Deli; social learnings: knowing the difference between the supervisors, managers, and expeditors, and their roles; as well as the skill learnings, listed out carefully and intentionally. Sherpas were provided to help each new trainee through the processes, introducing and developing the culture of interdependence. Expectations were clearly outlined; managers and supervisors clearly communicated (to the best of their ability) when those expectations were misinterpreted, missed, or met. Learning includes watching others apply the material, relating with those people, applying the material consciously, receiving feedback, even going back to question and reevaluate the original material. I see the Zingerman's perspective on learning modeled by this passport system. I see how this culture of learning is so different from academia. I see that while I was memorizing over 100 sandwiches, I learned a new way to learn. I believe that experience is extraordinary. I believe in the—plural—pages of learning.

Looking outside of the passport system I began to recognize patterns in the culture of learning at Zingerman's. I continued to notice how Zingerman's worked. I studied it. I tried to learn from it. Only when I applied to be a Staff Partner (which made me really consider and process the information about Zingerman's that had been collecting in the back of my brain) did I realize the bigger picture. I had been distracted by the "how" Zingerman's worked. And I needed to remember the "why." Now, I believe asking "why" is a very important question. Bringing it back to my own learnings, I wanted to know "how" to make a career. There are a lot of options out there and I was having a terrible time figuring out which one would work best for me. Only when I started to think "why" I wanted to make a career in the first place did things start to fall into place (though maybe I should change the tense to *are* starting to fall into place.) I believe that the Zingerman's way of working really considers the "why" we do things, not just "how." I think the "how" is the easy question. How do we create an effective supervisor meeting? We could talk to people and put a meeting time in their schedule, create an agenda and hope it works. But with our process for change [Bottom Line Change] we can't do that without first creating a list of compelling reasons—the "why." We can get more direction from the "why" than the "how."

So "why" are we doing "learning" differently at Zingerman's? I asked myself this and I realized something. It's like I had forgotten that Zingerman's is inherently a Business. And I realized another one of my beliefs had changed. Why do we concentrate on really learning? Because it's essential to our business. But wait, when I started at Zingerman's, didn't I believe that "Businesses" existed solely to make money? That Capitalism was destructive but that there was no way around it? But through my role as a Staff Partner, observing and participating in Partners' Group meetings, watching the interactions between Partners at offsites, and taking time to reflect, I realized that Zingerman's isn't just about making money. I mean, I knew that. I had taken Welcome to the ZCoB. But now I saw it from a different angle . . . And I believe that a person who takes the time to wonder why can learn an awful lot.

II. Someone Believes in Me

As an introvert, having a few close friends has always been very important to me, and in turn, close relationships have always been a huge influence on my life. There was a time in my life when every close relationship I had involved some sort of struggle, some negative aspect. And it was having a negative impact on my entire life. Then I met Ashley. From the moment I met her I knew she was a kindred spirit. We talked together for hours and hours. Her words reached right into my soul. But more than that, if I had told any of my other close friends or family, "Wow, your words reach right into my soul," they would have stared at me for a second, perhaps even laughed. Ashley wouldn't laugh. She would understand. I know my other friends and family have loved me, despite our struggles. But what I've never had was someone who actually sat me down, listened to all my troubles, and actually said, "I believe in you." And somehow, the world is a better place because Ashley believes in me. She believed in me so strongly she put it into words and told me directly. I see myself differently because I have heard those specific words. They echo in my head. I wish everyone in the world had their own version of Ashley. While my struggles didn't disappear, they somehow dissipated and became more manageable. Things have changed for the better since then, some of which I never thought possible. Is that the power of belief?

Maggie Bayless, Managing Partner, ZingTrain

Like you, my core beliefs about business have changed over the years. I now see business—and profit—as a means to an end. And rather than seeing all businesses as inherently bad, I see huge opportunity for businesses to create interesting, engaging livelihoods for the people who work there. And to make positive contributions to the communities where they operate.

I've also changed my beliefs about my personal ability to lead an organization and to effectively manage people. I spent years saying—and believing—that I would be no good at either, and it turns out I'm actually not so bad. :-)

brandon Clark and Vincent Pisoni in the kitchen at the roadhouse

Leading with Positive Beliefs

Letting Go of the Fourth Illusion

Given that positive beliefs lead to positive outcomes and that negative beliefs do not, it became increasingly clear to me that leading from a positive perspective was the only way we were going to build the kind of long-lasting, much-loved organization we want to be a part of. What follows is my attempt to apply this principle in all walks of our leadership life. Just the act of working on it has helped me stay on the positive path and to get more rewarding results. I hope it does the same for you.

Schumacher Shows Us the Way

There are a couple of patterns, ways of being, that seem common to everyone I've found who is living a great life, at least the kind of life I'm interested in leading. One is that these people are impressively true to themselves. Despite the imperfections of daily decision making and the inevitability of making mistakes, they still manage to craft a life and a way of being in the world that is somehow so uniquely *them*. They hold to their principles, to their identity, to their core beliefs in a way that, while I know it's often a struggle on the inside, looks quite graceful to the rest of us.

A second common characteristic is that they believe passionately in what they're doing. They don't stop at the superficial. They don't let society's naysaying nix their dreams. People living great lives regularly sow intellectual and inspirational seeds into the soil as they move through the world. The quality of their ideas, and the good energy that comes with them, means that those seeds have a high rate of turning into lovely plants that blossom in many different places. They study, work things out, pursue their goals and their learning, and determinedly push to get to the place they believe is right. In the process, they leave an inspirational legacy for the rest of us. I'm most interested in leaders whose ideas inspire others to live creative and generous lives themselves. They may not have won elections or made the most money, but they've had a huge impact, often on people who never met them personally.

E. F. Schumacher was one of those people. His book *Small Is Beautiful; Economics as if People Mattered*, published in 1973, was already a classic by the time we opened the Deli in 1982. Somehow, though, I failed to read it until a few years ago. I'm sorry I waited so long. The book is amazing and insightful. And like all good work of that sort, it got me thinking, strengthening many of my already existing beliefs and adding new and interesting perspectives at the same time. Schumacher's later book, entitled *Good Work,* is equally engaging and intellectually challenging.

Books, for me, are like seed banks. They hold ideas, safely and securely, sometimes for centuries, so that when the time is right, the idea can emerge. Seeds that have lain quietly for ages can, with a few months' work, sprout into beautiful plants with healthy root systems and fruit for others to benefit from. Although it took me 30 years to get to them, the ideas in *Small Is Beautiful* and *Good Work* have now grown for me into some strongly held and impactful beliefs.

E. F. Schumacher was born in Bonn, Germany, in 1911. His father, Hermann, was a political economist. His father's brother was an expert on Goethe and a professor of architecture—it's not hard to imagine that his uncle might have met anarchist Gustav Landauer, who lived in the same era, or been influenced by some of his work. Schumacher himself likely was. As Theodore Roszak writes in his introduction to the 1975 edition of *Small Is Beautiful,*

> *Schumacher's work belongs to that subterranean tradition of organic and decentralist economics whose major spokesmen include Prince Kropotkin, Gustav Landauer, Tolstoy, William Morris, Gandhi, Lewis Mumford, and, most recently, Alex Comfort, Paul Goodman, and Murray Bookchin. It is the tradition we might call anarchism.*

Schumacher's daughter, Barbara Wood, also described his views in a way that aligns them with a great deal of anarchist thinking. His approach, she said, "did away with the concentrations of economic power" and "gave people work that allowed them to be fully human. . . . Small-scale technology, small-scale enterprise, workshops and small factories serving a community and served by a community."

Schumacher has significantly influenced the beliefs of thousands of creative and caring thinkers around the world. Will Rapp is one of them. Rapp read *Small Is Beautiful* back in 1974, just a year after it came out. He started the creative company Gardener's Supply in Burlington, Vermont, in 1983 (a year after we opened the Deli), a business that has successfully encouraged people to get involved with the land and create healthy ecosystems, both at work and in nature. Here's what he wrote to commemorate Schumacher's passing in 1977:

> *Schumacher was a practical futurist and quiet revolutionary. His vision of a human-scale world, his common-sense understanding of the need*

for people to remain close to the land in their work and their values, his articulation of the importance of "natural capital" and the consequences of our squandering it (even before the first energy crisis in the 1970s introduced the public to the threat of "peak oil") were prophetic. I believe we must integrate his idea of an alternative economic system into our conventional economic thinking.

One of the many remarks of Schumacher's that resonated with me was his strong statement that the boom growth years of the mid-20th century in the West had run their course, that we were destroying the elegance of our ecosystem in the interest of economic wealth for a small piece of the world's population. Putting things into metaphorical context, Schumacher says that we lived the Industrial Age deluded

by three great magicians, illusionists. . . . One was the illusion that somehow, against all laws of nature, infinite growth in a finite environment is possible. The second entertainer said that by some strange law of nature there is an unlimited supply of people who are prepared to do mindless repetitive work for quite modest remuneration. The same sort of illusion that was once fostered in slave-owning societies about the slaves. The third illusion, which is still rampant, is that science can solve all problems.

The inverse of each illusion is a positive belief. Mindful and considerate growth is far more sustainable; everyone wants to engage in meaningful work; although science has important things to share with us, intuition, emotion, and the natural world are all integral to a healthy and rewarding existence. All three of these beliefs underlie our work here at Zingerman's.

I'd like to add another illusion to Schumacher's list. The fourth illusion, I suggest, is that we will be able to get great things to happen even when people do not believe in the work they're doing, in the people they're doing it with, or in themselves.

Think about it. Can you come up with anything that's gone really well in your life, something you worked hard for, whether at work or in a relationship, that you didn't believe in strongly? I can't. And I'm betting you can't, either. To be clear, I don't define "great" as in "made a lot of money," but rather in a holistic, well-rounded, spiritually sound sort of way. If the root system reflects what shows up in the plants that grow from it, then by definition, when we see something special sticking up from the soil, there must be positive, passionately held beliefs below the surface. Magic won't be made from mediocrity, and excellence will not emerge from average.

Here's what happens, according to a number of important voices, when positive belief is absent from the equation:

E. F. Schumacher: *That soul-destroying, meaningless, mechanical, moronic work is an insult to human nature which must necessarily and inevitably produce either escapism or aggression, and that no amount of "bread and circuses" can compensate for the damage done—these are facts which are neither denied nor acknowledged but are met with an unbreakable conspiracy of silence.*

Emma Goldman: *[I]f man is doomed to wind cotton around a spool, or dig coal, or build roads for thirty years of his life, there can be no talk of wealth. What he gives to the world is only gray and hideous things, reflecting a dull and hideous existence.*

Howard Ehrlich: *Everyday life in most organizations is stultifying. Rarely is there an opportunity to conceptualize anything better. So one does what one has to do. And by going about one's work, people reaffirm their negative self-conceptions and revalidate the organizational form as something positive.*

Ashley Montagu: *[Bad work] neither kills outright nor inflicts apparent physical harm, yet the extent of its destructive toll is already greater than that of any war, plague, famine, or natural calamity on record— and its potential damage to the quality of human life and the fabric of civilized society is beyond calculation. For that reason, this sickness of the soul might well be called the "Fifth Horseman of the Apocalypse." Its more conventional name, of course, is dehumanization.*

Tony Schwartz and Christine Porath, in the *New York Times* article "Why You Hate Work": *The way we're working isn't working. . . . Just 30 percent of employees in America feel engaged at work, according to a 2013 report by Gallup. Around the world, across 142 countries, the proportion of employees who feel engaged at work is just 13 percent. For most of us, in short, work is a depleting, dispiriting experience, and in some obvious ways, it's getting worse.*

Wendell Berry: *We can say without exaggeration that the present national ambition of the United States is unemployment. People live for quitting time, for weekends, for vacations, and for retirement; moreover, this ambition seems to be classless, as true in the executive suites as on the assembly lines. One works not because the work is necessary, valuable, useful to a desirable end, or because one loves to do it, but only to be able to quit—a condition that a saner time would regard as infernal, a condemnation.*

It's dismal. Only 30 percent of people feel engaged in their work? Wow. It's what happens, I know, when we let a drive for high yields, oversimplification, silo mentality, and monocropping (both agricultural and spiritual) overcome natural diversity, complexity, caring, and constructive collaboration. I can only start to imagine all the unhappy people—the pain is too great to stay with the thought. I know that if I let myself sink into the negative, then negative is what I'm surely going to get. As Peter Block writes, problem solving "just does not have the power to bring something new into the world." Too much time focusing on faults yields a faulty ecosystem.

I'm committed to going in the other direction. My vision is positive. My values are affirming. I believe that positive thinking makes a big difference —something we work hard to recognize and reward at Zingerman's. So if I believe, as I do, that everything works best when it's all in alignment, then I keep coming back to the same conclusion: If we want to make great things happen, we must start with strongly held positive beliefs.

The Upside

Here's what some Zingerman's staffers had to say about being part of an organization with a strong, deep root system of positive beliefs.

Anne Kellogg: *Something that changed for me when I came to work at Zingerman's was the knowledge of what it feels like to work for a company that cares—in a foundational way, not just person-to-person—about how we operate in the bigger picture: our footprint, how we treat people, the impact we have on community, who and what we're "responsible" for. This was entirely new to me. Certainly, other places cared about things, about their product, about their bottom line, about the experience they were creating. But it was not until I worked here that I'd ever heard people talking about environmental impact, about* *serving the people who need extra help both in our organization and in the greater community . . . the things most companies just don't get to.*

James Abercrombie: *I now believe in myself. I spent years going from job to job, giving my best, working to improve myself and the job, always giving great service. Almost never being recognized. At Zingerman's Mail Order, I have found a family that believes in great service and respect for all employees. My coworkers are fantastic; I get positive and negative feedback, always with the incentive: you can do it, you are doing it, you will do it. . . . [A]fter many years of work in various jobs, I have finally found a reason to believe in myself and believe that what I am doing makes a difference in this world. Lots of years behind me, hopefully many more ahead to make a difference, now that I do believe in myself.*

Maddie LaKind: *Perhaps the biggest belief that I articulated at Zingerman's was how customer service should be seen more as an interaction rather than a transaction. I've always loved talking with people, but Zingerman's was really the place that showed me how a simple "Hi, how's your day going? How can I help?" can go a long way. This belief has been instrumental for me in terms of my professional development and general personal happiness both in/out of work. As someone who doesn't have a particular fondness or natural affinity for sales, I've also found that this customer service has helped me sell in a way that feels natural and comfortable.*

Matthew Bodary: *Before I worked in the Zingerman's Community of Businesses, I thought that in business there was a necessary trade-off between doing right by your people and ensuring profitability. Working in the ZCoB has proven to me that a company can, in fact, improve financial results through, not in spite of, investment in people.*

It's an amazingly sustainable ecosystem to be part of. The positive beliefs of my fellow staff members enhance mine, which in turn gives me the energy to work harder to be helpful to them. Imagine the power of positive beliefs like that, multiplied many hundreds of times. In our 2020 vision, we talk about leaving our world better than we found it. Creating good work like this, teaching and modeling the power of strongly held positive beliefs, might just be one of the most important ways in which we can make that vision come true.

Are there other organizations from which one would get equally inspiring answers? Of course! Are we perfect? Hah! Not even close. What I do feel confident of, though, is that when we can align our positive beliefs—with each other, our work, our values, our vision, our mission—*everything* is going to go better. Energy, joy, generosity, effectiveness all increase. Belief isn't everything, but it sure makes a big difference. We will never get to greatness without it.

E. F. Schumacher asked himself:

> *How do we prepare young people for the future world of work?* . . .
> *[T]he first answer, I think, must be: We should prepare them to be able*
> *to distinguish between good work and bad work and encourage them*
> *not to accept the latter. That is to say, they should be encouraged to reject*
> *meaningless, boring, stultifying, or nerve-racking work in which man*
> *(or woman) is made the servant of a machine or a system. They should*
> *be taught that work is the joy of life and is needed for our development,*
> *but that meaningless work is an abomination.*

This belief, coming on the heels of those responses from frontline staff members above, has helped me get through more than a few difficult days. While I always have my doubts—the small seeds of concern planted somewhere in the back of my mind—I know something at Zingerman's must be working. All of these folks know the difference between good work and bad. They understand, through experience, energy, and hands-on education, what it means to be engaged, to enjoy, to be constructively challenged, to learn and grow in your work. In the same way that almost no one will go from eating great food or drinking great coffee back to mainstream mediocrity, except under extreme circumstances, I'm convinced that only under great duress would any of these good people ever dream of going back to bad work.

The Fourth Illusion

Life in the Fourth Illusion sounds like a scary late-night science-fiction film. It feels like one, too.

I'll repeat my premise: *The belief that we're going to get to greatness when either we or the people we're working with don't have strongly rooted, positive beliefs is an illusion.* We will never get excellence from either apathy or antipathy. Believe me. I've tried. And failed. More times than I'd like to admit. I'm guessing you can relate. Ever undertaken a big initiative that you were sure was beyond wonderful, but you just couldn't quite get others to work on it the way you'd imagined they would? Ever started on what you were sure was some super insightful, strategically brilliant piece of a project, but you couldn't get your staff to implement it? Or hired someone you were really high on, but they could never get their team to support them? I've experienced all of these things. On the odd chance you haven't, I can assure you they don't bring good feelings.

Maybe, though, you're not the owner of a business like I am. Maybe you have a midlevel position in a bigger company. Let's flip the coin of organizational authority and check out life from the other side. Ever been assigned a project by your boss that you didn't believe made sense, but you went along and agreed to do it anyway? Or been told to work with a new staff member whom you didn't believe would do a good job? Ever been given a client lead to close that you were pretty sure from the get-go wasn't going to work? Or on a more personal level, have you ever tried to quit smoking, improve your presentation skills, lose weight, or master mindfulness, but despite your best early efforts, you just couldn't get these new habits to stick?

Obviously, there are many factors that could have caused us to come up short in these endeavors. We might blame the failures on deficits of intelligence, lack of insight, insufficient funds, shortfalls in stick-to-itiveness, or subpar strategic planning. But one likely factor to add to your checklist when things aren't working well would be the subject of this piece, something that makes all the difference. High intelligence, big finance, and great plans will still fail when the people involved don't believe in what they're doing.

I've seen it so many times I can't deny it any more—I've seen the light, let go of the illusion. If people don't believe in a product, it won't sell. If they don't believe in their leader, they won't follow. If they don't believe in themselves, they'll trip up long before they can get to greatness. If they don't believe in people we hire, systems we install, ideas we agree to implement, then those won't work well, either. When the people working on a project don't believe in it, the odds of them doing exceptionally good work are somewhere between zero and none. The correlation is clear. They may go through the motions, but what they do will never be great.

"They" can, of course, include you and me. If we don't believe, we're not gonna get anywhere either. The halfhearted effort, the subpar performance, the so-so results are almost surely a reflection of what, in their hearts, the people truly believe. Remember what Alexander Berkman said: "You can't grow a rose from a cactus seed." Belief makes all the difference. As Berkman pointed out a century ago, "Permit (a man) to do the work of his choice, the thing he loves, and his application will know neither weariness nor shirking. You can observe this in the factory worker when he is lucky enough to own a garden or a patch of ground to raise some flowers or vegetables on. Tired from his toil as he is, he enjoys the hardest labor for his own benefit, done from free choice."

The Tinker Bell Effect

I'm guessing you remember the story of Peter Pan? Australian attorney Cameron Stewart quotes from the novelization of the play in his article, "The Rule of Law and the Tinkerbell Effect":

> *"'If you believe,' he shouted to them, 'clap your hands; don't let Tink die.'*
> *Some clapped.*
> *Some didn't.*
> *A few little beasts hissed.*
> *The clapping stopped suddenly . . . but already Tink was saved."* (Peter and Wendy *by J. M. Barrie, first published in 1911 by Hodder & Stoughton, London, England)*

> *Peter Pan was able to save Tinkerbell from poisoning, using the healing power of imagination. According to the laws of Barrie's tale, fairies cannot exist unless we believe in them. If we believe in them at first, but come to doubt them later, they will die.*

The "rule of law" that Stewart writes about works much like Tinker Bell. Both survive only as long as we believe in them. If we do not believe in the rule of law, then we will violate it regularly. Which, in turn, will lead others to believe it doesn't matter, and then, in turn, to undertake their own unlawful actions. "However," Stewart says, "I have argued that we should try to believe in it because like Tinkerbell, if we believe enough it might become real."

I think the same principle is true for just about anything. What we actively believe—at least in places where our own actions have a big impact (I'm not talking about forecasting the scores of sporting events of which we're only a fan, not a player)—is highly likely to happen. If we don't believe, our projects will bomb, our products won't sell, our people will fail, and our organization will surely suffer. As Tom Asacker writes, "If our hearts are not into it, if we don't truly desire the change, our heads won't either. We are not computers. We don't optimize our decisions. We decide, and believe, in order to feel good. And to avoid feeling bad."

On the other hand, when we do believe, when we consistently clap our mental hands for what matters most to us, the odds of it going well increase dramatically. To contribute meaningfully, to make our beliefs come true, requires significant, sustained, steady applause and effort—out loud, in our hearts and minds, singing, on stage, or in writing. Claude Bristol says, "Often belief empowers a person to do what others consider impossible. The act of believing is the starting force, the generating power that leads to accomplishment." Whether it's social change or a small sales game we're running at the Deli, it works only when it's based upon positive belief.

Sixteen Things You Can Do to Build Positive Beliefs in Your Business

When belief is high and deeply rooted in the cultural soil, you can feel it. In the same way that a healthy plant is alive and energized, you'll find similarly positive things in people. The energy that comes from it is beautifully grounded, vibrant and appealing. There's a good glow. I'm guessing you've experienced this in the presence of people in your life who are true to themselves, passionate about what they do, big believers in a positive future. It's a positive cycle to be part of. As Anese Cavanaugh says,

> *Belief leads directly to energy—when people believe in what they're doing, energy amps up, people feel good, value is added to the lives and the work of the organization. In negative scenarios, when people just go through the motions and belief is low, the individual and organizational energy both sink quickly.*

When we find a way to stay positive, it's a beautiful cycle to behold. Positive belief builds success, which then builds positive belief, which steadily creates a culture of even greater success and a healthy sense of security, trust, and stability. All of which, coming full circle, adds to the depth of the positive beliefs of those involved. The longer we stick with it, the deeper and wider the root system, the more cultural stability we get, the more grounded things feel. Even in adversity, we stand high odds of holding true to who we want to be. "Continuity," Rosabeth Moss Kanter writes, "breeds faith." This is one reason that winning organizations, healthy organizational ecosystems, are naturally stronger and more resilient. They have tradition on their side; people buy in and do the little things that it takes to help keep the organization's success intact. Because they believe.

Following are 16 things I've found to be hugely helpful in planting positive roots and growing a lovely, if imperfect, sustainable garden of a business.

1. FIND THE POSITIVES

It's not easy to stay positive in a world in which we're surrounded by cynicism, knocked down by tragedy in the news, trying to work through illness and uncertainty in our personal lives. But even a mindful and imperfect effort to keep moving in the right direction makes a difference. We feel better when we're walking the path we chose to be on, regardless of how hard it may be in the moment. Emotional resilience gains respect, which builds inner strength.

I'm all about win-win (see page 139), but emotion is essentially a zero-sum game. When a culture is filled with harsh criticism, naysaying, blaming, and behind-the-back baloney, there's not much room left for the light and upbeat. An environment like that is very vulnerable to disaster. The best way to move out the negative is to fill the ecosystem with affirmative and appreciative approaches. Weeds may still grow, but they're peripheral. The more we fill our spaces and our spirits with appreciation—the real thing, not inauthentic superficial sweetness that sends nice sentiments that we clearly don't mean—the better things are going to go. As Henri Matisse said, "There are always flowers for those who want to see them."

It's certainly proven true for us at Zingerman's. It's right there in the 12th Natural Law of Business: "Great organizations are appreciative, and the people in them have more fun." To quote positive-psychology professor Martin Seligman, "Positive mood produces broader attention, more creative thinking, and more holistic thinking. This, in contrast to negative mood, which produces narrowed attention, more critical thinking, and more analytic thinking." Data show a connection in positive work environments to lower staff turnover, better mental health, higher immune-system function, and fewer sick days taken. (If you don't believe all that, maybe skip ahead to Secret #43 and explore whether you might want to change that belief.)

If you believe, as I do, that there's some good and some not so good in most situations, it can be challenging to quickly identify the upside. I was raised to focus on finding the flaws first, then argue about the right answer, and finally fix what was wrong. I know I'm not alone in that. Rebecca Solnit notes, "Yiddish can describe defects of character with the precision that Inuit describe ice or Japanese rain." American Jews swapped Yiddish for English, but the thinking process didn't change. I learned how to argue, how to think quickly, how to push forward through adversity, how to have emotional resilience. But, still, I'm glad I moved on. Finding the flaws first—other than in an emergency where urgent action is the point—almost always leads to failure. Even in the darkest of days, there are plenty of positive things happening. Everything we know about our minds says that the more we focus on those positive things, the more positive things are going to happen. Wendell Berry suggests, "Maybe the answer is to fight always *for* what you particularly love, not for abstractions and not *against* anything: don't fight against even the devil, and don't fight to 'save the world.'"

A small story from my childhood comes to mind. When my grandmother used to go shopping, she was sure that most shopkeepers were out to cheat her. She was very diligent—watching their work for short weighting, or in case they should try to surreptitiously slip in some subpar product. She's not the only one—when I go to markets I often see people digging through piles of produce to find just the "right" piece of fruit or ear of corn. If you look up at the vendors while their customers are doing this, sometimes you'll see them smirking slightly and biting their tongues. My own approach is the opposite of my grandmother's. Instead of treating the farmers as potential antagonists, *I appeal to the farmer's expertise and integrity.* When they ask me which pint of peaches I want, I ask them to just give me the one they think is best. I can't *prove* that what I get is any better than what my grandmother got. But I'm confident that my life is less stressful and that going to the market is a much more enjoyable experience for me.

Practical Tips

- Use the Three and Out Rule. This is a little self-management mechanism I made up a few years back and wrote about in *Part 1* (on page 214, if you want to see it in the original). It's such an eminently effective tool that I couldn't stand to leave it out of this piece just because I'd already put it in print earlier. It goes like this: When I feel my energy sliding into the negative realm, I find someone around me—whether in person, on the phone, or via email—and I thank them. Sincerely. For something that they've done that I honestly appreciate. I always get back positive energy from doing this. Then I immediately find someone else and do it *again*. Bingo. I get back more positive energy. Within a matter of minutes, I repeat my act of appreciation *a third time*. Voilà! More good energy comes my way. In the face of all that positivity, I simply cannot stay in a bad mood. The smiles, the warmth, and the wealth of good feeling that others give me for having unexpectedly appreciated them *always* turns my day around. And, if my mood gets better, consider the impact on the rest of our organization. Talk about time as an investment. What better use of 10 minutes can you imagine than doing the Three and Out Rule? Try it out. Three and Out is great stuff!

- Try the Three Good Things exercise. I learned this one from positive psychologist Martin Seligman. Every day write down three good things that happened to you. Then, for each, answer these questions: Why did this thing happen to me? What does it mean to me? How can I have more of it in the future? I've used the technique myself and taught it to others, too. It works. Over time, people build the habit of seeing more of the good things that were there all along. And guess what? More good things start to happen all the time.

- Flood with positivity. Noting three good things daily works well over a period of weeks. But sometimes, when I'm in a dark space, I don't have time to wait. This technique can turn my day around in a matter of minutes. I just pull out my journal and start listing all the good things I have around me and in my life. It's the emotional equivalent of flooding rice fields. The water kills off the weeds. By the time I've listed like 20 or 30 great things, I'm usually back to a more centered place. The whole process generally takes me less than five minutes.

- Offer appreciations at the end of meetings. When you're getting ready to wrap up any formal group meeting, pause for four or five minutes of appreciations. Anyone in the room can appreciate anyone or anything they want. It's informal and no one is required to speak. Most people usually do, though. It's a great way to get ourselves focused on all the good around us before we head back into the day-to-day work world. (For more on how we do it, see Secret #13, in *Part 1*.) We've been doing this for 20 years now, and I swear by it. It's simple; it's free; it requires no software license; and other than possible awkwardness the first few times you do it, it can't fail.

Pretend Until You're Positive

There is something to be said for the "fake it till you make it" mindset. Maybe a better phrase would be "pretend until you're positive." This approach can work when we've already committed to swapping out our negative beliefs for a more positive set. I know that I've gotten myself going on more than a few mornings this way. But be careful. Strategically faking positive beliefs to gain popularity—as has become so common in politics—is likely to lead to failure. Insincerity won't cut it. Just saying the "right" things never works well if the energy beneath them is inauthentic. A garden of faux beliefs is like a hotel lobby full of plastic plants. They may pass from a distance, but they have no roots, no life.

2. Check Your Beliefs Regularly

In the accounting end of our businesses, we track every transaction with great care (I hope you do at least). We balance our books regularly; we tie everything out. When a cash drawer is short, we spend hours trying to figure out where the missing $15 might have gone. At the end of the year, we hand in tax returns to the IRS and financial statements to banks. I'm all for all of it. The regularity of our financial regimen, the routine and the discipline, are a big part of why it works. We still make mistakes. But the structure of the systems helps us identify our errors quickly and fix them fairly easily.

We could do the same with beliefs. Having been working on this book for a few years now, I've grown accustomed to reflecting on what I believe about almost anything I've got going. I've done the "This I Believe" exercise (see page 107) in relation to dozens of different parts of my life. Essentially, I've begun to regularly employ all the tools and exercises in this book. Finding my negative beliefs and constructively reframing and retrofitting them to be more positive is not a swift endeavor. But it does work. I believe (seriously) that you can do the same. I work hard now to mindfully choose positive beliefs about customers, staff, other businesses, myself, my girlfriend, the world. When I find myself slipping into negativity, I notice it right away. And when I catch it quickly, I've gotten reasonably good at turning my beliefs back to the positive without too much trouble. The longer we let negative beliefs go, the harder it can be to change them. Turning around a lifetime of learning, replanting a whole garden full of mental routines, is not an overnight activity. But if you work at it, you can steadily gain as much consistency and accountability as you have with your bookkeeping.

Practical Tips

- Dedicate 10 minutes a day to mindfully exploring your beliefs.
- Keep a belief journal to help track your progress.
- Schedule time on meeting agendas to talk about beliefs. Dialoguing about them on a regular basis can help people understand the different beliefs that underlie others' actions.
- Make dialogue around beliefs a part of your organizational routine *before* you undertake a big group project.
- Reread your vision, mission, or values. Extrapolate the beliefs that would best help you attain what you've already committed to doing. Check them out against your actual beliefs. If things don't tie together, something needs to shift.
- Craft an organizational belief statement. Like creating your guiding principles, mission, and vision, putting beliefs in writing may take time, but you'll end up with a powerful document that will help you in many ways going forward.

All of these practices have proven helpful to me. The key, as with financial work, is regular reviews. As a ZingTrain client put it a few weeks ago, "practice doesn't make perfect," but it does make "permanent." Mindfulness around beliefs makes all the difference.

3. BE THE CHIEF ENERGY OFFICER

This is, I realized a few years ago, a far better use of the acronym CEO. I don't even know what an "executive" does. It doesn't sound good. Executives execute? Ugh. So why not switch it to something more positive? Over the years, I've come to believe that the leaders of an organization that aspires to work in a holistic, sustainable, and successful way need, probably more than anything else, to be chief energy officers. If I do nothing else but exude grounded, positive energy all day, I'm confident that I will have contributed to our organizational health.

To be clear, I'm not talking about fake pep talks. I mean focused, real, honest, upbeat belief and the energy that comes from it. I've worked hard—ever imperfectly—to find ways to do this. Every day. All the time. Even when I'm struggling. Last year wasn't the easiest summer, emotionally. My dog Jelly Bean, whom I loved deeply for 17 years, died in the spring. Paul's father had passed away the week before. ZingTrain's Maggie Bayless experienced the death of her dad two weeks later. In my youth, we didn't talk about those things. But of course, the tension would come through anyway in everyone's energy. Learning how to share what I'm struggling with, in timely and productive ways, has been a huge help. I try to do it in a constructive way so people know why I'm less than at my best. From there, I can steadily work my way back to the level of positive energy I want to have. By the way, in a healthy culture, others will happily pick up the pace when you're feeling down.

Our energy is essential. Remember: 93 percent of what people take away from an interaction with us will not be our words. In essence, I'm talking about our vibrational energy (see page 172 for more on this). When we're exuding positive beliefs, others pick up on that. They follow our lead. The whole business's energy improves, and it passes through to customers, projects, and everything else.

The thing is, in an old-school hierarchical setting where the atmosphere is often adversarial (win-lose) with a number of disengaged or discouraged people, giving energy to others is exhausting. We give; they take. We're tired; we run out of energy. Frontline folks are already emotionally exhausted, so they have little left to offer to others. We need to get away to protect ourselves. But when we give energy in a sustainable setting, when we move away from hierarchy, when we teach everyone to lead and take responsibility for their own lives while also being creatively collaborative, the collective energy is invigorating.

Here's a real-life example that happened in the hour or so that I was recently working on a rewrite of this essay: A very nice compliment came in through our general email box. It was from a U of M grad who'd since moved back to the East Coast. She had some great things to say about us, and I happened to be copied on her compliment when it was circulated through the organization. Of course, I had about 100 other emails to get through, but I caught myself thinking I ought to write her to thank her. After all, if she took the time to share such positive thoughts, the least I could do was return the favor. And really, if she'd written to complain, you and I know that I'd have been spending even more time crafting a caring apology response and then working on figuring out what went wrong and how to fix it. So I took a minute to write to thank her. An hour later, here's what came back:

> *Hi Ari,*
>
> *Well, you literally just made my day! I'm thrilled that my note had such an impact, and that it meant enough to a busy guy like yourself to take a moment to write to me. We live in such a bash and trash society that I try to do my best to acknowledge the positive! If I lived in Ann Arbor, I would apply for a job at Zingerman's in a heartbeat. For now, I plan to take a class at the Bakehouse or the Creamery during my next visit in November. But if you ever open up shop in the New York City metro area, sign me up!*
>
> *All the best,*
> *Julie Mason*

A 60-second investment on my part, and her day was made. Which, in turn, made my night. I believe that when we truly believe in what we're doing, when we practice pushing that positive belief out through every pore of our bodies all the time, others pick up on it. They feel inspired. They start to do great work. Which inspires me. Which then inspires them.

One of the nicest compliments I've gotten in a long time came from a completely unexpected place. It was about this idea of positive energy and how important it is. I was presenting on customer service to a group in the medical field. They'd stayed on after work to hear me speak, so I knew it was a long day for all of them. To exacerbate the situation, it took place in a windowless room in an office park—no natural beauty, no lovely sunset, no trees or birds to brighten the evening. None of the people in the room had ever been to Zingerman's, and only a couple had even heard of us. Not an easy recipe for connection.

One older gentleman sitting to my left barely smiled for the entire two hours. No matter what I said or did to try to engage, nothing seemed to work. I launched into our explanation of energy management and brought up how much difference a simple smile can make—which almost always gets everyone smiling—but he stuck with the stone face. When we got near the end of the talk, I decided to have the group practice the Three and Out Rule. Why not, right? It gets people out of their seats, connecting and talking, and it gets them focused on appreciation. About five minutes into the exercise, the super serious gentleman walked over to me. "Can I tell you something?" he asked.

My anxiety went up. I had no clue what he was going to say. I tried not to slide into negative beliefs so that I wouldn't get defensive if he offered criticism. Attempting to follow my own advice, I took a deep breath and smiled softly. "Of course." I stuck out my hand to shake his.

"This whole evening," he said slowly, continuing to hold my hand, "has been fantastic. You are a blessing. I'm so glad I'm here tonight!" I was totally surprised and touched. And also curious.

"I'm honored," I said. "Why do you say that, though?"

He looked me in the eye. "Because every single thing you've said for the whole two hours has been positive. You're just exuding positive energy. And your energy has completely turned my energy around. I'm so glad I came tonight. Thank you."

Wow. Serious synergy. In a healthy ecosystem, everything is contributing to everything else.

Practical Tips

- SBA (Stop, breathe, and appreciate). When I feel like I'm losing it, this is one of the best ways I know to get myself back onto positive footing. It's as simple as it sounds. When stress gets high, when I want to blame others, I just stop, take a deep breath, and find someone or something to appreciate. It takes about 80 seconds and it works nearly 100 percent of the time.

- Teach and live the energy recipe. (See page 343.) Effective personal energy management can make a major difference. In a manner of minutes, we can swing our energy from negative or neutral to positive. While it won't eliminate all our organizational issues overnight, it will definitely start to make our organizational culture more upbeat and affirming.

- Get back to basics. If you're a baker, bake. If you love fishing, fish. Pouring water at the Roadhouse or standing on the selling floor at the Deli always gets me reenergized because it brings me back to the people and the products that got me inspired in the first place. As Emma Goldman once said, "When things are bad, scrub floors."

4. BE YOURSELF

When we're living in a way that's true to ourselves, when we're living out our dreams, when we own our lives in a caring and productive way, people can feel it. And it's inspiring for others as they pick up the vibe. The folks at the Center for Positive Organizations at the University of Michigan say, "Excellence is a function of uniqueness." When we're going for greatness in our own way while caringly helping others to do the same for themselves, the ecosystem is bound to benefit.

Stas' Kazmierski always tells me, "Everyone's truth is their own." I'll build on that: "Everyone's life path is their own." The challenge is to work through what that is, and the visioning process is a hugely helpful tool. (See Secret #47 for a whole lot of insight into the power of visioning and how to do it.) Finding a way past the beliefs of others, the pressures of society, your parents, your peer group, in order to do your own thing, is easier said than done. But as Mihaly Csikszentmihalyi says, "A joyful life cannot be copied from a recipe."

About 150 years ago, psychologist John Stuart Mill, whose writings on liberty inspired many anarchists, wrote, "Human nature is not a machine to be built after a model, and set to do exactly the work prescribed for it, but a tree, which requires to grow and develop itself on all sides, according to the tendency of the inward forces which make it a living thing." More recently, Julia Cameron wrote: "The voice of our original self is often muffled, over-whelmed, even strangled, by the voices of other people's expectations." It's not easy to overcome. Whatever I've achieved in the context of owning my life has been done, all imperfectly, over a long, long period of time. I've made lots of mistakes; backed away from what I really believed by letting others' beliefs override my own; and, at times, put pressure on others through the force of my beliefs in ways I wish I hadn't.

But I believe strongly that we can live our lives with beauty and grace, being true to ourselves most of the time. When it's working, others will feel it and, knowingly or not, respond positively. Christopher Alexander writes, "When you meet a person who is true to himself, you feel at once that he is more real than other people are." It's the feeling you get in the presence of greatness—not wealth or stardom, but the greatness that goes with being ourselves.

Claude Bristol described the phenomenon quite well over 50 years ago. "You always know," he says,

> when a man or woman is using the power within his or her life. Such people walk in the consciousness of this power which is in and behind their every thought and act. They are poised, self-assured, uninhibited

and magnetic in expression. They know where they are going and how to get there. They have pictured their future and are moving with resoluteness and conviction into that future. There is a spirit about them which is contagious. They tend to carry you along with them, to spur you on to greater efforts in your own behalf.

Practical Tips

- Write a vision for how you want your life to go, professionally and personally. This is the number one way I know to do this work well. (See Secrets #6 to 9, in *Part 1*, for more on how—and why—to write a vision statement.)

- Journal regularly. It has helped me enormously. I've been doing it for decades now. Although I didn't learn the technique from author Julia Cameron, I could have. Her book *The Artist's Way* beautifully lays out the benefits of journaling, writing what she calls "morning pages." I can't recommend it highly enough. If life is art, it makes sense to learn more about how artists live and work!

5. Cultivate Confidence and Positive Beliefs in Others

It's become a regular part of my day to express positive belief in those around me. Paul started teaching this to me 25 or 30 years ago. If we expect the best from folks and believe they're going to do great work, it's way more likely we're going to get it. It's the Wrights' self-fulfilling belief cycle in action. The more I tell someone on our team that I believe they're going to go on to do great things, the more they feel valued, the more confidence they gain, the more they care, the more they want to do. Which often leads to them doing higher-quality work. Which happily reinforces my belief in them in particular, and in people in general.

When I believe strongly in what I'm saying, people I'm talking to can pick up the confidence in my vibrational energy. As Rosabeth Moss Kanter says, "Confidence is real only when it is grounded in reality." Confidence is based on a combination of belief (in ourselves, our business, our colleagues) and a consistent pattern of positive performance results. It's also a virtuous cycle. With enough confidence, we can stay calm under duress. Which in turn means we believe we can make things work even when they're at their worst. Which, in turn, improves our results. Relationships, sales, service, and free-throw shooting are all enhanced when we have calm, grounded confidence.

I believe that we have a huge opportunity here to help our colleagues excel. When the leader's belief is high, it can help carry others through a time of uncertainty. When others start to waver, calm, confident, heartfelt words from someone they look up to can work wonders. Jeff Fleckenstein, who worked at the Bakehouse many years ago, shared: "I was a kind of rebellious teenager who loved the Detroit hardcore punk scene. Luckily, there were a few individuals, teachers, and machine shop owners, who really believed in me and gave me the confidence to engage in my interests and to pursue them."

There are many ways to do this work. Pulling someone aside, especially when they don't expect it, to tell them how much you appreciate their work and believe in them can do wonders. Written notes—especially if your communication is generally oral—will definitely get a good response. Amy Emberling, managing partner at the Bakehouse, reminded me that one way a leader can help is simply to take time to listen to others' beliefs. Just that can have a positive impact on people's feeling of belonging, as we affirm that their insights and ideas have value.

Practical Tips

- Express belief in those around you. Most people will rise to the occasion.
- Pick up on others' ideas and actively help get them implemented. The smallest sign that someone matters will likely not go unnoticed. Standing behind seemingly small things that a colleague proposes can work wonders to jumpstart a sense of belief in self, in leaders, and in an organization.
- Take time to point out small ways in which individuals have made a difference. As Masanobu Fukuoka writes in *The One-Straw Revolution*: "Treat one strand of straw as if it was important."
- Give people tools and resources that will help them with their work. And mental space, too. Showing faith through all our actions means a great deal.
- Come through with what you say you're going to do. In an unstable setting, every small action carries even more weight than it would in a more stable one. Do what you say every time in order to build trust.

- Achieve some quick wins. Do this by setting reasonable goals and then exceeding them. That slowly builds confidence in everyone around you.

- Do "comparison tastings." Staff can experience your products and services side by side with competitors so they can see for themselves just how much difference there is.

- Share the numbers. Customers often think we're making so much money that our biggest problem is knowing what to do with it all. If only that were true. Sharing the real numbers with staff increases the likelihood that they will believe good things about the organization. Even if the numbers aren't great in the near term, employees are likely to get behind what we're doing.

6. WORK FOR, AND BELIEVE IN, WIN-WIN

I was raised lovingly, of course, but with more than a bit of a scarcity mentality. (The incongruity of the concept—"an abundance of scarcity thinking"—does make me smile.) Given my grandparents' experiences being Jewish in Eastern Europe and then, after coming to the United States, living through the Depression and reading about the Holocaust in the news, it's not hard to understand how they arrived at those limiting beliefs. The world at large generally reinforces the idea of scarcity. Nearly every day, the front page of the paper talks about "winners" and "losers"—in politics, in business, in sports.

But here's what I've learned: Working with the belief that life is a win-lose process limits the amount of joy and excellence I can attain and help others attain. While those who perpetuate win-lose thinking might say that it's based on a positive belief—they believe they can win—I think it's a fundamentally unstable form of belief, built on a foundation of negativity. It implies that someone has to lose so that I can succeed. If you're talented and on top of things, this might work for you for a while. But it's not sustainable, because energy comes when others fail, and the belief that there are always winners and losers will inevitably bleed back into your own organizational ecosystem. Competition for jobs, resources, energy, and attention eventually turns ugly.

I so much prefer believing in the idea of abundance. Win-win (really win-win-win-win, and so on) allows us to feed off one another's good feelings. I've worked hard to find ways to build this attitude into my everyday life. The belief in abundance—that there's enough for all if we just work well together—is another seed that Paul planted in me early in our relationship, one that has grown into a large and amazing tree in my intellectual and emotional ecosystem. There are still a few thorny scarcity bushes in the back of my brain, but they've long since been subsumed in a healthy, positive forest of abundance. (Or maybe it's an "abundant forest of positivity"?) I'm now adamant that we can *always* come up with win-win solutions. If we use our creativity—and I believe that we are all born infinitely creative—we will surely find ways to help all involved do well.

The more we go for greatness, the more easily, I believe, we'll be able to share. As Gary Snyder writes, "The preserver of abundance is excellence." There's no limit to the good energy, positive belief, joy, and generosity that we can engender.

So how can this work in practice? Here's a quick story from a ZingTrain seminar. We had four attendees arrive from the wonderful Honey Butter Fried Chicken in Chicago. They're all longtime ZingTrain clients, so we know them well. At lunch on the second day of the seminar, I overheard them working together, going back and forth trying to come up with a name for a new product. Basically it was chicken tenders, but understandably they didn't like that name. They wore that look of frustration that comes when you've been working on something seemingly simple that you just can't quite figure out. I suggested we use the power of the group—do a brainstorm with all 25 seminar attendees. We waited until midafternoon when the usual postlunch slump started to set in, pushed pause on the seminar, and set up a three-minute brainstorm to help the Honey Butter folks come up with a name. It was classic win-win-win. In that three minutes, the group came up with about 50 names. The Honey Butter crew got help and reduced their own stress, and the thing that had them stumped suddenly became fun again. The group's energy went up, as it almost always does when you do a quick, structured brainstorm like that. And we got to teach the entire group how to use brainstorming in their own businesses whenever energy might be lacking.

Practical Tips

- Engage in group visioning. The collaborative nature of our visioning process is designed to incorporate win-win design. Rather than look for where we don't agree and then horse-trade to conclusion, visioning pushes us to find creative, inspiring solutions that help all the key players get where they want to go. When we were working on a rudimentary round of visioning years ago, Paul told me, "I think I need to leave the business." I was stunned. "Why?" I asked anxiously. "Well," he said, "I think I want to spend about half my work time in not-for-profits." While it sounded extreme, it turned out not to be. We simply agreed that's what he would do, and then set about figuring out—together—how we could make it happen.

- Remember Paul's saying: "When furious, get curious." The more we can back off of conflict and calmly ask good questions, the better shot we have at getting to win-win outcomes. Coming from a family where success came from outarguing the others, it's still hard for me to shift quickly to curiosity when I'm operating under pressure. But I know it works better. Paul is a master at it. "What are you worried about?" he'll ask. "What's driving you?" "I hear your concerns—how about we flip things around and see how everyone can come out on top together?" "If things were working really well, what would that look like? Feel like?" The curiosity can quell the anxiety and allow us the opportunity to move more effectively to positive outcomes.

7. Treat New Ideas Like First-Time Guests

FTG is an acronym we use at Zingerman's. It stands for First-Time Guests. I love that FTG has been well incorporated in our culture. The truth is that first-time guests—people who are new to Zingerman's—have special needs. They need an orientation to what we do. They need nurturing. They need to have hope and belief that good things are possible as they try to navigate our often busy, confusing world. They need a touch more generosity of spirit early in the interaction, perhaps a taste of something wonderful well before they actually place their order. If we simply treat them as we would someone who's been coming in regularly for years, the odds are low that they'll have the great experience that we're so committed to offering them.

Understanding all that means we can welcome first-time guests even more enthusiastically than our already generally positive greetings. That we can encourage them to enter our world even though neither of us knows how the relationship is going to go. If we see them as seedlings being planted into the complex culture and community that is Zingerman's, we know they need tending. When we do that work well, many of these new arrivals will grow into longtime loyal customers; some will even become integral pieces of our ecosystem.

The same is true for new ideas. This is an insight that came to me while I was working on Secret #39 on thinking in *Part 3* of the series. I realized that if I wanted us to be an edgy, creative, and innovative organization, I needed to make sure that I was responding to new ideas appropriately. In other words, if I wasn't upbeat and open to new ideas when they were coming my way, that closed-minded approach was likely to spread through our organization in an unhelpful way.

In order to help myself respond positively, I decided I would treat new ideas like new customers. They often show up at inopportune times, like when I'm busy, behind, or in the middle of three other things. I know that some of them may never end up doing much business with us. I may not be immediately drawn to them. But if I ignore the idea, or dismiss it because I don't have time to deal with it, it too will likely get trampled in the pall-mall madness that is the hectic, slightly crazy world of food service. So regardless of my initial emotional response, I try to still greet them with a welcoming attitude, in the belief that this is how good things come about.

One of the most rewarding of these near-misses-turned-into-meaningful-connection was with someone I met in passing at the University. Normally I'd have let our conversation lapse after a quick set of pleasantries. But with this new approach in mind, I decided to actively carry it further. Gina Athena Ulysse and I have struck up a mutually rewarding friendship in which we regularly share ideas and insights. Learning about her work in cultural anthropology, the history of her native Haiti, poetry, and performance art—on the surface, all unrelated to the food business—has led to a series of meaningful connections and helpful learnings. She introduced me to the thinking of Suzanne Césaire, the Martinique-born poet; to Suzanne's husband, Aimé Césaire; and also his mentor, André Bloch, a French surrealist and, it turns out, anarchist.

I've been especially energized, though, by Gina's passion for changing the world's beliefs about her homeland. Haiti has had a long and difficult history. In the process negative beliefs form, negative actions are taken, and . . . you know by now what the belief cycle is all about. Negative beliefs lead to negative outcomes. In her essay "Loving Haiti Beyond the Mystique," Gina writes: "I grew up in a country that most of the world degrades and continues to dismiss because it is broken." With that understanding and acceptance in hand, she set out to change the story. Her new book is then appropriately titled, *Why Haiti Needs New Narratives*. By shifting beliefs, she creates intriguing outcomes. "Imagine," she writes, "what Haiti would be like had it been supported and nurtured instead of disavowed and shunned in its [national] infancy." It's a powerful reversal—a whole new narrative. It inspires me to learn more about Haiti. And closer to home, it reminds me to imagine what would happen if all the people we employ had been supported and nurtured by businesses when they began their work.

Practical Tips

• Practice the 3 Steps to Giving Great Service (see page 201) when you hear suggestions, ideas, or possible innovations.

• Reflect regularly to keep a handle on how you're doing responding more positively. A simple daily score sheet of positive versus negative responses can provide useful feedback in only a week.

Four Styles of Responding

Martin Seligman's work on positive psychology has helped many people adjust their views of themselves and the world. I like a lot of what he has to say. The constructs below gives a frame through which to mindfully process the way we respond to others. The responding styles are listed in order of generosity of spirit, highest to lowest.

Active constructive: In this case, enthusiasm and encouragement are offered for what's been said. Even if we don't agree with all of the content, we can still come across as supportive. We could say, "Wow! That's a seriously interesting idea! I'm gonna give that some definite thought. Tell me more about how you got there." Julia Cameron calls those who respond this way "believing mirrors," people with whom it's a great idea to share an early version of your personal vision. The approach I've taken up of greeting every idea as if it were a new customer fits right in here. (See Secret #38, in *Part 3*, for more on this.) It's my intellectual version of the 10–4 Rule—when I get within ten feet of an idea, I make direct eye contact and smile. And when I get within four feet, I give it an enthusiastic greeting! This doesn't mean you can't offer input or insight about how to make someone's suggestions even more effective. But it does mean you start with good listening and encouragement, and then begin to actively support the person in exploring their proposal.

Passive constructive: Acknowledgement is given, but that's about it.

This is a less generous and less effective response, though at least it's not negative. It could be a simple "That's interesting" or "Good idea," but with no real follow-up. In the context of the intellectual 10–4 Rule, it would be like a head nod and an understated, dispassionate greeting. Smiles and nods aside, only minimal active support would emanate from this sort of response.

Passive destructive: The other person is tuned out in any number of ways that all send pretty much the same disengaged and unsupportive message. As Rollo May wrote, "Hate is not the opposite of love; apathy is." Even if our words are okay, our energy is not. We roll our eyes, step aside, and wait for the bad things we believe are sure to follow.

Active destructive: This least generous response finds the shortcomings in whatever the other person proposes and then actively undercuts that person's efforts. When I slip out of self-awareness, this is where I usually land—the critical voices, the spirit of family dinners from long ago. We find fault, fixate on flaws, erode enthusiasm. Sighs, sarcasm, squirms, smirks, denial of resources, and passive-aggressive behavior are all effective in this vein, to send energy flowing downward to leave the other person discouraged and disenchanted. As Brenda Ueland writes, "There is that American pastime known as 'kidding'—with the result that everyone is ashamed and hangdog about showing the slightest enthusiasm or passion or sincere feeling about anything."

I've worked hard to choose the first option as often as possible. Active constructive is, most of the time, the way I want to go. It's the most generous of spirit, the most energy building, and, I believe, the one most likely to get the best long-term business results. When we respond positively, we're way more likely to get a positive response. Which, in turn, means our own energy is likely to go up as well.

If you want to really work on this, one way I've found helpful is to set yourself up with a box score and keep track for a week or so of which method you use to respond. Given that you've read this far in the book, I'm confident that your good intentions, combined with a heightened awareness, will lead relatively quickly to more effective responsiveness.

8. Make Criticism Constructive

Do people perform poorly? Do we make mistakes? Of course. In difficult situations, I try to remember to always get onto the same side of a problem as the person to whom I'm bringing feedback. This kind of caring contribution can nurture the seeds of positive beliefs in others we work with—coworkers, colleagues, even our bosses. They start to believe in themselves, in you, in the organization. Effective leadership—or self-management, for that matter— keeps the creative tension in place, living in the space that German educator Thomas Senninger calls the "Learning Zone." We push people (or ourselves) and, in the process, express positive belief. If we start small, there are good odds of succeeding. Then we gently push again. I try not to push too far, too fast. Saplings don't turn into tall trees in two days.

When we're trying to deal with difficult things, the discussions will go better, and further, if we begin by assuming good intentions all around. When I maintain positive beliefs about people's intentions, it's infinitely easier (if still not necessarily easy) to effectively address difficult issues. It's just a mindful move to start with the upside. What I'm proposing tends to be received better. And usually gets much better results. Even when things are going badly, I try to assume the best. I agree with Isaac Asimov when he writes

> To me it seems to be important to believe people to be good even if they tend to be bad, because your own joy and happiness in life is increased that way, and the pleasures of the belief outweigh the occasional disappointments. To be a cynic about people works just the other way around and makes you incapable of enjoying the good things.

Practical Tips

- Mindfully take inventory of your beliefs before you meet someone, call, text, or send an email. You could do a quick "This I Believe" exercise in relation to the person themselves, the project, or the particulars of the situation.

- Then go ahead and check: Are the beliefs you're holding likely to get you to the outcome you want? If they are, outstanding. Keep going. But if they're not, give some serious thought to changing your beliefs. The self-fulfilling belief cycle is really an indicator of future outcomes. Many of us, understandably, believe we need to see evidence from others through better performance in order to change our beliefs. I've tried to teach myself to flip that around; I now change my beliefs in order to see better performance. It doesn't work every time, but it works far more often than you might think. Believe and the evidence you've been waiting for just might start to appear.

- Get clear on what sort of impact you want to have in the conversation. How would you like people to feel when you're done talking?

- Or to take it one step further, write out a short vision for how you would like to have the dialogue develop. Describe your feelings, the feelings you hope the other person will have, the outcomes you'll have achieved, how all involved did better because of the discussion. If you get anxious, you can always take out your vision and read it. I'll bet if you do, strong emotions will emerge. Tears commonly come when we read a written-from-the-heart vision out loud. The emotion, heartfelt as it is, will almost always lead to empathy and stronger connection.

9. Lead the Market with Positive Beliefs

Market leaders make their mark because they're able to effectively alter the beliefs of their customers. It could be about their product, the product category, the world, or themselves. When you've led them in changing their beliefs—and your leadership has been for real, backed up by high-quality actions—they're likely to stay loyal for a long time. Here at Zingerman's, I feel certain that we have successfully changed the beliefs of many of our customers about all sorts of culinary categories. With few exceptions, no one in town believed that their lives were going to be improved by buying handmade cream cheese, old-fashioned candy bars, or naturally leavened breads for five times what they were used to paying for standard supermarket offerings. Clearly that's changed, since we now have annual sales of over $60 million and those sorts of products are at the core of our offerings.

You can see the self-fulfilling belief cycle at work here. The roots of loyal customers' support for us are deep and strong. Their positive beliefs mean it's more likely that they'll see the good things we do and tell others about them. If we mess up, they're more likely to appreciate our humanity. And when we work to recover the situation, they're more likely to comment on how well we (nearly always) handle our errors. This positive approach reinforces our belief in the goodness of the world, that most customers are kind and caring and won't take advantage of us. Which then leads them to believe in us still more strongly.

Many people who enter the Zingerman's world with negative, or borderline negative, beliefs are likely to find what they're looking for. If they believe we're "overpriced," I'm sure they'll be able to find evidence of that. If they believe we no longer care about quality, I'm sure they'll discover proof for that, too. Once in a while, I'm sorry to say, we do fall short, and in the process shift someone from positive to negative beliefs. It's embarrassing and frustrating, and it's not at all what we want to have happen. But we're human. We make mistakes. We let people down. And not all of them give us another chance. My hope is that if we at least know that we've let someone down, then we still have a chance to turn things around. Because we believe so strongly that effective complaint handling works, we train on it extensively and take the issue seriously. We're confident that if we handle complaints well, we stand a good chance of bringing people back to positive beliefs. And if we do, they may well become or stay loyal for life!

Practical Tips

- Believe in yourself and your products. One of the most colorful testaments to the power of authenticity comes from the son of food writer Angelo Pelligrini. The elder Pelligrini's wonderful *The Unprejudiced Palate* is one of my all-time favorite food books. Pelligrini's writing had a powerful effect on people, with its down-to-earth approach (literally, really, since there's a lot about the positive power of gardening.) "It's almost like LSD," Brent Pelligrini says of his father's work. "People read his stuff and it changed them. That's the impression I got from all these old letters I read. My dad expanded people's minds—and it was all from his peasant upbringing."

- Spread knowledge. Well-trained, knowledgeable staff who believe in what they're telling you are about 10 times more believable.

- Focus on telling people what *you* believe, not on what they "should" believe. In so doing, you show respect for others, even if they don't agree with you.

- Offer a free sample of what you sell. The door to changing beliefs might be opened by the above strategies, but people are most likely to walk through, and feel good about themselves in the process, if they can experience what you're selling before they actually buy it.

- Guarantee everything. Confidence builds when people know we'll give them their money back any time they're unhappy with our products or services.

10. Watch Your Language

Language is far more powerful than most people realize. If we want to create a positive culture, we need to start by choosing our words wisely. As Peter Block points out, "If we have any desire to create an alternative future, it is only going to happen through a shift in our language."

Many of the language choices we make unconsciously each day cultivate negative beliefs. I was reminded of this while working with a group of talented and in many ways successful individuals who had failed to create the kind of collaborative, consistently caring culture they desired. "Why are we falling short when everyone wants it?" one group member asked me. "What are we doing wrong?" another wanted to know. When a third person exasperatedly asked, "Why can't we get this right?" it hit me—they were all focusing on the negative.

I politely suggested they reframe the question. "I hear you," I said. "I grew up in a very critical, if loving, family, so I can relate. But I've come to realize that we can ask the same questions but change the words so that we're coming from a positive place. What if you try it this way: 'What can we do to take our culture to the next level?' Or 'We're doing so much well—how can we build on that to make our team more collaborative and create more positive energy?'" It worked. They got the point. By the end of the session, I could see them trying to reframe their questions. And answers.

The same goes for the phrases I've come to reference so regularly around the idea of free choice. "I have to . . ."; "I should . . ."; "I can't . . ."—these are so common in our everyday language that we don't even realize how much they matter. But if we believe we have no choice, if we believe we're trapped, then we believe that we're helpless and we'll always act as if we're being forced to comply. Our energy will never be positive when that's the case. And we can never own our own lives when we act as if we have no say.

One more thought to add. When we as leaders choose first-person possessive pronouns to describe our work, we are unwittingly excluding others. Break the cycle. Rather than "my business," try "our business." Instead of "my staff" or "my people," it's "our team." You get the idea. Using first-person pronouns can build a belief in others that the business is not theirs. Based on that belief, they distance themselves from their work and from the organization's outcomes. When we use inclusive pronouns—and believe them—we're effectively bringing others into the mental mix.

Practical Tips

- We recommend a ratio of four parts praise to one part constructive criticism. Five or six to one is even better still. Successful organizations run a ratio of *at least* three to one. Keeping track of how you're doing can quickly help you get it right.
- Track your use of the following phrases: "I have to," "I should," and "I can't."

11. SEPARATE PEOPLE FROM PROBLEMS AND SUCCESSES

We also want to be cautious with the words we use when giving compliments or criticism. All too often we unwittingly convey or internalize our beliefs about others or ourselves through the language we use. I suggest that both compliments and constructive criticism are significantly more effective if we apply them to behaviors rather than to people. Here's what I mean:

"That's a really great idea!" versus "You're brilliant!"

"That was really unproductive behavior" versus "He's a jerk"

"Her work is really creative" versus "She's so creative"

When we equate the behavior with an individual's character, we're essentially expressing beliefs that are likely to become self-fulfilling. If we say "Jack is a jerk," we start to treat him accordingly. Even worse, he may believe it. In both cases, the self-fulfilling belief cycle kicks in. Over time, Jack will start to "become" that person. (We know, by the way, that criticisms of this sort are frequently projections of our own internal fears. We worry that we ourselves are jerks, and we deflect the discomfort by dumping the same accusation on others.)

You might be wondering, "But what's wrong with telling someone they're brilliant? It's a positive belief, right? What could be bad?"

Well, here's the deal. If you believe, as I do, that we're all good people trying to do good things, then when we say that someone is brilliant, a genius, or a natural leader, we're implying that their greatness comes from genetics, rather than—what my sense of the world and a number of influential studies say is really at issue—how and why they're working to be successful. Greatness and excellence are not (yes, that's my belief) about *who* the person is. They are instead reflected in the ways we show up in the world, how hard we work, and the way we go after what we believe in.

If you apply the belief cycle in this same way, both the person you've complimented and the others around them start to adopt your belief. Someone might say that "Bashar is brilliant." But Bashar is probably *not* brilliant. What he's done is implement some brilliant ideas. If Bashar is brilliant, how much pressure do you think he now feels the next time he wants to share an idea? *A lot*. And he starts to agonize and self-criticize over what's actually normal—we all have ideas that are good and others that aren't so good.

And here's what happens to the other people around Bashar. They begin to think, "He can do it because he's brilliant. But I'm not. What can I do? I'm not smart enough." The real big difference maker—effort—gets lost here. How hard we work at stuff is what makes the difference, not brilliance. It's how well we stick with things. It's the energy we bring. It's our beliefs. It's our behaviors. I'll bet you a lot of dollars to a dozen really good Roadhouse donuts that it is *not* about innate brilliance. By complementing Bashar's behaviors instead, I can constructively remind everyone else that they, too, can match his work.

Setting up others as geniuses or "naturals" is likely to lead to competitive, hierarchical, win-lose thinking. As soon as I say "Bashar, dude, you're brilliant," people around him whose self-beliefs are based on their relative rank to others will begin to compete. Which puts loads of destructive, win-lose energy into their world, Bashar's world, and—if they work here—our organizational world. For what?

On the flip side, here's another gain we make when we criticize someone's behaviors instead of taking a stab at their essential existence as a human. "You're a jerk" is hard to hear. Unless I believe that I'm a jerk, I likely will want to fight back. "I'm so frustrated with the thing you brought up at the meeting today" is easier. Now it's not about the person, it's about their behavior. Better still? "I was so frustrated with the way things went in the meeting today." This statement shares the responsibility; there's no direct judgment of the other person. It's way easier to hear, and much more likely to turn the issue at hand into something that people can work through together.

Note also that it's only a small step from assigning characteristics to a person's inherent nature to assigning traits to an entire group. If Bill is a "terrible listener" (rather than a person who does a poor job of listening on a particular occasion), it's not a big leap to say things like "Men! They're such bad listeners." And before you know it, you have assigned characteristics (more commonly known as stereotypes) to almost every group you can imagine. Which then, of course, means that any individual you assign to membership in that group must, by definition, possess those same characteristics. Which, we know, is wholly inaccurate. Wendell Berry calls this "condemnation by category." I love the phrase, but I hate the action for which it's named. I believe that every individual is a unique being. And identities can be taken up and chosen by each of us anytime we want.

Practical Tip

- Watch the language you use to avoid assigning identity to people. Instead, focus on their behaviors and give feedback accordingly.

12. GET GREATNESS INTO YOUR MISSION, VISION, AND VALUES

Peter Koestenbaum writes: "Philosophical greatness is the commitment to relinquish mediocrity forever." Settling for mediocrity never inspires; when we believe we need to settle rather than push for something special, we will seed that same belief in others as well. "Leadership," Koestenbaum says, "means greatness in all you do." Vision, mission, and values are all fantastic places to commit to do something special.

I highly recommend putting all of those organizational statements in writing. There's great power in it. As Julia Cameron says, "We should write because it is human nature to write. Writing claims our world. It makes it directly and specifically our own." Just the act of putting the words on paper—whether we're using a pen or a computer—makes them come alive in new ways. In our heads, everything is shifting. A hundred voices are talking at the same time. When we put our thoughts on paper, we gain and share clarity.

If you're going for greatness, please know that not everyone will like it. Leading a change in beliefs will rarely be popular at first. As Kierkegaard noted, "The truth is always in the minority." The process we use for organizational change (see page 540) is designed with this sort of thing in mind. It requires us to get clear and to write a positive vision of the future. As multiple people in the organization work on the change, their belief in the work will likely increase as well. Others' beliefs in themselves and in the world grow more positive as they participate and see success slowly unfold. In this way, we effectively and caringly spread the benefit of positive belief to others, all the while crafting our own vision. Done well, it's the ultimate win-win.

As Mikhail Bakunin said, "By striving to do the impossible, man has always achieved what is possible. Those who have cautiously done no more than they believed possible have never taken a single step forward." There's a bit of a paradox here, in that no innovative idea ever comes to fruition without its advocate believing in it. What Bakunin really means (I believe) is that "those who led the way to great things believed possible what *others* thought could never happen."

Speaking up for what one believes is right for the organization—whether you're the boss or a recently hired baker—might mean messing with the status quo, going against the rules, disagreeing with what the majority of the group believes to be true. Just because others say it "has to be" or "can't be" doesn't mean you have to agree.

How do we know where the hard edges of reality end and where we have a chance, with a lot of belief-driven work, to make a big difference? I believe that the answer is, "It's hard to say." We would do best to remember Emma Goldman's words: "[E]very idea in its early stages has been misrepresented, and the adherents of such ideas have been maligned and persecuted." I do know that if we don't believe in what we're doing—from the heart, with all we've got—it surely won't work. (Of course, we also need to work hard to make it happen, and stick with the changes for the long haul.) Goldman says, "The true criterion of the practical, therefore, is not whether the latter can keep intact the wrong or foolish; rather is it whether the scheme has vitality enough to leave the stagnant waters of the old, and build, as well as sustain, new life."

Practical Tips

- Write, or reread, your mission statement.
- Write, or reread, your organizational vision.
- Write, or reread, your guiding principles.

(See *Part 1* of the *Guide to Good Leading* for more on all three.)

13. FOLLOW THROUGH

The benefits of making bold statements of positive belief in our mission, vision, and values will be advantageous for only a limited time if we don't actually make a solid effort to implement them. Failure to follow through erodes energy. Before you know it, organizational actions are falling further and further out of alignment with our stated values or visions. In the process, negative beliefs form. And we know what happens then. Positive belief is best reinforced when we complete what we say we're going to do. When we come through consistently, people start to . . . believe!

Practical Tip

- Track your success on timely completion of commitments. It's no different from mapping your workout program at the gym. What I learn from the measurement isn't always what I would have expected. I'm not very competitive with others, but I hate falling short of my own standards. Mindfully tracking the results, I've found, improves my effectiveness at implementation.

14. TEACH THE POWER OF BELIEFS

As Peter Koestenbaum puts it, "To teach is to systemically help others learn to think and act as leaders do and to integrate leadership intelligence into the achievement of organizational goals." Teaching about belief, making it a mindful activity within the organization, and giving people access to the tools and support to see where and how belief impacts them will ultimately change the way people work. While most of the world plays dodgeball with data, argues incessantly over "who's right," or cites long streams of facts to show "who's at fault," people rarely dig below the surface to explore one another's, or their own, beliefs. The more they start doing so, the better they—and the business—are going to perform. Even in the relatively short time that we've been teaching the basics of belief here at Zingerman's, I've seen a significant number of light bulbs go off for folks!

Does all this focus on belief make a difference in the day-to-day life of an organization? J Atlee, an assistant manager at Zingerman's Mail Order, shared this story:

> *I recently started training two new people for a floor supervisor position. Both were current employees. I found that I was excited about*

training the one, while I was having trouble buying into the other's success in the new position. I realized, through the training I'd been through, that if I weren't bought into her success, I would be an obstacle to her succeeding. So I proceeded to realign myself, by acting as if I were bought in, like I believed in her. Even before starting the formal training, I started sharing tips and techniques with her for the new position. I also became uberconscious of how I carried myself around and towards her. By two weeks in, when we formally started training, I was completely excited to be working with her and completely convinced of the oncoming star I'd be working with. And she ended up doing really well!

Practical Tips

- Add a section on beliefs to any existing training you have in place.
- Consider an entire class on the power of beliefs.
- Use the self-fulfilling belief cycle, which has proven to be a particularly effective teaching tool.

15. FIGHT FOR FREE CHOICE

Beliefs about free choice, as discussed in Secret #40, aren't only an issue for us as individuals; the same cycle plays out all the time in organizations. In an old-school system, people at every level are generally (unconsciously) choosing *not* to own their freedom. They see themselves as "forced" by their "superiors" to follow along. They're "slaves to their schedules." They're "compelled by company policy," "held back by the boss," "doomed by data." In the same way that my energy was drained by acting as if I was being forced to do things, an organization in which people don't act freely will be on a slow road to failure. The culture will come to be dominated by what Rollo May refers to as "passivism." As G. K. Chesterton says, "Business, especially big business, is now organized like an army. It is, as some would say, a sort of mild militarism without bloodshed; as I say, a militarism without the military virtues."

Choosing choice and freedom changes everything. As May asks, "But what really is ethical about obedience?" I believe obedience is overrated. Instead of paying people to follow along, I believe we would do better to get everyone to step up, think, act, and believe that we're all leaders. Osho said, "I don't want followers, obedient people. I want intelligent friends, fellow travelers."

Many people we hire come to us with the belief that they make little or no difference, that their opinions don't count, that no one cares what they think. "The challenge," Peter Koestenbaum puts forward, "is to welcome and institutionalize the existence of freedom." Getting a large group of people to choose freedom and self-respect isn't easy. I believe that part of our role as leaders is to nurture this in everyone we work with.[13]

Embracing free choice moves us out of the old-school, paternalistic organizational model and takes us to a place where everyone is a respected equal with a high ability to learn, lead, and contribute. My belief is that an organization made up of mature, free-thinking, creative, opinionated, and collaborative colleagues is a far more effective and rewarding one in which to work. In this environment, people start to realize that if they want something to be different, it's up to them to take the lead. As Koestenbaum points out, "Freedom is a reality within your heart. Know it, acknowledge it, claim it, use it."

One of the relevant stories that comes to mind involves Sharon Kramer, a longtime server at the Roadhouse. Though not a manager, she regularly takes on formal and informal short-term responsibilities in work groups and in our open-book huddles (meetings). A few years ago she came to share a concern. It was true, and much appreciated, she said, that Zingerman's gave servers paid vacation. It's rare in the restaurant world. But because servers' regular wages are very low (compensated for by tips, which, I'm happy to say, take their earnings to the top levels of compensation in the food world), when they take that time off, their "vacation pay" is way less than what they normally make with tips.

I was caught completely off-guard. I felt bad, but I knew nothing about it. In my commitment to handling complaints and suggestions from staff in much the same way I do customers, I tried to handle Sharon's concern with grace. I managed to properly thank her for bringing it up and told her I'd check out the situation without getting defensive (as I kind of wanted to). I did a bit of investigating. How long had things been this way? Since we opened the Roadhouse in 2003, 10 years earlier. The problem? Essentially, it involved different beliefs. We, the partners, believed it was generous that we were giving any paid vacation time at all. On the other hand, there was Sharon's belief that the point of the program was to allow her to actually take time off—impossible when $3.50 an hour (server pay rate, sans tips) was all she got in her check.

I'm happy to say that with the help of a work group—which included Sharon—it all went well. I'm sure it took longer than she'd have liked (Natural Law #11: "It generally takes a lot longer to make something great happen than people think"), but we changed our beliefs. The Roadhouse decided to pay out paid time off at "regular" minimum wage—still less than servers' tipped pay would have been, but three times the "minimum wage for tipped employees." And because we're open-book management, everyone in the restaurant ultimately shared the responsibility for making it fit into the existing finances.

The idea of owning responsibility for our lives and our careers is a big shift. But as Rollo May writes, "There is no meaningful 'yes' unless the individual could also have said 'no.'" Most people believe their job is to get themselves hired, work hard, be loyal, and wait, respectfully, for a raise. Or work hard for a while, get frustrated, and then move on. Neither sounds good to me. What I'm advocating here is to go after an entirely different approach in which we each stand up and go for what we believe is right in a caring and collaborative way.

"When people are forced to face the reality of their own freedom," Koestenbaum points out, "and that management no longer possesses them, they see that their future is in their own hands." When it works, I believe changing to choice takes people out of the mindset of thinking like an employee and into one of thinking, acting, and believing like a leader. Koestenbaum says:

> *It is one thing to hear employees blame management for their lack of motivation or even performance; it is another thing for managers to swallow the bait and believe it. We have accepted the idea that managers are responsible for their employees' attitudes and behavior; so much so that in some organizations, managers are evaluated and paid based on employee ratings of their manager.*

A lot of this is about putting an end to the hierarchical thinking that's so much the norm in our society. Sure, we still have job responsibilities and some level of "hierarchy" in the formal org chart. But we would do well to remember that title has no correlation to quality of work, nor to knowledge. When we start acting like kings, we're in trouble.

Practical Tips

Choosing and owning freedom changes everything. It's one of the bases, I believe, for why people at Zingerman's so often act like owners. Owners (at least good ones) own their choices. I've already written a lot about this subject in Secret #32 on Free Choice (in *Part 3*) and Secret #24 on Stewardship (in *Part 2*). But here are some concrete ways that I believe we're making this idea of free choice a part of our organizational construct and culture here at Zingerman's:

- Our Training Compact, which holds both the trainee and the trainer equally responsible for the effectiveness of training
- "Trial shifts" to help both parties decide whether employment at Zingerman's (at this time, at least) will be a good fit
- Open-book management, where everyone gets involved in running the business and learning the finances
- Teaching the idea of free choice in our Managing Ourselves internal class and ZingTrain seminars
- Open meetings where everyone interested can participate
- The Bottom Line Change system, where anyone in the organization can initiate a change
- Starting performance reviews with a personal vision written by the staff member
- Teaching Stewardship, which encourages everyone to learn to dialogue and negotiate as equals (see Secret #24)
- Using the consensus process for our partner-level (and some other) decision making

16. VIEW PROBLEMS IN A POSITIVE LIGHT

None of this, mind you, is about living life as a Pollyanna. Problems occur, some people advocate for things others are completely opposed to, people get sick, economies fail, orders go awry. But our beliefs about those things can make all the difference. Without trying to play word games, we can have positive or negative beliefs about negative things. Our beliefs dictate the actions we take to respond to those things. While I was raised to believe in perfection, I've swung around to the other side. I believe mistakes are an integral part of a healthy human existence. As Errico Malatesta said, "There is no freedom if there is not the freedom to be wrong."

When we view problems in a positive light—as a natural part of existence, an opportunity to learn and grow—good things often emerge. I grew up in a setting where worry and problems (and even worse, potential problems) were the order of the day. I've pulled that belief out by the roots big time. Today, I'm aligned with Rollo May, who wrote, "Problems are the outward sign of unused possibility." If we make problems and mistakes a normal part of our organizational life, we acknowledge our humanity in a healthy way. Even nature is imperfect. I'm not saying we should accept error without action to correct it.

But if we hold ourselves to perfectionist standards and then beat up ourselves (or others) every time we fall short, we'll end up in a very negative cycle. By helping our staff accept that going for greatness means making mistakes, that even the greatest players miss shots, they'll understand that practice and the *drive* towards perfection, finding joy en route, are really the point.

Possible Problem	Negative Belief	Positive Belief
Economic crisis	We're screwed!	This will be tough, but it's a normal part of the cycle. It will help us get stronger in the long run.
Firing someone	We're so bad at hiring.	We gave it our best shot—no hiring process is perfect. Now we get the chance to learn and go forward together.
We lose a big order	You just can't count on customers to come through.	This will give us a chance to look at things anew and see what we can do to improve.
Disagreement with a partner	People are impossible to deal with. I should have done this alone.	It's a Natural Law that strengths lead to weakness—of course we frequently disagree; it's a healthy element of diversity.

The negative column will almost always lead us towards sadness, anger, despair, even rage. These beliefs do not, Peter Block points out, "have the power to bring something new into the world." The positive column will more likely bring us to calmer, more centered, reflective, and then proactive, places. We may react initially with anger, but we're able to quickly reflect and manage our reaction. In the words of anarchist-leaning writer Oscar Wilde, "We are all in the same gutter but some of us are looking at the stars."

Toby Hemenway reminds us, "Nature can be the gardener's ally. We still hold vestiges of an earlier time's regard for nature as an enemy, or as something to be conquered or restrained . . . the vast majority—90 percent or more—of all insects are beneficial or harmless." What's considered a problem in more traditional settings might actually turn out to be a positive. As Dan Barber asks, "Is a weed really a weed if it doesn't compete with the plant?" Many plants that mainstream agriculture consider weeds are actually excellent for cooking. I ask the same question here: "Is it really a problem if it just breaks the rules, but doesn't violate values or undermine vision?" In old-school organizations, employees who speak up are generally considered to be problems. Most of them (though, of course, not all) here turn out to be thoughtful people who are ready to start leading. In the process, we positively embellish our ecosystem.[14]

When I read it 25 or so years ago, Paul Hawken's book *Growing a Business* planted some very positive seeds about sustainable business. Among them was this one: "Good problems energize. Bad problems enervate." It's now Natural Law #9: "Success means you get better problems." In his list of good problems to have, Hawken includes "customers showing up on Sunday afternoon seeking a tour of the facility." I'm familiar with that challenge! And I'm thrilled to have it.

Practical Tips

- List five to ten problems you're facing; then fill out a chart like the one on page 158 to see how you're framing your thoughts about them.
- Use active coaching to help people in your organization reframe problems and view them from a more positive perspective.

A Small but Significant Story:
How Positive Beliefs Can Make a Big Difference

Does all this really matter? Here's a small, easily overlooked, but I would argue meaningful story to support the belief that it does.

Nearly one in five Americans is dealing with some sort of disability. One of the many challenges that brings is the difficulty in finding a job. At the same time, nearly every business owner I know is looking for loyal, hard-working, dedicated, high-energy employees. The connection is clear. If you look at things this way, it's literally a match made in heaven.

One key to making it work is being at a positive starting point for the self-fulfilling belief cycle. When employers look at prospective staff members who are less abled as a pain in the behind, that's what they're going to get. Even out of good intentions, when one sees someone with a disability as a charity case, that belief will be self-fulfilling. When, by contrast, you see someone as another caring human being who has some things they're good at and some things they're challenged by, someone who will benefit from positive, strong, supportive leadership, then in that sense they're just like everyone else you hire.

Positive beliefs make all the difference. If you believe that a disabled staff member can contribute to making the business better, while at the same time enabling you to contribute to the quality of their life, all sorts of good things can happen. Does it work well every time? No. But neither do things work perfectly with folks who are, by the world's standards, full abled. Are there challenges associated with employing disabled individuals? Of course. But that's also true for, in our case, the 700 others who work here. Over the years, we've hired any number of disabled folks to work in our various businesses. Most all of them have done great work.

Vincent Pisoni started at Zingerman's Mail Order five years ago. He's one of the sweetest, hardest working people I've ever met. He later moved over to the Roadhouse where he did dishes for over two years. In our drive to build a positive culture, Vincent is a key contributor. The guy is always in a good mood! He always makes a point of saying how great it is that we're busy! A year or so ago, Vincent started to do prep cooking as well as dishes. I see him regularly in the back of the kitchen cutting vegetables or cooking bacon. A while back, Brandon Clark, now a sous chef, decided to take Vincent under his wing and help him keep growing in his skill level by teaching him even more about cooking.

Best I can tell, Vincent is blossoming as he takes on more responsibility. And so is Brandon. Both are learning a lot in the process. Brandon explains: "Vincent reminds me how to be a consciously competent trainer. When he performs a task incorrectly, it reminds me how to explain even the most 'obvious' of tasks in more depth. Having Vinnie working here is of great benefit to those that recognize it." Recently, Vincent approached Brandon about getting a special dish on the menu. A month later the Pisoni Salad (see page 568) made its debut on the seasonal menu. Both customers and Vincent are loving it.

When I told Brandon I wanted to include this story in the book, he wrote me back to say, "It means a lot to know my work is inspiring to others. One thing that might make the story have more depth is referring to the work I do with Vinnie as 'cooking learnins' as that's what we call them. He always asks me 'Are we going to do any cooking learnins today?' And that's when I always say, 'Yes.'"

The benefits of Vincent's hard work and Brandon's positive beliefs extend far beyond the confines of the Roadhouse kitchen. Vincent's brother-in-law, Quinn Strassel, wrote me on Thanksgiving Day:

I've been meaning to write a note of thanks about the "Pisoni Salad." You have no idea how grateful the entire Pisoni family is and how much pride Vincent has taken in contributing to the menu. My wife was in tears when she heard about it. And now, everyone's talking about it at the Thanksgiving table. Which, I guess, makes this a good day to say a huge thank you to everyone who has made such an effort to provide such a great environment for Vincent. It means so much!

List the top 10 to 20 positive beliefs that you'd like to see embraced throughout your organization. Try a bit of dialogue with others to see how they feel. You'll soon get a good sense of how well aligned—or not—your organization really is.

NOTES FROM THE FRONT PORCH

Hannah McNaughton, Founder & Chief Envisionary,
Envision Marketing, Ann Arbor, Michigan

I am the daughter of a railroader and the granddaughter of a farmer, a preacher, and a factory worker. I come from a family with no college diplomas on the wall. I was raised on Southern cooking and gas station gizzards. I was brought up running through golden rows of corn and kicking up dust in a poor, blue-collar town of God-fearing farmers and factory workers, where one out of every six people lives below the poverty line.

I was raised to be polite, respect my elders, and get good grades. I was raised to pursue a better life than my parents, and a better life than their parents. I was raised to go to college, and to take advantage of the opportunities my parents sacrificed for. I was raised knowing that dreams are just dreams, and that dreams don't make money.

And so I followed the path that had been laid before me. I did all the "right" things. I went to college, got a degree, landed an amazing job at a wonderful company, and achieved society's version of success . . . and yet I wasn't happy. "Success" had taken me away from my family. "Success" kept me up at night and strapped me down on the week-ends. "Success" left me stressed, exhausted, and riddled with health problems. "Success" had pulled me far from my roots.

Driven by a feeling of losing my way, I did the only sensible thing: I threw myself from an airplane. I felt like I was floating through life, and I needed to feel alive—and I can say that at 18,000 feet in the air, I felt more alive than I ever have. Three miles above the earth, surrounded by nothing and everything all at the same time, life becomes breathtakingly clear.

The stresses of life disappear and the things that are important become unmistakably obvious.

When you feel like your chance of death is as close as your next breath, you realize that surviving isn't enough, and life was meant for living. To take from two Greek words for "life," I had gotten so caught up in existing (*bios*) that I had no time for living (*zoe*)—and I wanted more *zoe*!

In an effort to figure out the next steps, I started reading Ari's books. Through his words, along with the wisdom of a wonderful mentor, I allowed myself to admit that society's version of success didn't match up with my own . . . so two weeks before Christmas 2014, I jumped from the security of my "successful" job to start my own company.

It may not have been the most elegant of plans, but jumping out on my own taught me a thing or two about making things happen. I wanted to start off right by going through ZingTrain's Business Visioning course, because Zingerman's was the one place I could feel the joy radiate when I walked through the doors. I wanted to learn how to build an atmosphere like that—partially because I wanted more, and partially because I was afraid of building a company like the "successful" job I had just jumped away from.

When I started the course, I thought that I had already come so far, but I didn't realize how far I still had yet to go. Throughout the two days, Maggie and Ari pulled on the passions of why we were all there, and helped us to silence the voices in our heads that tried to sway us otherwise. They showed us that having a vision allows you to attract a support group that will help you move forward—both personally and professionally. They helped us to not only understand our "what," but to get at the heart of our "why."

So many people lose sight of why they chose a particular direction in life. Maybe they never pinpointed it in the first place, or maybe it got buried by simply surviving, but it's there, and Ari and Maggie can help pull it out. Visioning works, and has helped me to continually improve my life every day.

I'm not going to say that visioning is easy or that it solves all of my doubts and fears, but having a vision is an indispensable tool to keep me on track, and serves as a reminder of why I've chosen the path that I'm on. Through visioning, I have been able to accomplish more goals in the past year than I had in the previous decade, including building a company that supports a healthy work-life balance, becoming a contributor to a leading industry journal, getting in the best shape of my life, and spending more quality time with my family.

I am thankful to have grown up in an area where prayers grow like weeds along the roads. I received the kind of education that can't be learned from a textbook. I saw the exhaustion in my father's eyes as I tried to rub the stained grease from his hands. My parents wanted the best for me because of what they endured, and pushed me to demand more from my future. But I've learned that the best decisions are not fueled by fear or by others' ideas of success; the best, most rewarding decisions are fueled by passion.

I'm still not entirely sure where my life will take me, but I'm okay with that. Sometimes I feel like I'm still falling from that perfectly good airplane, but the surprising part is that falling wasn't frightening; as in life, making the leap is the hardest part.

Maybe you can no longer hear the voice of your passion, but I assure you, it's still there. It may have been buried by years of "can't" and "won't" and "shouldn't." It may have been drowned out by reasons to believe you're not good enough or strong enough or experienced enough. It may feel impossible to give up that comfortable life, but comfort is anything but comfortable when you always have the tiny voice inside you begging you to believe that there could be more—the ache inside your soul to go and passionately pursue.

So close your eyes, take a deep breath, and jump.

Mike White, Assistant Retail Manager, Zingerman's Deli

I took a moment to write a few thoughts. Short and sweet.

I don't want to be in the food business.

I want to be in the personal-development business that specializes in using food as a platform for creativity, interpersonal relationships, and self-actualization.

I wrote that five years ago, shortly after leaving my job at the Deli, not knowing that I'd return and achieve that aspiration.

Reading it now, I feel the hope of my younger self, searching for a meaningful independence. I feel grateful knowing that my current work embodies these personal ideals. I feel pride for this place that enables me to succeed on these terms.

I'm curious, too. How much of what I achieve is based on intention? To that end: what haven't I written? Which hopes—which other beliefs in a future self—will lead me next?

Steve Mangigian of Zingerman's Coffee Company,
sifting chaff from coffee beans

It's All About Alignment

Beliefs and the Importance of Congruity
in All We Care About

One of the things that appeals to me so much about anarchist thinking is the strongly held belief that the means we use to achieve something must be congruent with the ends that we want to achieve. Gustav Landauer writes, "a goal can only be reached if it is already reflected in its means." Although it's hardly the first thing most of the world thinks of when you mention the word anarchist, it's at the core of almost all anarchist approaches. In Alexander Berkman's view, "Means and aims are in reality the same: you cannot separate them. It is the means that shape your ends. The means are the seeds which bud into a flower and come to fruition. The fruit will always be of the nature of the seed you planted."

There's a lot of congruence there! I like it. Quite simply, the more things are in alignment, the more effectively they're going to work. It's true in nature, it's true in our bodies, and it's true in our organizations. We won't produce high-quality products if we don't buy high-quality ingredients. We won't grow grounded collaborative staff by grinding them into the ground. We won't get caring customer service by treating staff with severity. As Voltairine de Cleyre asks, "Did the seed of tyranny ever bear good fruit?"

I've spent many years now working to bring all of the various elements of my life into alignment. The more I do, the better things go, the better I feel, and the better our business does.

—

I was at physical therapy one morning when I asked Patrick Hoban, my friend and physical therapist, about alignment. His eyes lit up and he started sharing thoughts enthusiastically. "It's *all* about alignment," he said.

> *When things are in alignment, they're working well. But, in reality, the body is often a little bit out of alignment, here and there. Most of the time that's fine. We bring things back into alignment mostly just through our normal movement; things reset and we haven't even noticed it. But when things pass over a threshold, when they're too far out of alignment, we get pain. And when we have pain, it's the body's message that we need to do something differently, or get help.*

It's much the same for us as organizations. We're never perfectly in alignment in all areas. But in a healthy business, like in a healthy body, the normal day-to-day routines will shift things back to where they should be without a lot of upheaval. Small incongruences can be worked through without too much stress if we just stick to the system. Teaching people processes such as visioning, recipes for customer service, open-book management, open meetings, performance reviews, and organizational change provide them the tools to self-correct when alignment is out of whack. As architect Buckminster Fuller said, "Energy flowing through a system tends to organize that system." Ideally, we would actively work together to create harmony between all of the following:

Mission
Vision
Values
Systems
Culture/Actions
Beliefs

What follows is a basic framework, a diagnostic list for getting things better aligned. My hope is that if you're frustrated by something that's not working in your organization, this list will give you a way to start identifying the issues and thinking about solutions.

Getting It All in Alignment

In a healthy business, where people are working in harmony with the Natural Laws (see page 306), it's highly likely that most of the work of the business is in alignment. As Stephen Cope says in *The Great Work of Your Life*, a good life—both personally and organizationally—"is like a great yoga posture. Everything must be aligned around the spine." When we get out of whack, whether it's our back or our business, we're able to get through day-to-day discomfort and still function fairly well in the beginning. Over time, though, the pain gets worse. Without treatment, we begin to compensate in unhealthy ways—we stand at odd angles, walk weirdly, take pain meds. As the years go by, life becomes more about managing pain tolerance than it does about joy, generosity of spirit, and well-being. We grow accustomed to the dysfunction and discomfort, believing it's "normal," that there's "nothing we can do."

Emma Goldman called it "the Lack of Joy and Purpose in Work which turns life into a vale of misery and tears." The sad thing in the work world is that this chronic pain, so spiritually debilitating, has come to be accepted as the norm. People believe bad work is what work is. E. F. Schumacher observes, "It is interesting to note that the modern world takes a lot of care that the worker's body should not accidentally or otherwise be damaged. If it is damaged, the worker may claim compensation. But his soul and his spirit? If his work damages him, by reducing him to a robot—that is just too bad."

The good news is that the right physical therapist, chiropractor, surgeon, or other health care practitioner can often help you get your body back to where it wants to be. And the equally good news, organizationally, is that with some active awareness, a fair amount of self-reflection, and a lot of collaborative conversation, you can get your company back (pun only sort of intended) to where it wants to be, too. While you make the changes, there's likely to be much work, frustration, and short-term failure. Determination is necessary. Over time, burdens will be lifted and balance restored. And in the end, things are likely to flow a lot better, you'll feel a lot better, and life will become a lot more fun. If you believe in what you're doing, strongly and from the heart, the odds of your efforts succeeding go up significantly.

In a healthy organization, mission, vision, and values must be well aligned. If they're not, nothing is likely to work well. (Because these three subjects are discussed at length elsewhere in this series, I'm going to leave them alone here.) Similarly, if our systems don't help us realize our visions, and aren't aligned with our mission or values, they're not a good fit. I'd suggest in

> ### Conversational Clarity
> To calibrate language, you can look back at pages 80 and 81 in Secret #40 to find our definitions for mission, vision, values, etc.

that case that it's probably the system that needs to shift to fit the values and vision, not the other way around! I'll come back to culture in a minute. Now I'd like to focus on beliefs: to see how they fit (or don't fit) with mission, vision, values, systems, and culture; how they may (or may not) be aligned with reality; and how they can be used to change that reality.

As you might imagine, I've spent a fair bit of time talking about the role of beliefs in business. When I bring up my belief that many people or organizations have beliefs that are out of alignment with their mission, vision, or values, most people look at me quizzically. At which point, I give them some examples from my own experience. For instance, if you look below the surface, you might well find that

- Your values are all about empowerment, but you don't believe that frontline staff can be trusted with making big decisions about key customer interactions.

- Your values state that people are your top priority, but at the same time, you believe that only upper-level people are qualified to weigh in on important issues.

- Your values talk about the importance of continuous improvement, but people on the front line believe that expectation is only the work of upper-level managers.

- Your vision and values commit you to being a high-quality provider in your industry, but you don't believe that you can charge what you need to properly cover your costs.

- You've agreed to a new sales target, but you don't believe it can be hit.

- Your values state that you're committed to the success of others, but you don't believe your colleagues are doing good work or that they're interested in hearing your thoughts.

- You believe that the people in your organization should take responsibility for their own work, but you also believe it's your responsibility as a leader to fix things for them.

- You have a vision that says the business will be three times as large in five years as it is today, but you don't believe that your partners are capable of getting to the next level.

- You have people in key roles, but you don't believe that they're going to get the work done to meet your vision.

- You believe that your organizational structure isn't healthy, but you believe no one will listen to you if you try to change it.

- Your values say that education is important, but you believe that investing in training for frontline staff is a waste of time because they're just going to leave soon anyway.

- You're expected to keep raising sales every year, but you don't believe you can do it because the product line is so outdated.

- You want to grow the organization, but you believe that adding administrative staff will create too much bureaucracy.

That's a general list of things I've heard from a variety of business leaders over the years. And here are two more specific examples from within Zingerman's of moments when we realized that our beliefs were out of alignment, and we made some adjustments to address them.

- In 2013, we wrote a vision for the year 2020 that said (among a lot of other things) that we would have a zero carbon footprint by the year 2020. Two years later it became clear that some of the key upper-level players in the organization, people who I know are committed to the organization and to doing good work, didn't believe we were going to make it. As a result, we decided to adjust the timing by pushing the date on the vision back a few years.

- Our mission is to bring our customers and coworkers a great experience, but for a long time, we didn't give too much thought to people who applied for jobs at Zingerman's but didn't get hired. Once we realized this long-standing incongruity, we spent about a year discussing the issue and then started a work group to improve the quality of the service we give to job applicants. Changes included streamlining the application process, focusing much more closely on a timely and courteous response to applicants, and adding pay ranges to job postings to help those applying know what they might expect.

We all have ways in which what we believe isn't fully aligned with where we want to go and the way we work. When the list of shortfalls isn't too long, or the gap between what we believe and reality isn't overly large, we can manage through the challenges to get to success. When the gaps are too big, or we don't have the gumption to do the work that's called for to close the gap, then trouble is sure to follow—the odds of getting to greatness then are next to nil. Congruity counts. In the hopes of bringing the beliefs in our businesses into alignment, it makes sense to do a bit of an inventory.

1. Do We Believe in Ourselves?

Paulo Coelho wrote in *The Witch of Portobello*: "You are what you believe yourself to be." If we do believe in ourselves—in a grounded, humble way—so many things become possible. Calm, considered self-confidence comes through clearly in people's vibrational energy. You can feel it when someone has a mission (or purpose); when they have a clear vision of where they're going in the long run and are excited to go there; when they're clear on their values and live in synch with them most of the time; when they know what their beliefs are, and those beliefs are in alignment with their vision and values; and when reality is being pulled along in the updraft of their drive towards a better future.

There are countless examples of people like this in our lives. Some are famous, but far more are just folks we find at work, in the classroom, or at home.

Take a minute while we're on this subject and think about a "radiant" personality (or two) in your life. What draws you to them? What are the signs that tell you they're "onto something"? Better still, make time to talk with them—learn more about their life, their beliefs, their vision, where they've erred, and what they've learned from their missteps. I will pretty much guarantee that if you're picking up grounded positive energy from them (even in passing), they will have many favorable beliefs, an inspiring mission, and a vision to share. As former Yale president Timothy Dwight said, "The happiest person is the one who thinks the most interesting thoughts."

Most people who think poorly of themselves have had plenty of "help" in forming their negative beliefs—poor parenting, a lot of bad breaks, suffering as a result of social bias, lack of resources. But even when everything is in place for positive beliefs to take root, all too often self-doubt destructively limits what people can and will do. Rollo May wrote this 75 or so years ago, but I think it's still true in most workplaces and in much of society: "Most people now, therefore, are able to find good 'reasons' for their belief that as selves they are insignificant and powerless." Here is a lengthy list of self-limiting beliefs I've heard over the years:

- I'm not very smart.
- I'm very unlucky.
- Things almost never go my way.
- Others are out to get me.
- "They" won't let me go where I want to go.
- There's no chance for people like me.
- No one understands me.

- I can and should get things under control.
- I'm not attractive.
- I'll never figure this out.
- I can't stick with things long enough to see them through.
- I'm not a good friend/parent/lover/son/daughter.
- I'm not a creative type.
- I'm not organized.
- I'm not good at finishing things.

- I'm not a leader.
- I'm a loser.
- I'm a liar.
- I'm bad with money.
- I'm not an idea person.
- I'm not a good writer.
- I don't deserve good things.
- I'm not going to go very far in life.
- I'll never be anywhere near as good as (fill in the blank).

Consider what Osho said about the last one: "Always remember the basic rule of life: If you worship someone, one day you are going to take revenge."

I've believed some of the items on the above list myself over the years. Often they're slightly masked because I've said them with a smile and some self-deprecating sarcasm. But when it comes down to it, whether we say negative things like this with or without a smile, to some degree we believe them, and they don't do us any good.

There are also more covert beliefs—beliefs that we never speak aloud, or even allow into our own heads, but that also have a significant impact on self-limitation. As Osho said, "The belief can create an atmosphere in your mind, where, without knowing, you start thinking that you know." Negative beliefs, especially ones we don't even realize we hold, keep doors closed that could otherwise open onto interesting and enlightening spaces. At best, they hold us back a bit and limit our ability to become all that we could be. At worst, these incongruent beliefs become actively destructive. At some level, we may even fear our own success. As Søren Kierkegaard says, "There is nothing with which every man is so afraid as getting to know how enormously much he is capable of doing and becoming."

How do we get out of this unproductive box? The first step is to get to know our beliefs (see page 84). The second is to look at how these beliefs impact our lives. The third is to determine if our beliefs are aligned with where we want to go and how, from an ethical standpoint, we want to get there. If you like the results you're getting now, by all means, run with them. But if you don't, then it's probably time to make some adjustments. You can skip ahead (at any time) to Secret #43 and look at—and then start using—the recipe for changing your beliefs.

Making the change isn't easy. But, if you know that your current beliefs are causing big problems, and that the upside of changing them can be really rewarding, then why not make a break for it? A friend of mine who is a teacher shared the story of a colleague who repeatedly told her classes, "I know, I'm just so disorganized!" Lo and behold, when the end of semester evaluations came in, "disorganized" was one of the most common criticisms. When she realized what she was doing and stopped calling herself disorganized, the comments stopped coming.[15]

Some self-doubt, managed productively, is healthy. Learning to express vulnerability in a calm, collected, panic-free way can actually be used to build strength and resilience. Proactively sharing stress and seeking support, wisdom, and insight can have big benefits in the world of belief. As we talk, we usually gain insight and support from those around us. In the process, we build our belief in ourselves and our ability to gather up the resources to move forward effectively through difficult times. As Wendell Berry writes, "We do not have to live as if we are alone." In the process, we help others build belief in themselves; asking for insight and support shows trust and confidence in people's ability to contribute at high levels.

Sadly, there are many people in the world who were taught that demonstrating doubt and uncertainty is a sign of failure. They want to show self-confidence, but because their confidence is inauthentic, it comes across in an unappealing way. Pretending not to have any self-doubt is ultimately self-defeating. No one in the world is free of it. "Can we do it? Will we be okay? Do I really know how to make this happen? Will people poke fun at me? What if I fail?" All of these questions have run through my mind many times (even just in the last week). While letting the unbelieving voices rule your world unilaterally leads nowhere, pretending we don't have them is equally ineffective.

Often people are enmeshed in self-doubt, but they've learned to cover it up by being cocky or excessively upbeat. That sort of mostly-for-show bravado will always work its way through to the individual's vibrational energy. Some people they interact with probably won't notice right off. But eventually, a problem will present itself. It may manifest as an uneasiness, a feeling that's hard to put your finger on, a dis-ease that others experience when in the presence of a person like this. Such people often come across as contemptuous of others, but in fact, it's their self-contempt coming through from beneath the surface.

Isaac Asimov is known for his science-fictional descriptions of life on other planets; he also had some insightful things to say about life here on Earth: "And above all things, never think that you're not good enough yourself. A man should never think that. My belief is that in life people will take you at your own reckoning." Go into any difficult interaction (personal or professional) from a place of self-doubt and internal dissonance, and inevitably the other person will pick up on it. By contrast, go in with a calm, centered sense of self and interact with the same person, and the outcome for all involved is likely to be much more positive and productive.

Belief Bending

To consider the impact your beliefs can have on your business, try this little experiment. One day, when you're in a good and grounded place emotionally, try going into a meeting or approaching a problem with an intentionally narrow, intensely negative, set of beliefs. (Be careful—I don't want you to lose an employee or a friend over this, so experiment with something small and low-stakes, okay?)

Take note: How does your energy shift? How does it feel when you read negative nuance into almost everything that occurs? How do others react?

Then try it the other way. Go into the same sort of experience—even the same day—with positive, generous beliefs. Again, take note of what happens, how you feel, how others respond, etc. I'm pretty sure—actually, I believe—that you'll find the two experiences to be very different and the experiment very enlightening.

2. Do We Believe in Our Organization?

Most everything in an organization is going to go better when the people working in it believe in what the business is doing. When we believe, we work harder, we give more, and we put a level of energy and passion into play that's essential to creating anything great. With few exceptions, people long—I'm tempted to say "need"—to believe that they're part of a great organization, that their work makes a difference, that what they're selling is a good product, that the organization they're part of is generally doing good in the world. Our job as leaders is to make that scenario a reality. I believe we can. When we do, everything—from feelings to finance to food quality—will be more positive.

Please note that I'm not talking here about kooky cults or surreptitious sleights of organizational hand. I'm speaking of solid, grounded, positive belief systems. Where people feel like they make a difference, and that by acting on that feeling they actually *self-fulfill into a positive future* that people who are doing bad work might dismiss as some silly piece of utopian science fiction. But it's essential if we're going to get to greatness. As Peter Koestenbaum comments, "Each of us needs to believe that the organization is ours to create if any shift is to take place. . . . Indifference or compliance is a form of passive aggression." Sticking around, but not buying in, will kill you: it's an act of slow spiritual suicide.

Emily Hiber, a supervisor in our Next Door café, used to be a teacher but has opted to work here instead. "I was just talking to a friend of mine whose husband is just super unhappy with his work," she told me.

> *He's not earning very much, and he is feeling totally unfulfilled. I was saying that, while I'm not in the 'lap of luxury,' my work pays me a livable wage, and because I believe in it so much, and in the people that are involved with it, I'm really fulfilled in what I do. My commitment is really high, because I believe in the people that I work for and with. I think the people who work here are willing to buy in, because they really believe in the service we provide and the products that we're introducing people to. And also to our way of thinking about food and work and relationships.*

When I teach "visioning" at Zingerman's, I often use the analogy of a cathedral, the story of two guys working on the construction site of the Duomo in Milan. Asked what they're doing, one answers that he's "laying stone." The other, doing the same exact work, responds that he's "building a cathedral." The vision, as we define it here, is the "cathedral" that everyone in our organization is constructing. I don't believe that anyone truly loves just laying stone day after day; we all—at least in some part our lives—want to build cathedrals. We want to know that our work is going into something great, making a difference, contributing constructively to those around us. That even though we may only put down a few rows ourselves, in the end, "our" stone is going to be part of one really amazing structure that will be appreciated far and wide.

Starting to Seek Belief

What would happen, I started to wonder, if we could teach new staff members about the power and importance of beliefs before they even begin to work with us? What if we ran people through the "This I Believe" exercise early on in their work experience? What if they did it about themselves? About their organization? Their manager? Their coworkers? Would the increased awareness of how much our beliefs make a difference, and then the idea that we can change them to be more aligned with the outcomes we desire, add up to a meaningful difference? Can we plant new seeds earlier in order to yield fruit sooner? Knowing what I know now about all this, how could it not?

3. DOES THE ORGANIZATION BELIEVE IN US?

Working—and living—with people who don't believe in us is debilitating. It's hard to do great work when our organization or the people who lead it have negative beliefs about us: that we're "bad," "lazy," "selfish," "doomed," or "dumb" and "have no real future" or "will soon be departing." At times, we may be able to change those beliefs; sometimes great work performance, an emotional appeal to excellence, or a meaningful heart-to-heart conversation can do the trick. On rare occasions, that works. When it doesn't, though, it may be time to go.

Here's what David Nugraha had to say on the subject shortly after he started working at the Bakehouse:

> *The last few days I have felt speechless and grateful at what has happened. It feels really good that John [Rolfe-Chin, Bakeshop retail manager] hired me that quickly, to have someone believe in me so much. I feel like it is becoming a familiar feeling, since I have experienced that same positive belief expressed from you throughout our many interactions the past few months. It is the same belief Tracie Wolfe [who works in our Department for People] also has in trying to get me the job that I want, and the same belief I experienced when my coworkers were training me during my first shift.*

In my view, an individual's relationship to the place they work (maybe we could call the Deli a relation*shop*?) ought to be win-win. I have to believe that a healthy business and a healthy individual have similar interests for both to get to greatness. As anarchist writer Paul Goodman says, "The moral question is not whether men are 'good enough' for a type of social organization but whether the type of organization is useful to develop the potentialities of intelligence, grace, and freedom in men."

4. Do We Believe in the Boss?

If the team doesn't believe in the coach, if the musicians don't believe in the conductor, if the staff doesn't believe in their manager, most everything I've gone over above will start to slide as well. It doesn't mean that the business won't run at all—just that a layer of richness, a pivotal piece of a big puzzle, a key ingredient, is missing. It's like taking the vanilla out of your baked goods; the average eater might not even notice. But the difference is there, and it makes the experience of eating much less rewarding. And over time, the whole thing becomes less and less compelling.

When people don't believe in their leader, the business will almost certainly stagnate and eventually collapse. But it doesn't have to be that way. As Peter Block points out, when people complain to him about their boss, they would do well to own the impact of their beliefs. "Why are you creating that kind of boss for yourself?" he asks. It's a good question. Why not take a more positive approach and believe the best? Claude Bristol notes, "So remember, some of your enemies may be of your own making . . . merely a reflection of our own thoughts—the other fellow will consider us an enemy or friend according entirely to the picture which we ourselves conjure up."

Sorting Out Symptoms

Although a symptom may show up in one spot, the root cause of the problem might be a belief issue somewhere else. It's true in our businesses and also in our bodies. A few weeks ago I started having a problem with my right leg—my gastroc muscles were tight, and the tightness gradually worked its way up my leg into my hamstring. I was having a hard time extending my leg properly when I headed out for my daily run. I went for a massage, which helped a bit but didn't alleviate the problem. After a few days I made an appointment with my friend and physician, Jay Sandweiss.

Jay takes a holistic view of medicine—he's been trained in both Western and Chinese approaches—and he's able to see things in ways that others miss. He quickly figured out that the issue wasn't my leg but rather two vertebrae in my back that were out of alignment. They were pinching the nerves leading to my leg, causing the other issues. Twenty minutes of realignment work made an enormous difference.

The same is true in organizations—although symptoms may appear in one place, the real issue might originate somewhere else altogether. Poor service from frontline staff might be a particular employee's performance issue. But it might just as likely involve low belief in the staff member, or in the value of customer service, coming from the manager. Low sales of a product could be a quality problem or a bad market fit. But it might well be that the supervisor on shift doesn't believe that the product is worth what we're selling it for. Or the owners might not believe in training and might have sent staffers out to serve without proper preparation.

The more we learn to do in our businesses what Jay does so effectively with the body—trace things back so that we can find the deeper issues, rather than getting stuck on symptoms—the more effectively we can work, the less pain we're going to have, the more freedom of motion, the more fun.

5. Do We Believe in Our Coworkers?

If we don't believe in the people we've hired, they aren't ever going to be great at what they do. Disbelief almost always leads to distrust, and our working relationship is pretty much doomed to disaster. If we believe that a newly hired coworker is incompetent, we're likely to exclude them from our activities and hold back information—why waste time and energy on someone we're sure will never succeed? Our actions will likely lead the coworker to the conclusion that they have no shot at success in our organization, if others don't seem to like them or they're discriminated against because of who they are. Which in turn will likely lead the coworker to do as little work as they need to do to get by, to withdraw from the group, and to go through their weeks without engaging others effectively. And that, of course, leads us back to where this story began, reinforcing our original belief that our coworker was never going to work out in the first place. It's a horrible cycle to be caught in. The problem here probably doesn't stem from the new employee but rather from those who believe this individual is a lost cause.

Cutting—Out—the Grass?

I should warn you that when we check for alignment throughout our lives, we may find some incongruities in unexpected places. Having studied permaculture as part of my work on this book, it's become clear to me that the clichéd American dream home with the well-trimmed lawn out front presents us with some serious problems. If we're devoted to diversity, if we believe that congruence counts, if we want to live more in harmony with nature, then a good place to start might be getting rid of the lawn.

"Typical lawns are monocultures," Toby Hemenway explains. We know what that means in a natural ecosystem—lack of diversity leads to trouble. But, oddly, in our standard social belief system, the diversity we're now advocating for at work is discouraged in front of our homes and offices. "True diversity is unwelcome," Hemenway writes, "since it's defined as weeds, pests, and raiding birds or rodents. Nature's knack for spontaneity often means trouble, rather than enjoyment and improvement." How unwelcome? Radical urban farmer and artist Ron Finley was actually cited by the city of Los Angeles for growing fruit and vegetables instead of grass in front of his house. In the end he won—he kept his garden intact. He now calls himself an "eco-lutionary."

How did we come to believe that a lawn is what belongs in front of a well-kept building? A big lawn in England in the 17th century showed that you were well-off enough to afford sufficient sheep to do the "mowing." Lawns held high social value because they were a way to demonstrate that you had enough wealth to use land for mere ornamental purposes instead of for growing food. Today lawns are one of the silliest uses of energy one could imagine. "The average yard," Hemenway reports, "is both an ecological and agricultural desert." The way American lawn management works, we're constantly operating at cross purposes in a win-lose setting, where we're on both sides at the same time. In the long run, we go nowhere, which is, ironically, the essential intent of the process. Lawn maintenance actually stops nature's development by keeping grass short and forcibly excising the plants that would naturally appear as an ecosystem develops. "With sprinkler and fertilizer we're tromping on the accelerator," Hemenway says, "yet with tiller and pruning we're slamming on the brake."

Granted, I'm biased. I always hated cutting the grass when I was a kid. Now I feel vindicated (not really, but it's sort of funny to think about it that way). This is actually all too congruous with the way so many ineffective organizations are run. Speed up/slow down; follow orders/be bold and act decisively. Whether it's out in front of your home or in the home office, incongruity kills. As Hemenway says, "No system runs well under that kind of schizophrenic regime."

And yet, the long-standing American belief is that a well-trimmed, well-kept lawn is a sign of solid citizenship. If you let your land gradually go back to its natural state, you'll be punished. Think about what that says about our society and its relationship to nature. If we want dynamic, diverse, ever-evolving, environmentally friendly ecosystems—both at home and at work—it looks to me like we need to change our beliefs. The lawn just might have to go.

6. Do We Believe in What We're Working On?

Oftentimes people believe in what the organization at large is working towards, but they do *not* believe in the work they themselves are engaged in. They love the mission, the vision, the values, even their manager, but they're apathetic about their own assignment.

I've realized, belatedly, just how much of a factor this is in the success—or lack thereof—of any initiative we undertake. I can see now that I've far too frequently left people to work at things they didn't believe in. Regardless of logic, data, or how compelling a project may be to me, when the people who are doing the work don't believe that it's worth doing, or don't believe that the initiative has a reasonable shot at success, then guess what? The project is almost sure to fail. At best, it stalls; at worst, it makes the working environment worse. In any case, it's wasted effort, and none of us can afford much of that.

Sometimes the product itself may be good, but the individual involved—for reasons of taste, values, or cynicism—may not believe in it. Perhaps it's the work group they're skeptical about but agree to lead anyway. Or maybe it's a new hire they don't think is likely to be very good but on whose behalf others are advocating. I have, at times, contributed to the problem (if inadvertently) by pushing people to do work that I believe is beneficial but that they don't believe in. Yet they agree to take it on. Sometimes they mean well and don't want to make waves; sometimes they just want to play "flatter the leader"; sometimes they legitimately don't have the energy to argue; sometimes they don't even realize that they don't believe in what they're being asked to do.

I hardly think these "nonbelievers" are malicious, lazy, or evil. Nor do I assume that there's some flaw with my vision for the work I want them to take on or its importance to the organization. But that's the problem: I believe in it, they don't. And neither a long list of supporting data nor a forceful demonstration of authority is likely to change things. Generally, nonbelievers in a business will do what most nonbelievers under pressure to convert have done throughout history: a couple will become passionate converts; a handful will depart rather than compromise their principles; and the majority will pretend, stay passive, try to pass, and wait things out.

The bottom line? I'd say that a technically terrific strategy, in the hands of nonbelievers, is just about guaranteed to fail; by contrast, a B-level strategy, put in place by people who are passionate about what they're doing, is far more likely to succeed.

Culture and Beliefs

The other morning, I was talking to Patrick Hoban, sharing some of this work about beliefs with him, when he stopped me and said, "Sure! That makes total sense! Culture is really just beliefs."

I'd never thought about it that way, but it does make sense. If what we do is based much more than most of us think on what we believe, then our culture is mostly based on those collective beliefs. Mission, vision, values, and systems, perhaps, are based on *what we believe we should believe.* They're an idealized macro-level model. But culture is much more mundane and maybe more meaningful—it's really made up of day-to-day decisions about how we handle seemingly small and insignificant issues, and, to Patrick's insightful point, those decisions reflect a lot about our beliefs.

7. Do We Believe in What We're Making or Selling?

When we believe in what we're doing, the quality of our work almost always goes up. Anarchist Murray Bookchin reflects,

> *Greek thought maintained that to produce an object of high quality was a moral calling that involved a special relationship between an artisan and the object he or she produced. Indeed, to many tribal peoples, to craft a thing was to actualize the raw materials, a "voice," as it were, an expression that realized its latent capacity for form.*

In that model, you build a positive relationship with your products—you're committed to their success, the same way you are for a coworker you care about.

Ann Lofgren, currently at ZingTrain (but who's worked in most every part of our organization over the years), told me, "I can't go out and sell a product I don't believe in. And when I do believe in it, then the experience for me isn't 'selling,' it's sharing. I get paid for it, but it's really about sharing something I totally believe is great. I have never, ever thought of myself as a salesperson, and of course now the reason why is clear."

And as Deli staff member Emily Hiber puts it, "I believe that at Zingerman's I'm selling something good. When people are upset because they think our prices are too high, I'm okay with that because I believe in what we're doing. And I don't have to put on a pretense. . . . you're not in a place where you have to lie to the people you're selling to."

Positive belief added to the quality of the product and the service being sold will almost always amount to great sales. It's why I so commonly hear the refrain from Deli customers: "I came in to buy a couple loaves of bread, but the woman working on the floor started talking to me about her favorite olive oils. And then we started talking about vinegars and cheese and . . . and now I've leaving with a whole basket full of food." I was at a nice coffee shop in Palm Springs not long ago (Ernest Coffee, if you're curious), and I inquired about a nicely packaged chocolate on the counter that I was unfamiliar with. "It's really good," replied the woman behind the counter. She wasn't spinning stories. Her vibrational energy backed up her comment. "I think you'll like it," she went on. "Really, everything we sell here is good! It feels so much better to work somewhere where you believe in what you're selling and doing." Needless to say, I bought the chocolate. And it was indeed very good.

In many places, though, staff simply don't believe in what they're supposed to get customers to buy. At times, it's because we as leaders have failed to share with them why our products are so special, or to make clear how much impact their work has on the quality of life for their customers and coworkers, and on the organization overall. Worse still, many businesses won't let the staff sample what they're selling! It's imperative that we share the story behind great products. Without the "why," the sales and service work will almost always fall short. Often, unbelieving staff members will start to side with a customer who's complaining about quality or how the organization is out to rip them off. And that's never a good sign or a good cycle to be a part of.

Low belief could also be a signal that there's trouble at hand. In my experience, there are two broad categories at play here. We may have a product or service that simply isn't compelling (as it needs to be, per Natural Law #2). We need to improve our offering, or we'll never get the level of belief we're after. The other area of trouble is when our product or service is seriously excellent but falls outside the comfort zone of the staff member. It could be that it's a luxury item they can't afford, and they're frustrated by that fact; it could be a design they think is doofy; or it could be a service that they'd never pay for because they'd just do it themselves. It's not a good situation. If the items upon which we stake our reputations, or our signature lines, aren't things someone on staff believes in, the odds of us arriving organizationally at a successful, mutually rewarding future are small.

Belief, especially knowledgeable belief, may not move mountains, but it does move caring men and women. In the case of Kieron Hales, now the managing partner at Events at Cornman Farms, the move was literal. He came to Ann Arbor from Britain to be part of Zingerman's. What drove him? "I came in for dinner with my sister, and when the server knew more about the food at the Roadhouse than I did about the food I was so proudly serving in the kitchen I was running in England, I realized I wanted to come here to be part of this."

Beliefs Lead Reality

What do we do, I've been wondering a lot of late, when reality doesn't match up properly with what we believe is right? What happens when our beliefs are out of alignment with what's really happening? And we know it, but aren't willing to settle for the status quo?

If you believe, as I do, that there's a self-fulfilling cycle that begins with what we believe, then it follows logically that *our beliefs are leading change in the world around us as much as the world around us is changing our beliefs.* Which means that for meaningful positive change to take place, someone needs to have a vision of a better future. And they must believe strongly that they can make that vision a reality.

It's true in all areas. Someone has to step up with a vision for business growth, a healthier organization, better benefits, quality improvement, cost controls, and a strong belief that what they've envisioned can and will become reality. By definition, when someone comes forward with a big idea for improvement, there will be tension and pushback. It's an intuitive response. "Your friends may love you," Hugh MacLeod writes, "but they may not want you to change. If you change, then their dynamic with you also changes. They might prefer things the way they are, that's how they love you—the way you are, not the way you may become." Ironically, even critics of the present reality tend to defend the status quo when it's under attack from someone other than themselves. If we're going to get change to happen, if we want reform, revolution, or radical improvement of any sort, we will have to push our own envelopes.

The question I struggle with then is: How do we know when a vision we've developed or a program we want to put in place can really lead to the change we want to see? We believe. But can it really happen? Or conversely: How can we tell when our good intentions are nothing more than a fantasy that isn't ever going to succeed?

Ultimately, I suppose, it's the challenge of all change—can we make happen what others consider completely impractical or even impossible? My belief is that if we aren't willing to push for greatness, to do what seems nearly undoable, to strive for outcomes that surpass what common wisdom tells us we can do, then we aren't going to do much remarkable work in our lives.

The historical record is clear—going for greatness means pursuing a vision that nearly everyone else (usually including the experts) says is impossible. Everyone who's done something great in business, art, music, sports, or anything else has been told that their dreams are just that—impossible dreams. But as food-focused British philosopher Ilyas Kassam says, "If nature has taught us anything it is that the impossible is probable."[16]

Remember that almost every element of mainstream modern life was once considered absurd, out of the question. People long believed that the world was flat and that the sun rotated around the Earth. Slavery was a socially accepted practice in most of the world for centuries. The best marriages were believed to be those arranged by people's parents. The idea that women shouldn't vote, or own businesses, was commonplace in the United States up until late in the

19th century, and is still ascribed to in some parts of the world. Civil rights, space travel, cell phones, and pretty much everything else we now take for granted exist only because a group of people believed strongly that they could be made to happen, and then stuck with the work to make them an everyday reality. The only way to find out if something is possible is to make the effort. As writer André Gide said, "There are many things that seem impossible only so long as one does not attempt them."

Here are some more ways in which beliefs have clearly changed. Women in the United States were the legal property of their husbands until the middle of the 19th century and were not allowed to own property or even have access to their children without their husbands' permission. Native Americans weren't allowed to vote until 1924. Slaves in South Carolina weren't allowed to read. Jews were generally despised and kicked out of every country in Europe multiple times over the centuries. Changing these situations probably felt near impossible at the time—each in its own era—that so many people had to live within them. Science-fiction writer Arthur C. Clarke says, "The limits of the possible can only be defined by going beyond them into the impossible." And speaking of outer space, here's Commander Jean Luc Picard from *Star Trek: The Next Generation*: "Things are only impossible until they're not."

Making the seemingly impossible come true is much easier when we make it part of our day-to-day reality. Like anything else in life, the more we practice, the better we get. As writer Elbert Hubbard says, "No one gets very far unless he accomplishes the impossible at least once a day." The better we get at something, the more strongly we sink the roots of our positive beliefs. The more positive beliefs there are in our culture, the healthier our organizational soil, the more likely we are to make our dreams come true. I love the moment in Lewis Carroll's *Alice Through the Looking Glass* when Alice is talking to the White Queen: "Alice laughed. 'There's no use trying,' she said: 'one *can't* believe impossible things.' 'I daresay you haven't had much practice,' said the Queen. 'When I was your age, I always did it for half-an-hour a day. Why, sometimes I've believed as many as six impossible things before breakfast.'"

The more ways we can make great things happen, small things that exceed the everyday norm, the more everyone in the organization begins to a) believe it can happen and b) believe they can make it happen. Given the self-fulfilling belief cycle, you know what usually comes next? They make exceptional things happen all the time!

Pushing to Improve Our Reality at Zingerman's

Remember back to the opening of this essay: effective systems will regularly push us back into alignment in the same way that the body will fix minor disturbances just through normal movement. What follows are some of the internal systems we use here to creatively and constructively push our own envelope in the interest of improvement. The repeated practice and high level of success that come from them combine to increase the power of people's beliefs—in the systems, in the organization, and in themselves.

- Visioning can contribute greatly to this effort. It helps us see innovative, out-of-the-box futures and get moving towards them. Martin Luther King Jr. said, "Faith is taking the first step even when you can't see the whole staircase." Visioning is not being able to see the whole staircase but having already clearly visualized what it's going to feel like at the top. The stairs are the strategic plan—we take them one step at a time. But whatever happens en route, we're already clear on where we're going to end up.

- Effective planning and implementation work give us hope that we can make it happen.

- Our third step to great service—"going the extra mile" (which we define as doing something for the guest that they didn't ask us for)— encourages staff to plow new ground by getting customers some small taste of food, or service, that they didn't expect.

- That same service standard applies to coworkers as well, so that all day, people are going the extra mile for each other.

- The Bottom Line Change process allows us to normalize and systematize organizational change leadership.

What If Our Beliefs Are Off Base? How Far Can We Push?

What if, you might wonder, our beliefs are so far out of whack that they aren't ever going to come to fruition? At some point, we might likely accept that we need to change those beliefs in order to bring them into alignment with reality.

Just because we have popular support for our idea doesn't mean it's really possible. As G. K. Chesterton writes, "Fallacies do not cease to be fallacies because they become fashions." Of course, knowing which is out of whack—our beliefs and visions or our sense of the world—is easier said than done. I believe that

- Gaining an understanding of what's "real" and "really possible," and what are just our own, off-kilter concepts, is one of the main themes of our life's work.
- Embracing the idea that struggling to sort all that out is normal and healthy, and ultimately makes life far less stressful.
- Surrounding ourselves with others who can, and will, help in caring, nonjudgmental ways is one of the most important methods to sort it out.
- Reflecting on a regular basis can help enormously to clear some of the mental clutter.
- By working at it, we can get in touch with our intuitive, trustworthy inner voices.
- Asking people we may not regularly work with for insight can provide us with different perspectives while providing them with belief that their views matter.
- Writing a vision for anything we're trying to make happen can give us clarity on where we want to go.
- Approaching these sorts of discussions with concerns and hopes but not with answers allows for more interesting and productive dialogue.

It's hard to say how to "know" what's right for you other than to test, track your intuition, and talk to people who share your values and value you. Thinking out of the box brings creativity. Sometimes pretending the box doesn't exist allows us to break free; other times it leads to free fall. I'd say dream big, and believe in your dreams. Write them down and share them with others you respect. If you believe, and you get other good people on board, and you're willing to do the work, amazing things can happen! As G. K. Chesterton writes, "A thing may be too sad to be believed or too wicked to be believed or too good to be believed; but it cannot be too absurd to be believed in this planet of frogs and elephants, of crocodiles and cuttlefish."

What do you do, then, when things are out of alignment? In essence, I

think it comes down to Maya Angelou's statement: "If you don't like something, change it. If you can't change it, change your attitude." Except instead of
"attitude," I'd say "belief." (I see attitude as the energetic manifestation of our
beliefs; negative beliefs lead to a "bad attitude," positive ones to a "good attitude.") Acceptance and agreement about the situation is a good start towards
making change happen. If we can agree on our assessment of the situation, and
if we commit to a powerful, shared vision of the future, one in which we believe
deeply, almost anything can happen.

Beliefs in Business, 1902

Some social beliefs have, thankfully, changed drastically over the years.
Or maybe they haven't changed as much as we might like to believe. If
you went to have dinner in a restaurant in the South at the time that
Rocco Disderide constructed his building, your food might well have been
cooked and possibly delivered to your table by African Americans, but it
would have been illegal for them to sit down next to you to eat. Interracial
marriage and interracial eating were considered gravely dangerous to society, and public policies were put in place to enforce those beliefs. "Jim
Crow" laws were referenced formally in the New York Times in 1892, the
same year Rocco Disderide arrived in Ann Arbor, but they were based on
the highly restrictive "Black Codes" that had existed since the early years
of the 19th century.

In the North, the overt manifestations of these beliefs might have
been less formal, but they were still often very strong. In fact, history
would demonstrate that beliefs speak louder than laws. Willis Patterson,
professor emeritus of the U of M School of Music, grew up in Ann Arbor.
Speaking about the 1940s, he remembers a good restaurant that "was
on Washington Street. That was a fine, fine restaurant. There was never

As history professor Angela Jill Cooley writes in To Live and Dine in
Dixie, "Laws against interracial marriage and in favor of restaurant segregation regulated these taboos in southern society, but white families
perpetuated them by instilling these two prohibitions in children, usually
in nonverbal ways." The power of beliefs? Cooley points out that it was far
more socially acceptable for a white person to have a drink with someone
who was known to be part of a lynch mob than it was to share a Coke with
a successful, community-focused African American professional.

a sign that said No Blacks Allowed. And I don't recall anyone saying that they have been told that they were not supposed to go in there. But somehow or another, the African American community knew that we were not welcome in those places, so we didn't go." Same went for lodging. "The Allenel Hotel was the classic hotel in Ann Arbor. Again, we understood that that was not a receptive place to African Americans." In fact, in the entire town in that era, he says, "I am not aware of there being a restaurant that they could feel they were welcome."

This book is not a study in these beliefs, but there are many sources that are, including Cooley's. Laws around racial hierarchy ended nationally when Lyndon Johnson signed the Civil Rights Act in 1964. If you want to see just how extensively the beliefs were formed in informal ways, take a two-hour drive north from Ann Arbor to Ferris State University and visit the Jim Crow Museum of Racist Memorabilia. It houses over 10,000 pieces of commercial art that reinforce racial stereotypes and taboos. Strong beliefs, as we know, have deep roots; it took years of conflict in court to get local and state laws changed. But legislation only cuts the beliefs where they visibly spring out of the soil. The roots remain alive below ground. And as we know, negative core beliefs about race still spring up from below the surface with far too much regularity. Many of the pieces in the museum at Ferris State were produced in the last five or ten years.

One Life, No Balance, and the Story of the Three Sisters

With all due respect to the good people who are trying so hard to attain it, I'm not big on the idea of work-life balance. To me, it's a win-lose model. I don't believe it works. At least not well. I don't mean, of course, that you should be working round the clock, that you should forego vacations, or that you should ignore your children or significant other. I just believe there are more holistic, rewarding, and effective ways to bring things together. The framing of work-life balance feels so limiting. As if our "life" and our "work" are somehow at war with each other and the best we're likely to get is a ceasefire. It's a funny construct. A little too much "life," and "work" suffers, or vice versa. We worry that we work too much, and then we beat ourselves up for doing it.

The word "balance" makes me think of one of those teeter-totters I used to play on when I was a kid. I have this image of standing in the middle, trying to master the art of keeping both ends suspended in the air so that neither ever touches the ground. Win-win only happens for those brief moments when you have things perfectly balanced. And those moments never seem to last all that long, do they?

David Whyte writes,

> *Poets have never used the word balance, for good reason. First of all, it is too obvious and therefore untrustworthy; it is also a deadly boring construct and seems to speak as much to being stuck and immoveable, as much as to harmony. There is also the sense of unbalance that must take place in order to push a person into a new and larger set of circumstances.*

Nature is always slightly out of balance. It functions through regular and effective rebalancing, not achieving perfect stasis and then stopping. Enjoying "the ride" of our lives is basically learning to love the flow and the flaws as much as we appreciate those few moments where everything is in synch.

I still smile every time I reread Wendell Berry's articulate blast at the idea of work-life balance: "Only in the absence of any viable idea of vocation or good work can one make the distinction implied in such phrases as 'less work, more life' or 'work-life balance' as if one commutes daily from life here to work there." I couldn't agree more. I want to bring as much life and liveliness as I can to every single thing I do. Life is short. Why waste it? Berry asks:

> *Aren't we living even when we are most miserably and harmfully at work? And isn't that exactly why we object (when we do object) to bad work? And if you are called to music or farming or carpentry or healing, if you make your living by your calling, if you use your skills well and to a good purpose and therefore are happy or satisfied in your work, why should you necessarily do less of it?*

Segregation wasn't sound social policy, and I don't believe it works well in our personal lives either.

Of course, if I stay focused on my distaste for the work-life balance construct, then I'm stuck in a negative belief. Which I know, from what I've already written here, will yield only negative results. The key is to turn it into a positive.

I believe we all can create a holistic and rewarding existence of our own design, a setting in which each element of our lives can synergistically enhance the others. I may go to work, but I'm still very much myself when I'm there. Good work, as we're working so hard to create, helps us be more effectively ourselves than we might be without it. As Robert Henri writes, "When the artist is alive in any person, whatever his kind of work may be, he becomes an inventive, searching, daring, self-expressing creature. He becomes interesting to other people." And, I would add, to him- or herself!

The same thing, I believe, applies everywhere. When we do things well—when we pursue mastery in whatever draws our interest—we become ever more effectively ourselves. And because being myself means helping everyone around me be more themselves, I and everyone in my life hopefully are all doing well at the same time. We, it turns out, are all too often the missing link in the equation of work-life balance.

It's simple, really. If we don't take care of ourselves, if we fail to nurture our own spirit, if we don't make time for solitude and reflection, then our "work" and our "family," despite our best intentions, will both eventually suffer. But when people talk about "work-life balance," what most of them mean, in practice, is that they want to find quality time for their family while still effectively getting their work done. We need to reinsert ourselves into the equation. Instead of trying to make peace between two opposing forces, I prefer the idea of a holistic sense of well-being. I like harmony. Elegance. And positive energy. I like vocation (which is not, by the way, at all opposed to vacation). And I'm very high on the Three Sisters.

Three Sisters is the name for an ancient Native American model of agriculture. Instead of the modern industrial approach, in which farmers grow hundreds of acres of the same main crop in the interest of "efficiency," in the Native ideal with the Three Sisters model, corn, squash, and beans are planted together, each one right next to the other two. If you walk through a field, you'll see "triads" rather than long rows. The Three Sisters model may look inefficient to modern industrial eyes. But it actually works well. As Dan Barber explains,

> Three Sisters is the opposite end from how corn is typically grown, with its military-row monocultures and chemical-fed soil. The logic is to carefully bundle crops into relationships that benefit each other, the soil, and the farmer. The beans provide the corn with nitrogen; the corn stalk provides a natural trellis for the climbing beans; and the squash, planted around the base of the corn and the beans, suppresses weeds and offers an additional vegetable to harvest in the late fall.

I like the Three Sisters approach about 600 times better than the concept of work-life balance. Instead of corn, squash, and beans, I see the three crops as myself, the other important people in my life, and my work. Each of the three supports the others. The better one does, the better the other two do. When one of the three falters, the other two can carry the slack while it recovers. Since each provides sustenance, I'm never dependent on only one working. It's actually more efficient. As Toby Hemenway says, "Together, the Three Sisters produce more food, with less water and fertilizers, than a similar area planted to any one of these three crops in isolation."

It's the same in our lives. All three elements—the personal, family, and work—support each other. The growth of each enhances the development of the others. When we leave work feeling good, our time at home is happier. When we learn job skills (such as visioning and energy management) that enhance the quality of what we do outside of work, all the better. When we make time for ourselves to get grounded, our decisions get better, we treat others in our lives more positively, and we generate energy that supports positive change in our work and with our families. When we have good relationships, when our home life is enriching, energy enhancing, and intellectually stimulating, we carry that positive input back into the workplace. Which in turn makes for better business. Instead of win-lose, we get win-win-win. When all three areas of life are healthy and working, the energy is hard to beat.

Intercropping Increases Energy

It turns out that in agriculture, intercropping of this sort—i.e., growing multiple crops interspersed in the same field—actually improves the flavor of the fruits and vegetables. The root systems of the various plants interact supportively, enhancing one another's output. Single vegetables grown en masse on their own—the typical industrial monocropping—produces less flavorful product. The trend in farming runs parallel to that of our lives. Busier and bigger but perhaps with a lower sense of well-being? The typical American farm at the time that Rocco Disderide opened his store in 1902 was about 150 acres; today it's about 1,100. Happily, the number of small farms seems to have been on the rise over the last decade, and intercropping is starting to gain some momentum. The Three Sisters—or even more sisters than that—could again become a popular way to plant.

Part of the reframing process might also involve looking differently at the way we spend our time. Instead of the categories "time at work" and "time off," I suggest we look at "time spent in activities that distract us" and "time spent in energy-building activities."

The former includes those effective, often entertaining, diversions; watching movies, playing video games, listening to music, spending time on social media could all qualify. We enjoy them, and they take our minds off other issues. But we don't leave them more excited about life than we were before we began them. They're distracting but rarely invigorating.

I'd rather focus on activities that refresh and rebuild my energy. There are plenty of them, both at work and away from it. Like learning, for instance. Like helping others in a healthy, supportive way. Reading. Exercise. Solitude. Teaching. (The acronym for which, I just noticed on this 88th round of editing, would be REST.) After doing them, I generally have more energy than when I started. You, of course, have your own interests along these lines. The key is determining what these activities are for ourselves and then doing them regularly. The more we can weave energy-positive routines into our day—at home, at work, and on our own—the more rewarding our lives are likely to be.

Last, but definitely not least, my own stress decreased drastically when I realized that, by definition, almost anything in my life that I care deeply about will always be worthy of more time than I'll ever have. I want to spend 100 hours a week *each* with my girlfriend, at work, reading books, studying food history, testing recipes. Add in a few hours a day of running and stretching, journaling, and cooking, and a weekly therapy session, and I think that puts my optimal seven-day stretch at a solid 700 hours. Well, that's not gonna work, is it? Once I made peace with the reality that there will always be more great things to do than I will have time in which to do them, my life got a lot less stressful. I figure it's a good problem to have. So when I start to stress about time, I just breathe, stay centered, keep moving towards my vision, remember to reach out with generosity, and do the best I can.

How Can You Construct Cathedrals When You're Not the Big Boss?

If you're thinking, "I'm only a manager" or "I can't control what everyone around me is doing" (it's actually all out of control—see Secret #29, in *Part 2*), I'll counter by arguing that you can stop trying to change what you have little influence over and start working to create a "cathedral" of your own. In other words, act locally. Instead of struggling with the central office, you might start by writing a vision of the future that applies only to your own area, working constructively within the limits that come down from corporate.

Yes, I know, I haven't had to do this myself. But over the years, I've watched people who've come to ZingTrain seminars pick up positive pieces of what we do and successfully take them back to their own organizations even when they weren't the ones in charge. Surrounded by apathy or even opposition, they still seem to find a way to make positive things happen in their own areas. Before long, energy, commitment, caring, and quality in their corner of the organization all improve. It can be done—you can create a beautiful room inside a mundane corporate castle.

What If You're Starting to Believe You've Stuck with Something Too Long?

My artist friend Alex Carbone asked me, "How do you know when it's time to throw in the towel on something or someone?" The truth is that I don't know. One of my strengths is that I'm very stubborn—loyal, determined, and I don't give up on things (or people) easily. Not shockingly then, per Natural Law #10, which says that strengths lead to weaknesses, one of my weaknesses is that sometimes I would likely have been better off to have let go much more quickly.

In trying to figure out the best way to move forward on a path that's both productive and true to myself, I've found that my intuition tells me a lot. More often than not, when something just feels wrong about a situation, usually something is wrong. When I'm wondering if I've stuck with something too long, my next step is usually to check reality with others who know me and support me. They're what writer Julia Cameron, in *The Artist's Way*, calls "believing mirrors": "Put simply a believing mirror is a friend to your creativity—someone who believes in you and your creativity." These mirrors could be friends, family, colleagues, a professional counselor, or a pen pal (like my friend Alex) whom you almost never see in person. The key is that they believe in you, they know how to share their thoughts in a constructive and caring way, and you place high value on their views.

Another good way for me to take the measure of a situation is to do a vision check—often arguments appear over tactics when, in fact, we're going to totally different places. If our visions are in conflict, it's clear we've got a problem. Same with values; if you continuously err on the side of being overly generous and then catch flak from others around you for it, it's not unlikely that you simply have different ethical standards.

At Zingerman's, we will always err on the side of sticking with things too long, with the belief that putting in extra effort will often bring about big results. That said, there are times to let go. It could be a product that's not selling, a project that's not working, or a staff member who's not working out. If, having given it all we've got for an extended period of time (how long "extended" means is your call), nothing has improved, then it's probably time to consider calling it quits.

What to Do When You Don't Believe?

What do you do when you don't believe in someone you work with? We often have no real say in whether a particular individual comes on board our team. It's a tough situation to steer through. As Alexander Berkman said a century ago,

> *What we call a lazy man is generally a square man in a round hole. That is the right man in the wrong place. And you will always find that when a fellow is in the wrong place, he will be inefficient or shiftless. For so-called laziness and a good deal of inefficiency are merely unfitness, misplacement. If you are compelled to do the same thing you are unfitted for by your inclinations or temperament, you will be inefficient at it; if you are forced to do work you are not interested in, you will be lazy at it.*

Caring and constructive conversations are one positive way forward. Taking an empathic approach might well open the door to other insights, as designer and writer Debbie Millman says: "I believe that empathy improves our ability to see the unseen and to better know the unknown." Taking the time to hear where others are coming from, actively cultivating empathy and compassion, is nearly always a positive thing. When we're feeling frustrated, it's likely the other person isn't feeling great about things, either. Open up about your own hopes for a better future; learning to share your dreams and desires, and to do it without demanding any immediate action, can be a powerful tool. Even if the dialogue doesn't do away with all doubt, it can at least start to dispel a bit of the disbelief, and things will almost always get better from there. The belief pyramid on page 244 is one tool that can help. Another is to find a way—formally or not—to work towards a shared vision of what your work together could be like when it's going well.

And what about when you don't believe in your leaders? And you don't have a viable alternative? That's a rough situation, one that millions of people are in. In the long run, no one—neither leaders nor followers—will do well. We can attempt to hold caring conversations with our bosses, though those dialogues may be risky. I understand that there are many settings in which implying criticism or calling the company's values into question are like getting asked to be fired. But sometimes talking can work. Remember: if you hold negative beliefs about your boss, you can follow the belief cycle on your own to find out what you're likely to get. You might try starting the conversation with a statement of positive beliefs in your boss. After all, bosses respond well to positive beliefs, too.

When all else fails, I default to dreaming—writing a vision about what your work life will be like a year or two down the road can't really put you in jeopardy. Even if you're the only one who reads what you write, I'm convinced it can be a calming experience. Knowing that you're clear on where you want to go—even if you're not sure you can get there in your current setting—is better than agonizing in a cycle of self-doubt and blame. My experience with visions is that those who write them and then share them with others they care about significantly increase the odds of getting good things to happen in their lives.

In Alignment: A Case Study of Service at Zingerman's

When things are well aligned in our organizational ecosystems, it's likely that they'll work well. To test this theory, I started by considering customer service. Here's what I came up with.

Zingerman's Mission Statement

> We share the Zingerman's Experience
> Selling food that makes you happy
> Giving service that makes you smile
> In passionate pursuit of our mission
> Showing love and care in all our actions
> To enrich as many lives as we possibly can.

Excerpts from Zingerman's 2020 Vision: Radically Better Service

Even though our Community of Businesses has almost doubled in size since 2006, walking into any business in 2020 is as intimate an experience as walking into Zingerman's Delicatessen in 1982. We're amazed that we've actually been able to increase the level of service while growing into a bigger business. We make it so natural and comfortable for everyone involved it doesn't seem like work at all. Great service happens everywhere: every element of Zingerman's is a great experience. We are as charming, selfless, and accurate in our opening acts of hospitality towards a guest as we are when we recover from a problem. Our customers, our suppliers, our community, our fellow employees—everyone considers Zingerman's the standard bearer. We do the things everyone says a business can't do. We define great service.

Our commitment to serving others is inspiring, and it finds its way into everything we do. We make it happen in small but meaningful ways. A free brownie finds its way into a get-well-soon package. An accountant interrupts her regular work flow to go take out the kitchen trash. There are also extraordinary acts of service that surprise even seasoned veterans who thought they'd seen it all. A server volunteers to make things right by delivering a forgotten product to a guest's home. The cook smiles and happily makes something that's not on the menu and brings it out to the table personally.

Each of us recognizes that our work here is more meaningful because of the service we give to our guests and to each other. We really do make a positive difference in people's lives. Servant Leadership attracts individuals who thrive on giving exceptional service to everyone they come in contact with—staff, guests, the organization overall, and the community—every day. Service here is so pervasive it's contagious. You can't help but be caught up in its challenge and thrill.

We have a strategy for growth that is about the long-term economic health of our Community of Businesses and our local economy. When we talk about "great service," we refer not only to our customers, our community, and each other, but also to our planet; we push ourselves to go beyond basic compliance on environmental issues.

We know that we are a small presence in the universe; we make and sell food. Rather than focusing on a few grand gestures, we take hundreds and thousands of small actions with great passion and great love. We are changing the world with every transaction. Everyone who comes in contact with our organization—employees, customers and suppliers, people asking for donations, journalists and reporters, public officials—leaves with the perception that we exist in order to be of service. We invite you to join us.

People who shop with us know we listen and respond. While each business is world class in its approach to food and service, we feel like the corner store.

FROM OUR GUIDING PRINCIPLES: GREAT SERVICE!

If great food is the lock, great service is the key. Great service at Zingerman's means

We go the extra mile for our guests, giving exceptional service to each of them.

We are committed to giving great service—meeting the guests' expectations and then exceeding them. Great service like this is at the core of the Zingerman's experience. Our guests always leave with a sense of wonderment at how we have gone out of our way to make their experience at Zingerman's a rewarding one.

Our bottom line is derived from customer satisfaction.

Customer satisfaction is the fuel that stokes the Zingerman's fire. If our guests aren't happy, we're not happy.* To this end, we consistently go the extra mile—literally and figuratively—for our guests. The customer is never an interruption in our day. We welcome feedback of all sorts. We constantly reevaluate our performance to better accommodate our customers. Our guests leave happy or they don't leave. Each of us takes full responsibility for making our guests' experience an enjoyable one, before, during, and after the sale.

*1 out every 300,000 guests will not be happy no matter what. If you think you are serving this guest, please refer them to the Manager, Managing Partner, Paul, or Ari.

At Zingerman's, we believe that giving great service is an honorable profession.

Quality service is a dignified and honorable pursuit. We take great pride in our ability to provide our guests and our staff with exceptional service. Service is about giving and caring for those around us.

We give great service to each other as well as to our guests.

We provide the same level of service in our work with our peers as we do with our guests. We go the extra mile for each other. We are polite, supportive, considerate, superb listeners, working on the basis of mutual respect and care.

OUR 3 STEPS TO GIVING GREAT SERVICE

1. Find out what the customer would like.
2. Get it for them, accurately, politely, and enthusiastically.
3. Go the extra mile.

OUR 5 STEPS TO EFFECTIVELY HANDLING A COMPLAINT

1. Acknowledge what the guest is saying.
2. Sincerely apologize.
3. Do whatever you need to do to make things right.
4. Thank the guest for complaining.
5. Write it up.

I believe that our beliefs about customer service are in alignment with our practice. From the way we deliver service, internally and externally, it's clear that we mean it. We never get it all right, but in all due modesty, I know we do well most of the time. Still, we haven't actually written down our beliefs about service—until now. What I see from doing the following simple six-minute version of the "This I Believe" exercise is that the beliefs of the organization are healthily aligned with our guiding principles, vision, and mission.

We Believe	As a Result
It's best to empower and expect every staffer to fix every customer complaint, even if it's their first day on the job.	Staff feel fully responsible from the get-go. We encourage people to think rather just follow orders. Customers get better service. New staff members are learning leadership thinking as soon as they start working.
Counter to the way it's phrased most places, we believe that the customer is often wrong, but we commit to acting like they're right anyway.	We're "real" with each other but don't have to argue with guests over who's right.
We can turn almost any unhappy customer around.	We almost never give up on trying to make a guest happy. Sometimes it takes years, but we keep working at it. Only partners are authorized to make the decision to "fire" a customer.

We Believe	As a Result
Customer service works best when it starts with Servant Leadership.	Leaders learn quickly that our primary job is to serve staff, not to yell at them for giving poor service. Staff feel served and hence freed to give great service to guests.
Even if it costs a lot in the moment to make a guest happy, it's well worth it in the long run to keep them as a customer.	We don't get caught up in the short-term cost/benefit analysis that so many companies do when they're figuring out how to handle complaints.
Better training gives staff the tools to give great service.	We do a ton of training—eight different internal classes on service alone and lots of on-shift training. We help shape new staff members' beliefs about service right from the get-go.
Going out of our way to delight guests by "going the extra mile" has a positive impact.	Everyone who works here knows what it means to "go the extra mile"—it's the third step of our service recipe. We do it, recognize it, and reward it with great regularity.
Smiling and making eye contact matter.	We teach the 10–4 rule—at 10 feet, make eye contact and smile; at 4 feet, greet the guest. Making eye contact with and smiling at others leads them to do the same in return. Meaningful eye contact and smiling increase energy—in the process, we help everyone here stay pumped up to do great work all day.
Every little piece of the service interaction matters. Watch the details!	We train for, pay attention to, reward, and follow up on the little things.
Staff who give poor service need to be dismissed quickly.	We weed out people who don't share these values and beliefs.

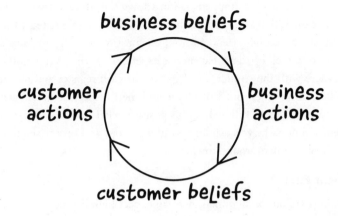

business beliefs

customer actions

business actions

customer beliefs

Of course, great service is not the norm. Here's a sadly common cycle of beliefs in the business world.

1. Business beliefs: "Customers are out to cheat us"; "staff aren't qualified to figure out what to do—that's why we have managers"; "headquarters will fire us if we give away too much."

2. Business actions: Handle complaints with some level of apathy and distrust ("I hope I don't have to do anything"); shunt responsibility ("You're gonna have to talk to the manager"); disown responsibility ("There's nothing I can do"); deny ("That's not what happened—I saw you take it").

3. Customer beliefs: "The business can't be trusted;" "the business is trying to take advantage of us;" "the business doesn't even trust its own employees."

4. Customer actions: Shop elsewhere when possible; don't recommend the business to friends; don't bother complaining even when something is really wrong; when they do complain, they do it out of anger, which makes it much harder for the staff member who deals with the complaint.

All of the actions by customers in this cycle simply reinforce the beliefs of those in the business that customers aren't loyal, can't be trusted, and mostly just want to make trouble. I can hear the comments of many industry colleagues over the years: "It's a good thing we're as cautious as we are in fixing complaints or we'd totally be out of business by now!"

On the flip side, I got stopped walking down the street today by a woman pushing a stroller. She was on the phone, but she was so excited to tell me something she asked her friend to hold on for a minute. "I just have to tell you," she said to me, "I had a great service experience at the Deli the other day. I was in there with the stroller, and I got to the cash register and realized I'd come without my wallet. But Bill Dever told me I could just come back later and pay. It was so great!" Bill had put his positive beliefs to work that she could be trusted, and now she was exuding positivity about us. I'm sure she'll be telling that story to others around town, too.

Alignment Pact

When things are out of alignment, we can expect high degrees of frustration, confusion, suboptimal operations, unwanted stress, and any number of other issues. Confusion reigns supreme, if only because it's hard to know what or whom to believe. As E. F. Schumacher observes, "A man who uses an imaginary map thinking that it is a true one, is likely to be worse off than someone with no map at all." It's like going to work in the organizational equivalent of a fun house—which, to my taste, isn't all that fun. People can literally start to lose their grip on reality. Paul Watzlawick writes, "The map is not the territory; the name is not what it names; an interpretation of reality is only an interpretation and not reality itself. Only a schizophrenic eats the menu instead of the food listed on the menu." The worse things get, the wackier we feel. Which is why, I've come to believe, so many people finish ZingTrain seminars with a sigh of relief. "It's so nice," they say, "to know I'm not completely crazy!"

Congruence makes so much more sense. We need to move through the world in the way that we would like our world to end up. If we want caring, we need to care. Gandhi, who was interestingly aligned with a lot of anarchist thinking, tells us, "Happiness is when what you think, what you say, and what you do are in harmony." When we're in alignment in all aspects of our lives, both our inner thoughts and our external actions, things flow smoothly. Our energy stays high, our productivity excellent—we feel like we're in the flow. As Krishna says, "There is a certain kind of action that leads to freedom and fulfillment. A certain kind of action that is always aligned with our true nature."

Five Ways to Check Your Alignment

What we each choose to do with all of this information is, of course, up to us. As poet W. H. Auden writes, "Choice of attention—to pay attention to this and ignore that—is to the inner life what choice of action is to the outer. In both cases, a man is responsible for his choice and must accept the consequences, whatever they may be." It's your call.

1. Check your vision, mission, and values for alignment. If you have a documented organizational vision, mission, or values (or guiding principles), it would be beneficial to go through them to see where items are in or out of alignment. If you find they're out of synch, you'll have a better understanding of why things may not be going as well as you'd like. And you'll have a good sense of where to start improving. If they're working well, you'll find the same sort of thing that I found with our customer service. Even then, it's important to make regular adjustments to keep things aligned.

2. If you don't have a vision, a mission, or values, make time to write them. Drafting any of the three will help. Doing all of them will help even more. Having just spent two days with an already healthy organization doing exactly that, I was again reminded just how inspiring and energizing the work can be. When you write the documents collaboratively, as these folks did, you stand very good odds of getting everyone involved into alignment. Those who are truly outliers—meaning that their vision, mission, and values are not aligned with the organization's—will end up leaving (hopefully, in a constructive way) either during the process or shortly thereafter.

3. If you have a written vision, mission, and values, and everyone is in alignment around them but you're still having problems, my guess is that there are below-the-surface beliefs that are incongruent with what you're trying to do.

4. One of the best ways to deal with this is to write an organizational belief statement to add to the vision, mission, and values you already have. We're working on ours right now. The Thriveal CPA Network has a beautiful one. Also see the start of Menlo Innovations's belief statement on page 400. And you have the beginnings of my own in Secret #40.

5. You can start the alignment process early by interviewing for beliefs. It's not foolproof, but it certainly can't hurt. Steve Dean is a longtime customer who's really interested in progressive business as well as the tech work that he does every day. He came to hear me speak one night on the subject of anarchism in business, then stayed afterwards for some quick advice. He'd been invited to participate in the interview process for an upper-level person at the company where he works. Not having a lot of interviewing experience, he asked for any thoughts I might have. Since I had beliefs on my mind, I suggested Steve ask the candidate what he believed.

Steve reported back:

> To set the stage, I was there with the VP who the position will report to, casually interviewing a potential candidate over coffee. . . . The VP asked the questions she had (general housekeeping and high-level technical). She then passed the baton to me, priming with "Steve always asks good questions." I had time for two questions. The first was a technical follow-up, which was okay. Then I asked, "What are your beliefs about Data Science?" It was electric. The candidate's mind completely changed gears, and we started to get honestly into who he was as a candidate. You were spot on. This question really let us know a whole lot more about how things were likely to proceed and what sort of value judgments the candidate would be making. Asking about beliefs is a keeper in any technical interview I am going to do going forward. It opens the door for me to discover more about where the candidate wants to go and what they will do in the future.

Sara Vander Zanden, Customer Experience Manager,
Stockbox Neighborhood Grocery, Seattle, Washington

Part 1: When Mission Becomes a Mask

I worked for a large nonprofit organization with a golden mission, and I got really good at telling the story. I had each line memorized, I had anecdotes lined up to make people swoon, and for a while I really believed that we existed to serve that story. (I could find all sorts of evidence!) I worked for this organization for three years, and over time, I began to notice unsettling discrepancies between our story and the execution of our work. At an organization that promoted community empowerment and change, there was a culture of distrust and micromanagement. In a department where programs aimed to reduce inequities, the association didn't make a real effort to hire minorities or pay their employees livable wages. I started to resent my work and my organization, and it took its toll. I'll never forget the sinking feeling of my employee telling me, "I used to think we were going to create change, but you've been bullied for so long that you're a bully now, too."

I saw many of my colleagues fall victim to a toxic culture that used lines such as "you're not in this for the money" and "unfortunately our board just won't approve those funds" and "it's for the community" to deny promotions and justify cutting corners that would adversely impact our neighbors, and to warrant endless hours of overtime without compensation. It's certainly a difficult thing to realize that a good mission doesn't necessarily equal a healthy culture or an honest organization.

Part 2: My ZCoB Credo

Before I worked for Zingerman's, I think I thought there was an inevitable dissonance between the things that comprised a good life and the things that made a successful business. I remember thinking in college that because I was in pursuit of a *good* life (a balanced life, a life not entirely dictated by greed, days full of curiosity and awe, meals with people, a little extra time), I was never going to have an *easy* life. I remember writing a blog post with tears in my eyes: "I'm choosing a life where I'll always feel guilty for a lunch not packed. I wonder if I'll ever be able to buy a sandwich without checking my bank account first."

Zingerman's taught me that my values weren't unreasonable; that they would exist in harmony with the beliefs of the *right* company; and that good business, like a good life, is usually fueled by a strong credo. I remember observing mentors (Ari and Maggie Bayless come to mind) and thinking, maybe for the first time, that it was possible to do well in life, to work for a successful company, and to still be a good and happy person.

As a result of working at the Deli, I also believe that spicy mustard can cure a cold, that chocolates wrapped in a bow can cure a heartbreak, and that the smell of pickle juice never really washes out of socks. I believe that I can, by willfully trying, avoid judging adults who order sandwiches with American cheese. I believe I can usually read people's minds (tell me you don't want the TNT Cowboy Reuben with smoked mozzarella . . . I dare you!). I do not believe in scooping bagels or in decaf coffee.

Lynn Fiorentino, Assistant to Paul Saginaw
and Tom Root, Zingerman's Service Network

In 1995, I had been working at Zingerman's Delicatessen for about a year. I worked in the Dry Goods department selling our packaged foods like olive oils and preserves and pastas and mustards—nonperishable foods that come in jars and boxes. Having spent enough time at the Deli to understand how our various systems worked, I came up with a few ideas of my own. Ari still spent a lot of his time at the Deli back then, so I wrote my ideas on some paper—three pages, back-to-back, with notes in the margins—and stuffed them into his inbox. I expected nothing to come of it; I just wanted to share some ideas in case any of them could be of help.

Instead, Ari asked me to meet with him to discuss my ideas. I was shocked. I was a 25-year-old entry-level employee earning a bit more than minimum wage, and the co-owner of the then $7-million-dollar company I worked for asked me to meet about MY ideas. What came out of that meeting were new projects for me, new areas of the business to explore, and new challenges to meet. I was thrilled.

I also got a new way of looking at my job. Rather than consider it as a mere stepping stone to something bigger and more important—that is, something just to pay the bills before I left food service altogether—I started to see my job at the Deli as an occupation worthy of my best creative work and attention. My interest was reinvigorated, and in addition to the new projects I was encouraged to initiate and complete, I started attending departmental and Deli-wide meetings with a sense that I had something valuable to contribute. I've worked for Zingerman's for over 22 years now, and I consider that conversation with Ari to be the catalyst for over two decades of loyal, grateful, and fun-filled employment.

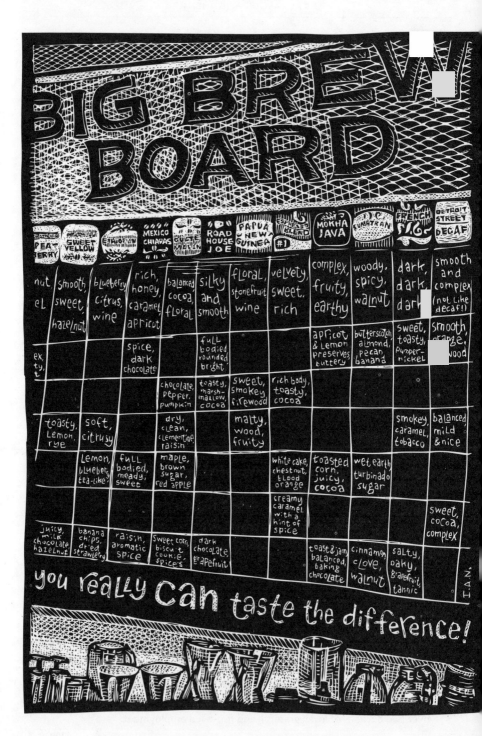

the big brew board at zingerman's coffee company

A Recipe for Changing a Belief

In Case the World Isn't Flat

As I studied, wrote, and reflected over and over again about beliefs in the course of working on this book, it became ever clearer to me that I wanted to make changes to some of mine. Many of my beliefs were positive pieces of what I've helped to create over the years. But others were unproductive. By this point in the book, it's likely that you're much more aware of your beliefs than you were back at the beginning. If you, like me, have found some beliefs you'd prefer to do without, the recipe that follows is for you. It's helped me a lot over the last few years. I hope it does the same for you!

I doubt you've ever heard of Claude Bristol. I hadn't until a few years ago. I stumbled onto his writing as I began the work on this book by doing a random search to see what would come up under the subject of belief. There were three publications listed under his name. The first, a small volume dating back to 1932, was *TNT: It Rocks the Earth*; the second, *The Magic of Believing*, an eventual bestseller, came out in 1948; the third, following soon thereafter, *TNT: The Power Within You*. Bristol died in 1951 at the age of 60.

Judging the books by their covers (which my mother specifically told me not to do), I was a bit unsure about what I was getting into. They're that "trade paperback" softcover-style printed on inexpensive paper. Not a terrible thing, but they certainly didn't give me great hope that I'd uncovered something of literary significance. I'd never seen Bristol quoted in another business book, never heard him referenced by anyone I know. All of which left me feeling hesitant about embracing his work as wholeheartedly as I might have.

Initial impressions, though, can be deceiving; what we believe at the outset of anything does not have to be where we end up. Although I was reading through a somewhat skeptical lens, the guy sure seemed to know what he was talking about. It had been 65 years since *The Magic of Believing* came out, but Claude Bristol's work on beliefs was shockingly spot on. I kept shaking my head in amazement, underlining like crazy as I read. Where did this guy get his stuff? And why hadn't I—book fanatic and serious student of leadership that I am—ever heard of him? Bristol was certainly singing much the same song about beliefs that I'd taken up in the previous months. If new beliefs grow deeper roots as we take to them more strongly, he certainly strengthened mine. "In every area of life," Bristol wrote, "there are winners and losers. What makes the difference can be summarized in one word: belief!"

After serving in the army during World War I, Bristol ended up in Los Angeles. The back of the book describes him as a "lawyer, lecturer, investment banker, and foreign correspondent." Clearly, he was intelligent, well spoken, and knew how to write. Bristol published his first booklet when he was 40 and went on to become a popular public speaker. He was apparently quite famous in his day—his lectures to financial groups won accolades. Yet I was still stumped—why didn't anyone I asked know about him?

Perhaps, I worried, his philosophy was superficial. Some sort of mid-century pop psychology—"just think good thoughts and they'll come true." But Bristol stresses over and over again that you have to work hard to make anything meaningful happen. "Success," he says, "is a matter of never-ceasing application. You must work at it diligently, or else it takes wings and flies away." I couldn't argue with that idea. He bases it all on the power of belief.

It's the constant and determined effort that breaks down resistance, sweeps away all obstacles. Often belief empowers a person to do what others consider impossible. The act of believing is the starting force, the generating power that leads to accomplishment. For some unknown reason it is still barely understood by the average person.

Yep, I certainly agreed with that. "Every person is the creation of himself, the image of his own thinking and believing. As individuals think and believe, so they are." I'm 100 percent in alignment.

I was about halfway through the book, enthused about nearly everything I was reading, but still having a hard time believing that Bristol's work was truly credible. Beliefs, even casually formed ones, can be hard to shake. It's interesting to note how even for me—open-minded as I'd like to think I am—it can be so difficult to let go of a seemingly small seed of doubt. The data say the book sold millions of copies. But data doesn't always lead our beliefs in the way you'd think they would. Sometimes a stronger belief overrides what the numbers say. For me, the book's popularity served only to make me more skeptical of it.

Since I'd never met or even heard of Mr. Bristol, my reaction had to have been driven by internalized judgments that had nothing to do with him. Bristol himself called me out on that: "It must be kept in mind that many of the thoughts we think are not ours at all, at least not of our own originating." Then I came on this bit about the formation of new belief: "Cultivate it, attend it, give it sunshine and water, and it grows into full life. Remember it always produces after its kind, be it single, or hybrid." Wow! Over 60 years ago, the man was using the same agricultural metaphor I had started to work with.

Bristol was well read. He referenced the writing of people I have a lot of respect for. Famous folks such as Emerson and Thoreau. Remember, there was no Internet back then, so finding the sort of supporting quotes he uses took more than the ten seconds it does now. And some were from far more obscure figures, such as Charles Fourier, an early-19th-century utopian socialist. Fourier was born in the town of Besançon in the Franche-Comté region of France, which is home to one of my all-time favorite cheeses, Comté. His positive beliefs about humanity's ability to live and work harmoniously inspired intentional communities all over the world. One was the town of Utopia, founded in southern Ohio in 1844, just seven years after the barn at Cornman Farms was raised. In 1847, the town came under the leadership of one of the earliest of American anarchists, Josiah Warren. Utopia became an intriguing experiment in cooperative and creative anarchism in action. It even had two "time stores," which operated based on Warren's belief that time, not money, was the currency in which we ought to be dealing.

The coincidences were starting to seem uncanny—Bristol even lays out the foundation of our approach to visioning! "Envision it is perfect, and you will be surprised when you see the realization of your mental picture." Remember, this is 1948, 20 years before Ron Lippitt began his pioneering work at U of M. Bristol encouraged people to focus, as we do, on the "what" of their vision and leave the "how" for later.

> *At the start you may have no idea of how the results are to come. Yet you need not concern yourself. Just leave it to the subconscious mind, which has its own ways of making contacts and of opening doors and avenues that you may have never even guessed. . . . Ideas useful in accomplishing your program will come at most unexpected times. . . . Whatever the idea is, follow it.*

Bristol even stressed the idea of taking ownership of our own lives: "Many employees hold to the idea that their work is given to them merely to further their employers' interests. They never entertain the thought that they are actually working for themselves, with the employer merely furnishing the tools and a place for them to work." He noted how the self-fulfilling belief cycle can play out in relationships: "If you wager, think and believe that the other fellow is a fine chap, that's what he'll turn out to be—for never forget that what you get back is a reflection of what you project mentally." And "remember, some of your enemies may be of your own making. Those friends or enemies are merely a reflection of our own thoughts—the other fellow will consider us an enemy or friend according entirely to the picture which we ourselves conjure up."

I was stunned by the depth and breadth of Bristol's words. How could he have done all this insightful writing without any of the high-end, well-read, well-traveled people I know in the world having heard of him? But Bristol wasn't done with me yet. He went on to describe the core of what we here talk about as "energy management," which I'd learned from my friend Anese Cavanaugh in 2005. Bristol was already addressing the subject 60 years earlier!

The atmosphere, the creation of the people habitually frequenting the place [of business] can be instantly detected as unsettling, disturbing, tranquil . . . the very walls themselves, all vibrate to the thinking of the persons occupying the room, and bespeak what type of thoughts they think. Whether the home is a mansion or a shack, the vibrations are always a key to the personality of those who occupy it. . . . Throwing around the proper aura—which is done by an act of imagination or an extension of your personal magnetism—will work wonders.

Bristol related how he had trained the staff in a cheese shop to believe in their products and themselves, and reported that sales increased dramatically in a matter of days. A bit further on in the book, he shared the story of a celery farm near his home. Now, I happen to be fascinated by the history of celery. Kalamazoo, 90 miles west of Ann Arbor, was once the national celery capital. When the train stopped there, vendors would hawk bouquets of celery to passengers who would buy them as souvenirs and gifts. Bristol told the story of his neighbor, who complained endlessly about how he couldn't compete with the Japanese merchants who were carefully washing each bunch and packaging it beautifully. His negative neighbor "never washed a bunch . . . packed it in secondhand crates and complained that his Japanese competitors were getting all the business."

The introduction to *The Magic of Believing* was written by another guy I'd never heard of, Nido Qubein. Again, I grew skeptical. Again, I was wrong. Qubein, it turns out, is president of High Point University in North Carolina, one of the most popular speakers in the country, a recipient of the Philanthropist of the Year award, and executive chairman of the board of Great Harvest Bread Company. And that's just a small slice of his CV. If I had any doubt that beliefs can get in the way of how we process the world, Bristol's book was sure proving my own point right back at me.

The final straw? Bristol basically described what we now know of as neuroplasticity. "Repetition," he wrote, *is the fundamental rhythm of all progress, the cadence of the universe. . . . The person with a fixed goal, a clear picture of his desire, or an ideal always before him, causes it, through repetition, to be buried deeply in his subconscious mind and is thus enabled, thanks to its generative and sustaining power, to realize his goal in a minimum of time and with a minimum of physical effort. Just pursue the thought unceasingly. Step by step you will achieve realization, for all your faculties and powers become directed to that end. . . . It's the repetition of affirmations that leads to belief. And once that belief becomes a deep conviction, things begin to happen.*

Now, if *The Magic of Believing* had just come out in 2012, none of that last bit about the brain would be noteworthy. In the large "library" of work piled up in my living room, I've got a dozen books that focus on neuroplasticity—the idea that the brain changes throughout our lives by repeated mindful practice done over an extended period of time. But in Bristol's day, such thinking was almost unheard of. In fact, at that time it was "well known" that the brain was a static entity, formed in early childhood and then staying as is for the rest of one's life. That belief—solid for centuries—began changing with new research in the 1970s, and the concept of neuroplasticity has emerged only in the last 10 or 15 years. Bristol seems to have been at least three decades—and indeed for a nonscientist, a good half a century—ahead of his time.

The story of my connection with Claude Bristol models many of the ways that beliefs can mess with our work, even in areas that wouldn't seem to make the slightest difference. I started with somewhat neutral beliefs when I found the first reference to Bristol online. But then I shifted quickly into a slightly cynical, negative approach. If I'd come to Bristol having heard that he was an expert on 19th-century anarchist thinking, a respected high-end retail consultant, or a well-ahead-of-his-time prophet of neuroplasticity, I'd surely have started reading with a totally different mindset. Fortunately, I also believe strongly in learning. And someone (my mother, maybe) planted the seed of the belief that if you start a book you should finish it. After 168 pages, I was completely sold; I might now be the biggest Claude Bristol fan in the country. (Though I'm guessing this essay will bring out a slew of other Bristolites—we tend to bond, of course, with people who share our beliefs. I'd love to hear your thoughts.) One other thing Bristol and I have in common: "It is a rare book," he writes, "that doesn't contain an idea or two useful in your own work."

Can We Really Change Our Beliefs?

Martin Seligman tells us: "One of the most significant findings in modern psychology in the last twenty years is that individuals can choose the way they think."

As with so much of our work, awareness is the first step to improvement. When we live without understanding what our beliefs are and how they impact our existence, it's as if we've turned our lives into a traffic circle from which we can't quite figure out how to exit. The faster we drive, the more quickly we go around in circles; effort and acceleration are of no help—round and round we go, but we still end up exactly where we began.

The way out of the traffic circle, then, is to drive slowly, carefully, respectfully turning the wheel so that we head out onto a new path, the one we would prefer to be on. The self-fulfilling belief cycle works in much the same way. As the Wrights make clear, "Only when we take action to break free from limiting beliefs and norms, do we become free to create our best life." With the recipe here and a good bit of the determination Claude Bristol called on us to give, we can change any belief that we truly want to change.

No one says it will be easy, though. We can't rewire 30 or 40 years in a week. To teach our brains a new set of beliefs requires many years of active work. Asked to share the most difficult thing she's seen her clients deal with in therapy, cognitive psychologist Judith Beck reported, "It varies from client to client, but generally changing their core beliefs, their most fundamental (negative and unhelpful) ideas about themselves, others, and/or their worlds can be difficult, if they've held these beliefs for a long time." Logical argument will almost never suffice. In fact, I usually find that the more I try to argue facts, the more others hold tightly to their beliefs. As Tom Asacker says, "Research has repeatedly shown that rational arguments are not very effective, since people's behavior is overwhelmed by their reasons—their beliefs and desires."

I've heard all of the following beliefs repeated in the business world over the years with uncanny consistency. They aren't my beliefs, and I'm betting they aren't yours, but they're part of a culture that underlies so many of the problems and frustrations that most businesses are struggling with:

- Employees are a nightmare.
- You can't find good people.
- Everyone's out to take advantage of you.

- Customers couldn't care less about you—they just want a deal, and as soon as another business opens up and sells stuff ten cents cheaper, they'll switch over in a heartbeat.
- If you don't watch out, everyone will be stealing from you.
- Millennials have a terrible work ethic.
- I could never take two weeks off—things would completely fall apart.
- Training is a total waste of time, since people are just gonna leave soon anyway.
- Businesses exist only to make money.
- People will never pay for quality.
- Business is out to screw employees.
- The economy is holding us back.
- Government gets in our way, so we can't get to greatness.

Pick any one of the above, follow the self-fulfilling belief cycle, and see what you get. It won't be positive. Nor pretty.

How about "Training is a waste of time?" Say that's the boss's belief. What actions follow? Minimal training, little guidance or direction, unclear expectations for new staff members. Which leads to . . . ? New hires feeling overwhelmed and believing the business isn't really interested in their success. The action they take based on that belief? They work only halfheartedly and start looking for other jobs. Which, of course, leads the boss to believe that it's a good thing so little time was wasted on training.

We Can Transform!

The good news is that even for people who "grew up" with those sorts of negative, limiting beliefs, it doesn't have to stay that way. As Drs. Bob and Judith Wright confirm in their work *Transformed!*, "We can literally change our brains and our minds, and what we believe, who we are, and how we live."

Here's a belief of mine that's changed in the course of working on this book. I've long held, as do many others, to the management dictum that past performance is the best indicator of future performance. More often than not the statement is true. The reason it's true, though, is not because the future is a mirror of the past. It's because as long as our beliefs stay the same, so too will the outcomes that emerge from our work. As author Kevin Bermingham writes, "[B]eliefs don't just create our map of past experience; they also form

218

the blueprints for our future actions." But—and it's a super big "but"—*if we change our beliefs, then the past no longer serves as a likely indicator of the future.* In fact, the future can become exactly what we want it to be.

Staying Calm About Complexity

Here's a belief that I've changed big time, and I'm coming out of the closet: I believe complexity is a good thing. I spent years trying to be patient while people rail against the increased complexity of the modern world. But I'm done with that now. Overemphasis on simplification is suffocating. Complexity, by contrast, is the natural state of the world. When we align ourselves with nature, things flow much more smoothly. Accepting that reality has lowered my stress significantly.

Nature, it turns out—people, plants, animals, the environment—is beautiful, but it's not simple. It's the opposite. As psychologist Carl Rogers writes, "there is a natural tendency towards a more complex and complete development." *Complexity—not simplicity—is the natural state of our existence.* The more we evolve, as Rogers explains, the more complex both we and our world will become. Human beings are the most complex life forms on the planet. Put a bunch of them together in a business, add in a lot of customers, the community, the country, and the influence of the rest of the world, and that complexity is multiplied many times over.

As Toby Hemenway writes, healthy ecosystems are "not merely flowery showplaces or ruler-straight arrays of row crops." Monocropping won't work in business either. Although key numbers, job titles, org charts, and strategic initiatives can help us hold short-term focus, it's my strongly held belief that no human being can fully comprehend or effectively orchestrate all that is happening (let alone what *will* happen) within our workplaces. Mind you, complexity doesn't need to be confusing. In the same way snowflakes or sunflowers have their own elegance, so, too, can our organizations and our lives. Each forms its own kind of complex order, in harmony with the ecosystem of which it's a part. Gary Snyder tells us: "Nature is orderly. That which appears to be chaotic in nature is only a more complex kind of order."

Remember: nothing in nature exists in isolation. Everything impacts everything else. (I called it the Theory of Relevantivity in *Part 3*—see page 379.) The same is true at work. Thinking of the pieces of our organization and its people as insular entities, all independent of one another's influence, is wholly inaccurate and, ultimately, unhealthy. While we can all impact what goes on around us, none of us, regardless of title, seniority, hierarchy, height, or hat size, can ever really control anyone or anything else. Ordering others to behave may sound appealing to some, but it's simply not sustainable. The idea, instead, is to collaboratively bring people and processes together so that getting organized becomes a creative act. As composer and lyricist Stephen Sondheim says, "Art, in itself, is an attempt to bring order out of chaos."

Buddhist monk Matthieu Ricard writes: "We have grown so accustomed to our faults that we can barely imagine what life would be like without them. The prospect of change makes us dizzy." But that change can also bring excitement, exhilaration. Even the act of engaging with the improvement will almost always ignite our energy. As Bob and Judith Wright explain, "Our brains respond with a flurry of neuronal activity when we open our minds to new possibilities, free ourselves of limiting beliefs, and perceive ourselves and our world in new and empowering ways." Realizing new things gives us the "power" to push for more learning, which in turn builds more good energy, which then leads us to learn even more. Osho said, "Every time one realizes something of the truth, there is a dance in the heart." It's easy to spot. You can read that dance almost every time in the eyes and in the energy of the person who's delighting in it.

New Beliefs Beget New Realities

Early-20th-century French anarchist Alfred Jarry was a master of inversion and insightful provocative humor. When the French government banned the Breton language, he spent years studying to become fluent. Jarry liked to get people thinking by telling a tale of an African gentleman who walked out of a Paris bar without paying for his drinks. Outrage ensued, and the police were called. Clearly, Jarry pointed out, people had the wrong idea: the man was simply an African explorer investigating European culture and had none of the local currency with which to pay for his experience. What beliefs about our own daily lives might Jarry be able to invert in the same way to completely alter our perspectives?

The Recipe

I can't say scientifically that this recipe for changing beliefs is foolproof, but it sure seems to have worked well every time I've tried it. It takes elements from the Wrights and others, blended into my own approach. The first time you use it, the recipe may well feel awkward. But, over time, like any other skill, it will likely get easier. Of course, it will work only if you believe that it will. Ready? Here we go.

1. IDENTIFY THE ISSUE

Getting in touch with what's going on is the first step of this process. We can't consciously change what we aren't aware of. Kierkegaard tells us: "There are two ways to be fooled. One is to believe what isn't true; the other is to refuse to believe what is true." Accepting and understanding present-day realities is the beginning of the work. Most of us have many issues; which is the one to start with?

A Six-Step "Recipe" for Changing a Belief

1. Identify the issue.
2. Backtrack to beliefs.
3. Do some homework.
4. Check the equation.
5. Mindfully adopt a new belief.
6. Erode the old patterns with new thinking.

It doesn't need to be a dramatic crisis—even a small, nagging uncertainty can signal something deeper beneath the surface at work, at home, in your heart, with your health. I'd suggest starting with something modest, less controversial, something that won't send your inner circle scurrying for cover.

So pick a problem, any problem that you're dealing with. It's not a card trick, but it will require a bit of shuffling and figuring out how to best play your hand. The more often you follow the recipe, the better you'll get at it.

2. BACKTRACK TO BELIEFS

Here's where we move past frustration and start to do some below-the-surface studying to get at the roots of the situation. How do we know what we believe? Here are five ways I know.

A. Read Your Reactions

We can learn a lot by paying close attention to what evokes strong negative responses in us and then work back from there. Intense reactions are signals that we've hit a sensitive spot. As Sam Keen says, "Where we stumble and fall, there lies the gold. Beneath the fault lies the virtue."

Much of this could be called shadow work: We project the parts of ourselves we're least comfortable with—both the desired and undesired—onto others. When others embody parts of ourselves that we don't like and have repressed, we tend to get angry. Or, alternatively, when others live out the dreams we don't dare to let ourselves live, we hold them high in admiration and are drawn towards them. "Shadows are projected on the wall and [we] take them for reality," Czesław Miłosz writes. Our reactions say more about us and our beliefs than they do about the person onto whom we're projecting.

Here are four examples I've dealt with of late that might help illuminate the process: one personal issue, one management challenge, one broader business problem, and one cultural image that seems to be an issue on a national level.

"Don't You Dare Change Plans." Let me start with myself. I get frustrated when people change plans on me at the last minute. The truth is that there's rarely anything wrong with them doing it, but it bugs me big time. My strong reaction isn't the end of the world, but it does throw me off my game at times. So backtracking from there, I reflected on what long-held belief might come into play for me to have such a strong reaction. I don't think I'd have been able to figure it out without going through the work about beliefs that's in this book. But now that I have, I sense that my belief is this: People who change plans regularly can't be counted on.

That, in turn, makes me wonder what belief lies beneath that one. I guess it's a belief that my own self-worth comes from being someone others can count on. The action that comes from that belief? I try hard not to change course without good reason and without giving fair notice. So when others alter plans, their action sets me off far more than the meaning of the actual schedule switch would indicate. *The issue, then, isn't anyone else changing plans— it's me!*

If I'm not happy with how much stress I encounter and cause when others change plans, I could consider changing my beliefs. I'm actually considering it right now while I write. You see, once you start working on this stuff and really paying attention, it's hard not to follow the clues and take constructive action.

Low Staff Morale. Let's say you have a manager who's consistently having trouble with employee performance. While many factors could come into play, one element to consider is to examine what they believe about employees. Maybe it's that frontline staffers are generally lazy, but that if the manager could just find the right people, everything would improve. A belief like that would likely lead the manager to give up too quickly on all but the best of new hires. And that action would likely lead other staff members to believe that the manager is impetuous and impulsive with hiring decisions. Which in turn might lead those personnel to act cautiously and start planning their own departures, which then just reinforces for the manager that most frontline people aren't very committed.

A belief that people are generally dishonest will also likely lead to trouble—instead of building on trust, we install surveillance cameras, limit staff freedom, and keep a tight rein on decision making. Again, staff members retreat to safety—they can tell where we're coming from, they believe they have no real future with us, and so they do as little work as they need to get by. Mostly they just want to stay in the shadows where no one will bother them. Results? The leader's frustration grows, the staff's engagement slows, we burn out, they leave. The solution? It's not the usual approaches of better hiring practices, better benefits, building a new break room, or setting up a staff retreat. While those are great and may end up happening and helping, the biggest change that's needed is for the leaders to let go of their old, unproductive, negative beliefs. Believe the best, and you're a heck of a lot more likely to get it.

The Pitfall of Underpricing. Here's another example that's all too common in the quality-focused segment of the food world in which we work here at Zingerman's. Contrary to the public's perception, most "high-end" food businesses are *not* making lots of money. Many owners are, in fact, perpetually frustrated with their lack of bottom-line financial results. I've heard much the same story everywhere, from the Lower East Side all the way to Ethiopia. Because money is tight, owners often limit their own pay and also that of others in their business. When profits are low or—worse—the bottom line is negative, it's hard to buy new equipment, afford to pay bonuses, or put anything away for a rainy downturn of a day. Over time, energy flags. People lose hope that there's a better tomorrow out there. When they don't have hope, they stop believing that their work makes a difference. The quality of the work starts to suffer, which depletes financial results still further. At some point, after this cycle has gone on long enough, energy or money runs out. Employees quit; owners eventually give up and opt out. The community loses an otherwise good business.

I've come to realize that the problem often isn't the public or the food. It emanates out from the beliefs and behaviors of the owners. *They believe that customers won't pay what it really costs for high quality.* As a result, they undercharge for their goods and services. Which means that they have insufficient resources to stay healthy and viable. The core of the problem, then, is not public perception—it's that we as owners don't believe we can charge what we really have to, and that customers don't care enough to put out the proper amount of cash for what we're purveying.

I can't tell you how many well-meaning businesses have gone under because of that negative belief. And here's the worst of it: by setting their prices too low, they also set the bar low for anyone else in the industry. That skewed reality means customers are likely to believe that anyone who's charging what they really need to is "overcharging." To go in the other direction—to charge more than one's competition—requires a belief that one knows what one is doing, that customers can tell the difference and will be willing to pay for it. Alice Waters writes, "I do feel like food should cost more, because we aren't paying farmers a living wage. It has to cost more."

The Struggle to Teach Service in Slovakia. After visiting Slovakia last fall to speak on our approaches to business, I came away impressed with how many positive things are happening in this small Eastern European nation 25 years after the fall of Communism. The country has come a long way in a relatively short time.

One theme that came up a lot, though, was that many progressive, forward-thinking new business owners have high frustration with their employees when it comes to customer service. "They just don't get it" was a common refrain. "Slovaks just aren't inclined to give service" was another. "I know customer service is imperative, but the people we hire just don't understand. They think it's phony, and they don't want to do it." I totally hear their frustrations, and I can see why they've drawn the conclusion that high-quality service can't work in their country.

There is, of course, truth to some pieces of what they're saying. But with beliefs big in my mind from working on this book, I tried to explain that it was, in fact, *their own belief* that "Slovaks just don't get it" that was probably creating the problem. I suggested reframing the issue. What if you said this: "Slovaks didn't have much experience with service during all the years of war and Communism. But I'm confident that with good training, good leadership, practice, and patience, they can learn to provide it, and will probably do so really well."

Which is, indeed, what I believe. And with that belief come inspiration, action, energy, and—I almost guarantee—good results over time. I believe that in the years to come, Slovakia could have some of the best customer service on the continent!

B. Try Out "This I Believe"

The "This I Believe" exercise I outlined on page 107 is an excellent tool for figuring out what we believe about any issue or area of our lives. It starts at the core by getting our intuitive answer to the question "What do I believe?" Many people I know who've done the exercise, even for only a few minutes, have stumbled upon troublesome, debilitating beliefs they hadn't realized were there.

C. Start with the "Shoulds"

As Sam Keen writes in *Inward Bound*, "The first task of introspection is to examine how we've been programmed by the shoulds and should nots of others." I know that my own childhood was chock full of them. Most folks I've met have quite a list that they've likely lived with, unknowingly, for a long time. "I should be more creative." "I should be more generous." "Nice people don't do that." "Showing anger is immature." "Real men shouldn't show emotion." "Women should stay home." "Leaders should never show fear." "Leaders are supposed to know what they're doing." "I should be able to figure this out on my own." "I shouldn't need help." "I shouldn't have to ask." "I shouldn't be stressed out at work." Any of those sound familiar? They do to me. I've lived with—and then successfully changed—them all.

I'm not here to argue that any of the beliefs that underlie each of those "shoulds" are bad, good, or otherwise. I want only to point out that when we're mindful of what our beliefs actually are, we stand a significantly better chance of changing them and, on the upside, actively endorsing the ones that serve us well. All of those basic, long-held beliefs are programming that we've gotten, unknowingly, from others. Understanding what they are and where we got them can help with our upcoming changes.

D. Listen Carefully to the Voices

Another way to get in touch with our beliefs is to mindfully, gently listen to the various voices that are active in our heads. I know you have them. I have a whole conference room full. There's my mother, there are all the partners at Zingerman's, there's Emma Goldman, just to name a few. Over the last year or so, I've tried to channel what Rocco Disderide might say. While they all have their opinions to offer, none of them, of course, are my own true voice. As Osho said, "Your whole idea about yourself is borrowed—borrowed from those who have no idea of who they are themselves. Listen to your being. It is continuously giving you hints; it is a still, small voice. It does not shout at you, that is true. And if you are a little silent you will start feeling your way."

There are many ways to do this work. Therapy, journaling, and meditation are all great tools. If you're one of the lucky ones who grew up believing from a young age that mindful reflection and self-awareness are healthy and important,

225

you might dive right into them. But if you're like many of us who were raised with little self-awareness, or with the belief that studying oneself was overly indulgent or that therapy wasn't for normal, healthy people, you might need a little more prodding. In fact, the act of engaging in those self-reflective activities in the first place may well require altering beliefs we've taken on from others.

"Therapy," one of the voices in my head told me, "is for people who are seriously psychologically screwed up." Another voice added, "Journaling is for high school girls." "Reflection is fine for Buddhist monks," a third chimed in, "but not for regular people like me." Over time, I changed all of those beliefs. In hindsight, I can see that I intuitively, awkwardly and uncomfortably at first, worked my way through all the steps of this recipe. It would have been a lot easier to have the steps in front of me, but fortunately, my strongly held belief that if I work at anything hard enough and long enough I can figure it out carried the day. Daily journaling is a great way to get at the voices, to separate the "shoulds" of others from what I believe is best for me. Therapy serves much the same purpose—talking aloud about what I'm struggling with often makes it clear how much I'm inadvertently confusing the views of others with my own. Doing reality checks with trusted friends works well too.

E. Illustrate the Issue

Another way to get at our self-beliefs is to use visuals. Amy Wenzel's article "Modification of Core Beliefs in Cognitive Therapy" shares a technique. Draw a pie chart, she suggests, and then assign percentages to what you believe would need to be present in the pie in order to make you a "successful" person. Go quickly, as you would with a "hot pen," so you don't overthink it. You can do the same for your organization. It's interesting to see what comes out. If what you draw the first time through feels out of balance, or out of alignment with your values or vision, that's a sign that it's probably time to change a core belief.

Assuming—for conversation's sake, at least—that one of these five methods has helped you uncover at least one belief you'd like to change, let's move to the next step.

3. Do Some Homework

Once you have an unhelpful belief in hand instead of just hiding in your head, you can start a bit of investigation. Knowing the origin of the belief doesn't change it, but it does help us understand, at a much deeper level, how we've arrived at where we are.

Since we weren't born with beliefs, we can be pretty sure that we learned them somewhere. But where? What was going on in my life at the time that I acquired this particular belief? How long have I lived with it? If you buy into my metaphor about beliefs being the root system of our existence, then we know that changing behaviors without digging all the way down to get the old roots out is a lot less likely to be successful. It's like snipping off a weed at the soil line—it goes away for a while, but it's only a matter of days before it reappears.

Unhelpful beliefs may have started in our childhood homes, they may have been imbued in us by a destructive role model, or they may have been planted in us by a group of peers. Often our parents' beliefs about themselves were passed down to us unknowingly, and those beliefs then influenced what we believe about ourselves. I can certainly see a lot of my mother's self-doubt in me. The homework helps. Without sharing 30 years of therapy work with you here, do you think it's possible that my parents getting divorced when I was only three years old just might possibly have something to do with my belief that changing plans is a sign that a person can't be counted on? Just a little, right?

We also all have beliefs about what constitutes success, what we "can" and "can't" do, what successful business leaders are like, how much money we should make. We've picked up beliefs from our old bosses, from books and seminars, from our friends. If you grew up in a family business, or follow in the same profession as your parents, you're likely to be carrying a lot of their beliefs with you as you go forward. Some will have helped, but others may be getting in your way.

The deeper you do the work, the more you follow the root system all the way down, the more effective change going forward is likely to be. Michelle Segar is a longtime Zingerman's customer whose professional focus overlaps the subject of beliefs and the dynamics of changing them. "Really understanding the old patterns is so important," she says. "It's not that it's impossible to change without really studying the past. But when you don't, it leaves you vulnerable to other old things coming up." It can be challenging work. But without it, we tend to make surface-level changes that have little meaningful long-term impact. Emma Goldman puts it this way: "Our institutions and conditions rest upon deep-seated ideas. To change those conditions and at the same time leave the underlying ideas and values intact means only a superficial transformation, one that cannot be permanent or bring real betterment. It is a change of form only, not of substance."

As Osho explained, "Truth is not to be found outside. No teacher, no scripture can give it to you. It is inside you and if you wish to attain it, seek your own company. Be with yourself." Once I realized it would help me to understand my family's past better, I started doing research the way any history major would. I started talking to people who were there, reading the views of professionals, reflecting, bouncing my learnings off of others I trusted. The results were hugely helpful. In hindsight, I can see that I changed many of my beliefs—about myself, about my family, about the world.

The same situation plays out on a social level. When we're raised in a community of any sort, it's highly likely that we've internalized beliefs about what's "normal," "right," or "appropriate." When we take those at face value as "truth," we will likely struggle later as we try to impose those "norms" on others for whom they are anything but. Whose reality is "right"? I've certainly been guilty of trying to convince others to come around to my side of things, but I know enough to know that unless they're open to the ideas, it's rarely effective. On top of which, it turns out, I'm often wrong. Pushing forward without care for others' (equally) deeply held beliefs might well be seen as a form of intellectual imperialism.

Learning to Confront Our Canons

I keep coming back to Rebecca Solnit's image of "the secret in the mirror." If you see what you want in a mirror, rushing towards it only gets you hurt. What you need to do is counterintuitive but correct: pause, get oriented, and then turn around and move in the exact opposite direction. It's an insight I had many years ago when I was first getting going in therapy. While they'd served their purpose in my younger days, many of my life-long habits—née beliefs—had become anything but helpful. Knowing that was true gave me some solace. But, of course, my brain had been shaped over 30 years of my life, and it wasn't going to be readjusted in a week, or even in a matter of months.

To help keep me moving in the right direction—when my "instincts" were sending me signals to do the opposite—I taught myself to imagine that the things I was going after were in a mirror. When the pressure felt highest, I learned, the most productive approach for me was almost always to stop, breathe, and reflect, and then turn around and go the other way. When I was afraid to be alone, I needed to find solitude. When I was afraid to tell anyone else what was going on, I needed to pick up the phone and talk. We often need to go towards the tension to get to the peace we're seeking. Errico Malatesta's magical statement sort of sums it up: "We must face the canons to get the corn."

Doing that work—facing our internal canons (which are often loaded and ready to fire a barrage of negative judgments at our soul)—requires us to get out of our comfort zones. As writer David Whyte puts it, "Not only can we become afraid of these internal questions, but also we can become terrified of the spaces or silences in which these questions might arise. The act of stopping can be the act of facing something we have kept hidden from ourselves for a very long time." Active reflection, setting aside time for solitude and study, is not what most of the world believes to be the keys to good business. But I now believe it's work that's essential to our long-term health and success.

4. Check the Equation

As much as we dislike an outcome we're getting from one of our beliefs, the ironic reality is that we're still probably getting something—often something significant—out of the status quo. Otherwise we probably wouldn't be pursuing it. If you look carefully at these outcomes, you can see the cycle of self-sabotage at their core. And you can then start the work required to make more productive decisions in your day-to-day life.

Try this example: We believe that if we're not present all the time in our business, things will fall apart. As a result, we never take time off. Employees buy into the belief as well and don't want to move up into management because they don't want "to be there all the time," and also because they believe that we have some special stamina or ownership incentive that they don't have. As a result, they don't lead; they just let others take care of everything for them. They believe that we don't really trust them, or else why would we be there all the time? So they no longer trust themselves; they doubt their own judgment and wait for us to come to the rescue. We the owners begin to burn out big time. Our belief that we're indispensable is reinforced. And to what end?

Is what you gain from your beliefs worth what they cost you? Are they getting you where you want to go? If so, keep going. But if the results you're getting aren't helping you attain your vision, live your values, or develop the relationships you'd like to have both at work and at home, it may be time to make some changes.

5. MINDFULLY ADOPT A NEW BELIEF

Knowing what you now know about the belief cycle and how self-fulfilling it can be, the next step is to make a decision to adopt a new belief. Take to heart William James's admonition: "If you want a quality, act as if you already had it." Try the "as if" technique, acting as if what you hope to change has already happened, and you'll at least be off to a good start.

Let's go back to the example that "people these days don't have a very good work ethic, and counting on them is a mistake." You've realized now that your read on the situation wasn't sound. That instead of your "staff needing you," it was actually *you using them* in order to feel needed. Whoa. That's not good. It's time for a change.

You can start the ball rolling in a new direction by changing your belief— *in this new preferred future, you start to believe that the people you hire are actually quite impressively capable.*

Many things can follow from this new belief. For instance, you might start to focus more on training, expressing positive belief in people's abilities, and being available to assist and support them as they start to take on more responsibility. Instead of getting on their case when they err, you reinforce how great it was that they took the initiative to make a difference. From that new approach, the staff start to gain more confidence. Over time, you're less and less "needed" in the day-to-day activities of the business. As a result, you're less exhausted, your decision making improves, and you're better able to step back and see the big picture. All of which leads you to set aside a couple hours every week to work on the business, developing new systems, training, and processes. And because you now believe that the staff are generally quite capable, you start to ask for their input on the changes you're making, which causes them to feel better about themselves, take more initiative, and grow even more effective in their work.

By the way, please don't use any of these examples to reinforce the negative self-image that you're a "bad manager." We're all human, we all have things we do well, and we all have things we can do better. Most of what I write about in the Zingerman's Guide to Good Leading series is stuff I learned by screwing up and then working hard to recover with some modicum of grace. And as my first therapist constructively pointed out, the unproductive beliefs and behaviors that I was becoming aware of and was then trying to change weren't totally unhelpful. Most had served me well at earlier stages of my life. I wasn't a "bad person" just because some of my beliefs were out of synch with the way I now wanted to live my life. I was just using out-of-date emotional "software" programmed into me by others many years earlier, in a different, and now long-past era.

The key at this current moment, my therapist made clear, was never to beat myself up about what I was doing "wrong." That would serve only to reinforce my original self-doubting beliefs. The idea was, instead, to replace criticism with steady care and confidence. Take my belief that I wasn't a good writer. When one sentence wouldn't come out the way I wanted, I'd get frustrated. Rip up paper. Rewrite. Agonize. Under pressure, I'd try again, but the results usually seemed even worse. All of which just reinforced my feelings of incompetence, which in turn raised my anxiety and reduced my effectiveness even further.

What changed? Instead of believing that "if you're a good writer, it comes naturally," I started to believe that writing was a skill that needed to be developed, *just like any other*. That being mad at myself wasn't going to get me anywhere. Rather, if I was going write well, it would take the same sort of work it had taken me to get good at anything else. I was going to need to study, practice, and get around people who knew more than I did and could teach me what they knew. Among other things, I read Brenda Ueland's amazing *If You Want to Write*, from which I learned—and quickly believed—that "writing is just talking on paper." Better writing, I realized, came not from being "born a good writer," but from lots of practice, patience, and persistence. It was, I came to believe, more important to *just write* than it was to worry about the quality of what I was writing. So when I feel frustrated or like I'm failing, rather than getting caught up in the frustration, the best thing I can do is just breathe deep and keep going.

In a business context, Edgar Schein's Stages of Organizational development (see Secret #34, in *Part 3*) helped me change my beliefs about what constituted the "right ways" for leaders to spend their time. In a start-up, as Schein discusses, it's highly effective to be hands-on nearly all the time. Since I'd begun that way, and believed that leaders who weren't hands-on were probably bossy and out of touch and that it wasn't right to ask anyone to do anything I wasn't doing, I just kept trying to do everything myself—to be on the front line all the time, to unload every truck, etc. In the beginning, that behavior was a plus: Paul and I put in a lot of hours, leading by example, inspiring others in the process.

Over the years, though, that way of working became increasingly ineffective. If we were on the front line all the time, who was going to work *on* the business? Answer: no one! In a much bigger, more mature business, the belief that effective leaders need to be ready to do everything themselves got me in trouble. Schein's teaching helped me change my beliefs about effective leadership. I started to realize that our organization now needed leaders who were going to be working much more *on* the business than *in* it.

Over time, I made peace with my new belief that at the stage of healthy maturity, the leader's most important work—one that few entrepreneurs truly embrace—is to develop effective systems and structure. I also began to believe that lasting change at this level takes a long time, and that even though things were likely to look like failures partway through, I would do well to stick with them. Without question, that change in beliefs is one of the keys to what has made Zingerman's what it is. Without it, we'd have burned out or sold out long ago.

Interestingly, these shifts required no changes in vision or in values. Those stayed the same. What changed were my beliefs and the behavior that followed from them. You can track the pattern here.

Old Belief	New Belief in a Bigger Organization
Managers need to be on the floor pretty much all the time to show that they're working with the crew.	Managers need to show willingness to do "the work," but they also need to spend a good chunk of time working *on* the business, doing systems design, training, etc.
Spending a lot of money on administrative positions sends a bad message to the frontline folks who do "the work" every day.	Hiring people with high expertise in administrative roles becomes ever more imperative.
Meetings are generally a waste of time.	How to run a meeting well is one of the most important things a leader at this stage needs to learn.

Taking a more detailed look at the last item in the chart, here's the old cycle: "Meetings are generally a waste of time," so we don't spend any time prepping for them and don't engage much in them, so others also believe meetings are a waste of time, so they follow our lead, come unprepared, and probably complain long and hard about "having" to attend. As a result, we waste a lot of time and effort, while communication grows ever more ineffective, and we have a lot of lone cowboys, each believing that they have the "answer" and advocating for their individual worldviews.

It doesn't work. With Schein's insight in hand, I changed to the belief that well-run meetings are one of the best resources a larger, healthy organization can have. I started to spend more time preparing for meetings, studying meeting management skills, and learning about facilitation. Once our meetings were better managed, others started to take them more seriously. Better meeting design, it turns out, leads to better communication and collaboration. It actually ends up saving time. That change is also one of the keys to our success at Zingerman's. Meeting frequently isn't one of our values, nor is it in our vision. It's a tactical tool, not an ethical issue. But I've learned that without effective meetings, it's impossible to run a big organization. And we now have a rotating team that ably takes turns facilitating our bimonthly Partners' Group meetings.

Change Now, Find Facts Later

Ten years ago I would have told you flat out that only the discovery of new "evidence" would have convinced me to change a belief. You'd have to "prove" to me that this new point of view was verifiably accurate, at which point I would give serious thought to it.

This recipe, though, is the opposite. The only evidence we're working with here is that we're not happy with something as it is. There is no particular proof needed that the new belief we're adopting will be better. We make the change to the new belief simply because we are convinced that it will effectively alter the outcomes we're getting.

Here's the funny thing: Given that what we believe drastically alters the data we notice, it's only *after* we change a belief that the evidence for its value will start to appear. In fact, it's only after I adopted this recipe that I had this realization!

6. ERODE THE OLD PATTERNS WITH NEW THINKING

Changing habits of a lifetime is a long and slow process. (If you believe that it can be done quickly, well, that might be a good belief to practice this recipe with.) When I first started going to therapy, I would regularly voice my frustration at my seeming inability to alter patterns of behavior I had realized were destructive. Fortunately, my therapist was more patient than I was. "You aren't going to be able to change 30 years' worth of habits in a week," he would remind me. "Even if you can do it in a year or two, that's a whole lot less time than it took you to build up the habits in the first place." Our brains are actually wrapped in such a way that we process things based on our beliefs without our even knowing it. One of my objectives in this book is to help readers (and myself) move to a level of conscious competence when it comes to recognizing our beliefs. So, if we want to change longstanding beliefs, we need to actively alter the way we interpret the evidence. Because we all filter information to fit our beliefs, most everything we take in will tend to reinforce what we already "know."

If, for example, we've been told our whole lives that men are emotionally inferior to women, we will find a great deal of "proof" out in the world to back up that belief. Every time we see a man do something insensitive, it informs our belief that men are clueless about how to navigate key relationships. To change that pattern, we have to actively watch for information that supports a new belief. We have to realize that assigning a stereotype to billions of humans is dangerous and destructive. As we alter our awareness, we can slowly start to change our belief; when we see a male do something insensitive, we remind ourselves it's just one man. And that we actually have no idea why he did what he did. Nor do we know whether it was a regular behavior for him or an aberration, whether he's had a lifetime of bad behavior or is just having a rough day. And conversely, when we see a man do something positive, we start to see it not as an aberration but simply as admirable.

Change like this takes a lot of focused attention and effort. "People are either not familiar with their history, or they have not yet learned that revolution is but thought carried into action," Emma Goldman tells us. How do you stay focused in order to make the change stick? Here are a handful of techniques that have worked well for me.

Write a vision. The single most effective way I've found to help alter longstanding beliefs is to start by writing a long-term vision of greatness. As Tom Asacker explains, "People don't venture down an unfamiliar path, unless they can visualize *their desired destination*." It could be a general vision of your life or your organization, or it could focus on a particular issue at hand. It could involve a specific behavior, a particular relationship, or a skill you want to develop. Visions themselves are based on positive belief—without belief, you don't sit down and write one!

Visions help us hold course; when there's internal or external pressure to slide back to our old beliefs, rereading the vision can help us keep moving in our desired direction. Visions can help us enlist support from others and internalize for ourselves the new future state we're going after.

Back when I was bogged down in perfectionism and ripping up papers while I was writing, I could have done a vision about what effective writing would look and feel like for me five years in the future. You might write a vision that details a newfound belief in your staff's ability to attain excellence. Or one that outlines how you're now charging what you need to charge to make your business sustainable while still serving super high-quality food. If I were the premier of Slovakia, I might consider a national vision that includes great service as the core pillar of the society.[17]

Reread your vision regularly and share it with others. When you're clear on where you're going and what it's going to feel like, sound like, taste like, and look like when you get there, it's a lot easier to hold course while you do the less-than-glamorous work to change beliefs. When you share your vision with others you care about, it's highly likely that they, too, will buy into this better future. Their support, assistance, and insights can make the difference between just starting to change and making a new routine stick.

Commit to journaling. Keeping a log of positive outcomes and self-assessments (done supportively!) can help keep us mindful. No team plays a perfect game every time. A daily dose of reflection can help keep us focused while we learn new plays to make the changes we've chosen.

Hang around people who share the new belief. One of the best ways I know to make a belief stick is to start spending time with people who share the new belief. They model the behavior we're trying to adopt, reinforce the wisdom of our choice, help us catch ourselves more quickly when we go astray, support us when critics attack, and share tips on how to handle adversity. Remember that "hanging around the right people" can also include what we read and what we listen to. Some of the best support I've gotten over the years has come from the work, and the words, of authors I've never actually met.

When I was working to change my beliefs about the value of well-run meetings, perhaps the most helpful thing I did was hang around folks who agreed that well-run meetings were a critical component of managing a healthy organization of our size. I'll never forget reading Peter Block's comment that "meetings are the family dinner of organizational life." There are, of course, many family dinners that don't prove to be much fun. But a healthy family dinner, in which everyone is engaged, honored, and uplifted, leaves all involved feeling connected and energized.

Conversely, hanging out with people who are still tied to the old beliefs that we're trying so hard to let go of can cause problems. Particularly early on in the change process, just spending time with them can be challenging. Their negativity can suck us down the rabbit hole of bad beliefs in no time flat. "Meetings are a total waste of time. What a disaster that was!" Though I'd be tempted to start arguing, I knew I'd never win that quarrel. Their beliefs are way too firmly rooted, and they aren't ready to change them. A better approach? Walking away politely with a quick "I gotta run" proved useful to me. Asking for input on how they'd have run the meeting instead might help, too, although it leaves room for a response like "Just don't have it in the first place." I like to keep in mind what Osho said: "If you live with unhealthy people, to be healthy is dangerous. If you live with insane people, then to be sane is dangerous."

Regularly reference success stories that support your new belief. When we're paying attention and when we believe we can really make the change we're trying to make, we will start to see evidence that it's working. Mindfully taking note of that new proof can help build positive momentum. The more we focus on stories of other folks living successfully with our newly developing belief, the more we find constructive role models, the easier it is to stay on course.

Sleep On It

I haven't tried this myself, but Claude Bristol swore by it, and it makes sense. If you're struggling (and even if you're not), why not give this a try? "Just before going to sleep at night," Bristol writes, "and upon waking in the mornings, concentrate upon your [desired] thoughts with added force. But don't stop with merely those two periods of the twenty-four hours. The more often you visualize your desire by this method (or by one of your own devising), the speedier its materialization will be." Thinking about what you want at least two times a day isn't that onerous, is it?

Repeat often! Claude Bristol advocates regularly writing down affirmations on index cards—essentially, short restatements of your new belief. "These repetitive words and phrases are merely methods of convincing the subconscious mind. It's the repetition of affirmations that leads to belief." As the Wrights assert half a century later, "We can rewire our brains." Psychiatrist Jeffrey Schwartz adds, "Attention density activates brain circuitry and, over time and with repetition, it actually alters the structure of the brain. In this way, 'the mind does change the brain.'"

Slowly but surely, using any or all these techniques, we can make headway. Statistics seem to say it takes somewhere between three and six months to change a deeply ingrained habit. That seems quick to me. I'd say it's more like two to three years. In any case, as Peter Koestenbaum admonishes us all: "Do not give up. Persist. Have faith. Today's heresy is tomorrow's dogma."

The good news is that starting to make a change will often unleash new energy. Per the Wrights: "When you're on a transformational path you achieve more, you feel more, you experience more." All of which contributes to the community around us—as each member of the group lives more in alignment with their own vision and values, that energy will collectively flow. As Paulo Coelho writes in *The Alchemist*, "When we strive to become better than we are, everything around us becomes better too."

Changing My Beliefs About Journaling

What follows is a personal example of the recipe in action.

Step 1. Identify the Issue: My problem—to put it bluntly—was that I was essentially making myself crazy. I was worrying, obsessing, ruminating, agonizing, and speaking to myself in harsh and disrespectful tones that were, in turn, contributing to problems in the way I was relating to others around me.

Step 2. Backtrack to Beliefs: My beliefs on the value of journaling (as you know from above) were at that time very negative. I'd long thought that journaling was silly, a waste of time, not for capable men. Those negative beliefs gave me good reason not to do it.

Step 3. Do Some Homework: Why did I believe that? I don't know for sure. Most likely it was just social norms. It's certainly not encouraged, and it may even seem unacceptable, for successful adult American males to spend time reflecting in a diary.

Step 4. Check the Equation: What did I get out of *not* journaling? Really, not much—at least not anything good. At a deeper level, I guess that a) I didn't have to face social pressure by doing something "guys didn't do"; and b) more challenging, not reflecting regularly allowed me to stay stuck in my old ways, in a world where harsh self-criticism, uncertainty, mental flip-flopping, and fear of failure were the primary beliefs. Once I started to look at the equation mindfully, as awkward as it felt there weren't too many reasons *not* to do it. So I started.

Step 5. Mindfully Adopt a New Belief: The new belief was that journaling was legit, a totally productive use of my time that would help me move forward.

Step 6. Erode the Old Patterns with New Thinking: I didn't write out a vision for my journaling (I didn't know anything about visioning back then), but in hindsight, I suppose I had one in my head. I wrote. It worked. Once I got going, I quickly settled into a routine of doing it nearly every day. Especially in the beginning when I had decades of indecision, uncertainty, and agonizing all bottled up inside me, there was a *lot* of internalized information to get out into the open. The more I journaled, the more I learned, the more I trained my brain to get at the real issues at play—to effectively sort through my feelings, the calmer I got, the more smoothly my day went.

The benefits have been huge. If I were to go back and recheck the equation —i.e., "how I benefited from doing it" versus "what I was getting out of not journaling," it would be about 10,000 to 1 (roughly 10,000 for each day that I've journaled). To make the new belief and routine stick, I tapped into my ability to stay on track with things that I mindfully decide to do. Experiencing the benefits of journaling—both in the beginning and in the long term— helped me stay the course as well.

Starting to teach and write about how effective journaling was for me sealed the deal; sharing a new belief with others actively helps imprint it in our minds. I suppose that is why our "fourth level of learning"—teaching—is so powerful when it comes to changing one's beliefs. By teaching regularly, one becomes the "spokesperson" for the new perspective. If the

Zingerman's Four Levels of Learning

1. Listening (or Reading)
2. Reflecting
3. Assimilating and Acting
4. Teaching (or Writing)

choice of the new belief was well founded—not something forced on you by others—and if the equation truly works out to show the benefits of the new belief, the teaching will significantly enhance the size, strength, and resilience of the roots of the belief. And in the process, the culture—the soil—is richer, better anchored, more stable around it.

I'm still, as of this morning, getting up every day and journaling. I can't imagine ever stopping. The cost? A couple boxes of black Pilot rollerball pens and a dozen or so fine-lined yellow legal pads (maybe $80 a year?), plus 10 or

20 minutes a day. The benefits? Enormous! Journaling pushes me to get at the root of other unproductive beliefs, or at least to mindfully consider many of them. It keeps me regularly in a reflective mode. I feel better about myself. I make fewer mistakes. I do more small acts of kindness. I'm calmer. I'm more generous to both myself and others. And I'm markedly more appreciative.

What Do You Do When You Want Someone Else to Change Their Beliefs?

This is one of the most common questions that has come up in my first few months of teaching this material. From the comments people have offered, they've learned a lot and have started to change things as a result. The University of Michigan's Kristen Kerecman wrote:

> *I've been meaning to write for a while and thank you for your seminar on beliefs. Since attending the session, I can now easily recognize the times (probably daily) where my beliefs are directly influencing how I react or feel about a situation. I think just that ability to check in and say, "Hey, this isn't really what's happening, this is what I believe is happening for these reasons" is incredibly valuable. It's helped me to be less defensive, more open, patient, and positive.*

What also comes up—not from Kristen, to be clear—is the common realization that others in our lives are stuck with unhealthy beliefs, beliefs that are causing their own difficulties or even despair. Which is why I think so many people have left the training and written to me two or three days later to ask "What do you do when you realize someone you care about is stuck in a bad cycle that starts with negative beliefs?"

It's a good question. I had to think about it for a while, and I'm not sure that even now I have a great answer. Here's one thing I realized, though: When we focus on others' behavior, we're not really tracking the belief cycle back to the beginning. The point isn't to see others' ineffective beliefs. It's to accept how much influence *our own beliefs* are having on *their* actions. It's by tracking the cycle back to the top, initiating change by altering what we ourselves believe, that we stand the greatest chance of influencing others around us.

If you do decide to try to get someone else to change a belief, it's not unlike trying to get a loved one to accept that they have an issue with, say, substance abuse. In essence, when we bring it up, we're asking them to face their denial—to reexamine the way they think, to look deeply at their lives, and ultimately to change years (even a lifetime) of beliefs about the substance, themselves, and their relationship with it.

I've always believed that we get at most one shot a year at that kind of conversation. More than that, and our well-meaning suggestions start to become a major annoyance, in which case (in my experience) many people just sink the roots that underlie their way of life even deeper. On occasion, this sort of approach can pay quick dividends. I remember a couple difficult conversations with friends that had significant results in short periods of time. The issue was raised, and they heard the concern, acknowledged it, and quickly took meaningful action. We never know what's been going on in someone else's head. Sometimes they're ready to change, and they just need that one last nudge. In those positive cases, it may be as Mikhail Bakunin says: "Revolutions are, so to speak, self-made. . . . They are a long time hatching in the deepest recesses of the popular masses' instinctive consciousness, and then they explode, often seeming to have been detonated by trivialities." All that those who want to bring on the revolution can do is to spread "ideas that are appropriate to the . . . instincts" and to be "true friends."

But more often than not, they don't make the change. The person with the issue just isn't ready to hear it. This is one of the hardest things I know of in relationships. What do you do if they give no weight to your observation? I don't have a great answer. I try to stay focused on making my own improvement, finding the positives in our time together, staying grounded, not getting angry. If things get really bad, distancing or adjusting the parameters of the relationship may be the only good option. I try to avoid giving the same advice over and over again, and focus instead on acceptance of the other person as they are, on my own actions and feelings, and on finding ways to be as supportive as possible in the process.

The Wrong Why

If we do put a lot of pressure on someone we know, we may get them to make some surface-level shift in what they say and, to some degree, what they do. But if the real reason that they're changing is to please others or comply with external pressure, it's highly unlikely that the newly adopted beliefs will stick. It's like a rose branch grafted onto a cactus—it may look nice for a few weeks, but eventually it will wither and die, leaving the original cactus plant pretty much as it originally was.

In her book, *No Sweat,* Michelle Segar discusses the difference between the "wrong why" and the "right why." Even when people are trying to make a much-needed change—to alter a habit, a routine, a relationship, an addiction, a way of life—the change, she shows us, will almost never take if they pursue it for the wrong reasons.

What's an example of the "wrong why"? Usually it's when we pursue something solely to make others happy because we believe we "should" rather than because we've really bought into making the change. We try to lose weight because our doctor told us to. We try to stop drinking because our significant other has threatened that they'll end the relationship if we don't. We take on a project because our boss wants us to. We try to exercise more because "we know it's good for us." When the "wrong whys" are at work, we'll almost always end up right back where we began. Eventually our efforts erode and we return to our old ways. After which, of course, we feel even worse, and a destructive cycle of negative self-beliefs starts up again.

My take? The "wrong why" comes when we try to make a change without mindfully swapping out our old underlying negative beliefs for the positive ones we need to stay focused on. Take losing weight: When we try to do it "because the doctor said to" or because "my wife and kids are on my case" or "I really should eat better," we're doomed. We may start, but we'll eventually slip back to old habits. The bottom line? Changing behaviors without changing the underlying beliefs almost never works.

The "right why"? It's almost always about pursuing the change because we believe it's the holistically sound thing to do. Rather than being motivated by getting someone else off our back, we do it because we believe that a meaningful positive future for ourselves can be gained by making the change.

Losing weight, for example, is most effective when it's built around a belief like this: "When I feel better about myself, everything around me will go better. I'm a good person, and getting into shape will help me do more good things for myself and everyone in my life. I can't wait!" A new work skill is developed not because it was touched on in our performance review, but because we're truly excited about the possibilities it opens up for us. We've shifted our beliefs about the action we're about to undertake. Michelle demonstrates this in her book with a great deal of data. The odds of attaining long-term success go up significantly when we start with the "right why."

While reading *Part 3* of the Guide to Good Leading series, Boona Pobst, who worked for us for many years, started to explore her own beliefs. They were, she realized, leading her straight into the problems she was simultaneously so frustrated with. "I had a *huge* personal moment," she told me.

I've been really listening and paying attention to my inner voices. And, man oh man, do they speak loudly and often! I had no idea the volume and magnitude of what was going on in my head on a daily basis. Today my daughter called and was ecstatic about getting an "almost A" in math. School has been really difficult for her, and she has struggled to keep afloat. This year, with a lot of extra help and the right environment, we have gotten her to a place where she is putting in the effort to do better.

In my head, the voice (my mother!) was saying, "Don't you celebrate mediocrity!" "Graduating from high school is not an accomplishment!" I have heard these expressions for years and years, but I did not know that I had been listening. Today I was able to override myself and really celebrate my daughter's accomplishment. I am so proud of her, and she really did work hard, albeit at the expense of other classes. What a life-awakening experience for me. I am now looking at my own definition of mediocrity and other people's definitions. They all matter. Who knew?

As Lao-Tzu laid out centuries ago, "Watch your thoughts; they become words. Watch your words; they become actions. Watch your actions; they become habits. Watch your habits; they become character. Watch your character; it becomes your destiny."

To build any or all of the above strategies into your personal process and into your culture will take time. But if you set some goals—say, "effectively expressing belief in others twice a day"—and stick to them week in and week out, two or three years down the road I guarantee that you'll have made great progress on all fronts. As Gustav Landauer wrote so insightfully a century or so ago, "Human relationships depend on human behavior. The possibility of [anarchism] depends on the belief that people can always change their behavior." I share that belief. So did Claude Bristol: "I am convinced that any intelligent person who is sincere with himself can reach any heights he desires." I'm confident that by working collaboratively, pursuing the positive, patiently learning to support each other's dreams, and sharing our vision and our values, we can make great things happen.

Just a Little Bit More Magic

One last funny story on this subject. Or maybe it's serious.

It wasn't until I was working on the 71st or so redraft of this Secret that I decided to add the material at the beginning of the essay about Claude Bristol. As you now know, I'd grown greatly enamored of his work, but I hadn't yet decided where to place it. Wanting to have my copy of his book in hand (I believe it enhances the effectiveness of my writing to have it front of me), I drove home from the Deli to get it.

Now, I'd like to tell you that I have all my books neatly arranged, alphabetically and by subject, but they've sort of taken over my house. There are piles of them everywhere. I was sure I'd seen Bristol's not that long ago, but I went through all 10 stacks on the table where I thought I'd seen it, to no avail. I started to get frustrated. But I've trained myself over the years not to totally stress out like I used to. I now believe that the thing I'm looking for will almost always turn up.

I searched the stacks again, trying to stay calm. Went to the kitchen to check there. Nope. Headed downstairs to look through the thousand or so books on the basement shelves. Couldn't find it there either. In the bedroom? No way. I decided to go back to the living room where I thought I'd seen it. I started going through one of the ten stacks on the center table—for the third time now—when, all of a sudden, the pile to its right toppled over onto the floor. I swore a few times, took a deep breath, and bent over to gather up the dozen or so volumes that I'd inadvertently sent flying. And darn if there wasn't Bristol's book *The Magic of Believing*.

Maybe it was luck. But I keep thinking about one of the many quotes I'd marked in Bristol's book. "At the start, you may have no idea of how the results are to come. Yet you need not concern yourself. Just leave it to the subconscious mind, which has its own ways of making contacts and of opening doors and avenues that you may have never even guessed at. You will receive assistance from the most unexpected sources."[18]

The Belief Pyramid

What follows is my adaptation of a technique I learned from Anese Cavanaugh. It's designed to help two people in conflict get to a place of understanding, better communication, and, hopefully, effective collaboration. I haven't done it enough times to tell you exactly how it works, but I'm turning the tool loose here like open-source software so we can all test it together. By all means, try it out in a somewhat safe setting; I don't recommend charging into your banker's office when you need a big loan and challenging her to some sort of belief showdown.

In the song "Angels," on his album *Mercy* (one of my favorites of all time), Sam Baker sings, "Everyone is at the mercy of another one's dream." Getting at our beliefs and how they fit or don't fit with what others around us believe is, I think, a positive step towards altering what Sam so astutely points out to be true in most of the world. If we recognize that other people are entitled to their own beliefs and that there's rarely a "right" or "wrong" dream, it's a lot easier to move past conflict and get to positive collaboration.

The belief pyramid helps people to hear each other and understand more about one another's beliefs, and to arrive more effectively—if still often awkwardly—at the best outcome for the organization. It creates a more balanced dialogue and organizes the conversation in a way that takes multiple sets of beliefs into account, while ultimately getting all involved focused on the big picture—which is what's right for business overall, not for us as individuals.

With any given issue that's in dispute, have each of the various parties start at the bottom of the pyramid and gradually make their way up to the top. The middle question, I'll tell you up front, frequently throws people for a bit of

a loop, but it's also often the one that brings out the most interesting answers. What comes out of this is sometimes uncomfortable, but I believe it's helpful.

Jen Mayer, Co-Founder, Honey Butter Fried Chicken, Chicago, Illinois

When I first started attending ZingTrain seminars and learning about the culture and business practices of the ZCoB, I had a very specific application in mind—my husband and I, along with our two business partners, were about to embark on the journey of opening a restaurant, Honey Butter Fried Chicken. We wanted to open out-of-the-gate with outstanding customer service, strong leadership skills and a culture that would be on par with the values and standards of Zingerman's.

We also owned graphic-design firm Kitemath. It was (and still is) small—at the time it was the two of us and one employee. As I went to seminars and learned about Zingerman's, I had tunnel vision of a sort—I saw how their philosophy and practices could benefit our restaurant and how it would apply to what eventually became 37+ employees and growing, but I dismissed it as being applicable to our tiny service-based business, thinking "That makes sense if you're managing a large staff" and "That would work in a retail environment" and "That's totally true for a food business."

But as I continued to immerse myself in the study of Zingerman's, and as we strengthened and refined our systems at Honey Butter, I started to realize that the "secrets" of Zingerman's and what they teach aren't just for mid-size businesses or big-businesses or food businesses or retail businesses. They apply to two- or three-person businesses. They apply to automotive-parts manufacturers, graphic designers, accountants, entrepreneurs, dreamers, and, ultimately—with the publication of *Managing Ourselves [Part 3]*—any one single person (yourself). Anyone with a passion to do it better. To be mindful and considerate of their actions and thoughts. To be lifelong learners and to never settle for anything less than great. That's my biggest takeaway from Zingerman's and I strive to apply that mindset to my businesses—big and small—and to myself every day.

Bob Bennett, Sous Chef, Zingerman's Roadhouse

When I started working at the deli 14 years ago, my beliefs were small and limited, as I really never took the time the ponder on what I wanted to believe in or who I wanted to be. I was a fifth-year college student, two semesters away from a bachelor but three months away dropping it for a career in cooking. My initial belief was that I didn't know what I wanted to be but I knew I wanted to be good at it. One day I was on the old back docks of the Deli, smoking with Lisa Clark, my supervisor on the line at the moment, and she had mentioned that I should think about going to the Roadhouse, and that Alex [Young, chef and managing partner] had said that I was one of the best line cooks he had seen. I was sold. Leading me to my next belief going into the Roadhouse: regardless of what situation I was in, I always believed that if my effort was strong and honest, it would be appreciated and rewarded.

I believe that a fulfilling career is never fully realized and changes day to day. Something I have been thinking about lately is "how did I get here." I have never been the one that says, "I am going to be this when I get older." Just never had that vision of myself. Which, looking back, I think is awesome! I have been able to go through life and practice and learn and take pieces out of many situations good and bad, to shape who I am, and what I do—could be beliefs about yourself, about food, about business, about leadership, service, quality, compassion, collaboration, visioning . . . anything, really!

I believe the qualities of being a good leader are almost the mirror of being a good parent. The hours, the constant active listening, guiding, coaching, and love.

Thinking back through your life . . . do you remember a time when someone really believed in you when most others didn't? And their belief really helped you keep moving forward through an otherwise difficult time?

Like so many others that I have seen through the years, Alex has helped me through tough times through his belief in people. I am a quiet person about my personal life, so it is rare that people know when things are off, but by having this real and honest place of work, where the leader of it has this intense commitment and belief that his staff will do the right thing in the moment, is such a righteous thing.

Last (and this will be cheesy but true), I believe that doing things/ reading things/eating things that give you goose bumps on a daily basis is as close to greatness as I may get.

This one keeps me going on a daily basis. When I was younger, my brother and I would literally watch ESPN for about three to four hours every day. One thing that always stuck with me was the now-classic Jimmy Valvano speech, where he says, "You think, you laugh, you cry and that's a full day, that's a heck of a day!" Still gives me goose bumps and brings me to the verge of tears to this day. And I go for that. I try to find work, music, books, and speeches that move me and inspire me.

And for me, that's fulfilling.

Thanks—felt weird and fulfilling to put it down into words.

ron Lippitt and Gustav Landauer sharing thoughts on freedom
and positive futuring on the bench out front of the deli

What I Believe About Anarchism and Business

Free Thinking and Caring Community in Action

My original interest in anarchist thinking goes back to my days in school at the University of Michigan. The ideas that came out of it lay dormant for most of the following three decades. But in the last six or seven years, I've become increasingly intrigued. I believe that there's a lot for those of us who are trying to run caring, progressive businesses to learn from anarchist ideas about free choice, respect for every individual, community-oriented collaboration, and the ability of everyone in an organization to contribute as much to leadership thinking and business management as they might to lifting boxes or laying stone. What follows is a look into those beliefs and how they came to resonate with me so strongly.

On Saturday morning, February 4, 1911, a short and stocky Jewish woman with wire-rimmed glasses walked (I imagine) up Detroit Street headed towards downtown Ann Arbor, where she was to speak later that day. She was coming from the train station on Depot Street, where she might well have been met by a handful of friends and supporters. Emma Goldman was 41 years old at the time and one of the most controversial figures in the United States.

Born in Lithuania in 1869, Goldman started working in factories at the age of 14 for wages of about $1.50 a week. She began fighting strongly held social beliefs at an early age, both at home and in Russian society. Her family was pushed into poverty by extreme anti-Semitism. Her Orthodox Jewish father, an innkeeper, had desperately hoped for a boy but got Emma instead. As a young teenager, she begged him to let her continue her education, but he angrily threw her French book into the fire and scolded: "Girls do not have to learn much! All a Jewish daughter needs to know is how to prepare gefilte fish, cut noodles fine, and give the man plenty of children." As is so often the case when we try to force someone to change their beliefs, opposition only makes the roots grow deeper. Emma decided to emigrate. She arrived in the United States a few years later. By the age of 20, she was already an avowed anarchist and had led her first factory strike. She went to jail for the first time four years later, something she continued to do regularly for the rest of her life. She was arrested so often that she learned to always bring a book with her whenever she spoke, in case she ended up spending the night behind bars.

Goldman arrived in Ann Arbor that February morning from Detroit, where she'd been lecturing for most of the previous week. By this point in her life, she was basically on tour all the time, vehemently sharing her views from the stage, five or six days out of seven, sometimes twice in the same day. By the time she arrived in Ann Arbor, she'd been lecturing regularly for over two decades. The week before, she'd spoken in Toledo, where artist Robert Henri was in the audience. He bought a copy of her newly released book, *Anarchism and Other Essays*, and read it on the train back to New York.

I'd imagine Goldman was a bit tense that day, though, as always, exceptionally determined. Despite international protests, in which she'd actively participated, and the fact that a dozen anarchists had been put to death by the Japanese government two weeks earlier. On her last visit to Ann Arbor the previous winter, she'd been faced with hundreds of angry students screaming epithets and trying to keep her from speaking. She'd spoken that year at Johnson Tent Hall at 109 North Main, about four blocks to the southwest of Disderide's. There were reports of "tables flying and stoves falling over." She wrote about the incident later that summer and, per her usual style, didn't mince words:

> *Ann Arbor! Brain producer of Michigan, hide thy face in shame! . . .*
> *Five hundred university rowdies in a hall, whistling, howling, push-*
> *ing, yelling like escaped lunatics. How infinitely superior is the rough-*
> *est element of workers, longshoremen, sailors, miners, street-cleaners. I*
> *have addressed them all; been with all. Men with not enough knowl-*
> *edge to write their names, men who have been harried and brutalized*
> *by drudgery and poverty. Yet all of them are as boarding-school girls in*
> *behavior and demeanor compared with the university rowdies of Ann*
> *Arbor, who packed the hall to create a riot.*

"A course on behavior and decency," she later concluded, "would not be amiss at the University of Ann Arbor."

As was her wont, she responded to the students that day—not with violence but by quoting playwright Henrik Ibsen. Which tells you a lot about Emma Goldman. Drama played a large role in her life, both because she was good at creating it and because she studied it in great depth. She was a big fan of George Bernard Shaw, Oscar Wilde, Ibsen, and others. Her book *The Social Significance of the Modern Drama*—perhaps her least known work—came out in 1914, three years after her visit to Ann Arbor. Great theater, she wrote in it, "is the dynamite which undermines superstition, shakes the social pillars, and prepares men and women for the reconstruction."[19]

Goldman was nothing if not provocative—intellectually and emotionally. She drew criticism from almost every corner of the country. One Baltimore paper deemed her a "Yiddish evangelist." Most of the mainstream press made her out to be a well-spoken version of the devil, a woman intent on destroying the country. In 1897, the *Detroit Free Press* had called her "the hysterical foe of organized government." The *Detroit News* chimed in: "Emma Goldman, the anarchist . . . rarely has an original thought. There is no appeal to a listener's intelligence. It is all passion."

Many of her supporters, conversely, saw her as an anarchist equivalent of Joan of Arc, a socially conscious saint who was willing to give her life for the cause of social justice. In 1912, writer Caroline Nelson called her "the most fearless woman in America." If Facebook had existed back then, she would surely have had millions of followers. In 1908, writer and editor William Marion Reedy sang her praises in the St. Louis *Mirror*. Emma Goldman, Reedy explains, is "[A]nything but what the papers say. She is not pretty, but when her face lights up the glow and color of her inner enthusiasm she is remarkably attractive." She was, Reedy writes, the "daughter of the dream, her gospel a vision which is the vision of every truly great-souled man and woman who has ever lived." And, he adds, "She is about eight thousand years ahead of her age."

To come back to 1911, as she walked the ten blocks or so to get downtown to speak, Goldman might well have come upon Rocco Disderide's shop. It's not hard to imagine that she stopped to get something to drink after breathing in the dust and dirt of the train ride. She'd likely have been carrying the large metal trunk of a suitcase she took with her everywhere, and it would have been good to set it down for a minute. Disderide could well have waited on her and offered pleasantries. He was ten years her senior, and at 6 feet 1 inch, he would have towered over her. By that point, the shop was nearing its tenth anniversary—a neighborhood institution in the making.[20]

I imagine that, perhaps, the two exchanged a few words in their differently accented English. He'd been in the United States longer, but her command of the language was far superior. Disderide was, it seems, almost always in a good mood, so he could well have smiled and slipped her a bit of peanut brittle. If he gave her back a few coins, their hands might have touched just a bit. And maybe, just maybe, that momentary meeting is somehow the source of the connections that crisscross my life: shop keeping and anarchism, working the counter and public speaking, small gestures of kindness and down-to-earth community building.

The students were much better behaved in 1911 than they had been the previous year. Feeling calmer, Emma might well have ended the evening on the other side of downtown at 1114 South University (between East University and Church), where Julius Seltzer and Eugene Chatterton ran a restaurant. Seltzer, like Goldman, was a Russian Jewish immigrant who had come to believe in anarchism. The two had met in Schenectady a few years earlier, where he arranged for her to give a speech. "An enormous success, with an overflow crowd," he later told historian Paul Avrich. Seltzer and Goldman, we know, met up again 15 years later in Toronto, where he and his brother-in-law owned and ran Dominion Knitting Mills. He became very successful in business but still stayed true to his anarchist orientation. Goldman called him "the only millionaire in our ranks." Seltzer, it seems, was a paragon of positive beliefs. "The ideal [of anarchism] is still floating all over the world," he said. "I have never been disillusioned. I am always optimistic."[21]

Goldman spent about half her time on the lecture circuit. In 1911 she reported: "In six months we visited 18 states and 50 cities," speaking to 50,000 to 75,000 people en route. The visit here that year was one of six that Goldman, by far the most famous anarchist of her era and probably of all time, paid to Ann Arbor. Her 1910 speech was her first; after 1911, she again came and spoke in 1912, 1913, 1915, and 1916. (A final scheduled talk in 1918—part of her farewell tour before being expelled from the country—was called off by order of the mayor and city council.) For some reason, she was always here in the winter. I imagine her stopping every time at Disderide's, a regular of sorts, en route from the train to downtown, and then later, again, to warm her hands a bit on the way back to the station.[22]

In 1916 she spent nearly a week here, speaking every day at Woodmen's Hall on the corner of Main and Washington. The hall was, Michigan anarchist Agnes Inglis wrote, "a very forlorn place down town, up two flights over a store." Goldman was nothing if not resilient. "She spoke twice a day, afternoon and evening and strange to say, the lectures were all well attended, which is a tremendous feat in as much as the students are worked to death and everyone foretold that eight meetings in Ann Arbor would prove a failure." Each day she dealt with a different Russian writer, including Tolstoy and Chekhov. You could buy a set of tickets for all six talks for $1. Pamphlets and books were also available for sale, the former for a nickel, the latter $1 or $1.25. The handbill for the 1916 talks says, "Emma Goldman's lectures have provoked a great deal of discussion through the Country. If you are interested in vital subjects and believe in thinking for yourself, Miss Goldman has a message for you." She—and her colleagues, it turns out—definitely had a message for me.

Comparing Quotes

There are so many great quotes with which to launch this Secret, I could spend a week worrying about which one is best. But since this is an essay about the ineffectiveness of hierarchy, I'm going to bypass my perfectionistic desire to pick the "top two." Instead, I'm gonna go with my gut: Here are a dozen quotes that speak to my beliefs about anarchism. My energy goes up every time I read through them. Ready? Here we go.

1. *The general contention that Anarchists are opposed to organization, and hence stand for chaos, is absolutely groundless. True, we do not believe in the compulsory, arbitrary side of organization that would compel people of antagonistic tastes and interests into a body and hold them there by coercion. Organization as the result of natural blending of common interests, brought about through voluntary adhesion, Anarchists do not only not oppose, but believe in as the only possible basis of social life.*

2. *The value of coercive power is inverse to its use—more so every day.*

3. *Our task is to push people to demand and seize all of the freedom they can grasp, to make themselves responsible for providing their own needs without waiting for orders from any kind of authority.*

4. *[Workers] will no longer need a "manager"; they can "manage" themselves.*

5. *Freedom is a reality within your heart. Know it, acknowledge it, claim it, use it.*

6. *Anarchism aims to strip labor of its deadening, dulling aspect, of its gloom and compulsion. It aims to make work an instrument of joy, of strength, of color, of real harmony, so that the poorest sort of a man should find in work both recreation and hope.*

7. *The revolution begins in our own hearts.*

8. *Each member needs to believe that the organization is theirs to create if any shift is to take place.*

9. *You are free. And we mean by this that you possess free will. Political freedom can be taken from you but your free will cannot.*

10. *The possibility of anarchy depends on the belief that people can always change their behavior.*

11. *I believe . . . that everyone, of whatever age and circumstance, is capable of self-transformation.*

12. *Humans have the capacity to freely and independently create a life that is their own. . . . No one lacks the ability, the disposition, the potential.*

There's just one catch—only *five of these twelve* are taken from anarchists. The others come from some of the best late-20th-century progressive business thinkers, none of whom, I'm pretty sure, would consider themselves anarchists. Yet the same themes—freedom and free choice, taking charge of our own lives, the importance of respecting every individual with whom you interact, an emphasis on the constructive role of healthy organizations, the importance of diverse perspectives—appear with roughly equal emphasis from all of them. The amount of overlap between the two groups took me by surprise. The anarchists? Quotes 1 and 6, Emma Goldman; 3, Errico Malatesta; 10 and 12, Gustav Landauer. The progressive business thinkers? Quote 2, Robert Greenleaf; 4, Dean Tucker; 5, 8, and 9, Peter Koestenbaum; 7, Peter Block; 11, business writer Warren Bennis.

My attraction to anarchism is both old and new. Or maybe I should say *re*-newed. One of the best parts of working on this series of business books over the last six or so years has been the rekindling of my fascination with anarchist thinking. It's not why I set out to write the books in the first place. But my increased interest has been an inspiringly beautiful by-product, an accidental but amazing outcome, informing my understanding of the world and my beliefs about business, life, and love. It's turned out to be quite a relationship—an alignment of already existing (even if previously unacknowledged) passions, and an enhancement of deep-seated but undeveloped beliefs that have made my work, my life, and my leadership significantly more rewarding and effective.

In case you don't already know the story of Ari and the anarchists (if I only had a band), I'll briefly share it here. Going back to the late 1970s, when I was making my way through the University of Michigan, I somehow stumbled upon the Labadie Collection on the seventh floor of the Graduate Library. I used to spend a good bit of time sitting at the long wooden tables and reading books, pamphlets, poems, and powerful manifestos written by people such as Emma Goldman, Alexander Berkman, and Peter Kropotkin. Most were published around the turn of the 20th century. Many were as aesthetically exceptional—lovely paper, great colors, incredible artwork—as they were intellectually interesting.

My worldviews were still being formed, but in hindsight, I can see that the spiritual seeds in what I was reading most definitely took root. I could relate completely to the idea that when we lived mostly as others wanted us to, feeling compelled to conform in ways that didn't feel right to us, that our lives and our work would end up being drab, boring, spiritually depressing, and, at worst, an outright disaster. And on the other hand, that when we lived in ways that were true to ourselves, respected others for who they really are, freely chose to contribute to our communities, tapped creative energy, honored human nature, and eliminated hierarchy, good things were likely to happen. I loved (and still love) Emma Goldman's view that "Anarchism is the spirit of youth against outworn tradition."

The Gentle Anarchist

Jo Labadie, the man whose name is on the collection, was born in 1850 in Paw Paw, Michigan. Descended from French Canadian and Native American ancestors, he moved east to Detroit as a young adult, where he gradually became more aligned with anarchist thinking. His granddaughter and biographer, Carlotta Anderson, described him as "handsome, debonair, well-dressed and well-groomed, sporting a Buffalo Bill–style goatee and slouch hat, Jo, as he was called, was commonly referred to as Detroit's 'gentle anarchist.'" He was, she says, "somewhat short in stature, but bearing himself regally, he had luxuriant black, wavy hair atop a big head, with penetrating blue eyes." Like me, he loved fresh whitefish, though he caught his himself in local lakes and rivers, while I find mine at the local fishmonger. "The prince of freshwater fish" is what he called it—an improbably imperial moniker coming from an anarchist.[23]

Like so many anarchists, Labadie had an aesthetic sensibility. He was a printer, a poet, and an all-around interesting guy. Unlike Emma Goldman, who caused so much controversy, Labadie was loved almost universally. When the head of the city water department dismissed him from his job one time, public outcry had him rehired in a matter of days. Labadie was not opposed to private property as long as it was in use by the owner (not just held for rental income from others who were truly using it), and felt that anarchism "admits of any kind of organization, so long as membership is not compulsory." In late 1888 and 1889, in a bold move of collaborative leadership, Labadie sent letters to 40 or 50 of the country's best-known anarchists in an attempt to get to consensus around a definition of the term that could be shared with others. Only about 15 responded, no agreement was ever reached, and there remains no consensus still to this day. I suppose the concept would be incongruent with the idea of anarchism anyway.

Given that all our beliefs begin to form somewhere, it's interesting to look back on Labadie's early years living among the Potawatomi people in the then lightly inhabited area of western Michigan. He described his impressions of the remaining folks: "Chiefs often had little power and no one was compelled to follow them. Individuals lived with the band in a voluntary community, sharing the food and work, but were free to go their solitary way or join another band. No one was subservient to another; no one dominated." The experience proved a formative influence; anarchistic seeds were planted in his soul early on. Anarchism, he later wrote, "claims that freedom, liberty, is the greatest factor in bringing material comfort and happiness to the people."

In the summer of 1911, six months after Goldman came to town, Labadie decided he would give his extensive collection of printed anarchist materials to the library at the University of Michigan. The boxes of books and pamphlets arrived in Ann Arbor in November of that year, but Labadie himself didn't visit until 1924. When he did, he would likely have taken the Detroit Urban Railway and, like Goldman, might have walked up Detroit Street on his way into town. He, too, could well have stopped at Disderide's. Both men, we know, were generally in good spirits, so it's easy to imagine the two laughing and talking a bit as Labadie made his way over to the library. At the least, he and Disderide would have appreciated each other's carefully coiffed moustaches.

Quote Comparison, Take Two

Want to try another quote quiz? One of these is from an anarchist and the other from a modern-day progressive business writer.

> *The best laws, the safest laws, and . . . the only laws necessary for the guidance of human action are natural laws.*

> *All successful organizations—for profit, not-for-profit, large, and small—basically live in harmony with the Natural Laws.*

The first is Jo Labadie. The second, as you may have guessed if you've read the other books in this series, is me. Now you might think, given all that I've written here, that I absconded with the idea from Labadie since his statement

257

was made over a century ago. But I never saw Labadie's line until last year. The idea of the Natural Laws came to me not from some past anarchist, but from my partner Paul.

My Own Beliefs

Sixty-five years after Jo gave his books to the University of Michigan, I sat in the Labadie Collection, some time in my sophomore year, looking through pamphlets and books by Labadie, Goldman, and so many of the other anarchists I've referenced in this book. It all resonated, but I wasn't sure what to do with it. The experience then was, for me, as Italian anarchist Leda Rafanelli writes of her own attraction to this way of thinking, "Something that I could not yet define . . . a secret impulse towards an ideal that I could not yet translate into action." In hindsight, I can see that I was drawn to the anarchists, in part, because what they were writing about was the work I wanted—and needed— to do for myself. We often, of course, seek in others what we are having a hard time doing for ourselves.

A few years into my work in restaurants, I moved into my first formal management position. As jobs went, this one was certainly reasonable, better than most. I'd met great people and come to love the food business. That said, none of my bosses were giving much thought to the creation of an egalitarian workplace. (They weren't headed where I was in terms of food quality either, but I'll save that for another story.) I tried to put some pieces of what I'd read in the anarchist books into action—doing my best to be kind, model good behavior, and generally leave everyone to their own devices—in the well-intentioned if naïve belief that people would just do the right thing of their own volition. The seed of this almost-anarchist approach was inspiring, but the soil in which I was planting it wasn't ready for what I was thinking. And I wasn't a good enough gardener to get anything to grow from my efforts. In hindsight, mine was probably not the most productive approach, but I was young. If my school studies came up for one reason or another, I would generally smile and tell people that I was a "lapsed anarchist"—I still believed in the principles, but I no longer practiced them.

The writer David Whyte says, "A life can often be measured against how sure we were in responding to the initial beckoning image." In that regard, I didn't do all that well my first time through. The fates—or more likely my own intuition—had invited me into the world of the anarchists. I was fascinated. But after a quick dabble, I'd left the party. Unable to figure out how anarchism could fit with my management job, I gradually let my attraction lapse. My friend Deborah Bayer asked me what I would say today to that younger me. The answer is, I suppose, "You're a lot less lapsed than you think you are. There's a good reason why you're so intrigued. Stick to your guns. There's spiritual gold at the end of that anarchist rainbow."

By the late 1980s, the Deli had grown to include 60 or so staff members. It became clear that I needed to get more serious about my leadership studies. I began to read progressive business literature—folks such as Peter Drucker, Robert Greenleaf, Max De Pree, Peter Senge, and Ricardo Semler. I learned about Servant Leadership, setting clear expectations, open-book management, "leadership jazz," and learning organizations. In the early 1990s, we wrote our mission statement, and then our vision for 2009. In 1994, we started ZingTrain, which got me teaching our approaches to leadership to other organizations. By the early 2000s, my work started to shift away from food-writing (which I still love) more and more towards business philosophy. I started to do more speaking at trade shows and business gatherings as well, which in turn pushed me to learn and understand leadership at ever-deeper levels. Although corned beef on rye remained the cornerstone of what we did, over the years Zingerman's became increasingly well known for our progressive approach to running a business.

One day in 2008, while I was working on *Zingerman's Guide to Good Leading, Part 1,* I was asked to speak at the Jewish studies department at the University of Michigan. The talk was scheduled for the following fall and was given the title "Rye Bread and Anarchism," a reference by department chair Deborah Dash Moore to my modern-day work with the former and my academic interest in the latter. Busy as usual, I didn't think much about the topic at the time that she invited me to speak. But over the course of the summer, I realized that although I'd recently written an in-depth article on the history of Jewish rye bread, I hadn't looked at anything to do with Emma Goldman in ages.

The Spirit of Rye Breads Past

The rye bread I wrote about, by the way, is the one that Emma Goldman would likely have been eating regularly in New York City so many years ago. She had good taste. As Candace Falk wrote, "She loved books, opera, beautiful scarves and earrings, buggy rides in the country, a neat home and well-prepared foods." I'm guessing she had some strong opinions about which bakeries had the best bread. Because our rye is made, in part, by adding some of the previous day's bread to the mix, the spirit of rye breads past is always carried forward. Given that the man who taught it to us, Michael London, learned his trade in New York City, where Goldman also lived, for all I know there's a tiny bit of an old loaf she ate from still present in what we do today.

Not wanting to embarrass myself in front of the well-versed professors who I imagined would be in attendance, I dug out a stack of my old anarchist books and started to reread them. What I found blew me away. The classic headline of anarchist beliefs—getting rid of government—was strongly present in what I was reading, but that's not what caught my attention. Government isn't something I have strong feelings about, one way or another. Instead, I stumbled onto a treasure trove of creative concepts that sounded surprisingly similar to the progressive business literature I'd been reading so much of over the years. And so many things that were integral to old anarchist thinking seemed to be embedded *already* in the way we were working at Zingerman's. The ideas that the point of an organization is to enhance the lives of the people who are a part of it; that involving more people in managing the work they're doing makes good sense; that there's wisdom in everyone who works in an organization; that when men and women don't believe in what they're doing, they don't do good work; that when people are treated like interchangeable machine parts, they aren't inspired to get to greatness; that anyone can learn to lead; that the point of the organization is to serve those who are part of it.

Quote Comparison, Take Three

Employees need to find meaning in work. They need to grow towards their fulfillment. They need to become self-realized at work. In short, they need to know that their organization's business objectives coincide with their own deep needs as human beings. These needs are four: (1) creativity, (2) an immortality project or legacy, (3) integrity and character, and (4) validation.

[Our] goal is the freest possible expression of all the latent powers of the individual . . . [which is] only possible in a state of society where

man is free to choose the mode of work, the conditions of work, and the freedom to work. One to whom the making of a table, the building of a house, or the tilling of the soil, is what the painting is to the artist and the discovery to the scientist—the result of inspiration, of intense longing, and deep interest in work as a creative force.

The first quote is from contemporary business writer Peter Koestenbaum, in 2002. The second is Emma Goldman, circa 1910—it's one of the quotes I came across in my reentry into the anarchist world that inspired me so much. The parallel was impossible to miss.

Second Chances

David Whyte writes, "Our ability to follow our star is also a measure of our belief in the original invitation." Sometimes when that initial invite arrives, we're too uncertain, not together enough, to take the chance. That's what happened to me; I let the original opportunity that was delivered to me lapse when I left the Labadie collection behind and started working in restaurants. But for whatever reason of luck or life, we sometimes get a second shot. The talk at the Jewish studies department was mine. This time I took it.

This new round of anarchist studies had me intrigued. For me, high interest can often lead to near obsession. Once I start studying, I don't ever want to stop. I get a buzz from reading good books. I pored over more material, gained more insight, read more, and more, and more. A couple hundred books later, I'm still studying today, still finding new insights. What once seemed sort of interesting but essentially irrelevant has now taken center stage. It's all come together quite remarkably. As Osho wrote, "What can you do with your music when you get into physics? It has become part of you; it is going to affect you whatsoever you do. Physics is so far away, but if you have been disciplined in music, sooner or later you will find theories, hypotheses, which somehow have the color and fragrance of music."

For me, replace "physics" with "business" and "music" with "anarchism." My approaches to leadership have the latent essence of the latter running through their branches. I love English writer Colin Ward's image of the ideas of anarchism in society sitting silently like "seeds beneath the snow" waiting for an intellectual spring to arrive. My anarchist interests began to germinate. As Gustav Landauer posited long ago, "Revolution is always alive. . . . It stays alive underground, it creates a complex unity of memories, emotions, and desires." I could probably now drop the "lapsed" part of my title—more and more, my belief system has come back to what I was unwittingly drawn to so strongly when I was a student.

Working on this book has taken that passion to another level. I've realized in the process that anarchism is basically a belief system, built primarily on a strongly held positive belief in human nature. As philosopher Rollo May wrote 50 years ago about his own work *Man's Search for Himself*, "the chief argument of this book is that the unique powers and initiative of each individual must be rediscovered, and used as a basis for work which contributes to the good of the community, rather than melted down in the collectivist pot of conformity." *My* anarchism is about a belief in human freedom and in the creative abilities of every individual to act responsibly when they know what's at stake and have a stake in the outcome.

What Is Anarchism?

Although I prefer to take a positive approach, it's sometimes easier to say what anarchism *isn't*. For me at least, despite popular perception to the contrary, it's not at all about chaos or confusion. It's not about violence. It's not about killing. It's not a free-for-all. It's not even about utopia. As Spanish anarchist Buenaventura Durruti said, "I believe, as I always have, in freedom. The freedom that rests on a sense of responsibility. I consider discipline indispensable, but it must be inner discipline, motivated by a common purpose and a strong feeling of comradeship." For me it's about living life in a way that's respectful of everyone and everything around us, all the while still staying true to who we are as individuals.

Gustav Landauer is one of the anarchists I didn't get to know until this second, more recent, go-round of study. He never visited Ann Arbor, and at the time I was in school, his work was available only in the original German. Thanks to the translation efforts of Gabriel Kuhn, this time I could read it in depth. I loved it. Landauer, I think, is the one who took all this to the next level for me. Born into a Jewish family in Germany in 1870, Landauer was a fascinating thinker—out of the box, even for an anarchist. He was forceful and funny, spiritual and solid, powerful but still a pacifist, all at the same time. One of his best friends was religious philosopher Martin Buber. An astonishingly tall 6 feet 5 inches, Landauer swam, spoke, and wrote regularly. His views on both spirit and the state were unlike any others I'd come across. His work resonated with me deeply. A pacifist to the end, he was kicked to death by the German army in 1919. In the spirit of seeing life as art, Landauer drew my attention when he said of anarchists, "We are poets." Interestingly, in this context anarchism is *not* a political program; as Landauer said a century ago, "We have no political beliefs—*we have beliefs against politics.*"

Quote Comparison, Take Four

The three cornerstones . . . are accountability, collaboration, and initiative.

The underlying themes of freedom, autonomy and cooperation remained consistent.

I cheated a bit on that one. The second is a quote *about* Emma Goldman, from the book *Emma Goldman: A Documentary History of the American Years, Volume 3.* The first is a direct quote from Rosabeth Moss Kanter's book *Confidence.* Kanter is another short, intelligent, insightful, outspoken Jewish woman who writes and speaks well. One significant difference between the two is that Kanter has long been a professor at the Harvard Business School and has won great recognition for her teaching and writing. It does turn out, though, that her PhD dissertation was on 19th-century utopian communes.

From "Freedom From" to "Freedom To"

Back in my student days, I got stuck at what Emma Goldman describes as "freedom from": "It is not the negative thing of being free from something, because with such freedom you may starve to death." Anyone who's angry and waiting to be liberated is going to have a long wait. Trying to convince others to get their act together, I'd say, is usually a waste of time. The more we live freely and find ways to be more respectful, inclusive, and receptive, the better things are going to go. Anyone who's focused mostly on making others stop doing something is stuck in reaction. And reactivity is rarely productive.

It is true that most anarchists have traditionally focused their energies on getting rid of government. But *I believe* that government is mostly peripheral to the problem. I don't mind paying taxes all that much—I make a free choice to do so in the belief that someone has to pave the roads, help people in need, and all that good stuff. But waiting for government to rescue us and blaming government for what it does or doesn't do are, I've realized, just two sides of the same unsatisfactory situation.

I look at it a different way. The society and culture in which we live and work is not a function of government; it's mostly just a reflection of us.

As Landauer put it, "People do not live in the state. The state lives in the people."We need to own our power and create positive outcomes, not just complain about the terrible things others have cobbled together. We can make a difference ourselves. The way we work every day matters greatly. We can actively support those in need in our communities ourselves. Like it or not, we, the people, are both the problem and, using a more positive belief system, the probable solution. We have the power. And to be clear, by "we," I mean mostly "you and me."

Gustav Landauer opened my eyes to a new perspective:

> *The State is a condition, a certain relationship between human beings, a mode of behaviour; we destroy it by contracting other relationships, by behaving differently towards one another. We are the State and we shall continue to be the State until we have created the institutions that form a real community.*

Zingerman's is hopefully one of those real—*imperfect as all real things are*—communities in action. Our work isn't just to dispute the injustices of others. It's to make a positive, proactive difference ourselves.

It's in that sense that, in the last few years, I've arrived at an emotional place from which I'm ready to focus on what Osho called "freedom to": "Real freedom, true liberty is positive: it is freedom to something; it is the liberty to be, to do; in short, the liberty of actual and active opportunity." I'm reminded of a short conversation I had one day last summer with my friend Meg Noodin and her 13-year-old daughter, Fionna. When I was thirteen, I remember lamenting to my mother regularly that I was "bored." I wanted freedom from boredom. That attitude was one of reactivity and helplessness. Fionna, for whatever reason of upbringing, genetics, or the fact that she's been eating at Zingerman's since she was born, started getting a bit of the restless feeling I used to get at the same age. But instead of complaining about being bored, Fionna chose *freedom to*. She adamantly told her mother, "I need an adventure," and then headed over to the main Deli—the part Rocco Disderide built back in 1902—to find one for herself.

Adventure, imagination, and active engagement are at the core of what draws me to anarchist thinking. The focus of this book and of *Part 3* of this series on managing ourselves, the work of my life and maybe yours too, is to liberate myself so that I can serve myself and those around me ever more effectively. As anarchist Émile Armand said a century ago, "I consider life as an experience, or rather a series of experiences, lived to secure the richest, the most abundant, the most varied possible." It's not about selfishness; it's about the understanding that my ability to serve others in a sound and successful way is contingent on managing my own health and happiness, about owning my choices and freely opting to do the right thing.

Beliefs About Anarchism

So if anarchism is about beliefs, what are mine? There are many that I've tried to incorporate into my life and my work, including the following:

- Anarchism is a belief system, a way of living life, not a political program.
- It's about freedom to, not freedom from.
- Effective leadership is important, but overemphasis on hierarchy is problematic.
- The means we use to achieve a goal must be congruent with the ends we're trying to arrive at.
- Everyone, regardless of title, age, race, gender, religion, eye color, or anything else, is a creative, capable, intelligent, and unique individual.
- While role definition and clarity of responsibilities are important, there is no correlation between hierarchical position and intelligence, creativity, or ability.
- People who are thinking and working freely, respectfully, caringly, and living in harmony with the Natural Laws will generally do good work. Creativity follows.
- Good things don't come from situations where people are forced to participate in anything—work teams, countries, classes, armies, political parties, ethnic groups, religions, athletic affiliations.
- Judging people badly based on any element of their personhood is always troublesome.
- When people live in harmony with nature, their natural abilities come out best.

- Organizations that are respectful, do the right thing, are inclusive, and encourage free choice—including the willingness to let people say no—can do exceptional work.
- Just because I'm the owner/manager/CEO/shareholder doesn't mean I'm any better a person than the newest part-time employee we just hired this week.

For me, anarchist thinking is about caringly and generously choosing freedom and spirit over status quo and conformity. It's about embracing the whole of each of us as humans, about ecologically sound ecosystem thinking—understanding that if I mess up everyone around me, I'm also messing up myself in the process. And vice versa. My version of anarchism is never about careless chaos or an unfeeling free-for-all. It's not "I get to do as I please, everyone else be damned." I believe, as Rollo May poignantly pointed out, that, "Freedom without compassion is demoniacal." If we don't truly care about others, care for them, believe in them, things won't work. "Without compassion," May continued, "freedom can be self-righteous, inhuman, self-centered and cruel." I believe his insight is accurate. Ultimately it comes down to what anarchist Errico Malatesta wrote: "We seek the triumph of freedom and love."

I agree, too, with former-Black-Panther-turned-anarchist-while-in-prison Ashanti Alston: "Anarchists see People as individuals with the will to live, learn, love, work out their own individual and collective destinies instinctively or spontaneously. Human dignity is key." For me, anarchist beliefs are very much about creativity, freedom, and positive possibilities. At its core, anarchism is always about a positive belief in people. As Peter Kropotkin wrote, "I believe profoundly in the future."

Permaculture and Anarchism

As I read Toby Hemenway's work on permaculture, I found myself taking many notes. Often, though, it was just one word: "Anarchism!" The parallels between the two worldviews were intriguing. I was journaling one morning after I'd finished the second of his two books when the thought popped into my head: "permaculture = anarchism." I thought through the two approaches. Both are really belief systems. Each honors the uniqueness of every element in an ecosystem, acknowledges the interconnectedness among all those elements, honors our interdependence, avoids hierarchy. Both believe that the healthiest ecosystems are the most diverse. That it's important to take the whole system, the whole community, into account when we're making individual decisions about seemingly small pieces of the ecological puzzle, but never doing it at the expense of the "small" contributors in the understanding that what might seem small by superficial statistical weight (bees and busboys, to use two examples) actually has a big impact. And that the more we can help every individual in the community to thrive, the healthier, more productive, and more resilient the community is likely to be.

This belief was bolstered for me by a dialogue I shared with Amanda Maurmann. Amanda started working at the Roadhouse about a year ago and then in the spring transferred out to work on our farm. Agriculture is one of her passions. Amanda emailed me:

> *As individuals become more effective, their individual niche becomes smaller, and the larger system becomes more diverse as there is room for more biological entities within the space. As individuals become truer expressions of themselves, other species thrive, and together they are able to continue to evolve in such a forgiving and dynamic environment. Each species becomes mindful of its place within the ecosystem and is able to coexist and live a richer life, surrounded by greater and greater resources. (Coevolution = a process by which species adapt to each other so that they can more successfully coexist.) Sounds like Eden, right?*

"Actually," I wrote back, "it sounds like anarchism." And a whole lot like what we're trying to do here at Zingerman's. As the ZCoB grows, and as Paul and I do our jobs effectively, our "niche has become smaller," but "there is room for more entities within the space." Amanda's entire statement fits almost perfectly with the way we're trying to run our organization. As Toby Hemenway writes, "This is the genius and elegance of natural systems design. It offers just enough order to create a functional framework but plenty of room for variation, spontaneity, and adaptation to the context. In a sense, this is design without design."

Anarchist Insight

Late-19th- and early-20th-century anarchists were actively engaged with this issue of beliefs a century ago. Emma Goldman was ahead of her time in explaining how beliefs are formed:

> *How much a personal philosophy is a matter of temperament and how much it results from experience is a moot question. Naturally we arrive*

at conclusions in the light of our experience, through the application of a process we call reasoning to the facts observed in the events of our lives. The child is susceptible to fantasy. At the same time, he sees life more truly in some respects than his elders do as he becomes conscious of his surroundings. He has not yet become absorbed by the customs and prejudices which make up the largest part of what passes for thinking.

Drawn to free choice and the idea of living my own life, I think I started rebelling even as an eight-year-old. The word radical, by the way, is linguistically tied to the idea of "going back to the roots." Where others often return to the cultural nest from which they flew when they get older, I reconnected with the anarchists.

What came first, the behavior or the belief?

I don't know. But it's clear that they've reinforced each other with good results over a long period of time now. The 16th-century Frenchman Étienne de La Boétie, an attorney by training, was an anarchist before there were people called "anarchists." In his *Discourse on Voluntary Servitude*, written in 1565 when La Boétie was all of 22 years old, he wrote, "The lies in which people believe have always been invented by themselves." He went on to note, "The natural may be as good as it is, but it disappears if it is not nurtured. Nurture will always determine us, whatever form it may take, and regardless of our nature." People working and living in hierarchical settings quickly start to internalize the beliefs of those in charge: "They turn themselves into the property of those who oppress them, because time has made this appear inevitable. In reality, though, time never rights a wrong but multiplies it endless times."

La Boétie wasn't all doom and gloom—he saw positive opportunities as well, with men who

possessed of clear minds and far-sighted spirit, are not satisfied, like the brutish mass, to see only what is at their feet, but rather look about them, behind and before, and even recall the things of the past in order to judge those of the future, and compare both with their present condition. Even if liberty had entirely perished from the earth, such men would invent it. For them slavery has no satisfactions, no matter how well disguised.

Ultimately, it's up to us as individuals to breathe and live and think as the intelligent free people we're wired to be. As leaders, we can encourage others who might have less than us—less power, less money, less experience—to claim their freedom, despite the disadvantages society has put in their way. They don't need to wait until they're "in charge" to make that choice. As Howard Ehrlich puts it: "To be free people must liberate themselves." Anarchism for me is about helping everyone to stand up for and create the life they want to lead, respecting all the while that others have different desires. Clearly, there will be conflict—within ourselves and with others—but I believe that if people stay positive and respectful, build empathy, think generously, and practice visioning, more often than not we can work it out. One of the most rewarding compliments I ever hear about Zingerman's is when someone who works here says, "It's great that I get to be part of all this and that I can be myself here at the same time!"

I believe, ever more strongly, that business can be a good setting in which to put anarchist beliefs into practice. While old-school anarchists railed against business barons, there was really no such thing back then as caring, constructive approaches to running a business. As Bo Burlingham wrote in the foreword for *Part 1*, "they had the right yoyo but the wrong string." Business, managed creatively and caringly, can be the string on which to spin these beliefs. Paul Hawken writes: "Being a good human being is good business." The inverse is true, too. Doing good business is about developing good human beings.

A Foundation of Free Choice

The more time I spent writing this book, the more it became clear to me that the foundation of all of this work is the belief that we are actively free to make choices in our lives. In my ecosystem metaphor, maybe free choice is the taproot—the one that feeds all the other roots in the system. Free choice won't eliminate all our problems, but it puts an entirely different spin on how we deal with them. As Kierkegaard says, "free choice is the key to defining our own existence and . . . being aware of our beliefs, versus those imposed on us, is essential to free choice." Awareness (per Viktor Frankl's "space" in Secret #40) of that choice and the willingness to own the choices that we make form the basis for a rewarding existence for anyone who embraces them.

I really like what Ashanti Alston has to say on the same subject:

> *What does it say about you, if you allow someone to set themselves up as your leader and make all your decisions for you? What anarchism helped me see was that you, as an individual, should be respected and that no one is important enough to do your thinking for you. Even if we thought of Huey P. Newton or Eldridge Cleaver as the baddest*

revolutionaries in the world, I should see myself as the baddest revolu-
tionary, just like them. Even if I am young, I have a brain. I can think.
I can make decisions.

To my view of the world, life without the freedom to shape what we do and how we do it is so limited. At best, it's constrained, controlled, constricted. As Robert Henri, who went to hear Emma Goldman speak back in 1911, writes, "Those who are 'imprisoned' work like prisoners. You can see where the heart is out of it." In which case, we end up living passively, frustrated that others won't do what we believe they should, feeling trapped, disrespected, misunderstood, forced to perform and conform. Mostly it's exhausting and it's certainly not much fun.

The belief that we're not free is generally based on a negative set of beliefs. I come across it all too often. I'm sure you've heard it, too: "If we're responsible, we have to behave properly." "Freedom is a phony—we're stuck with society's norms and there's nothing we can do about it." "The powers that be will always keep us in our place." "The world is way bigger than we are; we have little to say about how things go—our bosses, the government, the bigwigs, our better half are the ones who have all the power. All we can do is make the best of a bad thing." "Everyone else is doing it—no one cares what I think." "I have to go along with them." "There's nothing I can do."

Life through that helpless lens becomes burdensome, a struggle "against" others rather than a proactive pursuit of the life we want to live. I know because I spent parts of my early adult years living that way. It's not like I didn't do anything or accomplish anything. My life was hardly horrible. But feeling stuck and then reacting in kind was hard. Feeling "forced" to fit in, or to follow, is never fun. Without the understanding that we have free choice in the world, our beliefs will simply reinforce the roles and attitudes that have been assigned to us, the socially prescribed norms that others proffer.

The mainstream may be where everyone else is moving, but that doesn't mean it's right. As Hugh MacLeod says, "Nobody can tell you if what you're doing is good, meaningful, or worthwhile. The more compelling the path, the more lonely it is." After lots of therapy, loads of journaling, reading piles of books (and writing a few of my own), and making time to talk to people much wiser than myself, I realized that the decisions I was making were not being forced on me by anyone else. Of course, others had expectations and put some pressure on me to do things the way they wanted. But in the end, I had the power to push past anyone else's attempts to influence me. I just hadn't been using it. As André Gide writes, "The capacity to get free is nothing; the capacity to *be* free is the task." It took about three years for me to successfully change my beliefs. But I did it!

Free Choice and Fine Cooking

Owning my choices changed my life. And in a small-scale testament to the power of free choice and belief, when Emma Goldman was left to live her own life, she grew to love good cooking—the same skill she resisted so vehemently when her father demanded that she learn it as a way to limit her options in life. Blintzes were one of her specialties.

Building Free Choice into the Foundation of Your Business

If we want to work in ways that help those around us to go for greatness, to be themselves, to own their lives, it's essential that we cultivate a culture in which mindful free choice is the norm. As Osho says, "Freedom simply makes you absolutely responsible for everything that you are and that you are going to be."

Take a look at what happens when you follow the self-fulfilling belief cycle through on this issue of free choice. Our boss asks us for something we don't believe is right. Because we believe we have no choice, we follow their "orders." We may do all the little things we're "supposed to do," keeping our grudges to ourselves. Steadily, though, our anger builds, and apathy and disengagement follow. The boss then believes we're a poor performer and pushes us harder to fall into line. We go along for a while but halfheartedly—our lack of belief surely shows through. The boss begins to believe that we don't care and starts leaving us out of conversations. Which only reinforces our belief that we have no influence and that our views make no difference. Our anger increases until, eventually, we can't take it and quit, or get fired before we can bail out. "There's no choice," we believe. "This is what responsible citizens/parents/partners/ people like me have to do." Even if we keep our anger silent, we're still suffering. It's a poisonous cycle. "[A]nything that becomes destructive to freedom," Osho says, ends up with our "hating it."

On the other hand, free choice builds confidence, commitment, positive energy, and hope. Rollo May writes in *Man's Search for Himself*: "patient growth in freedom is probably the most difficult task of all, requiring the greatest courage." But it may also be the most rewarding task. With it, the cycle starts to shift us up, not down. As Robert Henri writes,

> *What you need is to free yourself from your own preconceived ideas about yourself. It will take a revolution to do it, and many times you will think yourself on the road only to find that the old habit has possessed you again with a new preconception. But if you can at least to a degree free yourself, take your head off your heart and give the latter a chance, something may come of it. The results will not be what you expect, but they will be like you and will be the best that can come from you. There will be a lot more pleasure in the doing.*

When we bring that positive, grounded, freedom-centered vibrational energy to our interactions, others are much more likely to believe that we know what we're doing, that we're "natural leaders." Which in turn leads them to take action by paying more attention to what we're saying, increasing the odds that they follow our lead, engage in more interesting dialogues with us, and are more open to our insights. Which then reinforces for us the "rightness" of living and thinking on our own path. I believe, with ever greater strength, that the more we mindfully make our own choices, the more the world becomes a calmer and more caring place. "[F]reedom is nothing but an opportunity to make the world a little more beautiful, and to become a little more conscious," Osho says.

The latest piece of learning for me about freedom was that we're not just free to make choices but also to choose our beliefs. When we understand that a) our beliefs shape our lives and b) we have the freedom to choose those beliefs, then it only makes sense that c) we would do well to at least consider choosing beliefs that are aligned with the way we want our lives to go, and d) we can write an effective vision of the future to bring all that together. As Claude Bristol says, "Often belief empowers a person to do what others consider impossible. The act of believing is the starting force, the generating power that leads to accomplishment."

None of this takes us as leaders off the hook. We too have full responsibility for how things go. As I learned a long time ago, responsibility goes up in multiples of 100 percent! But also, as Peter Koestenbaum says, "Leadership in an environment of freedom and accountability stands for each person being a manager, a leader, all responsible for the well-being of the larger world." Some might call that approach anarchism in action.

Staff Surveys and Social Satisfaction

Taking the idea of free choice forward, I've come to believe that we would benefit by making clear to all involved in the company that when it comes to culture and morale, we're all equally responsible. Responsibility, as we teach it here, goes up in multiples of 100 percent—a new staff member's responsibility for Zingerman's health and vitality doesn't reduce mine. Certainly, my job has a broader scope—experience, Servant Leadership, and ownership of stock shares all call for formally recognized leaders to step up, regularly and effectively. But I believe it's not our job to "take care" of the people we hire; instead, it's to help them build positive beliefs in themselves, in their teams, and in our organization, beliefs that tell them that if they take the lead, do good work, follow well-designed processes, communicate, and collaborate, they can make great things happen. The leader's presence is important, but everyone can—and needs to—take responsibility for the effectiveness of our organizational leadership. Peter Koestenbaum observes:

> When top management or a staff group conducts an attitude survey of employees that asks how they feel about management, they collude with the part of employees that does not want to be responsible for their own experience. It legitimizes the idea that employee well-being is in the hands of management. Plus, when top management gets the survey information, it is rare they can find really useful ways to act on it. . . .
>
> It is right and human for managers to care about the motivation and morale of their people, it is just that they are not the cause of it. Managers should ask for feedback from employees about how they can improve as managers, but they ask this out of their interest and desire to learn, not for the sake of the employees. If we decide to view employees as free and accountable, then we stop fixing them.

Stas' Kazmierski taught me many years ago that feedback from groups to the facilitator is mostly feedback the group needs itself. He used to tell us not to get too upset if post-training comments were critical, because "you just need to be a Teflon mirror and feed it right back to them. They're telling you as much about themselves as they are about you." I'd say the same thing about staff surveys. As Koestenbaum writes,

> *If we want to hold to the belief that managers and employees create each other, why do we believe that motivation only flows downhill? Who motivates managers? Does it make sense to believe that it is the employees' job to be responsible for the morale and motivation of those above them? If a manager is depressed, do we expect employees to ask what they are doing to depress that manager? Do we ever ask what new skills they need to increase top management's spirits? Not often.*

This makes solid sense. If people would like more positive feedback—and most of us do—why do those compliments count only if they come from a manager? I'm not saying that we as leaders don't have a responsibility to find the positives and to give praise liberally. I'm all about that. But seriously, if everyone is important, and we're all insightful and our opinion matters, why does the manager's opinion matter more than the new accountant or the long-time busboy?

It's also true with meetings. One of the most brilliant things I learned from Koestenbaum is that the evaluation question to ask at the end of one isn't, "How do you score today's session?" But rather, "How do you rate your own role in the meeting?" To which I add my own second question: "What will you do differently to be more effective?" The results can be big.

The bottom line? The blend of anarchism and business may sound surreal. But the surrealists, it turns out, were also inclined to anarchism. Business is an art. Anarchism is definitely about art. Bring the two together, and maybe we have something really big. I believe that Emma Goldman, Jo Labadie, and Gustav Landauer were well ahead of their time. I wish we could all have met once or twice for coffee. Apparently Goldman's was excellent. "In France, where I make my home," she told a reporter, "my friends call on me and I make them coffee. They always say, 'Emma, if you do not go down in history for your anarchism, you will go down for your coffee.' Visit me some day at home and try my coffee." Their lessons have had a huge impact on my beliefs and, hence, on the way I live my life. Maybe they'll do the same for you. Come by and talk. I'll buy the coffee.[24]

Finding Free Space in Action

Although few of us give it much thought, there are many areas of our lives that are already "governed" without formal authority. In a hierarchically focused society, we generally fail to take note of them—they're like the background in a painting where the featured hero is at the center. We see the main character, but we miss the perhaps more interesting bits on the side.

A few that come to mind include:

- the partnerships at Zingerman's (we come to a consensus on all partner-level decisions)
- my relationship with my girlfriend
- my friendships
- traffic circles (no one is in charge!)

Is power present in these settings? Sure. There's always power present. Sometimes it belongs to little kids who pull the strings in their families or to "powerless" passive-aggressive people adept at directing organizational drama from the sidelines. It's impossible to exist without some power at play—even inside my head there are power issues at work all day. Nevertheless, these things work pretty well without a structural hierarchy in place.

What about for you? Where are you already interacting at a peer level rather than waiting for formal authority to step in and take charge?

Brigette Christopher, Co-Owner,
Piper & Leaf Artisan Tea Company, Huntsville, Alabama

Thank you so much for the purpose and intentional direction with which you are influencing so many. When my husband, brother, and I accidentally started a little tea business just over two years ago, we had no idea what we were getting into. We suddenly found ourselves in a business partnership (something we had sworn never to do) with wonderful people working for us and looking to us for a vision and direction. Near the end of our first year, none of us really knew what direction we were going, how to bring order to our ever-growing organization, or how to keep everything as fulfilling and fun as the day we started.

In this critical time of growth we discovered your writings and example, first through the book *Small Giants,* and then through delving into many of your online articles and your wonderful books. I can adamantly say that Zingerman's, and you, have played a hugely important role in making Piper *&* Leaf Artisan Tea Co. what it is today.

When I first picked up *Building a Great Business,* our company had no vision, or rather had many ethereal undeveloped visions going every direction. Our systems were a mess, and proper training was almost nonexistent. Perhaps most importantly, our culture, which had started on waves of excitement with the quick success of our company, was at a turning point of continuing in a positive direction, or very quickly heading south.

We literally spent months reading more of your written wisdom and then meeting to discuss how each topic applied to our company and how we could make it happen. When spring of 2015 hit, we had our first draft of an employee manual ready to distribute. We were also now teaching our first new-hire training classes, and starting a new program of on-the-job training and tracking. And most importantly, we started that spring with our five-year vision in hand, which amazingly had been almost completely unanimously written by all the owners and managers. Once we actually took the time to think about where we were headed, we found that we all were actually going in somewhat the same direction; we just needed unification.

Visiting Ann Arbor and meeting you and some of the other Zingerman's partners just made the genuineness of everything you stand for even more real. The things you write about are not just half-baked ideas but rather concrete concepts that stand up bravely under the abuse of daily testing! I know this from more than just my short visit to the ZCoB. I know because we have put many of your concepts into our own daily practice, and they are working beautifully.

We still have so much to learn, practice, and implement, and I hope that you also will keep learning and writing so that we can continue to glean from your storehouses of knowledge. The success of Zingerman's was on all the faces of the people who work for you, from the new hires I met in your training class, to some of your seasoned partners. Thank you so much for all that you do and for penning your thoughts to share with others. You have no idea how many lives you have impacted just in our one little company. Your books are truly making a difference in the world.

Stas' Kazmierski, Managing Partner Emeritus, ZingTrain

My belief about organizations certainly has changed over time. My stint as a teacher in a small Michigan town was my first experience, as an adult, working in a "career."

This was in 1969 and the first year that teachers were unionized in that school system. The bureaucracy was solidly in place, and the management style was command and control. Neither the administration nor the teachers knew how to work collaboratively in a union environment, so the culture was quite militant. I left primarily due to low pay.

Then post-grad studies and lecturer at Eastern Michigan University. Best job I ever had! First day of the new semester the faculty went on strike. I wasn't union, so I worked anyway. Two years of teaching undergrad and grad classes with a really flex schedule and no required office hours. Went to an American auto manufacturer for much better pay and benefits. Back to the bureaucracy and really strict command and control. I was an automaton. It certainly wasn't hard work but stressful because of the way people were treated. I worked summers in college in a manufacturing plant, and working there was similar in the abuse laid on the salaried staff—it was just more subtle. Advancement was not by merit but the old boy network. Women in the nonsecretarial ranks were absolutely treated as sex objects (as were the secretaries)—harassed, belittled, and held back—unless they had a patron and had a professional degree in finance or engineering. They, in turn, were hated by the lower ranks for sleeping upward. Organizationally it was kick ass and take names. Never volunteer for anything and always cover your ass! Even though I was in product engineering we knew next to nothing about the product—only our narrow specialization.

It wasn't until the late 1980s that a chief engineer decided that we needed to work differently in order to compete with the Japanese. He was the father of one of the leading car designs and used a collaborative, team-based approach to work. Upper management was impressed, and we started developing team processes for vehicle development.

I'd had the experience of working and learning from Ron Lippitt in the early '80s and used my experience to help program managers stop managing programs and start managing people. Not only managing, but developing their staff. Team training went from "0" to "60" in two years. While teams were getting good training, the upper, upper levels were getting none. They were still operating at the command-and-control style, and kicking ass was still an acceptable method of managing. I [could] tell you real horror stories!

Leaving the auto manufacturer in 1991 and working as an independent consultant and ultimately with a consulting firm, I encountered some really wonderful people and organizations. I also worked with some really backward and constrictive organizations. Many of the organizations I consulted with that had a female CEO ([and there were] not many of these) were much more humane overall than those headed by males.

Working with you and Paul in the early '90s was really eye opening. I observed two white guys who were successful and wanted to do something exciting both for the business and for the people in the business who were not owners but plain old regular people. These guys are wacky, I said to myself. The fact that you offered to pay in food blew me away! Sure, I could have used the money, but having an account where I could just say "put it on my account" (and you guys kept cruddy records) was next to heaven. Thank you for that.

I was tremendously impressed that you ran your business in a way that was out of the ordinary yet not so funky that you'd go out of business by adopting the next wave of leaderless organizations. You guys were good and ran a solid business.

When, in 2000, you asked if I would be interested in exploring a partnership with Maggie, I was extremely flattered. I thought, "Wow, what a great opportunity to learn and try some new stuff." At that point I still didn't understand your business model, but what I did understand and admire was the way you treated people. You cared. You helped partners understand that they needed to care. Not just about the product or business but the staff who did the work and the customers that bought the product. After 34 years, Zingerman's still teaches what they live and live what they teach. Proud to be part of that history.

emily hiber behind the counter at zingerman's next door

Building
a Hopeful
Business

An In-Depth Look at How Much Hope Matters

People reflect regularly about what they hope will, or won't, happen. At times, they talk about "being hopeful," "holding out hope," or "hoping against hope." But discussion about the impact that having—or not having—hope has in business doesn't seem to come up a lot. I believe that's a mistake—without a hopeful attitude, very little positive, proactive work will happen. The more I've studied the subject, the more I've talked about it with others, and the more I've paid attention, the more I see how much hope impacts everything we do.

Hope, in my metaphysical metaphor, is the sun. Hopefulness is a consistent characteristic of successful people and organizations. It helps the plants that grow from the roots of our beliefs to reach upward. Low hope, on the other hand, is a characteristic of struggling (or often outright failing) businesses. Their organizational "sun" is blacked out—energy is exhausted, and work quality suffers significantly when employees are without hope.

I hope that sharing the thoughts that follow will be of value. I know that working on this essay has already helped me. I'm far more mindful of hope, and how I handle it, than I have ever been before. As anarchist Peter Kropotkin once said, "it is always hope . . . which makes revolutions."

The Tragedy of Fragile Hope Crushed

The story of how hope came to have a much bigger part in my consciousness isn't one that I feel super great about sharing. It grew out of a set of organizational screw-ups that I wish had never happened. (I'll explain more of the details shortly.) But trying to be positive about the whole thing, I'm working to see our goof-ups as a gift, not as the god-awful gaffes they felt like when the situations occurred. While in the moment my stress shot way up, I realize in hindsight that I was actually fortunate that they happened—it's really only because of our failures that my consciousness was appropriately raised. "Hope," as I'm now painfully aware, isn't just a passing moment of excitement for little kids looking forward to Christmas morning; it's an important and strategically sound part of building a successful business.

The incidents in question took place a while back, and I'm not here to point fingers or place blame. Truth is, it could just as well have been me that messed up—I'm sure I've done much the same thing, unwittingly, more times than I'd like to either know or admit. I apologize to those I've let down. The more I learn about the power of hope, the more I realize how seriously I might have unintentionally detracted from the quality of people's work experience by unknowingly squashing their hope.

Where does our relationship to hope come from? Psychologist Rick Snyder, one of the first people to do deep research on the subject, reports that "your childhood shaped the level of hope you have as an adult." Leading with the positive, I've chosen to believe that human beings are naturally hopeful. As anarchist anthropologist David Graeber says, "Hopelessness isn't natural. It needs to be produced." When we damage people's sense of hope, we don't just cause momentary hurt. When hope is crushed over and over again, we can seriously undermine our employees' entire existence—and, through them, our own. "Without hope," author Francis Moore Lappé warns, "we human beings die, if not physically, certainly spiritually."

Each of the unpleasant incidents that triggered this conversation occurred independently of the others—different people, different situations, on totally different days. The only connection between them was that they all served to damage—or even destroy—fragile hopes, and that each took place in *our* organization. To be clear, I was frustrated, saddened, and almost angry when I realized what we'd done. Thankfully, I'd long ago memorized my partner Paul's maxim: "When furious, get curious."

The statement itself embodies positive belief—the only reason we would pause to reflect rather than get angry at others is because we believe that we can benefit from a short session of mindful self-reflection. As a touchstone, Paul's saying has consistently helped me to catch myself and turn back from the criticism of others (or my own self-criticism) towards productive reflection. In this case, I began to examine what had taken place, to try to figure out how something I'd thought was so glaringly *not* good could have happened in our organization more than once in a matter of weeks. Clearly, we had some serious work to do here around the subject of hope management.

While the particulars were different in each case, the problem was basically the same. A staff member had come forward to pursue something—a promotion, a project, an idea, a new position, it really doesn't matter; it could well have been a poem or a new and improved version of Mr. Potato Head. The issue is that instead of responding with appreciation for the staff member who had the gumption to go after something bigger and better than the status quo, we basically shut them down. Our response in each case was essentially something along the lines of, "That's not going to happen because of *a, b,* and *c.*" Or, "There's no way I'm going to let you do that, because you aren't even doing *x, y,* and *z.*"

I want to be clear that I'm consciously using the term "we." Although it wasn't me who said what was said, I take responsibility—I hadn't ever shared my expectations about how to handle hope, and we'd never done any formal training on the subject. Looking back on it now, I wasn't clear about how hope worked within my own mind, let alone how to actively explain it to anyone else. I hadn't ever determined for myself how much the act of mindfully nurturing, cultivating, or even caring about hope matters.

I don't want to get into the details of what happened—it's not my intent to embarrass anyone, and I don't believe that any of those involved had bad intentions. The first incident occurred on shift; I just happened to be walking past and overheard a conversation between a long-time staff member and his manager. The staffer was saying how much he wanted to take on a project that he was excited about. I actually think it was a good idea for improvement, but that almost doesn't matter. The problem wasn't the employee's proposal; it was the manager's response. As soon as the staff member had made his suggestion, the manager immediately launched into a recitation of all the reasons the idea wasn't going to happen.

I'm sure there was some merit to the manager's concerns about the employee's performance that led him to respond so critically. The problem isn't that his reasons for being critical were "wrong"—it's just that he'd presented things in such a way as to scare the staff member off of ever sharing an inspirational idea again. While the manager talked, the staffer started looking down to the floor, shifting his feet back and forth, like a kid getting lectured by an angry parent. I can imagine that he was feeling both frustrated, as if he'd failed, and angry that the wisdom in his words wasn't being recognized. Hurt that his idea for improvement was being rejected. I know how *I* felt—I was embarrassed.

In her book *Confidence*, Rosabeth Moss Kanter remarks, "A loss is a crossroads, not a cliff. Winners make mistakes and encounter troubles all the time without falling off the edge. How problems are dealt with shapes whether they are just an interruption or a sign of impending doom, whether winners are resilient or are stuck in increasingly ineffective behavior." In this case, things sort of worked out. The employee had the courage to come talk to me about what had happened. I tried, per the principles of Servant Leadership (see *Secret #23,* in *Part 2*), to handle it as I would a customer complaint. I acknowledged what had happened and apologized on behalf of all of us. And then I set about "making things right" by working with him to try to accomplish what it was that he had his heart set on, trying not to totally undercut the manager in the process. Before we went our separate ways for the day, I thanked him for having the courage to come forward despite his frustration.

While I know empathy doesn't excuse what went down, I didn't just slough it off by blaming his boss. It's not hard to imagine that the manager was caught off-guard, busy, and maybe behind on his own work. Knowing how life goes, he was probably legitimately frustrated with the employee over five or six shortfalls the staffer had had in recent months. The manager ended up leaving Zingerman's before I had the chance to talk to him about the issue—he wasn't a good fit for our organizational values. But most importantly, the whole thing got me thinking about hope at a much deeper level than I ever had before.

I know, of course, that we're not the only organization to have made this mistake. To the contrary, what caught my attention here is that while the negative response we gave to the staff member's idea isn't (I hope) an everyday experience at Zingerman's, in the big-business world, from what I hear, it's more often than not the norm. Longtime Zingerman's customer Keith Ewing spent years struggling to stay positive in what sounds like a war-weary corporate world. Going to work in "the organizational killing fields" is how he describes it. Jobs aren't always easy to come by, and really good work is certainly the exception, not the rule. But still, work doesn't have to be that way. I figure if I share our shortfalls openly, it makes it easier for others to have hope. If we can screw up and recover with grace, so too can anyone else who's willing to own their errors and get to work on making things right.

In fact, one thing that contributes to building hope is showing people that others they relate to have made it through similar obstacles and have achieved success. That very approach—dealing with problems and finding creative and effective ways to move forward—is one of the signs of a hopeful mind. As Rick Snyder says, "When the going gets tough, the hopeful keep going." Hope helps us keep moving, when part of us wants to stop. As Scottish writer and reformer Samuel Smiles wrote, "Hope is like the sun, which, as we journey towards it, casts the shadow of our burden behind us."

What kind of hope do I hope for? I hope that tomorrow can be better than today; that our work will make a difference; that if we work hard and go after greatness, good things will happen. I hope that we can contribute positively to our emotional, intellectual, and financial improvement, and that of others around us.

Hope Helps

Not sure that this emphasis on hope actually makes a difference? Ask around. I doubt that you'll find a single person who's doing great work, in any area of activity, who's not already hopeful about the future. Even when difficult days cloud their horizon, hope soon reappears. Effective leaders are almost always high-hope individuals who have the ability to cultivate hope in others around them, with energy growing significantly in the process. It's clear to me that one reason Emma Goldman inspired so many people from the periphery of society a century ago is that she gave hope to those who'd had so little in their lives.

To paraphrase the old Coke commercial, "things go better with hope." Snyder reports that

> [C]hildren and adults who scored higher in hope have: (1) coped better with injuries, diseases and physical pain; (2) scored higher in satisfaction, self-esteem, optimism, meaning in life and happiness; (3) performed better in sports; and (4) excelled in academics (elementary to graduate school). What is especially compelling about these hope findings for sports and academics is that they have occurred beyond the predictions that are caused by natural abilities. That is to say, hope predicted sports performances even when the participants' natural athletic talents were statistically adjusted for. Similarly, when intelligence was corrected statistically, hope still predicted academic performances.

Snyder's former student Shane Lopez quotes his colleague Suzanne Peterson: "More hopeful employees are more likely to engage in and accept organizational change efforts." There's more, too. Higher-hope people show "less burnout on the job," are "more likely to exercise," and "do not perceive that events in their lives are as disruptive as do lower-hope people." Rather than "beginning to worry and ruminate about themselves, higher-hope people concentrate on the situation at hand to see what needs to be done." High-hope folks are also "more likely to be called on for leadership." Lopez concludes, "a high IQ is not essential to a good life. However, . . . we can't live without hope." All this, of course, is why actively investing time and energy into building hope in a business is such a big deal.

Hopelessness Hurts

Low hope works in reverse. It's another one of those cycles we're unwittingly a part of. People with low hope perform poorly. And people who perform poorly start to lose hope. Many of the people who make up the altogether too large deprived segments of society have, understandably, lost hope. It's hard to have hope when everything around you feels like it's falling apart. Natural Law #4 says that people do their best work when they're part of a great organization. The inverse is equally accurate—as Cesar Chavez, farm worker, civil-rights leader, and founder of the United Farm Workers, said, "in a damaged human habitat, all problems merge."

It's clear that low—or no—levels of hope in an organization lead to low energy, subpar service, and little engagement. We can talk all we want about needed change, but hopeless people are generally listening only to make sure that nothing even worse is about to happen to them. They slowly start to shut down, to withdraw *from*, rather than engage *with*, the world—they pull back into their hard emotional and intellectual shells where, not shockingly, they feel "safer." They may poke their heads out now and again, but basically, they just cut themselves off from most of the world as a method of self-protection. They feel—and act—like their efforts are essentially irrelevant. They may well toe our organizational line in order to avoid problems, but they'll almost never push hard enough to achieve greatness. Emma Goldman said a century ago, "No one is lazy. They grow hopeless from the misery of their present existence, and give up."

Over the years, I've come to explain it this way: Let's imagine that we have an employee who aspires to do something big, but whose current pace is not going to get them where they want to go. I look down the hall at the doorway towards which they're moving. The low-hope manager shuts them down—"At the rate you're going, you'll never make it. I'm locking the door." Once the door is locked, why would the employee keep busting their butt to do anything? They're going to be hurt or angry, shut down, do as little as they need to. I try to take a different approach: "At the rate you're going, you'll never make it. I really want to help you. Are you ready to pick up the pace? If you do, I think you can make it!" They may still not get there. But at least I'm encouraging them to attain the vision of the future that they've described. And you know what? They just might succeed!

When a staff member can't see a better tomorrow in our workplace, when the best they believe they can achieve is to just get by, hope is hard to have. Writer Brené Brown says, "Hopelessness is dangerous because it leads to feelings of powerlessness." The inverse is also accurate—feeling like an unempowered part of your organization (or community or family) leads to feelings of hopelessness. Unfortunately, there are far too many jobs that fall into that category. It's a vicious cycle. Good people, given little choice, take bad jobs—which over time just brings them down, which then makes for bad business and, ultimately, a hard life for those involved. Worse still, hopeless people generally get hired into hopeless settings, which just reinforces their belief that there's no hope. But as St. Thomas Aquinas put it, "there can be no joy in living without joy in work." It's an uninspired and ineffective place to be.

Surrounded by low hope, believing that they have no chance to lead change, people generally get even more depressed and more alienated with each passing day. Hopelessness becomes a way of organizational life. People who are hired into a low-hope or hopeless workplace will either quickly resign or eventually lose hope themselves—it's hard to stay upbeat when you're surrounded by cynicism, despair, and apathy. All of which just takes them further from believing in a more positive future. The extreme situations are akin to total darkness. Viktor Frankl writes, "The prisoner who had lost faith in the future—his future—was doomed. With his loss of belief in the future, he also lost his spiritual hold; he let himself decline and became subject to mental and physical decay." Most folks, though, are all too accustomed to that hopeless feeling. It's likely that they'll just keep on showing up, punching in, and checking out. But as philosopher Paul Tillich tells us, "Boredom is rage spread thin." A placid surface can surprise later in the form of sudden emotional eruptions. Being angry at the world around them starts to seem like standard operating procedure.

Low-hope organizations are running in an emotionally inefficient way, one that I can't imagine actually benefits anyone. "[L]ow hope can envelop a person's life," Snyder says, and it can also consume an organizational culture. As anarchist professor Mohammed Bamyeh writes, "[H]umanity then only loses interest in itself as it ponders, like an animal in a zoo, the [hopeless] impossibility of moving beyond existing structures and confines." In that context, hope has a limited scope; people's hope at work is that things will go smoothly enough, work won't be horribly hard, and Friday will come quickly. The quality of their contribution, of course, suffers significantly, which in turn leads to low energy and poor performance, both personally and organizationally.

Hopeless folks, by definition, will give up faster and fail more frequently. As José Joaquín Olmedo, both a poet and the president of Ecuador in the mid-19th century, said, "He who does not hope to win has already lost." In the end, organizations without hope are dying. No ecosystem can survive without sun.

We the People

Melvin Parson worked on the night cleaning crew at the Deli a few years ago. I'd seen him once or twice, but we hadn't done any work together. We connected over a book. *Part 1* of this series, actually. See, we have a standing offer out to everyone who works here at Zingerman's that they can get a copy of any of the volumes in this series if they're willing to read it and then make some donation (however large or small) of time or money to Food Gatherers, the local food-rescue program. My assistant, Jenny Tubbs, had been chatting with Melvin one day and encouraged him to take us up on the offer. A few days later I signed a copy of *Part 1* for him. We didn't talk, though, until one afternoon when I was out running. He was driving by, saw me, and stopped to say "hi" out the window. We chatted for a minute and he introduced me to his friend who was in the passenger seat. Lora, he told me, was about to open her own yoga studio.

Although Lora didn't work for us, I thought I'd help Melvin help her by getting her a copy of the book as well. It is, after all, about enhancing the ecosystem. Showing respect for her also demonstrates respect for him. So, in my effort to live by my "when in doubt, give it out" principle (see page 372), I got Lora a copy of the book. Jenny, who's becoming a bit of a Santa Claus for readers, delivered it. A bit later Melvin emailed to thank me—"I gotta tell you that having your book delivered made her feel really special and I believe she will take that experience with her in moving forward as it relates to making her yoga students feel special."

Eighteen months later I heard from Melvin again. He wanted to meet. This time we were sitting at a table at the Deli, not standing by the side of the road. It was the first time I'd listened to him deeply and noticed the nuance of his energy: grounded, interesting, engaged, insightful. I liked being in his presence. I also liked the project he came to tell me about. We the People Growers Association is in Ypsilanti, the town directly to the east of Ann Arbor. Although Ypsi (as locals call it) is its own place and was once very well off, in many ways, over the last half a century, it's become, you might say, a "less advantaged" part of our ecosystem. Many good things and good people are at work there, though, and I'd say it's on the upswing. A more positive perspective frames it as Brooklyn to Ann Arbor's Manhattan.

In a setting where many people don't have access to fresh food, where most are three or four generations removed from growing their own, Melvin's small project is making a difference. As he explains,

We the People is dedicated to using farming to empower people who lack access to resources and opportunities. We build community through farming. I believe that growing food grows communities. I want to use [urban] farming as a vehicle to create a different outlook for my commu-nity. Last year was my first-ever undertaking in growing vegetables. I inherited a 3' x 20' raised vegetable garden that had been tended to by a sweet woman named Verna. Sadly, Verna passed away last year and somehow I was chosen to grow vegetables in her stead; mind you I had no experience gardening. However, I was a gamer, so off I went pre-paring the soil, getting my hands dirty and loving every minute of it! I dedicated my first experience with growing food to Verna. This vision has led me to form We the People Growers Association. I don't just want to grow food. I want to create a sense of empowerment in the commu-nity and educate its members about food sustainability, nutrition, and other essential skills, which promote a healthy outlook upon self, and those about you. Our motto is "Grow Food and Get Strong."

I love it. Hope and hard work are making a difference. Melvin started with one raised bed, not knowing a darned thing about growing. Today it's 14 vegetable and herb beds that are 20 feet long and about 32 inches wide, tended to by dozens of volunteers, having fun and helping each other and the commu-nity. Melvin's work inspires me. It's inspired many others, too. We the People Growers Association is effectively building hope and seeding positive beliefs for those who haven't had that many of late. Melvin's generosity of spirit brings some much-needed sunlight to a part of town that has had more than its fair share of darkness over the last few decades. It's helping people learn the basics of growing their own food, a skill they can carry with them anywhere they go. It's helping to give them the sense of satisfaction that comes from hard work you care about, doing something good for yourself and those around you. And it's sending them home with healthy produce to boot.

Words and Hope

One of my favorite musicians, the late Kevin Coyne, once wrote a song called "Talking to No One" that starts out, "Talking to no one is strange, talking to someone is stranger." The way I see it, when we are talking to "no one"—i.e., ourselves—the quality of the conversation is a big indicator of our hopefulness about the future. The language we use says a lot. People who are consistently critical of themselves in their internal dialogue are unlikely to possess high levels of hope. When we say things, in our heads or to others, like "I'm an idiot"; "I'm a loser"; I'll never figure that out"; "They'll never hire me"; "That'll never work," we're working with a pessimistic picture of the future.

For those of us who were raised to believe (as I was) that cockiness and bragging are bad things, please understand that there's a middle ground between the kind of harsh self-criticism I'm talking about above and the sort of egotistical self-promotion that we're appropriately wary of engaging in. Self-deprecation is not the same as humble deference. We can treat ourselves with the same level of love, care, and consideration that we would anyone in our lives we care about and still be humble. In fact, the respect we have for ourselves, I believe, will carry over to conversations with others through our vibrational energy. The more we build our sense of grounded self-respect, the more likely it is that we'll convey meaningful respect to other people.

Another way to assess hope levels is to (literally) keep count of our words. The ratio of positive to negative comments we make says a lot about the way we view the world. Work in the field of positive psychology is showing that flourishing organizations, marriages, and individuals had a range of three to six parts praise to one of criticism. Below that level, odds of succeeding, and hence levels of hope, drop significantly. As philosopher Rollo May said, "Courage arises from one's sense of dignity and self-esteem; and one is uncourageous because he thinks too poorly of himself."

Why Counting Words Counts

I suggest that we could monitor that ratio in any number of ways to indicate to ourselves how hopeful we are about almost anything. You might, for instance, track the following:

- How many positive versus negative comments you make in a week
- The ratio of hopeful to unhopeful comments you make at work: When you talk about your organization, how many positive statements do you make? How many negative?

- What you say about your business partner, your direct reports, or your spouse

You can do this, of course, with anything or anyone, including yourself. The results will be an interesting indicator of your level of hope in that particular arena of life. If you mindfully improve the ratio over a period of months, I forecast that your level of hope will go up accordingly. And your effectiveness and enjoyment of life will likely follow suit.

Core Deprivation Leads to Low Hope

Every article I've read on the subject has shown that people who have low incomes, low access to health care, and minimal support networks also have relatively low levels of hope. And it's difficult to remain optimistic when you, and most of the people around you, don't seem to be able to break out of that cycle. The social implications of that reality are obviously important. If hope is one of the biggest indicators of one's future success, it's hard to imagine that cycles of poverty and prejudice can ever be broken without it.

The following excerpt from a beautiful piece by Ojibwe writer Bryce Stevenson, written for his Native American literature class at the University of Wisconsin–Milwaukee, drives the point home:

> *The fight for identity . . . is a fight that Native Americans have had for a very long time. To have nothing and feel like nothing is a devastating psychological experience for any human, but to live every day feeling incomplete and without a purpose is incredibly destructive. To have no hope and to exist for the sake of existing is difficult, and reservations offer little more than a place to eat and sleep and simply exist. They offer survival, but not sustainability. To create, love, and inspire are human nature, and not being able to do these things will completely kill a person inside.*

His words touch my heart—the struggle to find hope when others around you don't have it is a hard one. Mindfulness and learning can help clear a positive path forward. He has hope that the tide can be turned. This newfound hope, it seems clear to me, is altering his beliefs.

I have to understand the past and the present to figure out how to improve the future. Often, I feel as if I am only one of a very few that have a hunger for knowledge and resolve. This semester has changed me in a lot of ways. I've found minds much like my own that wish to learn and teach. In my mind, I see a small shift of perspective in regards to the Native American culture, and am hopeful that the more I learn and experience, the more I will inspire others around me to desire the same. If I can learn enough to pass on, I believe I can return to Red Cliff and find friends and family and even complete strangers that will sit and listen to what I have to say. I believe that I can help, even in the smallest way, to inspire the unparalleled and incredible essence of my culture in another person.

To state the obvious, a paragraph in a single essay in an off-the-grid alternative business book is a start, but certainly not a solution—the issue of hope deprivation in the world is really the subject for a national period of deep reflection and study. With that acknowledgment, I'm going to be briefer here than I might be, not because it isn't enormously important, but because this book is about how to build better workplaces, not how to work out all the many issues we struggle with in our society. But please don't let brevity belie the significance of this. Bryce's ancestors were living for millennia on the land where Rocco Disderide built his building before Europeans "discovered" America. They "discovered" the land, but they crushed the people. Which, I realize now, is a sad metaphor for what's happened in mainstream business.

Three central ideas come to mind in terms of hope building in the workplace:

1. When we're hiring someone who comes from a low-hope background, we would do well to be *extra sensitive* to how much seemingly small things might interfere with their sense of self-confidence and hope. Give support and caring, constructive structure. Be patient. It may take someone who's had very little in life more time to buy in, more time to believe, more time to start to be hopeful about their future in our organization.

2. With that in mind, I believe we should pay particular attention to creating a series of small successes early on in their training program. If we provide many small windows of hope, and caringly help them through (rather

than just waiting for one big one to be opened later on), the odds of getting the person onto a more hopeful and, ultimately, progressive path go up quite a bit.

3. The more we can raise entry-level wages (no small thing in our relatively low-paying industry), the more likely we are to increase hope levels in frontline folks we employ. Which should, according to the statistics, then improve their performance and, hence, our organizational output.

A few specific ways we might do this include:

- Taking care to show appreciation for new folks in meetings early on, or in writing, perhaps in our staff newsletter.

- Making sure that people see any "code greens" (our name for customer compliments) that were written about their work so they know it matters.

- Listening to them as much as possible. As Brenda Ueland writes, "When we are listened to, it creates us, makes us unfold and expand."

- Watching out for low-hope habits. For instance, people with low hope—i.e., a cynical or suspicious view of the future—will often smile and praise others for failing or for "getting in trouble." Though they may not realize it, this response serves to reinforce their negative view of the world.

- Being mindful that people who show high resistance to vision writing are often those with low hope levels. When you have low hope, it's hard to come up with a bold and creative commitment to the future, even when it's a future of your own choosing.

- Letting folks know about what we here at Zingerman's call our "Community Chest." Started a decade ago thanks to Paul's vision, each of our businesses contributes 5 percent of its net operating profit to a fund that can be tapped by Zingerman's staff members in financial crisis.

Rick Snyder listed a series of things that parents who effectively cultivate hope in their kids typically do. While I'm generally loath to pair leadership and parenting, I can't see anything on his list that wouldn't also be productive for us to do as managers to inspire hope in those we have hired. Snyder reported that parents—and, I believe, bosses—who effectively develop hope generally

- Demonstrate positive energy
- Show a steady determination to get to a positive future
- Successfully make things happen
- Are highly creative
- Stand up for what they believe
- Are dependable and can be consistently counted upon
- Think freely and independently
- Are consistently humble
- Encourage us to own our choices
- Offer regular reminders that our efforts have had an impact
- Praise regularly
- Criticize kindly and in context
- Teach positive self-talk
- Promote people's strengths
- Teach that running into roadblocks is normal (telling stories of how we got past them is a productive model for others)
- Encourage others to take responsibility
- Teach people how to do things for themselves
- Let others make mistakes but be there to support them throughout
- Encourage people to set goals
- Take care of their health and exercise regularly
- Talk *with* people, not at them

Shane Lopez says, "Nothing good happens when we're demoralized. The leaders who care about us most know this. That's why they work so hard to give us a glimpse of what's possible. And that is why people follow them." The more you and I can do any or all of the above, the more likely the subtle message of our day-to-day activities will lead to healthy, high-hope organizations in which bright, sunny days become the norm.

Living in a High-Hope Bubble

I'm *very* aware as I write this that I'm living in an exceptional bubble of extremely high hope. Not that we don't have people in our community who are

295

struggling or staff members who are having a hard time. But I understand that my experience with hope is not the norm—I'm about as hope-privileged as one can get. I'm part of a healthy organization, living a personal and professional life that I envisioned, worked hard to make happen and actively enjoy, in a creative, education-oriented, cosmopolitan small-town community. And the organization I'm a part of is selling products and services that people generally are happy to buy (as opposed to working in an emergency room or the cable-TV service center), selling mostly to people who are not generally scraping the bottom of their financial barrel every day to find a way to eat.

I understand that all that makes it far easier to be hopeful—and even to take the time to give so much thought to the subject in the first place—than it would be if I were an entry-level custodian working in the emergency room of an underfunded, hierarchically run, not-very-progressive inner-city hospital. Which means, if you want, you can take all that I've written here with a cynical grain of socioeconomic salt. But still, I believe the approaches to building hope—and to mindfully not destroying what hope already exists—will make a difference in any setting.

A small act of kindness and an affirmative and encouraging link to the future can mean even more to folks in a low-hope setting than to those in a relatively high-hope culture such as ours. Hopefulness is not a zero-sum game. The more we practice it, the more likely it is to spread to others we interact with. I've always liked Thomas Jefferson's quote about intellectual generosity: "He who receives an idea from me, receives instruction himself without lessening mine; as he who lights his taper at mine, receives light without darkening me." Take out "an idea" and add "hope"—the statement is equally powerful.

Melvin Parson's work with We the People is inspiring to me partly because he's operating in a setting where there are far fewer resources, where the sun shines (figuratively) far less than it does here, seven miles to the west. "I had this wonderful experience last Wednesday," he told me.

This kid pulls up on his bike. Well mannered. And he's like, "Hey can I help?" So I give him a hand trowel to do some work in the beds. But he doesn't really know what he's doing, and he's pulling plants that aren't weeds. So I stop to show him. He was going really slow, and he didn't do a good job. And that kind of agitated me a bit. So I said, "Thank you for coming out. This is your garden. Come out any time." He wanted to stay, I could tell. But I realized, out of my own frustration, I'd cordially blown him off. And then the universe said to me, "Asshole! This is his garden. You're supposed to make him feel comfortable here." So I started praying: "Please send him back." And he came back! I was like, "Man, I'm so glad you came back. Would you be willing to help me?" Because I realized it was about making a place for him. He said, "Yes," so I got him a bucket, and he started picking up the rocks . . . right away he goes in this area where I don't need rocks picked up. So I said, "How about over here?" He's missing a lot of rocks, and he's not doing a great job. But I realized it's not about that . . . this is about him and it being his garden. Anyway, the kid came over to talk to me. His name is Jamari. And he says, "I just turned fourteen today. Today's my birthday!" At first, I felt sad that he wasn't with his family. But that reminded me how important community gardens could be. He told me that he's not like a lot of his friends. He doesn't get in trouble. And how he wished he had a job. Wished he could go to U of M and study art. All day, every day, kids like that fall through the cracks because there's no one to help them. And that little thing really renewed my commitment to the garden, to We the People. He went on this tangent about being young and full of energy. "I do this, and I do this, and I still have all this energy." And then he says, "And that's why you need me."

By this point, Melvin is shaking his head, and I'm hanging on every word. Clearly, the man is making happen all the good things I'm writing about in this essay. The community is a brighter place for his efforts to help others to help themselves.

So I asked him, "Why do you need me?" And he looks at me, and he says, "Because you can show me what to do and give me guidance." He knows what he brings to the table, and he knows what he should be getting from the table. A few minutes later his younger brother comes and wants to help, too. Not looking for what they can take, but what they can give.

"You're giving him hope," I said to Melvin. He smiled softly and said, "I remember Jim Balmer, my sponsor and my friend, telling me that hope is the strongest currency we carry as human beings."

Building Creative Hope in Detroit

Like Melvin, Felisha Hatcher grew up in Detroit; she still lives there, along with her husband and daughter. Her project, Ec3 Lab, is a "social and cultural incubator for young creatives." It involves classes, training sessions, educational opportunities, leadership workshops, and entrepreneurial activities for young people to help them tap into their creative intelligence and put it to work for their own benefit and that of the community. She cares deeply about the kids. "It's not about me," Hatcher said.

> I'm just there to be a conduit for people. I've always been a dreamer. It all grew from seeing the hunger and the need in young people for something, or someone, to give them a sense of hope and purpose. Our answer to that call started by diving in to find ways to fulfill those needs. Often fueled by nothing but hope. Hope became the driving force to find creative ways to help impact the community.
>
> People ask me, "How have you been able to do it with no budget?" Well, we pour our personal money into it. I'm not gonna sit around and wait for someone to fund a dream that I want to make happen. The key is that we're all about serving. We're reaching the kids. It has to be about giving first. And then about serving with a foundation of love. This has been a great model for me in terms of how much I can give back to make sure that those seeds are planted and cultivated . . . to let them know that someone cares. I tell the kids, "I just need you to dream big!" I just want to leave the world a little bit better than I found it.
>
> Instilling hope became our mission. We host workshops that spark the imagination. We collaborate with community partners who highlight creativity. Any opportunity to positively impact a child that presents itself, we strive to be there. We utilize every event we can get as a teaching moment for the positive self-development of youth . . . using the world as a classroom! We're teaching [kids] that even within the word "impossible" lies "I'm-Possible." [This] continues to be at the core of what we do. For us, the rewards are priceless, and we couldn't think of doing anything else.

Hatcher's positive energy comes through in every conversation I've had with her. And I'm sure it shines brightly on the kids in the community as well.

Low Hope in School?

Many argue that this endemic hopelessness has its roots in our educational system. A school, after all, is an organization. If all successful organizations are living in harmony with the Natural Laws of Business, and if not living in harmony with nature results in an "energy crisis in the workplace," then it only makes sense that school systems would work, for better and for worse, in the same ways. Anarchist educators Isabelle Frémeaux and John Jordan write that when students are "[s]pending six hours a day for twelve years in a place where they have virtually no say in anything, where being governed is all they know, a profound passivity becomes normalized, the hopelessness of submission becomes fixed deep below the child's skin." When we hire people who've gone through that sort of educational upbringing, we need to expose them to some "healthy sunlight," give them a new perspective on themselves and on the world, and help them generate a good bit of hope.

Kids who get into more progressive schools (which are, knowingly or not, living in harmony with the Natural Laws) are more likely to have a greater level of hope. When we consider all the statistically demonstrated benefits of hopefulness, this means they potentially have an edge in most everything they engage in, including in the workplace. Referencing an anarchist school in Spain, Frémeaux and Jordan write that "Learning at Paideia is thus not simply about acquiring abstract knowledge—dates, facts, and arithmetic—but about encouraging a different way of being in the world, evolving the senses and deepening the capacity to connect with one's own potentiality and that of others." Kids at Paideia aren't just studying; they're actually learning to run the school, in much the same way that the people who work here are learning to run our business. It makes sense to me. As Emma Goldman once said, "Every child is an anarchist at heart."

Jeff Fleckenstein used to work at the Bakehouse. For the last 10 years or so, he's been part of a progressive school program in North Carolina. I asked him for his thoughts on all this. "I believe that although all school systems try to inspire students," he said, starting with a positive belief,

> *many don't succeed. With our program, North Carolina New Schools, we infuse hope into the education experience, by encouraging and supporting innovation. We try to be the "sandbox" where students can play and be creative and attempt new things all while reimagining their*

school experience. Students become excited and hopeful when those who are responsible for their success are also excited and hopeful. By working with teachers to imagine and create new engaging student experiences and then making the classrooms public, so that the change can be shared with others, [we help] work towards infusing hope.

It's not just about giving hope to the kids; it's teaching the students skills that, in and of themselves, build hope too. As Jeff explains,

When students are placed at the center of the learning experience and are asked to help create and execute lessons, students are empowered. We are doing our best to reconnect learning and doing, so that the knowledge of welding and the knowledge necessary for academia are once again both held in high esteem. In essence, we try to help infuse hope into students by radically changing the student's classroom and school experience from the traditional to the innovative.

And it's working. Through this approach, "many more students in North Carolina are now graduating from rural high schools with their diplomas. We do our best to be a thought partner who can push against the status quo and help others think differently about teaching/learning and student outcomes."

Hope For—and From—Reading

Not all bias is bad. I grew up with reading. I am, I know, beautifully biased in favor of books. I'm 100 times more at peace spending time reading an author's words on the page than I probably would be sitting with the actual person. My beliefs about books started early—my mother used to take us to the library with great regularity. Reading was part of our routine. If hope is the sun, sitting in a library is like a trip to the beach for me. For as long as I can remember, I've felt safest and strongest when I'm sitting quietly, alone in the sun, reading, suffused with hope. Being with a book was the place I felt most at peace. Books never criticized me, never told me what to do. I could take in their ideas and process them without feeling pressure to fit in. Plus, I could do it in pieces—one idea from one book, a different one from the next. And one book was never jealous when I learned something new from another.

It's almost impossible for me to imagine life without reading. Peter Kropotkin, Emma Goldman, and Alexander Berkman all write about being in prison and feeling their spirits saved when they were allowed access to books. I remember finding out about the Slave Act of 1834 in South Carolina. (It was the same year that the house at Cornman Farms was built.) As part of the continuing effort to dehumanize those in captivity, it became illegal to teach enslaved people how to read. I remember the sadness and fear that hit me as soon as I saw that. It was like a rush of creative claustrophobia. I could barely think about it, in the same way I can hardly process descriptions of horrible physical torture.

Active formal learning—for me, reading, but this can take a number of forms for different folks—is one of the best ways I know to shine some sun onto otherwise dark spots, to bring meaningful hope to those who need it. Gail Wolkoff runs a program here in town called Dedicated to Make a Change. Its mission is "to connect youth with the world to promote peace, greater understanding and a love of learning. Each program is created to focus on ways to give youth a variety of new and positive experiences needed to interrupt their acceptance of poor education in the local school system and to reduce their detention and incarceration rate." One of the program's top tactical tools is to teach and develop reading skills.

Through developing reading skills, hope starts to shine back into otherwise low-hope lives. Kids become more confident within themselves and more comfortable in the world around them. What Frederick Douglass said over a century ago is still true today: "Once you learn to read, you will be forever free." As Wolkoff explains, "I realized if the students had a school which failed them, essential academic knowledge was lacking. But reading will always make success. Once each person started reading (at first with a buddy, then on their own), they realized a book was filled with ideas instead of black dots which meant nothing." Here are a few testimonials:

> Justin: *From reading, I have acquired new knowledge that will help during the school year. I'm ready to go back to school and use all the new things I have learned.*

> Tay: *I am very proud of myself. I can read and pronounce words that I was not able to at the beginning of the summer. I have really grown to love reading. I am ready to tackle this school year, starting and ending strong.*

> Jasmon: *I used to find reading hard and complicated, until I started to read daily with Dedicated to Change's reading program. Now I can write sentences that make sense. I love to read.*

Jade: *As I've been reading, my constant improvement has boosted my self-esteem. The summer program made me feel like I could do anything as long as I believe in myself and never give up.*

Like I said, I'm biased. I've long loved books. But I've realized in doing this work just how important it is that books allow us access to other worlds, to other views. They connect us to realities that are radically different from, sometimes better than, the one we're currently stuck in. Often the sun is shining, but the tall buildings completely block it out. Books call up our creativity and our imaginations; they let the light in. With reading, you can see the characters, the setting, smell the sun. Each of us, of course, imagines them differently but that's part of the point. As Peruvian anarchist Manuel González Prada posited, "a book can demolish fortresses the cannon cannot."

Kurt Vonnegut writes, "Don't give up on books. They feel so good—their friendly heft. The sweet reluctance of their pages when you turn them with your sensitive fingertips. A large part of our brains is devoted to deciding whether what our hands are touching is good or bad for us. Any brain worth a nickel knows books are good for us." The kids in the program would agree. And so does Melvin Parson. "I got it from my grandmother," he says.

She was from Winn, Arkansas. She was amazing in her own right. Her dad sent her off to school. She had 14 brothers and sisters. She graduated from college at the age of 16, which was tough to do for a woman and a woman of color in that era. She poured a lot into me, sending me to private school for the first eight years. She taught me about reading. Opening up your mind. If you can't read, your mind is so limited. In 5th grade, I had a 12th-grade reading level.

It sounded great. I asked him what went wrong. "The soil around me," he said. "Not the soil in the home. It was stepping outside the home . . . it didn't nurture those things that my home environment was working to produce." It took 20 years, but Melvin is clearly back to the beliefs that his grandmother worked so hard to instill in him. And from those, he's now effectively spreading hope and positive belief to others.[25]

Effective and active learning is equally important in business. Leaders who don't do it rarely continue to lead with great effectiveness. Learning brings freedom and hope for a promising future. As Peter Senge says, "Through learning we re-create ourselves. Through learning we become able to do something we never were able to do. Through learning we reperceive the world and our relationship to it. Through learning we extend our capacity to create, to be part of the generative process of life." Books have given me the seeds of hundreds of insights. I'll never meet most of the authors of these books to thank them for their amazing gifts. I hope this Guide to Good Leading series serves as an expression of my gratitude.

Reading in Business

As I gathered all these insights into how reading helps build hope with young people in school, it started to dawn on me that the same must be true in the workplace. Per Peter Senge, "We will never transform the prevailing system of management without transforming our prevailing system of education. They are the same system." Getting people in business to read can open up all the same positive possibilities for employees that it does for young people (who, as Senge points out, we will later hire). Reading—or listening to books on tape, watching TED talks, taking classes, or going to seminars—opens doors to new options, facilitates new connections, increases self-confidence. And because one of the best ways to learn to write is to read other people's writing, it helps with a core business—and, it turns out, life—skill as well.

Here at Zingerman's we have the expectation that all folks in leadership roles will be doing, on average, two hours of formal learning per week. Do they all do it? Probably not. Does everyone who's doing it do great work? Probably not, either. But I do know that people who are feeling stuck, who aren't improving and growing in their work, surely aren't doing active learning about their products, people management, or any other part of their jobs. Students who aren't reading fall behind in school. I suggest that the same is true for anyone in our organization.

One of the most gratifying things about working on the books in this series is how many progressive business people I know have used them as part of a reading group at work. The Secret Pamphlets we've put out—as single-serving sizes, so to speak—have proven particularly positive tools for getting people who don't normally do it to read about business. It helps. In the same way that reading brings hope to 8th graders, it can also shine some light for the people with whom we work every day.

Revolution of Hope

Maybe music can do something similar. Many people I've asked about both belief and hope have listed music as one of their major influences. Like books, music allows us access to worlds beyond the one we're physically planted in every day. Revolution of Hope is a fascinating program that teaches classical music and orchestra skills to inner-city kids in Roxbury, Massachusetts. Their website explains: "An Orchestra is a model community where members must listen to each other and work together to achieve success. Mandatory parent involvement in the program will deepen relationships between parents and their children. This strengthened relationship will be the foundation for our goal of community renewal." The training was started by performer David France, who had learned a similar approach in Venezuela called *El Sistema*. The program is designed to do something similar to what we're trying to do here at Zingerman's:

> *To strengthen executive function skill development through collective musical ensemble learning, as well as to increase social capital through development of strong pro-social relationships with peers, parents and other adults. Finally, an additional goal is to promote civic engagement of Roxbury youth through the development of problem-solving and leadership skills that can be transferred into out-of-program contexts.*

If life is art, and music is art, then a great way to learn to live a healthy, community-connected existence is to be part of a collaborative musical setting.

Hopeful Writing

For me, writing has an equally amazing impact. Writing opens my mind. It makes me dream, notice, appreciate, connect, create. It's changed my life. I'm not sure how I would have undertaken writing without reading first. Reading, listening, tasting, touching, and the rest of real life are the raw material for anyone who does it regularly. I like what Julia Cameron says:

> *We should write because it is human nature to write. Writing claims our world. It makes it directly and specifically our own. We should write because humans are spiritual beings and writing is a powerful form of prayer and meditation, connecting us both to our own insights and to a higher and deeper level of inner guidance. We should write because*

writing brings clarity and passion to the act of living. Writing is sensual, experiential, grounding. We should write because writing is good for the soul. We should write because writing yields us a body of work, a felt path through the world we live in. We should write, above all, because we are writers, whether we call ourselves that or not.

Whether it's informal journaling every morning, food writing, business writing, essays, or books, writing has proven terrifically therapeutic for me. It keeps me learning, keeps me curious, keeps me figuring out how to adapt what I've learned to daily life. It helps me connect with other people's creative insights, which enhances our ecosystem and creates a hugely positive cycle. And hope. Lots and lots of hope.

Here are some practical ways that we're already putting this to work at Zingerman's. I can see the benefit of us doing even more of it in the years to come.

- We teach an internal class on managing ourselves, in which we encourage attendees to experiment with regular journaling.
- We actively engage staff to write articles for both our external and internal newsletters.
- Twice a year we run a writing group for interested staff members to give them a safe place to practice their skills.

Does Watching the News Reduce Hope?

Maria Popova writes in her great blog, *Brain Pickings*: "Carl Sagan saw in books *'proof that humans are capable of working magic.'* The magic of humanity's most enduring books—the great works of literature and philosophy—lies in the simple fact that they are full of hope for the human spirit." On the other hand, "News has become the sorcerous counterpoint to this magic, mongering not proof of our goodness and brilliance but evidence of our basest capabilities." When I read that, I realized I have almost completely stopped listening to the news other than to pick up the basics of what's going on in the world. (This, after years of religiously reading the paper and listening to the news.) The tone is generally so negative, the voices so critical, the hope levels so low, that listening just brings me down to the point where I have a hard time focusing on the things I can actually influence. Instead of sinking into worry and anxiety over things I can't impact, I've tried to put ever more energy into giving time and insight to those I can truly support in person.

How the 12 Natural Laws of Business (and Life) Make Hope Come Alive

Writer Victoria Safford says, "Our mission is to plant ourselves at the gates of Hope." I love the image. Sadly, so many people living on the periphery of society don't even get close, and if they do, the gates rarely open for them. Still, I have hope. When I look over the list of the 12 Natural Laws of Business, it seems clear that working in harmony with them is likely to consistently generate healthy, grounded hope. Working in a sustainable setting of that sort is like having the gates of hope opened for us. If we walk through, great things are much more likely to happen.

1. An Inspiring, Strategically Sound Vision Leads the Way to Greatness (Especially If You Write It Down!)

Having a positive picture of the future that's inspiring, strategically sound, written down, and shared is about as hope building as one can get. Especially when it's revisited and acted upon regularly.

2. You Need to Give Customers Compelling Reasons to Buy from You

When one's products and services are highly sought after, and customers are excited to buy them, the future looks very positive.

3. Without Good Finance, You Fail

Healthy finances generally lead to better pay rates, less worry about lack of money, and greater levels of hope in all involved.

4. People Do Their Best Work When They're Part of a Great Organization

Great organizations are hopeful. Hope is contagious. If you join a hopeful organization, you're likely to catch it, too. And when you become more hopeful, you do better work. Which in turn improves the organization further.

5. If You Want the Staff to Give Great Service to Customers, the Leaders Have to Give Great Service to the Staff

Giving service to staff is a statement of belief in their abilities and their value to the organization, as well as an expression of their importance as human beings. Hope grows as a result.

6. If You Want Great Performance from Your Staff, You Have to Give Them Clear Expectations and Training Tools

Clear expectations and training tools are all about a better future. Small training successes build confidence. People are more hopeful when they know what's expected of them and feel like they have the tools they need to do the work at hand.

7. Successful Businesses Do the Things That Others Know They Should Do . . . But Generally Don't

This one is all about appreciating the little things and understanding how much difference they make. It could be giving a struggling staff member just a bit more of a chance to turn things around; going out of our way to find—and pay more for—an especially excellent ingredient; or making time to connect with a customer to really get to know them and, as a result, serve them better.

8. To Get to Greatness You've Got to Keep Getting Better—All the Time!

Like visioning, this is a positive statement about the future. The more we continue to improve, the more we increase the odds of getting to greatness, the more hopeful we become.

9. Success Means You Get Better Problems

This is textbook hope building. Instead of seeing problems as peril, we organize them into desirable problems and undesirable problems. The more of the former we can find, the better we're doing. Good problems raise hope levels; bad problems produce worry, anxiety, and even all-out panic.

10. Whatever Your Strengths Are, They Will Likely Lead Straight into Your Weaknesses

Again, this reframes what most people fight with as a natural state of human existence. Rather than being discouraged, we can start to see these things as reasonable and realistic outgrowths of what we're doing well and then work to correct our course where we need to.

11. It Generally Takes a Lot Longer to Make Something Great Happen than People Think

This one helps people understand that sticking with good things is a big piece of what makes those things work. It's the opposite of the wishful thinking that lets people passively stand aside and "hope for the best." As Rick Snyder writes, "when the going gets tough, the hopeful keep going."

12. Great Organizations Are Appreciative, and the People in Them Have More Fun

When you're appreciated regularly, when you laugh a lot, it's safe to say that hope is shining brightly, and smiles will abound. In a healthy, affirmative setting, people essentially get a natural high from hope!

Stories of Hope

Stories are powerful tools for forming beliefs and for building hope. "I would ask you to remember only this one thing," says Badger in the book *Crow and Weasel*. "The stories people tell have a way of taking care of them. If stories come to you, care for them. And learn to give them away where they are needed. Sometimes a person needs a story more than food to stay alive. That is why we put these stories in each other's memory. This is how people care for themselves." Telling stories that seed hope—when we combine them with lessons of how to make our dreams and visions become reality—can be highly valuable.

Fending Off the Fear of False Hope

Cynics (or, as cynics would likely say, "realists") will be wary of building *too* hopeful an organization. Many would probably point out that we don't want to create a false sense of hope (for wealth, fame, or whatever else comes to mind) in the people we work with. "If we don't believe something a staff member suggested is really going to happen," they might well argue, "then why lead 'em on?" And "If they aren't really going to advance, why delude them? They're just going to end up angry and disappointed when what they want doesn't happen, anyway."

In the most literal sense, I actually agree with the skeptics—if we truly know that what the staff member wants to do isn't *ever* going to happen, then it makes no sense to nurture hope in them that it will. Clearly that would be uncaring and dishonest. But in the instances that I've mentioned above where we fell short and, really, in most of these sorts of situations in general, the leader shut the door to the future far too quickly. What could have happened instead is what I believe would be more effective: to help the staff member refine a positive, strategically sound vision of the future, and then put the pre-requisites the leader has in mind out in the open where the staff member then has a chance to either do them, or not, as they so choose. If they truly fall short over time, so be it. But then again, you just don't know—highly focused, smart, self-motivated folks can surprise a lot of people when they put their minds to something they care about. I prefer to take a chance on success, rather than to shut someone down before they can even get started.

Mind you, I'm not suggesting that leaders ought to toss hope around like some chew toy you use to keep your puppy happy. Belief in a positive future is not meant to be an organizational opiate that serves only to keep people quiet while steadily building an unhealthy emotional dependency. As Martin Seligman says, "[O]ptimism that is not accurate is empty and falls apart. Life defeats it." Giving false hope is, I suppose, a bit like sending people to the tanning parlor rather than letting them out in the sunshine to breathe the natural air—real hope and authentic purpose make a big difference.

To be clear, when I talk about hope here, I'm thinking about hope that we have something to do with. Not hope that your hometown team will win, or that you'll be saved suddenly by heavenly intervention, or that lightning will strike and love will appear during a dark, misty morning in May. I'm talking about hope for things we have some reasonable shot at—hope that we can make our lives more rewarding, that we can help others we care about, that our community might become a bit more collaborative, that our health might continue to be good. None of these, for me at least, are about magical hope for divine, parental, or a manager's intervention. As Russian dissident poet Nadezdha Mandelstam wrote, "The only good life is one in which there is no need for miracles." It's about doing good, grounded work to make positive progress, one small, hope-building step at a time.

There's no question that we want to be straight with staffers about how long it might take to make their idea a reality, or how much work is likely to be involved. It is, after all, Natural Law #11: it takes a lot longer to make something great happen than most people think. Here we have the Bottom Line Change process to put out as an organizational tool for folks to lead the change they want to see happen; the process can guide people onto a positive, grounded path towards the future they envision. It helps build what Rick Snyder called "waypower": the ability to actually move productively forward, not just wish for a magical solution. The change process can be frustrating; often, of course, there are more action steps to take than the staffer originally had in mind, or more people to gain support from than they may have ever considered. But as long as we're sincerely working to get to the same positive place, then why not work together?

The most important issue here is that when I offer hope to someone, I *really* have it—I really *believe* that we just might be able to make something amazing happen, that people can get to greatness, that the future can and will be better than the present. Most people are able to accomplish almost anything they desire if they're sincere, stay focused, and are ready to work hard over a long period of time. If we as leaders don't truly believe that employees can get where they want to go, we're probably doing everyone involved a disservice by letting them keep working in our organization.

How Servant Leadership Helps Build Hope

Being hopeful about the future is a prerequisite for anyone interested in effectively leading a healthy organization. But if we don't *communicate* that hope in inspiring and effective ways, our work will mostly have been for naught. It's like we ourselves are taking in the beautiful sunshine, but we've left everyone else in the basement with nothing but flickering fluorescent bulbs to light their way. Taking a positive, appreciative, authentic approach in all our communications always helps build hope. If we lead with dignity, empathy, generosity, and a commitment to great service, we are, in essence, effectively sending hundreds of small messages of hope out into our organization every day. As Oana Branzei writes, "Hopeful exchanges can set off chain reactions: sharing unexpected opportunities or revealing positive surprises spark additional '*as if*' acts that put new hope cycles in motion."

I am often asked which of the ZingTrain seminars is best for someone to take. While I'm happy to make recommendations, there is, of course, rarely one "right" answer. I've taken to saying that each of the seminars is essentially a different door into an amazing house. And that whichever door you enter through, you'll eventually end up in the same positive place. Many of the things we have already long been doing every day actively encourage the building of hope. Open-book management, customer service, visioning, and Bottom Line Training all contribute. In particular, though, our "Recipe for Servant Leadership" (see Secret #23, in *Part 2*) is pretty much guaranteed to encourage hope among all but the most determined of disengaged cynics. Take a look at each of the elements of this recipe, and you'll see why.

1. Provide Vision

It's hard not to feel hopeful when there's an inspiring and strategically sound vision of a better tomorrow in place. By definition, a vision like that is all about hope. Larry Lippitt writes, "Deep within each of us is a desire, a hope, for a better future. It is engraved deep in our souls. Whether we can articulate it or not, there is a desire for something better, something closer to our preferred future. It is hope that moves us into the future." Hope for a better business; hope that we can make a difference; hope that, if we work together, we can create great things; hope that we'll be learning and earning; hope that our lives will be made better in the process.

2. Provide Service to the Staff

When employees are treated as valued "customers" in the company, that encourages a sense of optimism, a belief that they matter, that the leaders in the organization see employees as valued contributors. When servant leaders handle staff suggestions or complaints with deference and dignity, the way we would respond to product requests or critical comments from customers, staff members are left hopeful. It's like spreading sunshine wherever we go.

The response to suggestions for improvement—from staff or clients—can be simple and sincere, along the lines of "Wow, that's great that you want to go for that. I'm really thrilled that you're thinking about this. In fact, this sort of improvement is what we're all about. Why don't we get together, and you can tell me more about what you're envisioning?" The staffer still may not get to make the change they were seeking—there aren't, after all, any guarantees, and effective organizational change takes time, even when you're the one in charge. But their sense of hope will, at the least, likely be fed for having been listened to.

What I've outlined above follows from one of our tips for giving great customer service. When a customer asks for something (no matter how odd or annoying it might seem), the most effective way to respond to them is to start by just saying, "Yes!"—and then get to work figuring out a creative solution that will make some of the guest's dreams and desires come true. It's infinitely easier and way less stressful for all involved when we start with a "yes," as in "Yes, we'd love to work on that with you. I'm not sure how we're going to do it yet, but let's see what we can come up with together." Which is so much more encouraging than the polite, but completely unproductive, standard service response of "I'm sorry, we don't do that." I've come to think of this as cultivating a hopeful culture, one in which it's far more likely that people will grow and thrive.

3. Manage in an Ethical Manner

When we do, our integrity will always increase. Working with people who do what they say they're going to do is what positive belief and hope are built on! Values-based leadership builds hope in humanity and encourages people to stay in the hopeful, grounded, true-to-themselves place where most everyone would ultimately like to be.

4. Help Staff Succeed

If I'm supporting a staff member's efforts to get themself to greatness, how can they not have hope for a better future? I'd rather fall short helping them live their dreams and make a difference, hoping they'll do something significant, than to instantly dismiss their good intentions out of hand. The more we engage, the more we give, the more we believe in them, hold them caringly accountable, the better they're likely to do. It's not foolproof, but when it works, it's amazing to experience. To quote Brenda Ueland, "The only way to love a person is . . . by listening to them and seeing and believing in the god, in the poet, in them. For by doing this, you keep the god and the poet alive and make it flourish."

5. Learn and Teach

By actively learning all the time, we demonstrate that there's a positive future towards which to move. Reading and formal learning, as I've already reviewed above, are closely correlated with levels of hope. By teaching what we learn, we actively share that knowledge with our organization. In the process, the spirit of intellectual generosity models that we can—and will—improve in all we do. (On the flip side, I find over and over again that leaders who aren't learning or actively sharing what they know in a meaningful and connected way have, themselves, secretly lost hope in a more positive future.)

6. Say Thanks

When staff members know that their work is valued, hope that it will be even more valued in the future is sure to increase. Saying thanks—for little and big things alike—makes a huge difference to the people to whom we've expressed gratitude.

It all adds up to what anarchist anthropologist Harold Barclay says: In "natural leadership," "one is accepted as an authority in some particular endeavor because he possesses acknowledged expertise in that endeavor. One does not seek to dominate others through his or her authority. He seeks to share knowledge so that others might be raised to the same level of ability." And that's what Servant Leadership is all about.

Helping Build Hope at All Levels

Although most frontline people tend to forget it, bosses are human, too. It's just as important for folks in formal leadership roles to know that their work matters as it is for someone who just started a frontline job. I know it's true for me. Fortunately, I find hope most everywhere I look. To wit, there was a nice family having dinner at the Roadhouse one spring Sunday. Grandparents, parents, and kids—the whole multigenerational thing in action—to celebrate Father's Day. The grandfather was the formal guest of honor for the evening, but it took only two passes by the table to realize that the person upon whom most of the attention was centered was his wife, the grandmother. Apparently, she'd been ill and hadn't been eating well, and everyone was concerned for her health. They were clearly hoping that a nice meal might help get her appetite up again.

Their hopes were fulfilled. She really liked the collard greens. We cook them for five or six hours with ham hocks and plenty of bacon. They're very much comfort food for folks—like her—who grew up with them. Excited that she was eating with some enthusiasm, her daughters asked if they could get another order. We got her more, and followed that by gifting her a pint of pot likker to take home. Non-Southerners won't know it, but pot likker is basically the broth from the long-cooked greens. It's said to cure all of sorts of ills and boost spirits, and it's highly nutritious; the Southern equivalent, best my Northern self can tell, of chicken soup.

She loved it! Her eyes, which had been dull in the way they often are in people who aren't feeling so great, came to life. You—or, at least, I—could see the hope rising throughout the meal. And the whole family felt better for it. The grandmother gave me a big hug when I helped her out to the car after dinner. While hope wasn't listed on the menu, it was certainly on the line throughout—and it was confirmation for me that our work truly does make a difference.

Start Building Hope in Your Business

- Use Rick Snyder's characteristics of hope builders (pages 294 and 295) as a checklist. Keep track weekly to see how you're doing.

- Start a reading club within your organization or with peers in the community.

- Begin regular journaling and encourage your colleagues to do so as well.

- Make a point of treating staff like customers.

- Teach the Natural Laws of Business to your colleagues.

Try Cooking Great Food

This one is so much a part of my daily life—both at work and at home—that I nearly forgot about it. But here's the thing: Intentionally preparing a great meal brings all the elements of hope into play. It requires us to imagine sitting down to something really delicious; we then go out and get the ingredients; and if we're not dining alone, we rely on healthy collaboration with others. It's even better when you push yourself to make something new—it adds learning to the mix. Private group sessions at BAKE, our school for home bakers, are a wonderful way to build hope in teams of coworkers. Same with private cooking classes. If you're not comfortable with cooking, keep it simple; the idea is to build success! When you get to savor what you've prepared, you get the feeling of satisfaction that goes with doing anything you mindfully chose to do well. And the good news is that, hopefully, it's only a matter of hours before you're going at it again! (See the recipes beginning on page 556 for some ideas.)

Chad Brummett, Director, Division of Pain Research,
Department of Anesthesiology, University of Michigan
Medical School, Ann Arbor, Michigan

It is just better—everything is better. Before, we did not have a common vision, so people were just doing a job. Now everyone is working as a team towards the ambitious goal of personalizing pain medicine. Most importantly, we have created a positive culture where we consciously recognize and log the many wonderful things that happen throughout a normal workday. Then these little nuggets of positivity are blasted out via email every Friday afternoon, which we call Good Vibes. People in the team frequently note that they leave work feeling better than when they started that morning—no more TGIF. We also engage in positive service as a team supporting local charities and organizing medication "take back" days to help keep prescription medications off the streets. This positivity has spilled over to other groups around us. Satisfaction, retention, funding, and productivity are all up!

Whereas the effort to change our approach took time and commitment, it does not feel like "work" to keep it going. I am very aware of how we have grown and what we owe to Ari and the ZingTrain team and do not take these things for granted. I love my job and my team and am very proud of what we have become.

Lauren Korany, Master Merchandiser, Zingerman's Deli

The months prior to working at Zingerman's were some of the hardest moments in my life. I had recently left a toxic work environment to take care of two hospitalized parents who had been foreclosed on a few months earlier. They hadn't prepared much for the foreclosure due to being sick, so I was simultaneously tending to them while trying to pack up my childhood home before it was turned over to the bank. My bills were piling up, and I had no income to support myself or my family. My sense of hope was dwindling, but in order to get through the hardest patch I knew that I had to be a light at the end of the tunnel. During those months, I applied for so many different graphic-design positions. I received only one interview. It was for a Merchandizing Graphic Designer at Zingerman's Deli. That was my first hope. During the interview process, I was so impressed with the Merchandizing team. I knew off the bat that this was unlike any other design job I had held in the past. It didn't seem sterile. The people interviewing me were real people; everyone was *happy*. When I was called about a job offer, I was more than thrilled. I think I would have been excited to work anywhere at that point, but I was extremely fortunate to end up here at Zingerman's. I started working in a positive environment. I felt respected in my career for the first time. My opinion mattered; it was one of the first times where I was no longer the "yes man" to a head honcho. The sense of community and employee empowerment is still so rewarding. That empowerment is the hope that has kept me going. The hardest times turned into the best: my parents got better and found a home, and I felt like a weight had been lifted off my life. I can honestly say that this is the first job that I am happy to show up to work for, and I don't think I could go back to anything else.

Shawn askinosie and mr. Livingston at the cacao coop in tanzania,
after mr. Livingston gifted Shawn his warrior bracelet

A Six-Pointed Hope Star

Systemically Shining the Light of Hope Across Your Organization

As I grew ever more conscious of the power of hope, I started to consider how we might work to weave it more effectively into daily life at Zingerman's. Many of our long-standing organizational recipes already help to build it in indirectly. The Six-Pointed Hope Star that's illuminated below is a more direct way to do it. The Star provides anyone who's interested with a practical, repeatable, and extremely effective tool to help make hope happen. Just knowing it's out there and putting it into use as part of my daily routine has increased my own hope, and I believe it will do the same for you.

Amos Arinda started working as a busboy at the Roadhouse when he was 17. Over the last 10 years, he's steadily advanced and has become a consistently big contributor to our organization. He trained to wait tables and, from there, started to supervise. For two years, he led our Zingerman's-wide coffee quality group, and then went into the kitchen to learn how to cook the line. He worked with us for three years learning to master Tunisian cooking at a high level of excellence and currently tends bar at the Roadhouse. Amos has done well at most everything he's engaged in. He's hard working, happy, intelligent, caring, attentive to detail, devoted to our organizational cause, and, importantly for us, possesses a great palate.

One day Amos and I were chatting when, as he so often does, he came out with something amazing: the original seed of this essay, perhaps. Out of the blue, he brought up the idea of "moments of hope." He explained,

> *It's a brief window. You take an interest in somebody that you believe has potential but may not yet have the tools to perform at a higher level. By showing interest in them, you actually help 'give' them the tools—and the hope—that they need to grow. In truth, they might have already had those tools but just didn't realize it.*
>
> *My moment of hope was when I was bussing at the Roadhouse and one of the managers came up to me and asked me if I wanted to start training to be a server. It truly made me think that maybe this job was something more than what it had seemed. And then the second moment was when I got asked if I wanted to be part of the work group for the Zingerman's 2020 vision. I was just a busboy, and I was getting asked to participate in a rollout of the long-term vision of this organization.*

I was like, "Wow." It really got me interested. That's basically what changed my trajectory here.

Amos usually shares this stuff in a mellow, rather matter-of-fact manner, so much so that I think people might miss what he's saying because he's just calmly and considerately delivering deep, meaningful insights. If you're listening, thoughtful people like Amos have a lot to say.

It's my belief that every organization has competent, quiet folks like Amos who they don't realize are ready to engage at a higher level. I take heart in the Taoist image that Gary Snyder shares: "sages disguised as melon growers in the mountains." These people don't make headlines with their steady, thoughtful performance; they don't make a lot of noise, and they aren't provoking big problems. But they're far more thoughtful than you might think. Helping them find a window of hope to climb through can make all the difference. "I feel like we have those moments with lots of people, but if we keep ignoring them when they come up, we lose the employees," Amos reflected more recently. "But when we do it right, it gives the person more of a sense of self-worth and a lot more confidence in general. The best leaders can recognize those moments and take advantage of them. It helps the individual, the organization, and, really, everyone." With Amos's admonition in mind, I'm now on the lookout for folks at Zingerman's who might be ready—people who, although they may not come with a fancy résumé, have the energy, the attitude, the shared values, the work ethic, and the wisdom to make great things happen.

It's especially important, I believe, that we mindfully create moments of hope for folks who might be fearful that they won't fit in. People who feel like outsiders, who for whatever reasons might have historically been or felt excluded, people whose self-image might be something like, "I could never succeed at that level." They, more than any of us, can benefit from the opening of one of the windows Amos got me thinking about.

In the context of our service work (see *Zingerman's Guide to Giving Great Service* for more on this), we would call these "moments of truth." Barely noticeable inflection points where a situation can either be propelled to great success or decline into a difficult and dismal failure. Where, suddenly, someone realizes that "somethin's happenin' here," even though, as the old Buffalo Springfield song says, "what it is ain't exactly clear." When we embrace the moment, with the right person, at the right time, people light up. The shift in energy is palpable—you can see it in their eyes. They suddenly start to fire on all cylinders. And they begin to engage in their work at a higher level, usually with much more passion and often with better results as well.

While moments of hope don't always work out the way we want (what does?), I know that if we can help the person move forward in a positive way, then the possibilities for future gain for both the staffer and the organization are endless—there's a lot more talent out there in the workforce than we're currently tapping. *Our responsibility as leaders is to help create more of those moments and to then act to make those moments of hope matter.* It works. As Oana Branzei writes, "Hope is renewable. The more it flows, the more it becomes cognitively, affectively, behaviorally, and spiritually energizing." Organizations that access this hopeful energy—in this case, through the act of creating a sincere, positive, and grounded sense of possibility—are, simply, a lot more likely to succeed.

A Six-Pointed Hope Star

Now that we've explored hope from a conceptual aspect, the next and probably most important question is: How can we *concretely* help make hope happen?

I think it comes down to continually opening windows, letting sun shine into previously dark places, and then helping people to see that they can effectively climb through and begin to live in the light. Having clear steps helps me; I hope it helps you too. This Six-Pointed Hope Star is a systemic, teachable, and repeatable way to help start some new, more positive relationships with what's to come.

1. HELP PEOPLE SEE A BETTER FUTURE

The fact that we're talking positively about a better tomorrow, that we're thinking about it and are excited about it and care enough about the people we hire to engage them in the dialogue, is a huge "hope builder." It's the opening of the window Amos is talking about. It's a way in which we can show people the possibility of a future in which they feel better, do more, learn more, contribute more, earn more. They are more appreciative and more appreciated; this is a future in which they are an important part of what they do and they are happy to be doing it. It's soulful work, work that matters, work in which the spirit isn't crushed, but cared for. If today is totally terrific, positive, grounded hope could be the belief that tomorrow will be just as exceptionally good as today!

Mind you, "better" or "more rewarding" doesn't necessarily mean making more money, getting a big raise, or acquiring a corner office. Everyone's dream, by dint of the reality that each of us is a unique and special being, is different. For some, cash is king (or queen), but for many folks, a positive future might mean that they're learning more, having more fun, feeling more recognized, giving more to others, or enjoying being part of a successful business. For some, perhaps all of the above. For others, a "more desirable future" might be the chance to work less and spend more time with their kids, to travel more, or to work on more interesting accounts. Each of us has to decide what a "better" future is for ourselves. Our job as leaders in this regard is to consider the future that our staff members aspire to and connect it, if we can, to the organizational vision of the future. When the two are congruent, great things can happen.

Remember that what might be a better future for you as the leader may not be at all appealing to others. Forty years ago, when the restaurant group I was working for as a kitchen manager began talking about national expansion and developing district managers (I'd need to take my earring out, of course), I knew it was time to leave. To be clear, there was nothing wrong with where they were headed; it just wasn't a good fit for me. Being a suit-and-tie-wearing regional manager for a large restaurant group was *not* the future I wanted, and the only thing it "inspired" in me was my two months' notice.

Hope can effectively be inspired by a strategically sound long-term vision. (See Secret #47 for more on our visioning process.) For folks who have a hard time imagining anything more than a month down the road, shorter-term visions of the future can help. A vision could detail a better life for the individual, a healthier organization, or a more positive picture of the future for any community we care about. Even just talking regularly and confidently while we're on shift about how the end of the day, or the end of the week, or even just the completion of the task at hand is going to help make things better for all involved is a good thing to do. Feelings as well as facts matter—talking about how happy, or relieved, or excited, or energized we're likely to be when we get where we're going may be far more important than sales figures or salaries.

Even a couple of caring, seemingly casual, questions can make a big difference. As Adam Grant explains in *Give and Take*, "By asking people questions about their plans and intentions, we increase the likelihood that they actually act on these plans and intentions." (He does warn us that this "only works if you already feel good about the interaction that the question targets.") We do this already on all our training shifts, ending them with the "liked best/next time" tool that Maggie Bayless taught us 20 years ago. (The trainee and trainer each share what they liked best about that day's shift and then discuss what they're going to do differently next time.) Shane Lopez talks about using a technique with his young son that he calls "nexting": they regularly dialogue about what comes *next*. It systemically gets his son thinking positively about

323

the future. "Nexting" (just the term alone makes me smile) is also at the core of the weekly forecasting work that's so critical to our open-book management because it teaches people to look ahead to a better tomorrow.

Confidence counts, too. Oana Branzei writes about the importance of the leader acting "as if"—the more we calmly and confidently talk about the future as if it's going to happen, the more others around us can relax and tap their natural creative potential. Interestingly, this is the style we recommend when writing a vision: we use the present tense "as if" it's already happened ("It's 2026, and we're doing better than ever"), not the future tense ("In 2026, we will be doing better than ever"). The more we stay focused on positive outcomes, the higher our energy, and the better we do. As Ralph Waldo Emerson wrote over a century ago, "We are never tired as long as we can see far enough."

How we do it here: regular visioning work, weekly forecasting as part of our open-book management process, our energy recipe, the "liked best/next time" training technique, and our Bottom Line Change recipe.

2. HELP PEOPLE SEE HOW THEY MIGHT GET TO THAT FUTURE

What makes hope *happen* is the belief that there's a real and reasonable shot at successfully doing the work to get where we want to go. Positive psychologist Rick Snyder, the man who began researching hope many years ago, refers to it as "waypower," which, he says, "reflects the mental plans or roadmaps that guide hopeful thought." It is, he adds, a "capacity we can call on to find one or more effective ways to reach our goals." It helps us stay the course. As modern-day anarchist author Noam Chomsky writes, "Optimism is a strategy for making a better future. Because unless you believe that the future can be better, you are unlikely to step up and take responsibility for making it so."

Interestingly, there's a lot of talk on the workplace circuit of late about how positive thinking "doesn't really work." I guess backlash to everything is inev-

A Six-Pointed Hope Star

1. Help people see a better future.
2. Help people see how they might get to that future.
3. Show people how much they matter.
4. Help people see how much their work matters.
5. Help people see how small steps are the keys to success.
6. Show people how they fit into a larger whole.

itable. See *Rethinking Positive Thinking* by Gabriele Oettingen or *The Positive Power of Negative Thinking* by Julie Norem if you want to read more about it. Not my thing, but I don't want to be negative. Maybe you'll like them. Not surprisingly, there are data to back up the critical theories. The data show me that positive thinking must be attached to an action plan and hard work to be beneficial. Otherwise, positive thinking is just wishful thinking. Or as Shane Lopez says, "mental fast food." To be clear, I'm not saying we should assure people of total certainty in achieving their visions and goals. There is no safe, perfect path forward. I think that's the point. Healthy hope says we know obstacles will arise, we know we will make mistakes en route, but we still believe we're gonna get there anyway.

Showing people that there's more than one way to get where they want to go is an important element of healthy hope. Knowing there are multiple paths that we might travel builds resilience and helps people steer clear of despair when they encounter resistance or make a wrong turn. We can help people learn how, and why, not to put all their (hope) eggs in one imperfect basket. When we expect some setbacks on the way to success, when we know that there are other options to pursue when one particular path seems to be closing, or when we're confronted by resistance or confusion, we learn to take a deep breath, pause to appreciate, and get grounded before we keep moving.

Rick Snyder said that to learn hopefulness, children need relationships that are characterized by healthy boundaries in which they get consistency and support from their parents. I'd say the same thing is true at work—boundaries, consistency, and active support, set within a positive and encouraging context, are likely to build hope in your workplace.

The world at large seems fascinated by sexy young superstars in sports, music, or software design—"heroes" who have loads of "natural talent." The reality is that these examples rarely help. For a moment, they take your mind off your own issues, but later leave you feeling worse than ever. They fill your head with fantasy, but they don't lead to fulfillment. When we compare ourselves to the people society places at the very top, most of us will feel like failures. Any time we spend imagining that we'll wake up next Wednesday as a wealthy superstar is time that's not spent doing constructive work to move forward.

On the other hand, when younger, less experienced, or less hopeful, people hear how other folks have overcome comparable obstacles and made progress despite the disadvantages that they experienced, hope builds in positive, meaningful ways. People are more hopeful when they meet, see, hear, or read about men and women to whom *they* can relate. If you have a story like that and honestly most everyone does—tell it! When you share your struggles and recoveries from failure, people will be much more likely to get behind you and to build an effective action plan of their own.

Which, by the way, is why it's so important that Paul and I teach our new-staff orientation class. I want everyone at Zingerman's to understand that we (and pretty much everyone who's been here for a while) have been through many ups *and* downs over the years. Success comes not from "natural ability" but mostly from sticking with things and working collaboratively to get to a better place. I believe this understanding helps give people hope.

Remember that our own behavior as leaders has a large impact. When we come through on our commitments, other people's confidence builds as we demonstrate to them that good work done, day in and day out, moves us closer to the future we desire. When we consistently act in caring ways, when we take the time to go the extra mile, to encourage learning, to make the most of each moment for every member of our team, to appreciate others' actions, tiny sparks of hope are igniting. And, of course, our own level of hope is contagious in itself—the more we have, the more others will have as well.

How we do it here: our Training Compact and Training Passports, our annual planning work, following up on commitments we make, performance reviews, and guiding staff towards making their visions come true.

3. Show People How Much They Matter

One of the first responsibilities we have as hope-building leaders is to demonstrate daily to everyone in the organization how much we value them for who they are. Taking time to learn their story—where they're from, what their family life is like, what they want for their future, what sort of music they listen to, what they do when they're not at work—helps us honor them as the unique creative individuals they are. Asking how their significant other is, inquiring how their kids are doing in school, or discovering their favorite food (assuming we listen attentively to their answers) may seem minor, but it can have a major impact.

Hope levels go up every time that we as leaders actively envision each person we hire as a potentially great contributor. As Pulitzer Prize–winning Native American author N. Scott Momaday says, "We are what we imagine. Our very existence consists in our imagination of ourselves. Our best destiny is to imagine, at least, completely, who and what, and that we are. The greatest tragedy that can befall us is to go unimagined." Many people are viewed by their boss as a pain in the organizational ass, an interchangeable part hired to fill a long-term hole, or maybe as a moderately competent role player. I try to do the opposite—I imagine them as amazing. I want to help find the artist in everyone we hire: to inspire them to greatness and help them find their passion and their power. Everyone wants to matter. And I believe they do.

How we do it here: appreciations, Service Star awards, orientation classes, Bottom Line Change, open-book finance, open meetings, stewardship, Servant Leadership, 3 Steps to Giving Great Service, 5 Steps to Effectively Handling a Complaint, and authorizing everyone to do whatever they need to make things right for a guest.

Bringing a Bit of Sun to Yourself

One of the things I love about teaching is that it helps me learn as much as it helps those I'm teaching. The first time I taught the subject in this Secret to anyone in a formal setting, it dawned on me that we can apply the six points of the Hope Star to ourselves. Now that you're learning how to effectively build hope in others, you can do it for yourself as well. Just address each of the six points—remind yourself about how the future will be better; think through your action plan for getting there; honor yourself for the unique, creative human being you are; appreciate how much your work matters every day; acknowledge the little things (stuff others might dismiss as dreadful drudgery) that matter; and reconnect in some way with a part of the community you care about (family, coworkers, French club).

---

4. HELP PEOPLE SEE HOW MUCH THEIR WORK MATTERS

Once we've honored those we work with for *who they are*, the next point on the Hope Star is to show respect for *what they do*. Knowing that our efforts have an impact changes everything. When they don't, what's the point? Victor Frankl wrote, "Ever more people today have the means to live, but no meaning to live for." Whether it's in work, life, art, or anything else, *lack of purpose leads to problems.* As Sam Keen says, "We demand more from our work than subsistence. We want meaning and a sense that we are serving others and creating something of value." When there is a purpose (a "why") and meaning and value behind what we're doing, it's more likely that we're going to believe in the work and the organization. Hope and emotional resilience increase accordingly. As Friedrich Nietzsche wrote, "He who has a why to live for can bear almost any how."

This is not "happy talk" or "soft skills" hocus-pocus. In his book *Using the Power of Purpose*, Dean Tucker lists "purpose" or "meaning" as the first of four "innate drives" that all humans have. (The other three are autonomy, mastery, and acceptance.) He provides data to show that purpose-driven businesses (which are surely, according to positive psychologist Rick Snyder's studies, also high-hope businesses) simply do better: they show statistically higher profits, productivity, longevity, and loyalty.

In my ecological metaphor, purpose is air; without it, we can't breathe. Quite simply, we suffocate and die. In the case of our work, the death will be spiritual. As anarchist Rudolf Rocker wrote, "Organisation is, after all, only a means to an end. When it becomes an end in itself, it kills the spirit and the vital initiative of its members and sets up that domination by mediocrity which is the characteristic of all bureaucracies."

Purpose is woven into our culture at Zingerman's so completely that hardly anyone here talks about it. Like oxygen, it's easy to take it for granted when you have plenty of it all the time. It starts in our mission statement. These are the four questions mission statements are meant to answer: 1) What do we do? 2) Why are we doing it? 3) Who are we that's doing it? and 4) For whom are we doing it? The answer to "Why are we doing it?" is our purpose. Our purpose is in the last line of the mission:

> We share the Zingerman's Experience
> Selling food that makes you happy
> Giving service that makes you smile
> In passionate pursuit of our mission
> Showing love and care in all our actions
> To enrich as many lives as we possibly can.

It's also embedded in our Guiding Principles. As longtime customer, professor of public health, and author Vic Strecher says, "Core values are the pillars—the scaffolding—of a life purpose." It's also an integral element of writing an inspiring vision of the future. Simon Sinek writes, "*Directions* are instructions given to explain how. *Direction* is a vision offered to explain why." When you feel like your work matters, it makes all the difference—it's infinitely easier to push through the daily challenges that life presents, to go forward when we feel like stopping, when we know how much others are impacted by our efforts. Sinek points out, "People don't buy what you do, they buy why you do it." Hope builds. Hope brightens our days. And hope helps us keep going. .

How we do it here: sharing "code greens" (compliments), offering appreciations, giving extra mile awards, engaging in direct dialogue with guests, using open-book management, conducting staff surveys, committing to training, and using our Training Compact.

5. HELP PEOPLE SEE HOW SMALL STEPS ARE THE KEYS TO SUCCESS

Shane Lopez says, "Hope is created moment by moment through our deliberate choices." What most of the world perceives as a powerful bold stroke of genius is nearly always a composite of many thousands of little things. If you take anything that you do well and break it out into the individual action steps that are required to do it, I'll bet you'll find there are actually a dozen or two components to what you've casually considered as a single task.

Just cooking a simple pasta dish requires learning enough about pasta to know what to buy, getting the right water into the pot (and enough water—too little and the noodles can't absorb enough liquid), adding sufficient salt, using good sea salt (iodine in commercial salt makes for bitter results), stirring the pasta right after it goes into the boiling water so it doesn't stick (and the stirring needs to be gentle so as not to break the pasta into pieces), checking it regularly while cooking so that it doesn't overcook, getting it out of the water before it's overdone, dressing it appropriately, having warm bowls ready so it doesn't cool off too quickly—you're getting the idea, I'm sure. It's no big deal when you're used to doing all that—I've been doing it two or three times a week for 25 years so it seems simple to me. But if someone who's never done it thinks that they're going to just go out and put a world-class pasta course on the table without doing all those little things, well then they're engaged in magical thinking. And their initial elation will quickly end up with about as much substance as a bowl of overcooked mushy macaroni. The little things, the small steps, the seemingly unimportant decisions all matter.

I love what Frances Moore Lappé writes: "Hope, I learned, is more verb than noun. It is action." Hope isn't just a way to think about the world; it involves taking a deep breath and actively doing the little things that add up to (our version of) greatness. We want to help people who work here understand that success is most often attained through a long series of small actions. Even the most majestic cathedral is built one brick at a time. It's Natural Law #7 in action: successful businesses (and people) do all the little things that everyone else knows they should do but don't feel like doing. As Martin Seligman says, "The real leverage you have for achievement is more effort."

People who lose hope rarely understand this. Rather than beginning to take action, they wait endlessly for the right moment. The longer they wait, the more the sun sets on their horizon. In his preface to E. F. Schumacher's *Good Work,* his colleague George McRobie wrote, "Schumacher would invariably get asked by someone, often overwhelmed, in the audience, 'But what can I do?' His simple answer was 'Do three things, one after the other, one leading into the other. Inform yourself. Support others who are already at work. Initiate where you can and how you can. Start where you are. But start. Don't wait for the perfect situation.'"

Meaningful hope (not the magical, miraculous variety) is intrinsically intertwined with impact. As leaders, our job is to make sure that people realize that all the little things they do every day add up to big results. It's important for us as leaders to notice the small stuff—to see the beauty when a customer complaint is handled with grace, a bit of ad copy is skillfully crafted, the crust on a baguette is beautifully baked, or the *crema* atop an espresso is nearly perfect. It helps keep us going when the going gets tough. As Nelson Mandela writes, "Part of being optimistic is keeping one's head pointed towards the sun, one's feet moving forward."

How to go about communicating this? Personal stories that show how many small steps it took you to get to the level you're now at can help. Or it could be a comparable tale about someone else you know, or know of. The more the example is about either a task or an individual to whom the staff member can relate, the more meaningful it's likely to be. Like the story of Paul memorizing flash cards of cocktails when he first applied to be a bar manager years ago. Or how many test batches it takes to get a new bread at the Bakehouse before we're ready to roll it out. What I want to do is make clear that although the world judges success from awards and headlines, those are really only hood ornaments; they look good but matter very little. The real work is the daily practice, the study, the rehearsal, the mindful improvements in small but meaningful parts of our lives that get us to greatness.

I'm often asked what our biggest success or biggest failure has been. I usually answer with a non-answer. I just don't think about our work like that. I try to focus on the tiny details, both the successes and the stuff that we can do better. Because greatness in science, sports, or curing salami is attained not from one master stroke of genius, but from steady, mindful work to master the little things. Anyone you know who's a master in their field has spent countless hours practicing and putting effort into whatever it is they're now good at. They didn't give up when they failed at it the first few times. Reminding people that all those little things matter and add up to success, that they're modeling positive behaviors for others, and that they're benefitting customers, coworkers, and the community helps to make the point.

Slowly but surely, in this way we build hope, and hope enhances emotional resilience and attention to detail. It may be hard to see in the moment, but in the long run, it adds up to big things. As Howard Zinn writes,

> *Revolutionary change does not come as one cataclysmic moment (beware of such moments!) but as an endless succession of surprises, moving zig-zag towards a more decent society. We don't have to engage in grand, heroic actions to participate in the process of change. Small acts, when multiplied by millions of people, can transform the world. Even when we don't "win," there is fun and fulfillment in the fact that we have been involved, with other good people, in something worthwhile.*

How we do it here: acknowledge that small steps add up to big things; compliment people's contribution, no matter how small; use product-quality scoring; and perform constant quality checking.

6. Show People How They Fit into a Larger Whole

People's level of hope tends to increase when they connect—and feel connected—in a meaningful way to something greater than themselves. It's a group within which you feel grounded—at home. As Gary Snyder says, "To know the spirit of a place is to realize that you are a part of a part and that the whole is made of parts, each of which is whole. You start with the part you are whole in." The key, to me, is that the group be one of our own choosing—not something assigned by society. For this sixth point of the Hope Star to succeed, *each of us must be able to mindfully pick* "the whole" that we want to be part of. A big piece of what makes Zingerman's Community of Businesses work is that most folks here feel a part of something positive. For many, it's the first time in their lives that work has ever filled that bill.

It's interesting to note that there's a natural tension between Point 3 ("Show people how much they matter") and this sixth point. At either extreme, the two can be in conflict. The more tightly we connect to a particular group with which we identify, the higher the chances that our individuality will be lost. If we take it too far, we get into trouble the other way: We can lose ourselves in the mass of the larger entity. But if we keep too much distance, we can end up alone, isolated from others. Psychologist Marilynn Brewer calls it the principle of *optimal distinctiveness*: We look for ways to fit in *and* stand out. A popular way to achieve optimal distinctiveness is to join a unique group." Terry Tempest Williams tells the same tale more poetically: "Can you be an insider and an outsider at the same time?" she asks. Her answer is also my own: "I think this is where I live."

Hope, by the way, is contagious—if you want to increase your own, one of the quickest ways to do it is to join a group of hopeful people. You're likely to become more hopeful, essentially by emotional osmosis. Conversely, hanging out with cynics and critics can bring your hope down to dangerously low levels in a relatively short period of time. If you're already hopeful, it's almost painful to be in their presence. I suppose a cynic would say the same about getting stuck with a bunch of enthusiastic optimists.

One of the hardest things to deal with is that when we're discouraged and down, desperately needing connection the most and feeling our hope sinking, it can be most difficult to reach out to others in a meaningful way. Few of us are raised to connect constructively under pressure, to calmly express vulnerability and uncertainty during difficult periods in our lives. To the contrary: when we're feeling high stress, when failure is walking our way (or, harder still, has already arrived), when undesirable outcomes are upon us, most of us tend to withdraw, worry, or lash out in anger. I grew up pulling away under pressure, but I know plenty of people who revert to rage. Neither response is very productive.

Hope stays higher when we know that we're supported, encouraged, and cared for. Reaching out to others for help is one of the best ways I've found to juice up my level of hope. If you believe that people are generally good and want to assist (which I do), and that the most successful organizations and individuals are the most collaborative (as opposed to cutthroat and competitive), then connecting with your community (again, you get to pick what that community is) can help enormously. Sure sounds like good business to me!

How we do it here: Welcome to Zingerman's orientation class, Zingerman's 2020 vision, mission and guiding principles, other Zingerman's-wide classes, One + One work, open meetings, sending huddle and committee notes out to the whole organization via email, annual planning work, open-book management, business- and organization-wide "games."

Leading the Way Towards a Hopeful Culture

What if each of us in a leadership role simply made a point of doing each of those six things for the people we work with every single day? Within a few weeks, hope levels would certainly go up. By the end of a year, hope would be deeply embedded in the culture; the climate of the organization couldn't help but be significantly sunnier than it was before you started.

Although the benefits of that work would be enormous, it shouldn't be all that hard to do. For each person who works an eight-hour-or-so shift, we'd need to:

1. Make a positive statement about their future.

2. Share one thing they might do to help make that future (short or long term) happen.

3. Appreciate their positive, creative presence.

4. Recognize at least one thing they did to touch someone else's day in a meaningful way.

5. Compliment them on some small but significant piece of work they did that day.

6. Connect them with some other part of our work community. It could be as simple as introducing them to someone from another department or a vendor, or showing them something on the intranet.

I like it. I think I can do it, and I think I'll start teaching it. It seems tangible and tactically sound, and I feel like the results would be terrific. Regimens—for me, at least—really help. If you like visuals, it wouldn't be hard to make a simple scorecard for yourself. I'm betting money—actually, our business's health—on my belief that using the Hope Star will make a big difference.

Hope in the Classroom

Jeff Fleckenstein shares a similar approach that his progressive-school program in North Carolina is now using. "Our expectation is that *every* child reads, writes, thinks, and talks in *every* class, *every* day." It works. He adds: "When students are empowered to exercise their voices in the classroom and in the school, a transformation takes place, and the educational experience then becomes transformative." Swap out "student" for "employee" and "school" for "organization," and I'm betting the regimen would work just as well in the work world.

Sometimes It All Works, Part 1: Life in a Hope-Building Culture

As I've grown more conscious of hopeful constructs in the last couple of years, I've started to notice many small but meaningful positive actions that help to build hope.

One morning not long ago I was sitting Next Door at the Deli. It was early, about seven-thirty on a Monday morning, so it was relatively quiet. Out of the corner of my ear, I heard Emily Hiber, a long-time Deli supervisor, talking to Elliott Rose, a sandwich maker. He'd just walked over from the other building (where the sandwich line is located) to bring a couple of the premade, wrapped sandwiches that we sell in the café space for customers who are in a hurry and don't want to wait in line for something custom made. As he handed her the pile of peanut-butter-and-jelly (which are very good—Koeze peanut butter from Grand Rapids, strawberry jam from Eric Farrell here in town, and challah bread from the Bakehouse), Emily lit up.

"You know, I was watching this little girl eat one of these the other day, and it was amazing!" she said. Emily is generally low key, but she was enthusiastically telling the story. "She was so cute. She was eating it so seriously. By the end of her lunch, she had peanut butter all over her face. It was totally the way a peanut-butter-and-jelly sandwich should be eaten!" I could see Elliott engaging with Emily's excitement—he's a caring guy, and how could you not smile hearing a story like that about a sandwich that you or one of your colleagues had made?

About half an hour later, I heard Emily spreading hope yet again. She was chatting casually with a new staff member she didn't know while he got some coffee for himself. At the end she asked his name (it's Mo) and then introduced herself. She stayed engaged for an extra minute or two to explain to him the fairly complicated method by which Deli staffers can pay a particularly low price for their coffee. I realized as she was talking that for a new employee, the interaction was like a little bonanza of hope. Emily put all six points of the Hope Star into action in under two minutes. In that short window, she showed Mo:

1. There's a positive future for him here (good coffee on shift that he can buy at our cost. I'm confident it's not why he took the job, but it's a nice benefit).

2. There's a clear path he could go down to get the best coffee pricing possible (a seemingly small thing, but when you're starting a new job, so much can feel intimidating and confusing. Plus, I'd imagine, when you're starting a frontline food-service job, money is generally tight, so saving a few bucks a week makes a difference).

3. Even though he was new and in a different department, he mattered enough as a person for someone to stop and chat to try to help him.

4. The many sandwiches the crew crafts every day are truly appreciated!

5. Small, friendly interactions are important, and we put a lot of thought into the pricing of a cup of coffee.

6. He's working with a caring crew of coworkers.

In this spontaneous and unscripted way, Emily helped Mo envision a better future and see how he might get there, showed him that he mattered, affirmed that his work made a difference to others, reinforced that the little things have big impact, and identified him as part of a larger whole. Kudos to Emily for making that small but super significant moment of hope happen.

What's in a Name?

One of the most important ways we can help people feel honored and valued for being the unique and important individuals they are is simply to know, and regularly use, their names. It's something I've been working at for many years. I just never quite realized how much it mattered until I began this work to promote higher levels of hope.

I'm not even sure why I originally started being so mindful of people's names other than it just seemed like the right thing to do. Maybe it's because so many men and woman I've met have pronounced my name incorrectly, often despite the fact that I'd told them exactly how to say it two minutes previously. I'm not without empathy—it's not easy to articulate words we're not familiar with. But reflecting back now, in this context, it always seemed like I must not matter much if they couldn't even get my name right.

There's a lot more in a name than many of us might consider. Walt Whitman wrote, "Names are the turning point of who shall be master"—he altered his own from the more formal-sounding Walter Whitman, Jr. to be more aligned with his down-to-earth views of poetry and society. I don't know the name of every single one of the 700 people who work here, but I do know most. And I see it as my responsibility to learn the others. Uma Sickles, who hostesses at the Roadhouse, came up to me one night to tell me she appreciated my knowing her name on her second or third day of work. "It just made me feel like I was special," she said. "I felt like I really mattered." Here's the thing—*she does.*

John U. Bacon, a nationally known sports writer, local high school hockey coach, and University of Michigan instructor, tells how he does the same thing in his college classrooms. "I have big classes. Like 150 students. And I can tell you, if I don't know a student's name, they almost never talk in class. But as soon as I learn their name, they start to open up!" How does he learn them all? "When most professors ask who you are, they aren't actually listening. They're already thinking about the next thing they're going to say, so they never actually hear your name. I just try to pay close attention." Bacon's technique is to repeat their name back to them: "'Sameer, it's really nice to meet you!' Saying the name aloud truly helps. The next time I call on them, I use their name again, and after that, I've pretty much got it."

I have a similar technique. I try to introduce myself to every new staff member I see. Remember, I'm a shy introvert, so meeting people regularly requires me step well outside my comfort zone. Mostly, when I see someone new, I just want to hide and hope they don't see me. But instead, I try to make myself go up to them and do as John Bacon does—extend my hand and say, "Hi! My name is Ari." To honor them as an individual, if time permits (and it usually does), I'll ask them where they're from or where they used to work. Then, when I see them next, I say "Hi," and I *use their name* almost every single time I see them. The more thought I've given to this work on hope, the clearer it's become to me that this simple act helps people feel recognized and honored, with hope for their day and for their future. And for what it's worth, the energy and quality of their work improves in the process.

I've had a lot of people tell me that they worked in other jobs for years—often in much smaller businesses than ours—and the owner never learned their name. That's disheartening. It makes people feel like they're unimportant, as if they essentially don't exist. And guess how they act when they feel that way? Mostly as if they don't exist, or as if they're completely unempowered—they allow problems to unfold, customers to leave angry, and product-quality issues to pass without mention. Pronunciation is powerful—even attempting to use the right accents for a staff member with a name in a language we don't speak shows respect.

Many upper-level execs, people who lead large organizations, tell me that they "just aren't good with names." But it's hard to imagine that people who've learned finance, mastered complex production systems, and studied detailed methods of quality management can't remember the names of the people who work with them. Is it fair to ask our staff at Zingerman's to learn the details of literally hundreds of products but feel that we as leaders can't commit to remembering their names? On top of which, we now know (per Secrets #40 to 43) that if people have the belief that "they're terrible with names," it will likely be a self-fulfilling prophecy. Those who tell themselves they can't remember names won't.

On the other hand, believing that a) learning and using people's names matters and b) you're more than capable of learning them leads to you doing so. You start looking for techniques like John Bacon's to help you. Of late, realizing that there are only going to be more and more people's names for me to remember, I've started writing them down. I now keep a list in my journal, which allows for quick reference of people I've only recently met. And, of course, the more you work at learning names, the better you get at it.

In Native American tradition, names are an important element of tribute. Robin Wall Kimmerer, whom Maria Popova calls "a Thoreau of botany," and whose ancestry goes back to the Bear Clan of the Potawatomi (the same Native tribe, you might recall, with whom anarchist Jo Labadie lived as a youth), writes, "It is a sign of respect to call a being by its name, and a sign of disrespect to ignore it. Words and names are the ways we humans build relationships." Practice doesn't make perfect, but it does make permanent. There are any number of small but significant ways to put people's names to work.

I've become much more conscious of writing someone's name into an email instead of just saying, "Hi." I'm careful (though definitely not perfect) about referring to people who aren't present by their names, rather than just saying "he" or "she" or "the baker." It helps people feel seen and valued as important individuals. The more they feel like they matter, the more hope they're likely to have, and the better their work and their lives are likely to be.[26]

Sometimes It All Works, Part 2: Cacao and Hope in East Africa

I first met Shawn Askinosie about 15 years ago. He'd been a successful trial lawyer for the first half of his adult life. As he moved into his middle years, he decided he wanted to do something that would make more of a positive difference in the world. He chose chocolate—and beautifully so. His bars, made with beans he buys directly from growers in Honduras, Ecuador, the Philippines, and Tanzania, are truly exceptional. I eat them and frequently recommend them. If you like good chocolate but haven't yet had any of Shawn's, try it ASAP. It might just change what you believe about one of your favorite foods. It might also help build hope halfway around the world.

In fact, Shawn has spent most of his recent years spreading positive belief, hope, and the spirit of generosity among the cacao growers with whom he works. He's taught them what it takes to improve quality, he guarantees them higher prices for better beans, he visits them regularly, and he shares his passion and his belief in a positive future. He practices open-book finance all the way to the growers, so they can see how their work impacts Askinosie Chocolate as a company; when Askinosie makes money, the growers get a bonus. And he's brought the farmers finished chocolate made from their beans (almost unheard of 20 years ago) so that they can taste the difference their attention to detail makes.

Shawn's efforts in Tanzania have been particularly powerful. He's taught our visioning process to the cacao growers there, with great results. He's developed a program for them to export the local Kyela rice (which is delicious; we sell it, and I cook it at home regularly), through which they have begun to earn income to fund their school. Because the school had no books, he raised money to buy computers and then uploaded thousands of instructional YouTube videos onto them to help the students learn. All of these actions enhance the levels of hope in a setting where there was once very little.

In the summer of 2015, Shawn and his daughter Lawren decided to try teaching our visioning process to the 200 girls in the school. He wrote me at the end of July to ask for advice. I was stumped. I've taught visioning to thousands of business and nonprofit leaders, loads of Zingerman's folks, and even to hundreds of college students. But 200 schoolgirls in rural Tanzania? No experience whatsoever. I gave it a bit of thought and, not feeling sure that I was helping, sent him some questions he might use to focus the teaching.

> Can you remember a time you imagined a future, and it happened as you imagined it?
>
> What's something you're already really good at?
>
> What can you do to get a good result with anything you try doing?

Six days later I got this note from him:

> *I'll give you details later, but the vision session with the girls went well. Far beyond what I could have hoped. I used your questions. Brought two volunteers up to ask. The first girl—a 7th grader—said she had really never imagined anything in the future, and could I come back to her. I was so sad when I heard that I almost could not stand up. I kept it together, and when I got back to her, as she stood with me up front, she said she imagined "going to fetch some water," and that she did then go and do it. Her vision was to take a bath to feel clean. I almost lost it again but was able to turn what she said into an incredible lesson in vision for these very, very poor girls. We said, as you teach, that vision brings hope. A vision and a plan to lead build hope. She had both. I'll never forget this day. Ever.*

He was still blown away by the experience six weeks later. "I started with ambivalence," he said. "I didn't really think it was gonna do anything. But then when she said she couldn't come up with *anything* that she'd thought about in the future and then done, it really affected me emotionally."

"What was the feeling?" I asked.

"Almost like despair. My knees were weak. I thought I might just fall down. But I thought, 'I can't do that in front of these girls.'" *Despair,* by the way, is just another word for *hopelessness.* It's only Shawn's strength—a lifetime of positive belief, hard work, caring, and determined hope—that helped him stay on his feet.

Things started to turn around from there.

Another girl was able to talk about her vision for reading a book. And then she said she actually had read it. Upendo is her name. It means "love" in Swahili. By getting them talking, all the other girls were able to connect to that. And relate. That opened up a lot of discussion. They were asking me a bunch of questions, things that I know they would never have asked if we hadn't gotten this conversation going with the original questions. Like what my greatest challenges were, what happened to me in school, and what my vision was. They're people who are so radically different in their circumstances, but they were asking the same questions as we ask here. What happened in those couple hours went from me worrying it would have no effect whatsoever to me believing it was one of the best days of my life.

The girls left him inspired and hopeful. And he helped give them hope and inspiration as well.

Like Emily Hiber, Shawn unconsciously touched on all six points of the Hope Star:

1. He helped the girls see a much better future, both through the talk that day and through the work he's done with the cacao cooperative and the school.

2. He taught them techniques—learning, business, a focus on quality, and now visioning—that help them imagine how they might be able to get there.

3. In spending so much concentrated time with them, he's demonstrated that they matter.

4. By acknowledging examples such as bathing and reading books, he's demonstrated that the little things they do make a big difference.

5. He's helped them see how much their own efforts matter in making those visions—small as they seem—come to fruition.

6. By coming to Tanzania in the first place, bringing volunteers from Missouri to help in East Africa multiple times now, he's shown Tanzanians how they fit into a larger whole, one that would likely otherwise have been almost inconceivable.

Listening to Shawn tell the story—more than once now—I can feel the bright light pouring out of him. His work has helped many in the cacao-producing regions. And the energy, insight, and positive example he sets helps do the same for people like me (and you?) back here at home.

Anarchists and Hope

Hope, I've come to realize, is at the core of anarchist thinking. Anarchists such as Emma Goldman and Peter Kropotkin instilled hope in people on the periphery, people who'd previously had little of it. Through speeches, books, and pamphlets, they gave them the belief that, with social changes, there could be a better future. Attilio Bortolotti saw Goldman speak many times. "I went to hear her," he said, "and was flabbergasted by the way she spoke, with her energy, with the beauty of her sentences. When she spoke, with that fire in her, you forgot everything." Another young anarchist, Sarah Taback, says that Goldman was, "a good speaker, a powerful personality. She possessed you when she spoke." Historian Candace Falk writes that Goldman ended each speech "with a rousing articulation of a vision of hope for a better world within reach."

Kropotkin's style was quieter and gentler, but in his own way, he made the same hopeful impact. He was a wise soul who knew his subject inside and out and believed deeply in what he was doing. One listener remarked, "His evident sincerity and his kindness held the attention of his audience and gained its sympathy." Anarchism itself is based on the hopeful belief that there's a better future to be had. We just need to make some significant changes in the way we live and work to get it. As Leda Rafanelli wrote, "It is inside of us, in our thoughts; the hope that these things will materialize one day in the future."

Cantril's Ladder

I first learned about Cantril's Ladder by reading Shane Lopez's fine book *Making Hope Happen*. Although the model was new to me, it's a well-known survey and measurement methodology that's been around for over half a century.

Aside from the tool itself, I was intrigued by Hadley Cantril, the man who came up with it. Ivy League–educated in psychology, he became a national leader in statistical sampling work. He has a long and impressive CV, but what caught *my* eye was that he was the main author of *The Invasion from Mars*, published in 1940, an academic study of the panic caused by Orson Welles's *The War of the Worlds* radio show. In the late 1950s, he developed what he called a Self-Anchoring Striving Scale, which others started calling by the catchier name Cantril's Ladder. The survey work behind the test was originally designed to comparatively measure the hope levels of people in different countries around the world, but it's now employed regularly in all sorts of individual and group situations. It's easy to use and pretty darned interesting.[27]

Here's how Cantril's model works: Imagine a ladder with ten rungs. Where on the ladder (0 to 10, with 0 being horrible and 10 being fantastic) would you put your life as it currently is today? And then, using the same scale, in five years where do you believe your life will be? The Gallup Organization puts the two scores together to create its Well-Being Index. Before you read on, assess where you see yourself on the ladder.

People who have a high sense of well-being, who are thriving in their lives, are very hopeful. They show current scores of at least 7 and future scores of at least 8 (the score has to go up as you look ahead in order to demonstrate hopefulness).

Those who are "standing" on the middle rungs of the ladder are generally struggling to make it. They would be the ones with scores of 6 or 7, and also people who, for whatever reason (illness, age, loss), have a higher score today and a lower score for their future. They may not be super pessimistic, but neither are they particularly hopeful. Lower still are the folks who enter scores of 5 or 6; Gallup says of these people: "They are either struggling in the present, or expect to struggle in the future. They report more daily stress and worry about money than the 'thriving' respondents, and more than double the amount of sick days. They are more likely to smoke, and are less likely to eat healthy."

According to Gallup, those who score their present or their future at 4 or below are those who are really suffering. They're in dire straits today and, not shockingly, have little hope for a better tomorrow. People who are living at or below the poverty line are more likely to have low hope scores—the harder it is to pay the rent, the less confident you are that there will be cash for food next week, the lower your level of hope is likely to be.

The good news is that with enough nurturing, consistent care and support, regular infusions of positive energy, work towards raising entry-level pay rates, and actively using the Six-Pointed Hope Star, scores can be improved. Hope can be both taught and learned.

Cantril's Ladder and Zingerman's Energy Recipe

As I was reflecting on the beauty and simplicity of Cantril's construct, it dawned on me that the energy recipe we teach at Zingerman's does basically the same thing on an everyday basis. It's a beautiful parallel, one that made me realize the importance of our focus on energy management (thank you to Anese Cavanaugh for teaching it to us 10 years ago). If you aren't already familiar with it (see Secret #21, in *Part 2*, for more details), our recipe looks like this:

> **Step 1—Read It:** On a scale of 0 (where 0 is horrible) to 10 (which is super great, calm, Zenlike, and positive), where would you currently score your energy level?
>
> **Step 2—Vision It:** At the end of the shift (the day, interaction, meeting, or whatever else you're engaged in), where do you want your energy to be, and where do you believe your energy will be?
>
> **Step 3—Manage It:** Do what you need to get from where you are to where you want to be. Even if the number is the same— "I'm a 9 now and I want to stay there all day"—there's still energy management to do.
>
> **Step 4—Repeat It:** As soon as we arrive at the energy we envisioned, we need to be ready to repeat the whole thing; like it or not, customers, complications, and complaints are coming at us all day long. We need to respond effectively to get where we want to go.

And I now see that when we use the recipe well, hope levels here at Zingerman's and for each of us individually can't help but go up. By teaching energy management and making clear that each of us is responsible for choosing the quality of the energy we bring to work every day, we actively support and increase levels of hope. Looking at life through that lens, the energy recipe can do the following:

* Lay out a performance expectation that people who work here will have high energy.

- Teach staff how to put a hopeful frame on things every day.
- Show people that they're responsible for how they "show up."
- Give staff a simple, repeatable tool to use to be successful.
- Reinforce that people's energy is an important piece of our group success and will have a big impact on customers, coworkers, product quality, and, ultimately, the health of the entire organization.

Things *Not* to Do if We Want a Hopeful Organization

If you want to help people in your organization increase their levels of hopefulness, there are a few things to avoid. Unfortunately, they're all too common in the workplace. Each time we do them—intentionally or not—we reduce hope in everyone around us and, in turn, decrease people's effectiveness, hurt sales, lower the quality of customer service, and reduce group morale. All of which, of course, then adds to our burden as leaders. A meaningful investment in more effective self-management to eliminate the actions below can pay big dividends.

- Don't ignore *anyone* who works in the organization.
- Don't dismiss people's ideas out of hand.
- Don't dump your anxiety on others.
- Don't overemphasize what's wrong.
- Don't swing to the extremes. Over-the-top elation or descent into passive worry and active panic almost always end up causing problems.

Hope and Worry

Two years ago I would have told you that the opposite of hope is hope*less*ness. I would have been wrong. According to those who've studied this much more than I have, the opposite end of the hope spectrum is actually fear.

It's only when we have grounded hope for a more positive future that we also fear what we can lose. Rebecca Solnit says, "To hope is dangerous, and yet it is the opposite of fear, for to live is to risk." By contrast, people who are truly hopeless are generally also no longer afraid. Hopelessness is a "giving up," a surrender to circumstance, one that Gustav Landauer described in 1919, just before he was killed, when the short-lived German Revolution was being crushed. The end, he knew, was near: "There is nothing more to hope and nothing to fear; it is here."

As I worked to sketch the model that follows, I realized that I prefer the word *concern* rather than fear. The latter seems extreme, and I can't imagine any situation, other than an emergency one, where intense fear is helpful. The word *worry* doesn't work that well, either—it seems to me to be about dwelling on what could go wrong. (As Rick Snyder writes, "Instead of beginning to worry and ruminate about themselves, higher-hope people concentrate on the situation at hand to see what needs to be done.") Concern, though, seems more constructive; it's essentially about mindfully considering what might go wrong and then preparing properly for possible problems.

It makes sense. As hopeful as I am, I'm still concerned that:

- We need to always be careful to avoid complacency.
- We want to continually improve our customer service, our food quality, and the standards of our workplace, lest we lose focus and falter.
- I might be too dominant as a leader in the business, but I'm wary of being too laid back.
- We're not being bold enough in our work. But perhaps we're so far out there with what we're trying to do that we'll never get where we want to go.

There are other concerns, of course, but you get the idea.

The hope–fear format appears in my mind now as a continuum. People tend to pair the two that are equidistant from the center. In other words, those who get instantly elated also bounce all the way back over to panic mode. More in the center of the spectrum are those with well-founded, healthy hope, who also have a grounded sense of reasonable concern.

As you imagine the model, starting at the far left and moving towards the center, picture the following:

Magical Unachievable Elation: "This is great! We've got it made! Our problems are over forever!"

Full-On Fantasy: "Maybe tomorrow angels will come pick me up and fly me to a bank in Bratislava, which will tell me I've inherited all the money we need for the business."

Repeating the Present but Hoping for a Different Future: "If I work just a little harder at this than I have the last ten times, we can do it." All the while, you ignore a decade's worth of data that show otherwise.

Wishful Thinking: "Maybe sales will really turn around next week. After a year of being in decline, something good is due to happen."

In the center, where I'd prefer to spend most of my emotional time, there is:

Grounded Hope: "I'm pretty confident that if we review our plans one more time, then get going and do what we've agreed to do, we'll start seeing sales increasing sometime in the next six months."

Reasonable Concern: "I'm concerned that a lot of the staff aren't fully grasping the financial risk we're headed into, and as a result aren't making the best day-to-day decisions."

Continuing on to . . .

Wistful Memories of the Past: "Things in the old days were so wonderful. We'll never get there again."

Persistent Worry: "I just can't stop the wheels from turning in my mind. If we run out of cash, there are so many problems that will come up! How will we pay the bills? What if we have to lay people off? How will I tell my family?"

Intense Fear: "I'm so anxious I can barely function. All I can think about is what's going wrong and how bad it's going to be!"

Outright Panic: "We need to get out now. I'm going to put the business on the market ASAP and sell it before we lose everything!" Or, in the case of Cantril's book about *The War of the Worlds*, "We better get the heck out of here within the hour before the Martians make off with us!"

It seems clear that the more we expend our energy living on the extreme ends of the continuum, the harder it gets for us to function effectively. On the other hand, the healthy place for us to be most of the time is somewhere in the center, in the vicinity of grounded hope and reasonable concern. We will all, of course, shift from hope to concern with great frequency; it's a normal part of keeping our perspectives in balance, a bit like standing in the center of a teeter-totter trying to keep each end from hitting the ground.

Still, some people have a hard time staying present in the moment. Instead, they obsess about the past or worry about the future as a way to avoid taking action in the present. As Rollo May writes, "Living in hope for the future is said to be the usual escape of unsophisticated people, so living in the past may be the common escape of sophisticated persons." However, the present is the place from which we're most likely to take positive, proactive steps to address any issues at hand and move towards our vision of the future.

Teaching this sort of healthy hope/concern construct to our staff can only be a positive thing. Giving people some context in which they can frame their anxiety and their ambition in a productive way is a valuable practice. Mindful, focused action towards an agreed-upon future is an effective way to overcome anxiety.

And hopelessness? *It's off the chart altogether.* When we've lost hope, life is almost unbearable. The sun has been extinguished. Imagine going through the day with no affect, no mood, no drive, no nothing. I've never been there, and I hope never to be. From those I've talked to who are clinically depressed, it's devastating. People do come back, but it takes a lot of long, hard work and a good support system. As Voltairine de Cleyre writes, "[The] resolution to hope in the face of hopelessness, that song on the edge of the abyss, marks a courage even greater than that of the idealist." Staying centered, grounded, and hopeful in a healthy and realistic way is the place from which I want to experience the world.

A Hope Chest of Ways to Build for the Future

The tradition of hope chests dates back many centuries. Young girls gradually accumulated useful goods that they'd want for the day that they, hopefully, got married. Without getting into all the stereotyping and gender issues at play, what follows is a conceptual list of stuff we can do to stock our "organizational hope chest," to build optimism and cultural strength that will contribute to a better tomorrow for all involved.

1. Teach Hope

Since people are rarely *consciously* working at building hope, bringing its import out in the open can only help. Teach it in classes, on shift, in formal training, and in casual interaction. Actively sharing the Six-Pointed Hope Star with everyone in the organization is nearly guaranteed to increase levels of hope.

2. Actively and Consistently Provide Hope by Recognizing the Little Things

While upper-level leaders and business owners often have high patience for long-term gratification, most of the people we hire are far more focused on the short term. By showing that we notice the little things, we give hope. I'm talking about small, specific appreciations for work done well: "Beautiful foam on that cappuccino today!" or "Love the way you got the break room cleaned up!" As long as our comments are sincere, only good things will come from the compliments.

3. Ask Questions That Cultivate Hope

Simply by building the positive use of the word *hope* into your regular dialogue, you will make a difference. Hopeful inquiry helps. Here are some questions you can ask.

- What do you hope for the future?
- What helps you feel like you matter?
- What's the best compliment you've gotten lately?
- What gets you most energized?
- What are your hopes for today?
- What are you hoping will happen tomorrow?
- Are you hopeful about our new hire? About the new product? About your career?
- What are you looking forward to?
- What's your vision for the future?

4. Watch for Moments of Hope and Celebrate Them When You Can

When you see an opportunity to help someone take a big step forward, to go where they never imagined they might go, seize it. Every time you help a staff member to higher levels of engagement, it's a win for the organization, for the individual, and for society at large. When you can, acknowledge the ways in which people around you express hope.

5. Share Success Stories of Hope in Action

Many people learn well from stories, whether the stories are tales of people who've succeeded in the organization way beyond expectations, or about interactions with customers and how we may have contributed to their lives. The Chicago-based nonprofit program City Years systematically encourages people to share "ripples of hope," actions they took that encouraged or built hope in others. Given that we've had such great success with using "appreciations" at the end of all our meetings, I wonder if we might do well to start each morning with "ripples."

6. Expect Hope

For years now, we've been teaching everyone at Zingerman's about the importance of asking for help. But now I believe it's time for us to also start asking for hope! If we're doing our part by building a positive organization, it's totally okay—actually appropriate—for us to ask the folks that work here to be hopeful, to think positive thoughts about the future, to have hope about the impact that their work will have and their ability to make a positive difference. See, if hope is a two-way street, and if it's our job as leaders to provide it, nurture it, cultivate it, and care about it, then the staff's side of all that is to actually have hope. An important part of working here is to bring hopeful, optimistic energy to work every day.

7. Practice Being Hopeful

Practice makes permanent. To quote from author Barbara Kingsolver, "The very least you can do in your life is to figure out what you hope for. And the most you can do is live inside that hope. Not admire it from a distance but live right in it, under its roof." Mindfulness matters. When you realize you've slipped towards the hopeless end of the emotional spectrum, see what you can do to get back under hope's happier "roof."

8. Help Reduce Hopelessness

Kingsolver's image is poignant. A roof, of course, provides shelter—in this case, from the dark hopelessness that's laid waste to so much of the work world. If you've never seen the face of someone who'd lost hope light up when they start to feel it reappear, it's an amazing experience. The six points of the Hope Star are all active ways to make this happen.

Hopeless Shelters

We talk a lot about the issue of homelessness these days. And for good reason: it's a big problem. Certainly, folks who give of themselves to work with people in need know how much of a role hope—or the lack thereof—plays in the psychology of helping the homeless. Writing this essay is making me think that we might also pay attention to the problem of hopelessness. Maybe, I start to wonder, we should have something akin to "hopeless shelters" for people in need to find succor and get back on track towards future success.

After all, if we can reinstill reasonable levels of hope in those who have lost it, nearly everything in their lives is likely to get better. When people have hope, when they get those glimmers that there's more to our presence on the planet than "just trying to get by 'til I get to the next thing," the mental and emotional lights go on. To quote from Robert Greenleaf's classic book, *Servant Leadership*, "[H]ope . . . is absolutely essential to both sanity and the wholeness of life."

9. Hire the Hopeful (But Don't Forget We Can Still Help Those Without Much Hope)

You can, I've realized, actually interview for hope—as Ralph Waldo Emerson encouraged us, "judge a man's wisdom by his hope." Asking questions that call into the open people's sense of hope, or the lack thereof, will help us do a more effective job of getting more positive people into the organization. According to Shane Lopez, the best indicator of future performance is not just past performance but a combination of "history and hope." Cantril's Ladder or Rick Snyder's Adult Hope Trait Scale test would both be interesting tools to use when interviewing.

What else can you ask to assess hope levels? One thing that comes to mind is the question that Tom Walter and the crew at Tasty Catering in Chicago ask applicants: "How many days a week would you wake up happy if you worked here?" Correlating to Cantril's Ladder, it seems like you'd want to get people who expect to wake up happy at least five days a week. And of course, the next question would be: "How many days a week do you wake up happy *now*?"

Beyond that, I come back to the idea of interviewing for the elements of the Hope Star. For example, you could ask the following:

- What can you tell me about the future you've envisioned?
- What are some ways that you've made a positive future happen?
- How do you feel about yourself?
- How have you mattered in past jobs?
- Tell me about how your work contributed to the success of the company and to the customer's experience in past jobs. Can you share a few stories of small things you've done that have had a big impact?
- In what communities do you feel most at home and why?

If you try it, let me know how it goes, and I'll do the same.

Within a positive, hopeful culture, there are ways we can help someone who's been beaten down by society and left relatively hopeless. Hiring too many hopeless folks at one time is likely to bring down the organization's energy, but ignoring them altogether turns us away from the chance we have to help those in need. By bringing in one or two employees with low hope, we stand a strong chance of helping to change their lives for the better.

Putting Hope to Work

I've long been inspired by Meg Noodin's passion for her native Ojibwe language. Though historically it's only a spoken language, Meg has worked hard to help keep it alive, both by writing it down and by getting people to use it in everyday conversation. I've learned a few words, and so too have many of the staff at the Roadhouse, where she's a regular customer. I think our ability to speak some Ojibwe words, minimal though it may be, has given her a bit more hope that the language will stay alive and vibrant. We're just a small speck in the world, but hey, if hostesses at a popular restaurant know how to greet Ojibwe guests by saying "*Aanii*" (meaning "Hello!"), then hope rises a bit.

"It's worth noting," Meg told me, "that we have no exact equivalent word for 'hope' in Ojibwe. The word we use is *bagosenim*, which is a verb, meaning 'to wish for someone.' And a word close to it, *bagdinimaa*, means 'to be set free.' So 'hope' in our language is something that one does into the future, directed towards or with another, and it sings of the sound of freedom." I like the idea of hope setting us free. Hope illuminates a positive future and shines its warmth and light and stimulates growth and health.

Perhaps best of all, hope is not a zero-sum game. Each bit of grounded hope helps encourage more of the same in those who come into contact with it. By building hope here at Zingerman's, I know that we're slowly sending positive ripples out into the work world. We impact those who work here, their friends and families, our community, and other organizations around the country. Just as it's hard to go back to eating bad food when you've experienced full flavor, living without hope once you've had it is almost unimaginable. To quote the poet Vaclav Havel, former president of the Czech Republic, "I can hardly imagine living without hope. As for the future of the world, there is a colorful spectrum of possibilities, from the worst to the best. What will happen, I do not know. Hope forces me to believe that those better alternatives will prevail, and above all it forces me to do something to make them happen."

I'll close with a quote from Peggy Kornegger, an anarchist from a small town in Illinois, who writes, "I do believe that what we all need, what we absolutely require, in order to continue struggling . . . is HOPE, that is, a vision of the future so beautiful and so powerful that it pulls us steadily forward. . . . If we abandon hope . . . then we have already lost."

Putting the Hope Star into Practice

The more mindfully we practice implementing the six elements of the Hope Star, the more effectively we master it. On the chart on the next page (which you can easily recreate for repeated use), run through the first blank column and list one action you've taken in the last week that exemplifies the element given. Then go to the next column and try listing one thing you're going to do in the coming week. If you want to take the practice further, fill out the six boxes with an action step you'll take for one particular person you work with. My belief is that we could do all six for nearly every person that we're working with on shift in exactly the same time we're working now. It doesn't require working harder or longer, just being more mindful.

Remember, the work we do with this has big benefits: each time we increase the hope of someone in our organization, the effectiveness of their work goes up, they feel better, and the business does better. For me, the work isn't exhausting at all—it's energy producing. I'm inspired and given hope by the growth and learning of those around me.

Hope-Star Point	Past Examples	Will Do
1. Help people see a better future.		
2. Help people see how they might get to that future.		
3. Show people how much they matter.		
4. Help people see how much their work matters.		
5. Help people see how small steps are the keys to success.		
6. Show people how they fit into a larger whole.		

NOTES FROM THE FRONT PORCH

Mary Lemmer, Founder,
Iorio's Gelato & Foodscape, Ann Arbor, Michigan

Whether you recognize it or not, both you and Paul have been instrumental in my personal and professional growth over the past eight years. Bear with me, it's a long thank-you letter. Could've been longer, as there is a lot I could say about the impact you've made on my life.

For the past several years I have been living mostly in San Francisco, with scattered visits to Michigan to visit family or for business. Whenever I visit Ann Arbor I go on a Zingerman's binge, visiting as many of the businesses as possible as often as possible, as Zingerman's has been a significant part of my life since the first time I met Paul at the Net Impact event where he spoke. Certainly your products made an impact in my life (I ran from my dorms to the Deli to buy loaves of whole-wheat farm bread to take back to my dorm for myself so I didn't have to endure the thin, weak white bread the cafeterias served, and for my neighbors in my hall). But even more so, the Zingerman's experience and your leadership positively influenced me in ways I continue to realize as I grow older and gain more life and professional experience. Experiencing Zingerman's as a customer, an employee, and forever an evergreen supporter has shaped me into my own unique leader.

At Zingerman's I learned more than I learned at business school. I've seen companies of many shapes and sizes struggle to create as impactful and strong a community and experience. After graduating from U of M, I spent a few years working at RPM Ventures, where I had the opportunity to be part of several high-growth, highly valued companies. Most of them haven't figured it out. I've been part of multibillion-dollar companies that still don't know how to treat their team members, build a positive culture, and keep people staying year after year.

Something I've recognized as my former employees get older and move on to other ventures, is that I love hearing from them, about what they're working on now and what they remember most about their experience working with me. Similarly, I'd like to share with you some of my fondest Zingerman's memories and experiences . . .

- Paul's talk to the Net Impact chapter. It was this moment that I was initially drawn to Zingerman's and was the initial inspiration to be an avid customer and work with Zingerman's in any way I could.
- Ari's leadership workshop, where we created a positive change for Zingerman's and went through the Bottom Line Change process. To this day I cite *The Corporate Mystic* and reference my experiences in that seminar.
- Selling tickets to raise money for Food Gatherers, demonstrating how businesses can do good for the community in big ways (and developing sales skills I have used in so many capacities).
- The partners' meetings where I learned about how real businesses hold leadership meetings (versus just reading about it in textbooks), understanding how decisions are made, how communication happens, which metrics to track, and so forth. These meetings helped me set my own business meeting agendas in a way that was aligned with our values, inclusive, and helpful for the business.
- Making movies to share at the Zingerman's annual meeting. I remember filming at the Deli in the middle of the night, riding a tricycle through the Deli, wearing a Donald Duck hat, to put together our Zingerman's version of *Dr. Strangelove*.

Over the past year working with Steve and the team at Zingerman's Coffee, and serving Zingerman's coffee in my gelato shops, has been a lovely reminder of the spirit of Zingerman's that has infiltrated my life since first experiencing it. I feel incredibly blessed to have been and continue to be a part of a community of people. Thank you for making all of this possible and for continuing to positively impact my life!

Dana Laidlaw has been working the counter at Zingerman's Bakeshop for the last couple years. She consistently offers me great insights into life, work, and how we might do what we do in more caring and effective ways. She hasn't had the easiest circumstances in life, so having—or not having—hope is not just an intellectual activity for her. She was kind enough to give some thought to the issue of hope in the workplace. What follows are ways she consciously works to be sure she stays positive and lives hopefully every day.

Dana Laidlaw, Counterperson, Zingerman's Bakeshop

Let go of the bad energy. Every day—ideally every customer—is a brand-new game. You can't let the bad stuff accumulate. My best days at work, when I'm in the "Zone," the day seems to flow. I'm alert, handling problems as they arise with confidence, and my confidence accumulates as I make a succession of good choices and spread good energy. On my worst days, it's the opposite. I do something stupid early on, which makes me mad at myself, flusters me, erodes my confidence, and sets me up to be hard on myself each subsequent time I mess up or lose focus. Hopefulness means not hanging on to the bad energy and assuming that the rest of the day can still go right.

Get your energy up. It's really hard to be hopeful if you are tired, sick, in pain, or otherwise not in peak form, so try to be healthy for yourself and the people around you.

Stick with stuff. Perseverance and hopefulness go hand in hand. Sometimes persevering when everything seems to be going wrong is a form of hopefulness—you are assuming that if you can just make it through the next minute/hour/day/year, things are bound to get better. Other times the hopefulness is pulling the cart—you are willing to make hard choices or decisions that benefit long-term planning because you're hopeful that the future will be better.

I'm a hopeless geek, but I keep thinking of Frodo and *The Lord of the Rings*. J. R. R. Tolkien had a lot to say about hopefulness, and Frodo and Samwise were the embodiment of hopefulness, as were all the good guys. Tolkien coined a term, "Eucatastrophe." Basically, it was the opposite of a catastrophe. Instead of things suddenly going all wrong, it was the situation where things suddenly go all right.

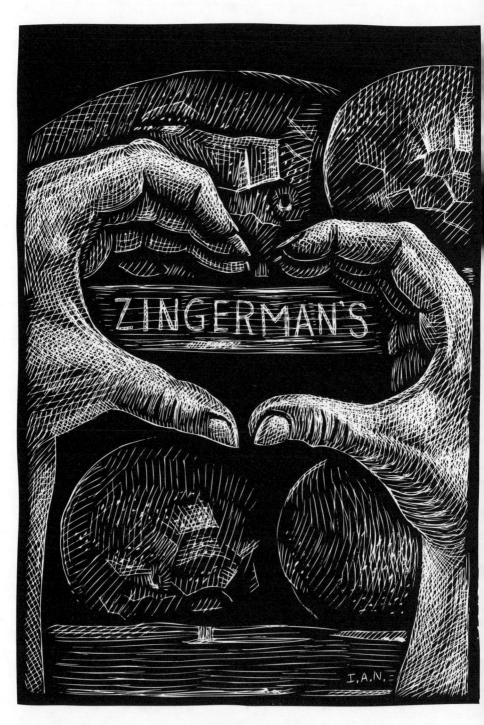

selling food that makes you happy; giving service that makes you smile

The
Spirit of
Generosity

---

22 Techniques to Weave Generosity into Your
Work and Build Your Bottom Line by Doing It

Like its philosophical fellows, belief and hope, the spirit of generosity is an essential element in developing a sustainable organization. My organic metaphor, as you know, positions beliefs as the root system of our lives and hope as the sun. The spirit of generosity I've come to view as water; when we don't water our soil regularly, our culture dries up, and even the hardiest of plants will have a hard time surviving. Rainwater softens the soil and brings out the bright colors that are waiting to emerge in a drought. Think about the morning after a rainstorm, the sun coming up in the newly clear air, and the colors of the plants made more vibrant by the previous evening's moisture. Generosity in an organization can do the same thing: it manifests in the smiles, bright eyes, and renewed energy of the people who are part of it.

Permaculturist Toby Hemenway says: "Without water, there is no life." Without generosity, there will be no work. At least not good work. Without the spirit of generosity, there would be no sustainable businesses, no well-being, no rewarding lives. We at Zingerman's would have no organizational success story to share. And speaking of stories, if Rebecca Solnit is right that starting a story is dipping a cup in the ocean, then without generosity, there would be no story to start. The cup would come up empty every time.

The spirit of generosity is rarely the lead topic in strategic-planning sessions. When it does come up, most of the world perceives it as a desirable but all-too-often-undependable source of sustenance. Icing on the community's cake; gilding the business lily; hosting a charity ball; donations and fundraisers, sharing something of what we have made with those unfortunates who have less. It's generally delegated out to the marketing department or the person in charge of charitable giving. But to me, that sort of generosity is too little and, more often than not, too late. It's reactive. The spirit of generosity, as it follows here, means so much more. It's not about writing another check to your local charity; it's a way of life. It's worth watching. The spirit of generosity—or the lack of it—might well be one of the best indicators of organizational health we have.

U of M medical student Rana Kabeer explains it nicely in this note he sent me following a ZingTrain session on visioning that we ran for him and his fellow first-year med students (all 250 of them) at Cornman Farms. I share it not to toot our own horn, but rather because Rana says it so well. "When people think of successful companies giving back to the community," he writes, *maybe they think of building a new rec center, a community garden, or something along those lines. But for you all to take aspiring doctors based in your hometown and teach us from your playbook personally, in hopes that we get inspired to be greater leaders in turn—that's huge and remarkable. I get the sense that you truly care about us, Ann Arbor, and the potential that we at University of Michigan Medical School have for changing the world, as you also continue to do. Thank you for hosting us, and committing yourselves to help form the leadership that your own community generates, so we may impact others around the world someday.*

Designing a Generous Ecosystem

Toby Hemenway posits that we can mindfully build gardens to almost, if not totally, ensure that water will always be present. "With a conscious ecological design," he writes, "water becomes an integral part of a landscape, designed *in*, not added *on*." It's the same in business with the spirit of generosity. The framework that follows is a way to take Hemenway's admonition to heart, ensuring that we infuse generosity into every aspect of our own existences, all our relationships, *and* our organizational ecosystem.

In the garden, good design dictates that the soil should retain sufficient water at all times. You may not see it, but it's there, below the surface, keeping the earth supple and open, holding nutrients so that they can later be pulled up by the plants that grow in it. The image works well. A rich, moist soil in the garden would correlate with a gentle, healthy, rich company culture. Water retention, Hemenway explains, is enhanced as well by a deep root system. The deeper and broader the roots grow, the more the soil is aerated, the more water the soil can hold. Plug in "beliefs" for "roots," "culture" for "soil"," and "generosity" for "water," and you're sitting pretty. To take it all further, in a natural ecosystem the plants will pull water out of the soil and share it, generously, with the air, which later returns it in kind in the form of rain. If the plants are akin to the people who work here and the products we produce, then perhaps the clouds are customers and the rain is our clients generously choosing to share their hard-earned cash with us.

The cycle is positive and sustainable. In Hemenway's language, our organizational garden becomes nearly 100 percent "self-watering"—water should rarely have to be piped in, except in extreme situations. When we effectively do the work that's outlined below, we can create the same sustainable cycle with our organizations through the spirit of generosity. We build a culture in which generosity moves out from us to our community, which in turn gives us back support with which we can generously reenergize our own work. You may not be able to measure it, and most people won't even consciously notice it, but it's there all the way along. There's more than enough generosity going around to keep all our energy high and still give a good bit to our community.

Kropotkin and the Collaborative Community

In the fall of 1902, three months or so after Rocco Disderide opened his grocery in Ann Arbor, Peter Kropotkin, an avowed anarchist and former Russian prince living in exile in London, published *Mutual Aid*. One of a dozen books and many more pamphlets that the prolific scientist put out in his lifetime, *Mutual Aid* went on to become a classic in the anarchist community and a topic of great study in much of the scientific world as well.

Although Kropotkin, like all anarchists, was the focus of a great deal of critical attention, he was generally considered to be the exception to the typically negative stereotypes held by mainstream society. He certainly didn't come across as one of the evil-eyed demons being portrayed in the press. With his flowing white beard and a fringe of white hair, kind eyes behind wire-rimmed glasses, and a gentle manner appreciated by all he came across, he was more like your grandfather than someone who wanted to bring down the government. Even those who criticized Kropotkin usually did so apologetically. His vibrational energy, we would say at Zingerman's, was grounded, giving, appealing. Definitely generous.

Praise came from people in nearly every walk of life. Oscar Wilde said that Kropotkin had "one of the most perfect lives I have come across." Anarchist printer Joseph Ishill observed, "All the works of Kropotkin . . . are permeated with his faith in mankind." Danish writer Georg Brandes said, "He is the man of whose friendship I am [most] proud. I know no man . . . whose love of mankind is up to the standard of his. In good society, no matter where, one only needs to say 'Peter Kropotkin,' and regardless of political or social convictions, everybody will arise, moved." In 1899, the political magazine *The Outlook* called Kropotkin "a great idealist" and "a generous spirit."

Late-20th-century scientist Stephen Jay Gould described him this way:

> *Kropotkin was a genial man, almost saintly according to some, who promoted a vision of small communities setting their own standards by consensus for the benefit of all, thereby eliminating the need for most*

functions of a central government. . . . Kropotkin is one of the brightest
stars in the firmament of famous revolutionists. In him is seen the ideal
rebel exemplified.

Given all that, it's easy for me to imagine joining Kropotkin in the back corner
of the Next Door at the Deli where I like to sit, sharing an inspiring cup of
coffee and a couple of interesting anarchist insights.

Mutual Aid came out when he was just a few weeks shy of turning 60,
and it was the culmination of many years of study, research, and writing. It
was Kropotkin's controversial and extensive response to British biologist
Thomas Huxley's popular book *Man's Place in Nature*. Huxley's extrapolation
on Darwin's idea of natural selection was that each living being was essentially
in conflict with every other to get hold of its share of limited resources. The
theory, as Huxley saw it, was that only the "fittest of these individuals would
survive." This idea remains as one of the underlying beliefs in mainstream cap-
italist theory: that the world runs on constant and aggressive competition. The
theory is basically, as athletes have come to say in the seventh game of a playoff
series, "win or go home."

Kropotkin wasn't having any of it. A diligent and passionate scientist
who traveled extensively to study nature, animals, and humans alike (interspersed with some severe stretches serving terms in Russian and French prisons), Kropotkin found both the original trigger, and much of the proof, for
mutual aid in his extensive studies of the wildlife of Siberia. *Mutual Aid* takes
us through all the elements of the animal world, including humans, to demonstrate how mutual aid works. Ashley Montagu, the great humanist and teacher,
called it "one of the world's great books."

Kropotkin's ideas are, like Huxley's work, built on Darwin's theory of survival of the fittest. But he comes to an entirely different conclusion. "I failed to
find, although I was eagerly looking for it, that bitter struggle for the means of
existence among animals belonging to the same species, which was considered
by most Darwinists (though not always by Darwin himself) as the dominant
characteristic of the struggle for life, and the main factor of evolution." Yes,
Kropotkin concurs, the fittest survive. *But the fittest, he found, are not the most*
competitive, but rather those that are the most collaborative.

Kropotkin explains,

> *If we . . . ask Nature: "who are the fittest: those who are continually at*
> *war with each other, or those who support one another?" we at once see*
> *that those animals which acquire habits of mutual aid are undoubtedly*

363

the fittest. They have more chances to survive, and they attain, in their respective classes, the highest development of intelligence and bodily organization.

Collaboration and care, Kropotkin argues, aren't just desirable by-products of success, or something given by those who "have" out of sympathy for those who "have not"—they are sound social strategies to attaining success. This, he writes, is well in line with human nature. "The mutual-aid tendency in man has so remote an origin, and is so deeply interwoven with all the past evolution of the human race, that it has been maintained by mankind up to the present time, notwithstanding all vicissitudes of history." Mutual aid is most important, and most commonly practiced, when people are under pressure. Hence, he says, we need, "to find out the best ways of combining the wants of the individual with those of co-operation for the welfare of the species." Just as in nature there is no life without water, Kropotkin says, "without self-respect, without sympathy and mutual aid, human kind must perish." [28]

Kropotkin's beliefs are well aligned with ours at Zingerman's; I've long felt that those who succeed in our organization are the most collaborative, and also the most self-reflective. We're constantly—both culturally and systemically—looking for win-win-win solutions in which all involved come out ahead. Whether it's visioning, open-book management, handling difficult customer complaints, or coming to consensus in the Partners' Group, we've worked hard to share wisdom and resources and to work towards outcomes from which everyone can benefit. In our 30-plus years in business, we've made hardly more than a handful of enemies (I think). And we have a whole lot of friends and supporters. Educator and business coach Bob Wright smilingly told us, "You guys are probably the most pacifist organization I've ever worked with." Sure, there are struggles, problems, frustrations. We're not utopia. But working collaboratively, we believe, we can figure out almost anything. It's a belief Paul planted in my head not long after we opened the Deli, and I stand by it now more strongly than ever. Mutual aid works well.

Mutual Aid for the Modern Era

One hundred eleven years after Kropotkin's book was first published, Adam Grant, a former U of M grad student, long-time Zingerman's customer, and management and psychology professor at the Wharton School of Business, came out with a book that in its own well-presented, statistically detailed,

21st-century way argues much the same thing. It's called *Give and Take: A Revolutionary Approach to Success*. While it's likely that Kropotkin never made it to Ann Arbor, Adam spent four years here in school, during which time he visited Zingerman's regularly. He's remained a Mail Order customer ever since. (He once told me the Deli was his "favorite place to buy gifts!" Coming from someone who teaches about generosity for a living, that's an important endorsement!)

Adam is about half the age Kropotkin was when *Mutual Aid* first made its way into print, but he's well on his way to attaining comparable acclaim and appreciation. Unlike Kropotkin, he has a shaved head and no beard, and I don't think he'd consider himself anything remotely related to an anarchist (though I do notice now that the subtitle to his book calls for a "*revolutionary* approach to success"). But surface-level differences aside, the two men have a shared passion for study and social science and a seemingly omnipresent positive energy that makes others want to spend time with them. And they both hold the positive belief that generosity and collaboration are likely to lead to greatness.

I'm one of about 200,000 people who have bought a copy of *Give and Take* (actually I've bought eight, keeping one for myself and giving the others as gifts). While you may not want to work through all of Kropotkin's lengthy scientific tome, I would *highly recommend* giving Grant's work a read. Or two—it's loaded with impactful insights. Although Adam didn't study wildlife in the woods of northern Michigan, he has devoted a great deal of energy to studying people. What he found, to my read, is very similar to what Kropotkin concluded a century earlier. The people who are the most generous of spirit and helpful to those around them—assuming they manage their generosity effectively and are genuinely generous—turn out to be successful.

Give and Take is filled with statistics, stories, examples, and anecdotes that explain how one can make generosity an effective and energy-building part of one's life. "Every time we interact with another person at work," Adam explains, "we have a choice to make: do we try to claim as much value as we can, or contribute value without worrying about what we receive in return?" He believes "when giving starts to occur, it becomes the norm, and people carry it forward in interactions with other people. . . . When the groups included one consistent giver, the other members contributed more. The presence of a single giver was enough to establish a norm of giving." Sounds like the kind of organization we're trying to create at Zingerman's.

Given the anarchist belief that "the means must be congruent with our desired ends," it's good to see that Adam Grant gets it right. He is as generous and positive in his daily presence and his scientific work as the people he writes about. Rick Price, a retired professor and formerly head of the organizational-studies program at U of M, says, "Adam has the rarest of gifts among scientists—the ability to inspire and at the same time remain rigorous about the evidence. He offers us a powerful message about how best to do our work and conduct our lives." The *New York Times* reported, "Helpfulness is Grant's credo. He is the colleague who is always nominating another for an award or taking the time to offer a thoughtful critique or writing a lengthy letter of recommendation for a student—something he does approximately 100 times a year. His largess extends to people he doesn't even know."

We both, it seems, give out our email addresses regularly and correspond with far more people than most would think possible. (Kropotkin did the same in his own era—sans email—meeting with and helping many, many people.) "For Grant," the *Times* says, "helping is not the enemy of productivity, a time-sapping diversion from the actual work at hand; it is the mother lode, the motivator that spurs increased productivity and creativity." I couldn't agree more. Both he and I will tell you the same thing: We gain as much energy as we give—*and very often a lot more*. It's essentially what Paul taught me back when we first opened the Deli: the more you give, the better things are going to go.

Just before I sat down to work on this essay, I traded notes with Vince Gabrielle, who owns a gym in Berkeley Heights, New Jersey. We've never met in person, but he got my email address from *Part 3* of the series (yes, I publish my direct email in the books). Night before last, he wrote me to say

> *I have been reading your book* Managing Ourselves, *and I just wanted to thank you for writing it. You have an outstanding way of writing where it makes it so easy to understand and take action. I wrote my personal vision today, and I set a time to go back and add more. I truly appreciate the care and time you put into this exercise; it helped me tremendously. Thank you for your contribution to the entrepreneurial world; you are truly making a difference. Vince.*

How could I not be energized by that message?

I wrote back relatively quickly, thanking him and offering any help I could give on his vision work. I think I surprised him. "Thanks so much for responding," he wrote. "You are the real deal." He sent me his draft vision, and within a day, I sent him back notes; it doesn't take long to do, and clearly, I've worked on a lot more visions than he has. An hour later I got back another note:

> *This is awesome! Really helps! Thank you! I just finished the section on Edgar Schein's four stages of organizational growth (Secret #34). It's crazy how many times I read about myself in that chapter. I have been looking for something like this after reading* The E-Myth *and* Ready, Fire, Aim, *but the way you explained Schein's model was outstanding and much clearer. The basketball-team scenario was clutch. Thanks so much for your help, Ari; definitely would love to make it out there and see it all come together. I am making it a 2016 goal! Have a great night, Ari. Thanks for making me better.*

It'd been a long day—not bad at all, mostly good, but definitely long. And yet, after reading Vince's notes I was totally charged up to dive into writing. It was, for me, a great, completely down-to-earth, real-life example of Kropotkin's *Mutual Aid* and Grant's *Give and Take* in action. Start the story where you like, but here's what I know: Vince is feeling better than ever about himself and his business; I'm feeling more confident in my writing; he now feels better about his vision and his future; I feel better about this book. It could well be that the energy I gleaned from the exchange has upped the effectiveness of my writing here, which I hope will help you and thousands of others to lead better lives. Maybe you'll go on to be a bit more effectively generous this week, which in turn will benefit others in your life and community. One of you might even live in Berkeley Heights, New Jersey, and you'll now go out and join Gabrielle Fitness to work out and tell Vince that you read this story. Which will build his confidence, while your commitment to working out will enhance every other element of your life.

How would the story have gone elsewhere? For people like me and Adam Grant, it's the norm. The issue, in many ways, comes back to beliefs. Most folks I've met seem to believe that email is a nightmare, a burden, the biggest bane of their existence. They sigh and their spirits sag at the mere mention of it. Had I been worried about being bothered and interrupted more than I already am, I probably wouldn't have put my email address in the book. While Vince still could benefit from the reading, his learning would stop there. I wouldn't gain from his insight and experience; my energy might flag a bit after a long day at work; this essay might be a bit less effective; you might learn less. If you live in Berkeley Heights, you'd probably miss out on the best local gym training program you could find, and your life would be a bit less loving for it. Vince might never come out to a ZingTrain seminar, so he'd lose learning, and we'd lose sales. And he'd miss the chance to go to the Deli and draw energy from Rocco Disderide's generous building.

Beliefs and Mutual Aid in Action

If we *believe* that collaboration, abundance, and assistance are going to benefit everyone, we will *regularly* and routinely act in ways that demonstrate generosity. Which will infuse a positive feeling in those we're sharing with, who will surely pick up on our energy. They will then be much more likely to act generously themselves. And, later, the odds are high that we will in some way benefit, directly or indirectly, from their generosity, which will reinforce our original upbeat beliefs and encourage us to be even more generous of spirit in the future.

On the other hand, a belief in scarcity, constant competition, and impending shortages will create the inverse cycle. We act selfishly, protecting our own interests (or perhaps those of our "tribe"), in the belief that there's not enough to go around. From that action, others form the belief that they too better hold tight to what they have, and they begin to eye some of ours. They start acting more aggressively, focusing on their own gain, even when it's overtly at the expense of others. Which just reinforces our original belief. *Give and Take* shares a quote from Cornell economist Robert Frank: "The fear of exploitation by takers is so pervasive . . . that by encouraging us to expect the worst in others it brings out the worst in us: dreading the role of the chump, we are often loath to heed our nobler instincts."

Remember: We can change our beliefs. I've consciously worked to choose generosity. I believe that living the spirit of generosity is the ultimate and easiest contribution we can make to a sustainable and fulfilling life, both organizationally and personally, for ourselves and for everyone around us. Whether you first heard the concept from your parents, your professor, your priest, Peter Kropotkin, or Adam Grant, the idea is the same: the more we give and share, freely and generously, the better everyone around us, and we ourselves, will do. The spirit of generosity, lived in a healthy way, is at the basis of the entire idea of synergy; the more we give to others in our "system," the more we, unwittingly, will ultimately get back for ourselves. Everyone wins.

The spirit of generosity also makes solid business sense. And cents. As Paul said in our commencement address at the University of Michigan in May of 2015, "Generosity follows the natural law of the harvest—you *reap* more than you *sow*. When you *give*, you get *more* back." Recommending generosity as a way to improve profitability may sound counterintuitive in the context of the modern business world. The return on a spiritual investment is intangible and hard to pin down. The spirit of generosity, after all, is not something that shows up on a financial statement. It won't get you a tax credit, nor does it get your logo listed in an ad in the *New York Times* the way sponsorship for some big and well-deserving nonprofit might. No one sends you a formal "request for spirit" (though maybe we should set things up that way and start supplementing RFPs with RFSes in the business community). In a standard workplace setting, the spirit of generosity is rarely even acknowledged.

There's a whole host of people—like my partner Paul—to whom this approach seems to come naturally. I don't think I'm one of them. I have to move mindfully through the world each day in order to be good at it. But maybe, because I have to be so mindful to make generosity happen, I'm able to teach it more effectively to those who are interested. The good news is that all it takes is understanding, commitment, effort, and a series of small but meaningful actions. We can *all* do it, starting today. Making the spirit of generosity a key element of your emotional existence and your daily actions takes nothing other than mindfulness and effort. As E. F. Schumacher says, "T.L.C. is the only fertilizer that really works. Don't inquire where you can buy it—you can make it yourself."

In the long run, I believe the spirit of generosity will end up making you more money seven or eight times out of ten. You can disbelieve me if you like. But if you're up for a bit of an adventure, stick with me for a page or three before you move on. I truly believe that putting the spirit of generosity to work in your life and in your organization will get you back far, far more than the expense of the time it will take to read the 10,000 or so words that follow. As Robert Henri writes, "Those who wish to give, love to give, discover the pleasure of giving. Those who give are tremendously strong."

They're also very loving. I was talking one morning with Eli Genisio, a five-year-old regular customer. I was in the early stages of working on the book you now hold in your hands. Although I hadn't thought about it at the time, even taking the time to speak regularly with five-year-old customers is a good example of the spirit of generosity in action. I took two minutes to talk to a cute kid who loves our food; I got back a brilliant response that will resonate with everyone who reads it.

"Eli," I asked, "what should I put in my next book?"

"How about you and me?" he responded, smiling. Then, looking to the left at his big sister, whom he clearly loves (as do I), he restated his plan more generously. "You and Maia and me," he corrected himself.

"What should I say about you?" I asked.

"That I love you," he responded shyly, his long eyelashes closing down on his cheeks.

It was said with such sincerity, so spontaneously, that my heart melted.

22 Techniques for Weaving Generosity Into Your Workplace

What follows is a list of tips and tools that have helped me make the spirit of generosity more than just a pleasant piece of marketing material. Any or all of these (plus other ways you've already developed on your own) will create a culture that like Hemenway's ecological garden is richly self-sustaining. Each technique on its own will help; the more of them you use, though, the more each will build on itself to create a holistic and wholly generous organization. It's my 22-point plan to help put Kropotkin's and Grant's great work into action to lead a more generous existence.

1. Begin with an Abundance Mentality

I'm convinced that the spirit of generosity works best when it's based on a *belief in plenitude*, not an old-school fear of penury. It is, as my partner Paul posits, "a belief that there's plenty to go around," not the fear of getting the short end of the organizational (or social) stick. Instead of the old "the more you get, the less I'll have" (which has long been a core belief in the business world), the idea here is the opposite: "the more I give to you, the more there'll be for me later, and, actually, for everyone else as well." In this sense, I stand by my theory that when we live in harmony with the Natural Laws of Business, good things are likely to happen for everyone involved. As E. F. Schumacher says, "There is incredible generosity in the potentialities of Nature. We only have to discover how to utilize them."

Where does this concept come into play? Hopefully, everywhere. Many places are what you might expect—profit sharing, community giving, employee ownership. Others are a bit more nuanced, less frequently found in the world. For instance, in our 2009 vision, we developed the idea of having managing partners who would own part of each new business we opened. And although we owned more than they did, we chose to make partner-level decisions by consensus. Today the entire organization is run by consensus of the 24 partners. Last year we added three Staff Partners—frontline folks who are considered part of the Partners' Group—in the belief that their perspectives will enhance the effectiveness of our dialogue and our decisions.

Beginning with an abundance mentality leads directly to our choice to focus on our own improvement at Zingerman's and almost never on that more negative angle of "beating the competition." We work hard to make the "market" happy, but we're not all that worried about others eating into our share of it. We've always believed that if we do our work well, deliver great experiences, constantly improve, take healthy risks, try new things, and make a great place to work that serves amazing food and delivers incredible customer service, we stand a good shot at succeeding. It's a focus on healthy sharing, rather than just increasing our own share.

Kropotkin said over a century ago:

> "Don't compete!—competition is always injurious to the species, and you have plenty of resources to avoid it!" [Mutual aid] is the tendency of nature, not always realized in full, but always present. That is the watchword which comes to us from the bush, the forest, the river, the ocean. "Therefore combine—practise mutual aid! That is the surest means for giving to each and to all the greatest safety, the best guarantee of existence and progress, bodily, intellectual, and moral." That is what Nature teaches us; and that is what all those animals which have attained the highest position in their respective classes have done. That is also what man—the most primitive man—has been doing; and that is why man has reached the position upon which we stand now. . . .

In essence, this is all about synergy, something we specifically wrote into our 2009 vision. Anthropologist Ruth Benedict first defined the concept when she was studying Native American societies. She found that the tribes that defined success in terms of generosity, rather than accumulation of wealth, consistently did the best. High social status in those settings went to those who gave support to others. In synergistic environments of that sort, no one is left out or left behind; everyone willing to help is encouraged. It's almost impossible not to contribute. If I do something for another, I inadvertently help them, and vice versa.

2. When in Doubt, Give It Out

I have a far better shot at changing old habits and mastering new methods when I create catchy little ways to keep my mind from drifting too far from what I want it to be doing. Our 10–4 Rule ("smile and make eye contact at 10 feet, greet the guest at 4 feet") has been hugely helpful to us in our service work. So, too, the idea of Three and Out has helped me enormously in effectively managing my moods and my energy (see page 129). With the spirit of generosity, what's proven most productive has been the catchphrase "When in doubt, give it out."

I've been using it over the last few years with good results. Here's how it works: Let's say I have the thought to do something nice for someone. I'm not talking about anything extreme. I'm referring to the sort of small stuff that (I think) everyone ponders. Should I tip $24 or $25? Treat that regular customer to dinner tonight? Give a book to Bill as a gift? Send a thank-you note to Nancy? Buy a small token of appreciation for Antonio? Take flowers home for Tammie? When I begin to have second thoughts on things like that, I now just call up this little saying: "When in doubt, give it out." In which case, despite whatever critical voices may arise to tell me why I don't "need" to do it, *I've been trying to make myself just go ahead and take action anyway.* It pushes me to default almost daily to small acts of generosity that I would probably otherwise have let pass.

Yesterday I had coffee with a very nice guy in Ann Arbor. I don't know him well, but he asked to get together, so I did. Although he's high achieving and is extremely intelligent, he's in a difficult job, newly charged with running a large organization in which, let's say, the spirit of generosity might not be the order of the day. Anyway, we had a nice chat, and I headed to my car to go back to work. As I was walking, I had the thought that he could benefit from some of the stuff in the Guide to Good Leading series. Now, he's hardly indigent, so my second thought was something along the lines of, "Well, I don't need to give away books to a guy who makes more money than I do." But then I caught myself—*when in doubt, give it out.* For all the prestige of his position, the man could use a hand. So I pulled copies of *Parts 1, 2,* and *3* from my car, signed them, and dropped them off as a gift. A small thing, but maybe it'll make a big difference.

The Gift of Learning

During the economic recession in 2009, ZingTrain was probably hit harder than any of our businesses. When times are tough, training is one of the first things companies tend to cut. (Here we actually increased our training focus and budget, but that's another story.) About three weeks before one of our regularly scheduled seminars, signups were so low that we started to talk about cancelling it. We almost never call one off, but doing a whole two-day seminar with two instructors teaching four people just doesn't make sense. Needless to say, folks at ZingTrain felt down, already stressed about low sales, and now they were facing cancellation of one of their key events.

But Maggie Bayless, ZingTrain's managing partner, used the spirit of generosity to turn the entire experience around for everyone. Her suggestion? Rather than cancel, she said, "Let's open the seminar to a whole series of local nonprofits. They all need help with organizational development, too. And when the economy is bad, they're strapped for funds and can't afford training at a time when the demands on their services are probably higher than ever." So that's what we did. ZingTrain offered the seminar seats to nonprofit leaders at no charge. We did the two days of training. The nonprofit folks were all excited to go back and use what they'd learned. And the giving energized everyone at ZingTrain as well. In dark days, when we understandably feel the inclination to restrict our resources, sometimes the spirit of generosity can lighten the load and, in fact, brighten everything around us.

3. UNDERSTAND HOW HOARDING HURTS EVERYONE

If "sharing is caring," then the opposite is probably true as well. I'll always remember hearing the jazz cornetist, playwright, and actor Olu Dara speak at the Southern Foodways Alliance Symposium six or seven years ago. He said about 16 super insightful things in his half-hour talk, one of which was, "Racism doesn't scare me. It's harmful to the person who has it, not so much to the person at whom it's directed." The statement still gives me pause all these years later. Taking his wisdom one step out, the same applies to the spirit of generosity. If the opposite of the spirit of generosity is greed, then putting Olu Dara's powerful insight into play, I'll say that "Hoarding mostly hurts the hoarder." The good news is that we have the power to turn things in the right direction. Don't hoard—give help! Cut a coworker some slack. Help someone in need succeed. Be generous with energy, information, and ideas. Share credit. Be kind. Everyone wins when we do!

Say Thank You a Lot

Adam Grant's popular research on how givers are often more successful than takers suggests that givers are more grateful when they receive something from others at whatever point. If you're grateful, that makes people want to continue giving to you and to others. You're making everyone a little bit more of a giver every time you express gratitude. Gratitude takes people out of narrow thinking (which often involves only near-term gains) and into bigger-picture thinking (which often involves long-term gains).

In the workplace, we can be grateful for everything, even criticism. You can be grateful for the value of other people and their experiences and think of their criticism as an attempt by them to help you get better. If you're a manager, thanking people for just doing their job makes sense. After all, these people are spending their days contributing to the growth of the organization and helping everyone reach their goals. There's a special power in handwritten thank-you notes. Both ZingTrain and Zingerman's Mail Order use these regularly, and they get positive comments on the cards they send all the time. Send some this week and see what happens.

4. GIVE GREAT SERVICE AND LIVE THE SPIRIT

New beliefs we know will grow more quickly in the nutrient-rich soil of a positive culture. The spirit of generosity will always get moving more effectively in an organization that already has a strong service ethic. At Zingerman's, if we simply live our long-standing commitment to great service, then we're getting this spirit of generosity stuff into play right from the get-go. The third of our 3

Steps to Giving Great Service is what we refer to as "going the extra mile." This means doing something for the customer that they didn't ask us to do. Usually, it's small stuff that makes our guests leave their interaction with us feeling some form of "Wow! That was so nice of them to do that." And because we believe and teach that our steps to great service apply not just to our work with customers, but also to how we deal with our coworkers and our community, the spirit of generosity is actively in play all day long.

There are so many great stories of how this happens here. The way the Bakehouse found out about a customer's love for our coffee and had a special pot of it ready when she came to one of our baking classes. The way that Mara at ZingTrain went outside when it started to snow during an evening program and cleaned off the windows of every car parked out front. People here who've made the decision in the moment to send food over to the hospital with customers who are in town to visit a sick relative. Our Mail Order crew shipping a box of Bakehouse treats to a hurricane victim who called to cancel her order because money was suddenly tight. It's all small stuff, but it adds up to make a big difference.

Going the extra mile regularly starts another positive, sustainable cycle. As Adam Grant explains, "[O]n days that people helped others out of a sense of enjoyment and purpose, they experienced significant gains in energy." It's one reason, I realized, why our staff at Zingerman's can maintain their positive energy despite long hours in a high-intensity service industry. "If you spend the money on yourself, your happiness doesn't change," Grant reports. "But if you spend the money on others, you actually report becoming significantly happier." It's a beautiful thing to be part of—the more effectively we help others through our good service work (see *Zingerman's Guide to Giving Great Service* for much more on the subject), the better our guests' experiences will be, and the better our sales. And much to the shock of the everyday work world where customers are all too often considered an intrusion and an impediment, our service work—combined with the good energy we get back from guests—turns out to be fueling our own energy as service providers.

In fact, when we act generously for an extended period of time, it actually begins to change our brains. The more we think of ourselves as service providers in all facets of our lives, the more likely we are to carry generosity into everything else we do. Better service takes more work, but simultaneously, what we do generally reduces stress and buttresses our spirits against burnout. When people know their work is helping, we all benefit.

Bob and Judith Wright's Seven Rules of Effective Engagement

This list gives me a good framework for staying centered and generous in any challenging conversation. Like all the recipes we use here at Zingerman's, it's eminently practical in any group activity.

1. Accentuate the positive

2. Minimize the negative

3. No one gets more than 50 percent of the blame

4. We each get 100 percent of the responsibility

5. Express and agree with the truth, always

6. Fight for, not against

7. Assume good will

---

5. LEAD WITH GENEROSITY

To make service and giving into a way of organizational life, *the spirit of generosity has to start at the top.* The "higher" we go in the organization or in society, the more incumbent it is on us to give at ever-greater levels. Natural Law #5 says that if we want our staff to give great service to our guests, then we as leaders need to do the same for our staff first. By serving others, we serve ourselves as well—when I give generously and freely it renews my own spirit. Instead of the old model in which almost everyone is exhausted, Servant Leadership creates a sustainable cycle. Thinking back to Secrets #44 and 45, business writer Margaret Wheatley says, "[W]hen we serve others, we gain more hope. We gain energy."

If we want to lead with generosity (which we do), then the work of "Managing by Pouring Water" (Secret #25) takes on a whole new, deeper meaning. The leader pouring water means that we're leading with generosity. And it also makes me look anew at the lovely little Marge Piercy poem "To Be of Use," which closes with the lines: "The pitcher cries for water to carry / and a person for work that is real."

Open Your Mind and Your Meetings

By giving weight to staff perspectives in decision making, we help employees develop, and we put Kropotkin's mutual aid and Grant's "give and take" into action in real life. So everyone comes out on top.

6. ACT IN KINDNESS

"Kindness is free." That's what I said to a schoolroom full of 1st and 2nd graders a few years ago. It just sort of came out of my mouth. I think I was probably more nervous talking to those 100 or so little kids than I am presenting to five times as many upper-level business executives. I don't have kids myself, and I had a hard time figuring out what a shy CEO was supposed to tell a bunch of six- and seven-year-olds. I ended up just sharing my personal story and encouraging them to be themselves, to learn a lot, and work hard at whatever they want to do. I shared my belief that it's totally normal to want to be mad at your sister or your parents or the teacher or some kid on the playground. And then, at the end, I added in what just happened to pop into my head: "The best way to make the world a better place is just to be kind to everyone around you—kindness is free."

As Lao-Tzu told it, "Kindness in words creates confidence. Kindness in thinking creates profoundness. Kindness in giving creates love." You can put kindness to work anywhere you want: tip big, smile broadly, open doors, let someone get in front of you in line, stop cutting off every driver who radiates rudeness to "show them who's boss." Simply sending a few more thank-you notes, assisting seniors in crossing the street, helping parents with strollers to squeeze through doorways—it works wonders.

While I was writing the original draft of this essay a few years ago, we sent a scone and a cup of coffee out to a driver waiting by his limo while the VIPs he was transporting were inside the Deli ordering sandwiches. I don't share the story because we're so special; only because it's a real-life example of an incredibly easy, inexpensive way to put generosity into action. I mean, why not do something nice for the guy? As you might imagine, he was pretty excited. And so was Elin Walter, who worked at the Deli then and brought it out to him. When I mentioned something to Elin about taking the driver something as a gift, she reacted as if it were the most normal thing in the world and got on it immediately. Generosity is well ensconced in our culture.

A Not-So-Random Sidebar

The phrase "Practice random kindness and senseless acts of beauty" was coined by a woman named Anne Herbert, who wrote it on a restaurant placemat in 1982, the very same year we opened the Deli.

While all this theory may be inspiring, the important thing is to *do it*. Kindness is free, and it's actually almost covert—no need to announce a new program or engage anyone else. You could try it right now. Put the book down (you probably need a break anyway) and find someone, in person, online, or on the phone, someone you know or someone you've never met, and do something small but meaningful for them. If you want to do this at an advanced level, find a person with whom you share tension in your relationship (we all have them) and do something nice for them right now. I guarantee that you'll get good results.

I've been using this principle of late when I teach time management. To show how much good can come from a single, often wasted minute, I ask people to take out their phones and text someone they know to thank them. The only guideline is that the thank you has to be sincere. And specific. Within minutes, responses start coming back. There is an occasional "Why are you telling me that? Are you ok?" (Remember—when you pour water onto really dry soil, at first, it just runs right over the top.) But 99 percent of the responses are positive, some tear-provokingly so.

If you want to make this exercise into an advanced version of the Three and Out Rule, you can do three generous acts in a row. If you want to completely seal the spiritual deal, and you're driven by data, Adam Grant's research seems to show that doing *five generous acts one day a week* will get you the best emotional energy boost (better than doing one a day). Apparently, this practice builds a reservoir of good will and positive energy that stays with us for the rest of the week.

7. HAVE EMPATHY AND COMPASSION

Empathy and compassion, like an abundance mentality and a commitment to great service, are at the core of the spirit of generosity. Rather than investing energy in blaming, accusing, antagonizing, or out-arguing, empathy can help us put our energies into working to understand what others around us are going through. We don't have to love the way they've handled a situation, nor must we agree with everything they've done—effective leaders can retain their own views while still being empathic during a difficult interaction. I like what Rollo May wrote: "[M]oral courage has its source in . . . one's own sensitivity with suffering of one's fellow human beings."

Empathy, to me, means I take time to get a sense of what others are struggling with. It means being in "beginner's mind," to remember as best I can how it felt to be a new dishwasher who didn't know anyone else in the building and had no clue how to do his job. To relate back to what it feels like to be a new manager who's suddenly bombarded with 80 million conflicting demands while trying to stay in balance personally at the same time. To be patient with a new customer who's just come in and is confused. To remember, every time I pass a person living on the street, that I am not all that far removed from living on the street myself. To put myself in the place of anyone who's first coming to the idea of better managing themselves. When I slip, I try to be mindful that, even after decades of working at it and writing all these books, it's still hard for me to effectively manage my emotions and interpersonal interactions.

To be clear, effective empathy and compassion are *never* paternalistic. It's not about pity. As Buddhist teacher and author Pema Chodron puts it, "[C]ompassion is a relationship between equals." I believe this is a critical construct. Caring parenting is great at home, but it's completely different from healthy peer-to-peer interaction at work. This is about understanding and constructive support, not sympathy. In the end, I remember Robert Greenleaf's admonition: "The servant [leader] always accepts and empathizes, never rejects." This approach always helps. At the least, it slows me down enough to keep me from getting myself into trouble; at best, it does help me to see things differently and do the "right thing" to arrive at a win-win solution.

3 Stages of Empathy

This is a simple and practical way to work empathy into your day-to-day life, distilled down to three easy-to-remember options. When confronted with conflict, in his book *Work as a Spiritual Practice*, Lewis Richmond recommends:

1. Try not to make things worse. At the least, let's not fan the flames or provoke things any further.

2. "Stand sideways," minimizing the odds of conflict happening by acting your best and hoping that your "adversary" will follow suit.

3. Get on the same side of the problem as the other person. The more it's "us against the issue," the calmer and more collaborative everyone will probably be.

An anecdote told by the composer John Cage might relate to the idea of "standing sideways." Like Cage's famous composition 4'33", it means starting with silence, saying nothing in the face of negative beliefs. Don't argue. Just breathe and be quiet. Cage told the story of getting into a cab in New York City where the driver went off on one bad thing after another. Cage decided to keep his mouth shut rather than respond. He said the driver eventually ran out of emotional gas. By the time Cage got out of the car, the driver was saying rather nice things about the world around him. Empathy for others has enhanced my own life—it's expanded my emotional horizons and softened my edges, to both my own advantage and that of others. As Osho says, "As you become more sensitive, life becomes bigger."

8. Be Generous with Your Time

It may seem crazy, but I try to find a way to make time for almost anyone who asks. I'm not saying everyone else needs to do the same—time is limited, I don't have kids, and I like to work. What I am saying, though, is that if there's a way to fit in a few minutes for someone who wants to talk to you, it's a generous thing to do. And in my experience, it's usually a worthwhile investment as well. I can think of probably half a dozen great folks working here whose now long-standing presence in our organization started by me agreeing to a meeting, at their request, knowing nothing about them. The story of Vince Gabrielle, the New Jersey gym owner, is just one of many. A number of other folks here do this as well, including Paul, who gives freely and generously of his time (and resources). Just this week I talked to probably four or five students to help them with business-related projects. The last one took maybe 20 minutes. At the end of the meeting, the student thanked me like three times for talking to him. And while it's not why I did it, I'm confident he's going to go out and sing our praises to 40 or 50 other people in his class.

Making time is not always easy to do. There are days when I'm tired, wiped out emotionally, and not in the mood to deal with one more person who wants to talk. And I'm also careful to protect my time for journaling, running, some solitude, and cooking dinner with my girlfriend, Tammie Gilfoyle. But talking to people, listening to what they're thinking and feeling, *is my job*. I try to breathe deeply and then delve into the well of energy inside me. Thanks to the help of the highly supportive, positively energized people around me, it's a deep one. It's what makes it possible for me to pull off this time sharing more often than not. Seriously, whatever I give will almost always come back to us organizationally—frequently in ways I'd never have imagined or expected— many times over. I hear ideas; I can build hope in smart people; I can contribute something small, but meaningful, back to them; I learn what's going on in the marketplace and in people's minds; customer relationships are nurtured; and the community is better for it.

Here's a simple story from a few years ago. A frustrated frontline staff member asked me to meet with her. In most organizations, I doubt she'd even ask. And if she did, I don't know what would happen. I'm the CEO, and she works about 30 hours a week on the counter making coffee drinks. But following this guideline, I went ahead and met with her the next morning. All I can say is that I'm glad I talked to her. With help from others, we found out fairly quickly that, rather than being some complainer who just wanted to vent about something silly, she had good reason to be frustrated—we'd actually been unwittingly messing something up with her pay rate for months. As is so common, she was starting to slide into ascribing bad intentions, beginning to think ill of our organization, assuming the worst about her managers. No one—not me, not her, not anyone really—can do their best when they feel like they're getting the short end of the stick. But to her credit, rather than retreating into isolation and eventually probably quitting in anger and telling this negative story to friends and family, she chose the more generous path of emotional maturity. She had the courage to share, and so we collaborated and corrected course. She got the raise she was asking about, we paid up the hours she'd worked at what should have been the higher rate, and she began having more fun at work. Customers, I'm confident, got better service, and her coworkers gained a more collaborative colleague.

Sometimes It's Okay to Give it Away

Most of this piece, appropriately I believe, is focused on those of us who've achieved a lot in the world learning to be generous with what we've gathered. But there's also something to be said for being generous in order to *move up*. In other words, when you have next to nothing financially, being generous with your time and ideas can help you feel good, while at the same time, leading to some positive steps for your career. Even when it means being generous to those who, on paper, have far more than you might. I can't tell you how many people with fancy résumés, high billing rates, and highly credible credentials—often well-known individuals—have related stories about how they kicked their careers into gear by offering to give their work, skills, insight, and ability away for free in order to learn and to prove themselves to those they wanted to work with.

I know this runs counter to common wisdom and current government regulations, which were, appropriately I believe, created to protect innocent interns from being taken advantage of. But still, a *lot* of people I know have turned to giving out "free samples" of their good work to get themselves a foothold. The reality of the world is that if you want learn to speak, speaking for free can get you going; if you want to write, your "career" usually commences with writing for some small publication without pay. And if we want to lead a life suffused with generosity, doesn't it make more sense that we start by sharing liberally, even with those who have more than we do?

Aaron Clay at Amy's Ice Creams in Austin, Texas, tells the story of how he showed up for an interview for a marketing job with a bunch of sales-building ideas on a thumb drive for Amy's to use if they wanted. "I told them that they could have the ideas, whether they hired me or not," he said with a smile. He actually got the job, and it proved a good match—a decade on, he's still there and thriving.

One of my favorite new musical acquaintances of the last few years is Providence-based musician Allysen Callery. In a recent enewsletter, she suggested that her fans mark September 25, her birthday, on the calendar—rather than get gifts for her birthday, she decided to give some. "You might want to remember that date, because I'm going to make all my albums free for digital downloads for that day." If you're drawn to good singer-songwriters and artists, take a quick break from your reading and check out her music right now!

Similarly, John T. Edge, head of the wonderful nonprofit Southern Foodways Alliance, is adamant about not pushing too hard for fundraising. While they need money, like all nonprofits, he prefers leading first with their "product." Edge says, "I want our work to be so good that when people come to the symposium or see a film or listen to an oral history, they want to call us and contribute." We've been giving money and support to SFA for well over a decade now.

It may seem unfair that those with little should give away their personal resources without monetary compensation. But, if you believe that there's such a thing as intellectual capital, and that good investing can help get something going, then why not use yours to jump-start your career?

9. Be an Active Listener

Listening—really listening, without judging—is an exceptionally generous act. I was going to say that it's not hard to do, but that's actually inaccurate. If you were raised like I was—which is to have your answer ready long before the person you're talking to completes their question—it's not easy to just shut up, sit still, and pay full attention. I've been working hard at it for 20 years, and I still have a long way to go. Listening with sincerity, listening without judging, listening with empathy, and listening to learn more—all are skills I still (and always will) work at enhancing every single day for the rest of my life. To quote Robert Greenleaf, "To be open, one needs first to accept that unless one has made a conscious effort to learn to listen, one probably isn't a good listener." Listening well takes energy, and it takes time, but I believe that it's very well worth the effort.

Think about what happens when we *don't* do it. If you and I as leaders aren't paying close attention to the folks around us, you know we're going to be headed for trouble. Staff members tune out, they lose hope, they disengage. "We should all know this," Brenda Ueland says, "that listening, not talking, is the gifted and great role, and the imaginative role. And the true listener is much more beloved, [more] magnetic than the talker." I've been fortunate to witness Paul prove her point regularly over our 30 years together.

Good intentions matter. Even offering to listen can be a good start. Opening a door to dialogue is far more productive than sitting behind a closed one, wondering why no one is coming in to visit. Actively listening to those who want to be heard is where the rubber of the soul meets the road of real life. This is no small thing, to let in what the person is saying with all its nuances, to really hear them where they are. Taking the time to be an active listener, to pay attention to intonation, to tune into the details—the spirit, the suffering, the enthusiasm, and the energy behind what the other person is saying—makes a difference. It can be hard work, but it's well worth the effort. Good listening always leads to positive energy. As Ueland writes, "It makes people happy and free when they are listened to. And if you are a listener, it is the secret of having a good time in society (because everybody around you becomes lively and interesting), of comforting people, of doing them good."

Let Your Pen Do the Listening

One technique that's helped me listen is to take notes. Clearly, this is not ideal for many situations—I wouldn't suggest you try it at the dinner table. But at work, it works well. At the least, it forces me to focus in order to write down what others are saying. In the end, I try to remind myself regularly of spiritual teacher and author Ram Dass's insightful statement, "The quieter you become, the more you can hear."

10. SHARE THE POSITIVE ENERGY

Speaking of energy, if you've already read *Part 2* of this series (Secrets #19 to 21, in particular), you know that my awareness of energy in the workplace has grown ever higher over the years. I'm deeply appreciative of Anese Cavanaugh for teaching this to me. To have a great organization, the leaders have to be the positive-energy spark plugs who will effectively ignite the passion and inspiration naturally present in everyone in the business. Energy, like the spirit of generosity, is basically self-generated. Kropotkin was conscious of this as well: "Overflow with emotional and intellectual energy, and you will spread your intelligence, your love, your energy of action broadcast among others! This is what all moral teaching comes to." When we radiate positive energy in our daily lives, we start a virtuous cycle, one in which we almost always get back what we put into it, and usually a lot more.

Per the previous few paragraphs, listening is a great way to do this. Ueland writes, "When we listen to people there is an alternating current that recharges us so we never get tired of each other. We are constantly being re-created." If I give an extra 10 percent and, as a result, everyone else ups their energy even half that much, and we multiply the 5 percent increase times the 700 folks who work here, it's clear that I ought to try to ratchet up my efforts even further!

While I certainly have hard days here, I'm surrounded by so many good people putting their creative leadership skills to work that it's impossible to stay down for long. If I'm open to their generous spirits, others around me are likely to give me a big boost. Feeling like our work matters, giving and getting positive reinforcement, and learning new things are all good ways to inject more energy into our personal (and then organizational) systems.

It's hard to give good stuff to others if our own energy is exhausted or has turned down into a cynical or negative space. Feeling a bit drained is fairly common. Especially in the old-school hierarchical world, it's lonely at the top, and it's exhausting to be the sole source of leadership insight and creativity. Many leaders run out of emotional gas. What's critical is that we deal with being drained in a productive way—take time for ourselves, do some random acts of kindness, learn some new things, and be generous of spirit. Giving—energy or anything else—and being able to see, hear about, or feel the impact of our giving at work can make all the difference. As Adam Grant writes, "Giving itself didn't affect energy: people weren't substantially happier on days when they helped others than on days that they didn't. But the reason for giving mattered immensely: on days that people helped others out of a sense of enjoyment and purpose, they experienced significant gains in energy." Note that the impact may not be instantaneous; Grant explains that the energy often didn't manifest until many hours after the act of generosity took place.

I learned long ago that my stress was a lot lower, and the organization's chances for success a lot higher, when I gave whatever it was I was giving with no expectation of it being returned in kind. I choose to do things freely because they're congruent with who I am, in line with my values, not because I'm hoping to get anything back a few minutes later. I'm not talking about fairly negotiated agreements with suppliers, or about a staff member who was promoted and got a raise as part of the package, or when we sent an employee to a training class. Those are different: there's an overt agreement up front for both sides to contribute something to a more positive future. I'm thinking about anything from an offer to cover a work assignment for a colleague, to going the extra mile for a customer or a coworker, to volunteering to do the dishes or clean the kitchen at home. When we consciously make the choice to give freely of our own volition, our energy is always higher.

Focusing on the positives, while mindfully steering clear of unconstructive criticism, is another good way to put the spirit of generosity into action. Having grown up in a high-achieving family that considered it an act of love to share with you where you were falling short, I know how easy it is to be critical. But criticism without a healthy balance (four or five parts praise to one part constructive criticism is a productive ratio) rarely creates the kind of positive progress that we care most about. We can, I'm completely confident, manage the ways we respond to others. I love Russian poet Josef Brodsky's beautifully stated philosophy: "I permitted myself everything except complaints."

I'll add that to be effective, the good energy we give needs to be authentic. While it's no doubt preferable to be generous in an inauthentic way than to be authentically stingy, things won't work as well as they can unless generosity comes from the heart. Inauthentic energy is easy to spot—it feels fake, phony, ungrounded. People respond to us in kind. If you're somewhere in the middle, I'm fairly certain you'll get mostly middling results. Ultimately, I believe it's about making peace with ourselves and living life as we want to. As Christopher Alexander writes, "[W]hen a person's forces are resolved . . . we feel relaxed and peaceful in his company."

The Eyes Have It

I'm increasingly convinced that our eyes speak louder than words or, for that matter, anything else. I've come to realize that we can convey almost any emotion simply by concentrating on it and actively expressing it through our eyes. When I feel grief, I can sense it physically first in my eyes—there's a heaviness, a hurt I feel under my eyelids that reminds me that though I might be acting like things are fine, I'm sad about whatever it is that's hit me. I know now that I can convey my compassion more effectively if I mindfully focus on expressing it through my eyes. Love, loss, anger, rage, empathy, excitement. You can, literally, see them all in the eyes. Ralph Waldo Emerson said, "One of the most wonderful things in nature is a glance of the eye; it transcends speech; it is the bodily symbol of identity." Modern science says the same thing; the eyes are believed to offer more information about someone's state of mind and intentions than any other organ. And, of course, when we want to be sure that someone is listening to us and speaking the truth, we might say to them, "Look me in the eye."

It's amazing how many articles about Emma Goldman describe her eyes, often in great detail. It is, I suppose, common with people who have intense energy that it pours out through the eyes. One of my favorite descriptions of Goldman's eyes is from the Des Moines Register and Leader, April 26, 1914. She had spoken that afternoon at the Trades Union Hall. "She has eyes that are like the sea," the paper reported, "gray, gray blue, cold, piercing with an occasional sunny half-light."

If we work at it, any of us can excel at the art of communicating by eye. But like any other skill, it takes mindful practice. Claude Bristol shares a technique that I'd never considered but could work quite well. "Remember," he writes, "that your own gradation or position in life is marked by what you carry in your eyes. So develop eyes that bespeak confidence." How do you do that? Practice! "The mirror will help you."

Knowing this, I've begun to use my eyes to lead my emotion. When I catch myself falling short in my energy output, the first thing I do is take a deep breath, and the second thing is to open my eyes wider and softer, make them more open to the world. A smile follows almost instinctively. And then, almost instantly, things start to get—and go—better. Science backs all this up: wider pupils are a sign of a more positive response. Which we know, in turn, increases the odds of getting more positive responses from others.

11. Lavishly Share Information

Being generous with information is, I believe, one of the most meaningful ways to live the spirit of generosity. Rather than the old "need-to-know basis" model, here, we start at the other end of the information highway. We work to share everything unless there's some real reason why the information isn't appropriate for others to have access to. (There are, of course, some issues of a personal and private nature that need to stay that way.) Our commitment here at Zingerman's is to what we call a "lavish sharing of information." That means telling people more than they would probably ask for, in the belief that the better the information our coworkers collect, the better the quality of the decisions they're going to make, the better off the entire business is going to be. Actively sharing what we're doing, what we're thinking, how we're feeling, what data we've gathered, why we're doing what we're doing in productive and positive ways—not dumping it randomly to relieve our stress—is a good organizational deed.

Our training business, ZingTrain, has based its entire existence upon being generous with information. That often means sharing systems, ideas, and techniques with others, including people who are direct competitors. I'm doing it right now—writing for publication is really just teaching on paper. Teaching internally is certainly a key element of information sharing; it provides an organized way to convey key information to our crew. Interestingly, like so many other aspects of the spirit of generosity, teaching is nearly always inspiring. I finish most classes I conduct totally jazzed—when the students are learning, my own energy is lit up in the process.

Effective generosity of information also means productively sharing our struggles. When we as leaders retreat under pressure, rather than open up, others fill the information gap by making up stories about what's going on. When things are bad, the people around us will all too often assume the worst. While the boss worries in silence, others figure that their leader just doesn't care. Constructively sharing the stress is an act of faith—we demonstrate belief in those around us and help get them involved in making things better, rather than treating them like unimportant bystanders. Terry Tempest Williams poetically challenges us to "speak through our vulnerability with strength." Remember: tears are water, too—leaders who are willing to cry in front of others (assuming the sentiment is authentic) are also generous of spirit. Admitting uncertainty while owning responsibility and asking for help without abdicating our obligations are powerful, honest, and effective forms of leadership.

Probably once or twice a week someone from outside the organization asks me why we would share all of what we do so openly. The answer has always been what amounts to the basis of the spirit of generosity: we believe in what we're doing, we believe that it works, we like to teach, and we believe that sharing it strengthens our ecosystem and makes us and everyone around us better. Poet Gary Snyder says, "Of all moral failings and flaws of character, the worst is stinginess of thought." This approach is the opposite, designed to share our thinking in constructive ways on a regular basis. (The emphasis is on the constructive—freely blurting out every critical sound bite that enters your mind is neither generous nor helpful.) Per Secret #39 on Creativity, we get back so many great connections with wonderful people and outstanding organizations, and all sorts of positive energy, that I can't actually imagine working any other way.

I'll be honest, though—while it's easy to talk about the idea of "sharing," at times it's tough figuring out where to draw appropriate lines in the informational sand. Knowing how much to share with the outside world can be a struggle for me. People seek me out a lot, wanting my time and information, and while I want to offer it to them in the spirit of everything in this essay, it's hard to balance that with the fact that we have a business—ZingTrain—that makes its living selling the same time and the same information. But even with those reservations, I try hard to push myself back to generosity and to stick with my rule: When in doubt, I usually give it out.

12. Share Social Capital

When I asked for Paul's input on the subject of generosity, an area in which he excels, "sharing social capital" was one of the first things he brought up. Honestly, I didn't know what he meant, but he was generous enough to explain himself and his point. In essence, it's about freely sharing your connections so that others can tap them too. "Your contact list is a big resource," Paul told me. "You can help people who work for you to get a meeting with a banker or a lawyer or a doctor. People who are successful in society don't realize how much their willingness to help make those introductions for others who are less fortunate matters." This small act of no-cost kindness can make a major difference in people's lives. If the meeting results in, say, a small reduction in a mortgage payment or a slightly lower cost on a big purchase, that can be a big deal. All we have to do is connect the dots; how things go from there is up to the two parties we helped bring together. And as Paul pointed out, "The social capital doesn't wear out. You can use it over and over again." Your generosity with these connections will likely come back to you and to the community many times over.

Paul is an expert at this. My guess is there's rarely a day that goes by that he doesn't help someone coming from lesser circumstances to connect with a resource who could help them. I try to follow in his generous footsteps. Sometimes the connection is one that a staff member has asked for. Other times it involves connecting someone to people or ideas that they haven't even yet realized they want. A book that would be of help; a key leader in the community or in the industry; a supplier whom they've never met but whose product they sell very regularly; someone else in our organization whom they might like and get along with. The opportunity to make these connections is so common it's easy to miss, but it's so powerful and so meaningful that I now probably do it many times a day.

Roots Connect

Not long ago I was working with Maggie Bayless to coteach our two-day Creating a Vision of Greatness seminar. For all the reasons listed in Secret #47, it's an extremely powerful couple of days. Insight and inspiration abound. At this particular session, we had five people from the much respected local software design firm Menlo Innovations. James Goebel and Rich Sheridan, the owners, generously sent their staff members to work on their own personal visions in the belief that the better their crew were doing, the better the business would be doing, too. Menlo is a great neighbor—another sustainable organization here in town that's also become a destination spot for creative business people. Rich's book, *Joy, Inc.*, is highly recommended. We've shared many ideas with them back and forth over the years.

David Minnix was one of the Menlo staff members at the seminar. Sometime on the afternoon of the second day, he commented that "Menlo and Zingerman's sure seem to have a lot of shared DNA." His comment triggered something I'd read in Toby Hemenway's book on permaculture about a particularly great old tree in a garden. "A tree's roots, researchers have shown, can graft with those of its kind nearby, exchanging nutrients and even notifying each other of insect attack." If roots are beliefs, and organizations such as Zingerman's and Menlo share many of the same ones, then it only makes sense that our roots would link up. While you may not see it on the surface, ideas and energy are regularly moving back and forth from one of our businesses to the next. It all fits together. And, as Hemenway writes, "We start to see how tightly enmeshed is a simple tree with all the other elements in a landscape." If Ann Arbor is an ecosystem, Menlo is one of the loveliest tall shade trees in town.

13. Compound Connections with Generosity

The more generous we are, the more each connection and relationship we have is multiplied to create more positivity. Starting relationships with an act of generosity can be beneficial for all involved. When a big group comes in for dinner, why not begin the evening with a gift from the kitchen? If we have a major catering or training event coming up, why not send a little "extra mile" gift a week or two in advance? If someone comes in for a job interview, why not begin by buying them something to drink or eat?

The Deli's facilities manager, Nancy Rucker, is a master at building connections. "I actually get a lot done in my job because I lead with my heart," she told me.

I'm not a mechanical wizard. But because I connect from my heart and do things for others, I get a lot of extra, often difficult, things done. I connect the dots and eventually things come together in a great way. I have a million connections. I've just done it by engaging with people. By taking that extra moment to say, "Do you want a bagel or something [else] to eat?" Or, "How are your kids?" I'll go way out of my way to get a cup of coffee for the guy who comes to clean the sewers here. It allows them a minute to open up. And then, because we have that connection and that opening, something will come out in conversation that they wouldn't have brought up if there hadn't been that time in which to do it. My friends call me a "social chemist."

Everyone wants to feel acknowledged for who they are. I got the electric-company guy to come out here to do something that everyone else said would never happen. But I "made the impossible happen" because once I offered the guy a cup of coffee and I talked to him for a few minutes. And then two years later, when I needed something, he was here to help in a couple days when everyone told me it would take months. Most people would have dismissed him. But, because I'd talked to him, we got things taken care of really quickly.

It's sort of a boomerang approach, I guess. You just throw positive connections out there, and if you do it well, they come back to you in kind.

The Reciprocity Ring

Developed by Cheryl Baker (founder of Humax Corporation in Ann Arbor) and her husband, Wayne Baker (head of the University of Michigan's Center for Positive Organizational Scholarship), this is a simple but powerful exercise. Basically, the Bakers put together groups of 10 to 20 people and have each of them take a turn asking the group for help with something they're working on. The Reciprocity Ring works well whether it's personal or work related. Because everyone is asking for something, the Rings remove the stigma of requesting help. From what I've heard from Wayne, the Rings work every time—it's amazing how many resources emerge when everyone in the group puts their heads together.

---

14. Create Ever More Opportunity

With abundance in mind, one way to put the spirit of generosity into practice is to focus on finding meaningful growth opportunities for the people in your organization. What those opportunities actually are is up to you—and them—to figure out. But the key is that people have a chance to do more, learn more, get more, and be an ever more important part of what we do. While this sounds simple enough, I don't think it's the norm in most places. But in a sustainable, healthy organization, opportunity is essential at every level; it's one of the major sources of hope. And when the opportunity becomes reality, it builds belief, both in the self and in the organization.

History here in the United States and around the world is loaded with examples of situations where people got "into the club," "hit the big time," or got a long-awaited promotion, and then suddenly didn't want to make room for anyone else to enter alongside them. The placement of the "bar" or the barrier to entry was plenty fine when they went over it, but it seems like some folks want to raise it even higher as soon as they're on the other side. Though I guess I'm "in the club," I want to take down the barriers altogether and help everyone around me gain and grow as best they want to and can. Many of our staff, I know, will later leave here to do something with food on their own, and some of these endeavors could be in competition with Zingerman's. But in my view, the more people who go out to do good things in the world, the healthier our ecosystem, the more we all benefit.

15. GIVE THE BENEFIT OF THE DOUBT

So much of the world is caught up in assigning blame, figuring who's at fault, and then finding ways to punish them for their failure. We make up stories about who screwed up and then set out to find evidence to support the tale we've told ourselves and others. With the understanding that negative beliefs lead to negative outcomes, it's clear to me now that this approach is a surefire way to cycle ourselves into failure. Nothing good can come of it. As Peter Block writes, "Retribution by its nature serves to fragment community and reduce social capital."

I like to take things in the opposite direction: assume the best and give the benefit of the doubt. This is, I've realized, an "inside job"—it's almost all about us as leaders being able to self-manage more effectively. When I start to spiral into frustration, exhaustion, or exasperation, I try (if not always successfully) to stay on what Paul calls "the higher spiritual plane." Often all that means is giving people the benefit of the doubt. Rather than assuming the worst right off—"they did this on purpose," "they aren't committed to the company," "they're incompetent"—I try to start by believing the best (harkening back to what I wrote about belief): that they messed up unknowingly and unintentionally.

One of the best things I learned of late was in an essay in the Frances Hesselbein Leadership Institute magazine, *Leader to Leader*. I can't recall right now who wrote it, but the author taught me "never to ascribe intentions" to anyone else. That bit of wisdom has turned out to be exceptionally helpful; it saves me emotional energy, and it keeps me from heading into a hellhole of organizational dead ends. I'm sure there are some seriously conspiratorial types out there in the world, but my personal experience is that there's usually a lot less malice behind what people do than others want to believe is there. Nine times out of ten, the "ill intent" that those who are looking expect to see is actually just neglect, a different way of seeing the world, lack of information, a misunderstanding, or plain old failure to follow through.

Interestingly, the stories we make up might say more about us than they do about anyone else. Maria Popova of *Brain Pickings* writes, "The assumptions people make about the motives of others always reveal a great deal more about the assumers than the assumed-about." In other words, the stories I make up about others' intentions say more about me than they do about anyone else. Next time you start to imagine something sinister about someone else, try turning the inquiry around—it might be an opportunity for increased self-awareness.

By getting clearer on what's (most likely) going on, we stand a significantly better chance of making something positive out of frustration. Martin Seligman calls it our "trauma narrative." Trauma leads to what he refers to as "a fork in the road"—if you move on the road of anger and feeling victimized, trouble and tension will almost always follow. But if you can stop, breathe deeply, get centered, and assume good intentions, you can turn things back to the positive quickly. I have come to believe that being able to start by giving the benefit of the doubt is the spirit of generosity at its simplest and best. It costs nothing to do it, and it just might reap you big rewards.

16. Give People a Chance

Here's my leadership take on John Lennon's antiwar anthem from long ago: take out "peace," and put in "people." You can sing it in your head or hum it aloud if you're shy: "All we are saying is give 'peeps' a chance." Seriously, it's amazing how quick most companies are to cut people off. Often, even before they get to the pass, a new employee has been sent packing. Yeah, yeah, I know—one can take generosity too far and let people keep working after they've demonstrated that they aren't able, or willing, to do well or play as part of the team. But it's hard to get it just right, and we mindfully opt to err on the side of giving people too many chances rather than on the side of giving them too few. Sure, sometimes we screw it up. Then there are the other times—when somebody slips up again and again, but when we help them one last time instead of shoving them out the door, something clicks. And when it works out well—as it has quite a few times at Zingerman's—those people go on to become key contributors who add a lot to our organization for many years.

It's also about giving folks an opportunity to get going in the first place. So many people never get hired to begin with because they don't seem, at first glance, to fit. You can fill in any of 50 reasons why that might be the case—race, religion, gender, criminal history, education (either lack or surfeit of it), past personal relationships, physical disabilities, previous failures, previous successes (they're "overqualified"), or any others I'm sure you're familiar with. This element of the spirit of generosity is at the core of positive, meaningful diversity work. It's about giving everyone who's eager and interested a shot at contributing, and helping people who haven't had the social advantages that so many of us, often unknowingly, have been able to build on. We've taken people on that other organizations have turned away, who then go on to become positive contributors for years to come. We've got lots of them here. In fact, Paul and I probably are a pair of 'em ourselves.

17. Make a Point of Taking, and Giving, Second Shots

Here's a personal story from my past. My grandfather Jack Perlis came here in 1916 with his parents and younger sister from a shtetl in what's now Belarus. It was the middle of World War I, and he was 15 years old. He was the second youngest of seven kids, and the other five had already come to the United States, one or two at a time, over the previous decade. When my great-grandparents arrived, along with my grandfather and his younger sister, they had a stack of Russian rubles with them—their life savings. Trying to decide what to do with their cash, they asked the advice of my grandfather's older brother Abe, who'd been the first to arrive in the United States. He recommended that they hold on to the rubles, believing that the currency would appreciate in value after the war ended. Abe's advice turned out to be terrible; a year later, in the fall of 1917, the revolution put an end to the empire, and any value the tsar's Russian currency could have had evaporated quickly. My grandfather's parents were so angry at Abe that they didn't speak to him for decades afterwards.

The extreme absurdity of this all-too-true family story drives the point home. The tighter you hold it, the more the grudge gets hold of you. What you'll end up with is actually a not-very-rewarding long-term relationship with the grudge, and in the process you'll lose a good bit of emotional freedom. Holding grudges poisons our energy and brings unneeded negativity to our organizational existence. In the context of "kindness is free," how about an equally easy-to-remember rule: "Holding grudges never helps."

I've tried to teach myself to turn what could be a grudge into a gain. In basketball, they track something called "second-chance points": the instances when a team scores after rebounding its own missed shot. It's not a classic statistic, but those in the know look at it when they want to really analyze what's going on in a game. I'm starting to think we might want to track second-chance successes in business, too. How many times did we rehire an employee who left on less than great terms but now sees things in a new light? How often have we reengaged with a supplier we cut off because they screwed up a few too many times? While it doesn't always work out, some of the best people and best products we've got didn't do well their first time around. There's little reason not to go after these second chance opportunities. In basketball, the other team is doing everything it can to keep you from rebounding your missed shot. But in business, the only thing keeping us from picking up the "loose balls" and going back in and scoring is our own obstinacy.

We probably have at least a half-dozen high-contributing people in the organization who'd been fired for poor performance at an earlier point in their employment here. Giving them the second chance, more often than not, has turned out for the best. Here's what one of them wrote me the other day, after I appreciated his growth and contribution aloud in a huddle.

> *I wanted to thank you again for the very kind appreciation in the huddle today. When I was first hired, my life was in disarray. Getting fired for my actions was the best thing that could have happened to me. It has helped me reevaluate my life's direction and strive to be a better person to myself and others. I truly love working for such a great organization and I look forward to many more years of service to the Zingerman's Community!*

By the way, forgiveness isn't just the right thing to do. A lot of science is showing that it brings benefits to the forgiver and whatever personal or professional group they're a part of. Frederic Luskin, psychologist and author of *Forgive for Good*, reports, "The practice of forgiveness has been shown to reduce anger, hurt, depression and stress and leads to greater feelings of hope, peace, compassion and self confidence. Practicing forgiveness leads to healthy relationships as well as physical health. It also influences our attitude, which opens the heart to kindness, beauty, and love." Forgiveness has also been tied to longer life span and higher immune-system function. We know it reduces conflict that when unaddressed creates a toxic, unsustainable work setting. And at worst, it costs a lot—so much time wasted, energy misdirected, people working to undercut instead of collaborate. In the end, forgiveness starts with us as individuals.

This sort of work is often derided as soft stuff, shoved aside in the interest of strategy and new-product initiatives. But I think it's at the core of everything we do. I might argue that the success of a project means more to the organization when it's achieved by someone who's failed and been given a new shot at things than when it's done by someone on the fast track. As Sam Keen puts it, "[T]he ability to act rather than merely react, to forgive and begin again, is precisely what defines a human being." Osho adds, "Bitterness is a state of ignorance. You have to go beyond it, you have to learn the awareness that becomes a bridge to take you beyond. And that very going is revolution."

Go Back to Go Forward

The founding father of positive psychology, Martin Seligman, recommends thinking of someone still alive who years ago did or said something that changed your life for the better. Someone whom you never properly thanked, and could meet face to face next week. Write a letter to this person. It should be concrete, about 300 words long, specifically articulating what they did and how it affected you. Deliver the letter in person without disclosing in advance your purpose for meeting. When you see the person you're grateful for, read the letter slowly out loud in person. "Gratitude can make your life happier and more satisfying," Seligman reminds us. "But sometimes our thank you is said so casually or quickly that it is nearly meaningless. In this exercise, you will have the opportunity to experience what it is like to express your gratitude in a thoughtful, purposeful manner."

18. SHARE THE CREDIT

While it may be hard to borrow from your bank, it's hardly ever difficult to share credit liberally with those around you. The person who takes all the credit seems selfish, and everyone around them is left feeling unappreciated. Anger and antipathy are the common outcomes. I'd advocate the opposite: spread around the credit for success, liberally. The truth is that whatever we've done or achieved, we'd have had no shot at that success without the support and contribution of others in our lives. Without waiters, even the best chef's food never gets to the guest. Without payroll clerks, even Fortune 500 companies can't function.

It's easy when things are going relatively well for any of us to think that we—as individuals, as a unit, as a division—are the ones who've made (or are making) the organization successful. I've tried to train myself to stay away from even going down that mental drive. Divisiveness and blame almost always result. Everyone contributes in their own way, and it's impossible to allocate the accolades with any level of honest exactitude. None of us would be here without the other.

Take this insight from E. F. Schumacher. I'd never really been opposed to taxes, but this simple statement completely changed my belief. Although businesspeople like us often take full credit for our contribution and complain about paying taxes, as Schumacher points out, "The truth is that a large part of the costs of private enterprise has been borne by the public authorities—because they [the public] pay for the infrastructure—and that the profits of private enterprise therefore greatly overstate its achievement." He's right. Trucks arrive on roads, and cities support the infrastructure that allow our staff to live close enough to work here. Why be stingy giving credit when you can share the emotional success with everyone you can? I keep coming back to Masanobu Fukuoka's marvelous metaphor: "It is like clapping your hands and then arguing about which is making the sound, the right hand or the left."

I also appreciate this lovely little anecdote from science-fiction writer Isaac Asimov's autobiography. After Asimov had won any number of awards, he gave credit to his elderly father for raising him in a way that made all his achievement possible.

> *"How did you learn all this, Isaac?"*
> *"From you, Pappa," I said.*
> *"From me? I don't know any of this."*
> *"You didn't have to, Pappa," I said. "You valued learning and you taught me to value it. Once I learned to value it, the rest came without trouble."*

Credit is anything but a zero-sum game. We can all share it widely—in fact, the more we spread it around, the more likely we are to repeat our successes in the years to come. The focus here is on actively finding others to appreciate. To honor the high-energy busser, the new counter person, the itinerant hostess, the barely-just-started baker, and give *them* the recognition. This desire isn't selfless, nor is it cold and calculating. It's just good. Good for them. Good for business. Good for building positive belief and increasing levels of hope. Good for the world. *And* good for me—I feel better for having done it.

Appreciating Appreciations

One of the best ways that we systemically share credit at Zingerman's is by budgeting a few minutes at the end of every meeting for what we call "appreciations." The full story behind how I learned about this beautifully basic technique and how we put appreciations in place is in *Part 1* of the series, in Secret #13. But in a generous nutshell, what we do is simply slot a few minutes for anyone who's moved to share an appreciative thought. Speaking up during that time is totally optional. It could be about something work related: "I want to appreciate Jenny Tubbs for all her work on this book." Or, "I appreciate my good friend in North Carolina, Lex Alexander, for teaching me how to do appreciations 20 years ago." Or it could be something personal and not work related at all. "I'd like to appreciate Jay Sandweiss, Jeff Sanfield, and Patrick Hoban for all their medical insight and guidance." The point is just to create a regimen around appreciation. Because every formal meeting we have ends this way, we regularly put positive energy and acknowledgement of others' efforts out onto our organizational table. I feel confident stating that the more you share appreciations, the better your organization will get. The return on the time investment is always a good one. Thinking of financial statements, *appreciation* clearly appreciates.

19. GO FOR GREATNESS, NOT VICTORY

The business world is loaded with war and sports analogies: "Beat the competition." "Dominate the market." "Take no prisoners." "Win market share by taking it away from the enemy." I don't look at it that way, and I never have. For better or for worse, I'm just not wired that way. And the more I think about it through the lens of the spirit of generosity, the more it seems like the military-based business model might not be the most constructive way for anyone to work. The simple truth is that that approach is based wholly on a win-lose worldview. I'd rather work towards win-win. Our gain does not have to come at the expense of others. As Sam Keen suggests, "The only just war is the battle against our tendency to do battle."

Menlo's Innovation

Believing in win-win solutions is a great start. Designing systems that support such solutions, that essentially train our "branches" to grow in the ways that we envision, adds enormously to the effectiveness of our work. Rich Sheridan, James Goebel, and the crew at Menlo Innovations are doing just that. Their mission is to "end human suffering as it relates to technology." Any project Menlo takes on is assigned to a two-person team that works collaboratively to get to greatness with the client. The different perspectives and the support of the teammates for each other help to reinforce their belief in collaboration.

With the client, they've come up with an equally innovative system. Menlo often agrees to take lower fees in return for long-term equity in the client's business or royalties on their product. It's an excellent example of win-win at work. As Rich and James shared,

> We believe so strongly in our approach that, in many cases, we are willing to trade away significant cash for equity or royalty. In other words, we are willing to bet that our approach will deliver business results while delighting users. This portends the highest degree of trust between a client and a vendor. The only word we know that applies in this circumstance is "partner." Many of our clients feel as though they are a part of the Menlo team; they start using the word "we" when they talk about our efforts together.

20. Design a Programmatic Approach to Community Giving

Community giving—whether in the form of cash, an in-kind donation, or volunteer time—is a positive thing. The need in all our communities is high, the resources ever limited. I'll share a brief synopsis of what we do here at Zingerman's just to get the dialogue going. My partner Paul has led our work in this area with amazing ability, insight, and expertise. He and Lynn Fiorentino, and now Robby Griswold, have managed the day-to-day coordination of all our community giving for many years. Together they've developed a clear and cogent set of materials through which we're better able than ever to effectively help those in need around us.

With community work and practicing the spirit of generosity every day, Paul is about as good as it gets. I'm sure there are others out there who've done comparable work (remember, it's *not* a competition), but he's set the bar high for us. He believes, and lives, what he told me when I asked him to comment for the purposes of writing this piece. "Nothing that you possess is worth much of anything. Its value is when you give it away." In that spirit, he and Lynn led the crafting of a written vision for what we at Zingerman's are committed to do in the community. Robby has taken it further still. We've also got a well-worked-out process for handling the many requests for donations that come through every day. Our donation request form can be found at zingermanscommunity.com.

One belated glimpse of the obvious on this subject came to me from reading entrepreneur Yanik Silver's helpful little book, *34 Rules for Maverick Entrepreneurs*. The final item on his list is about giving forward. Silver points out that most businesspeople have good intentions when it comes to giving. But because so few ever create a regimen or a budget for their giving, they rarely do it at the level they might initially have considered. They fail to follow through, he writes, because they don't have "a systemic, regimented giving plan."

Our formula for budgeting our community giving is that we set aside at least 10 percent of the previous year's operating profit for donations in the following year. I say "at least" because, realistically, there have been years when the bottom line here has been less than we'd have liked, but for better and for worse, we usually ended up spending in excess of that budget guideline anyway. Beyond that, we also put an additional 5 percent into our Community Chest, a fund for staff members who find themselves in crisis. When frontline folks fall on the ice at their house, have their car totaled, or find themselves victims of other extreme circumstances, the Community Chest can be all that stands between them and eviction. Paul was saying the other day that when he shares the story of our Community Chest program with others at conferences, many are amazed but confused about how they might make it happen. "Wow, that's a great idea. How do you do it?" He responds, "Well, it's really not all that hard to get going . . . you just set the money aside and start working out the details of how to help those in need."

21. GIVE BACK TO THE BUSINESS, TOO

In our personal contexts, as you know, I'm a big believer in using the Three Sisters metaphor. We ourselves, our work, and our connection to friends and family all need to be healthy for us to do well. Here, I'm adding a fourth sister to the mix: if we work as part of an organization, it too must be healthy or little else in our lives will hold up. If you believe in the value of the spirit of generosity, then it only makes sense that you need to be generous to the business itself.

How do you do that? In the moment, what strikes me is the importance of setting aside savings, of regularly putting time and money into improving infrastructure, training, and people. This reinvestment could be in the form of renovations (sprucing up a tired work setting), quality of product (a better oven), service improvements (a better phone system), or a better workplace (computer access for our staff, a nicer break room). And definitely training—reinvesting in our learning is paramount. At Zingerman's, we give out quarterly staff scholarships to encourage outside education.

The alternative, where you take everything out personally and put nothing back in, might make you money in the moment, but it leaves the world around you worse for your having entered it. It's the organizational equivalent of strip mining or bottom-dragging trawlers. If the key players extract everything they can and leave nothing behind to care for the business itself, the organization is going to suffer a lot in the long term. The situation is, in fact, very much like the difference between high-intensive monocropping and old-school sustainable agriculture. The former, made possible only with large inputs of artificial additions, leaves the soil depleted. As Dan Barber writes, "Monocultures . . . impoverish life and all its fantastic little ecosystems. They depopulate landscapes." Regenerative supportive settings, on the other hand, enrich the ecosystem, leaving all the life forms that are part of it in at least as good and often better shape than when the growing began.

This all works best when the people in the company are freely giving of themselves to make the organization into something special; while the culture and systems can, and hopefully will, reinforce things, it means the most when we leave the decision to be generous up to individuals. Grant writes, "[A]s people make voluntary decisions to help colleagues and customers beyond the scope of their jobs, they come to see themselves as organizational citizens." And as with every other area of this work, the more we give, the more we'll get back. Former coach of the Chicago Bulls and Los Angeles Lakers Phil Jackson writes in *Sacred Hoops*, "[C]reating a successful team . . . is essentially a spiritual act. It requires the individuals involved to surrender their self-interest for the greater good so that the whole adds up to more than the sum of its parts."

22. BE GENEROUS OF SPIRIT WITH YOURSELF

For many, I'm sure it would be easy to do all 21 items above and then leave this last point off the list. The incongruity of that, though, would cost them later. For the spirit of generosity to be effectively sustainable, we need to treat ourselves with the same generous spirit that we're sending out to everyone else. Terry Tempest Williams offers great insight on the subject: "When we don't listen to our intuition," she says, "we abandon our souls. And we abandon our souls because we are afraid if we don't, others will abandon us. We've been raised to question what we know, to discover and discredit the authority of our gut." She concludes, "I regret whenever I abandon myself."

The key to this, then, is to give generously to others while still watching out for your own spirit and means of sustenance. Doing both in tandem seems to get the best results. Grant writes, "[S]uccessful givers are *otherish*: they care about benefitting others, but they also have ambitious goals for advancing their own interests." If we don't do things for ourselves, both inside our heads and in our day-to-day lives, a counterproductive harshness of spirit will quietly but consistently undercut the generous acts we're carrying out on the outside. According to Grant,

> *Research shows that people who failed to maintain an equilib-*
> *rium between their own needs and their partner's needs became*
> *more depressed over the next six months. By prioritizing others'*
> *interests and ignoring their own, selfless givers exhaust themselves.*
> *. . . [W]hen people give continually without concern for their own*
> *well-being, they're at risk for poor mental and physical health.*

A leader who's out of synch with themself is likely to end up hurting others around them. Knowingly or (more often) not, they will inflict on others the "punishment" that they are internally imposing on themselves. By contrast, when we treat ourselves respectfully, don't hold grudges, stay positive, and are actively giving and appropriately forgiving, we're far abler to evoke a similar spirit in those around us. The two go together synergistically—giving to others helps us to find ourselves.

Playing the Giving Game: Support for Spiritual Economics

E. F. Schumacher wrote a piece called "Buddhist Economics," which was published in 1973 as part of *Small is Beautiful*. "Spiritual health and material well-being," he says, "are not enemies: they are natural allies." The story that follows is one small example of how that's worked here.

Back when I first started to think about the spirit of generosity in depth, it was somewhere in the summer of 2009, in the midst of the worst years of the economic recession. The more I studied the subject, the more it seemed like we ought to be talking nationally about using the spirit of generosity to jumpstart the economy. It appeared to me that we didn't need to wait for the federal government, majority control of Congress, the Small Business Administration, big business, overseas investors, or an upswing of the stock market to make it go. All we needed was for each of us to be generous enough of spirit to be the one to start our own cycle heading in the right direction. If you're waiting for your boss, your brother, the next President, your colleague, or the new line cook to be the one to get it all going, that sort of defeats the purpose. If we each committed to a significant increase in generosity of spirit right now, I think we could get the country headed in the right direction.

At Zingerman's, to help ourselves keep focused organizationally on doing the right things, rather than getting reactive and sliding down into the seeming insanity of the rest of the world around us, we rolled out what we called the Giving Game. We did this in December 2008, a couple of months after the stock market had sunk to new lows and at a time when we were approaching what was still supposed to be by far our busiest few weeks of the year. I don't think the Game was the linchpin in helping us successfully survive that year's insanity, but it certainly helped. Over 200 of the 500 folks who worked here at the time participated.

The Giving Game listed nine areas in which a "player" needed to take a positive action step in order to "win." The list included stuff like giving particularly exceptional service, watching the daily details in our work, more actively living our open-book approach to finance, and going out of our way to be especially kind to customers or coworkers. None of these things, on their own, were likely to be life altering. But small though they might seem, all were meaningful actions that helped keep things going in the right direction, especially when everything seemed to be in a downturn. For everyone in the organization who "played," we donated an additional $10 (above our existing commitment) to Food Gatherers, our local food bank. It's not like that 10 bucks was going to resolve the issue of hunger here in our area. It was just one small piece in an effort to keep from slipping into the vortex of finger pointing and fear that so many businesses were, understandably, getting caught up in. The top item on the Giving Game "scorecard," I just remembered, was none other than the "spirit of generosity."

Generous Conclusions

I can say with confidence that compiling this collection of 22 techniques has been helpful for me in my own self-management. I've realized a good number of things that I hadn't consciously thought of before I wrote the essay. I now have a checklist that has already helped me to more effectively make the spirit of generosity a part of my daily life. I know I have a long way to go to get to where I ought to be, but at least I feel like I'm living Ram Dass's credo: "I help people as I work on myself and I work on myself to help people."

It's often said, "Money makes the world go round." Maybe that's true in the mainstream business world. But in the natural world, from a more holistic perspective, money is merely a tool. What really makes our world work is generosity. Money matters, but generosity is generative. "Water," Leonardo da Vinci said, "is the driving force in nature." I agree. We can make a difference. Let's do it. As the late Nick Drake once sang so beautifully, strumming his acoustic guitar softly in the background, "And now we rise, and we are everywhere." [29]

The Spirit of Generosity Checklist

To give a bit of structure to your work in bringing the spirit of generosity to life, here's a simple grid you can fill in and follow along with for each of the 22 tips.

Technique	Action Taken
1. Begin with an Abundance Mentality	
2. When in Doubt, Give It Out	
3. Understand How Hoarding Hurts Everyone	
4. Give Great Service and Live the Spirit	
5. Lead with Generosity	
6. Act in Kindness	
7. Have Empathy and Compassion	
8. Be Generous with Your Time	
9. Be an Active Listener	
10. Share the Positive Energy	
11. Lavishly Share Information	
12. Share Social Capital	
13. Compound Connections with Generosity	
14. Create Ever More Opportunity	
15. Give the Benefit of the Doubt	
16. Give People a Chance	
17. Make a Point of Taking, and Giving, Second Shots	
18. Share the Credit	
19. Go for Greatness, Not Victory	
20. Design a Programmatic Approach to Community Giving	
21. Give Back to the Business, Too	
22. Be Generous of Spirit with Yourself	

Sarah Okin, Director, The Herb Amster Center,
Jewish Family Services, Ann Arbor, Michigan

I'm an Ann Arbor native; Zingerman's Deli sandwiches are as much a part of my assumed truths about life as is gravity.

After college I left Ann Arbor as quickly as I could for the bright lights and shiny opportunities New York City promises every rose-colored-glasses-wearing, motivated twenty-something. I left New York to pursue bigger opportunities (in a stronger currency) in London, England for about five years. London was where my career in entrepreneurship really began, and during which time I discovered the magic of motivating employees.

My personal dogma in business has long been that happy, productive employees are the secret to achieving and maintaining growth and profitability in business. This may not be so paradigm shifting to the readership of this book, but it is not necessarily a widely held belief amongst the general public. It's also not the easiest thing to implement in a traditional business setting. Even as an entrepreneur, I fought fires on a daily basis that took my attention away from shifting our company values to treating employees as partners (not subordinates) as much as I would have liked. It just wasn't as practical or as easy as it should have been to achieve this culture shift.

Upon moving back to Ann Arbor after ten years, I discovered the wonders of the ZCoB. Truly, I was bewildered by the choice this profitable, *famous* organization made to remain small. I was in a bit of culture shock professionally and personally, having come back to Michigan from cities that favored "bigger is better" and "growth equals success" mantras.

Why this organization chose not to expand was an enigma . . . the

407

opportunities available to ZCoB would result in not just incremental revenue, but spectacular growth in size and profit that (surely) every business owner wanted! So what were they thinking?

By asking questions, reading Ari's books, attending the Zingerman's Experience ZingTrain course and learning about Zingerman's values from Ari and Robby Griswold (who looks after ZCoB's Community Partnerships) it became clear: this phenomenal organization chose, time and time again, to prioritize employee engagement and to do good locally.

They truly walk the walk: every single employee at the ZCoB prioritizes both internal and external customers as well as the good of our community over growth and expansion. Furthermore, they hold fast to the belief that profitability is not the only goal: this triple-bottom-lined organization is as concerned with fighting hunger in our community as it is with whether you receive your fried chicken how you expected it. This unique model has proven to be successful for Zingerman's, and I believe can be for every organization that chooses to emulate it.

Learning from Ari and the ZCoB has enabled me to further develop and validate my own managerial style and convictions, and to even launch a business based on the principle that happy, productive employees directly impact businesses' productivity and profitability. I'm now in a position to share strategies to achieve productivity and profitability through employee engagement with organizations interested in ZCoB's style, too. Emulating ZCoB's values and following their lead has enabled my organization (and my clients!) to be better, and to know that better can be more significant than bigger.

Lisa Roberts, Product Manager, Zingerman's Mail Order

The tenets of the 12-step program are a core value match for several of our principles in practice here at the ZCoB. Service is one of the three main tenets of the Alcoholics Anonymous program, and it's also obviously a big part of our experience here. Servant Leadership, internal service to each other, and great service to our customers all emphasize an outward focus. "Give it away to keep it," as they say in 12-step programs.

For myself, Zingerman's was the first job I'd had in two or three years. My addiction was such that I was simply unemployable before that. I felt lower than low. I had been homeless and crashing in public spaces around Detroit and Toledo. I was referred to a women's transitional housing and treatment facility, where I began my road to recovery. It was the beginning of a journey back to myself, and Zingerman's has been an integral part of that journey.

From my first day at the Deli, I have felt supported and safe. I was treated with the dignity and respect that every person should experience. I experienced great internal service! I was so grateful to be accepted, grateful to be employed, grateful to be treated like I had value and something to contribute. That last part was the hook for me. In my addiction, I was in taking mode. At Zingerman's, I felt like I could give back.

Something about the open-book finance and the sense of ownership and responsibility it espoused in me supported my recovery. To my family and last several employers, I did not have a great track record of showing up when I said I was going to and doing what I said I was going to do. Here was an opportunity, a second chance to start over and prove to myself

409

that I could be trusted and that I could contribute or be of service in some way. I began to learn about the products we sell and the relationships we have with our vendors. I began connecting with other people, and I felt a pride growing for this new organization I was a part of. Step by step, my life began to have meaning again. I had a purpose. Like the AA program, Zingerman's believed in me until I could believe in myself.

My sobriety date is January 8, 2001. I was employed at Zingerman's later the same month. For this reason, the two will always be intertwined for me. I am and always will be grateful to Zingerman's for the beautiful life I have today.

Every time we have the opportunity to hire an employee in recovery, my heart swells thinking about the new possibilities their life may hold. I want to gush about the incredible journey my life has been since I started here at Zingerman's, but I know it's up to each of us to find our own path. I'm going to keep on looking for opportunities to serve in small ways every day and watch the miracles unfold around me.

The Secrets that follow are systemic strategies we use regularly at Zingerman's. Having spent the last few years working on this book, I can see now how they all contribute significantly to helping shape positive beliefs, cultivating hope, and encouraging the spirit of generosity. I believe that all can be adapted and then put in play in any sort of organization. Hopefully they'll bring you as many positive outcomes as they have us.

mara ferguson at work at zingtrain

Visionary Roots

Strongly Held Beliefs About Visioning

I've already written a lot about our approach to visioning. And yet the more I study it, teach it, write about it, and use it, the more I believe that visioning can make a positive difference in so many parts of our lives. For many, it is clear to me, visioning is the "missing piece." What follows is new learning, realizations that I've had since I first started writing on the power of visioning in business in Secrets #6 to 9, and then again in Secret #35 on personal visioning. To get a fuller understanding of the ways we use visioning at Zingerman's, you might want to head back to those essays before you read this one. If you're even a little bit familiar with our approach, the pages that follow will hopefully build on your understanding of the process and how and why it works. As you'll see, I believe more strongly in the power of visioning than I ever have!

I keep coming back to my metaphor from the beginning of the book, looking at organizations as ecosystems. The more I think on it, the more I teach it to others, the more I like it. Beliefs are roots; hope is the sun; the spirit of generosity is water; and organizational culture is the soil. The mission statement is the North Star. Purpose is air. New ideas and people are seeds planted into the organizational soil, which we hope will develop deep and positive roots and grow into healthy additions to our community. The ecosystem comes together quite effectively with creative constructs and instructionally sound imagery. There's one thing still to be added, though. It's the organizational concept we probably talk about here at Zingerman's more than any other, something that's essential to the way we work, without which neither Zingerman's nor I would be anywhere close to where are now: visioning.

Everything else in the model—roots/beliefs, soil/culture, seeds/people and ideas, water/generosity, sun/hope—holds equally true for an unwalked part of the woods or a pristine wild prairie as it does for anything we're actively working in and on. Animals—and I love them—mostly exist within an environment, living their lives, changing only in the way their genetic coding tells them to. Beavers build dams, birds build nests, and lions make lairs. But they don't develop new constructs, and they don't, as far as I know, really innovate—they only repeat what's been done and has worked well for the hundreds of generations that came before them. Humans are different. As anarchist geographer Élisée Reclus suggests, "Humanity is nature becoming self-conscious." We don't just string beads following the pattern that everyone before us used; we can choose to add them in an order that's true to us. We have the ability to imagine institutions, design things, construct cathedrals, dream up new projects, develop pioneering products.

Businesses, of course, aren't like wild mushrooms—they don't just spring up in the night after a big rainstorm. Someone had to have had a dream, a vision. And then they had to do the work to make that dream a reality. As architect Christopher Alexander writes, a vision of greatness "is, quite simply, the desire to make a part of nature, to complete a world which is already made of mountains, streams, snowdrops and stones, with something made by us, as much a part of nature, and a part of our immediate surroundings." Vision is what makes all of what we do into something—operating in harmony with nature as we hope it is—that moves beyond what's naturally present on the planet. It's the way we take what we've imagined and actively build it into something tangible and, we hope, terrific.

So what is a vision? That's a question I've addressed a number of times in earlier parts of this series. Secrets #6 to 9 and 35 all get into what I know about the process, why it works, and how to put it to work in your organization or your personal life. In a nutshell, vision at Zingerman's is when you describe success at a particular point in time in the future, with enough richly engaging, emotionally meaningful detail that you'll know whether you've arrived. We've all become increasingly clear—when we don't know where we're going, it's hard to end up where we want to be. A vision describes the future of our dreams. It needs to be both inspiring and strategically sound. At Zingerman's, we document our vision and share it with everyone involved.

We write visions here in greater detail, far, far more than most business strategists generally suggest. (Our vision for Zingerman's 2020, written in 2007, is approximately nine pages long.) I believe this way of doing it is about 10,000 times more meaningful than mainstream methods. We write visions for everything here—every business, every project. Nearly every long-term staff member will have written one themselves or participated in writing one with their peers. We teach it internally, and we teach a two-day ZingTrain seminar. Visioning, it's clear to me, has changed my life. I wouldn't be here, and Zingerman's wouldn't be what it is, without it. It's the most positive, practical, easy-to-put-into-practice (if you're willing to work at it) process for creating your preferred future that I've ever come across. Working towards an agreed-upon vision brings purpose and engagement to all involved. We often describe it here as the difference between "laying stone" and "building a cathedral." And I know very well which of those two I'd rather do. As Peter Koestenbaum writes, "Vision . . . is the crowning achievement of human evolution."

Visioning, Zingerman's style, is all about creativity—a powerful, natural, if often untapped, tool. It's about imagination. As Wendell Berry writes, "To imagine is to see most clearly, familiarly, and understandingly with the eyes, but also to see inwardly with 'the mind's eye.' It is to see, not passively, but with a force of vision and even with visionary force." It's about effectively putting our ingenuity into concrete action. Vision is the future we *want* to create, the life we dream about, the legacy we want to leave, the cathedral we're working to construct.[30]

Four Elements of an Effective Vision at Zingerman's

Inspiring

Strategically sound

Documented

Communicated

Lost and Found

Fundamentally, I look at the visioning process as a tool with which we can begin to build the future we want to create. But it's also a great technique to help us find a positive way forward when we're feeling lost. While I don't have any statistics to support my supposition, I gotta believe that people get lost (in a geographical sense at least) a lot less often than they used to in years past. Even seven-year-olds now have cell phones. With GPS, self-driving cars, and satellite tracking in hand (literally and figuratively), I'd imagine we find ourselves lost far less frequently than we used to when I was growing up.

In case you haven't gotten yourself lost lately, let me remind you that it isn't a great feeling. Whether you're a kid or a corporate executive, it's not a whole lot of fun. Panic starts to set in, often swiftly. If there are others around you who aren't lost, they all seem to be calm and confident. You feel like you may never find your family and friends again. The only thing that's truly certain is that everything that seemed solid has suddenly turned to sand.

I can still recall being something like six years old and losing my mother (or did she lose me?) in Marshall Field's, Chicago's very busy, very large, once world-famous downtown department store. I was scared out of my mind. I was already an anxious kid, and being lost brought my fears quickly to the fore. Totally unsure of where to go or how to get there, I think I tried to look composed. I was the kind of kid who tries to act calm even when he's not—and I'm not all that far removed from him today. My body was still, but my mind was moving a mile a minute. Me, small—and feeling even smaller—totally uncertain, in the middle of the shopping madness, surrounded by fast-moving adults in big overcoats, but very much alone, feeling scared, sad, stupid, ashamed, close to tears (though trying not to cry). We'd all heard stories (to scare us into behaving?) of kids who disappeared, who were kidnapped, or were sold into some sort of 20th-century slavery. "What if that happens to me?" I worried. My Marshall Field's story has a happy ending—I stayed put until a nice woman who worked there spotted me and helped me find my mother.

Feeling lost when you're running a business, or trying to run your life, is equally intimidating. It's just a lot easier to admit to your uncertainty when you're six than when you're a CEO. And lost little boys are far more likely to accept help than most high-level adults would ever be. The two most common tactics I've seen for leaders who have lost their way are a) just staying put, the way I did at Marshall Field's, waiting for someone or something to show up and save them; and b) alternatively, racing around, almost frantically, trying to find a quick solution to the stress.

While standing still was a successful strategy for me at six, I wouldn't recommend it for any organization. Nevertheless, lacking a clear sense of themselves and unsure of their future, many simply settle into a routine. Work continues apace; sales still come in; staff get hired, fired, and promoted. There's plenty of day-to-day activity to keep everyone busy, but the deep sense of purpose, the power of pursuing something unique and special, has long since been lost. Anxiety precludes bold, affirmative action. Every possibility for significant change starts to seem too risky; uncertainty leads to hesitation, hesitation leads to waiting, waiting leads to worry. Everyone knows things aren't ideal, but the status quo feels safer than anything else. Stagnation ensues.

Then there's the other group. The ones for whom running hard to somewhere, anywhere actually, is preferable to feeling lost. Rollo May says it well: "It is an ironic habit of human beings to run faster when they have lost their way." When they don't know what to do, they hide their insecurity by racing out to find a quick fix. Afraid of appearing indecisive, they dive in, move faster, worry more, all the while trying to act calm and in command. When the first escape route doesn't play out properly, they quickly reverse course and try to get out the other way. Leadership coach Art Petty refers to it as "flailing and then failing." He observes, "When senior managers are frustrated over a lack of quick results, they'll lash out in pursuit of new initiatives. Projects are started and abruptly stopped, and new projects are heaped upon the existing overload of work. Eventually the organization grinds to a halt." In the corporate world, the results of this race to no place in particular often show up in the form of "burnout."

Making Good Time but Going Nowhere

I shared Dr. May's insight with a ZingTrain client who then related this story. "My husband and I were in Provence years ago on a cycling trip," she told me. "We were covering long distances every day. One day we were so lost that we really had no idea where we were. Finally, I told my husband that we needed to just stop and ask directions. He rolled his eyes at me and said with a bit of a regret, 'But we're making such good time!'"

Feeling lost in our organizational lives is a particular problem for individuals and businesses that have already had some level of success. The initial vision of their business (often unwritten, but effectively internalized over many years) has been finished. They did what most of the world told them they'd never be able to do. Offers to expand or sell out start to come in regularly. Expectations are high. Advice, of course, abounds. But listening to others while losing ourselves is never effective. From the outside looking in, things seem like they couldn't be better. But on the inside, uncertainty is the order of the day.

Historian Robin D. G. Kelley writes, "Without new visions, we don't know what to build, only what to knock down. We not only end up confused, rudderless, and cynical, but we forget that making a revolution is not a series of clever maneuvers and tactics, but a process that can and must transform us." Visioning, as we do it here, is just such a process. It has saved me from the slow spiritual death, existential burnout, and emotional bailout that happens to people who lose their way in life.

Winchester Mansion: When the Workmen Just Keep Coming

Every successful organization started with a vision. Even if that vision was only clear in the founder's head, someone had to have a sense of something special, a "cathedral" of meaningful import that she or he was determined to build. Many fail, some succeed. If things do go well, that original vision will be brought successfully to fruition. At which point, it's as if the founder's original mental blueprint has been successfully completed.

If their business was a construction project, the work would, literally, come to an end. But in organizations, it just keeps going. Vision, or no vision, day-to-day operations continue apace. In essence, even the though the original plan has been seen through to fruition, the workmen just keep coming. With no clear end in sight, they continue to find work for themselves, adding on to what was originally imagined, embellishing already finished elements of the design, long after the original plans were completed. Each new thing they build, viewed in isolation, may seem to make sense. But in the process, the elegance, coherence, art, and harmony of the founder's original vision gets buried under a hodgepodge of ad hoc additions. The work continues but things are ever more offbeat. Rhythm is lost. The results are rarely pretty.

If you want to see what can happen in a rather extreme example of that scenario, visit the Winchester "Mystery House" in San Jose, California. It was built by the widow of the man who made his fortune inventing the Winchester rifle. Sarah Winchester, so the popular story goes, was told by a psychic that in order to keep the souls of those killed by her husband's rifles at bay after his death, she needed to continue the construction of their home without stopping. She kept it up for almost forty years. Because the point was to keep building rather than to complete a blueprint, the house grew way beyond anything the original architect ever imagined. When she died, the house had spread over roughly five acres, had 160 rooms, 47 fireplaces, two basements, and three elevators. There are staircases that end with no exit, windows that weirdly look into the next room rather than the outside. It had a number of bathrooms but only one actually worked—the rest were decoys that served only to fool evil spirits. The design makes no sense.

All of which is, I suggest, a superb metaphor for organizations that continue adding on for decades without ever taking time to sit and write out a new, inspiring, strategically sound vision of greatness for their future. Their daily operations might look impressively busy from the outside, but their work has lost its coherence. You can spend days inside, and get increasingly more lost the longer you walk. The pieces no longer fit with the whole. Like the Winchester mansion, what results may be look impressively large, but it will lead nowhere.

Tapping the Power of Positive Pace

Effectively working towards an inspiring and strategically sound vision, as we do it here, is about pace. Steady as you go, moving mindfully, neither too quickly nor too slowly. It comes up a lot in the work of many people I respect. They call it walking. It's a way to access our intuition, to stay in touch with nature. Rebecca Solnit says, "Walking is the intentional act closest to the unwilled rhythms of the body, to breathing and the beating of the heart. It strikes a delicate balance between working and idling, being and doing. It is a bodily labor that produces nothing but thoughts, experiences, arrivals. . . . It leaves us free to think without being wholly lost in our thoughts." The image alone is evocative. Even reading about walking gets me more in rhythm.

It's true in agriculture, too. Wendell Berry says, "The gait most congenial to agrarian thought and sensibility is walking. It is the gait best suited to paying attention, most conservative of land and equipment, and most permissive of stopping to look or think. Machines, companies, and politicians 'run.' Farmers studying their fields travel at a walk." Moving steadily, mindfully, calmly forward seems to be quite conducive to finding, and making, one's way in life. (Given the anarchist belief that the means need to be congruent with the ends, maybe I should add the idea of taking a good 10-minute walk before writing to our vision recipe?) Poet Wallace Stevens says, "Perhaps the truth depends on a walk around the lake." It's no coincidence then, I suppose, that a great deal of the conversation Paul and I had that ended with our writing our 2009 vision took place while walking circles around the neighborhood.

Learning from Ron Lippitt

I never had the pleasure of meeting Ron Lippitt in person. At least not that I know of. He passed away in 1987, which means that I might well have unwittingly waited on him in the early years at the Deli. I hope I did. If I could meet him now, I would thank him profusely. His work, conveyed to us primarily through what Stas' Kazmierski learned from him, has helped make many thousands of people's lives better.

Lippitt grew up in rural Minnesota, raised by his grandparents. If walking is the pace that most effectively approximates working towards a vision, Lippitt came to love its rhythm early in his life. Stas' shared: "Ron told me he loved to walk from the farmhouse to the mail box in the snow in his stocking feet. He loved that feeling of cold and wet on his feet." Lippitt studied in Europe and then took a position at the University of Iowa, where he worked with pioneering organizational psychologist Kurt Lewin. I don't have the sense that Lippitt would have called himself an anarchist, but he was clearly fascinated with tapping the power of people at every level of the organizations he worked with. His doctoral thesis was about democracy in boys' clubs. He went on to found the National Training Laboratories in Maine, which is where Stas' first met him. Lippitt later moved to Ann Arbor, where he was a big part of the Institute of Social Research at the University of Michigan for many years. Stas' was working at an American auto manufacturer at the time when Lippitt was brought in to design a process to increase employee engagement. Much to Stas' good fortune (and later ours), the two were assigned to work together.

Lippitt definitely did not follow the path most others were on. Even in little things. Stas' told me that Lippitt was known for wearing bolo ties— not an everyday look in Ann Arbor. He'd been in New York years earlier with his wife, Peggy, and a handful of others, and they were all going to dinner at a fancy restaurant. The restaurant required that gentlemen wear ties, but Ron didn't have one. So he walked down the block and found himself a bolo he liked. He put it on and was then allowed into the restaurant. Stas' reports, "He wore a bolo tie on all similar occasions thereafter!"

Lippitt's study of community building led him to explore group dynamics in an effort to figure out how to help people get to a more positive future. Nearly every group he monitored seemed to bog down, descend into the details and logistics, splinter into opposing factions who settled in for long fights, or just gave up, feeling more frustrated than they had when they began. Lippitt had the brilliant insight to turn things around. He suggested they stop trying to solve problems and, instead, turn their attentions towards describing the future of their dreams.

"Don't worry about what's wrong today," he would say. "Instead, imagine you're in the future of your dreams. Tell me what's going on when it's all going really remarkably well." When people started to, again, descend into arguments over what tactical steps needed to be taken to move forward, he would gently bring them back. "Let's stay in the future," he would say. "We'll work on 'how to get there' later." The results were powerfully impressive. Energy went up, creativity emerged, people found productive ways to blend their individual dreams and desires into win-win "visions" of the future in which everyone could come out ahead. Lippitt called his approach "positive futuring."

Thirty years after his death, Lippitt's work around what he called "positive futuring" is at the core of everything we now know, teach, and practice as "visioning." Although we never knowingly met, it sounds like we did connect culinarily more than a few times. "Ron had a regular meeting at his house called the 'Lippitt Cluster,'" Stas' said. "I started going in about 1982—same year you opened the Deli. If you attended, you were expected to bring a dish to pass. Bringing Zingerman's food made you a hero!" Lippitt's work has made heroes out of *us* many times over. The seeds of the visioning work that he planted half a century ago have grown into a wonderful forest, filled with tall, healthy trees; plenty of sun; and a rich, moist, resilient soil.

Convincing those who are lost to be emotionally bold enough to take a few long walks, and then to sit quietly and write out a description of where they actually want to go and what it will look and feel like when they arrive, can be challenging. While we've taught many, many people and achieved powerful results, the truth is that there are still some who, though they like the concept, never sit down to write their vision. I've often shared the story—usually off the record—of talking to a friend of mine who was perpetually frustrated that he and his partner were arguing again and again about where to take their successful business next. Each time we talked, he'd tell me about another possible plan they were considering—open a new unit, sell one of the old ones, hire a new executive team. Trying to be helpful but not intrusive, each time he'd start the story again, I would gently, patiently, suggest they might consider quelling their confusion by taking time to write a long-term vision together. Each time he would offer me a good reason why this wasn't the right moment in which to write one, or how they were still thinking about it, or that they didn't have time. Meanwhile they went ahead and opened another place, started another new product line, and hired a new set of managers. Lost and confused, they kept speeding up, but they remained as unclear as ever on the ultimate goal and purpose of their work.

Times to Speed Up

In the right settings, a sense of urgency certainly plays a positive part in organizational life. I'm all about getting moving. But having thought about this for a fair bit now, it's clear to me that this approach—reflecting and looking back towards beliefs rather than charging first into reactive, autocratic action—is a much more grounded and positive way to go.

I've started to see it in the same way we view "Slow Food." Fast food is quick and low cost, but it's not good for you or for the environment. Same goes for reactive decision making. In the long run, neither is very rewarding, nor is it really going to sustain you. Slow Food is all about embracing complexity, diversity, reflection, nature, and nurturing. Ultimately, it's a mindset, not a standard operating procedure. There are still plenty of places where speed in food and cooking are critical, though: getting olives from tree to press in a matter of hours; a 29-second shot of espresso, consumed within a minute of being made; freshly picked spinach leaves given only the briefest of sautés in great olive oil; fish going from sea to sauté pan in under an hour.

Same goes for the work world in general. No one who's worth their business salt would suggest that we dally when responding to customer complaints, greeting guests, returning phone calls, or getting to market with new hi-tech innovations. Moving more quickly would help big companies that won't adapt to a changing consumer base, organizations that fail to innovate, leaders who vacillate and won't make decisions when they're needed, staff members who "can't" decide if they want to stay or go. So, yes, in the right situations, speed is essential.

The work in this book is a far less frequently traveled road forward. Ultimately, it's about choosing reflection rather than acting without thinking. It's about learning to dig deeper rather than dumping our anxiety on those around us; taking time to build hope where others have unwittingly crushed it; trying to figure out how to give, rather than racing ahead to get more for ourselves. It's about learning to look beneath the surface at our beliefs when society says to skip over them and just work on strategy. It's about moving steadily in the direction of our dreams rather than just "playing it safe" and standing pat with the status quo.

In a sense, it's about accepting that even as mature adults who are supposed to know what we're doing, we're often confused, frustrated, angry, and out of touch with what's happening inside us. It's hard to admit, but that doesn't make it any less true. Like it or not, we get lost. The Persian philosopher Rumi has a wonderfully helpful saying: "When you're drunk and near a cliff, sit down." To adapt his saying here, "When you're lost and in business, sit down and write (or reread) your vision." If we put that principle into practice, we would save a lot of companies and maybe even some lives.

You know the story of how Paul and I made it through this stage. He intuitively knew we needed to stop and take stock. Had we known then what we know now, it would probably have been a whole lot easier. Fortunately, we stumbled and struggled our way through. We took a lot of long walks together. Over the course of a year's worth of challenging conversations, we came up with what we called "Zingerman's 2009"—a creative, powerful, and effective vision that helped us take our organization to a better place. In fact, that place is almost exactly what we wrote about in the vision back in 1994. In the 22 years since we finished writing the 2009 document, I've learned a whole lot more about visioning. Every day I learn more still.

Stuck in Space

This decision to vision or not to vision, to speed up or slow down or get stuck altogether, seems like another application of Viktor Frankl's "space between stimulus and response." Those who race forward when lost are reacting to the stress and anxiety of uncertainty. Movement, almost any movement, feels less scary than sitting with discomfort. Those who worry but never make a decision get stuck, in essence, in Frankl's space. They enter it same as you and I do, but they agonize so much that they can't ever decide how to exit. It's a bit like bring trapped in a fun house. Things feel increasingly insane, but after a while, you get used to it. Few ever leave.

Today I believe more strongly than ever that *visioning is one of the best tools we have to get unlost*—a construct we can use with great consistency to get clarity on where we truly want to (and then *will*) be, on a future in which we will feel fulfilled, have fun, and help others we care about do the same.

Beliefs and Visions

Something I'd never even heard of 25 years ago has grown to be one of the most extensive, relied upon, and religiously practiced parts of my life, both personally and professionally. When we craft positive, ethically anchored, inspirational visions in which the individuals who are part of them are respected and honored for who they are, we create what I believe Wendell Berry is referring to when he writes, "This work would be worthy of the name 'human.' It would be fascinating and lovely." The more I use it and teach it, the more strongly I believe visioning to be one of the most powerful, life-changing leadership tools I've learned. And there's a lot more.

1. *I believe that visioning is one of the best ways we have to infuse hope, positive belief, and the spirit of generosity into our organizations, our lives, or really anything else we're engaged in.* Taking the time to write down the future we dream about is sure to build positive belief. Working effectively towards that future is a near-certain way to increase hope. Sharing our dreams with others is a generous act; asking for and incorporating their input is more generous still. The more people work on a vision, the more their voices are heard, the stronger their belief in the future, the more hope they have, the more they experience generosity of spirit. And as they then step forward to lead, to draft and share visions of their own, they repeat the same positive process with others in their lives.

2. *I believe that visioning is a great tool for restoring vitality to a failing culture, to enrich otherwise depleted organizational soil.* Vision isn't everything, but it certainly makes a big difference. If you look at any of the major issues in the world—racism, the conflicts in the Middle East, environmental problems—it's clear that there is nothing remotely resembling a shared vision (nor shared beliefs) among those involved. Without shared vision, violence and war will surely, I'm afraid, continue to be the order of too many parts of the world's day. Conversely, we could acknowledge that we have different beliefs and even different values, but still manage to agree effectively on a vision of a respectful and peaceful existence and then move steadily towards it.

3. *I believe that the visioning process is one of the most effective ways we know to find the "passion" that people so often implore us to "follow."* While their advice is well meaning—it's far, far better to work with passion than to put up with

something you don't care much about—telling people to "relax and just follow their passion" is generally not all that helpful. Ironically, what's intended to inspire often intimidates. Those who already have their passion in hand will likely nod their heads and smile affirmatively. The other 96 percent of the world—still searching for *theirs*—will respond mostly with wonder and worry. They start to believe that there's something wrong—with them, with their world, with their job—because they can't figure out what their passion is.

They *want* to answer poet Mary Oliver's challenge: "Tell me," she asks, "what is it you plan to do with your one wild and precious life?" But they simply don't know what to say. I believe that the visioning process can help people solve that problem. It will, more than any other approach I've used, open the door to the dreams we all have inside us but have long since learned to let go of. Instead of going for the greatness we're so hungry for, we allow fear of failure, social pressure, and strong self-doubt dominate. But it's in those dreams, I believe, that our excitement and engagement, our purpose and our passion, are found.

Visioning helps us move aside the other "voices" that can be so active in our heads (the ones that advise us on how we "should" live) and regain access to our own. As Thomas Merton puts it, "Every man has a vocation to be someone: but he must clearly understand that in order to fulfill this vocation he can only be one person: himself." Although making your vision a reality will require a lot of work, the work will be rewarding because you're doing what you feel called to do, creating a future that you're inspired to create. *Your* future. Not mine. Not your mother's. Not one you made up to please anyone else.

4. *I believe that visioning is the best way to enhance each of our unique and amazing, one-of-a-kind, individual existences.* As designer John Todd explains, we do our best work when we create "elegant solutions predicated on the uniqueness of every place." I'd apply his principle to every person as well: We do our best when what we do honors on our distinctiveness.

Unfortunately, the usual ways that we're taught to define our desires strike me as oddly one-dimensional. We're given distinct categories into which we're trained to believe we *should* fit, but they don't seem to support individuality or creativity. And they're so maddeningly multiple choice—pick your passion from the list on the page: "I'm going to be a banker." "I'm going to have children." "I'm going make a lot of money." "I'm going to be a businessperson." "I'm going to be an academic." Each item on its own says little about you.

My friend Faith Kyunghee-Chen explains:

It's scary how often we let the titles we take as our identities take over. Perhaps this is why when they're stripped away, we often feel a sense of loss. At least I do! I need to let my head give my heart permission to lead. My heart is filled with things that excite me—photography, art, management, serving people, food, autonomy, words, quietness, cultures. Sometimes it overwhelms me, because it seems like too many passions without any connection from one to another. I have to trust in its journey.

I believe she's correct. Her first name is well suited to the visioning work. When we trust the process, we can bring all the passions that society says are incompatible into a congruent, uniquely compelling construct.

That uniqueness is a beautiful thing to behold. Everyone has it in them. Osho says,

Nobody is superior, nobody is inferior, and nobody is equal either. Everybody is unique. Equality is psychologically wrong. Everybody cannot be an Albert Einstein and everybody cannot be a Rabrindranath Tagore. But that does not mean that Rabrindranath Tagore is superior because you cannot be him. [Remember,] Rabrindranath cannot be you either.

No one can. You are one of one, and writing your vision seals that deal. While some of the main themes of what you write about could, of course, be common to what others have put down in theirs, the combination of nuances and details any vision comprises will result in a picture of a life that only you will live.

Try it. Sit and write your vision, with feeling, as if you're in the future, already living out what you're writing about. Describe your dreams, pick your passions, share your emotions, talk about what tickles your spirit. Reflect on a difference you've made in the world, how others responded to it, how you've grown and learned and contributed and collaborated. Add anything else you want that feels meaningful—music, family, food, friends, animals, achievement, education. Add a nice building or an interesting anarchist if you like. But whatever you do, string the beads of your story the way *you* want to string them.

Visions, as we write them here, are essentially then the DNA of our existence—each, without exception, will be unique. No one—*no one, I promise* —will ever publish a vision that's *exactly* like yours. Creating a future of our own design is so much more inspiring. I recommend it. Visioning puts the meaningful details—the love and the passion and the feeling and the strange, but significant, specifics of our dreams—into play. It gives us a tool to describe the totally exceptional future each of us deserves. The folks at the Center for Positive Organizational Scholarship at the University of Michigan write, "Excellence is a function of uniqueness." Which means that the more you become yourself, the more elegantly excellent your existence is likely to be.

5. *I believe that the* process *we use for visioning counts more than the* content *of any particular vision.* I'm in alignment with designer Bruce Mau's belief that "process is more important than outcome." Our conscious brain excels at knowing what we could or should do, but our unconscious is, more often than not, radically clear on what we really, in our heart of hearts, desire. Visioning is a way to work out our dreams, to stop the self-editing and self-deprecation that we've come to live with, to cut out the overthinking we're all trained to do. Robert Henri writes, "There are moments in our lives, there are moments in a day, when we seem to see beyond the usual—become clairvoyant. . . . Such are the moments of our greatest happiness. Such are the moments of our greatest wisdom." And that is exactly what the visioning process is all about.

The key of the work is *writing*. Not thinking. It's the discipline of what we at Zingerman's call using the "hot pen"—sitting down and just starting to write, for anywhere up to an hour, straight through. What the process *doesn't* allow is pausing. No stopping to self-edit, no taking time to "think things through," no holding back while you "assess the options." The faster you move your fingers, the better the whole thing will go. The movement essentially forces out most of those "shoulds," the critical concerns and "helpful advice" that we've internalized from others over the years.

The "hot pen" process is all about us, our authentic voice in action—it hotwires our hearts and our hands so that what comes out is as close as we can get to what we actually want. It pushes us past the status quo, away from the life everyone else might have us live. It gets us out of the comfort zone and into what German educator Thomas Sennenbacher says is "the learning zone," but without letting us fall off a cliff. The key is to catch our creativity within effective boundaries. As jazz musician Duke Ellington says, "It's good to have limits."

I've watched the visioning process work with thousands of people over the years. Many have a hard time writing at first. Worry and overthinking start to get in the way. But the discipline of the "hot pen" always takes them to the next level. As Pablo Picasso points out, "One doesn't paste one's ideas on a painting. . . . One simply paints." Time after time I've seen the change in their faces—eyes come alive, smiles soften, energy is increased. All from 40 or 50 or 60 minutes of free writing. The process is the point. The pen becomes the paint. You are the painter.

6. *I believe that not tapping our individual—or organizational—uniqueness, not being true to ourselves, harms us and deprives everyone around us of our special gifts.* When we live a life that's not our own, when we fail to fulfill our potential in any part of our lives we truly care about, we deprive ourselves, our business, and our community of the unique contribution we're capable of. Poet Mary Oliver writes, "The most regretful people on earth are those who felt the call to creative work, who felt their own creative power restive and uprising, and gave to it neither power nor time."

How do we continue to hold our out-of-the-box, slightly crazy, offbeat dreams in high esteem when there's so much social pressure to fit in? It's not easy. The pressure to conform is part of everyone's existence. But as Julia Cameron admonishes, "To kill your dreams because they [seem] irresponsible is to be irresponsible to yourself." Naysayers will always needle us, critics will still complain, but the positives will always be there for those who choose to find them. Visioning works. I'm with Robert Henri who writes, "The individual says 'My crowd doesn't run that way.' I say, don't run with crowds." I agree. Be yourself as best you can. Over time, good things will follow.

7. *I believe that visioning is a great way to push past the all-too-common fear of finding out what we really want, along with its cantankerous cousins: the fear of failing and the fear that we won't be "allowed" to get where we want to go.* We hold ourselves back as protection, in the misguided belief that it's better to scale back expectations than it is to fall short. I know the drill—I've done it. Julia Cameron explains: "Rather than trust our intuition, our talent, our skill, our desire, we fear where our creator is taking us with [our] creativity." The certainty of the status quo certainly feels safer, even when we're suffering. "Blocked," Cameron continues, at least, "we know who and what we are: unhappy people."

At which point, the self-fulfilling belief cycle kicks right in—we believe we can't cope with failure, we hold back in our efforts, others don't respond well to our halfhearted work and hold back in turn, and then our original fears are reinforced. We say, "It's a good thing I didn't go all out. Look how lame things ended up anyway." My friend, actress and artist Alex Carbone, describes the dance: "In the past, sometimes the pattern has been to try less than I really should so I have that margin of error for excuses. Like, if I had really tried, I could've done better." Clearly, she's changed her beliefs and, with them, the results. After a recent acting audition, she reported, "I tried really hard and it felt so good to succeed." By the way, if you write your vision to address this challenge you might say, "It's five years into the future. Unlike the old days, I now routinely give my best to everything meaningful I engage with. Although my fears still arise, I mostly just plow ahead anyway. The results have been amazing."

8. *I believe that the clarity of a written vision will help us hold course over the long haul, filled, as it always is, with many ups and downs, disappointments, and achievements.* We all have our moments of doubt. Problems drag us down; opportunities entice us off course. But with a well-documented and shared vision, we can stay true to our dreams.

It's a good problem to have, but most every achievement will likely lead to more enticements to leave the path we've chosen. It's inevitable—when we do well at what we wanted to do, the sirens of success start calling out: "Move here! Open there! Free rent! Franchise! Go public! You've got a goldmine—sell out now!" Staying on track to our vision—or writing the next one when we've successfully finished the first—isn't a guarantee of success, but I far prefer to fail going after my own dreams than to have my life derailed by socially acceptable advice from others.

On the downside, when things feel like they aren't working, the pressure to change paths can be intense. Uncertainty may haunt us. We pass through what we call "the zone of doubt and blame." The doubters can take you down. "Why did we ever start this project?" "Whose idea was this, anyway?" Having a written vision—and better still, sharing that vision with others we care about—keeps us going for greatness and helps us avoid the natural tendency to abandon ship or slide back to the status quo. It puts our personalized peg firmly in the ground, marks out our destination to the world, sets the bar on our high jump. It helps us hold true to where we want to go when the rest of the world would be happy with us going back to the way things used to be. G. K. Chesterton puts it beautifully: "Progress should mean that we are always changing the world to fit the vision."

9. *I believe that everyone who's interested can learn visioning and that everyone has the ability to be a visionary.* Some will take to the process more quickly. Others of us will struggle at first but remain more than capable if we're willing to stick with it. Everyone, I believe, *can* do it, and no one who tries will do a

bad job. I've taught visioning to 2,000 or 3,000 people over the last few years, and every single vision I've read is seriously inspiring!

Society tells us that only a select few, the brilliant heroes of their era, are special enough to be true "visionaries." I take the opposite tack. *Everyone* has inspiring insights and plenty of creative ideas. Most people just don't know how to take them beyond random appearances in their heads. I believe that the best way to address this situation is to teach visioning to everyone who's interested. In the process, we help everyone learn to think like a leader, and we unlock otherwise underutilized human potential, creativity, caring, and ingenuity. It's a sustainable energy source the world would greatly benefit from. I'm fully aligned with Ashanti Alston, who says, "You all can do this. You have the vision. You have the creativity. Do not allow anyone to lock that down."

10. *I believe that when people learn to do visioning well, they are also, in essence, learning to effectively engage in "time travel."* Visioning, it turns out, has the power to alter our experience of time. When we follow the recipe faithfully (see Secret #8, in *Part 1*), we move through past, present, and future rapidly over the course of an hour (or less), and in the process, we rearrange the presumably linear relationship between them. Instead of operating in isolation—the past is over, the present is now, and the future is yet to come—the visioning process weaves the three time frames so they come together collaboratively in new and creative ways. As time becomes whole, so do our lives.

We begin the process by going back to the past, listing what we call "prouds." We spend a few minutes actively recalling and writing down things we feel good about having achieved in our lives and the feelings we experienced when those things were happening. It's an easy step to skip over, but don't—our willingness to select and honor the positive feelings and accomplishments we've already had will have a huge impact on what will happen in our future. Focusing on the positives helps tap our intuitive creativity.

And then, after that, we start the vision process by writing in the *present tense, as if we're settled into the success of the future that we're actively describing.* That's right—without getting out of your seat, you suddenly transport yourself into the future. You pick your date and then get grounded in it as if you'd already arrived. If you're writing about 2022, then imagine your kids at whatever age they'll be; you doing what you want to, feeling how you want to feel; your favorite team winning the world championship; your organization transformed into the blessedly beautiful place you'd like it to be.

From there, we return to the present moment, in which we start to take action to make our vision come true. Where we've decided to go in the future alters what we decide to do today. Which means that, as psychologist Paul Watzlawick points out, "In this sense it was the future—not the past—that determined the present."

One of Marge Piercy's poems begins, "We are trying to live as if we were an experiment conducted by the future." By using visioning, I believe we can bring the tenses together to form a whole and healthy life. As her predecessor in poetry Carl Sandburg put it, "Yesterday and tomorrow cross and mix on the skyline." At which point, we can go about our days differently, feeling calmer and more confident, breathing deeply and walking steadily—we know where we came from, and we're clear on where we're going.

11. *I believe that when we're pursuing a vision of our own creation, our energy is more positive, and, as a result, everything around us is likely to improve.* Designing a life, and then making that life a reality, is an enjoyable experience. As Robert Henri writes, "The fun of living is that we have to make ourselves, after all." When we're doing our own dream work, living the lives we want to lead, others want to be around us and will find ways to contribute to our causes. Is it risky? Of course. Everything is risky. But I believe that it's far more fun and more rewarding to work, risk in hand, towards a future of our own creation and choosing than it is to settle for a prefab profession chosen for us by others. As Matthieu Ricard writes, "Freedom means taking the helm and sailing towards the chosen destination." It's a good feeling.

And it's likely to work. Studies led by psychologists Kennan M. Sheldon and Linda Houser-Marko show that "Individuals in the process of pursuing goals for intrinsic, personal reasons had grade point averages higher than those predicted by their American College Test scores. . . . [P]eople who can identify sets of goals that well represent their implicit interests and values are indeed able to function more efficiently, flexibly, and integratively across all areas of their lives." Similar studies showed benefits in both physical and psychological health as well as faster recovery from trauma.

It's worked well for David Nugraha. The time he's spent as part of our organization seems to have had a positive impact.

Meeting with you that morning has had an enormous impact on me; it has changed me so much. On the outside, I appear much the same. I am just as energetic, as enthusiastic, and as curious as I was back then. But internally, I am completely different in so many ways. I think overall the root cause of what is different and improved about me is that I have much greater belief in myself. These days, I have a much greater belief that I am a creative person, that I have great ideas and can make the right decisions, that I am personable and capable of being well liked, and that my future will be brighter because I want it to be so.

Can you imagine a company—or even a country—filled with people in that frame of mind?

12. *I believe that when we practice visioning regularly, we train our brains to focus on the positive.* Rather than just waiting to see what's wrong, we start to move "automatically" to what we want. And because that new focus builds positive beliefs, hope, and a spirit of generosity, it makes us more open to the beginnings of other good things as they start to grow and develop. With practice, we can experience what Martinique poet Suzanne Césaire describes as "Permanent readiness for the marvelous." When we look for the positive—in both people and projects, in the past, present, and future—we are sure to find it. So many people who've done visioning start to say things like, "It's wild, but it's all starting to happen just the way I wrote it." Things start to come together in surprising ways. Julia Cameron explains it this way: "As you move towards a dream, the dream moves towards you."

What Comes Out Can Change the World

A while ago I was asked to write my "American dream" for a photojournalism collection entitled "The American Dreams Project" that a photographer named Ian Brown is putting together. Here's how I replied: "My American dream? I don't really have an *American* dream. Maybe a universal dream? I dream, I hope, I envision that people all over the world can come reasonably close to making their own dreams come true, to live the lives they want to lead, to make their visions a reality, and, in the process, to leave their own creative and caring mark on the world." In other words, my vision is that everyone gets to come close to making their vision come alive.

Philippe de Vienne is our amazing Montreal-born-and-based spice merchant. He and his wife, Ethné; daughter, Marika; and son-in-law, Steve, buy and sell some of the most exceptional spices I've ever encountered. Their wild cumin, their incredible Indian cloves and cardamom, the special selection Spanish paprika—these are just a few of their aromatic and amazing offerings we now have on hand at Zingerman's. Aside from successfully changing the entire spice world, Philippe is one of those "geniuses" who's been visioning, "naturally," on his own his whole life. He's what those in the training world would call "unconsciously competent." Nonetheless, he decided, with perhaps a grain of Gallic salt in his spirit, to come to the two-day ZingTrain visioning seminar. He realized early on in the training that although he'd essentially always been visioning, he'd never understood what he was doing, never taught it to others, and hadn't put its power to work in his organization. Two months or so after the seminar, Philippe wrote me this note:

> One of the first things we did upon our return was to explain visioning to our core people. We gave them an assignment to do a personal "hot pen" vision for the business. Well I was moved by what we heard. The oldest (in his 50s), the most cynical of our people, a guy who has been abused by previous employers (broken promises, fired when he could be replaced more cheaply . . .), actually had to clear his throat and hold back the tears when he read us his vision. And he has been with us for only a year. [Everyone's] visions are amazing and are being taken into account as some of the descriptions are great and inspiring, not to mention the great practical ideas. The immediate consequence was a palpable energy in the office; somehow, in one week, files that had been lingering moved ahead or were completed. People left late and came in early.

Here's another anecdote, this one from Ann Arbor–based digital marketing expert Hannah McNaughton:

> The visioning seminar was of more help than you know, and I would like to say again how thankful I am for the last couple days. I can't even explain to you how optimistic I am now. I feel at peace, but I also feel like I'm finally waking up from a daze. I am suddenly examining everyone around me, and [I] have the urge to make them happy. The gas station attendant at Costco. The cashier. The gentleman pushing in carts. Even the woman who hurriedly closed the gap in two merging lanes so that I couldn't merge on the way home yesterday. I want to show them joy, because I feel that the reason so many people feel unhappy is because they have no vision for their lives. How incredibly depressing it must be—and how incredibly discouraging it once was—to only be sure of life's end, and to be treating the middle like a Magic 8 ball considering life trivial. When the only vision you truly have for your life is death, the work of each day can understandably feel quite pointless. Perhaps the blue skies and shining sun in the middle of this Michigan winter

have also affected my judgment, but I truly believe that some clouds have been lifted from my perception. I believed I was nearly there when I walked in on Monday morning, but I was much further away than I had realized. I know I don't have it all figured out just yet, but I feel confident that I can dare to dream and firmly believe that my aspirations are possible.

And, since the third time is believed to be the charm, let me share this story from Tanzania in East Africa. Cacao there, like Rocco Disderide here, is an immigrant. It arrived in East Africa around the time of Tanganyika and Zanzibar's independence from Britain and merger in 1964. About fifty years later we began getting shipments of wonderful Tanzanian chocolate from Shawn Askinosie. His work to help the people in the communities he buys his cacao beans from is exceptional. (You can read more about his work in Secret #45.) Among the many things he's done to support the development of the cacao growers has been to teach them the visioning process he learned here. Referring to the visioning work, Mr. Livingston, one of the growers, said:

Shawnie comes once a year and teaches us strategies to achieve our goals. It makes me feel like a young man again. We have to talk in present tense about our goals, like they have already happened. The first time, one of the men said, "I woke up this morning and I had a mattress, and I looked up and I had a ceiling in my house. My wife was so happy because she was able to go to the store and buy what she wanted at the market." Tears were streaming down his face as he spoke.

Next time Shawnie comes I want to get more training on how to improve our funding and get better tools so I can work better and get more out of it. Right now I have a big goal: Buy a tractor. I believe I'm going to get it. Shawnie's teaching has helped me use my money more efficiently. He's helped our community in other ways, too. He helped build three classrooms, so instead of studying under a tree in the rainy season, the children can study in a classroom. The students now have textbooks and laptops with videos and can learn better. For a long time, the children in our village of Mababu starved, and the girls dropped out of school to sell themselves in exchange for food. Shawnie heard about this when he first came to our country. We grow the most wonderful rice in Mababu, and he sells it in the United States and gives us 100 percent of the profit for school lunches.

I agree with Mr. Livingston about that rice—it's ridiculously good! I'd write you a recipe, but all you need to do is buy some (from Askinosie Chocolate or from us), boil it with salt, and eat it. You also have the recipe for visioning in the following exercise. It's a bit more involved, but the results, I believe, will be equally excellent. One summer Saturday morning, our regular five-year-old customer, Eli Genisio, was showing me the "crystals" he'd brought with him in a box. "What do they do?" I asked him. He picked them up carefully to show me. "When you hold them up to the light," he said, "they look *really* cool." The same is true for the future when we stop long enough to write and then bring our vision to the fore. When you hold your dreams out in the light of the organizational day, they're as lovely and beautifully illuminated and marvelously multifaceted as one of Eli's crystals. If we get clear on the details we desire, if we collaborate and then concur on a vision of greatness as a group, we can achieve almost anything. As de Vienne forecasts, "The impossible is possible if the circle of your vision is wide enough."

Follow the Recipe for Writing a Vision of Greatness

For a much more detailed description of how to write a vision, check out Secret #9.

Ingredients for Effective Visioning

- Belief in the process
- Your gut
- Some time
- Willingness to make yourself vulnerable
- Readiness to do something great
- You've gotta wanna
- The willingness to stick with the process

Procedure

Step 1: Pick Your Topic.

Step 2: Pick Your Time Frame. I'd recommend going at least three, or probably five to ten years out.

Step 3: Put Together a List of "Prouds." They may be both facts (things you've achieved already that will help you get to greatness in the future) and/or feelings (how you felt when you experienced success in the past). This small step helps get us thinking positively, which helps in turn to open the creative door to more effective visioning.

Step 4: Write the First Draft of the Vision. The first time through is only a DRAFT! Write what you like—you can edit it later many times! Just sit down, get ready, and write with the following in mind.

- Go for Something Great. Don't hold back. It's the only life you're likely to get, so make it a great one!

- Write from the Heart. Put the passion, the feeling, the dreams, and emotion into it!

- Get in the Future. We always write our visions as if they've already happened. So, if you were writing today (in 2016), you might start by saying, "It's December 31, 2020, and I'm heading home from work. I'm more excited than ever about . . ." and then move on from there. Keep remembering to write it as if it's already happened.

- Go Quickly. On the first draft, don't edit at all. Just write what comes to mind. If you hate what you wrote later, you can always throw it out.

- Use the "Hot Pen" Technique. Once you start writing, just keep writing. Whatever it is that comes out of your head will be helpful. The key is to keep the computer keys or the pen moving!

- Get Personal. Add adjectives, names, places, tastes, smells, etc. that mean something to you.

Step 5: Review and Redraft. Set the vision aside for a few days and then take it back out and reread. Feel free to adjust.

(Optional) Steps 6-A, 6-B, and 6-C: More Redrafts. Repeat, as in Step 5, a few times so you can continue to refine your draft.

Step 7: Get Input from People You Respect. Share your vision and listen to what others say, what questions they have, etc. At some point—usually much sooner than anyone with perfectionist tendencies will want to admit—you're done!

Step 8: Let's Go—Start Sharing the Vision.

Here's the rough outline of the vision from the cacao-growing village where Shawn Askinosie has been giving so generously of himself, his ideas, his time, and his insights. There's more work to do on it, but you can see already how inspiring it is.

7 August 2014 at Mababu Primary School

Facilitator: Shawn
Translator: Kellen
Transcriber: Daudi

2024

1. We have our office with computers and many other things.
   - "At my office, I turn on the computer and take a look at our records of past years, and I am able to show my children these data."
2. All stakeholders are able to educate all of their children.
   - "The secret that enabled me to educate my children is cocoa sales."
   - "When I was a young man, I was a businessman with a milling machine. Now I feel better than ever because even though I didn't get far in my education, cocoa enabled me to give my children the opportunity to go to school."
   - "I educated my children, now one is working in the U.S. That one came home for Christmas and I told her the way cocoa made her to be able to reach for lofty aspirations."

3. We will have a big tractor, one lorry, and two power tillers.

- "I am in the field, and I'm telling our workers, 'Be careful with our machines over there!'"

4. Our community profits through us.

- "This morning I met a farmer. I explained to him how high-quality cocoa can get him a better price, so that he can get a better profit and a better life."

5. A good house for every member.

- "I left that old thatch-roofed house behind. Now I park my car by the door of my new luxurious house. I told my wife, 'Don't ride your bicycle to the market, we'll take the car.'"

6. We help nearby schools.

- "I told my daughter how today we took more than $4,000 worth of textbooks to the school in Mababu. I taught her that she should have a generous heart for giving."

7. We own wood projects: a chainsaw and a lumber milling machine.

- "Today, on the 7th, I woke up and drove my car to the workshop and I found a big problem when I got there: There were so many customers, I had no idea how we would get to them all."

8. We have a power (electricity) project.

- "I'm telling my children that we have uninterrupted power that doesn't go out, and it's because we got a very good customer. I want my children not to stop where I managed to reach in life, but to keep pushing forward."

9. We help widows and orphans.

- "Once upon a time, we got an American customer, and since then we have been able to help orphans, who are now members of Mababu CCF." [In case you're not fluent in Swahili, CCF stands for "Farmer Business Group."]

david marshall serving up a cappuccino at zingerman's coffee company

One + One = A Lot!

How a Bit of Unorthodox Math
Can Make Your Business a More Rewarding
and Productive Place to Work

If I told you I had a small, inexpensive, ethically oriented, and innovative idea you could implement in your organization, something that would reduce turnover, improve staff satisfaction, build bonds across all parts of your business, and over time improve your financial performance, would you take it? Most moderately active leaders in an open-minded organization would snap up such a proposition. As far as I'm concerned, One + One is the most rewarding organizational algebra I've done since my 8th-grade math class. It is, in its simplest sense, about engaging the people in your business in some additional part of the organization. We do it here in the interest of getting them—and nearly everyone around them—feeling better about themselves, their peers, our organization, their work, and the world at large. I can't say exactly how much One + One will equal in your organization, but I can guarantee you that it will be far greater than "two."

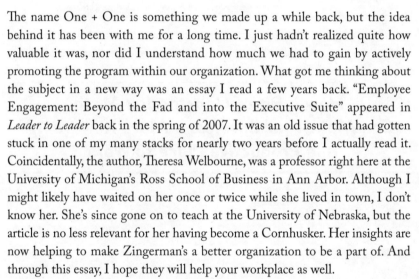

The name One + One is something we made up a while back, but the idea behind it has been with me for a long time. I just hadn't realized quite how valuable it was, nor did I understand how much we had to gain by actively promoting the program within our organization. What got me thinking about the subject in a new way was an essay I read a few years back. "Employee Engagement: Beyond the Fad and into the Executive Suite" appeared in *Leader to Leader* back in the spring of 2007. It was an old issue that had gotten stuck in one of my many stacks for nearly two years before I actually read it. Coincidentally, the author, Theresa Welbourne, was a professor right here at the University of Michigan's Ross School of Business in Ann Arbor. Although I might likely have waited on her once or twice while she lived in town, I don't know her. She's since gone on to teach at the University of Nebraska, but the article is no less relevant for her having become a Cornhusker. Her insights are now helping to make Zingerman's a better organization to be a part of. And through this essay, I hope they will help your workplace as well.

Welbourne's entire article is helpful—it shares how-to tips on getting staff more engaged in an organization, something we're always working to do ever more effectively here. But one particular insight struck me—and stuck with me—more than any other. About halfway through the piece, she writes, *"Employee engagement improves when employees are successful in both the core job and the non-core job roles."* I knew right away what she was talking about, and I knew that she was right. People feel a lot better about being part of an organization when they're actively engaged in a second piece of work, one that takes them outside the bounds of their regular daily duties.

For context, let me say that while we're tiny by the standards of national chains, we're not exactly a "small business" anymore either. The Zingerman's community includes over 700 employees working in 10 different businesses in the Ann Arbor area, all operating as one organization. So while I know that "work groups" and committees aren't exactly the norm in small businesses (like we were when we opened in the early 1980s with just two employees), they've long been fairly standard around our organization. Up until I read Welbourne's piece, our drive to solicit staff members to participate in "non-core activities" had been focused just on finding ways to get good people to do good work. ZCoBers were usually asked to become members of work groups because we thought they had some expertise in the area a committee was focused on and, hence, could contribute to the "cause." But Welbourne's article planted the seed of a whole new belief: that having as many people participating in groups as possible could, and should, be a high organizational priority.

I'd always figured that most of the work group and committee members were among our most committed staff members. It's just that I'd incorrectly assumed the reason they were involved in the work groups was that *they were already engaged*. Now I realize that the inverse was equally important. The employees who got into work groups or, to use Welbourne's language, took on "non-core work," consistently *became* more engaged simply because they were immersed in that second level of activity. I came away with an entirely new perspective on organizing work. We call it One + One.

One + One in Practice

Here's how it works. The first "One" in the equation is the staff member's core position. It's what we hire them to do, the job that takes up the bulk of their workweek. By definition, it's the role that most likely taps into a significant part of their skill set. Being a baker, a sandwich maker, a line cook, a member of our catering crew or our HR team—you get the idea. The second "One" (we call it the "+ One") is less obvious. It's an additional piece of work, something outside their core day-to-day activity. The + One could find a staff member joining one of our organization-wide work groups that focuses on service, training, benefits, etc. They might teach a class about our products, food safety, merchandising, management, service, sales, or sanitation. They might take responsibility for leading a project. They could also "own a line" in our open-book finance system—it's a longer story than I have room to get into here, but that means they're taking "ownership" of managing a key "number" that might involve sales, product quality, cover counts, check average, or service scores, to name a few. There's really no limit to what they could do, since we have so much going on, and most anything of consequence here is done collaboratively.

The point of the + One is that while it's also work, it's a *different* activity from what the staff member is doing during the bulk of their week. Most of the time it draws on different skills from what they do every day. And it will certainly put them into a different role in the organization, one in which they interact with people outside their regular daily orbit and in which others start to see them in a new light. It's not hard to understand how that starts to change things up. When they do One + One work, they use a different part of their skill set, meet other people, and learn new things. In the process, we enhance creativity, connection, caring, communication, and commitment.

My ever stronger belief is that one reason staff get so bonded to each other and to an organization when it's in the start-up stage is that, in brand-new small businesses, One + One work happens naturally, out of necessity, every day. In the craziness of those early months and years of getting going, most everyone starts to do a bit of everything just because that's the only way you can make things work. If you've been part of a start-up, I'm guessing you have a good sense of what I mean. While it's stressful getting through, those who do survive usually end up with great memories, a strong sense of camaraderie, and a lifelong commitment to the business, even if they go on to do other things. In a way, One + One is just replicating what most of us went through unconsciously during our early years of getting off the ground.

As we grow, most of this overlapping organizational behavior is "straightened out" and jobs become increasingly specialized. Where everyone used to do some HR, now we hire an expert. While everyone worked on every product, now we have folks who do only one part of the work. And in the process, organizational "depth perception" gets lost. People's lives are less rewarding, their perspectives narrow, their chance to learn, grow, and contribute tends to decrease.

But with One + One, we go in the other direction. All sorts of out-of-the-box things start to happen. A frontline staffer who might be baking 40 hours a week gets to assess health-care proposals. Someone who's making sandwiches at the Deli by day might be working in our Training Engineers work group by night. A server might wait tables most of the week, but every Wednesday they "own" the line for Total Sales on our whiteboard, which means they're responsible for reporting and forecasting revenues and also delivering on their forecasts with great results. A bartender might do a yearlong stint on our Benefits Committee, where they're fielding proposals from various insurance providers, assessing options, and making a plan for how our organization will address insurance needs for the coming year.

Getting people engaged in that + One, that other element of the organization, the place where they use different skills and build relationships with different people, makes for a far richer and more expansive work experience. So much so that we've begun crafting a bit of new-age business math.

One + One = 170

No, I haven't forgotten everything I learned in math class; I do teach ZingTrain's two-day open-book finance seminar. And yes, it's also accurate that we're working to turn One + One into 170. With all of what I've outlined above in mind, a few years ago we set an organizational goal of having 170 people—close to a third of our staff at Zingerman's—involved in One + One work by the end of this year.

The target of 170 was about twice as many people as we had doing it the previous year. What drove us was, quite simply, our belief that the more One + One work we got going, the healthier our organization was going to be. There's the business benefit from the work people do in their secondary role. And for the staff members themselves, there's the opportunity to significantly enhance their work experience. One + One is definitely win-win.

Here are the first two steps of the process we use for organizational change, which we call Bottom Line Change (BLC), as presented for this One + One approach (written in 2011 when we were just getting going with it).

BLC Step 1. Compelling Reasons DRAFT— ONE + ONE = 170

To enhance the quality of more ZCoBers' work experiences while simultaneously helping the ZCoB.

Three legs on a stool are more stable than two; relationships are the same way. The relationship that any of us have to our workplace is more stable, more resilient, and more enriching when we are active in parts of the business beyond the specifics of our day-to-day job responsibility. The more people get involved in an additional element of the organization—their own job + another work group or project —*the higher the quality of their experience* here tends to be. They meet other good people. They learn from those people. They have a wider support network to depend on in both good and challenging times. They learn best practices, tips, and tools that can make their own work better. Turnover goes down, energy goes up, we tap into more creative brains, the culture improves, and new staff have a better shot at finding out early that they can get involved. Everything and everyone feels—and is—more supported. Relationships are more rewarding and more resilient.

In September 2010, 90 people reported that they had a One + One activity. In March of 2011, 106 did. Now we're going for 170, or one-third of our organization.

BLC Step 2. Vision Draft

It's the end of September 2011. Over one-third of the people working in the ZCoB are now on board with One + One—they've got their own "regular" job, plus they're engaged in some other active and ongoing job responsibility, one that might tap somewhat different skills in a different setting, in which they get to do work that's different from what they do every day. We've generated, agreed upon, and actively promoted a list of what those "+ One" activities could be —participating in committees, coming to Partners' Group, owning a line at a huddle. From that work, everyone gains. Over one-third of us have the benefit of the stronger bonds and learning that comes from the secondary, supporting layer of learning. As a result, people's sense of connectedness is higher, as is their feeling of being able to make a difference. And their actual ability to make a difference is increased, too—they learn how things "work," so that when they want to make improvements, lead change, or help the organization as a whole or their part of it, they know how to get started doing so. They know more people in the organization—crew members have been connected and now communicate with ever-greater effectiveness. We've helped to build an informal network behind the scenes. As more and more people know each other, there's "someone to call" in the other ZCoB businesses when help is needed. Energy is up, turnover has stayed low, staff survey scores are up—almost everything has improved as a result of this seemingly small change.

Why Employees' Job Experiences Are Better with One + One

Having now worked on this plan for five or six more years, I can add to the list of compelling reasons.

THEY GET TO BRING FORWARD MORE OF THEMSELVES

With One + One, people's work experience improves, quite simply, because they get to switch on parts of their skill set that they probably would never otherwise use on the job. You don't have be an HR expert to figure out that most everyone has a wide-ranging set of abilities and interests that, almost inevitably, go to waste in their particular role at work. Very few jobs call upon all the different talents we each have to offer. As Peter Block writes, "there are too many people in our communities whose gifts remain on the margin." By getting people involved in another area, we maximize the odds that they get to put their full selves—or at least more of their full selves—to work. As a result of which, they feel more fulfilled, more appreciated, and more valued.

THEY GET MORE VARIETY

When you do them day after day after day, all jobs can feel drudgerous. Even if we like what we do, it still starts to get old after a while; it doesn't much matter if you're the business manager or a busboy—most jobs are mostly made up of repetitive tasks. One + One work gives people a way to break out of their regular routine, add variety and interest, and help keep energy up without abandoning the work that they're particularly good at in the first place.

THEY CONTRIBUTE MORE

Everyone likes to know that their work makes a favorable difference; it helps build positive belief and increases hope. One + One work offers both in a convenient organizational package: because the work brings a change of pace, people get to contribute in a whole way. And since the organization does better in the process, its employees feel all the better for being part of a successful group.

THEY MEET NEW PEOPLE

One + One gives the staff member a new peer group to be a part of, new people to learn from, new friends to connect with, and new coworkers to commiserate with. Don't write this off just because your organization is small—One + One work might well put staff members into contact with a different group of customers or suppliers than they usually interact with. Meeting new people builds their support group; they learn things from peers that they might not be ready to hear from their boss, and they add to their network of friends and community.

They Learn New Things

People who are doing good work want to learn. And getting them into a secondary side of the work of the business will make it far more likely that they're learning regularly and consistently. Everyone does better when their minds are moving. And because what they're learning is being directly applied, it's often more meaningful than something they'd get in a straight academic setting. It's so easy in our day-to-day job responsibilities to lose sight of the importance of learning. One + One constructively forces us back into the learning zone. And we know how powerful that is: active learning builds hope; it gets people thinking and engaging in new and different ways.

They Develop New Skills Without Having to Give Up What They're Good At

I'm not a big believer in the Peter Principle, which says that people will consistently be promoted until they reach the level of their own *in*competence. But it is true that sometimes good staff members will go after a promotion or change jobs because they're bored and want a change of pace or a way to get extra income. One + One work gives them a chance to get that variety, test out some new skills, and add a little boost to their pay package, without having to leave their old position altogether.

New Experiences Are Energizing

While learning new skills is often challenging at first, once we get moving it's almost sure to build energy. Adam Grant writes: "Two hours a week in a fresh domain appears to be the sweet spot where people make a meaningful difference without being overwhelmed or sacrificing other priorities." He also points out that it's easier for us to give additional energy when it's done in a different setting. "The logic behind it? Change of context made giving feel fresh."

Why One + One Adds Up to Better Business

One + One isn't just good for the staff members who do it—the business benefits as well in the following ways.

STAFF BUILD MORE RESILIENT RELATIONSHIPS WITH THE ORGANIZATION

In most work settings, an employee's main tie to the company comes through their manager and their immediate coworkers. If those bonds are good, things stay strong. But if the manager (or a close colleague) grows cynical or starts acting like a victim, it's likely that the employee will do the same. One + One builds a much wider range of relationships so that the staff member is solidly engaged with other parts of the business. This makes it easier to handle stress, improves interdepartmental communication, and increases empathy.

TURNOVER IS REDUCED

Generally, if a manager leaves, their top employees are likely to leave, too. One + One work increases the odds of other staff members staying, which means lower costs, less stress on the remainder of the staff, and more stability.

WE TAP INTO NEEDED SKILLS

Frontline people in most businesses have far more to offer than their organizations realize, let alone access. One + One significantly increases the odds of tapping into that underutilized natural resource. Getting a bit of copywriting from an English major who's already engaged in some other part of the business and having a sandwich-making biology major teach food safety to the staff are easy ways to put One + One to work. Cab-driving carpenters could also build shelves in a new office. It's win-win-win—the business gains because needed work gets done; the staff member wins because they're getting paid to do something they're good at and probably really enjoy; and leaders benefit, too, because we have fewer things to do ourselves!

PEOPLE WHO DO ONE + ONE START THINKING MORE AND MORE LIKE OWNERS

Because One + One work gives employees a much broader, organization-wide perspective and puts frontline people into leadership roles they might not otherwise get into, everyone increasingly makes decisions with the thought of "what's good for the overall business?" in mind. And that can only help us get better results, better buy-in, and better everything else!

DEPARTMENTS LED BY LESS-THAN-EFFECTIVE MANAGERS CAN BE MORE STABLE

This isn't a subject most people want to talk about, but it's the reality of organizational life. At any given time, some managers won't be operating effectively. It could be that they're new to their job, they could be experiencing personal issues at home, or they might be overwhelmed by changes in the marketplace. By building a wider peer group and grounding staff members in parts of the organization other than their primary "address," One + One gives a staff member who's serving under an ineffective manager a way to get needed support, both technically and emotionally. The benefits of the One + One work also reduce pressure on new managers who tend to be overwhelmed in their first few months.

THERE'S DIVERSITY OF WORK FOR A DIVERSE WORKFORCE

We like diversity. The healthiest ecosystems in nature, we know, are the most diverse. Different people with different backgrounds see, hear, and experience things differently. Which is helpful and holistic, both. But I've realized of late that there's another, rarely acknowledged part of workplace diversity. One piece is a serious, long-term effort to recruit from groups who aren't well represented in your business's workforce, and to make your business as welcoming and inclusive as you can. But the other side is that by offering a diverse range of ways that employees can engage with the business, we honor the fact that all of us have complex, multifaceted minds. I've started to envision it as a kaleidoscope, needing two parts to work its full magic. One holds a panel of colored glass pieces, each of which on its own is colorful and interesting. But it's when you put the revolving lens on, hold the kaleidoscope up to the light and turn it, that you really see its full majestic force!

WE'RE IN ALIGNMENT WITH NATURE

With all the attention I've given to working in harmony with nature, I shouldn't have been surprised to discover that the One + One approach is totally true to what happens in an ecologically sound natural setting. It's a setup that's well aligned with nature. As Toby Hemenway reminds us (see page 49), every element of an ecosystem is connected to many others—those connections contribute to the system's health and resilience. One + One helps to systematize just such a structure, since everything in a healthy ecosystem does more than one thing.

> *If you look at what a tree is doing in any natural system, it is producing fruit, it is producing shade, the leaf litter is building soil, the roots are breaking up heavy soil, it is harvesting rain and channeling it somewhere. It is habitat for a zillion different kinds of creatures. And, that is the kind of thinking that permaculture recommends. And so we put it into a principle of every element should serve multiple functions.*

Which is, of course, exactly what happens when we put this program into place.

A Testimonial from Another Industry

Patrick Hoban runs Probility Physical Therapy here in town; it's smaller than us in size, but it's growing very nicely to the point where they now have 12 locations around Ann Arbor. While they haven't started to formalize One + One the way we have, they have been doing it informally for three or four years now. Patrick is a big believer in its value. "You just can't really know what skills people on your team have until you get them into other settings," he said. When his business first started doing One + One work, he was concerned that the staff would be losing billing time—every half hour that a certified therapist isn't working with patients is theoretically billable time lost to the business. But after trying it, Patrick told me he found that it was extremely productive to get people engaged elsewhere.

One + One Works in a Small Business Too

If you only have half a dozen people on staff, each will almost certainly have skills, dreams, and desires that aren't going to be fulfilled by doing only their regular duties. And conversely, the organization will always have needs that would be well met by people who might not be formally expected to work on them in their regular job assignments. All the same benefits apply—

cross-training, greater resiliency, increased satisfaction, and all the other good stuff I've outlined above.

The Manager's Role in Making One + One Work

In her article on employee engagement, Theresa Welbourne warns that One + One–type activities won't be successful unless leaders learn to create the appropriate culture. If a manager believes that the One + One work is a waste of time, we know from the self-fulfilling belief cycle that they will almost certainly ensure it will fail. When a staff member comes back to their core job after spending some time on a secondary task, all the cynical manager has to do is say something along the lines of "Okay, can we get back to some real work now?" to have the employee go from feeling excited to ashamed. A skeptical manager can also make it hard for the staff member to find time in their schedule to do the work. To add insult to intellectual injury, the manager can completely ignore the content of the work by never showing interest, never asking what the staff member is learning, and never expressing any appreciation for the extra effort taken to do the work. Discouragement and disillusionment follow. Hope levels decrease. With an unsupportive leader, One + One may equal *less* than zero.

We want the opposite: managers who want the staff member engaged in the One + One activity to feel appreciated and encouraged. At Zingerman's, we ask leaders to play the same sort of positive role with One + One as we do with other training, what we refer to by the acronym CRU, which stands for "Context-Reinforce-Use." Although the examples that follow are specific to One + One, the approach would be the same for any training or noncore work that might come along. Here's how we put CRU to work.

CONTEXT

The manager frames things for the staff member. Usually, this conversation takes place when we have the initial dialogue about One + One. Something along the lines of, "We love having you here, and I want to make sure that your work experience is as rewarding as possible. We've found that getting involved in this One + One work really helps enhance the quality of the experience of our best staff members (of which, of course, you're one). Based on what I know about you, you've got some great skills that we're not tapping into during your everyday activity here in the department, and I'm hoping this will let you put those skills to work. I think it's gonna be great for you, and for the organization too." Obviously you could add in any or all of the benefits I've listed above. The key is backing up the significance and value of the One + One work, so the staffer knows it's important and why.

REINFORCE

This typically happens right *before*, and then again shortly *after*, the One + One work commences. It could be as simple as the manager saying, "I'm so glad you decided to get on that work group. It's really valuable for the organization. I'm sure you're gonna get to know some great people and learn some interesting stuff." Or, "This is great that you're on that work group. I'm looking forward to you teaching everyone else in the department about it." Or maybe, "I'm happy this worked out. It's really gonna help your career growth here down the road."

USE

Although the One + One work may not be directly related to an employee's everyday responsibilities, the likelihood is high that they're learning things of value to their home department. For instance, if the One + One activity is with our Great Service Group, it could be that the participant shares service trends with their sandwich-making peers. If the work involves teaching a class on personal finance, they might end up more regularly assisting others in the department with finance-related issues. If they're learning about benefits proposals, perhaps they'll join the HR team in speaking to the rest of the staff about the new health-care plans being rolled out. The point is that we want to use what people learn in their One + One work and apply it to what they're already doing every day.

Anarchist Angle

With anarchism's focus on aligning with nature, it's no surprise that there's a good deal of support for the idea of One + One in anarchist circles. Anarchist geographer Élisée Reclus charged his students to "avoid overspecialization." Peter Kropotkin points out that

> *if scientists were to clean sewers two hours a day they would invent so many improvements that it would become a comparative pleasure to work in sewers. . . . The ideal society . . . is a society of integrated combined labour. A society where each individual is a producer of both manual and intellectual work: where each able-bodied human is a worker, and where each worker works both in the field and the industrial workshop.*

In Spain, these anarchist principles have been put to work at the Paideia school. It was started in the late 1970s in the town of Mérida, in the western region of Extremadura, which we know at Zingerman's for its wonderful sheep's milk cheeses, smoked paprika, and aged Ibérico ham. In line with the belief that the means we use must be congruent with the ends we want to achieve, on the school's wall is painted: "Be careful with the present that you create because it should look like the future that you dream," a quote attributed to Mujeres Creando (a Bolivian anarcha-feminist street-art group). In the spirit of One + One work, the students of all ages—yes, including young kids— get involved in managing the classroom, their education, and even what they eat for lunch. They're learning to collaborate, be accountable, and think both big and small from the time they're five or six. What happens when you go to a school like that? The same sort of thing that happens in any other healthy organization of this sort. One visitor wrote, "In Paideia one of the many things I learnt was that being free is fundamentally about taking individual responsibility and being able to collaborate fluidly in a collective community." If scientists benefit from cleaning sewers, and our staff members gain from being a big part of running Zingerman's, then it only makes sense that students who are learning how to run their school will do remarkably well.

One + One Conclusions

One + One makes far more than two—it helps the people who work with us, it helps the organization overall, and it creates a very strong and steady stream of positive energy and best practices across the business. It enhances the development of favorable beliefs, builds hope, and encourages the spirit of generosity.

By getting One + One up and running, we're giving everyone here a better chance to keep learning, to use a different part of their skill set, and to gain knowledge and experience. Putting One + One in place isn't some bold and brilliant new business innovation. But it is a solid and ultimately significant bit of background work that has helped—and is actively helping—our business and everyone in it!

NOTES FROM THE FRONT PORCH

Ludo Gaberon, Designer, Ann Arbor, Michigan

Changing Perception About People and Life in General

I come from a traditional French family with a relatively conservative upbringing.

I went to medical school and graduated in physical therapy, worked as a professional for a few years, and immigrated to the United States in 1996.

My story is not mainstream America, and it is probably not any different from any other foreigner's: it's about challenges and finding ways to overcome them.

I started working in Ann Arbor as a dishwasher in one of the cafés downtown. I quickly moved to positions with more responsibilities and found myself after a few weeks in charge of the closing shift (mid-afternoon to close), managing the staff, interacting with customers, doing daily accounting, and participating in the cleaning duties at the end of the day.

I did not have any prior managerial experience. Physical therapy is not about managing active people but managing patients. It is very different, and my summer jobs when I was still in school were insipid, mostly spent as a staffer in an accounting department of a privately owned bank in Paris. So when I was given a team to manage here in the U.S.—even though it was a small one—I felt inspired.

Unfortunately, I did not find the ground—I should say the soil—for my skills to grow. Consequently, I quit less than a year within.

At that time my wife was giving French lessons to Tommy York's family—Tommy was at the time manager of Zingerman's Deli. She told him about my experience and he suggested I stop by for an interview. I recall the interview with Matt Morgan to be less than formal. It actually fit very well with the environment surrounding me. I was struck by the craziness of the place. When I say "craziness" I mean a Deli spreading over what used to be two single houses, filled with thousands of different smells, covered with thousands of different stickers and boards filled with thousands of colors telling thousands of stories about thousands of products. Maybe I was the one a bit crazy that day . . . but it was the impression I had.

I instantly knew I had found Ali Baba's cave and its treasure to be revealed with the use of a magic phrase: the Zingerman's experience!

The Zingerman's experience was to me like a trip to the Frontier, an outpost in a new world of culinary culture and professional management. To my French archaic and rigid perception of the world, these new grounds were populated by "Indigenous people," real people, with a set of specific ways to proudly proclaim their cultural distinctiveness: in the way they presented themselves, expressed themselves, interacted with others, and thought about food and business.

Quickly the filters I used to rely on to perceive "others" unraveled. I discovered that most of my preconceived ideas on the notion of being "different" were in need of a refresh.

There was a high level of professionalism in all those "characters." They all became true friends and I learned a lot from them.

"A manager has the ultimate responsibility to serve to the best of his abilities his employees so that in turn his employees will serve to the best of their abilities the customer or client." is the most insightful comment I remember from Ari during my time at Zingerman's. I remember thinking how forward thinking such an approach to managing that was. This inverted hierarchical pyramid is the key to enable, to empower employees, and to make them feel inspired.

There lie two crucial notions, freedom and trust: Freedom to the employees to make the organization's values theirs and to act, portray, and promote those values in their own way. And trust on the part of the employers to let their staff carry the flag and to let them be brand ambassadors, reassured that they will act in good will. Achieving, in the process, genuineness, which is the pillar for sustainable business.

Business is commerce. It is transactional. This notion of exchange, of giving and receiving, where values are being transferred from one hand to another . . . Through my time at Zingerman's, I came to realize this was, as many other activities man engages in, just really about human interaction. It is not systematic nor mechanical.

It is just about behavior. Economist Hersh Shefrin defines three prevalent themes in behavioral economics; the one that I got myself immersed into without knowing while I was helping customers at the Deli was mostly *framing*. Framing, according to his definition, is the collection of anecdotes and stereotypes that make up the mental emotional filters individuals rely on to understand and respond to events.

That is the secret I learned during my time at 422 Detroit Street in Ann Arbor. The emotional DNA, the secret to do business right. The personal history one brings to the deal will condition the output, whatever is being traded; it is what makes *us* that will make the deal a success or a failure.

Because it is only when one resonates with true emotions that genuine behavior will be expressed and honest behavior will be diffused and perceived.

I remember my first class at the Bakehouse, I felt pretty comfortable as we gathered around the flour-dusted tables. After all, I grew up in a culture where people were consuming an average of one loaf of bread per day. I didn't anticipate the roller coaster I was about to ride. Frank Carollo, the man in charge, told us the story about the first sample of yeast that was used to make the first loaf of Zingerman's bread back in the 1990s and how this mixture was kept and cultivated since then to make today's bread. . . . I was literally crying, overwhelmed by my emotions. Authenticity, dignity, ponderance. The subject could have been trivially delivered; the passion made it powerful. Once again my cultural foundations were blown to pieces. Why? Because I took food and the culture of food for granted. I did connect sensorially with it throughout my earlier life but never emotionally. There was no emotion in buying a piece of cheese in my life before. At Zingerman's I filled the void. Following those "Indigenous people" around and learning from them I was able to link my sentiments to my senses and vice versa, to finally involve myself wholly. That was only achievable because these people were true to themselves and to their passion.

Below are some comments from folks at Zingerman's who've done One + One work. Next to each name you'll see their main, everyday position and then next to that, their additional, or + One, work.

Joanie Hales, marketing and events manager at the Roadhouse, + ZingTrain trainer, instructor of a number of internal Zingerman's classes, and member of our Training Engineers work group

Reading the books, teaching class, doing ZingTrain gigs—it really does just reinforce how much One + One matters. Doing other things beyond my current job makes me more engaged, more interested, and I think more of an asset to the organization.

Sara Whipple, marketing manager from the Bakehouse, + leader of our Zingerman's Southside work team, member of our Marketing work group, Staff Partner, and former coordinator of customer feedback for all the Zingerman's businesses

I gained a greater understanding of the other businesses and I can share that with my coworkers. I see and hear about opportunities to give better service or increase sales in my business. I learn best practices from others in the organization. I strengthen my leadership skills by using them in new situations. I get to practice our recipes, writing visions, project management, time management, and our Bottom Line Change recipe when doing the work of these groups.

Betty Grattop, with our Mail Order Business,
+ member of our Diversity work group, and LEAN instructor

It's fun. And when I have fun, I love my job more! Being on a committee puts me in the position of being an active learner. It makes me engaged, and I feel more a part of the whole ZCoB. There's a regular opportunity to share and gain best practices. It allows me to ask for help from folks from other parts of the organization, because I get to know people I'd normally never call.

Sharon Kramer, Roadhouse server, + owner of the "cover count" line
at the Roadhouse huddle

It helps me pay attention to the finer details. It's easy to know the day to day, but this is something I'm interested in that goes beyond that. I'm always thinking about how I can make my line (cover count) better. I look at which areas of the business we can improve and where we're doing better. After being here for five years, it would be easy for me to stagnate, but owning the line helps me keep trying to get better, and helps me focus on what my goals are for the Roadhouse. It helps keep me and the restaurant moving forward at the same time.

James Christie, Roadhouse server, + teacher of our internal service class
and former member of the Great Service Group

It's taken me outside of the Roadhouse. It's made the ZCoB "smaller" (in a good way) and more accessible. Before I started doing the One + One work, the Roadhouse was Zingerman's. I used to think about it as if the Roadhouse was the Earth, and all the other businesses were the rest of the solar system. But then, after I started teaching and doing work on the Great Service Group, I realized the ZCoB wasn't so disparate. Everyone in the ZCoB has pretty much the same problems and the same guests. It's definitely an opportunity to learn new things, too. And I learned that there are a lot more resources in the ZCoB that I could tap.

Carole Woods, Deli–HR liaison, + leader of the Deli Culture Club,
and trainer of our Zingerman's Employment Experience
and M.O.R. money classes, to name a few

One of the things I like best about working with the Culture Club is the opportunity to connect with coworkers outside of the regular day-to-day work. We just don't have the time during a busy shift to really talk about what we can do to make the Deli an even better place to work. I enjoy our meetings because they are both fun and productive. I'm always reenergized after one, even if I'm sort of dreading it beforehand—you know, in the "ugh, not another meeting" frame of mind. By meeting together as a group, we discover different strengths than we might otherwise see in our everyday work. For instance, we have someone in the group who is great at facilitating, someone else who takes great notes, and someone who always comes up with the crazy idea none of us had considered. These people don't get the chance to use these specific strengths every day, so this group is a great way to help bring them out.

Why (Paul or) I Still Teach Orientation for New Staff Members

Building Positive Beliefs, Hope,
and the Spirit of Generosity from the Get-Go

While it hardly wins big headlines, the act of teaching this orientation class for new employees is, without question, one of the most rewarding and productive parts of my job. If you want to make a big difference in your organization—large or small, for- or not-for-profit—a class of this sort is one of the most practical and effective tools I know of.

As Zingerman's grows, it's appropriate and important that Paul and I continue to hand off various aspects of our work to others who can devote more time, or better skills, to tackling a particular part of the organization's activity than we can. That said, one of the last things we'll give up in the steady and sustainable march of our organizational progress is the orientation class we teach for new staff members—a class we call Welcome to the Zingerman's Community of Businesses, or more colloquially, Welcome to the ZCoB. If you aren't already personally teaching some version of an organizational orientation (whether for your business overall or your department or division), and you want to make one meaningful change in your culture this year, I'd give a class of this sort serious consideration. I often say that the yellow legal pads I buy to journal on provide *the* best return on investment I can make. Teaching this class, I believe, comes in at a close second. Everyone who's a part of it (and even their peers, parents, and partners who weren't there) will benefit from it.

Given that I've probably taught our orientation a couple of times a month for nearly 30 years now—which, if my math is right, is well over 500 times—I suppose I'd have good reason to be bored with it. To the contrary, I'm anything but—the Welcome to the ZCoB class is one of the most positive parts of my work. Why? Because literally every single time I teach it, I finish feeling recharged, excited, challenged, and more motivated than ever to go out and excel in all I do. My belief system on the subject—as you'll see—is deep, strong, and positive. I love it!

If I told you I'd achieved that same excellent personal impact after spending a couple of two-hour sessions with a high-level business coach who costs me $1,000 or so a month, you'd probably say I had a good coach. You might even ask for a recommendation and contact information. The coaching in this case is coming from our newly hired crew, and the inspiration is what their enthusiasm, interest, and dedication to doing good work in the world calls up from inside me. And unlike the considerable price tag associated with expert executive coaching work (though I'm supportive of good coaches), all this class costs us is the time I spend teaching it, the expense of photocopying the eight-page workbook, and the hourly rate of the employees who attend. While you might not be inclined to seek inspiration by adding two or three hours of teaching to your already busy schedule, I'll argue adamantly that these are some of my most productive hours.

Why It's So Much Better When the Boss Teaches This Class

In smaller organizations, it's rare that there's any formal "welcome" class of this sort. The orientation generally happens one-on-one with whoever is training the new person in their area of focus. In most organizations of our size, the orientation class—if there is one—is taught by HR staff (here, our Department for People) or some official training-type person. From what I've heard, these sorts of sessions usually give a bit of historical overview and focus a lot on benefits, how to get paid, and how the organization's policies and personnel systems work. All of which is important stuff. For what it's worth, we have a comparable class for that as well. Neither Paul nor I teach it. One of our very able HR folks does, and they do an excellent job. It's a very helpful way to orient everyone to the operational basics of being part of our organization.

What Paul and I teach is something totally different. It's the intellectual, emotional, historical, and ethical story of Zingerman's, and some of the key ways we work to make it all happen. I want Welcome to the ZCoB to focus on business, passion, commitment to excellence, and effective energy management. When new staff members leave our class, I want them to feel valued and excited about the job they've chosen to take with us and the opportunity they now have to be an important part of what we do. Essentially, I've realized of late that the class aspires to build positive beliefs about our business as well as to encourage positive belief in each individual's sense of themselves.

In essence, it's not a whole lot different from a two-hour talk about Zingerman's I might give to a couple hundred leaders of progressive organizations. Welcome to the ZCoB is about substance—real people, real food, real customers, real coworkers, real money, real insights; it's about real problems, real recoveries, and real-world realities. The whole thing is about being real (see Secret #29, in *Part 2*). I want to share thoughts on how we (which now includes them) can effectively run a sustainable business. I want them to walk away with a good understanding of who we are—as individuals, as leaders, as an organization. I want our new crew to know where we've come from (personally and professionally) and to understand where we're going and how we're working on getting there. I want them to have some sense of where we've messed up and how we've learned to move forward anyway. And I want them to understand how they fit into all that and how they can contribute to helping the organization—and themselves—be successful.

There's a simple, but very important, message that's sent when the owner of the business (or the leader of a given department or unit) sits—in person, not a prerecorded picture on a video screen—with all the new staff to review this stuff. The way I see it, we're asking the people we hire to work their butts off to help create organizational excellence; the least I can do is bring them up to speed on what we're doing and how it's going. By taking the time to teach the orientation, we send a clear message: we value everyone who works here. What we've long believed is congruent with what Peter Koestenbaum writes: "The true teachers must be those persons who are in charge of the organization. The bosses, ideally, should be the teachers."

Having done it for nearly 30 years, and having seen many friends and ZingTrain clients start doing something similar in their businesses, I guarantee that teaching an orientation class will have a hugely positive impact on your organization and on the people who are a part of it. Its effect may well, very seriously, stay with them for the rest of their lives. Teaching a class of this sort works in every size business. In large organizations, it allows owners and leaders to connect firsthand with the people they've hired. It may seem extraneous in small businesses, but the truth is that not many people really get this level of in-depth orientation attention, even in workplaces that have just a few people in them. In the smallest of businesses, the "class" becomes a one-on-one get-together. In those that are geographically spread out, it can, I'm sure, be done using Skype or some other technology that will be invented soon to connect people all over the globe. My strong belief is that the bigger your business gets, the higher the risk of people feeling excluded and ignored or of carrying negative beliefs or low levels of hope with them from previous jobs. All of which only increase the import of teaching this class as you grow.

How Does It Work?

Most every manager or owner that I tell about this class thinks it's a fine idea; they just can't imagine how they'd find time to implement it. I think about it the other way—I can't conceive of what it would be like *not* to have it. The cost of staff possibly getting "dis-oriented" by others in the organization is so high that that alone gives this work great value. From a practical perspective, Paul or I teach the orientation for new staff at least twice every month. At the holidays, we do it about 15 times in six or seven weeks in order to get all our seasonal folks up to speed. Staff usually take the class sometime during their first few months on the job—on occasion, in their first few days; more often than not, somewhere between weeks one and eight of their work experience.

To back up a bit, for years we required new staff to attend this Welcome class before they could begin working. There's a pretty clear logic to that approach: get everyone up to speed before they start. But as we grew and had a harder and harder time finding qualified staff, it became almost impossible to stick to our "no-class, no-start" requirement. In the real-life world in which we operate, new crewmembers were being hired on different days, working totally different schedules, and experiencing different degrees of urgency to get things in order. A manager short six people on next week's schedule understandably needs to get new folks working, cooking, baking, and taking care of customers, not having them on hold waiting for me or Paul to schedule an orientation. So in practice, people began to start working without having taken the class.

Finally, about 15 years ago, Paul and I gave in—we accepted what was happening in the real world of our workplace and altered our expectation accordingly. Today we simply teach a couple of Welcome to the ZCoB classes a month, and new staffers come when they can. If someone isn't able to make one of the prearranged times, Paul or I will do our best to set up an alternative session they can come to. Sometimes we have only one or two attendees; other classes can have up to 20. When we hold classes in the preholiday Mail Order ramp-up, some have 60 or 70 people in them.

Although changing the timing of the class so that it came after most folks had already begun working a bit came out of convenience—not some brilliant, strategic HR maneuver—it has significantly increased the effectiveness of the experience. Getting oriented to something you've never done isn't unhelpful, but it can't really ever resonate in the same way as giving context, meaning, and depth to something you've already been experiencing. Before the switch, we were sharing nice ideas, but people couldn't really connect the conversation to what they were about to start doing for work. In hindsight, the disconnect is clear. Adults generally like to learn by doing, Maggie from ZingTrain would remind me. Now, because most folks have somewhere between a week and a few months of real-life work experience in our organization before they take the class, most everything I'm talking about will a) seem at least slightly familiar, b) give the background and thinking behind what they've already experienced, and c) give meaning to their work. The entire two hours is now generally filled with the workplace equivalent of "amens"—comments like "Oh, that makes sense!" "Yeah, I've seen that." "Wow! That's why . . ." "Yeah, we learned that in . . ." It's much more meaningful when the work is already underway than it ever was when it was entirely conceptual.

A Recipe for Putting Together a Kick-Ass Orientation Class

Incorporating the items below into the class outline is pretty much assured to lead you towards a successful orientation session. I'm so confident of this that I'll offer a guarantee to back up that statement: If you do this class and staff don't respond better than they have to your *not* doing one, I will seriously send you a bag of our Magic Brownies or a couple of handmade candy bars to pay you back for the time it took you to read this piece. (Actually, let's make it more positive. If you begin teaching an orientation like this and it goes well, let me know what you learned, and I'll send you a brownie anyway.) The examples I use here are drawn from the organization-wide orientation that I teach, but *the recipe is equally applicable to comparable classes done for specific departments within a business, too.*

With that in mind, here's what we do in the class.

1. PROVIDE A CHANCE FOR THE LEADER TO GET TO KNOW NEW PEOPLE

Good relationships almost always start by sharing stories. Given that we're going to work together for quite some time (I hope), it only makes sense that new staff members and owners/managers get to know each other. So after I move through a quick overview of the class, the session starts off with a round of personal introductions. I specifically say that I want to know more than just their name and where in our organization they're working. I want to hear their stories—what their backgrounds are, where they grew up, what they're doing here. And usually I'll ask them to tell the group something strange or interesting about themselves that we wouldn't normally know. Gets 'em thinking and gets me learning. Knowing that they're on the rowing team, read mystery novels, have three kids, spent two years abroad in the Peace Corps in Cameroon, or whatever is meaningful information. They all have deep roots from before they arrived here, and the better I understand their beliefs and passions, the more effectively I can help them grow and succeed in their time with us.

Stas' Kazmierski taught me many years ago that it is essential when running a meeting to get everyone's voice into the room. Once people speak aloud, the emotional ice is broken and the odds of them speaking again go up significantly. On the other hand, if they begin in silence, most people will stay that way out of uncertainty, shyness, doubt, or deference. (This is the same experience John U. Bacon talks about in greeting and learning the names of students in his U of M classes.) If Peter Block is correct, as I believe he is, that meetings are the family dinners of organizational life, then getting everyone to speak in the Welcome to ZCoB class is like welcoming everyone to the organizational family. Once people have spoken aloud in a formal setting, they will hopefully feel comfortable speaking their minds as they go forward with their daily work. And as Terry Tempest Williams writes, "In a voiced community, we all flourish."

Servant Leadership says that new staff members are, in essence, new customers, and it's hard to meet your customers' needs if you don't know what's driving them, who they are, and how they got here. I'm so used to this level of connection to new staff members that I can't really even imagine it any other way. And if the organization is going to be completely committed to the success of each individual in it (see Tenet 1 of Secret #29 on Anarcho-Capitalism), and I'm one of the cofounders and key leaders, it only makes sense that I spend some time getting to know the people working here. As they tell their stories, it's hard not to be intrigued. The last group of new folks included one guy who collected comic books, another who bred geckos, and a third who emigrated from Ireland and whose father-in-law was one of our first customers back in 1982. Then there was the woman who spoke Thai, the guy who graduated from Texas Tech, a woman who loved home renovation, and another still who studied event planning and was extremely interested in traveling to Haiti. Oh yeah, and there was a former U of M football player, someone who was in recovery, and another guy who played both bass and piano. Everyone at the orientation had an interesting past and, I believe, a chance for a really positive future. The more I knew about them, the more they felt honored for who they were, the more likely it was that good things were going to come from our collaboration.

Our mission at Zingerman's says that we show "love and care in all we do." This early interpersonal engagement makes that statement into something real, not just another irrelevant line of corporate mumbo jumbo to put into a PowerPoint. If nothing else, this intro makes clear to your new coworkers that you believe in them, that you think they have something significant to contribute, that you care what they think, and that you care about them—which goes a long way towards getting people to buy into the organization.

Please don't underestimate the power of this personal interaction. It's enormous. For most of our new staffers—coming as they do from, shall we say, less-engaged environments—it's like lighting the fuse to reignite their personal energy. Thinking back to what I wrote about "the energy crisis in the workplace" (see Secret #19, in *Part 2*), I'll quote Brenda Ueland again, who says that if we listen, love, and connect, we can preserve the "joyful, imaginative, impassioned energy" that's naturally present in everyone.

Once I've made the connection with new staff members, it's about 10,000 times easier to make their ensuing work experience meaningful. I can ask about their hometown; I can inquire as to how their family, friends, or pets are doing; I can send them articles that I think would be of interest; I can watch for organizational opportunities that might arise for them. These small, meaningful moments may radically alter the quality of their work experience. Through which, I will also guarantee, the cost of the class will get paid back to our organization about 80 times over every week each of the attendees works with us. When people feel cared about, connected, and included, guess what? They act like they're part of the organization, not like replaceable robots who don't have the tools or training to handle any situation more difficult than showing people where the bathroom is. My job is to get to know people who work with us so I can help bring out as much of their inherent intelligence, insight, and innovative energy as I can! Ralph Waldo Emerson wrote, "The secret in education lies in respecting the student." This class is all about it.[31]

2. OFFER AN OPPORTUNITY FOR NEW STAFFERS TO GET TO KNOW THE FOUNDERS/LEADERS

The average employee, even if they're optimistic about life in general, is still likely to believe that the owners of a business of our size will mostly be focused on making money—maneuvering big bank deals, leveraged buyouts, stock sales, and key strategic decisions—not on new hourly employees. At best, I'd guess they'd stereotype us as bigwigs who might be nicer than bigwigs in other industries, but still we're the bosses. What most new employees in an organization with more than 10 or 12 people almost never have the chance to learn, I think, is what their new boss is actually about. Which is why I take time early in the class to cover our backgrounds, our beliefs, what drives us, what makes us crazy, what our families are like, what we like to eat, and why we love food, creating good work, and living in Ann Arbor. The truth is that "bosses are people, too."

I want new staff to know where I'm coming from, what I care about, and also what I struggle with. To know that I don't have all the answers and I need all the help I can get. I want them to know Paul, too. When I teach the class, I ask who's met Paul already. If they haven't, I give them homework—to write, call, or connect with Paul in person and introduce themselves to him. "It makes no sense to me," I tell them, "to be working for someone and not have met them."

If all we did in the class were the two things I just went over—me getting to know them, and them getting to know me—it would already be a big win. The personal connection is pretty much priceless. If you don't yet do an orientation, just ask your HR staff for a list of new employees, and then make your way around the organization and introduce yourself. Spend five, maybe ten, minutes to talk—or go wild and take twelve. I guarantee that your organizational "game" will change completely and that people's loyalty to the business will be way higher than it was before you took time to chat. Look, no one—let me repeat, no one—wants to work for an abstraction, a press photo, or a bio on the company intranet. Good people want to work for good people; when we give new staff the chance to get to know us, we're giving them, and us, a far better shot at getting to great things!

3. Introduce Our Approach to Training

Since this class is training, in and of itself, and since training is such a big part of what we do here (so much so that, as you probably know, we went out and started ZingTrain, our own training business!), it only makes sense to explain to new employees why we do training and how we do it, and to clarify our respective roles as trainers and trainees. Our approach to training is summed up in our Training Compact.

Zingerman's Training Compact

The Trainer Agrees to:	The Trainee Agrees to:
1. Document clear performance expectations.	Take responsibility for the effectiveness of their training at Zingerman's.
2. Provide resources to do the work.	
3. Recognize performance.	
4. Reward performance.	

Every time I teach the orientation, I ask the attendees how the way we organize training here with Zingerman's Training Compact is different from how training was organized in their previous jobs. Probably six or seven out of ten respond with some version of "We didn't even have training." Even for those who got some training in earlier work experiences, the way we approach it here—where both the trainer and the trainee take full responsibility for its effectiveness (100 percent each)—is significantly different from the way it was done elsewhere. The peer-to-peer approach that we use in training is the same one we apply to most everything else. It means so much that we take time to talk in person instead of sending someone to represent us.

4. RELATE OUR HISTORY

This is what I've written about in Secret #8, "Vision Back." When people know where we've come from and how we got here, it's not surprising that they feel significantly more connected to the company they're now a part of. Zingerman's may be famous in the food world, but I never assume that new employees know much of anything about who we are, either personally or organizationally. One new staff member shared at the class that although she grew up going to Zingerman's and can't remember a time before the Roadhouse, she really had no clue what Zingerman's meant to others until she heard her mother enthusiastically telling everyone that her daughter was working there!

· The story I tell is not a dry detailing of irrelevant old information, but rather the telling of a living history, which they are now actively participating in enhancing. "We have to reintroduce ourselves to history," contemporary anarchist Paul Cudenec says, "not as observers but as participants." The more I can make that history come alive, the more I believe we help people buy in to what we do, the more effectively they can communicate with customers, the better the guest experience, and the better our business will be.

I start out by sharing my own background, how I came to be in the food business, how I met Paul, why we started Zingerman's, why I love my job, etc. As I tell the class, I grew up in Chicago, came to Ann Arbor to go to school, and studied Russian history with a special emphasis on the anarchists. After graduating, I had no vision and little idea of what I would do next. Mostly, I just knew that I didn't want to move back home, and in order to make that hope a reality, I would need to get a job. While I was in school, I had driven a cab part-time to make money, but that wasn't much fun. One of my roommates was working in a restaurant in town, and he seemed to like it, so I went in and applied to be a server, too. After waiting a few weeks without hearing anything, I went back and reapplied. "Maybe I could start as a busser and then get promoted to server later if I do good work?" I suggested. Two weeks or so later, still not having been offered a job, I went back and offered to do any work the restaurant needed done. They asked if I wanted to wash dishes. I said yes, and that is how, unwittingly, I stumbled into a life in the food world!

As I tell the group, I got lucky. I really had no interest in much of anything other than paying my bills and not having to move back to the suburbs (where I was super worried I'd get stuck for life like so many others had seemed to do). I also got lucky because I met great people—Paul was the general manager; Frank Carollo (one of our partners at the Bakehouse) and Maggie Bayless (managing partner at ZingTrain) were also working at the restaurant. I didn't have a passion for food, I explain to the class. I grew up on a diet of Kraft mac and cheese and fish sticks from a box. I gradually learned to prep, I tell them, then to cook, and finally to manage kitchens. In the fall of 1981, I decided to leave and gave two months' notice. Two days later, Paul called me to talk, and we opened up the Deli together in March of 1982.

Granted, as a history major, I'm biased towards the importance of sharing background. But how can the crew have a good sense of perspective on things when they don't have any idea where we've come from? Or how we've successfully arrived where we are today? I talk about where and how we've succeeded, when we've failed, and how we've recovered from those failures. Hearing those tales—and hearing them from someone who's been through them—gives a richness to our organizational story, a depth of character to who we are that will never come just from reading (or being read) policy guidelines and principles.

Our organizational history is really one of the most meaningful parts of the class. It's actually what a lot of trainees remember most. Yes, it's true—they could just go and read it online. But what resonates more with you? Stories your grandfather told about his own experiences growing up or a textbook that takes you through the key political events of that same era? While both have value, my experience is that the stories, the history, generally mean more when they come from someone who actually was there and lived through it. In our case, the start-up phase of the business, the early struggles, the stranger-than-fiction stories probably wouldn't make it past most corporate HR departments' edits.

Alex Young, chef and managing partner at the Roadhouse, teaches a comparable class for restaurant staff there: Welcome to the Roadhouse. Alex says, "I love telling the story of how we got here, and how so many people have influenced who we are now, and what an opportunity it is, because of who we are, to make a stand for food quality. And then how being an open-book company is the ultimate opportunity to learn and help to improve our workplace." The emotion, energy, personal perspective, and humor we can put into the history make all the difference.

It's quite funny to hear some of the stories people have heard about the business. Many think that Paul and I went to college together, sat in our shared dorm room scheming about ways to make money, designed this little deli, and then went out and did it and, of course, were an overnight success. The only problem with that story is not a single part of it is true. Others imagine that Zingerman's was started a century ago, somewhere around the time Rocco Disderide was getting going. They're shocked that the owners are still alive.

Setting the story straight brings some smiles, but it's also good business. If they're going to represent us—and themselves—well in the world, staff members need to know who we are and how the heck we got here. The history we share in the class, combined with the employee's personal experience of our business as a customer—sometimes extensive, sometimes nonexistent—basically *is* Zingerman's to new folks. And if they don't hear it from us, they're going to get some other version of history from someone else, perhaps a cynic who's all wired up about something.

Talking about how we recovered from failures is an important subtext in the session. I want people to understand that success doesn't come quickly and easily. To the contrary, I tell them, I've personally screwed up almost everything I'll be talking about in the class at some point in the past. I want to normalize failure and show how we can all recover if we stick with things, stick together, and steadily keep moving towards the vision we've agreed to pursue (more on that in a minute). All of which, I believe, helps build hope and teaches emotional resilience, both of which are essential to people's success at work and to their lives at large. In the words of Gustav Landauer, "history is not only revolutionary, it is revolution."

5. Emphasize Our Mission

From there, I move forward to a review of our mission statement. In a nutshell, a mission as we see it here answers the broad, but very important, questions: "Who are you? What do you do? Why do you do it? And for whom do you do it?" I explain why, how, and when (in 1991) we wrote the mission in the first place, sharing the history of what it means to me, and how I believe it impacts our daily work (if you want to check it out, see page 198), and that there's an entire essay on the idea behind it in *Zingerman's Guide to Good Leading, Part 1* (see Secret #5). Although each of us here has been hired to do a particular job—make coffee drinks, cook, bake, serve—we need to understand that regardless of job title, we're actually all here at Zingerman's for only *one* real reason: *to bring everyone we interact with a great Zingerman's experience.*

To emphasize the point, I tell them that if they take only one thing away from this orientation class, it's the seriousness of that statement—that while we clearly need to do baking, accounting, and sandwich making well, I *need* them to understand the most important part of our work is to make great experiences happen for literally everyone we come into contact with—customers, coworkers, suppliers, or anyone else we might meet. This approach is so different from what most staff members have been taught in other jobs that I usually reiterate it two or three times. And you know what? They get it. And you know what else? They go out and do it! I guarantee that the mindset behind the mission actually alters the way most everyone here looks at their job. When people comment (which they do regularly) that our employees act like owners, the acceptance and internalizing of the mission among those who work here is one of the main reasons why.

I also tell the story of how we wrote the mission: it was drafted by a work group of eight people (including me and Paul) who spent six months developing it, along with our guiding principles. We got about 80 of the 100 or so people who worked at the Deli involved. I want our new staff to understand that the mission wasn't made up at some anonymous corporate headquarters, that it didn't emerge on paper overnight in finished fashion, and that many of their predecessors worked hard for many months on it. Most importantly—per Natural Law #11—the lesson is that good things take a lot longer to create than most people think, and they are generally the product of a lot of challenging conversations.

6. SHARE OUR VISION

If you don't have a vision, I can't recommend doing one highly enough. For more on writing effective visions, see Secrets #6 to 9, in *Part 1*, and #35, in *Part 3*, or skip back to Secret #47 in this book. For conversation's sake, we'll just act like you have one even if you don't and talk about why you want to share it.

Here's the deal: People like to be a part of something greater than themselves, and the vision is one way we make that happen. It's the cathedral we're all building, the marvelous and majestic structure we're working so hard every day to collaboratively construct. Sharing an inspiring vision of the future gets people excited and helps them feel a part of something special. And almost everyone likes that feeling!

I tell the group the story of how Paul and I came up with the vision for Zingerman's 2009 back in 1994. (It's become a bit scary for me to consider that an increasing segment of our staff now *weren't even born back when it was written*, but I remind myself that this is a good problem—most places don't stay in business long enough to have it.) I tell them how we had, unknowingly really, fulfilled our original "vision" of the Deli from back when we opened in 1982. Paul intuitively realized that had happened and that we had reached a point that I now equate to "organizational midlife." I describe how he sat me down on a bench in front of the Deli one summer day in 1993 and asked me where we were going to be 10 years down the road, and that I had no clue—either personally or professionally—what the answer to his question should be. And how we then spent a year talking and disagreeing, continually coming back to the table, to come up with our six-page vision for Zingerman's 2009.

When we shared it, both the business world at large and people inside our own organization were skeptical; many thought we were nuts. That was also true when we opened the Deli in 1982, and then again when we started the Bakehouse in 1992. And we pushed ahead anyway, and look what happened with these now nationally known culinary icons. When we're doing something really great, I tell the class, we know that hardly anyone may believe it will work at the start. But I want them to know that about 90 percent of what we wrote in that vision came to pass.

From there, I fast-forward to 2006, when we began writing the 2020 vision, which involved direct input from over 200 staff members, went through a number of revisions, and was completed only after all 19 managing partners had reached consensus. I want new staff to know that when you work here, you really can make a difference, and to believe that it's *all* of our responsibilities, regardless of seniority, specialty, and schooling, to help make the vision a reality. I review each of the vision's nine bullet points, with a bit of a story behind each, encouraging them to read the entire document on their own. As I talk about the vision, I tie it to their work, sharing examples that have day-to-day meaning.

Finally, I ask for questions and pose one of my own. "What do you think?" I ask. Then I pause and wait for them to speak. The pause is important—staff members usually think any questions the owner or manager asks in a class are rhetorical. The responses are almost all along the lines of "I love it!" or "It's amazing!" I don't like to stop at the surface, though—I usually press them for more details. The responses that follow are almost always thoughtful and often exceedingly insightful. And it's not that hard to understand why the vision appeals. Few people, if any, will have worked at a place that has a vision, let alone have had the founder of the company take the time to share it with them. They're caught off-guard by the fact that profitability is only one small (if still significant) piece of it. And, fundamentally, the language is inspiring, and they can relate to almost all of it. Sharing this vision with everyone, right from the start, goes a long way towards building positive beliefs about us and changing beliefs about business in general.

The 9 Key Strategic Elements of Our Vision for Zingerman's 2020

1. Changing Our World

2. 12 to 18 Vibrant Businesses

3. Radically Better Food

4. Radically Better Service

5. Radically Better Finance

6. Intentional Technology

7. We Put the F U in Fun

8. ZCoB as an Educational Destination

9. Opportunity for Everyone; Responsibility for All

To read the full vision, head on over to http://www.zingtrain.com.

I also mention what businesses we might be opening next, and I remind them that most of the managing partners in the organization came from within the ZCoB. And that our sincere hope is that *they* might, one day, become one of those partners. I invite them to talk to me or Paul about any idea they may have for a Zingerman's business. Many have them. I know that only a few will actually follow up. But just the open invitation helps to build hope and belief and to get folks thinking differently about both themselves and their work. "I took a job here washing dishes because I needed to pay my rent, and now you're telling me to come talk to you about being a partner in a Zingerman's business that I would help create?" Yep. You got it!

7. Present Our Business Perspective Chart

I then take a few minutes in each class to review our Business Perspective Chart. By the time they've been here for a month or two, most staff members will have heard it explained three, four, five, or more times. It's essentially a visual representation of how we believe our organization, and really any organization, fits together. (For a full explanation, see Secret #4, in *Part 1*).

I tell folks that the chart was one of the first things Maggie from ZingTrain pushed us to create back in the mid-1990s, because, as she said, "Different people learn in different ways, and you would benefit from having a visual model of how the organization works." She was right. It resonates with people. The chart shows mission, vision, systems, culture, principles, and bottom lines. I explain to the class what each term on the chart means and how and why it's important for us to use. I also always tell people that it took Maggie, Paul, me, and others about a year to finish the chart. Again, I want them to realize that good things take time, and that most are born out of disagreement and the ensuing dialogue, almost never from some divine poof of congruity that comes out of the cosmos.

If some of the folks in the class have worked here for a couple of months already, I may ask if they're willing to try teaching the chart before I do. Many are up for it. Even though they weren't "prepared," I like to put them into a leadership and teaching role right off—it shows that everyone is capable of comprehending this stuff and that it's safe to step up and try it. It also sets the bar high for the other attendees. While I pretty much always embellish on the student's original explanation, I always thank and credit them for being willing to start a discussion of the material, and I acknowledge the many parts that they presented well.

More than anything else, explaining the chart gives people a language to talk about the workings of something that most know next to nothing about when they first start working here. Remember that very few of the people we hire have any business training. But when we review the chart, they're all learning the basic key concepts, and now they have words to talk about business, as well as a fairly common understanding across the organization of what those words mean. I've seen frontline people who've been here for four or five

Zingerman's®
business perspective

the zingerman's experience

vision

↓

principles

culture   systems

↓

results

great food! great service!
great finance!

the zingerman's experience

©zingtrain 1996

months present these concepts more effectively than upper-level executives elsewhere, just because they all have the same understanding of things like "mission," "vision," and "culture." Psychologist Rick Snyder says, "As we impart word power to our children so too are we instilling hope." The same is surely true for new staff members.

8. Explain Why We're Here

Purpose, you might remember from the ecosystem metaphor I wrote about in the introduction, is air. Without it, we suffocate and die. In their old jobs, most of our employees got only a long list of tasks they were supposed to complete. It's hard to breathe well, let alone think or exercise, in such a stifling environment. By contrast, I want new staff to start their work here with a nice burst of fresh air. The mission and the vision fill the all-important need that people have to know why we're here—why we're committed to delighting our guests, delivering amazing food every day, operating in a financially sustainable way, and contributing to the community and to the quality of one another's lives. Without that "why," what's the point? When we have no purpose, our work just degenerates down into ways to make money, in which case, honestly, other than paying the bills or saving for retirement, who really cares?

We're in the food business, where your average employee is likely to approach work as merely a way to make a living while they wait for a "real" job to materialize. While more people are inspired by the culinary world today than back when we opened in 1982, for most folks, food is not the focus of their life's ambition. All of which makes it imperative that they know *why* we're working so darned hard to do what we do, and how it could have meaning for them even if they might only be here for six or eight months. Reading right from the mission, the answer is actually: "to enrich as many lives as we possibly can." Getting further afield, it's to work together to attain our 2020 vision and in the process, as it spells out, to contribute positively to the lives of everyone who works here, our customers, our suppliers, and our community. Believe me, knowing *why* makes a world of difference. To quote business writer Simon Sinek, "Average companies give their people something to work *on*. In contrast, the most innovative organizations give their people something to work *toward*."

9. Lay Out the Bottom Lines for the Organization: How We Measure Success

While having spiritually sound missions and visions can be uplifting, and sharing our history can be inspiring, I want new staffers to understand that we also need to get results. Unfortunately, few frontline employees in America (or I'd guess anywhere else) have any clue how business actually works. While you're probably thinking about how in the heck you're gonna pay your bills, they're thinking about how rich you must be. We need to deliver results, I want them to understand, in order to stay in business, pay our bills, and pay them. If you don't know how the team you're on keeps score and what that score actually is, it's awfully hard to make good decisions every day, let alone win, right? So if knowing the "why" gets people fired up, then knowing how we're doing helps keep them focused. This is why we're so adamant about all our new staffers knowing how we measure those results.

At Zingerman's, we've been working with not just one but *three* bottom lines for nearly 20 years now. Food, service, and finance are of *equal* import to us. Service means service to each other and to the community as well as to the guest. I go over with them brief explanations of each, giving specific examples throughout. We have full-on, in-depth classes we teach on each of those subjects, where they'll hear far more than I can fit in here. But I want them to have some sense of what we measure, why we measure it, and how we all go about trying to get it every day. I try to tailor the examples I use for each area to the particular businesses and departments in which the attendees work, so that they can leave with concrete ways to connect what I'm teaching to what they're doing every day. While I was editing this essay, I ran into Iris, who just recently started working at the Deli. We exchanged greetings, she asked me what I was working on, and I gave her a 60-second version of this book. She responded by reflecting on the bottom lines question. "Yeah, I was telling my friends how we have three bottom lines here, not just one. And now that's kind of in vogue with companies who are realizing, 'Wow, maybe we should have more than one bottom line!' It's a different way to think about business."

10. DESCRIBE THE KEY SYSTEMS

If there are any really important systems that are essential to your success, this class is a great place to bring 'em up. I explain how our systems contribute to our three bottom lines, and I highlight the most important times to use them. Inevitably, you have way more systems than you're going to cover here—the point is to pick the top two or three, the ones that you care most passionately about, or that are most integral to the success of the business, or most helpful to newly arrived staff members. In our class, I give a brief explanation of our 4 Steps to Great Food, 3 Steps to Giving Great Service, 5 Steps to Effectively Handling a Customer Complaint, and 3 Steps to Great Finance. They'll hear more about all of them elsewhere, but the repetition is helpful. Meanwhile, I want new folks to understand that we know we're not perfect, that part of their job is to help figure out how to improve, and that the improvement is a collaborative activity for everyone here, not just the responsibility of owners and managers.

Explaining Positive Energy

One thing I've added to the content of the class in the last few years is a review of our recipe for energy management. You can read much more about it in Secret #21, in *Part 2*. Back in 2011, we adopted "positive energy" as our professional definition of fun at Zingerman's. Having an agreed-upon, well-understood organizational definition allows us to honor the reality that each of us enjoys different things, while at the same time agreeing on one specific meaning that applies when we talk about having "fun at work." (For a quick version of the energy recipe, flip back to page 343 in Secret #45.)

The recipe allows us to make clear to every new staff member that *the energy we bring with us to work every day is our own choice*. It's a performance expectation in our organization that, other than those above-mentioned sorts of exceptions, we all need to mindfully choose to bring a high level of positive energy. *If we can't, I remind them, it's probably better not to come to work.* Why? Because per all six points of the Hope Star (see page 322), the energy each of us brings to work for the day—and to every interaction we have—has an enormous impact on the way the business works and on the quality of our lives as individuals.

To illustrate the point, I give an example or two, usually tailored to the work that the attendees on any particular day might do. Say, for instance, that a host or hostess has less-than-enthusiastic energy at the front door at the Roadhouse, or that the first person a guest interacts with at the Deli fails to smile and greet the customer enthusiastically. "What's going to happen to the guest's energy?" I ask. They all understand that the guest's mood is likely to be lowered as a result. "And what comes next?" They can pretty much all figure it out. The customer will likely be slightly on edge. If the customer was a bit cynical or upset about anything else when they arrived, they probably now start *really* looking for trouble. And when they're looking for trouble, they'll find it.

I like to take the story all the way through, though, just to prove the point. You may come to work with us feeling like a small piece of a very large puzzle, but when things are framed like this, it's hard to miss the reality: every tiny action you take makes a big difference. "Let's just imagine that one little thing goes wrong with their sandwich," I say. "Then what?"

The customer is already looking for trouble and, of course, they've found it. We all know that they're now pretty likely to complain, often in a negative and unproductive way. That, in turn, will drag the service person's energy down if they're not careful. It could also cause the manager to leave what they're doing and focus on our unhappy guest, who now needs extra attention. Which, if the manager isn't doing a great job of staying grounded, can quickly lead to other problems. Before you know it, if folks aren't really on their game, the whole shift can go downhill. And all simply because the first person to see the guest greeted them in a halfhearted, or robotic, or unwelcoming kind of way. Believe me, everyone gets the point.

11. Cover Our Core Values

While our guiding principles, or values, aren't "why we're in business," they detail how we're going to work together, with the world, and with our community en route to our vision. In the class, I review our ethical guidelines, with the belief that they'll help shape the decisions that new staff make all day, every day. If you can stick in a few real-life examples to illustrate your points, I guarantee that will go a long way towards helping people understand what your guiding principles actually mean.

For instance, I always talk about how our definition of quality at Zingerman's is a) full-flavored food and b) traditionally made food. And how those two criteria—not what the market wants, not what we make the most money on—are what drives our decisions of which items to serve or sell. I might give them the example of our Jewish rye bread—how it arrived here from the Polish part of the Russian empire in the late 19th century with the large waves of immigrants who came after a series of brutal pogroms. I tell them that I prefer the large, 2-kilo loaves, because they were common back in the days when my great-grandparents would have been eating it, and also because bread in big loaves tastes better. If someone's interested in the anarchists, I might add in that it's also what Emma Goldman almost certainly was eating in New York City a century ago.

I also like to talk to them about our commitment to making Zingerman's a great place to work. And I emphasize that although we'll do everything we can to make that happen, the reality of daily life is that how they treat each other minute to minute will be more meaningful than any fancy benefits plan.

Random acts of generosity towards coworkers—as simple as getting someone a cup of coffee or emptying the trash cans in a different area—can make all the difference in more than one person's day.

Here are some other key elements of our guiding principles that I mention.

- Nearly all our food—with a couple dozen exceptions (balsamic vinegar is one)—has roots as poor people's food. A couple of fun facts: Caviar used to be given away free at bars to get people to drink more after consuming so much salt; New England law once forbade serving salmon to indentured servants more than three times a week.

- We value learning, and offer opportunities for learning everything from leadership to finance, to food history, and much more in the form of internal classes, scholarships, a staff library, seminars, etc.

- We're committed to each other's success, which means that when we're frustrated with a colleague, we have an ethical obligation to be direct with them (as well as, of course, to offer help and coaching).

- We like long relationships, so when people leave the organization, we really appreciate it if they give fair notice. It's not uncommon here for people who know they're leaving to give three, six, even twelve months warning. We want to continue to build our relationships even after a staff member has left the organization.

- We take community giving seriously, donating 10 percent of the previous year's profits. And a customer who would like to request one can go online (at zingermanscommunity.com) to ask us to make a donation to their cause.

- With four exceptions (see page 541), we believe that it's ethically important to break the rules when we need to get great service to a guest. This last note always gets people's attention. What does it mean in practice? Well, for example, we don't typically take reservations at the Deli. But if a group of senior citizens is coming in for lunch, we can figure out a way to hold a table for them, and have someone go take their order there, rather than requiring them to wait in line like everyone else. I remind new staff that we have 700 creative and intelligent people working here (which includes them), and I'm confident that if we put our heads together, we can almost always figure out a way to make a great experience for any guest.

12. OUTLINE THE CURRENT STRENGTHS AND WEAKNESSES OF THE ORGANIZATION

As an open-book management company, we share all the financial information with our staff. So in the Welcome to the ZCoB class, new hires get a quick synopsis of the performance of the organization as it's reflected in the current year's scorecard. I show them the same sheet of numbers that the partners get every two weeks at our leadership meeting, and then give them a quick idea of how to read it. Think about the meaning of that act for a minute: one of the founding partners of a "successful" organization of our size sits with a new frontline cook (or baker or box packer or anything else) and goes over the current performance of the business. That's quite a difference from anything they're likely to have experienced elsewhere. By the end of the class, the attendees know the score across our organization: how we're doing on all the key financial measures, service scores, inventory levels, etc. Imagine, on the other hand, joining a new team where they give you no sense of the team's standings or overall issues, but just send you out on the field to play your own position. Kind of scary!

I remind folks that although our intentions are good, we will fall short in some ways on some days. I apologize in advance for our errors and remind them that no one is ever messing with them on purpose. When the shortfalls come, when they're frustrated or feeling let down, I ask them to take a deep breath, honor their anger, and then start working on what we all need to do to make things right. (For more on managing our emotions, see Secret #31, in *Part 3*.) We're all responsible for coming up with solutions together.

13. MENTION PET PEEVES AND PERSONAL QUIRKS

Let's be real—we all have pet peeves and strange personal quirks. You can try to minimize their impact, but you rarely leave home without them. And since sooner or later, new staff members are going to find out what those quirks are anyway, why not save all involved a lot of aggravation and confess 'em up front so they can be ready? It's fine to tell folks the three things that totally make you crazy or, better still, the six that make you really happy. Why hold back?

New employees might actually work to avoid unintentional faux pas and, in the process, make your day better and save themselves some unnecessary stress.

Now, I'm guessing, you're wondering what mine are. I have a really hard time when people who work here don't greet each other enthusiastically with a smile. Another pet peeve is when someone walks right past paper or food that's lying on the floor. I try to remind folks to practice mindfully taking in as many details as possible, to spot both trouble signs and successes while they're unfolding, not to wait until it's too late to manage them effectively in the moment. There are also what I guess you could call "pet preferences." I tell them about my standing offer to buy lunch for any staff member about whom we get a customer complaint saying that they were too enthusiastic! It happens so infrequently I want to free them from even worrying about the "problem"— just be as enthusiastic as they can imagine! I've got your back when the one guest in 500 that will be bothered by it complains.

The Power of Pronouns

I'm adamant in my belief that pronouns will tell you a lot about whether a person has really "joined" our organization. People who are already thinking of themselves as a real part of our organization will pretty much always say "we" when talking about themselves, their department or business, or our organization in general. People who don't really feel on the "inside" are often quick to disassociate themselves from a problem rather than own it. Which is why, whenever a new staffer says something like, "At Zingerman's, they . . .," I'll always gently correct, "You mean 'we,' right? You're now the 'they' that you're talking about. You're part of *us!*" I believe this seemingly insignificant shift has a major impact on the way people think about themselves and their work.

14. Offer Resources Available to Assist the New Trainee

Everyone who comes to work here is going to be overwhelmed at some point. I still feel it regularly, and I started the company with Paul over 30 years ago. When new people feel lost, confused, or concerned about their career or the company's integrity or any of the 800 other things that could be bothering them before they finish their fifth day on the job—well, it's hard to bring great energy and stay super focused when you're fearful. Even worse, I think, is feeling that fear and having not the slightest idea of what you might do about it.

The corporate-fantasy scenario generally pretends those issues aren't going to arise. "Not at our company, at least." But how can you not come to work somewhere new—especially somewhere like Zingerman's with very high standards, 700-plus high-powered personalities, and a highly complex ecosystem of an organization—and not get frustrated? Right from the get-go, we're working to counteract the cultural norm that "strong" people don't need help (they do); that good organizations don't have problems (we do); and that if we had a perfect training program, we'd be able to combat everyone's stresses (we can't).

We provide people up front with a list of the resources both inside and outside the organization that they can look to for help: our Employee Assistance program, our HR folks, additional training programs, etc. I also give out my email and cell phone number—if we're truly here to give service to our staff, it only makes sense that I make it as easy as possible for them to get ahold of me if they have a problem. And lest you worry, if you decide to do the same, that you'll be overwhelmed with bothersome bits of business minutiae, I'll just say that I've never felt hassled at all. Mostly people get in touch to say positive things about the class and the quality of their work experience, or to ask questions about where they can learn more about a product, service, or process. Often they have a customer that they're trying to help and need a hand with information. And if something troublesome is on their minds, if they're frustrated and feeling like they've been treated poorly, honestly, it's much better that they tell *me* than everyone else. If this little orientation-based bond gives me the chance to catch a couple of problems a month more quickly than I would otherwise, then I'd say, on that basis alone, the class pays for itself.

How Can We Afford This Sort of Investment?

When the subject of the orientation comes up, as it usually does at ZingTrain seminars, there's almost always an attendee from another organization who asks, "Why bother taking the time and spending the money to teach this way when turnover in our industry is so high?" It's true that there's a very real cost in doing a class like this. For Paul and me, it's a combined investment of about four hours a month, plus the not-insignificant cost of paying the new staff members for attending.

But I defer to Russ Vernon, of the nationally known West Point Market in Akron, Ohio, who I heard many years ago respond to a similar question with an inquiry of his own. His response—and now mine—was to pause thoughtfully and then say quietly, "I like to look at it the other way." He'd then pause, put a little twinkle in his eyes, and add, "What I worry about is, what if they stay?"

Russ is right. What if new people end up staying for a while, and we haven't taken the time to go through all this information with them? I'll tell you flat out, it's trouble—they don't know where we're coming from, they don't know where we're going, they don't know why we're here. (Which always makes me think of the line I heard once about Columbus: "He didn't know where he was going when he left, he didn't know where he was when he got there, and he didn't know where he had been when he got back.") If they don't hear otherwise, the odds are high most people will project onto us all the bad things they've read, heard, and experienced elsewhere about bosses and businesses—we're rich, we're greedy, we're unfeeling finance freaks who don't care about employees, the environment, or anything else other than the economy, our kids, and our cars. Lord knows what one reads online, and the truth is that there are more than enough bad bosses out there living some or all of those stereotypes to give people good grounds for projecting it all onto us as well.

But since none of that is true here, it's well worth the investment of time and energy to show people what we are about. I teach this class very solidly in the belief that *staff are actually going to stay*. My experience is that when they take this class, the odds increase that they're going to be with us longer, and more successfully, than they would have otherwise.

And If You Still Aren't Convinced . . .

In case I haven't already gotten you to believe that teaching a comparable class in your company is a good idea, let me close with some more valuable things I think it can do.

INCREASE EFFICIENCY

Even if you only do it for the sake of finances, it's worth considering teaching an orientation of this sort, where you share information with a group of 10 rather than doing it one person at a time. These new arrivals also learn a lot more from each other's stories than they'd ever get just by hearing me talk to them alone. They meet folks from other parts of the organization, people whom they might typically never see otherwise. They build bonds, developing a support system to reach out to if tensions should arise between their department and another. Our organizational ecosystem becomes more effectively and meaningfully diverse and sustainable.

And since we've shared our organizational background, vision, and values with new staffers, they generally start contributing positively to our work much more quickly than if they had to figure things out on their own. It's not rocket science—the more they're contributing, the more efficiently we can operate.

GET PEOPLE TO "BUY INTO" THE ORGANIZATION

I believe that we need our staff more than they need us, that there are 100 other jobs out there that they could choose other than ours. It's important to remember that people who work here represent us to our customers all day long, and thus, they're making many, many decisions that have a drastic impact on our organization's future, though they may often be quiet, unspoken, or unseen (by us, anyway).

When new staff members leave the class, they're going to go out into the world and talk to their friends, family, coworkers, and customers about what we do. Since I believe strongly in what we do, and since everything I'm telling them is from the heart, the odds are high that the class will make them feel far more connected to Zingerman's. You don't have to be a marketing expert or give talks on the "tipping point" to know that people who work here are a lot more likely to be out there actively promoting our organization—both as a place for customers to come and for other people to work—after they have attended an orientation class.

MAINTAIN A CLEAR AND CONSISTENT MESSAGE

We all know how hard it is to get any group on the same page. By bringing every new staff member through the same orientation class, with Paul or me presenting, we increase the odds that they're going to be able to speak with one voice when they interact as our organizational representatives with the community, customers, suppliers, and other new staff members coming in down the road. The mere act of repeatedly teaching a class on this (or really any) subject also pushes us as instructors to clarify our message. Repeating that message at least two dozen times a year means that I also get pretty consistent and comfortable with it. In fact, one way to increase consistency if you have shared leadership in your organization is to have people take turns teaching the orientation—everyone, of course, working from the same outline and the same set of notes.

HELP ME HOLD MYSELF ACCOUNTABLE

This isn't the point of the class, but it's a really positive side benefit. Just the act of getting in front of these nice people every couple of weeks to talk about how we work, how much the little things matter, our vision, our mission, our values, service to each other, and food quality, how can I *not* go out and work harder to keep my behaviors aligned with our organizational beliefs? When you revisit the basics and restate your beliefs regularly, in public, it can't but help increase the odds of your actually doing your best to follow what you believe. And, hey, I can use all the help I can get!

OFFER A POSITIVE VISION OF THE FUTURE THAT GOES A LONG WAY

Let me say it again: *everyone wants to be a part of something greater than themselves.* I think it bears regular repeating. The other day a new prep cook at the Roadhouse attended the class (along with eight other folks from various Zingerman's businesses). His reflection afterwards? "I can totally see how my day-to-day work contributes to each one of those parts of the vision! I love it!" That comment inspired me as much as the vision had inspired him.

BUILDING (AND REBUILDING) BELIEFS

What I've come to realize in working on all of this is that a big piece of our work at Zingerman's is to shape—or, equally often, reshape—people's beliefs about work in general, their workplace in particular, and themselves within it. The sad reality is that not many of the people in one of the Welcome to the ZCoB classes have previously had a positive work experience. Many come to us believing that business is a way for bosses or wealthy people to take advantage of those in need in order to make even more money. Even fewer have had a job in which they're motivated, encouraged to be themselves, believe that they actually matter, and feel inspired to go for greatness.

To the contrary, most have gone from one so-so work experience to another. Far more often than not, they've been beat up by past jobs or let down by other leaders, or have emotionally opted out of other organizations that promised a lot but delivered little. Not surprisingly, many of them come out of those experiences with at best neutral—but more often than not, negative— beliefs about jobs, business, systems, customer service, work, and themselves. Many have told me that they left other jobs discouraged, demeaned, apathetic, or even angry. Our work here is to change all that. If they've been lucky enough to have a really good work experience, we applaud their previous efforts and then reinforce that we want that and then some here. If they've had bad experiences, we acknowledge those and invite them in to be participants in our more positive, more engaged, and creatively active ecosystem.

My commitment in this class is go below the surface, to examine the beliefs that people rarely realize have anything to do with their problems, and invite them to change those beliefs. This class does a good job of starting the belief ball rolling. (And, of course, we must continue with it in the work environment; if we pump up positive beliefs in the class but then let people down everywhere else, they'll be even more cynical than they were before we hired them.)

In many ways, I hope that their experience here—with this class as one important element—will change people's views about work and beyond. None of this is an exercise in implementing some recently read study about how to increase "employee engagement." If we're effective in helping to plant these beliefs in people's hearts, it's because we really believe them.

Why I Like Repeats

Although the class was designed for new members of our organization, I regularly encourage anyone who's been to the class in the past to make a bold move and come *again*. The suggestion never works as much as I want it to, but even a few folks showing up again here and there makes a difference. Some have been three or four times, and they've said they got new things out of it on each occasion and felt energized by the experience. I like having them there as well, because their presence, leadership, and insight add to the richness of the new staff members' learning experience. It's proven extremely valuable for people who've worked here for a long time, too. Let's face reality—it's just too easy to slide into survival mode, doing your day-to-day work in the interest of getting by rather than remembering to go for greatness.

Final Thoughts

Lest I doubt the wisdom of my decision to continue to teach it, I have only to wait until the conclusion of the next class to be reminded of how important it is. Watching the energy that grows within people reflected in their eyes as the class unfolds, hearing their stories, listening to the perceptive comments they make and the questions they ask, I'm consistently blown away by the insights, the awareness, the intelligence, and the passion of the new folks that come on board here. I'm reminded every time of how fortunate we are to have the opportunity to work with them. Writer Neil Gaiman writes, "good stories should change you." A great orientation class does exactly that—connection, caring, and great stories told in ways that will change the people sitting around the table. And both you and the people you are teaching are better for the experience.

Annie Kopicko, Former Zingerman's Catering Staffer

Attending Welcome to ZCoB was, quite simply, the moment I knew I belonged at Zingerman's. If I wasn't convinced before the class that Zingerman's was something extraordinary, after Welcome to the ZCoB I was not only convinced but evangelizing. Everyone who would listen heard a dozen reasons why this place is amazing. I was completely awed that every new employee at Zingerman's—even temporary holiday help like myself—was personally trained by one of the founders. From day one, I felt as though I was a part of something bigger than myself, something worthwhile and meaningful, but yet not something so big that I would be lost or unheard. Welcome to the ZCoB taught me that Zingerman's is an organization with a purpose beyond just making money, an organization with personality and heart.

As someone who cares a lot about intangible things such as "meaning" and "purpose," I have often felt that my personal vision is at odds with the business world. Making a positive contribution and treating others with love and respect are goals I consider worthy of primary importance, not just background appearances when they don't conflict with the other things I have to do. Sometimes, in the working world, these priorities have led me to feel like the odd one out. I cannot express emphatically enough how much it meant—and means—to me to find myself a part of an organization that actually dared state "showing love and care in all our actions" as a part of its mission statement. And, perhaps more importantly, this was an objective important enough that the actual founders took personal time to explain and teach the mission statement to each and every new employee. We're setting out to enrich as many lives as we possibly can, and we're stating it boldly! Because of Welcome to ZCoB, we all begin our time at Zingerman's with the same introduction. We are all invited to be a part of the same community. We can all be held accountable for upholding our vision.

Thank you for all that you have done to make that a reality!

Tracie Wolfe, Recruiting Specialist, Department for People, Zingerman's Service Network

I think it's INVALUABLE to every new staff member to not only have the Welcome to the ZCoB class, but more importantly that both you and Paul teach it. Getting to meet one of the cofounders and hear the history, the principles, and our values right from one of you is an incredible service that you both provide. It has now been three years since I took your class in the Swanky Café when I first started; I still remember it like it was yesterday. That's how impactful it was to me. I have worked in other organizations that either didn't have an orientation program or did, but this is the only one that has it taught by the owners. It's fantastic! I have implemented orientation programs at other jobs, but could never get an owner to participate. I am really appreciative of how it works here. It really shows new staff that you and Paul care he/she is here and succeeds—it really highlights how focused our organization is on servant leadership.

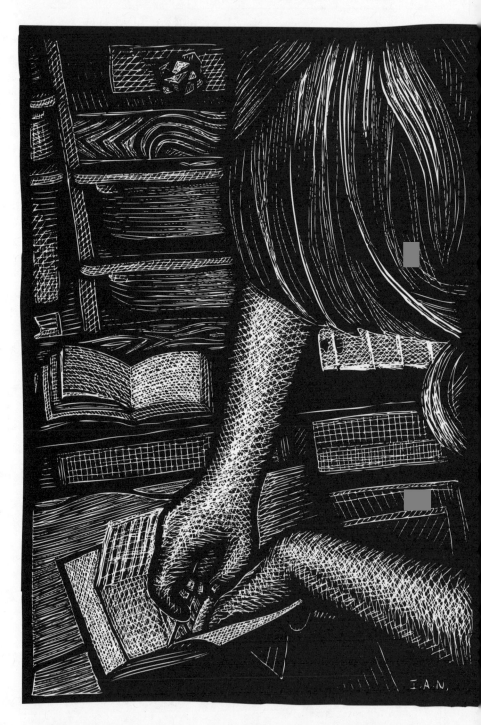

jenny tubbs doing traditional book making by hand at zingerman's press

The Art of Business

Why I Want to Be an Artist

Here's an idea. Next time someone asks what you do for a living, try telling them you're an artist. Watch their response. My forecast? They will pay far more attention when you start to share more about your life. So, I'm pretty sure, will you.

Don't worry. I'm not trying to get you to tell tall tales. I believe it—even if you're not an artist by trade today, I have full faith that you might already live an artistically inspired life. If you don't now, I'm confident that you are more than capable. Accountants, actuaries, and astrophysicists—regardless of profession, we all have the ability to live our lives as if we were artists. And when we choose to live our lives creatively, to make the most of the days and months and years we have on the planet, to be true to ourselves as best we can and as often as possible, then our lives—and our organizations—are truly art as well. Most of us, I know, haven't conceived of ourselves as artists. But I'm guessing that if we start imagining ourselves in this new light, our lives will likely become richer and more rewarding. Excellent, if imperfect, works of art in the making.

If "artist" doesn't feel quite right, you could try saying you're a poet. "Real poetry opens all doors," Jim Morrison once said. "You can walk through any one that suits you." To Morrison's point, there are many we can go through. We get to pick the door we're best suited for, based on what we believe, our dreams, and our desires. The path it leads to may be difficult, challenging, anything but easy. But at least we're on the right road. I far prefer to fall short going after the life I want to lead than to succeed on a path that others say I should have chosen. With that in mind, I opt for the door that leads to an interesting and meaningful life, to more creativity, to helping others around me be themselves; the door to learning, to loving; the one that opens to appreciating the nuance, the shading, the surprise. All of these, I believe, make for better business as well.

Don't panic. I'm not going to make you present half a dozen poems in PowerPoint. Whether you put your poetry to paper or not isn't the point. I agree with Osho, who conveyed, "When I say be creative, I don't mean that you should all go and become great painters and great poets. I simply mean let your life be art, let your life be a poem." I don't write poetry. But I do try to live poetically. Poet Robert Duncan said "poetry must have music and magic." I'd say the same is true for a great life. I look for them wherever I go. The crema on a freshly poured cup of espresso; the smell of real Spanish saffron; the caramelized crust on a dark loaf of Roadhouse bread; the look of amazement on a customer's face as they take their first bite of a Reuben at the Deli. They're all pretty poetically powerful to me.

Which door we opt for is our decision. As Robert Henri writes, "Be yourself today, don't wait till tomorrow." Pressure and problems are always present. Your sister, your soul mate, and society can all have their say. But, in the end, the choice to live an artistic existence is ours alone to make.[32]

Alternatively, you might try saying you're a musician. Rhythm, harmony, pitch, powerful solos within a dynamic band collaboration—these things matter in business, too. As businessman and writer Max De Pree writes, "Jazz, like leadership, combines the unpredictability of the future with the gifts of individuals." Whatever lingering doubts I might have had about this comparison were erased when Lo Rowry, the new cleaning manager at the Bakehouse, came to our bimonthly Partners' Group meeting for his formal introduction to the rest of the business. It's something we do with all new managers—they share their story and they get to meet the key players in the ZCoB. It also helps them to get their voice, so to speak, "into the organizational room." I hadn't met Lo till that morning, so I really didn't know anything about him. Turns out he grew up in Ann Arbor, went to high school next door to the Deli, and actually worked for us briefly a number of years ago. He moved out of town and was gone for quite a while before coming back this year. "Zingerman's was the first place I applied," he said. "I knew it was where I wanted to work."

Lo, it turns out, is also a jazz musician. Mostly plays bass, but he's learned piano and drums as well. "So, is cleaning the Bakehouse a lot like jazz?" someone in the group asked, probably expecting to get a chuckle before we moved on. But with total seriousness, Lo responded, "It *is* like jazz. You never know where it's going, it's all over the place." "How has the job been for you for the first few months?" came another question. "It's been great," he said. "Most places, when you're in cleaning work, you can experience a separation. People don't even look at you. It's like you don't exist. But it's not that way at the Bakehouse. People care about us, and they pay attention to us, and they talk to us." His answers were music to my art-attuned ears.

When Paul and I were working on our University of Michigan commencement address, it occurred to me that what everyone asks when you graduate from school could well be the wrong question. "What are you going to do now?" seems so narrow. A far more powerful and infinitely more interesting way to frame the inquiry might be to ask: "What kind of life do you plan to create?" There are as many "right" answers as there are human beings in the world. Visioning, of course, is one of the best ways we know to get clear on an answer. Because when we write a personal vision of greatness, the profession we're planning for ourselves—doctor, designer, software developer, or donut maker—is just one part of what we're about. There's so much more to our lives than what it says on our business card. The beauty, the depth, the artistry, I believe, are in the details. Remember, it's the fine brushstrokes in the background that bring the foreground into focus. We can, I'm confident, all live a creative and an artistic existence. The more we help everyone in our organization to do the same, the more rewarding their lives will be and the better our business will become. As Robert Henri says, "In every human being there is the artist."

Although Henri was born in 1865, I've known him for only a few years. That we even met is a testament to the spirit of generosity and the positive belief that when you're spending time with creative people, you're going to gain interesting insights. A few years back, I'd offered to meet with a group of journalism fellows at the University of Michigan, including a *New York Times* reporter by the name of Laura Holson. Afterward, she emailed to thank me for the talk. Based on what I'd said during the presentation, she recommended Henri's book *The Art Spirit*. "While he wrote about art and teaching," she said, "his message is this: To be an artist, one has to live a life artfully in every aspect. It is a gorgeous message wrapped up in painting technique and instruction, but one I have always loved."

I took Holson's suggestion to heart and looked him up. Henri was well known as both an artist and a teacher. He was also, it turns out, active in anarchist circles and was an admirer of Emma Goldman. Emma described him as "an anarchist in his conception of art and its relation to life." My interest, of course, was piqued. Henri (pronounced Hen-rye) was born in Cincinnati in the same year the Civil War ended. As a child, he lived in Nebraska and Colorado before his family moved to New York City in 1883 (one year after Rocco Disderide arrived from Italy; they might well have passed on the street in Manhattan), then on to Atlantic City. Henri started painting professionally, traveled extensively in Europe, and came back to Philadelphia, where he started to teach. He also formed a group called the Philadelphia Four, whose members read and discussed the works of Whitman, Thoreau, Emerson, and others. In 1902, the same year Disderide's opened its doors, he began teaching at the New York School of Art, where his students included two of my favorite artists, Rockwell Kent and Edward Hopper.

Early in 1911, Henri took the train out to Toledo, where he heard Emma Goldman speak, and bought a copy of her newly released book, *Anarchism and Other Essays*. He read it on the way back to New York. Later that year, he began teaching at the anarchist Modern School (also known as the Ferrer Center, named after the Spanish anarchist educator who'd been executed by the Spanish government in 1909). Others who taught there included Alexander Berkman, Jack London, Upton Sinclair, and Goldman herself. *The Art Spirit* was published in 1923, when Henri was 58 years old, the same age I am right now as I write this. Mostly the book is a collection of the lessons he taught in his art classes. But like Brenda Ueland's *If You Want to Write* (published in 1937), it speaks as much about making an artful life for oneself as it does about doing art. Hanging out with caring, creative people brings one's care for creativity to the fore—even if they're people who passed away many years before you got to meet them. Both books have given me insight into how to effectively design a great business, what I can do to be a more inspiring and effective leader, and how I can bring the key elements of a creative life into my everyday existence.

Henri fascinates me. How could you not want to get to know a guy who was the leader of something called the the Ashcan school of art, an approach that portrayed the lives of everyday people in New York rather than the more typical portraitist, who tended to paint only the who's who of society's upper crust? Like me—and, I'm betting, you—Henri was a strong proponent of each of us walking our own creative way in the world.

There's great energy that comes from living artistically, as Henri advocates. Creating a life of your own design, even when others raise their eyebrows in doubt and disbelief, can be challenging in the day to day. But ultimately, it's invigorating. It brings our unique passions to the fore. Whether it's baking or business (or, in our case, both at the same time), believing deeply in what you're doing makes all the difference. As Henri writes,

> When the artist is alive in any person, whatever his kind of work may be, he becomes an inventive, searching, daring, self-expressive creature. He becomes interesting to other people. He disturbs, upsets, enlightens, and opens ways for better understanding. Where those who are not artists are trying to close the book, he opens it and shows there are still more pages possible.

It seems to me to be what great business is all about—well-crafted, original art in our products and services; engaging language in our marketing materials; compassionate, kind, community-oriented workplaces; and in our case, high-quality food with distinctive character. That creative, caring, engaging energy is a lot of what gets people lining up to spend time and money in unique businesses such as ours. It's why people talk about us, post about us on social media, and become exceptionally loyal customers for long periods of time.

To be clear, I'm not talking about art as some kind of cute accessory, an unnecessary bauble to brighten up our business. It's actually the opposite. I'm saying that we're all already creative, *and approaching life as art can bring that natural creativity to the fore*. Designing our businesses as if we're artists invites us to pay more attention—to listen for harmony and rhythm, to choose original products and free-thinking people, to check the colors, and to embellish the corners—in ways that we probably wouldn't when we're "just going to work."

All else aside, it's a far more fun *and* effective way to be. "Art cannot be separated from life," Henri writes. "It is the expression of the greatest need of which life is capable, and we value art not because of the skilled product, but because of its revelation of a life's experience." The same, I would argue, is true in business. Through business, we reveal ourselves—the way we treat our newest staff member, how we deal with our most difficult customer, the care that goes into every product we produce says a lot about us. I can't help but relate Henri's credo back to our mission statement: "We share the Zingerman's Experience." When we live artistically, we become far more mindful. We care more deeply. We notice the nuances. We pay more attention to seemingly small but still special things that others skip past without thinking.

In fact, let's try it right here: a small workout for your imagination. This is quick—not a full-on visioning exercise. Just a little stretching for your spirit. Stop for a second and consider some of the little things that you have in your life, the seemingly mundane details that can make your day so much better. Not like a big promotion or a fancy boat. I'm thinking small and generally low cost. Many are free. Grab a pen. Or maybe a colored pencil. You can make notes right now in the margins, which is actually where most of these things show up in our lives and our businesses anyway. If you're inspired, do some sketches on the side of the page to illustrate your ideas. I'll bet your day gets better just by doing it.

Here's what's on my list this morning: the brickwork on Rocco Disderide's building. Eating oysters outside in the sun. A piece of Shawn Askinosie's Tanzanian chocolate melting on my tongue. A lovely note of appreciation from a long-time staffer at the Roadhouse (thank you, Aleta). The new harvest olive oil that's just arrived from Michael Zyw's Tuscan farm, Poggio Lamentano. (Michael really is an artist *and* a farmer—look up his watercolor and glasswork online.) And David Nugraha's work experience here at Zingerman's.

You might remember David from the introduction. He came by to have coffee with me after hearing Paul and me give the address at Michigan's commencement in May of 2015, and then took a position at the Bakehouse soon after. Six months later, he wrote me to say:

> It's been a pleasure working at Zingerman's; it has surpassed any expectation that I had prior to working here. I am so surprised how much of myself I can be at work! On occasion, I will run into an old college friend that recently graduated, too. Many of them are happy to learn that I now work at Zingerman's, but they all say the same thing: "I wish I could find my passion, too," or something along the lines of, "I wish I wasn't so worried about money," or, "I wish I could just do what I love." I now realize that my friends say this because they don't have any belief in themselves. They don't believe that they are capable of achieving the life that they really want. I challenged most of them

on this negative way of thinking, and a few of them were inspired to leave their banking jobs, their consulting jobs, to now start working in the field that they have a passion for. So don't think you are just affecting a few of the 50,000 people at the Big House who emailed you about visioning after your commencement speech last spring. You have inspired me to inspire others, so the indirect impact that you have could be way bigger than you could imagine!

In a healthy organization, every person matters, every interaction matters. David Nugraha. Lo Rowry. You, as you read this book. The delighted look on a customer's face; the crust on a perfectly cooked piece of Great Lakes whitefish (the local fish that Jo Labadie so looked forward to eating); a wonderful sliver of Parmigiano-Reggiano cheese; the passion of an ex-employee talking, 20 years later, about how much he learned here and how he still puts it to work in much bigger, fancier-sounding businesses; the two-year-old excitedly exclaiming, "There's Zingerman's!" to his parents as they walk up the block towards the Deli. All inspire me. Each brings joy. Each is important. All are art. "Every factor in the painting will have beauty," Henri points out, "because in its place in the organization it is doing its living part." Most people wait for big headlines, but I prefer the subtle, small brushstrokes that come together to make a little magic in business.

I realized not long ago that the self-fulfilling cycle we've been talking about around beliefs is also true for passion. While most artists (whatever they do for a living) struggle with the same sorts of self-doubt that everyone else does, their passion for their craft helps them keep going when others give up. It's certainly the same in business. When we're enthused about what we're doing, we find more things that excite us further. Study harder, stay longer, push past the places other people pause. Passion from the heart makes people around us pay attention. Which, in turn, fuels our belief in what we do and our drive to do it well. It is, I believe, a far more rewarding way to live. As Henri says, "The artist is teaching the world the idea of life."

Creative organizations—such as Askinosie Chocolate, Menlo Innovations, Épices de Cru, and hundreds of others—are doing exactly what Henri was writing about. Pop artist Andy Warhol said: "Being good in business is the most fascinating kind of art. Making money is art and working is art and good business is the best art." It doesn't matter if you're an electrician, an engineer, or an educator. When we do business with passion, we make great art. Which, in turn, makes you a great artist. The two seemingly separate walks of life then come together to become one.

Soup Cans and College Football

Andy Warhol, by the way, brought business and art together beautifully—he won worldwide acclaim for his painting of the same Campbell's soup can that, 60 years earlier, was an award-winning culinary innovation Rocco Disderide would have stocked on his shelves at the corner of Detroit and Kingsley Streets. Coming back to the influence of football on business, the red and white of the Campbell's can came after the company's general manager admired the colors of Cornell's football team. In the fall of 1901, the season that led up to Michigan's first-ever Tournament of Roses win, Cornell had a record of 11–1 and allowed no points until the eighth game of the season.

Even just the idea of approaching each action we undertake as artistry has an enormous impact. For one attendee at a ZingTrain seminar last month, it was his biggest takeaway from the two-day Managing Ourselves seminar. "I work in manufacturing," he said. "I'm an engineer. I've been trained to think of things as black and white, to be logical all the time. But I keep coming back to what you said about business being art. And it's really got me thinking about things differently." You could see the impact in his eyes. He'd been pretty buttoned down when we began the session on Thursday morning. But when we did the debrief two days later, he was smiling, his energy lighter and livelier.

When you're looking for them, joyful little things like that show up all over the place. Today, while working on my writing, I got an email from Patrick-Earl Barnes, a New York City folk artist who I met 12 or so years ago while I was walking down the street in Soho. It was on the corner of Spring Street and West Broadway. I'd never seen anything quite like what he does—everyday people painted onto pieces of wooden produce crates. His work is full of life and personality. I imagine that Robert Henri would have loved it. I certainly did. I bought three of Patrick-Earl's pieces, wrapped them carefully, and took them home with me on the plane. It was surrealist poet Suzanne Césaire's "permanent readiness for the marvelous" in real time. I've since bought many more of Patrick-Earl's paintings. On the enewsletter he sent this morning, there's a painting of a woman with the caption "Art is how you think" inscrolled across the top of the canvas.

Unfortunately, a lot of organizations are run in rather artless ways. Art is something they view at a museum or that they pay someone else to install in their lobby. At best, they see art as an oddity, a pleasant pastime that people don't believe is in their purview. As Masanobu Fukuoka writes, "There is no time in modern agriculture for a farmer to write a poem or compose a song." Sadly, I would say that the same seems to hold true for most of the modern business world. The problem is endemic.

Even seemingly inspiring workplaces, ones with world-class art on the walls, aren't immune. A woman I met last year told me about taking an administrative job in one of the best art museums in the country. While the museum's mission and community-based values sounded great, its organizational culture wasn't very creative or constructive, and shockingly, the folks who worked there weren't all that appreciative of the art hanging on the walls. Within a few days of starting the job, she told me, she started regularly using her breaks to go visit the collection. With her belief in art, learning, and positive appreciation of her surroundings—all of which had led her to look for work in an esteemed art museum in the first place—it seemed an obvious thing to do. Oddly, though, her new colleagues, having lived a long time in an unhealthy culture, reacted with near-hostility, challenging her choice. "Why do you keep going out there all the time?" they would ask. She left the job, completely disenchanted, not long after she'd enthusiastically begun.

We can, as individuals and organizations, do so much more. Each of us, I'm convinced, has cool and inspiring insights, paintings to paint, poems to write, interesting lives to lead. If I ever doubt it, I only have to wait a few minutes before someone in our ecosystem generously shares their creative spirit. Not long ago, it was Jim Pawlicki, a dining room manager in a restaurant in Detroit, who'd sat rather quietly through most of the two days of the ZingTrain visioning seminar. All of a sudden he raised his hand. Quietly, he began to talk about his passion for writing, how he'd learned to write screenplays through the exercise of taking dryly written newspaper articles and making them come alive, adding emotion and putting them into the present tense—in the same way, he pointed out, that we teach visioning here at Zingerman's. Then it was the story I heard from Christina Carmichael who came to the same visioning seminar as Jim. When her eight-year-old son, Solomon, heard what she was working on, he insisted on writing out his own four-page-long vision about Legos. I loved it. I start each day with pretty high expectations. And, yet, I'm still surprised by 100 small, wonderful things that happen every day.

Poet Gary Snyder came to visit Ann Arbor a few months ago for a reading. He's studied Japanese drawing and Chinese poetry, and he used to hang out with Allen Ginsberg and Jack Kerouac. He's been called "the poet laureate of deep ecology," does environmental work, and has also published a good bit of insightful prose, including an essay that particularly resonated with me called "Buddhist Anarchism." As I write, he's in his 85th year. He was born ten months after Robert Henri died. I'm honored that Gary chose to eat at the Roadhouse (as he did on his previous visit as well) on the evening of the event. Over 500 people came to hear him read poetry on a farm 10 miles west of town. Wow. Snyder shared his belief that "[c]ommercial art is when you do something to respond to a demand in the marketplace. That's not a bad thing. But when you do something because it's what you love, and then you figure out how to get people to buy it, even though they didn't know they wanted it until you made it, now that's really great art." It's what we've tried to do here at Zingerman's for 34 years now.

Just for context, it might help to know that in many cultures, art and life haven't taken leave of each other in the way they have in the United States. In her essay "Rasanble," anthropologist, performance artist, and my friend in the making Gina Athena Ulysse interviews Haitian poet and playwright Lenelle Moise. "What Americans call art really, in Haitian culture, is just what you do," Moise says. She cites her mother as an example, remarking that when her mother "is really pissed off, she doesn't say anything. She doesn't say, 'I'm pissed off.' She starts singing some old spiritual. And you can hear all the anger and all the nuance in the song she's singing. Art is life." Zingerman's and Haiti, it turns out, have something significant in common. What you've read in this book is about business and life lived in an artistic way. I believe that given the desire and a bit of support, *anyone can do it.* "It is not as if the artist were a special kind of man," early-20th-century Ceylonese philosopher Ananda Coomaraswamy says. Rather, "every man is a special kind of artist."

One of the most interesting interview questions I've learned to ask an applicant is, "What's the best compliment you've gotten in the last six months?"

Their answer tells you a lot about what they value. Here's what I'd say if you asked me that today: probably the best one I've received in the last couple of years came from Brandon Clark, a line cook at the Roadhouse. He told a bit of his story in Notes from the Back Dock in *Part 2* of the series. In a nutshell, he came to work in the Roadhouse kitchen while in recovery from substance abuse. After a reasonable run of good work, he relapsed. Failed to show up for a bunch of shifts. Got fired.

The good news is that his story didn't end there. After a while, he reapplied and got rehired. Why? Essentially, all the things in this book. The leadership team at the Roadhouse didn't hold a grudge. They believed Brandon could turn things around; they offered him hope. They were generous with him, and he returned the generosity in kind, volunteering for all sorts of projects, working on our farm, gradually stepping up both his cooking skills and his leadership work. He got onto our Governance Committee, became a supervisor, and most recently a sous chef. Throughout his work, Brandon built on positive belief in himself, overcoming self-doubt and moving forward with grace and a willingness to put himself out there for the success of the business and everyone around him. Not long ago, out of the blue, Brandon wrote me to say, "Thanks for helping so many people be artists in such a great organization." Brandon's note built up my hope for the future, increased my energy, and reinforced my already positive belief in the goodness of humankind. Brandon is making an artful life and helping others around him do the same. Andy Warhol, Robert Henri, Patrick-Earl Barnes, and all the others would likely be happy to hear Brandon's message. I know I was.

I hope what's written in this book has gotten you thinking, wondering, crafting a business, and leading a life of your own design. Doing work that matters deeply to you and to those with whom you do it. As Robert Henri wrote, "All I can hope . . . is to incite you to do something for yourself—to create something. What it is, I can't guess. I'm eager to see." Send me a note and let me know.

Postscript: Back to Buildings

You might remember, way back at the beginning of the book, Brenda Ueland's helpful admonition to write "like a child stringing beads in kindergarten—happy, absorbed and quietly putting one bead on after another." For me, one of those beads was the idea of a spiritual connection between Zingerman's and Rocco Disderide, the Italian immigrant who opened a shop on the corner of Detroit and Kingsley Streets in the early 20th century. It popped into my head, and I picked it up and put it into the preface. It seemed a little strange, but strange things lead to interesting outcomes, so I thought, "Why not?"

Then, one evening, while I was pulling the last pieces of this book together, I finally read the copy of architect Christopher Alexander's *The Timeless Way of Building* that I'd bought about a year earlier on a friend's recommendation. I was reading away, when I bumped into this: "We need only ask ourselves which places—which towns, which buildings, which rooms, have made us feel [alive] like this—which of them have that breath of sudden passion in them, which whispers to us, and lets us recall those moments when we were ourselves."

And so it turns out that my "crazy thought" was a connection that had already been made and written about. Buildings impact businesses, which in turn impart something of their essence to the building. Alexander is adamant about this: "[T]he connection between this quality in our own lives and the same quality in our surroundings—is not just an analogy, or similarity. The fact is that each one creates the other." It is, perhaps, like a wine barrel—the wood impacts the wine, which then leaves some of its essential elements in the wood, waiting to be imparted into whatever is next stored inside it. Good energy in a building, Alexander believes, begets good energy in us.

> *Places which have this quality, invite this quality to come to life in us. And when we have this quality in us, we tend to make it come to life in towns and buildings which we help build. It is a self-supporting, self-maintaining, generating quality. It is the quality of life. And we must seek it, for our own sakes, in our surroundings, simply in order that we can ourselves become alive.*

The self-fulfilling cycle at the core of this book—*that what we believe is likely to happen, which will, in turn, reinforce our beliefs*—turns out to be relevant to what occurs in buildings. The designer brings their spirit to what they build, the building passes it on to the business, which then passes it to the people who work and shop there, who, in turn, infuse good energy back into the building, and so on.

Which just reminds me to add that, as you write *your* vision, as you design the artistic existence you desire, you might want to pay particular attention to the space in which you're doing whatever it is you're doing. The more the building reflects what you want your life to be like, the more likely it is that you're going to make it all come to fruition. Alexander says, "this quality can only come to life in us when it exists within the world that we are a part of. We can come alive only to the extent the buildings and towns we live in are alive. The quality without a name is circular: it exists in us, when it exists in our buildings; and it only exists in our buildings, when we have it in ourselves." The cycle on the corner of Detroit and Kingsley Streets has been working, I'm happy to say, for 114 years now.[33]

Understanding now that the future is playing as big a part in the past as the past does in what is yet to come, sharing generously and appreciating those who came before us as we do those who will come after, I only wish I could meet Rocco Disderide right now, sit out front on that bench, share some stories and a few laughs, learn more about him and about the building, uncover a few interesting beliefs, and watch life go by in our little corner of the world.

the two oldest members of the class of 2015
finally getting their advanced degrees from the university of michigan

Extra Bonus Stuff

More Notes from the Front Porch	508
More Notes from the Back Dock	516
Suggested Reading	522
What is Zingerman's, Anyway?	530
Paul and Ari's University of Michigan Commencement Address	533
A Handful of Organizational Recipes	539
Time to Eat! Nine Recipes to Cook in Your Own Kitchen	545
An Epicurean Epilogue: Anarchist Eating in Greenwich Village	574
Endnotes	577
Appreciations	586

MORE NOTES

FROM THE FRONT PORCH

Philippe de Vienne, Co-Founder, Épices de Cru, Montreal, Quebec

Things I Have Learned from Zingerman's in One Year

After our visit to the ZCoB and ZingTrain we realized that we were not that crazy. It seems we had been visioning for years; we just did not call it that, or even realize that we were doing it.

What we did NOT DO then was write it down. We are French so we talk . . . ceaselessly, which is great as it refined our goals and reinforced the culture within the company. However, as we have found out, there are additional advantages to writing down.

It formalizes the process, and it becomes a tool for all to refer to. It makes the long-term objectives available and clearer to all. Visioning also helps to solve small and not-so-small problems.

When people know where we intend to go and agree with the vision, they change the way they work by themselves, individually or in groups. Also boring everyday tasks acquire a broader meaning. Goals are more easily set and reached in the face of adversity. People know why they are doing stuff, so they keep at it!

Our employees are now more involved in decision making at all levels, from the seemingly mundane to the profound. This question now comes up regularly when a decision is being made: "How will that help us accomplish our vision?" As a consequence less time is lost, fewer efforts are wasted, and money is saved. The result is greater efficiency and improved morale.

A year into the process of switching to trust and track, the net effect is liberating to all levels of the company. We still have a long way to go. However, considering the progress that has been made so far, not bad. Ari's guesstimate that it takes three years to make such changes seems to hold water. Employees, rightfully, feel empowered and simply work better. Managers' tasks are changing from constantly directing people to channeling enthusiasm in the right direction. They are slowly becoming leaders. The owners have a lot fewer mundane decisions to make and a lot less frustration. They have a lot more time to do what they love and be creative. Basically we have reached more objectives and made more positive changes in the past year than the previous five.

A ZingTrain prediction that came to pass: "People in your organization will be changed, most will become motivated and happier, and some will simply leave of their own accord, as they do not want to be part of the vision." Within three months of consulting every employee and crafting our vision, 15 percent of our employees had left. We did not replace them, and we did not fire anybody. Surprisingly, productivity increased without adding to individual workloads. We were all working smarter, not harder.

With a clear vision, what's important or superfluous becomes obvious to all. Given the power and a process, people of good will make the right decisions (for the most part; certainly better then average). There is less wasted effort, and all are pulling in the same direction, vastly improving morale and creating a virtuous circle. People working towards a clearly defined future are far more productive, responsible and happy.

Like the Einstein equation it's simple, profound and elegant.

Equally, it's not obvious at first glance. So WRITE IT DOWN and keep talking about it!

Not bad for the first year; now all we have to do is master all the other stuff in Ari's books. ☺

Lisa Barnwell Shirtz, Marquette, Michigan

Thank you for offering the free webinar on visioning. Last night I decided to follow your example by teaching visioning to my fellow Toastmasters in a seven-minute speech. It wasn't a lot of time, but I did my best and shared handouts they could read later.

Giving that speech reminded me of how powerful visioning really can be. The two-day visioning workshop I took in January was energizing, to say the least. It made clear to me that I needed to tie up loose ends before I could proceed further. Since then, amazing things have happened rather quickly. We sold our Marquette house the first day it was put on the market in July. Those proceeds allowed us to buy outright the Harvey house where we are living and complete its needed maintenance. No mortgage has freed me to leave the library, take a master gardener class, and use my expertise to plant 21 aronia shrubs in a fenced 1,800-square-foot organic garden (also new) on our five acres. At maturity these bushes will yield about 400 pounds of fruit, the sale of which will help to fund my women's projects. Thank you for teaching me visioning. It was a good investment. Many blessings to you and your ZingTrain staff in the coming year.

Preston Mckee, Owner, Morris-Baker Funeral Home, Johnson City, Tennessee

At first, I didn't know what I would have to say, but then I realized one result of the vision I started in your seminar years ago is right in front of me today.

The vision included my wife joining me in the Executive Health Program at the Mayo Clinic. Two years after that part of the vision became reality: they found the early-stage breast cancer our local physicians missed. Mayo just did her surgery a week ago, and today they told her that though she will face some reconstructive surgeries, she is essentially cured from cancer.

To you, the connection may not be clear, but to me it's one more example of positive ideas that have been ushered into reality aided by a clear vision of priorities, values, and beliefs.

Wayne Mullins, Ugly Mug Marketing, Alexandria, Louisiana

Understanding the need to change my beliefs has been at the core of my transformation.

For several years I had a business coach who keep telling me that I needed to give up my limiting beliefs. Beliefs (specifically, limiting beliefs) were never intended to be the center of our conversations, but somehow they always ended up there.

I'm stubborn, which in many ways has served me well as an entrepreneur. My stubbornness has kept me pushing forward when others would have likely quit. On the other hand, my stubbornness caused (and still causes) me to hold on to beliefs that may at one point have served me well—but no longer serve me well.

For me, it was particularly difficult to even acknowledge that my beliefs could be a part of the issue. But that's the thing about beliefs: we sincerely believe them, and that makes it extremely difficult for us to identify beliefs that may be hindering or even preventing us from achieving or accomplishing what we're after.

After countless conversations with my coach, I finally began to slowly understand that it was indeed my beliefs that were causing the issues.

Like with so many things in life, it took a serious event to cause me to seriously question my beliefs. For me, this event was severe depression. Not just any depression, but depression that led (and remained for some time) to suicidal thoughts. As a result of working through this debilitating depression, I began asking tough questions of myself.

The beautiful thing about life is that results usually don't lie. For example, if you're broke financially—that's the reality, and it was created by inputs (or neglected inputs). But most of us get caught in the trap of believing that the results aren't fair, or they're unjust—which they may indeed be, but that doesn't change the reality.

Two random things that really helped me with regard to my beliefs:

Stoicism—learning and embracing this philosophy.

Cognitive Biases—learning and understanding that our thinking often deceives us.

Jeff Fleckenstein, Director, Client Services, Rural Innovative Schools, NC New Schools | Breakthrough Learning

As soon as I learned that I was going to take part in our [NC New Schools/ Breakthrough Learning] New Leaders yearlong seminar, I immediately went to Zingerman's and then to ZingTrain and ordered your second book on Being A Better Leader. I had to chuckle when I started reading and got to Secret #26, "Beekeeping and Leadership," as I had just got started with my new hobby of beekeeping (with two, then four, and now eight hives)! So I had to start reading right there, and I must say I connected with your writing and philosophy right away. With that said, I'd love to add my perspective on beliefs and how my Zingerman's experience has helped both form and change them.

When I initially came to the Bakehouse, I was leaving my job as an aircraft mechanic (almost across the street), and I remember Jake asking me, "Are you sure you want to do this? I can only start you washing buckets." My response was, "Sure, show me what has to be done, and I'll get to work." Right away I knew that the Bakehouse and ZCoB were run differently. I was told that I was empowered to make things right by the customer. That even as a new employee, I could do what I believed to be the best course of action to make sure that any customer had an exceptional experience. That was definitely a new experience for me, the trust in my decision making, coupled with the expectation that I employ empathy, was inspiring. I found myself reflecting on how I would like to be treated as a customer in an ideal world, or what were my expectations as a customer if I could expect exceptional service. I began to "see" the world of service through a slightly different lens. I now thought that it was possible and preferable to give and expect great service, simply because that's how we should all live our lives and that would help to create the world in which I want to live. I started to look for ways that I could serve others in a way that would exceed their expectations and "surprise" them. I'll never forget seeing the smiles emerge on a group of Bakehouse visitors who were peering through the window at a couple of afternoon bakers when I just had to launch into a furious guitar solo with the bread peel to some Bon Jovi song! Fusing passion with work became my goal . . . I also came to believe that one could simultaneously work towards profit and honor the work of individuals. That one did have to exploit people to get them to work hard and strive for a successful/profitable business. A person and a business could "work hard to do good!"

By fusing passion with work, I have enjoyed a life dedicated to education and food. I have been able to build a cob oven in my backyard to bake bread and now have ventured into beekeeping. Frank taught me the difference between eating and tasting. I now use that skill when trying to determine the floral source of the harvested honey. Is this predominantly sourwood, tulip poplar, or basswood honey? I look, smell, taste, and really taste the way Frank taught me . . . Yes, that's sourwood for sure! I now also apply this patient, deliberate method of tasting to listening. When working with school districts that are trying to innovate and be true to the accountability imposed upon them by others (dream and do simultaneously), I try to listen carefully, with patience and with empathy. I am listening for values and for understanding. In a way very similar to how I try to taste for understanding.

I was a kind of rebellious teenager who loved the Detroit hardcore punk scene. Luckily, there were a few individuals, teachers and machine-shop owners who really believed in me and gave me the confidence to engage in my interests and to pursue them. To employ the same energy I got from music to other endeavors. I have used their belief in me to fuel my optimism. I try to see future potential as opposed to the challenge or struggle. This has helped me in my pursuit of equity in education. I try to open new opportunities for students and not hold their academic past against them. Although their academic record may not "show" or "prove" that they can be successful in college, I believe that with proper support (affective and academic), students can rise to high expectations and succeed. I have witnessed countless instances when this was true. I continue to look for win-win situations daily. This helps me in my work as I try to help good school districts become great and to advocate for rural education innovation.

Thank you again for taking the time to respond, and if you would like, I will continue to answer This I Believe . . . I should do this as an exercise anyway. I did recently reflect on my "core values" kind of a belief system/list:

- Universal opportunity
- Personal responsibility
- Value of education
- Determination
- Individual and collective integrity
- Leave the world better than how you found it

Heather Gray, Business Owner, Columbus, Ohio

"Face the Facts," Ari Weinzweig writes in *Zingerman's Guide to Giving Great Service*. "We need customers far more than they need us. In an era of ever-increasing sameness, something as simple as a smile, the competent delivery of goods, or even just a little enthusiasm can make a lasting positive impression on customers."

I purchased *Zingerman's Guide to Giving Great Service* online hoping to read something I could apply to my six franchise locations, whose staffs seemed to be struggling to wrap their minds around how to consistently treat customers well—especially the customers who weren't so "easily pleased." And customers, as many business owners know, are the only reason we exist. Without them and their commitment to what we provide, we would be forced to shut our doors and would fade away into the background. So it is imperative that we do treat them well and that they continue to return. But how do we do this?

The moment I began reading *Zingerman's Guide to Giving Great Service* I knew it wasn't just another "business self-help guide" full of empty statements without actual service backing them up. Firsthand, I had the opportunity to experience these business practices in action. My very first experience at Zingerman's Roadhouse, I had a chance to meet Ari. I was on a business trip that was taking me a few hours away from Ann Arbor and into the late Sunday evening night. I had purchased the Lapsed Anarchist Series of books and Ari had taken a few moments to meet with me and sign them—while he was assisting in helping pour water to all of the guests at the Roadhouse. As I gathered my items to leave, Ari wouldn't let me go without a complimentary cup of coffee for the road. I was taken aback and pleased by his gesture of a free cup of coffee. And that one cup of coffee has made me a Zingerman's customer for life. Of course, it wasn't just about the cup of coffee. It was about what the coffee represented, about the impression. I felt valued and important; that someone cared that I stayed awake during the rest of my trip.

Ari mentions that as service providers we need to make each customer believe that they are the best thing that has happened to us. That single cup of coffee made me feel as if I were something special, that I mattered even though Zingerman's services thousands of customers.

When it comes down to it, that is really what great customer service is about. As a service provider, it is my job to convey to my customers that they are special and that I am going to do everything that I can to satisfy why they came in to see us; getting to know my customers and developing an understanding about what will make their experience better, what will make them feel as if they are the best thing to happen to me.

Since my personal experience with Zingerman's and after reading the *Guide to Great Service*, I keep a copy in my work bag. I don't want to be caught without it. I reference it frequently when speaking with my management team and we have even created quarterly training meetings that implement applicable parts and pieces from it. Each member of my management team is given a copy and we discuss points within its covers often. Ari breaks down customer service into viable parts that are easy to understand and translate in any service industry. "The bottom line here," Ari states, "is that the work each of us does as an individual service provider with an individual customer—one interaction at a time—is what it's all about. From both a personal and business perspective, I truly appreciate the opportunity to make such a difference a reality." Witnessing stellar customer service from the man who wrote the guide about it certainly makes it easier to implement a plan of action in my own businesses. It is a challenge I am willing to accept because I know it is possible. It is now my responsibility to take what I have learned [and] ensure that my customers have the same experience I had by reminding myself and my employees that it truly is about one customer at a time and working towards going the extra mile for them, remembering who they are and greeting them with a smile. Breaking it down in those terms makes the task feasible, and I have already seen vast improvements with not only my employees but the customers as well.

Mack Davison, Routes Captain (Supervisor), Zingerman's Mail Order

I have had to do a bit of soul searching myself, and call into question my own beliefs, albeit with the assistance of the government and treatment programs at times; nonetheless it has come about. Currently, my take on the matter is as follows:

1. I will do no thing without thought. For me this includes any facet of being human, such as: a. Form beliefs, b. Attain feelings/emotions, c. Develop desires, d. Perform any action whatsoever. Thus, I believe I do well to be conscious of my thoughts.

2. My current thought/belief on my own beliefs is as follows: "My beliefs are prepackaged thoughts regarding how I will respond to a given person, place, or situation." A very generic statement, I realize things like context and self-awareness in the moment of truth, among other things, will play on my actual response. So very much to your point at Zingerman's Mail Order, self-efficacy of my beliefs is predicated on the belief that I can't look at the other guy in the situation to understand how that situation played out as it did; I can only look at my inputs into the situation, and those inputs started with my own beliefs.

3. This brings us to the workplace. If what is true at the core of my thinking/beliefs, the systems that dictate my beliefs in general, then necessarily these systems will dictate in the workplace as well. Generally, in my 20s (I'm now 41), I believed the workplace was nearly a parent/child relationship. You, the employer, agreed to provide me a livable wage, and in exchange I provided my time, learning ability, existing skills, and work ethic as a service (worked for a pager company—service industry). Very myopic view, of course. It was almost as if I believed I was owed a means of surviving, and that my employer was

responsible for conveniently providing me a way to "learn" my way to the top. Coworkers were a means to this end. At one point, my manager who hired me even said she felt like a big sister to me.

Today, however, I do not believe that a parent/child relationship of any kind will benefit me, and thus anyone I come in contact with. I cannot take accountability for my own beliefs under this one systemic belief. As a result, I consistently have more gratitude for the fact I have a job, for the interactions I have with the individuals with whom I work, and am more willing to say yes to tasks outside of my normal function and do them with more gratitude than I would have in my 20s. I also believe my managers recognize this about me.

Kristen Beckett, Host, Zingerman's Roadhouse

I've worked at the Roadhouse for 10 years, so I've been doing it a while, but it still takes me some preparation. A constant interrelationship. I like to make sure I am receptive enough to be aware. It is going to be busy at the restaurant. How am I showing up today?

I will be present.
I will breathe.
I will listen.

I have found that Setting My Intention is a strong contributing factor to the lessons my day will manifest. How have I been influenced by the time I have spent with Zingerman's? Many of the thoughts I have had already today have been fostered and encouraged by the people and the ideas I have encountered in this community. I have heard and experienced Anese Cavanaugh share her magnetizing work with energy. I have listened to the Spice Trekkers Ethné and Philippe de Vienne share life wisdom gathered from all over the globe in their travels to nourish the stomach and the soul. Nancy has told me many a great joke or story (No!) that puts a twinkle in my eye every time I pass her on the floor. There is a web, a supportive net, the strands of which we have interconnected here. We create a nourishing collective experience that is built from taking the time to invest in love for ourselves. By focusing on the development of the individual, we elevate the experience of the group. If you are hungry, it is hard to feed others. Belief in the idea that our compressive strength is only multiplied by ensuring the tensile strength of each individual is at the maximum.

Every day I am amazed at the motivation and creativity gathered in Ann Arbor. Every day I see people with whom I work directly make choices that benefit the community as opposed to the individual. We volunteer. We babysit for free. We give rides. We shovel your car out of the snow. We make piggy crayons that can make your day. We tend the land. We teach kids how to make great food choices. We do yoga before event shifts, we dress as superheroes on Halloween, visit you in the hospital, raise money so you can take three months off to be with your newborn baby. We have flash mobs, bowling parties, farmers' markets. We perform in choirs, in concerts, plays, have art shows, dinner parties. We comfort one another, we fight, we talk about how to improve, we try to better understand one another and celebrate our varied histories, traditions, and tastes. We gift food to our friend sick at home and we hand-deliver the scarf you left last night at the restaurant. We feed the hungry. We source incredible food and bring together the artisan merchants from various countries to make culinary magic. We meet with inspirational people who provide insights to great service and to teach us from the wisdom gained through their experiences. We exchange with other farmers who believe in the value of love and care for the land, and have respect for the many gifts life provides. We are asked to give the speeches at the commencement ceremony of the Big 10 university that enriches our city. We travel to the White House to affect the laws that govern our country. We do all these things where we live because this city, this Earth, is our family. It extends universally. We have love in common. We arrive, we leave, adventure, expand, change faces, forms, share lessons.

Are there times when I question if I am in the right place, or ask if I am I doing the right thing? Without a doubt. Inevitably, there will be something that doesn't flow as smoothly as it could, but this is one of the great things I appreciate about being a part of the ZCoB: When challenging circumstances try to cement my feet to a sinking stone, I am given the tools with which to help me rise to the surface of the moving waters; I get paid to take classes to make me better at budgeting my bills and investing my money; I get discounts at many local businesses; I get delicious food and delicious information. Our service recipes are great guides for any type of human interaction, occurring anywhere, but the living, breathing element of those recipes are the people, and I am loving the people with whom I am spending my time. If we need someone to help with some food prep for three off-site catering events, Peter will help. Then he'll jump behind the dishtank and wash all those dishes he just prepped for two hours without being asked because things were starting to pile up. Afrim will *do everything all of the time*. Mason will go get your hat from the farm on his day off so you don't get burned while you garden, and Emma and Mandie will both volunteer to watch your dog while you go out of town. All of these exchanges, originating in my Community, contribute to my sense of my connectedness; to growth and love; set me up for success so I can share that love with others. Life and work for me are not separate entities. It is all one, and when I am here, I feel valued. I feel wholly cared for and appreciated.

As I walk in the back door, I smile, not having "put on" layers, but removed them. This is the dance I love. I tape a piece of paper with my three shift vision ideas to the screen of the OT computer: Be present. Listen. Laugh.

For me there is no mountain on which I stand solo at the crest, though I often feel elevated. I am reinforced by the stable base of my coworkers, systems, recipes, love, intention, and energy, plus 6 or 1,000 other things that contribute to the high plateau on which is built our Community. Reaching Further. Outward. Inward.

There is always light here, no matter the time of year, and the comforting smells that remind me (and so say many others) of a place where I am home. Trusted to make my own choices, supported in my individual quest for development, educated, challenged. A Community of which I am proud and honored to be a part.

Alex Young, Managing Partner, Zingerman's Roadhouse

I believe that we can't give enough, and that giving from the Roadhouse creates a sense of importance to all of us here.

I believe that your spirit of generosity has impacted all of us in a tremendously important way.

I believe that your faith in all of us has spread and makes Zingerman's an even safer place for all to contribute.

I believe that our generosity has paid us back ten times over in spiritual wealth.

Jamie Hull, Server, Zingerman's Roadhouse

As far as personal beliefs go, I think mine have definitely evolved over the years. I spent a large portion of my 20s getting over my childhood, accepting my sexuality, and trying to figure out how to "adult." I believe this is fairly common, and rightfully so. Gaining confidence in yourself is not a skill they teach in school and for me it was something I had to make a conscious effort to work on. Changing my beliefs about how powerful I am and knowing I deserve happiness took the help of many friends, family, life experiences, and working in multiple fields with a lot of diverse people. I work on this every day.

One of the biggest obstacles for me was learning that I am a product of date rape. Knowing this messed me up for many years and I struggled with self-worth for longer than I would like to admit. I still sometimes struggle. What helped me was changing some of my beliefs about life. I believe we are all here for a reason. I believe we are all connected and gravitate towards those who have similar vibrations or a vibration which we are trying to attain or are attracted to. I believe life is a series of events that are meant to help you learn about yourself and the world. I believe in the wheel of Samsara and the pursuit of enlightenment. I believe failure is actually success because at least you tried. Oh and something like, without messed-up stuff happening to you, you can never truly appreciate all the blessings you have. Serving can be a test to these beliefs but also a great way to practice at being a better person/servant. I make plenty of mistakes and I am always honest with my tables. I find this is the best policy because everyone can relate and if the problem is fixed quickly most people are just happy it's fixed and that effort was made on their behalf.

I have been serving for a little over two years now and most of that time has been at the Roadhouse. I started serving at another local restaurant and boy oh boy was that a completely different experience. The management there was not supportive and the environment was hostile. When I came to the Roadhouse everyone was so nice I thought there definitely must be a catch or lots of drugs in the water. It took some getting used to, but now I really appreciate the systems in place that promote success. By no means is the success easy to attain, there is definite work you must put into it but there is always someone there who is helpful or has a kind word. The Roadhouse may not always run as smoothly as we would hope, but I believe people do have good intentions and that can be very powerful.

I think this kind of support is what helps build confidence and therefore the belief that your self is strong and capable of handling life's difficulties. Empathy is also crucial. Without it we would not be able to be of good service to each other or our customers. Sometimes when customers have what we perceive to be silly problems, it can definitely be hard to empathize. We definitely cater to some interesting folks and having support in those moments is invaluable. I have definitely learned a few new moves on how to handle these sensitive situations.

Charlie Frank, Managing Partner, Zingerman's Candy Manufactory

It's like learning to ride a bike—a two-wheeler—for the first time. Your mom or dad is behind you, and the belief is that they will be there, right behind you all the way. You believe/HOPE that they will not let you fall to either side because the training wheels are off. At some point they let go but you don't know exactly when because you are focusing forward—as you should be. When you get to where you've decided to stop and you look back, you realize you did most of the trip on your own, and Mom or Dad let go without you knowing when they did. So after they let go and before you stopped, you were believing and HOPING not to fall. When you stopped the bike, the belief changed into a KNOWN. Experience was the proof that I could do it. That's how it was for me, anyway. When I knew I could do it I didn't have to believe in falling anymore. Belief is hoping.

Suggested Reading

*It is what you read when you don't have to that
determines what you will be when you can't help it.*

—Oscar Wilde

*I've referenced, I know, many books throughout this book. What follows are some of
those that have particularly inspired me, given insight or triggered good thoughts
and interesting conversations. Many—though certainly not all—of the insights and
ideas in this book have been prompted by things I read in them. I have dozens more
stacked up to read, some of which I'm sure will land on a future list. (Let me know
what you've been reading so I can add to it!) Apologies to every book that has influenced me but has unintentionally been left off these pages.*

ANARCHISM

Carlotta R. Anderson, *All-American Anarchist: Joseph A. Labadie and the Labor
Movement*

Paul Avrich, *An American Anarchist: The Life of Voltairine de Cleyre*

———, *Anarchist Voices: An Oral History of Anarchism in America*

Mohammed A. Bamyeh, *Anarchy as Order: The History and Future of Civic
Humanity*

Alexander Berkman, *Now and After: The ABC of Anarchism*

Murray Bookchin, *The Ecology of Freedom: The Emergence and Dissolution of
Hierarchy*

———, *Remaking Society: Pathways to a Green Future*

———, *Towards an Ecological Society*

John Clark, editor, *Anarchy, Geography, Modernity: the Selected Writings of Elisée Reclus*

Michael Coughlin, editor, *Jo Labadie and His Little Books*

Lee Alan Dugatkin, *The Prince of Evolution*

Candace Falk, *Love, Anarchy, and Emma Goldman*

Emma Goldman, *Anarchism and Other Essays*

———, "Anarchism: What It Really Stands For"

———, *Living My Life*

———, "What I Believe"

Paul Goodman, *The Black Flag of Anarchism*

David Graeber, *Fragments of an Anarchist Anthropology*

Peter Kropotkin, *The Conquest of Bread*

———, *Fields, Factories, and Workshops*

———, *Mutual Aid: A Factor of Evolution*

Étienne de La Boétie, "Discourse on Voluntary Servitude"

Gustav Landauer, *Revolution and Other Writings: A Political Reader*

Peter Marshall, *Demanding the Impossible: A History of Anarchism*

Erich Mühsam, *Liberating Society from the State and Other Writings: A Political Reader*

Sharon Presley and Crispin Sartwell, editors, *Exquisite Rebel: The Essays of Voltairine de Cleyre—Feminist, Anarchist, Genius*

James Scott, *The Art of Not Being Governed: An Anarchist History of Upland Southeast Asia*

———, *Seeing Like a State: How Certain Schemes to Improve the Human Condition Have Failed*

———, *Two Cheers for Anarchism: Six Easy Pieces on Autonomy, Dignity, and Meaningful Work and Play*

Benjamin Tucker, *Why I Am an Anarchist*

If you're looking to buy anything of an anarchist nature, check out Bolerium Books in San Francisco; they have a great collection. Publishers PM Press, across the Bay in Oakland; AK Press in Chico, California; and Black Rose Books in Montreal do as well.

BUSINESS

The books that follow aren't likely to be found in any of the anarchist bookstores. All have helped me to arrive at where I am.

John Abrams, *Companies We Keep: Employee Ownership and the Business of Community and Place*

Ichak Adizes, *Corporate Lifecycle: How and Why Corporations Grow and Die and What to Do About It*

James Autry, *Confessions of an Accidental Businessman: It Takes a Lifetime to Find Wisdom*

——, *Life and Work: A Manager's Search for Meaning*

——, *Love and Profit: The Art of Caring Leadership*

Wayne Baker, *Achieving Success Through Social Capital: Tapping the Hidden Resources in Your Personal and Business Networks*

——, *United America: The Surprising Truth About American Values, American Identity and the 10 Beliefs That a Large Majority of Americans Hold Dear*

Peter Block, *Community: The Structure of Belonging*

——, *The Empowered Manager: Positive Political Skills at Work*

——, *Stewardship: Choosing Service Over Self-Interest*

Bo Burlingham, *Finish Big: How Great Entrepreneurs Exit Their Companies on Top*

——, *Small Giants: Companies That Choose to Be Great Instead of Big*

Anese Cavanaugh, *Contagious Culture: Show Up, Set the Tone, and Intentionally Create an Organization That Thrives*

Chip Conley, *Peak: How Great Companies Get Their Mojo from Maslow*

Stephen Covey, *Principle-Centered Leadership*

Max De Pree, *Leadership Is an Art*

——, *Leadership Jazz: The Essential Elements of a Great Leader*

Peter Drucker, *The Effective Executive*

——, *The Practice of Management*

Jane Dutton and Gretchen Spreitzer, editors, *How to Be a Positive Leader: Small Actions, Big Impact*

Carol Dweck, *Mindset: The New Psychology of Success*

Robert K. Greenleaf, *On Becoming a Servant Leader: The Private Writings of Robert K. Greenleaf*

———, *Servant Leadership: A Journey into the Nature of Legitimate Power and Greatness*

Paul Hawken, *Growing a Business*

Rosabeth Moss Kanter, *Confidence: How Winning and Losing Streaks Begin and End*

Peter Koestenbaum, *Leadership: The Inner Side of Greatness*

Peter Koestenbaum and Peter Block, *Freedom and Accountability at Work: Applying Philosophic Insight to the Real World*

Danny Meyer, *Setting the Table: The Transforming Power of Hospitality*

Gifford Pinchot and Elizabeth Pinchot, *The End of Bureaucracy and the Rise of the Intelligent Organization*

Daniel H. Pink, *Drive: The Surprising Truth About What Motivates Us*

E. F. Schumacher, *Good Work*

———, *Small Is Beautiful: Economics as if People Mattered*

Ricardo Semler, *Maverick: The Success Story behind America's Best-Run Companies*

Peter M. Senge, *The Fifth Discipline: The Art and Practice of the Learning Organization*

Richard Sheridan, *Joy, Inc.*

Simon Sinek, *Start with Why: How Great Leaders Inspire Everyone to Take Action*

Jack Stack and Bo Burlingham, *The Great Game of Business, Expanded and Updated: The Only Sensible Way to Run a Company*

———, *A Stake in the Outcome: Building a Culture of Ownership for the Long-Term Success of Your Business*

Vic Strecher, *On Purpose: Lessons in Life and Health from the Frog, theDung Beetle, and Julia*

Dean E. Tucker, *Using the Power of Purpose: How to Overcome Bureaucracy and Achieve Extraordinary Business Success!*

AGRICULTURE

Dan Barber, *The Third Plate*

Mario Batali and Jim Webster, *America–Farm to Table: Simple, Delicious Recipes Celebrating Local Farmers*

Wendell Berry, *The Art of the Commonplace: The Agrarian Essays of Wendell Berry*

——, *Life Is a Miracle: An Essay Against Modern Superstition*

——, *Our Only World: Ten Essays*

——, *The Unsettling of America: Culture and Agriculture*

——, *The Way of Ignorance and Other Essays*

Masanobu Fukuoka, *The One-Straw Revolution: An Introduction to Natural Farming*

Toby Hemenway, *Gaia's Garden: A Guide to Home-Scale Permaculture*

——, *The Permaculture City:* Regenerative Design for Urban, Suburban, and Town Resilience

David Mas Masumoto, *Epitaph for a Peach: Four Seasons on My Family Farm*

Angelo Pelligrini, *The Unprejudiced Palate*

Alice Waters, *The Art of Simple Food: Notes, Lessons, and Recipes from a Delicious Revolution*

LIFE, BELIEFS, HOPE, PERSONAL DEVELOPMENT

Christopher Alexander, *The Timeless Way of Building*

Tom Asacker, *The Business of Belief*

Isaac Asimov, *It's Been a Good Life*

David Bayles and Ted Orland, *Art & Fear: Observations On the Perils (and Rewards) of Artmaking*

Sharon Begley, *Train Your Mind, Change Your Brain: How a New Science Reveals Our Extraordinary Potential to Transform Ourselves*

Kevin Bermingham, *Change Your Limiting Beliefs: Three Steps to Achieve Meaningful Goals*

Robert Bly, *A Little Book on the Human Shadow*

Claude Bristol, *The Magic of Believing*

——, *TNT: It Rocks the Earth*

Julia Cameron, *The Artist's Way*

Stephen Cope, *The Great Work of Your Life: A Guide for the Journey to Your True Calling*

Viktor Frankl, *Man's Search for Meaning*

Natalie Goldberg, *Writing Down the Bones: Freeing the Writer Within*

Daniel Goleman, *Emotional Intelligence: Why It Can Matter More Than IQ*

Adam Grant, *Give and Take: A Revolutionary Approach to Success*

——, *Originals: How Non-Conformists Move the World Forward*

Robert Henri, *The Art Spirit*

William James, *The Principles of Psychology, Volumes 1 and 2*

——, *The Will to Believe and Other Essays in Popular Philosophy*

Steven Johnson, *Where Good Ideas Come From: The Natural History of Innovation*

Jon Kabat-Zinn, *Mindfulness for Beginners: Reclaiming the Present Moment— And Your Life*

——, *Wherever You Go, There You Are: Mindfulness Meditation in Everyday Life*

Sam Keen, *Fire in the Belly: On Being a Man*

——, *Hymns to an Unknown God: Awakening the Spirit in Everyday Life*

——, *Inward Bound: Exploring the Geography of Your Emotions*

Robin D. G. Kelley, *Freedom Dreams: The Black Radical Imagination*

George Lakoff, *Don't Think of an Elephant! Know Your Values and Frame the Debate*

Anne Lamott, *Bird by Bird: Some Instructions on Writing and Life*

Lawrence L. Lippitt, *Preferred Futuring: Envision the Future You Want and Unleash the Energy to Get There*

Ron Lippitt, Bruce Westley, and Jeanne Watson, *The Dynamics of Planned Change*

Shane Lopez, *Making Hope Happen: Create the Future You Want for Yourself and Others*

Hugh MacLeod, *Ignore Everybody: And 39 Other Keys to Creativity*

Dawna Markova, *I Will Not Die an Unlived Life: Reclaiming Purpose and Passion*

Dawna Markova and Angie MacArthur, *Collaborative Intelligence: Thinking with People Who Think Differently*

Rollo May, *Freedom and Destiny*

——, *Man's Search for Himself*

Debbie Millman, *Look Both Ways: Illustrated Essays on the Intersection of Life and Design*

Osho, *The Book of Understanding: Creating Your Own Path to Freedon*

——, *Creativity: Unleashing the Forces Within*

——, *Gold Nuggets: Messages from Existence*

——, *Life, Love, Laughter: Celebrating Your Existence*

Massimo Pigliucci, *Answers for Aristotle: How Science and Philosophy Can Lead Us to a More Meaningful Life*

Matthieu Ricard, *Happiness: A Guide to Developing Life's Most Important Skill*

Lewis Richmond, *Work as a Spiritual Practice: A Practical Buddhist Approach to Inner Growth and Satisfaction on the Job*

Carl Rogers, *A Way of Being*

Michelle Segar, *No Sweat: How the Simple Science of Motivation Can Bring You a Lifetime of Fitness*

Jean-Louis Servan-Schreiber, *The Art of Time*

Gary Snyder, *The Gary Snyder Reader: Prose, Poetry and Translations*

——, *Nobody Home: Writing, Buddhism, and Living in Places*

——, *The Practice of the Wild*

Gary Snyder and Jim Harrison, *The Etiquette of Freedom*

C. R. "Rick" Snyder, *The Psychology of Hope: You Can Get Here from There*

Rebecca Solnit, *A Field Guide to Getting Lost*

——, *Hope in the Dark* (along with every other book she's written!)

Claude Steele, *Whistling Vivaldi: And Other Clues to How Stereotypes Affect Us*

Nikki Stern, *Hope in Small Doses*

Brenda Ueland, *If You Want to Write: A Book About Art, Independence, and Spirit*

————, *Strength to Your Sword Arm: Selected Writings*

Paul Watzlawick, *The Invented Reality: How Do We Know What We Believe We Know?*

David Whyte, *The Three Marriages: Reimagining Work, Self, and Relationships*

————, *Crossing the Unknown Sea: Work as a Pilgrimage of Identity*

————, *The Heart Aroused: Poetry and the Preservation of the Soul in Corporate America*

Judith Wright and Bob Wright, *Transformed! The Science of Spectacular Living*

What is Zingerman's, Anyway?

As I write this, the Zingerman's Community of Businesses (ZCoB) includes

ZINGERMAN'S DELICATESSEN

Newly renovated and expanded (for the fourth time), but still on that same spot at the corner of Detroit and Kingsley, the Deli is still unique, still crowded, still confusing for first timers, still hard to find, still short of parking, and still, I think (biased though I obviously am), pretty special. Now led by managing partners Grace Singleton, Rodger Bowser, and Rick Strutz, the Deli continues to deliver all the same sorts of sandwiches, traditional Jewish dishes, artisan cheeses, oils, and vinegars that it has for more than three decades; along with other great foods from all of the Zingerman's producers (Bakehouse, Creamery, Coffee, and Candy). Only now, I think, it's better than ever.

ZINGERMAN'S CATERING AND EVENTS

From the far corners of the Deli kitchen comes catering for all occasions. We offer corned beef to caviar, potato salad to smoked salmon, for business meetings, bar mitzvahs, weddings, and whatever else—delivered down the block on Detroit Street or all the way into downtown Detroit.

ZINGERMAN'S BAKEHOUSE

We started the Bakehouse in 1992 with our partner Frank Carollo to finally get bread for the Deli like the stuff I'd been bringing back from Paris and San Francisco for years. Working under the tutelage of master baker Michael London of upstate New York's Rock Hill Bakehouse, we learned to craft traditional hearth-baked breads true to French, Italian, and old Jewish recipes. Later we added a whole range of butter-laden, full-flavored, know-fat (get it?) pastries and baked goods. Amy Emberling, who was one of the original crew of six bakers before she headed off to Denmark and from there to Manhattan (where she earned her MBA), later returned to the Bakehouse as a second managing partner. Today, the Bakehouse sells bread and pastries to more than a hundred wholesale accounts across the state.

BAKE!

The Bakehouse's much-loved teaching kitchen, offering classes on breads, pastries, cakes, biscuits, croissants, pies, and much, much more. Not to mention the special weeklong BAKE-cations.

Zingerman's Creamery

Just up the sidewalk from the Bakehouse, Ann Arbor's only creamery makes fresh hand-ladled cream cheese, a variety of fresh goat- and cow's-milk cheeses, incredible gelato, and more. Aubrey Thomason is the managing partner. The Creamery has one of the country's best little cheese shops on site as well.

Zingerman's Mail Order

Ships all those full-flavored and traditionally made foods to people like you all over America. Led today by a trio of managing partners—Mo Frechette (the original Mail Order man, who packed boxes in the basement of the Deli nearly 20 years ago), along with Toni Morell and Tom Root (who together led the work to create the first Zingerman's website back in 1999). Check out their work by mail or online at www.zingermans.com.

ZingTrain

Offers training and educational seminars on subjects like those covered in this book, as well as our approach to service, management, merchandising, and other engaging subjects. ZingTrain does custom consulting, too. Maggie Bayless is the managing partner who pushed the organizational envelope to create ZingTrain back in 1994.

Zingerman's Roadhouse

A full-service sit-down restaurant serving really good American food. Alex Young is the James Beard Award–winning chef and managing partner who does everything from expert organic farming to very fine work on the fryer to put together a well-crafted menu of ground-fresh-daily burgers, whole-hog barbecue, Memphis-style fried chicken, Maryland crab cakes, and a wide selection of American beers, bourbons, wines, and cheese. The Roadhouse is also home to the Roadshow, a 1952 Spartan aircraft aluminum trailer permanently parked out front of the restaurant, where customers can get great drive-up coffee, homemade doughnuts, sandwiches, Bakehouse bread, and pastries. The Roadhouse also has its own farm (see below).

ZINGERMAN'S COFFEE COMPANY

Sourcing, roasting, and brewing really good beans right here in Ann Arbor. You can sip the Coffee Company's craft roasts at the Deli, Bakehouse, Roadhouse, and Roadshow, as well as at other leading cafes, restaurants, and retailers around the country, and now at our new retail space. Our managing partner is Steve Mangigian.

ZINGERMAN'S CANDY MANUFACTORY

The Manufactory crafts candy bars by hand, as they would have been made in the early days of the last century. Charlie Frank, now the managing partner, started making the amazing Zzang! bars while working as the pastry manager at the Bakehouse, and we later spun the idea out into a business all its own. Zzang! bars are now sold in specialty shops all over the United States, as are the peanut brittle, halvah, and other craft confections.

ZINGERMAN'S CORNMAN FARMS

The farm comprises a farmhouse dating from 1834 and a barn built soon afterward, as well as acres of crops and animal pastures. Both structures have been restored and renovated to accommodate a wide variety of events, including weddings, private dinners, cooking demonstrations, and meetings, with managing partner Kieron Hales. The farm's fields have yielded exquisite, pesticide-free heirloom tomatoes, peppers, onions, garlic, carrots, squash and more for Zingerman's Roadhouse for the past eleven years, and the rolling pastureland sustains cattle, hogs, and sheep.

Paul and Ari's University of Michigan Commencement Address, May 2, 2015

PAUL: When most people think of Zingerman's success, they picture a line of people stretching from Detroit Street to Division. A sandwich so big it takes two hands to pick it up. And when you finally bite into it, the Russian dressing rolls down your arms. Reporters write about our vision, our values, and our marketing skills.

ARI: There's huge value, of course, to each of those things. But what very few folks ever ask, what reporters rarely write about, and what hardly anyone seems to really be all that interested in, is what we believe. While vision, values, quality, customer service, marketing, and making money are all important, we believe . . . that what we believe . . . makes a big difference! The beliefs that we choose—or those we hold, but don't acknowledge—will form the footprint for everything else that happens in our lives. As writer Claude Bristol said 75 years ago, *"As individuals think and believe, so they are."*

PAUL: To be clear, it's not for us to tell you what to do with your lives once you leave here.

ARI: But we can share with you some of the key beliefs that underlie all that we've done in our organization, beliefs that have laid the base for us to build a healthy business that provides meaningful employment to over 700 people. Beliefs that contribute positively to our community in many, many ways. Beliefs about people and processes that are being adapted in places as far afield as Australia, Slovakia, and Ethiopia. Beliefs that have helped build a business that—33 years later—we both still love working in, literally, every single day. Paul?

PAUL: I believe it's rarely a good idea to read the comments others make about you on social media, but who can resist? Right after we were named as commencement speakers, I read this post: "WOW, WHOEVER WAS THE FIRST CHOICE MUST HAVE BACKED OUT." I laughed, too, but it hit me what an immense honor and opportunity this was. In the interest of reciprocity, I committed to give to you the best of what I have to offer . . . other than a $16 Reuben.

To do that, Class of 2015, mentally pull up your Must Have list for success and scan it. Really, take it out and give it a good look. Raise your hand if joy is at the top of that list. It wasn't on my list when I graduated from this fine institution. Joy is not the typical yardstick of success. Will the bank ask for your joy quotient when you renegotiate your student loans? Not likely. So why would you want joy on your list, and what *is* it, anyway?

Joy is a feeling so profound that it sits at the top of the human-experience chart. Just above love and just below peace and enlightenment. To feel joy, you don't have to wait until you're old, like us, I believe you can have it now, starting today. How? Generosity. Generosity leads to joy. It's simple and it's guaranteed.

Generosity follows the natural law of the harvest—you reap more than you sow. When you give, you get more back. Minimally, you get a joy buzz. Research tells us that generosity kicks off a "feel good" hormone in your brain called the "helper's high" that can last up to two hours . . . and it's legal. Even outside of Ann Arbor.

I am not telling you to take a vow of poverty. Earn money, as much as you like. See the world. Buy a nice car. Get rewarded for hard work. Just know that these things don't bring joy like being generous does.

Another natural law of generosity is that it's self-perpetuating—just like the yeasty starter the Bakehouse uses to bake zillions of loaves of Zingerman's rye and sourdough breads. What applies to bread applies to people. The mother starter of Generosity is also passed down through generations. This was proven in a study by the National Academy of Sciences where one person's act of generosity inspired others to be generous, spreading to dozens, even hundreds, of people, known and unknown. I've got my own proof for you: three true stories from my life illustrating the natural laws of generosity.

I'll begin with "my starter"—my grandfather Ben Sherman. We called him Zadie. That's Yiddish for grandfather. I think about his big smile and hearty laugh, how he warmed me with his presence. I realize now that he was joyful because he embodied generosity. In my early teens, I worked at his machine shop in a rough part of Detroit. Frequently, homeless men wandered into the shop looking for a handout, and Zadie invited each one to go next door to Joe's Bar and Grille, saying, "Get yourself a hot meal and put it on my tab." Zadie told me two things I'll never forget: *"Half of what you have belongs to those who need it,"* and *"If you're successful, make the people around you successful."* With this wisdom in mind, Ari and I added the crucial ingredient of generosity into Zingerman's business plan from day one.

My second story has Mrs. Johnnie Mae Seeley as the "starter." She is a tiny, elderly angel in our neighborhood who got the Deli to bag up our unsold bread and rolls every night for her church to parcel out. Her generous act inspired Zingerman's to found and launch the nonprofit Food Gatherers in 1988 with a mission to eradicate hunger in our county. Twenty-seven years later, Food Gatherers distributes over 6 million pounds of food every year to our neighbors in need. Every day I feel profound joy for the work Food Gatherers does in our community.

My final story demonstrates how Zingerman's Community of Businesses, our partnership model based on Zadie's advice of making those around you successful, was put to the test in 2001. Ari and I had pledged a quarter of a million dollars to build a shiny commercial kitchen inside the county's new homeless shelter. Our funding was to come from a business venture slated to open at Detroit's new McNamara Terminal. Several days after 9/11, the airport project folded, and our kitchen funding vanished. When I heard this, I actually had to lie down on the floor of my office for over an hour. Ari and I had to break the news to all of our Zingerman's partners in the wake of the national tragedy. It was agonizing. How were we going to honor our commitment? What happened next would have made Zadie and Mrs. Seeley weep with joy. Our partners shocked us with their decision to take on the entire quarter million dollars. I was stunned and overcome with joy—our partners had now become the next generation of starters. Seeded by their generosity, today that kitchen prepares one hundred thousand hot meals each year.

So . . . when you leave here today with your Must Have list, I invite you to measure your success not so much by what you gain or accomplish for yourself, but rather by what you contribute to others. I believe practicing generosity is the way to joy. It's free for the taking. Or should I say . . . for the giving.

Ari? I told them what I believe. What do you believe?

ARI: I believe that active, engaging, interesting learning is very clearly at the core of a great life. Probably the one thing that this amazing institution—of which everyone in this very big emotional and intellectual house, is a part—has been trained in, more than any other single thing, is how to learn. The challenge, though, is that when you leave here today, there are no more grades to be gotten, no more professors to pass judgment. And when there's no one pressuring us do to it, there are a hundred reasons not to open a book, not to go to an interesting lecture, not to read a poem. Working hard at learning doesn't win headlines, but it's clear to me that the people who keep doing it regularly almost always live powerfully positive lives.

I believe that our lives are radically more rewarding when we actively own our choices. I wish I'd understood this the day I graduated; unfortunately it took me another fifteen years to figure it out. Owning my own choices changed my life. The reality of the world is that everything I do, everything you do, is a choice. No one made us go to school, no one makes us to go work, or read a book, or be kind. No one makes us do anything. We can choose to be generous, we can choose to care, we can choose to make a positive difference. Perhaps most powerfully of all—if we choose to pay attention—we have the power to choose what we believe.

I believe that, although history focuses mostly on the big headlines, it's really the little things that matter most. Your grandmother's hug today. The notes you took on your favorite book assignment this year. The small gesture of generosity you did to help someone in need. A thank-you note to the people who clean the rooms, and run the phones, and make this university go, so that you and I could go to class and get grades and graduate. In that sense, I believe with great strength that everything matters and everyone matters. The people who are least likely to be consulted in a company, or included in society. The sky. A smile. The stars. Your mother. This moment. Your dog. The person you walked by on the stairs on the way in, and the one you walk by again on the way out.

I believe that simple kindness matters more than most people will admit. That if instead of getting angry at others, we appreciate; that instead of blaming, we give blessings; that instead of keeping score, we live out the generosity of spirit that Paul just detailed so powerfully. Kindness is free, and kindness counts! We believe what Paul Hawken wrote: *"Being a good human being is good business."*

I believe that—contrary to what much of the world would say—hard work can be one of the most rewarding things one ever engages in. Not just any work, but good work, work you believe in, work that brings the generosity and joy that Paul just talked about so beautifully; work that makes a positive difference for you, for the world; work that matters, work that you care about. Hard work like that may not get the glamor, but it is almost always exceptionally rewarding.

I believe that perhaps the hardest work we have to undertake is the work no one else sees, and that no one else can ever do for us. It's the lifelong challenge to manage ourselves effectively, to make peace with ourselves and turn our natural ability into a positive and powerful presence in the world. Although it almost never comes up in postgraduate conversation, it's at the core of everything else we will ever do for the rest of our lives.

I believe that everyone—everyone—in the world is a unique, caring, creative individual. Walking our own way while still respecting the world around us is no small feat. Holding our own course can be uncomfortable, but it's essential if we're going to truly live lives that we—not everyone else who has input—really own. Despite what higher-ups in the hierarchy might tell you, I believe what Rollo May wrote, that *"The opposite of courage in our society is not cowardice, it's conformity."*

It was hard for me to comprehend when I was 21 but I believe, ever more strongly with each passing day, that every single minute really does matter. Life, when it comes down to it, is very, very short. There are a thousand reasons to sleep in, to drink another beer, to put things off till tomorrow or two weeks from Tuesday. But I believe what author Annie Dillard said, that, *"The way we spend our days is the way we spend our lives."* Every minute we spend worrying, every minute we spend waiting for someone else to improve, is a minute we don't spend doing something meaningful for the people we care about, for the world, for ourselves.

I believe that going for greatness, greatness as you—and not everyone else in the world—defines it, is energizing. I believe that uniqueness like that is exciting. Empowering. Emma Goldman says *"When we can't dream any longer we die."* Choosing greatness, choosing to push your own envelope, to find ways to be more generous, to find more joy, to learn more, study harder, and make a more positive difference is what leads to a great life.

I believe that one of the best ways to makes our lives into the artistic, positive, amazing existences we want to them to be is to write out a vision of what that life will look like when we've successfully made it a reality. I believe that any one of you who is willing to push "pause," and to gently ask the voices in their heads to step aside for an hour so you can write out that kind of personal vision of greatness, their true dream, can come darned close to making that life a reality. They may not make the most money, they may not have the fanciest car, but they will find fulfillment, and equally importantly, they will help many others find it as well. The visioning process, the initial work on which was done here at U of M fifty years ago, is the single best tool I know to make that happen. And I'm happy—though it might take a while if you all take me up on it—to meet with any graduate who wants help with the visioning process. I believe that anyone who does that work will pretty surely lead an amazing life.

Most importantly for today's purposes, I believe in YOU—by dint of the fact that you have done what you have done to earn the right to be here today, both you and the world know that you have the intelligence, you have the emotional resilience, you have the connections, you have the capability to do great things. To help make the world a meaningfully better place than it was yesterday. You have the power. As African American anarchist Ashanti Alston said: *"You all can do this. You have the vision. You have the creativity. Do not allow anyone to lock that down."*

PAUL: Class of 2015, congratulations! Be generous!

ARI: Be joyful!

PAUL: Be great!

ARI: Make a difference!

A Handful of Organizational Recipes

3 steps to giving great service

1. Find out what the customer would like.
2. Get it for them, accurately, politely, and enthusiastically.
3. Go the extra mile.

5 steps to effectively handling a complaint

1. Acknowledge what the guest is saying.
2. Sincerely apologize.
3. Do whatever you need to do to make things right.
4. Thank the guest.
5. Write it up.

5 steps to effective bottom line change

1. Create a clear and compelling purpose for change.
2. Create a positive vision of the future and develop leadership alignment around that vision.
3. Engage a microcosm to determine who needs to know and how to get the information out.
4. "Officially" present the vision and create an action plan.
5. Implement the change.

zingerman's 4 steps to productive resolution of your differences

1. **Go direct.** That's right, speak directly to the individual involved and express your concerns and work towards resolution. Don't know how to say it? Sign up for D4P's (Department for People) class in Courageous Conversations or ask your manager for help.

2. **Put it in writing.** Address your concerns in writing to the individual involved (with a copy to their supervisor/manager and managing partner) and then meet with them again. If you still aren't satisfied with the outcome, then . . .

3. **Put it in writing and meet with a manager present.** Follow up in writing (copy to supervisor/manager and managing partner) and ask for a meeting with you, the other individual, your supervisor, their supervisor, and/or the managing partner. If that meeting still doesn't meet your needs, then . . .

4. **Present your issues at the Partners' Group.** Follow up in writing again (copies to everyone) and ask for time at the Partners' Group where you can both present your case and ask for help. The Partners' Group is the final spot to reach resolution.

4 rules not to break under any circumstances

Among the most important things you should know are 4 things that can get you fired:

1. Working under the influence of drugs or alcohol
2. Stealing
3. Being rude to a customer
4. Being rude to the food

twelve natural Laws of business
from zingerman's Guide to Good Leading, Part I: a Lapsed anarchist's approach to building a great business

1. An inspiring, strategically sound vision leads the way to greatness (especially if you write it down!).

2. You need to give customers really compelling reasons to buy from you.

3. Without good finance, you fail.

4. People do their best work when they're part of a really great organization.

5. If you want the staff to give great service to customers, the leaders have to give great service to the staff.

6. If you want great performance from your staff, you have to give them clear expectations and training tools.

7. Successful businesses do the things that others know they should do . . . but generally don't.

8. To get to greatness you've got to keep getting better, all the time!

9. Success means you get better problems.

10. Whatever your strengths are, they will likely lead straight to your weaknesses.

11. It generally takes a lot longer to make something great happen than people think.

12. Great organizations are appreciative, and the people in them have more fun.

Secrets #1-18
from zingerman's guide to good Leading, Part 1: a Lapsed anarchist's approach to building a great business

#1 Twelve Natural Laws of Building a Great Business

#2 Contrast, Composition, Content

#3 Creating Recipes for Organizational Success

#4 The Zingerman's Business Perspective Chart

#5 Building a Better Mission Statement

#6 Revisiting the Power of Visioning

#7 Writing a Vision of Greatness

#8 Vision Back

#9 An 8-Step Recipe for Writing a Vision of Greatness

#10 A Question of Systems

#11 Writing and Using Guiding Principles

#12 5 Steps to Building an Organizational Culture

#13 Creating a Culture of Positive Appreciation

#14   *Why I Want to Finish Third*

#15   *Building a Sustainable Business*

#16   *28 Years of Buying Local*

#17   *A Recipe for Making Something Special*

#18   *Finally, Some Food!*

Secrets #19-29

from zingerman's guide to good Leading, Part 2: a Lapsed anarchist's approach to being a better Leader

#19   *Fixing the Energy Crisis in the American Workplace*

#20   *Raising the Energy Bar*

#21   *Defining Positive Energy*

#22   *We're All Leaders*

#23   *A Recipe for Servant Leadership*

#24   *The Secret of Stewardship*

#25   *Managing by Pouring Water*

#26   *Beekeeping and Leadership*

#27   *The Entrepreneurial Approach to Management*

#28   *Moving Your Organization from V to A*

#29   *Twelve Tenets of Anarcho-Capitalism*

Secrets #30-39

from zingerman's guide to good leading, part 3: a lapsed anarchist's approach to managing ourselves

#30 *Why Managing Ourselves Well Matters*

#31 *Managing Ourselves*

#32 *It's All About Free Choice*

#33 *Mindfulness Matters*

#34 *Schein On, You Crazy Diamond*

#35 *The Power of Personal Visioning*

#36 *Making the Most of Our Lives*

#37 *Time Management for Lapsed Anarchists*

#38 *Thinking About Thinking*

#39 *Creating Creativity*

Time to Eat!

Nine Recipes to Cook in Your Own Kitchen

My Beliefs About Cooking

Food and cooking are clearly central to my life. They've taught me to pay attention, to appreciate aspects of the world that I've never before noticed; significantly increased my sensory awareness and my sensitivity to smell, touch, and taste; and demonstrated how joy in little things can make a big contribution to so many other elements of our lives. They're at the core of what Zingerman's is all about. Traditional food and food traditions are both intellectually fascinating and culinarily compelling for me. They've given me a path by which I can bring my interest in history alive in ways that make it meaningful to others. Back a few hundred pages, I shared a recipe for changing one's beliefs. What follows are some beliefs that might change the way you approach recipes.

Beliefs are just as much at play in the kitchen as they are anywhere else. What we cook and what we put on our tables are basically the sum total of a series of interlocking and overlapping beliefs. The beliefs of the people who grew or produced the raw materials we buy (fresh, canned, bottled, milled, or dried) and the beliefs of the those who sold them to us at the store, at the farmstand, or online. If you grow your own ingredients, that says a lot about your beliefs as well, whether about gardening or gathering in the wild or farming 40 acres. If we take Claude Bristol's quote about beliefs and bring it into the kitchen, the principle is equally applicable. Bristol said: "As individuals think and believe, so they are." I'll extrapolate: "As individuals think and believe, so they cook." Our beliefs don't cook our food, but they do call our culinary shots.

My own beliefs have changed drastically over the decades. I grew up with rather unremarkable feelings about food and almost none (that I can remember, at least) about cooking. Like every kid, I liked what I liked, wouldn't eat what I didn't. Best I can recall, I was neither particularly picky nor overly adventurous. I grew up eating off a list that I can now see was essentially the epitome of mid-20th-century industrial menu making. Kraft macaroni and cheese in the dark blue box; Mrs. Paul's frozen fish sticks (with the tartar sauce in the little plastic packets); pale orange American singles (first in layered stacks, then as plastic-wrapped slices); presliced loaves of white bread; boxes of cinnamon-frosted Pop-Tarts; fruit cocktail out of the can; Tang, Tater Tots, and Twinkies; Nestlé's Quik or, my favorite for a while at least, the less famous but fabulously pink Strawberry Quik. None of which, of course, would be remotely considered nowadays for a Zingerman's menu. I have no desire to eat any of them today. But their memory makes me smile.

Back then we ate so matter-of-factly industrial. At the time, it all seemed completely unremarkable, which tells you a lot about the beliefs about food and cooking in middle America in the middle part of the 20th century. In our family, the idea of "local" referred mostly to area codes or the lanes (as opposed to "express") on the highway that allowed you access to exits. I have no idea if a farmers' market existed anywhere within 100 miles of our house. We shopped at either "the Jewel" or at Dominick's. Meals were consistent if not even close to the quality standards I've come to count on every day in my full-flavored bubble of an ecosystem here at Zingerman's. Food was sort of mundane, really—hardly central to our existence other than the human requirement to eat. And Jewish holidays. Every Friday night my grandmother used to cook all the traditional Eastern European Jewish dishes—chicken soup, chopped liver, potato kugel, and the like. Same for Rosh Hashanah, Passover, and latkes at Hanukkah. Other than that, it was pretty much a midcentury, mostly modern, all-American meal plan. Happily, we never went hungry. One twist on the construct is that we had a kosher home, which meant that many foods (as well as many combinations of food) were completely out of bounds. I was very focused on what I'd now call "freedom from" those culinary codes. Mostly the restrictions just made me mad—I *really* wanted to eat a cheeseburger. But it's interesting how deeply sunk the roots of some beliefs can be, even when we don't know it; as rebellious as I was, the idea of eating exceedingly illicit options like bacon or oysters back then was so taboo as to be almost unimaginable.

My mother was a caring and considerate woman who was trying to do the right thing for her family. She graduated from the University of Wisconsin, read widely, taught school, and gave generously of everything she had. Cooking, however, was neither her passion nor her forte. She did, at times, experiment with "exotic" foods such as zucchini, but I think she mostly just got pushback for her attempt to get out of the box and quickly withdrew to what we were willing to eat without whining. Mostly, our meals were mainstream.

Others out there, I know, ate more interestingly, but we were certainly not alone. Food writer and historian Laura Shapiro explains that "in the late 19th century Americans were pushed to think differently about food—to be scientific, to simplify cooking without regard to taste, to adopt the first industrial products such as ketchup and Jell-O." Prepacks started to replace made from scratch. These are the types of commercial "innovations" that I can imagine Rocco Disderide somewhat uncertainly stocking on his shelves back in 1902. For more on this, check out Shapiro's superb book, *Perfection Salad: Women and Cooking at the Turn of the Century*.

In her next book, *Something from the Oven: Reinventing Dinner in 1950s America*, she continues the story. She details how women of my mother's era were pressured to change their beliefs about food and cooking. Many, like my mom, had grown up with their own immigrant mothers cooking the foods of the old country—in this case, the stuff my grandmother prepared so regularly. But in the postwar years, mass marketing pushed homemakers to drop the "messy" foreign foods of the past and feed their families properly by choosing industrial consistency and control in lieu of the low-quality variability of the rough-around-the-edges peasant foods they'd had previously. By that point, Shapiro says, "it wasn't just ketchup or canned soup, it was packaged food moving right to the center of the plate. The change in thinking was already pretty widespread, and now Americans were ready to accept that macaroni and cheese could mean opening a box."

Backing up to the late 19th century, farmers who went to town to shop would often have gone to general stores, spots that sold everything from groceries to animal feed, seed, clothing, and linens. There were also specialists. The *1887 Jubilee Cookbook*, published in Ann Arbor, has ads for "fine teas, coffees and spices" at the Palace Grocery on North Main Street; Edward Duffy's Coffee opposite the post office; Walter Toop, a baker and confectioner; and another of the same, known as L. Gerstner. T. E. Nickels, "the leading dealer in fresh, salt and smoked meats," was billed as "the finest meat market in the city." Mr. Nickels's legacy lives on—the Nickels Arcade remains a landmark today, off State Street, on the west side of Campus.

"Corner groceries" such as Disderide's were somewhere in between the general store and the specialists—small neighborhood shops in which the owner worked the counter, knew the clientele, and often (as the Disderides did) lived upstairs or maybe just down the block. The proprietor, or their family, frequently waited on the customers themselves. House accounts were commonly carried for locals, which would be settled up either weekly or monthly. The industrial 21st-century version of the corner grocery is probably the impersonal, shop-in-a-box convenience store, often fronted by gas pumps. Corner groceries, of course, still exist in old neighborhoods in big cities and also in some small towns. In many ways, when we opened the Deli, we functioned as one. Large self-serve supermarkets of the sort my mother shopped in converted to "cash and carry"—no more personal accounts, no more owner to serve you as you did your shopping. For me, mid-century city kid that I was, those big grocery stores with dozens of long aisles, glass-doored freezer sections, and tall shelf fixtures were the norm.

The shift to supermarket shopping changed everything; as Laura Shapiro says, many people—city folk at least—reduced the odds of culinary error by shifting to factory-made standardized products. The perceived rough "out-of-control" edges of earlier eras were squared off, and the variability of seasons subverted in favor of straight lines and consistently, tightly sealed plastic packages. In some ways, buying food this way reduced the workload and stress of the housewife. What could go wrong when dinner was made by combining cans or when dessert meant unwrapping a package of Twinkies? Increased "consistency," lower prices, and better packaging became the order of the day. I can only imagine what Emma Goldman—who loved well-prepared food— would have had to say on the subject. If she'd been born 50 years later, she and I might well have met at some Slow Food event. It's not hard to imagine her preaching forcefully about protecting heirloom apples instead of advocating for anarchism.

Unlike me, writer Mimi Sheraton grew up in a family in which full-flavored food and skilled cooking were greatly valued. She went on to become one of the best-known food writers of our era. And yet, the social pressure she felt as a kid to straighten things out was still very strong. Talking about her love of the Old World food her mother made, she writes, "I remember the embarrassment I felt [at school] at the rye bread sandwiches and how I wished for neat, squared-off sandwiches on packaged white bread, which I considered more American and, therefore, classier." Going back to Rollo May's "the opposite of courage is conformity," the mainstream American kitchen lost courage—more and more home cooks conformed to mass-market consumer trends. The belief that we're supposed to fit in is a powerful force. Even—or maybe especially—with food. As Sheraton explains, "The problem with the rye bread was its shape, the standard loaf that tapered towards both ends. My mother cut it on the diagonal to make large slices, and no two slices were the same size, so the edges of my sandwiches did not match. They were, I thought, sloppy Jewish sandwiches."

In order to fit in, many women changed their beliefs. "What happened in the '50s," Shapiro says, "was that for the first time probably in the history of the world, it became possible for ordinary, not-rich women to decide whether or not they *wanted* to cook. The food industry was eager to step in and make that decision for them, of course, and the advertising was pretty powerful." That was the setting in which I grew up in the suburbs. Processed foods ruled the day. Millions opted for industrial. Industry, in turn, made millions. Monocropping and mass-market manufacturing followed. A half-century later, the country is still in recovery.

Fortunately, there were some holdouts. There was, Shapiro says, still "the appeal of real food—ingredients you could touch and smell and taste. The American kitchen became a battleground of beliefs about love, family, health, responsibility and status." My mother wasn't one of them, but there were women who never strayed from what they'd learned from their mothers and grandmothers. Much of it would have been the kind of cooking that's now held in high esteem in so many parts of the culinary ecosystem. (It was, of course, mostly women; men in that era, it was commonly believed, should not be cooking, other than an occasional holiday barbecue.) Shapiro says that those women "held firm, long enough to give Julia Child and Alice Waters and a lot of other people—you at Zingerman's included—the time and space to create the alternatives and niche markets that now make it possible to find honest food, not everywhere but in a lot more places than we would have dreamed possible half a century ago." The result? Thirty-four years after we opened, a whole lot of people believe that the full-flavored, traditional food that is the focus of everything we source, sell, and serve at Zingerman's is worth the time, effort, and cost. Those "sloppy Jewish sandwiches" are now the centerpiece of the Zingerman's world. And that embarrassing rye bread with the rounded ends and rough edges is one of our signature products.

My own beliefs about food and cooking have clearly come a very long way during the course of my life. What was once a rather unremarkable routine that ensured survival is now the centerpiece of my existence, something that sustains me physically and financially, intellectually and emotionally. Everywhere I go now, good food is an essential element of my existence. Here are a few of the beliefs that I hold that drive my—our—work with food at Zingerman's and my own cooking at home.

- The best cooking is a lot like leading a good organization. If you get great ingredients—i.e., people—together, get to know them, honor them for what they are, and use effective basic processes that let their personalities shine through, good things are likely to happen. In business, it can make for a healthy organization. In the kitchen, it might well just make for a delicious dinner!

- Anyone who's interested can fairly quickly tell the difference between bad, good, indifferent, and excellent. Many people I've met say they can't. But guess what happens when you have that belief? You got it! If you believe you won't be able to taste the difference, the odds are high you won't. If you change those beliefs, and open your mind to appreciate the differences between delicious artisanal fare and mediocre industrial offerings, I'm confident you will. In fact, I'd say it's almost impossible not to. Given the choice between marvelously good and run-of-the-mill mundane, anyone who's attentive will be able to tell the difference in a heartbeat.

- Trinidadian historian C. L. R. James said, "Any cook can govern." I agree with him. I also believe the opposite to be true: "Any governor—no matter their political affiliation—can learn to cook." Cooking is a skill anyone with an interest can do well. It starts with beliefs. If we're afraid of cooking—as we are of so many unfamiliar things in our lives—we will find mostly faults: in our own ability, in the recipe we're trying so hard to follow, or in the quality of the ingredients we bought. When we're looking for trouble, we will quickly see where we fell short; many of us just worry and wait for culinary miracles that never come. By contrast, when we have a positive belief that anyone who's interested in learning and willing to work a bit can easily learn the basics, good food will likely follow.

- The anarchist belief that *the means we use must be congruent with the ends we want to achieve* applies in the kitchen as well. Trying to make something super tasty out of stuff that doesn't taste good on its own is nigh impossible. It's about 8,000 times easier to cook delicious food if you start with great, top-notch, full-flavored raw materials.

- Good cooking is, ultimately, about being ourselves and letting the ingredients be themselves. Alice Waters says, "When you have the best and tastiest ingredients, you can cook very simply and the food will be extraordinary because it tastes like what it is." I agree 100 percent! Her short sentence sums up 34 years of Zingerman's culinary history.

- If you stick to simple, down-to-earth, delicious stuff, then really anyone with some access to good ingredients can make marvelous meals. By contrast, fancy dishes—ones that are beyond our current cooking ability and acumen—all too often fall flat. When they do, confidence erodes and belief falters. Mediocre meals generally follow.

- Knowing the story behind the food is, I believe, essential to being able to cook it in a way that honors what it is and brings out its best. In the same way that one can't manage people without knowing who they are and what moves them, I don't think one can really do culinary justice to even the simplest ingredient and their own cooking without taking time to find out more about how the food came to be what it is. Studying the history, the geography, the politics, and the economics that go with every ingredient and every recipe, bringing food, cooking, and culture alive, takes time but it's well worth the effort.

- Learning the foodways of any people is one of the best methods I know to honor who they are. Reading cookbooks is an intriguing way to enter the belief systems of cultures around the world. When you learn the cooking and eating traditions of a given culture, you're honoring the people who are a part of it, and you will come much closer to understanding their struggles, successes, and sensitivities. Both empathy and good eating will probably ensue.

- Putting together a really great meal—not fancy, just delicious and well suited to the occasion—is really about the self-fulfilling belief cycle. Alice Waters, writing about Chez Panisse chef David Tanis, said, "He understands that creating a meal means creating your own reality."

- Good ingredients almost always emerge from good ecosystems. It's hard to find delicious food grown sustainably over a period of years without it coming from people who care about their soil, their community, their crops, quality, and flavor. Dan Barber's farmer friend Jack says, "Industrially produced grains, vegetables, and fruits taste of almost nothing because the nitrates [in the soil] have crowded out the minerals." The good news? It can be much better! "The development of flavor, and the health of the plant, are the same freakin' thing. You don't get one without the other. If I treat the soil's microorganisms right, if they have everything they need to prosper, they'll do the work for me. At that point you just need to put it on the plate, basically."

• Better food will almost always cost more money. It's not true that all expensive food tastes good. But it is true that low-priced products are less likely to be amazingly delicious. Is there a range of workable quality levels for those who have limited food budgets? Of course! How do we make the best-tasting foods more affordable? I don't have an easy answer. My approach is to try to create more jobs that pay better so people can afford to buy food that's sustainably grown.

• One way around the cost issue is quite simply to grow our own. We trade our time in the garden against lowered costs. This is why projects such as Melvin Parson's We the People Growers Association are so positive—they let people with limited financial resources have access to land on which to grow something delicious and nutritious.

• Just to show you the correlation between good cooking and so many of the other beliefs in this book, here's a bit more from Alice Waters, sounding a lot like an anarchist: "The most common way people give up their power is by thinking they don't have any." And speaking of radical change, check out the title of one of her recent (and highly recommended) books: *The Art of Simple Food: Notes, Lessons, and Recipes from a Delicious Revolution.* Calm confidence in the kitchen makes a big difference. Anxious cooks press too hard and then feel like failures when what they prepare seems somehow less than perfect. They tentatively try to follow recipes as if they were adhering to standard operating procedures for safety in a nuclear plant. But cooking is a craft—it's no more an exact science than is managing your employees. Enjoyable, not exacting and exhausting. Learn the basics of cooking; take time to taste, practice tasting, learn to trust your palate, be patient and pay attention to what you're experiencing, and let your intuition help you bring together flavors that work well. If you need to choose between what tastes right to you and what the recipe says, close the cookbook and go with your gut.

- Starting simple will lead to increased odds of success. A great grilled cheese (good bread, good cheese, and a frying pan) with a nice salad (vegetables from the farmers' market) with good olive oil, vinegar, sea salt, and freshly ground pepper make an amazing meal. Overreaching—trying to follow recipes for fancy dishes you've never before experienced—is like buying a violin to play Beethoven for the first time in front of 500 friends and family on Christmas Eve. It's too much! Try it alone first, or with a close friend, where you can keep calm and let the cooking come slowly and gently without a lot of pressure to perform.

- For me, cooking is a personal thing. Eating is an intimate act. Honoring your palate and your preferences, getting to know your own cooking, with care and dignity, becomes then an act of mindful self-awareness. It's also all about art! And as artists David Bayles and Ted Orland write, "In large measure becoming an artist consists of learning to accept yourself, which makes your work personal, and in following your own voice, which makes your work distinctive."

- Like anything else, learning to cook and eat well takes intention and practice. We don't get good at anything without working at it. Cooking and eating are no different. The more we pay attention over time, the more wisdom we accumulate. It's not magic— just mindful practice. Gary Snyder says, "[R]epetition is not necessarily an enemy. Because every time you do something it's different. . . . Being too interested in always having things new and interesting is to miss the point." When it comes out of a box or a can, repetition can be boring—we know what we'll get every time. But when we use artisanal foods, fresh produce, or heirloom vegetables, nature contributes complexity—the tomatoes taste different, the texture of the bread changes with the weather, the flavor of our coffee is impacted by the water and method used to brew it, the choice of salt for our salad alters the entire eating experience.

- With that in mind, though, I've learned that repetition in the kitchen can turn out to be riveting. If you caringly cook scrambled eggs 18 days in a row, you'll surely notice the varying nuances with each day's dinner. Your eggs will be lovingly different every single day. If you start with good eggs, the odds are they will taste even better. Actually, why not try different eggs every evening? Each detail matters. As Snyder says, "We need attention to doing things well." I agree. If you want to really get into it, take notes: the utensil you use; whether you add cream, milk, water, or nothing at all; the heat and shape of the pan; the fat in which you cook; the pepper you grind (or don't) to sprinkle on top. As Gary Snyder adds, "It's what the artist brings to it in a new way." By the 18th evening, you will nearly be an expert.

- I believe very strongly that simple dishes, made with great ingredients, prepared by cooks who respect their raw materials and have even a modest understanding of the basics of cooking, will almost always taste terrific. Some of my favorites include:
  - Slices of artisan bread, toasted and topped with a fantastic extra virgin olive oil, eaten while still warm.
  - A bowl of stone-ground oatmeal topped with your choice of natural muscovado brown sugar, real maple syrup, artisanal cane syrup, or great butter—a beautiful way to start your morning. (Rocco Disderide, by the way, loved oatmeal and ate it nearly every day.)
  - Fresh vegetables from the farmers' market tossed with good olive oil, sea salt, and a bit of fresh garlic, then oven roasted at about 450°F for half an hour or so.
  - Two slices of great bread and some farmhouse cheddar grilled till it's golden brown and eaten hot from the frying pan.
  - A pound of locally dug potatoes, steamed or boiled till they're tender, smashed and eaten with good butter or olive oil, some sea salt, and freshly ground pepper.
  - Top-notch artisanal pasta tossed with really good Parmigiano-Reggiano cheese, an excellent extra virgin olive oil, and some freshly ground black pepper.
  - Great salad greens, a pinch of sun-dried sea salt, a small bit of well-aged naturally converted vinegar, and a bit more of that good olive oil.
  - The Tanzanian Kyela rice that we get from Shawn Askinosie, the proceeds of which go to provide school lunches for kids at

the Mababu Cacao Cooperative, cooked simply in water with some sun-dried, natural sea salt.

- Same goes for the grits from Glenn Roberts at Anson Mills or the polenta from the Marino family in the Italian Piedmont. They take time to cook, but the cooking couldn't be simpler. And they taste terrific.

- A BLT made with Nueske's bacon (or any other artisanal bacon), ripe summer tomatoes, good bread, and four leaves of fresh lettuce.

- A few slices of well-made salami or cured ham (served at room temperature, where their flavors will best come through) and a little salad with a good loaf of bread.

- Fresh fish, sprinkled with the Indian fennel seed we score from the folks at Épices de Cru, sautéed at medium heat till it's just done, then dressed with a touch of delicate olive oil.

- A couple squares of Shawn Askinosie's dark chocolate laid between two slices of buttered sourdough bread, fried in a medium hot skillet till its golden brown and the chocolate is soft—best dessert ever!

There are thousands of other options—different cuisines, different ingredients, different days. The key again is starting with good stuff and taking it from there. Are any of these meals impeccable? Of course not! Perfection sounds inspiring, but it's almost impossible. Gary Snyder says, "Art is never perfect." Neither is great cooking. It just tastes really terrific! So, in the same way that I learned to get past my perfectionism by writing more quickly when I get anxious, I'd recommend the same strategy for cooking. When it starts to feel uncomfortable, don't cut back—relax if you can, buy better ingredients, cook more. Take in the smells. Savor the flavors. Appreciate the colors and the sounds. Enjoy.

In the meantime, try out a couple of the recipes that follow. I believe you'll enjoy them. Happy cooking!

(For more on this approach to cooking, see *Zingerman's Guide to Good Eating*.)

ROCCO'S SPAGHETTI
WITH BASIL AND BUTTER

I learned about this recipe while gathering stories from Rocco Disderide's great- and great-great-granddaughters. It's a simple, delicious spaghetti dish. One hundred twenty years after Rocco and Catherine arrived in Ann Arbor, it remains an emotional and culinary favorite in the family. The prominent use of fresh basil is a practice that would have come from Rocco's hometown on the Italian Riviera—the region in which pesto originated. The eyes of all four of the women at the table lit up when they started to tell me about this dish! Be sure to use high-quality spaghetti—traditional producers such as Martelli or Rustichella offer great options. (Industrially made pasta has neither the wonderful wheaty, full flavor nor sturdy texture that you get in a well-made artisanal offering.) Be sure to use fresh basil—dried basil will *not* work here! And you'll want to warm the serving bowls before you start; this should be served immediately.

Sea salt, for the pasta cooking water and for seasoning later

½ pound spaghetti

¼ cup (4 tablespoons) good butter

1 cup loosely packed torn fresh basil leaves

Freshly ground black pepper

Freshly grated Parmigiano-Reggiano cheese

Bring a large pot of water to a boil. Add 1 to 2 tablespoons salt and stir well. (The water should taste like the sea!)

Add the spaghetti, stir gently with tongs or a pasta fork. Bring the water back to a boil, stir gently, and keep cooking till the pasta is *al dente*. (Refer to the timing on the package, but more importantly, taste a strand as it gets near the end.) When the pasta is ready, drain it using a colander.

Just before the pasta is ready, heat a skillet over medium heat. Melt the butter in it. Add the hot spaghetti and toss gently. Cook for a minute or so, stirring occasionally to keep the pasta from sticking and to get the butter better integrated with the noodles. Sprinkle on the basil and stir it in gently. Add pepper and salt to taste. (If the butter is unsalted, you'll likely want to add more salt.)

Serve in warm bowls.

Add some grated Parmigiano-Reggiano cheese to each bowl, as much or as little as you like.

Serves 2 generously

CHOCOLATE-DIPPED ESPRESSO STARS

It's very important that your butter not be cold, in order for the dough to come together.

½ cup (8 tablespoons) butter, at room temperature

¼ cup granulated sugar

½ teaspoon fine sea salt

1¼ cups all-purpose flour, plus more for rolling

2 tablespoons ground espresso coffee beans

Dark chocolate, 58% or higher, chopped

Gold luster dust (optional; available in stores that sell cake decorating supplies)

Preheat the oven to 300°F.

In a mixing bowl, beat together the butter, sugar, and salt until the sugar is blended in. (If using an electric mixer, use the paddle attachment and mix on low-to-medium speed.) Add the flour and coffee. Mix until the dough holds together.

On a lightly floured surface, roll out the dough to a ¼-inch thickness. Cut out shapes using desired cookie cutters. (We recommend a 1½- to 2-inch star cutter.) You can roll out the dough that remains and cut more stars and still have a nice-textured cookie. You should end up with 3 dozen cookies.

Very lightly grease 1 or 2 cookie sheets, or line them with parchment paper. Lay out the cookies on the cookie sheets, not touching.

Bake the cookies for 30 minutes. The tops should look dry, and the cookies should be slightly browned.

Remove the cookies from the oven and let cool to room temperature.

Melt the chocolate in the top of a double boiler. (You can make your own double boiler with a metal bowl that fits over the top of a saucepan.) Fill the pan about one-third full of water and bring the water to a boil. Reduce the heat to medium and place the bowl, with the chocolate in it, on top. Make sure the bottom of the bowl is not touching the water. Stir the chocolate until melted. Scrape the sides to avoid burning. Once the chocolate is melted, remove it from the pan and set it aside to cool a bit.

Lay out a sheet of waxed paper or parchment paper on the work surface. Dip ⅓ of each cookie into the chocolate and lay them flat on the paper. Let the cookies sit at room temperature until the chocolate hardens.

If you like, lightly brush gold luster dust over the hardened chocolate (we recommend using a new, clean paint or makeup brush). This will give the cookies a particularly festive look.

Store in an airtight container for up to a week or freeze for up to 3 months.

Yields 3 dozen cookies

MACARONI AND 3 PEPPERCORN
GOAT CHEESE

This is an easy-to-prepare and tasty macaroni and cheese dish. The creaminess of the goat cheese is set off beautifully by the spiciness of the peppercorns. I like the diversity of peppercorns in color and in flavor. The better the quality of the peppercorn, the better the dish—as we generally do, I rely on the complex, full flavors of the pepper we purchase (and sell!) from the folks at Épices de Cru in Montreal.

The quality of the macaroni is also critical to the quality of the dish. You can really taste the difference as a result. I recommend using macaroni from the Martelli family in Tuscany, but Rustichella, Faella, and Baia are all top-quality brands we use regularly at Zingerman's.

At the Roadhouse, we serve this dish with a slice of Zingerman's Creamery Aged Chelsea goat cheese, breaded and pan-fried, atop the peppery, creamy macaroni, giving the dish an enjoyable contrast of textures and flavors. You'll want to fry the cheese rounds just before serving, so have your ingredients ready.

For the macaroni

Coarse sea salt, for the pasta cooking water

1 pound macaroni

2 tablespoons butter

¼ cup diced onion

1 bay leaf

2 tablespoons all-purpose flour

1½ cups whole milk

¼ cup heavy cream

1 teaspoon Dijon mustard

2 cups fresh goat cheese

¾ cup chopped roasted red peppers

2 teaspoons freshly and coarsely ground black peppercorns, plus more for seasoning

1 teaspoon freshly and coarsely ground white peppercorns

1 teaspoon freshly and coarsely ground green peppercorns

½ teaspoon coarse seal salt

For the Aged Chelsea

1 large egg

2 tablespoons whole milk

4 ounces aged goat cheese (such as Zingerman's Creamery Aged Chelsea), cut into 4 disks or squares, each ½-inch thick

1 cup dried breadcrumbs (preferably homemade)

1 tablespoon butter, for frying

To make the macaroni, bring a large pot of water to a boil. Add 1 to 2 tablespoons salt and the pasta and stir well. Cook for about 13 minutes (if using Martelli) or until it is almost *al dente*. Drain the pasta in a colander.

While the pasta is cooking, melt the butter for the sauce in a large heavy-bottomed pot over medium-high heat (be careful not to scorch the butter). Add the onion and bay leaf and sauté until the onion is soft, about 5 minutes.

Remove the bay leaf. Add the flour and cook for a minute or so, stirring constantly.

Slowly add the milk, a little at a time, stirring constantly to avoid lumping. When the flour and milk have been completely combined, stir in the cream. Keep the mixture at a gentle simmer (not at a high boil) until it thickens, 2 to 3 minutes.

Reduce the heat to medium. Stir in the mustard, goat cheese, red peppers, peppercorns, and salt.

Stir the drained pasta into the cheese sauce. Taste and adjust the seasonings if necessary. Cook for 1 to 2 minutes, stirring regularly, so the cooked pasta absorbs some of the sauce. Cover and remove from the heat.

To fry the Aged Chelsea, beat the egg and milk in a shallow bowl until just combined. Spread the breadcrumbs on a plate. One at a time, dip each cheese round in the egg wash to cover, then completely coat it in breadcrumbs, pressing them lightly to stick. Set the cheese aside on a clean plate and coat the others.

Melt the butter over moderately high heat in a heavy-bottomed skillet. Fry the cheese round about 1 minute on each side, until golden.

Divide the macaroni among serving bowls. Serve each bowl topped with a golden Aged Chelsea round. Dig in!

Serves 4

Zingerman's
maiL order.

OCTOPUS AND COUSCOUS (OCTO-COUS)

This is one of my favorite dishes—octopus, couscous, harissa, and beans simmered together to make a wonderfully delicious stew. It's hearty enough to be great on a cold Michigan winter evening, yet still light and fresh in the summer, too. If you start with cooked beans and cooked chickpeas—I confess to using canned more often than not for convenience—it's about an hour of cook time, most of which is unattended so you can do whatever other inspiring things you want while the stuff is simmering on the stove top.

As with every recipe you'll get here, I'll put a plug in for high-quality ingredients. The Mahjoub family has been making olive oil and other traditional Tunisian products for over a century. They grow olives for olive oil, wheat for couscous, and peppers and tomatoes for their amazing harissa. Everything we get from them is exceptional. Their couscous and harissa will drastically elevate the quality of this dish.

The texture you're looking for in the finished dish is that of a thick stew so I'll let you judge, but starting with ½ cup of couscous will be fine. To put the picture into your mind's cooking eye, it's more a tomato-based bean and octopus stew with couscous, not a bowl of lightly fluffed couscous with bits of octopus in it.

3½ cups water

½ cup tomato puree

¼ cup tomato paste

3 tablespoons extra virgin olive oil, plus more for serving

1 rounded tablespoon harissa (preferably from the Moulin de Mahjoub)

1 teaspoon chopped garlic (preferably sun-dried garlic from the Moulin de Mahjoub)

1½ cups cooked chickpeas (one 15-ounce can), drained and rinsed

2 to 4 meaty octopus tentacles (about 1 pound), sliced

1½ cups cooked baby fava beans (one 15-ounce can), drained and rinsed

½ teaspoon ground caraway seeds

About ½ cup couscous (preferably M'hamsa—hand-rolled— couscous from the Mahjoub family)

Coarse sea salt

Bring the water, tomato puree, tomato paste, olive oil, harissa, and garlic to a boil in a large heavy-bottomed pot. Stir in the chickpeas and the octopus and bring back to a boil. Reduce the heat so it all barely simmers, cover, and simmer for about an hour, until the octopus is tender. The result will be a light and flavorful tomato broth.

Stir in the fava beans and ground caraway and bring back to a boil. Add Mahjoub's amazing couscous. Stir well, turn off the heat, cover, and let rest for 12 minutes or so. The couscous will cook in the broth.

Taste for seasoning and adjust accordingly. You can adjust the seasoning with more tomato, garlic, caraway or harissa, and salt to taste.

Serve in warm bowls with a crescent of olive oil drizzled atop each bowl.

Serves 4

Zingerman's
CORNMAN FARMS

TOMATO 'N' N'DUJA SAUCE

N'duja is the wonderful spicy, spreadable pork sausage of the Italian region of Calabria. I'm particularly partial to the one being made by Antonio Fiasche in Chicago (under the N'duja Artisans brand). It's got a unique and almost addictive flavor—you can spread n'duja on toast, make sandwiches with it, or eat it as an appetizer. It's also delicious added to this simple tomato sauce that comes alive first from the quality of the ripe tomatoes and then from the spicy sensuality of the n'duja. You can adjust the amount of n'duja based on how much spice you like.

You can use this sauce on pasta, fish, or other seafood (it's great with mussels); over eggs; or with rice, chicken, pork, or polenta.

2 tablespoons extra virgin olive oil

2 to 3 large, ripe heirloom tomatoes, chopped (in the off-season, substitute one 14-ounce can diced tomatoes, undrained)

Sea salt

Parmigiano-Reggiano rind (optional)

2 to 4 ounces n'duja sausage

Pasta cooking water (optional)

Heat the oil in a large skillet over medium-high heat. Add the tomatoes and a pinch of salt and simmer for 5 minutes or so. If you have a piece of cheese rind, add it to the sauce. (It adds flavor like a bone adds to soup stock.)

Stir in the n'duja and cook a few minutes more. If you're making pasta, add a few tablespoons of the cooking water; the starch in the water will gently thicken the sauce just a bit. Reduce the heat to low and let simmer, stirring occasionally, until it's slightly thickened. Remove the cheese rind before serving.

Yields about 2 cups

ZINGERMAN'S SQUARE CHALLAH

Challah is the traditional bread baked for the Jewish Sabbath and holidays. It's been a staple at the Bakehouse since we opened back in 1992. You, of course, can make it any time you like. Great for everything from festive occasions to a tasty peanut-butter-and-jelly sandwich.

¾ cup water (room temperature)

5 egg yolks (room temperature)

2 tablespoons plus 1 teaspoon corn or olive oil, plus more for the containers

2 tablespoons plus 1 teaspoon honey

1½ teaspoons instant yeast

3 cups plus 2 tablespoons all-purpose flour

1½ teaspoons fine sea salt

1 egg, lightly beaten with 1 tablespoon water

In a large bowl, mix the water, egg yolks, oil, honey, and yeast thoroughly with a wooden spoon. Add half of the flour and mix until the mixture becomes a thick batter. Add the remaining flour and the salt and mix until the dough comes together. Scrape the dough out of the mixing bowl onto the work surface.

Knead the dough for 6 to 8 minutes, scraping the work surface if it keeps sticking. The dough will become smooth and elastic during kneading. Lightly oil a large container. Put in the dough and cover with plastic wrap or a damp towel. Ferment the dough for 1 hour at room temperature.

Turn the dough out of the container onto the work surface and divide into 8 pieces. Round each piece of dough, cover them with plastic wrap, and let rest for 5 minutes.

Lightly oil a 10x5-inch (or thereabouts) loaf pan. Arrange the balls of dough in the pan in two rows of four, seam side down.

Brush the loaf with the egg wash, cover with tented plastic wrap, and allow to rise for about 1½ hours at room temperature, until it has nearly doubled in size. To test if it's ready, press the dough gently with a finger. The indentation should spring back slowly but remain visible.

While the loaf rises, preheat the oven to 350°F.

Brush the loaf again with egg wash. Bake for 35 to 40 minutes or until golden brown and the center is 190° to 200°F.

Cool completely before enjoying.

Makes one loaf

PISONI SALAD

This wonderful salad is the invention of Vincent Pisoni and Brandon Clark, who work together in the kitchen at the Roadhouse. For more on the story behind their collaboration, see page 160. For more on the salad, see the recipe below! I love it. The creaminess of the blue cheese and richness of the pistachios are offset by the fresh spiciness of the arugula.

For the vinaigrette

2 tablespoons plus 1 teaspoon balsamic vinegar

1 teaspoon coarsely chopped fresh rosemary

1 teaspoon coarsely chopped fresh flat-leaf parsley

1 teaspoon Dijon mustard

1 teaspoon minced shallot

½ teaspoon minced garlic

½ teaspoon coarse sea salt

½ teaspoon freshly ground black pepper

½ cup extra virgin olive oil

For the salad

2 ounces arugula (about 4 cups)

⅓ cup toasted pistachios

1 Asian pear, cored and diced

½ cup diced roasted red pepper

½ cup crumbled blue cheese

A few slivers red onion

Combine the vinegar, rosemary, parsley, mustard, shallot, garlic, salt, and pepper in a medium bowl or small food processor. Drizzle in the oil and emulsify the oil into the mix. (Use an immersion blender if using a bowl.)

Place all the ingredients for the salad in a medium bowl. Add about ½ cup of the vinaigrette and toss to coat.

Serve immediately, with any extra dressing on the side.

Serves 2

ZingTRAIN

FINE E MEZZI: AN ANARCHIST APPLICATION TO PASTA COOKING

Errico Malatesta was one of the great figures of the anarchist world in the late 19th and early 20th centuries. He was from the province of Caserta in the Campania region, on the Italian west coast, south of Rome. When he was 10, his family moved south a bit, to Naples. Later he spent years living in exile in England, some time in South America and the United States, and a decade in Italian prisons. Throughout his life, Malatesta wrote and spoke extensively, usually quite forcefully. He was known to be an inspiring leader and drew attention—from both anarchists and the authorities—wherever he went.

The last few decades of the 19th century were a time of great upheaval in Italy; social unrest, bad harvests, and inflation ruled the day. Rocco Disderide, having come to the United States from the northern region of Liguria in 1882, must have been feeling good about his decision to move to America. He'd freely chosen to leave Italy to look for a better life; Malatesta, working to make life better for many by fighting the government, fled to London to keep his freedom. While Disderide was trying to fit into the mainstream of American existence, Malatesta was trying to turn it upside down.

In 1892, the same year that Disderide moved with his wife and daughters from New York to Ann Arbor, Malatesta published an article in England entitled *"Fine e Mezzi."* It translates in English to "ends and means." The import of ends and means being congruent will likely already be familiar to you from essays earlier in this book (see Secret #43.5 for more on the subject). But the day I was reading Malatesta's piece, I happened to be thinking more about cooking than organizational culture. What caught me when I saw the article was that, anarchist beliefs aside, *Fine e Mezzi* sure sounded like a marvelous name for a pasta dish. Malatesta, after all, grew up in Naples, the home of Italian pasta making. Born in 1853, it's sure that young Errico would have eaten pasta, probably—as it was then done—with his fingers, purchased from street vendors. It's just as certain that in the summers he'd have walked by wooden racks of spaghetti drying slowly in the sun. (Pasta in those days was made seasonally—you needed warm weather in order to dry it properly. Mechanical drying didn't really get going until early in the 20th century.) In fact, it's around the time of Malatesta's youth that tomatoes—having arrived in Italy from the New World a few centuries earlier—were first beginning to be paired with pasta.

With all that in mind, inspired, I decided to invent an appropriately anarchistic pasta dish to fit the title of Malatesta's article. Because *Fine* means "ends," I imagined something that would use up all the various bits of orphaned pasta shapes that I almost inevitably have on hand. You know, the ones left behind when you don't quite finish a whole bag so that there's not enough left to use for a full meal, but what you have is still too good to throw out? I started to think about putting all these misfits together in one communal pot, which struck me a fine way to do a culinary homage to anarchist beliefs—making something special out of what is so commonly discarded; moving away from the uniformity of cooking pasta of all one size and shape; and, in the process, bringing diversity to the fore, highlighting difference instead of hiding it. And so, Pasta Fine e Mezzi was made.

In total, you'll want about 4 ounces of dried pasta per person for a dinner portion, a bit less for lunch. Remember, of course, that the better the quality of the pasta, the better the dish will be. The concept will be equally applicable to noodles of any caliber, but the quality of the eating will be dramatically enhanced by using great artisanal pastas (Rustichella, Martelli, Cavalieri, Faella, and Baia are some of my favorite brands). I began with a large pot of rapidly boiling salted water like I would any other pasta dish. Then I added the thickest, biggest pasta shapes first, i.e., the ones that would take the longest to cook. In my case, it was paccheri—large, thick tubes. It was just coincidence—it's what I had on hand—but it's a good choice for this dish, since it's a shape that's typical of Malatesta's home region of Campania. After stirring gently and giving them a few minutes to get going, I then added the next-thickest. For me, it was maccheroni. And then the next-thickest still—some whole-wheat shells—and on down the line (spaghettoni and then spaghetti) till they were all added to the pot. I broke the longest pastas into 4- or 5-inch-long pieces to make it easier to eat them with the short shapes. Gentle stirring throughout kept things moving. I worried that it would be hard to cook the different shapes and sizes to a consistent level of doneness, but then I realized that maybe they didn't have to be. If every person is a unique individual who brings their own personality to the table, why wouldn't every piece of pasta do the same?

Given the different cooking times that would be called for if they were each prepared on their own, it was hard to judge when to take the pasta off the stove. But I just kept checking and tasting until most of the pastas were around the level of *al dente,* tender but firm, doneness that I'm so fond of. Then I drained them all in a colander. I figured it would be best to keep the dish simple in the spirit of the food Malatesta would likely have had. I poured the pasta quickly into a large bowl, dressed it with one of the best full-flavored extra virgin olive oils I had on hand, and then added some grated Parmigiano-Reggiano cheese. (Remember, excellent ingredients, combined simply, generally yield great results—the means need to be congruent with the ends!) In honor of the anarchist colors (black and red) and always in favor of flavor, I finished each bowl with a generous dose of both black pepper (freshly ground Tellicherry from the folks at Épices de Cru) and red pepper (I used the Gorria pepper flakes, also from Épices de Cru). I then tossed the whole thing into warm bowls and ate it while it was hot!

For this first test, I used six different pastas, but you could use more or less as you like—that's the point! Short, stubby, small, long, thick, thin, whole wheat—really anything will be good as long as it's of high quality. Don't discriminate. Each contributes its own unique qualities. Every mouthful brings a range of different textures. And because of the quality of the ingredients—artisanal pasta, Parmigiano-Reggiano, top-notch extra virgin olive oil, great pepper—it tastes terrific.

To be clear, while the means were completely congruent with the ends, the outcome is probably a bit outrageous by most people's standards. But Fine e Mezze, it turns out, is marvelous. It messes with mainstream methods, but tastes terrific. It looks messy, but eats beautifully. (In fact, to a non-Italian-speaker, the name might easily be misconstrued to mean "a fine mess," which is linguistically inaccurate but exactly what it looks like!) Making the dish pushed me to pay attention in new ways and made eating dinner more interesting. Creatively disruptive cooking in action. It shows, as Malatesta would surely have appreciated, how something special can be created from what most of society would consider its castoffs. Diversity and deliciousness, economy and excellence all working together in one warm bowl.

Fine e Mezzi now makes regular appearances on the dinner table at our house! I thought about naming it for Malatesta, but he was always so adamant about not making heroes of individual leaders that doing so seemed incongruous. So I'm keeping it simple—Fine e Mezzi. Just the title of Malatesta's article. A core belief of anarchist thinking. And now, after this piece hits the press, a really delicious pasta dish. Every time I make it I think of Malatesta. I'm betting he'd be a big fan.

GRILLED HALVAH
AND CHOCOLATE SANDWICH

Halvah is a popular Middle Eastern confection, generally made from sesame as well as other nuts along with honey and sugar. We've been making one by hand at Zingerman's Candy Manufactory for many years now. It's great nibbled on its own and excellent with espresso. Here we put it in a sandwich—an idea I came across at a nice Turkish cafe on the West Coast. As simple as this seems, it's truly a delicious dessert or afternoon snack. Some chocolate fiends even fry 'em up for breakfast. By definition, the better the chocolate, the better the sandwich. Shawn Askinosie's would be delicious! I like it with a dark chocolate, but you can certainly make it with any good milk or white chocolate as well.

1 tablespoon butter

2 slices sourdough bread, ½-inch thick

1 ounce halvah, crumbled

1 ounce (about 2 large squares) dark chocolate

Butter the slices of bread on one side. Sandwich the halvah and the chocolate between the nonbuttered sides.

Place a small skillet over medium heat; the pan should be hot enough to toast the bread to a golden brown and melt the chocolate. When the skillet is hot, place the sandwich in the center.

Set a bowl or plate on the sandwich to weigh it down. Cook until the bottom of the bread is lightly browned, 2 to 3 minutes. Turn the sandwich over and repeat. Eat it while it's warm.

Makes one yummy sandwich

An Epicurean Epilogue

Anarchist Eating in Greenwich Village

Our beliefs, as we know, direct us into the lives we lead. Mine steered me towards this story. It brings together so many things that are important to me—restaurants, food, anarchists, art, and a lot of the free thinking insightful people from whom I've learned so much.

Robert Henri's beliefs led him, when he wasn't painting, teaching, or traveling, to frequent Polly's Restaurant in Greenwich Village in New York City. The place was run by anarchist Polly Holladay, along with her brother Louis and her lover, anarchist author–cum-line-cook, Hippolyte Havel. Holladay was originally from Evanston, Illinois, home of Northwestern University and a few miles east of where I went to high school in Skokie. Polly's was located originally at 137 MacDougal Street (between West Fourth and West Third) from 1913 to 1915 and then around the corner at 147 West Fourth Street from 1915 to 1917. A third location followed at 5 Sheridan Square, where the Holladays and Havel had a pair of dining rooms and a basement grill. Polly's original space had, half a century earlier, been the home of Nathaniel Currier, founder of Currier and Ives. Havel was better known as a writer (he wrote the foreword for Emma Goldman's *Anarchism and Other Essays*) than a restaurateur, but as a partner in Polly's, he cooked and waited tables. He didn't quite have the Zingerman's service ethic—he's said to have regularly taken delight in creatively insulting any customers who didn't fit with his views on society.

If you were an advocate of the avant garde in that era and spent time in Manhattan, it's a good bet you'd have been eating at the restaurant as well. Emma Goldman most certainly did. It's easy to imagine her sitting down for supper with Henri. He might have successfully broached the idea of painting her portrait while talking at one of Polly's tables. The painting was finished in 1915, so initial discussions could well have come at Polly's, which opened in 1913. Brenda Ueland likely ate there as well. She also lived in the Village in that era and hung out with Goldman, radical writers John Reed and Louise Bryant, and artist Mabel Dodge, all of whom would have been found frequently at one of Polly's tables. Eugene O'Neill was close to the Holladays and was a regular at the restaurant. (Havel was the basis for the character Hugo Kalmar in O'Neill's *The Iceman Cometh*.) Polly's was also the meeting place of a club called Heterodoxy, which artists and founding member Mabel Dodge described as "unorthodox women, women who did things and did them openly." Suffragist Marie Jenney Howe said of the group, "We intend simply to be ourselves, not just our little female selves, but our whole, big, human selves."

Memoirist Agnes Boulton, a friend of Eugene O'Neill's, describes Holladay herself as "tall, dark-eyed and calm" (sounds like me) "with an interesting and receptive mind, she gave the place the air of a club, and people who went there didn't think of it as a restaurant." Really, they mostly seem to have gone to hang out with friends. Writing in *Inside Greenwich Village*, Gerald McFarland says Polly's was "the first of many Village bistros to be run by a self-identified bohemian owner for a bohemian crowd." Early-20th-century author Alice Anna Chapin called it a "sacred institution" in the neighborhood. She wrote, "In many minds, 'Polly's' and the Village mean one and the same thing." It was apparently quite the scene. Writer and editor Arthur Bartlett Maurice marveled:

> It remains, through fluctuations and fads, the most thoroughly and consistently popular Village eating place extant. It is, outwardly, not original nor superlatively striking in any way. It is a clean, bare place with paper napkins and such waits between courses as are unquestionably conducive to the encouragement of philosophic, idealistic, anarchistic and aesthetic debates. But the food is excellent, when you get it, and the atmosphere both friendly and let us admit frankly inspiring. The people are interesting; they discuss interesting things. You are comfortable, and you are exhilarated.

Polly's was clearly what we would now call "a third place" (see Secret #14, in *Part 1*). Jessie Tarbox Beals, the nation's first female photojournalist, scrawled this on a photo she took of the restaurant: "When life is very strenuous and spirits are down you'd better go to Polly's in little Greenwich town for there the clans are gathered—it's there you'll find 'em all. The artists and the writers ranged against the wall."

Speaking of artists, Clara Tice was a painter who had trained with Robert

Henri, assimilating many of the lessons that later appeared in *The Art Spirit*. A series of female nudes she'd painted were put on display in Polly's dining room. Conservative crusader Anthony Comstock, founder of the New York Society for the Suppression of Vice and a regular annoyance in the anarchist world (he led the seizure of a great deal of printed matter, which resulted in any number of long court battles over free speech), appeared in the restaurant and demanded that the paintings be removed. From the way it was reported in the press, it was a drama of which Eugene O'Neill might well have been enamored. Diner Allen Norton took a break from whatever he was eating and, on the spot, bought the entire collection and rescued the paintings.

Tice ended up gaining a good deal of fame from the incident and came to be known as "the Queen of Greenwich Village." She cut quite the figure. According to the *New York Times*, in 1908 she'd been the first woman in the Village to bob her hair, then considered quite a radical act. Henri had helped to organize her first show, the exhibition of independent artists, which opened on April Fool's Day 1910. In an act unheard of in its day, it was art for art's sake—the show was set up to be free of juries and awards. Over 2,000 people came to the opening. Tice was known for her unorthodox attire as one of the early advocates for short skirts and rolled-up stockings. She was seen regularly walking the Village with her large Russian wolfhound. The two were quite the contrast—she herself was thin and only about five feet tall. Tice's line drawings, especially her erotica, became quite famous. To my layperson's eye, her work really is quite exceptional. If Paul Klee is correct that "a line is a dot that went for a walk," then each of Tice's lines was like a Broadway production. Gallery owner Meredith Ward wrote that, "Tice had an extraordinary ability to capture with a few simple lines the grace and agility of the human body in motion, and she approached her subjects with an irreverent and naughty wit." She also designed menus for restaurants, though I'm still on the search to determine which ones. Later in her life she published a lovely children's book entitled *ABC Dogs*, in which she drew a different dog for each letter of the alphabet. Throughout her life, Tice seems to have walked her own way, taking Henri's early advice: "The better or more personal you are the less likely [your works] are of acceptance." Remember, he advised, "you are painting for yourself, not the jury." Sound advice, great art, interesting people. All of which one might well have experienced on any given evening by stopping off at Polly's Restaurant for dinner.

Endnotes

Preface

1 John Nueske—the great-grandfather of Tanya Nueske, who runs the business today—arrived in the United States from Germany in 1882, the same year that Rocco did. Perhaps they shared a sandwich at Castle Garden Immigration Center. If they did, their memories are now meeting up every day at the Deli. I know for sure that for well over 30 years now, Nueske's bacon has been contributing to the aromatic ambiance of Rocco's building.

2 The belief that "nation states" are normal is a relatively recent one. Up until the time of the French Revolution, what we think of as "countries" were mostly divided into smaller parcels of land ruled by princes and dukes and other local nobles who ultimately reported to kings and queens in faraway capitals. Four centuries ago, the idea that Liguria, where Rocco's family lived, would be more connected with Calabria, 600-plus miles to the south, as opposed to Provence, 120 miles to the west in what is now France, would have seemed very strange.

3 Italians were an aberration in Ann Arbor in that era. My copy of the 1877 *Jubilee Cookbook*, a collection of recipes contributed by the women of the town, shows not a single Italian surname. I doubt any African American women would have been included, either. All the last names listed appear to have been German, English, or Irish.

4 Beliefs change quite a bit. In October of the previous year, Booker T. Washington became the first African American to "dine" in the White House. Others, of course, surely ate there. But they were kitchen staff who supped behind the scenes, not as Dr. Washington did, sitting down to be served dinner at the same table as the president. A hundred and seven years later, Barack Obama was inaugurated as the first African American president of the United States.

5 For context, Ann Arbor's population in 1902 was about 15,000, less than a third of the number of people who were in Michigan Stadium to hear Paul and me give the U of M commencement address in the spring of 2015 (see page 533). In 1901, the year before the building was built, Ann Arbor's first auto dealership was established. The Staebler family, already established bicycle sellers, saw an opportunity to stay on the cutting edge of technology and took on sales of the Trimoto, a three-wheeled automobile built by the Toledo Steam Carriage Company. Its maximum speed was 12 miles per hour, and it apparently had a good bit of trouble getting up some of the town's hills. The next year, President Theodore Roosevelt was the first

American president to ride in a car (which, by the way, was electric). By 1906, there were still only six cars in town. But again, beliefs—and with them, buying patterns— progress: in 1929, Ann Arbor had more cars and telephones per capita than any city in the world. Perhaps it was a sign of things to come, an indicator of Ann Arbor's current role as a center of high-tech innovation.

On a personal level, 1902 is the year that my grandfather, Jack Perlis, was born in a small shtetl town in what he called "White Russia," know today as Belarus. In Ann Arbor there were only a handful of Jewish families, and in 1902, the same year that Rocco Disderide built his building, Lansky's Junkyard was established by one of them. Eighty-five years or so later, the Lanskys' grandson Aubrey, living in the Detroit suburbs but commuting to the junkyard in Ann Arbor to work every day, offered to pick up our rye bread at Modern Bakery. We'd been driving there and back—it was in Oak Park, 45 minutes or so to the east—to get bread every morning for our first four or five years in business. In the sort of win-win solution we've come to specialize in, we paid his gas and gave him a truck to use, and he saved us a trip. That arrangement lasted until 1992 when we opened the Bakehouse, and the by-then-legendary bread run came to an end. Around the same time Disderide and Lansky were getting their businesses going, another Jewish businessman, Jacob Ingber, opened an auto parts business for the newly emerging auto industry. His granddaughter Molly used to bake cheesecake for us in the early years at the Deli.

In 1920, the Ann Arbor Foundry opened on North Main Street, co-owned by Charles Baker, an African American, and Tom Cook, a Russian Jew. Maintaining a very progressive management, they actively shared profits with their staff. The business survived until 1972.

6 Another demonstration of how beliefs can change: Back in 1982, we allowed smoking in the Deli. We also sold cigarettes—at a low price, in the hope that it would bring in business from the neighborhood. Perhaps it was unwitting deference to Mr. Disderide's lifelong love of smoking that led us to put the cigarette rack on the wall behind the original cash register.

7 When St. Thomas church up the block from Disderide's purchased new pews, Rocco took some of the wood from the old ones and handcarved it into replicas of his fellow Genovese adventurers' three ships—the Niña, the Pinta, and the Santa Maria. Columbus, of course, is a testament to the power of perspective on the way we experience what goes on around us. For Europeans, he was a brave explorer who "discovered the Americas." For Native Americans, he was an invader whose unwanted arrival presaged the end of thousands of years of successful cultural existence. For Africans, he was an intruder, one of the people who put slave trading into the forefront of history. Given the geographical proximity of their origins, I wonder if Rocco imagined his own story of sailing across the Atlantic to have started with Columbus. The three model ships he carved are still "afloat"—each of Rocco's three great-grandchildren has one.

8 There's a wonderful program at Mott Children's Hospital in Ann Arbor called Beads for Life. It's designed to help kids struggling with difficult health issues to stay focused on the positive and to remember they are making headway even when recovery can feel slow. In the program, beads are used to represent strength and courage. The programmers explain, "Just like medals, ribbons and certificates, many ancient and modern-day cultures use beads to show bravery and accomplishment. They have long

been used to protect warriors from natural and supernatural enemies, along with lending special magical protection for heroes during long journeys."

9   Many African Americans, already living as free citizens, made great contributions to the community. In 1872, Elijah McCoy earned a patent for his graphite lubricator cup for trains. It was a big success and spread quickly across the country. The phrase "the Real McCoy" was a reference to people who wanted his original product, not a low-quality replica. In 1890, George Jewett was the fastest sprinter in the Midwest. He entered medical school the same year.

10   I-94, which runs right past both the Bakehouse and the Roadhouse, is one of the longest highways in the world. It actually began in 1941 just to the east of Ann Arbor, near Ypsilanti, not too far from where the Aray family was farming a century earlier.

11   The University of Michiganania (as it was originally called) was established in Detroit in 1817 and is actually 20 years older than the state. It moved to what was then known as Annarbour in 1837.

Secret #40

12   The Disderides' parish church, St. Thomas, was built in 1899 after an aggressive eight-year-long fundraising campaign by Father Edward Kelly. I wonder now if Rocco's desire to build the building in 1902 was inspired and influenced by Father Kelly's belief that new construction was an important and timely piece of the neighborhood's development.

Secret #41

13   An attorney by training, Étienne de La Boétie wrote his exceptional essay "A Discourse on Voluntary Servitude" in 1552, when he was about 22 years old. If you have a few minutes, look it up online. Here's a snippet of his amazing insights:

> Place on one side fifty thousand armed men, and on the other the same number; let them join in battle, one side fighting to retain its liberty, the other to take it away; to which would you, at a guess, promise victory? Which men do you think would march more gallantly to combat—those who anticipate as a reward for their suffering the maintenance of their freedom, or those who cannot expect any other prize for the blows exchanged than the enslavement of others? One side will have before its eyes the blessings of the past and the hope of similar joy in the future; their thoughts will dwell less on the comparatively brief pain of battle than on what they may have to endure forever, they, their children, and all their posterity. The other side has nothing to inspire it with courage except the weak urge of greed, which fades before danger and which can never be so keen, it seems to me, that it will not be dismayed by the least drop of blood from wounds.

La Boétie's belief was reinforced for me again a few weeks ago. We used the Three Good Things exercise we learned from Martin Seligman in the ZingTrain "Managing Ourselves" seminar. When I asked the group what they had noticed about the "good things" people read aloud, one of the participants raised his hand. "Almost everything that people wrote down as a good thing that had happened to them was something they had freely chosen to do."

14 More often than not, if we shift our core beliefs, what we've long believed to be weeds turn out to be terrifically interesting. Even elegant. Check out this description of the dandelion from anarchist anthropologist and geographer Élie Reclus:

> *This flower which is a little sun, becomes a milky way, a world of stars after blooming. It passes from green to yellow, and then to greyish-blue. Everything about it is unity and radiation, the leaves as well as the flowers and the fruit. The dandelion represents a complete and harmonious idea; everywhere revealed as an incarnation of unity and constitutes an eloquent image of perfection in beauty and simplicity. Nothing resembles the sun more closely. Contemplating an Alpine meadow, one sees a vision of immense skies with thousands of constellations and millions of eyes.*

What was the bane of life when trying to fulfill my childhood lawn-care responsibilities, an annoying weed that just wouldn't go away, turns out, when you turn the lens a bit to the left, to be quite beautiful.

Secret #42

15 Brenda Ueland's advice in *If You Want to Write* helped me make peace with some of my negative beliefs around writing. "If you are going to write," she says, "you must become aware of this richness in you and come to believe in it and know it is there so that you can write opulently with self-trust. Once you become aware of it, have faith in it, you will be all right. But it is like this: if you have a million dollars in the bank and don't know, it doesn't do you any good." By putting an end to my worrying and self-criticism and just letting myself say what I want to say, trusting in good editors and good friends to help me, the results of my work improved drastically. (Though, of course, the doubts never fully go away—I can still hear the self-critical voices saying I shouldn't even write this for fear that you'll say this entire book is baloney.)

16 Kassam specializes in congruity. On his website he says, "I work closely with restaurants and other food companies to develop menus and products that strongly reflect the brand, work in symbiosis with the aesthetic, and deliver undeniable deliciousness." His London pop-up restaurant, the Thinker's Balcony, develops menus designed to "evoke the philosopher in you."

Secret #43

17 It turns out the Slovaks are actually working on just such a thing. I believe, as I said above, that there are great things to come in that country! Here are a couple of paragraphs excerpted from the 2020 vision of the Pontis Foundation, a wonderful community-minded nonprofit based in the capital of Bratislava. The Slovaks, I'd say, are setting the pace for the rest of us.

> *We are making a big difference locally and a small difference globally. We have never been afraid to think big and set ambitious challenges for ourselves*

in Pontis Foundation. We challenge ourselves to make Slovakia a good country, a place for free and responsible people trying to improve their lives and the world around them. We wish to have a prosperous country which works well and, at the same time, sustainably, and which is a good "global citizen." We want [a] country in which people work to be better, learn, where people are active and able to get a job or start a business. We want [a] country where it is possible to run a business fair and square and enjoy it. We want [a] country where smart, creative and hard-working people do well rather than oligarchs and corruption. We want an affable environment for weaker ones, for the ill and for people with disabilities who feel accepted here.

We are well aware this is a long-term ideal. Still, in the last five years we have managed to get a step closer to this aim together with our partners from the business sphere, NGOs as well as from public administration authorities. We have managed to make many people enthusiastic about the idea that is not only possible to have a better life in developed foreign countries—that it is achievable even here, in Slovakia. And that the responsibility for our situation lies not only with the state, politicians, and white-collars. All of us—people, companies, and organisations—can make the change by owning the initiative and by doing myriads of small steps.

18   Oddly—or maybe not—two days after I finished this essay, a regular customer named Julie Parrish walked up to me at the Coffee Company while I was journaling one morning. "Have you ever heard of a guy named Nido ..." She paused, trying to remember his last name. I looked at her with total amazement. "Qubein?" I asked. I'd never heard the man's name spoken by anyone in all the years I've been studying business. "That's it! How did you know that?" Julie exclaimed. I just shook my head and smiled and sent her the draft of this essay.

Secret #43.5

19   The period of 1910 to 1915, during which Goldman's visit to Ann Arbor took place, was one of the most violent in American history. Negative beliefs were whipped up into overwhelming rage. African Americans were being lynched, on average, one man, woman, or child every third day. Union organizers and anarchists were regularly beaten, tarred, and feathered.

20   Emma Goldman's suitcase now resides at U of M in the Labadie collection. It was donated, in the same year I was working on this book, by Spanish-born anarchist Federico Arcos, who had received it many years earlier from Emma's compatriot Attilio Bortolotti.

21   I came upon the reference to Seltzer's Ann Arbor restaurant—called Seltzer and Chatterton—in Paul Avrich's wonderful oral history, *Anarchist Voices*. I couldn't find anyone in town today who'd ever heard of it, but the restaurant does show up in Polk's City Directory for 1911. (Rocco Disderide, his family, and his shop at 422 Detroit Street are all also listed.) As is true with so many food businesses today, the restaurant didn't last long—Seltzer moved to Toronto, and the restaurant was closed by the following year.

22   Emma's visits proved to have a lasting impact on Ann Arbor. In 1911, she

wrote, "I have the pleasure of knowing, that my last year's visit has induced a Professor to announce a course on Anarchism for this year." The professor was Robert Mark Wenley, who went on to write and teach about the subject. Born in Scotland, Wenley came to Ann Arbor and taught in the philosophy department at the University of Michigan. The 1904 version of *The Ann Arbor Cook Book*, compiled by the Ladies' Aid Society of the Congregational Church, included recipes for Scotch Soda Scones, Scotch Shortbread, and Scotch Bun contributed by his wife. In 1913, he published *The Anarchist Ideal and Other Essays*, one of over a dozen volumes he wrote.

Wenley was highly regarded on campus and was the commencement speaker at Michigan State University in Lansing in 1919. Upon his death in 1929, university president Clarence Cook Little said, "He will stand in Michigan's annals for all time as one of her greatest teachers and scholars. The University has added a lasting figure to its history but at the cost to many of us of a good and true friend whose passing leaves us in the most profound sorrow and with a sense of enduring loss." Today there is a Robert Mark Wenley memorial stained-glass window in St. Andrew's Church on Division Street, a few blocks from the Deli, and a Wenley House in the dorm at West Quad on campus.

23   A good number of anarchist books from Carlotta Anderson's personal library are now in a "Little Labadie Collection" at ZingTrain. She generously gifted them to us a year before she passed away in 2015.

24   Historian and biographer Candace Falk writes of Emma Goldman: "She enjoyed the sensory experience of a flower, a fragrance, a cup of freshly ground morning coffee. Goldman's blend was described by her friends to be dark as the night, strong as the revolution, and sweet as love." Our French Roast would probably be the best approximation of the darkness of her beans. You'll need to bring the revolution and the love.

Secret #44

25   Candace Falk reports that Emma Goldman was also "a voracious reader who found traces of anarchist ideals in almost everything."

Secret #45

26   Why I Don't Love Name Tags: Though I know they're not the worst things in the world, I've never liked name tags. There are, of course, places where they're helpful. We use them at ZingTrain seminars where 30 or so people who have probably never met are together in a seminar room for two days. And they're helpful at Zingerman's Mail Order at the holidays, when we bring 300 people together for only five or six weeks. Still, there's something so impersonal about them. No, I don't believe that banning name tags would radically alter the state of our society. But they just seem like a shortcut, a substitute for learning what we know we ought to learn, and not really a means towards spreading hope and recognition where it's so badly needed.

Imagine asking an employee at a Zingerman's business a question about a product. Before they answer, they look up at a monitor on the wall and read to you word for word whatever it is they find there. It's certainly more helpful than if they knew nothing. But what about a different scenario, hopefully the one we deliver to you now, an experience where you ask something, and the employee's eyes light up? If they then immediately launch into a passionate description of the product you've inquired about, *it completely alters your experience as a customer.* The same thing applies to name tags. I think my positive influence is far higher if I make the effort to learn, actually know, and then use the person's name—and get to know them and their unique personality in the process—rather than just reading it off their name tag.

27 In 1955 Cantril founded the Institute for International Social Research with Lloyd A. Free (no relation to the former Philadelphia 76ers shooting guard Lloyd "World" B. Free). In his research, Cantril noticed the paradoxical polling result that a majority of Americans opposed "big government" but were simultaneously supportive of expanding social programs. Remembering Secret #42, "It's All About Alignment," we know that this sort of incongruity in beliefs and values is highly ineffective.

Secret #46

28 Best I can tell, Kropotkin never came to Ann Arbor, but he did give a speech in 1897 in Detroit, where he visited with Jo Labadie and spent a day being shown the workings of the Detroit sewer system.

29 **The Insight of Saint Augustine:** Saint Augustine and Peter Kropotkin lived 15 centuries apart. In many ways, they were at opposite ends of the theological spectrum. Augustine was a key figure in developing organized Christian thought; Kropotkin was an anarchist who wanted to free society from organized religion. But both believed generosity was at the core of a great life and a successful society. In his *Enchiridion on Faith, Hope, and Love*, St. Augustine wrote:

> *And now as to love, which the apostle declares to be greater than the other two graces, that is, than faith and hope, the greater the measure in which it dwells in a man, the better is the man in whom it dwells. For when there is a question as to whether a man is good, one does not ask what he believes, or what he hopes, but what he loves. For the man who loves right no doubt believes and hopes aright; whereas the man who has not love believes in vain, even though his beliefs are true; and hopes in vain, even though the objects of his hope are a real part of true happiness; unless, indeed, he believes and hopes for this, that he may obtain by prayer and the blessing of love. For, although it is not possible to hope without love, it may yet happen that a man does not love that which is necessary to the attainment of his hope.*

When you put all the pieces together, the spirit of generosity is just positive belief and grounded, strongly held hope put into tangible practice in our daily lives. To Augustine's point, it's positive beliefs and hopefulness made real—one might, I suppose, donate money while remaining cynical, merely to conform socially. But I can't imagine living the spirit of generosity, as it's outlined here, for any length of time without a positive belief in people and a hope that each of us can contribute to making our communities more sustainable.

An Anarchist Santa Story: Kropotkin's saintliness and his belief in generosity and mutual aid inspired the creativity of modern British anarchist professor Ruth Kinna. She put two and two together to make up a great story that didn't happen but sure could have. Building on Kropotkin's commitment to mutual aid, Kinna created an interesting connection between the anarchist, the Christmas holiday, St. Nicholas, and the spirit of giving.

Kropotkin's noble roots trace back to Rurik, one of the early Norse kings of Russia. St. Nicholas, better known in the United States as Father Christmas (the real St. Nicholas, not the cartoon character we know as Santa Claus), was historically revered in Russia as a defender of the poor. He too turns out to be descended from Rurik. As Kinna fancies

> Nicholas's branch of the family had been sent out to patrol the Black Sea. But Nicholas was a spiritual man and sought an escape from the piracy and brigandage for which his Russian Viking family was famed. So he settled under a new name in the southern lands of the Empire, now Greece, and decided to use the wealth that he had amassed from his life of crime to alleviate the sufferings of the poor.

Kinna's imaginary Kropotkin admired his saintly ancestor and went on to write about him and the holiday with which he was associated. "If you are one of us," he continues in Kinna's tale, "you will realise that the magic of Christmas depends on Father Christmas's system of production, not the stores' attempts to seduce you to consume useless luxuries." Kinna describes the sprawling workshops at the North Pole, where elves work happily all year because they know their work will result in peoples' pleasure. Noting that these workshops are strictly not-for-profit, purpose driven, and craft based, and run on communal lines, Kropotkin treats them as prototypes for the factories of the future (as he actually outlined in *Fields, Factories and Workshops*). Bringing his subversive ways to the surface in Kinna's creative story, he issues a challenge: "Infiltrate the stores, give away the toys!"

Secret #47

30 A funny historical note. A Toronto reporter asked Emma Goldman in 1939 about having visited palaces: "'Hmmmph,' snorted the rugged stocky little woman. 'Lots of them. But I didn't find them especially interesting. I like cathedrals though. Some of the cathedrals in France and Spain are marvelous.'"

Secret #49

31 To quote Spanish anarchist educator Francisco Ferrer, whose work to found the Modern School in Barcelona in 1901 is a story unto itself: "The real educator is . . . he who can best appeal to the child's own energies." The core principles of Ferrer's approach to education were based on treating kids as intelligent individuals, and it only makes sense that the same approach would work here. My work as a leader is to find out what and where a new staff member's energy is and then "appeal" to it in a way that helps both them and us get to where we want to go!

Epilogue

32 If you want to read poetry and business in action together, check out the books of both David Whyte and James Autry. See the reading list for titles.

33 Would I ever have noticed all this in Alexander's book if I hadn't already put forward my belief that Disderide's building was a big influence on our work? We'll never know. But, in the spirit of the future creating the past that Paul Watzlawick opened my eyes to understanding (see page 432), I actually went back and put another quote from Christopher Alexander into the original preface after reading *The Timeless Way of Building*. The parallel, the positive nature of the cycle, was too good, and too well aligned to overlook.

Appreciations

I'll begin by appreciating Paul—without him there would be no Zingerman's, and without his positive belief in people my food service career would likely have ended shortly after it started. Being partners productively for this long is a special thing, one that I never take for granted. His patience and persistence and positive vision of a better world are an inspiration to me and many thousands of others. Thanks to our first-ever staff partners: Larry Robillard, Sara Whipple, and Arianna Tellez. Much appreciation to all the managing partners: Alex Young, Amy Emberling, Aubrey Thomason, Charlie Frank, Frank Carollo, Grace Singleton, Kieron Hales, Ji Hye Kim, Maggie Bayless, Rick Strutz, Rodger Bowser, Steve Mangigian, Tom Root, Mo Frechette, Toni Morell, and Ron Maurer. Thanks too to everyone at Zingerman's. It's a 700-person project! Not to mention the 300-plus people who share a few months with us to make Mail Order's holiday season go so smoothly. Every one of their efforts matters. None of what's in the preceding pages would be worth much without the wonderfully delicious, day in, day out crafting of great food, and the amazing service it takes to deliver.

Thanks to everyone who's worked on making this book—the fourth in the series, there are many who have contributed to the whole collection. *Migwetch* as always to Meg Noodin for great editing, insight, support; to Deborah Bayer for her always gentle and enormously insightful editing; to Polly Rosenwaike for her fine line editing; Suzanne Fass for copyediting; Ann Grahl and Hillary Parsons for proofing; and Liz Lester for layout. Thanks to Nicole Robichaud and Liz for great design, and Ian Nagy and Ryan Stiner for the superb scratchboard drawings that have become such a signature in this series.

Thanks to everyone at ZingTrain, without whom very little of what I've written about would have been put into such teachable and adaptable form. Thanks for Stas' Kazmierski, retired as the co-managing partner at ZingTrain a few years back, who taught me the vast majority of what I know about visioning and organizational change. And thanks to Ron Lippitt who taught a lot of that good material to Stas'!

Very deep appreciation to Claude Steele for being willing to carve time out of his busy schedule to write such a wonderful foreword.

Huge thanks for friendship, advice, insight, and good emails to Lex Alexander, Molly Stevens, Alex Carbone, Rich Sheridan, James Goebel, Marifer Calleja, Lea Chansard, Rob Pasick. I appreciate as well the entire de Vienne family, Shawn Askinosie, Melvin Parson, Gail Wolkoff, Glenn Roberts, Felisha Hatcher, and Candace Amori for their help and support in working on the book, and for everything else they do for their communities and for Zingerman's. Additional appreciation to Wayne Baker, Gretchen Spreitzer, Jane Dutton, Chris White, and everyone at the Center for Positive Organizational Scholarship. Thanks to Teddy Araya from the Center for African Leadership Studies for sharing his quiet wisdom. Special thanks to Bob Wright, for sharing both his knowledge and insight.

Thanks to Peter Koestenbaum, Dawna Markova, Dean Tucker, Edgar Schein, Jack Stack, Chip Conley, Gary Snyder, Adam Grant, Rick Price, Robert Greenleaf, Peter Block, John T. Edge, Jay Sandweiss, James Scott, Victoria Johnson, Walter Sowden, Daphne Zepos, Randolph Hodgson, Makale Faber Cullen, Carrie Davenport, Tricia Gatza, John Abrams, and a fair few other folks whom I'm sure I'm forgetting but can't recall right now. Extra and well-aligned appreciation to Patrick Hoban for his generosity, friendship, and good leadership dialogue, and for helping make our ecosystem ever more positive. Thanks to Wayne Mullins for all your support over all these years. Thanks to Christina Carmichael for so many good conversations over coffee.

Appreciation still, nearly four decades down the road, to professors William Rosenberg, Arthur Mendel, Roman Szporluk, and Carl Proffer, for teaching me history many years ago. Thanks to Jan Longone for all her help with the culinary components of the work. Thanks to Gina Athena Ulysse for great conversation and insight. Thanks to Ben Lewis and David Nugraha for all the insightful, in-depth dialogues.

A few thousand freely given thanks to all the anarchists who've lent their words, insights, and ideas to the world. Emma Goldman, Ashanti Alston, Paul Goodman, Alexander Berkman, Mikhail Bakunin, Peter Kropotkin, Voltairine de Cleyre, Nestor Makhno, Rudolf Rocker, Robert Henri, Étienne de La Boétie, Murray Bookchin, Paul Avrich, Joseph Ishill, Gustav Landauer, Élie and Élisée Reclus, Rebecca Solnit, Ammon Hennacy, Errico Malatesta,

Buenventura Durruti, and all the other insightful anarchists who were writing about this stuff so long ago. You got me thinking! Thanks to Julie Herrada at the Labadie Collection for all her help in tracking down relevant anarchist writing. Special appreciation to Bo Burlingham, another modern-day lapsed anarchist, for insight and inspiration. Thanks to Jo Labadie, the peaceful and inspirational Michigan anarchist who donated his archive of books and pamphlets to the University of Michigan in 1911. Thanks to Agnes Inglis, who worked for many years to make the Labadie Collection a living archive that people like me could access. And thanks to Carlotta Anderson for sharing her anarchist books with us.

Super special, great gratitude to Jenny Tubbs for keeping tabs on, and leading, the behind-the-scenes work that has made it possible for you to be holding this book in your hands.

Thanks to Richard Kempter and Marge Greene for imparting much of the insight that's helped me to grow and learn about myself over all these years.

Very big thanks to Marsha Ricevuto for all the behind-the-scenes support that makes it possible for me to spend so much extra time working on books like this one.

Thanks to Jelly Bean for being an amazing and loving companion for 17 very special years. I miss her very much. Thanks to little Bean Sprout for joining our family. Extremely large, super long and very loving appreciation to Tammie Gilfoyle for all of her love, patience, positive energy, encouragement, insight, and smiles that are spread throughout the book. Best coadventurer ever!

So many people have contributed to the contents of this book over the course of my life, and more directly, over the last 34 years here at Zingerman's— many will be missed on this list, but I appreciate them nevertheless. Everyone matters, and every little thing matters. Thank you for reading and for sharing thoughts.

ZINGERMAN'S GUIDE TO GOOD LEADING, PART 1

A Lapsed Anarchist's Approach to Building a Great Business

"Zingerman's is a utopian version of corporate America in which the company leaves added value everywhere it does business. The design is a beautiful virtuous cycle in which each of Zingerman's stakeholders wins: employees grow; customers are delighted; communities flourish; suppliers thrive and profit."

—**DANNY MEYER**, CEO, Union Square Hospitality Group

hardcover
$29.95

ZINGERMAN'S GUIDE TO GOOD LEADING, PART 2

A Lapsed Anarchist's Approach to Being a Better Leader

"Expanding yet again beyond his brilliant careers as both the finest deli-man in the Midwest and also as a savvy business strategist to closet Fortune 500 types, this book is Ari's magnum opus in the key of smarts about how to properly lead your team for fun and profit. Clarifying the intuitive, he's fine tuned early 20th century anarchist ideology into an effective recipe for 21st century leadership. This magnificent tome will help anyone interested to learn how to do the right thing (and increase sales) without selling out to the man."

—**MARIO BATALI**, Chef and author of *Molto Gusto*

hardcover
$29.95

ZINGERMAN'S GUIDE TO GOOD LEADING, PART 3

A Lapsed Anarchist's Approach to Managing Ourselves

"*Zingerman's Guide to Good Leading* turns the accepted wisdom about business on its head, or tail. You won't find any pep talk here about swimming with sharks or taking Genghis Kahn as your mentor. Here, Ari Weinzweig shares a wealth of practical advice about managing a life and a business from one of the founders of the country's most progressive businesses."

—**SAM KEEN**, Author

hardcover
$29.95

ALSO AVAILABLE

ZINGERMAN'S GUIDE TO BETTER BACON

Pork Bellies, Hush Puppies, Rock 'n' Roll Music, and Bacon Fat Mayonnaise

Ari guides you on a personal tour of bacon's long and curious history. You'll head to the farm and learn about 19th-century drovers who were crucial to the hog trade. Ari's story shows how bacon moved from delicious farm staple to a huge-selling flavorless commodity—and how it's going back to its roots today. There are loads of delicious, well-tested recipes, from chocolate gravy to cheddar bacon scones.

hardcover $29.95

"An essential guide-book for any bacon-enthusiast."

—SARA KATE GILLINGHAM-RYAN, ApartmentTherapy.com

"A real bible of all things smoked pig, an engrossing, affably rambling, borderline obsessive one-stop swine seminar."

—CHRIS BORRELLI, *Chicago Tribune*

paperback $19.95

ZINGERMAN'S GUIDE TO GOOD EATING

A deeper discussion of good food

Ari has collected stories, recipes, and pearls of wisdom into this tome of culinary knowledge. A must for serious chefs and weekend cooks alike. Not only does the reader understand the ins and outs of formerly mysterious foods like balsamic vinegar and great olive oil, but its approachable writing makes it easy to become an authority on practically all things artisan.

"[B]rilliant. Certainly anyone who seasons with salt, cooks with olive oil, bakes bread, or loves chocolate should have it in the kitchen."

—DEBORAH MADISON, chef, restaurateur and author of *The Greens Cookbook*

"Ari Weinzweig is my favorite go-to source for every single great gastronomic treasure on the planet, both for information and for the actual stuff itself."

—MARIO BATALI, chef, restaurateur and author of *Molto Gusto*

"This is the book for all who lo to eat. Your copy will end up ju like mine, dog-eared and staine always the sign of a keeper."

—LYNNE ROSSETTO KASPER, host NPR's *The Splendid Table* a author of *How Eat Supp*

ZINGERMAN'S GUIDE TO GIVING GREAT SERVICE

"When it comes to service, few establishments can rival Zingerman's." —*Saveur*

Eighty percent of complaining customers are unhappier after they complain. Why? How do you deal with tough customers? Or really good ones? Here's our quick guide to treating customers like royalty. It details our recipes for giving great service and for effectively handling customer complaints. There are plenty of usable, teachable tips and tools that are applicable for service providers in organizations of any size, in any industry.

Also Available in Spanish

paperback
$16.95

Customer Service Training DVDs

$350/ea. or all 3 for $750

ZINGERMAN'S 3 STEPS TO GIVING GREAT SERVICE

We share our core customer service concepts from The Art of Giving Great Service Seminar in a fun and memorable lesson that will get your organization started building great service skills and culture into every single element of your organizational activity.

Last year, I showed it to my employees at the start of our busy season, and we saw an 8% increase in sales! It's the best tool I've found to encourage great service."

—DIANE RIEHM, RIEHM FARMS, TIFFIN, OH

ZINGERMAN'S 5 STEPS TO EFFECTIVELY HANDLING A COMPLAINT

Our service recipe will help take the stress out of one of the most challenging encounters in customer service. With practice, and using Zingerman's easy-to-follow recipe, you can start seeing complaints as gifts rather than as trials.

"We recently purchased the 5 Steps to Effectively Handling a Complaint video and have incorporated it immediately into our customer service training for our frontline staff."

—PERRY SPENCER, UNIVERSITY OF MICHIGAN HOSPITAL SECURITY

ZINGERMAN'S 3 STEPS TO GREAT FINANCE

We believe Open Book Management has been key to our financial success and one of the "secrets" behind how we were able to thrive during the recession. This DVD is all about Zingerman's rules of finance, keeping score and sharing success. You'll see Zingerman's staff in action and hear them explain in their own words why creating an Open Book organization is a better way to work— and the way of the future.

AVAILABLE AT WWW.ZINGTRAIN.COM

Can you name the one

NATIONALLY RECOGNIZED

LEADERSHIP TRAINING PROGRAM

☞ that ☞

wins rave reviews from:

- Bootstrapping Entrepreneurs
- Corporate CEOs
- Nonprofit Leaders
- Bankers
- Busboys
- Creative Attorneys
- Public School Teachers
- Successful Restaurateurs
- Psychology Professors
- Booksellers
- Food Co-op General Managers
- MBAs
- Nationally Known Business Writers
- Naval Engineers
- Bartenders
- Training Professionals
- Liberal Arts Majors
- Anarchists
- And Food Lovers from all over the world?

Only one that we know of!

ZingTRAIN

www.zingtrain.com

notes

notes

notes

notes

notes

notes

notes

jelly bean (1998-2015); she was the paragon of positive belief,
hope, and the spirit of generosity

2001

zingerman's creamery opens up in manchester, mi and cheesemaker and managing partner john loomis begins making fresh cheeses.

2003

"inc." magazine calls us "the coolest small company in america."

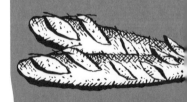

chef alex young becomes managing partner and executive chef as zingerman's roadhouse opens up in the old bill knapp's building on ann arbor's far west side.

"zingerman's guide to good eating" by ari weinzweig is published and written up in "fine cooking," "saveur," "the chicago tribune," "the new york times," and other national publications at the top of their holiday book gift lists.

zingerman's coffee company opens and roastmaster and managing partner allen leibowitz starts selling zingerman's coffee throughout the zingerman's community of businesses and to wholesale customers across the country.

2009

zingerman's candy manufactory, a wholesale candy maker creating old-fashioned american sweets by hand, opens with charlie frank as managing partner.

zingerman's "guide to better bacon," ari weinzweig's tome on pork (featuring bacon history, recipes and lore) is published.

zingerman's coffee company opens its retail and café space on plaza drive down the walk from zingerman's bakehouse and creamery.

2008

zingerman's coffee company manager steve mangigian joins allen as co-managing partner of the business.

zingerman's is featured on oprah's sandwich episode and #97 lisa c.'s boisterous brisket is oprah's favorite, rating an "11" on a scale of 1-5.

2011

zingerman's delicatessen breaks ground on their long-awaited expansion.

zingerman's roadhouse chef alex young is named best chef in the great lakes region by the james beard foundation.

2010

Publication of "a lapsed anarchist's approach to building a great business," the first part in ari weinzweig's leadership series.

rodger bowser moves from chef to co-managing partner at zingerman's delicatessen.